T0293166

THE CORPORATE LIFE CYCLE

THE CORPORATE LIFE CYCLE

BUSINESS, INVESTMENT, AND MANAGEMENT IMPLICATIONS

Aswath Damodaran

PORTFOLIO • PENGUIN

PORTFOLIO / PENGUIN
An imprint of Penguin Random House LLC
penguinrandomhouse.com

Most Portfolio books are available at a discount when purchased in quantity for sales promotions or corporate use. Special editions, which include personalized covers, excerpts, and corporate imprints, can be created when purchased in large quantities. For more information, please call (212) 572-2232 or e-mail specialmarkets@penguinrandomhouse.com. Your local bookstore can also assist with discounted bulk purchases using the Penguin Random House corporate Business-to-Business program. For assistance in locating a participating retailer, e-mail B2B@penguinrandomhouse.com.

Illustrations by the author.

LIBRARY OF CONGRESS CATALOGING-IN-PUBLICATION DATA

Names: Damodaran, Aswath, author.
Title: The corporate life cycle : business, investment, and management implications / Aswath Damodaran.
Description: [New York] : Portfolio/Penguin, [2024] | Includes index.
Identifiers: LCCN 2023056658 (print) | LCCN 2023056659 (ebook) |
ISBN 9780593545065 (hardcover) | ISBN 9780593545072 (ebook)
Subjects: LCSH: Corporations—Finance. | Valuation. | Corporations.
Classification: LCC HG4026 .D33 2024 (print) | LCC HG4026 (ebook) |
DDC 658.15—dc23/eng/20240416
LC record available at https://lccn.loc.gov/2023056658
LC ebook record available at https://lccn.loc.gov/2023056659

Printed in the United States of America
1st Printing

BOOK DESIGN BY TANYA MAIBORODA

To Michele, Rebecca, and Kendra,
who, as amazing schoolteachers, work much harder in the classroom than I ever do,
and to Noah and Lily, two of my favorite people in the world!

CONTENTS

Value and Price across the Life Cycle

Investing Philosophies and Strategies across the Life Cycle

V

Managing across the Life Cycle

PREFACE

IN EVERY DISCIPLINE, PRACTITIONERS search for a framework that helps them explain the whys, the why nots, and the what ifs of that discipline. In corporate finance and valuation, there have been many attempts to build such universal theories and, in my view, the structure that offers the most promise is the corporate life cycle, where companies go through the cycle of being born, growing up, growing old, and eventually perishing. It is one that I have found myself coming back to repeatedly as I try to understand the behavior and misbehavior of businesses, differences across investing perspectives, and the allure of the "next big thing."

The Corporate Life Cycle

The place to start this journey is with an understanding of how companies age and the transitions they go through, and I try to provide that in the following picture:

PREFACE 1.1 | The Corporate Life Cycle

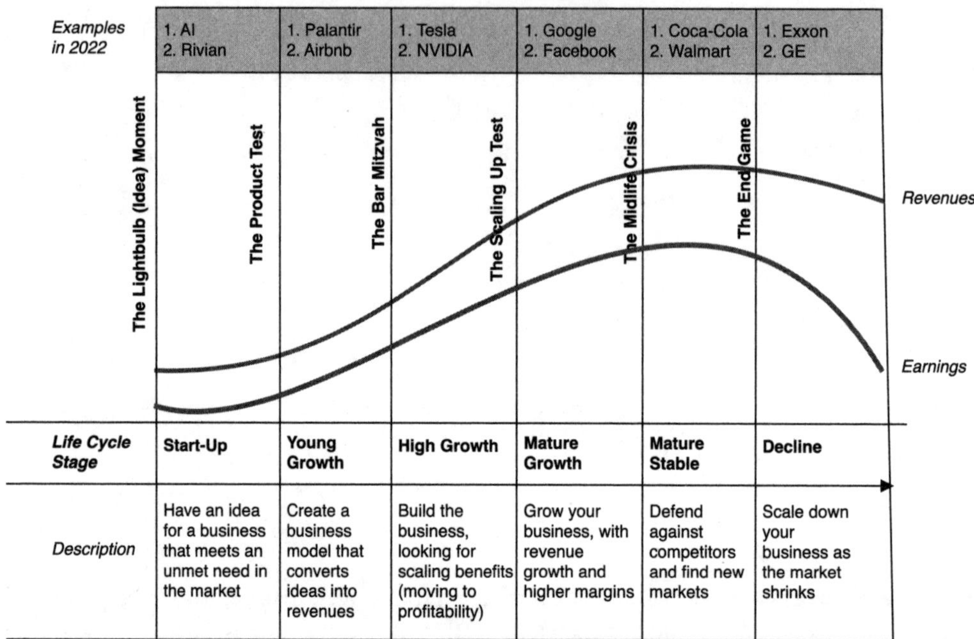

A business start-up is like a baby with a high mortality risk. Despite the care and attention paid to it, if a new business makes it from concept to product, it is already an exception, and in young growth it tries to find a business model that works with all the logistical challenges involved. If successful, it enters the high-growth phase, with revenues accelerating (though profits usually lag), and the business will require capital infusions to keep growing. The most successful of these companies will be able to build working business models, wherein profits start to catch up to revenues, and not only will these businesses be able to self-fund, you will see the beginnings of cash-flow payoffs to owners and other capital providers. While the very best of these mature businesses can extend this phase of glory, middle age eventually comes to every business, bringing slowing growth but solid profits and cash flows.

Being middle-aged is far less exciting than being young, but after middle age comes worse. As businesses age and find their markets shrinking and profits fading, they reach their end. The corporate life cycle resembles the human life cycle in its arc, and just as humans try to fend off aging and death with plastic surgery and personal trainers, companies do the same, with consultants and bankers offering them expensive and fruitless ways of becoming young again.

A Journey through the Book

In the first part of this book, I describe the corporate life cycle, including the markers that tell you where a particular company falls in its life cycle and the forces that determine how the shape and timing of life cycles vary across different types of businesses. I also look at the transition points where businesses move from one stage to another in their life cycle and the challenges they face in making these changes.

PREFACE 1.2 | The Corporate Life Cycle: Drivers and Determinants

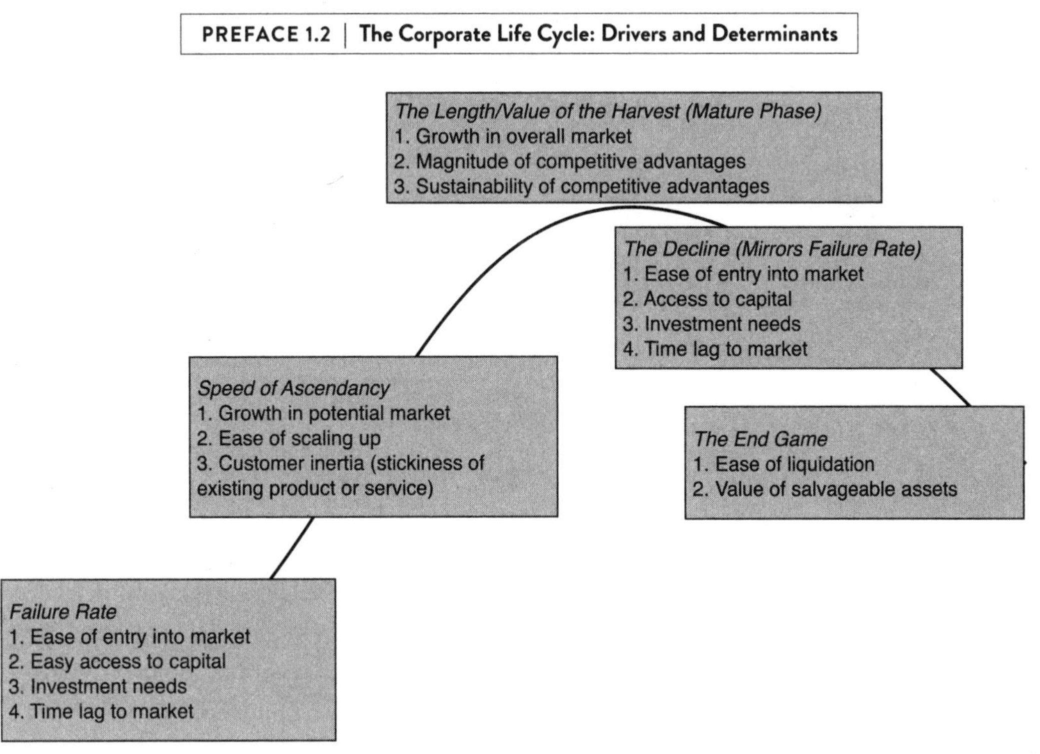

In the second part of the book, I use the corporate life cycle to explain how and why the focus of a business should change as the company ages, with young companies ideally being almost entirely centered on finding good investments, mature companies looking at changing financing mix and type, and declining companies deciding how to return cash most efficiently. I use this framework to argue that the most destructive acts in business occur when companies refuse to act their age, behaving in ways that are incompatible with where they are in the life cycle and often spending large sums in this endeavor.

PREFACE 1.3 | Corporate Finance across the Life Cycle

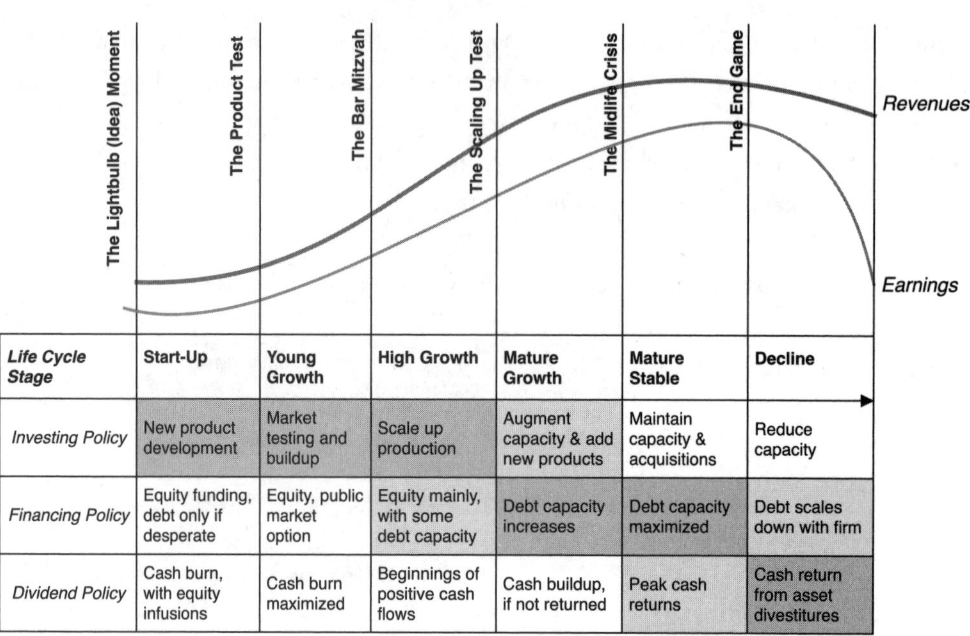

Life Cycle Stage	Start-Up	Young Growth	High Growth	Mature Growth	Mature Stable	Decline
Investing Policy	New product development	Market testing and buildup	Scale up production	Augment capacity & add new products	Maintain capacity & acquisitions	Reduce capacity
Financing Policy	Equity funding, debt only if desperate	Equity, public market option	Equity mainly, with some debt capacity	Debt capacity increases	Debt capacity maximized	Debt scales down with firm
Dividend Policy	Cash burn, with equity infusions	Cash burn maximized	Beginnings of positive cash flows	Cash buildup, if not returned	Peak cash returns	Cash return from asset divestitures

In the third part of the book, I use the corporate life cycle to illustrate the challenges of valuing businesses as they move through the life cycle. With young companies, the biggest barriers are the absence of information on the workings of their business models and the uncertainties about how these models will evolve in the future. With mature companies, the main challenges are an overreliance on past information and the assumption that what worked in the past will continue to work in the future. With declining companies, the key struggle in valuation is the unwillingness to even consider the possibility that, over time, companies can shrink and go out of existence. In response, analysts often concoct shortcuts and turn to pricing companies and the use of pricing metrics, where the scalar changes from users and subscribers (for young companies) to earnings (for mature businesses) to book value (for declining firms).

PREFACE 1.4 | Narratives across the Life Cycle

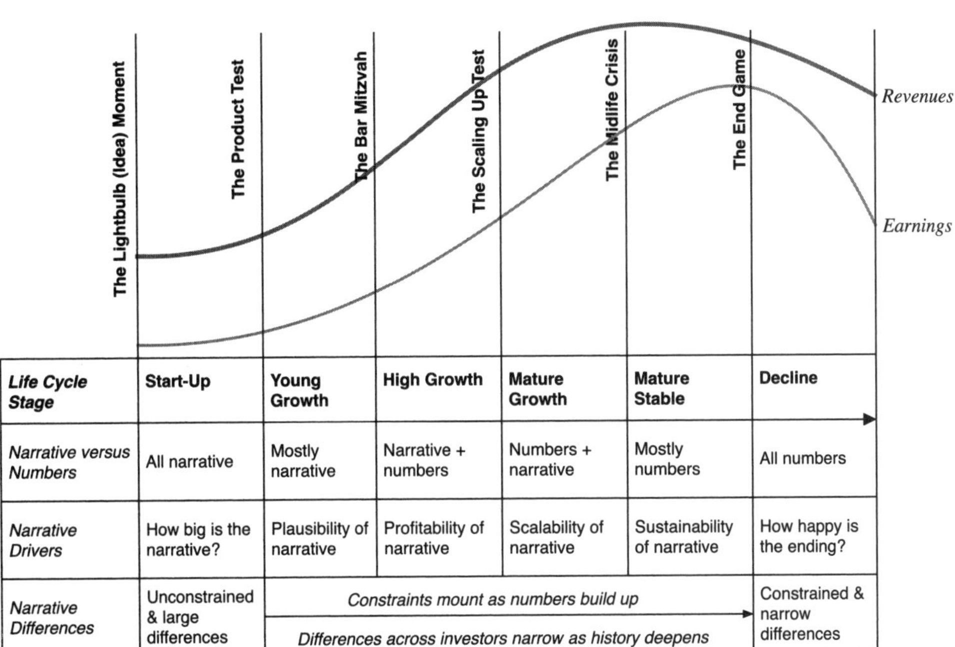

Life Cycle Stage	Start-Up	Young Growth	High Growth	Mature Growth	Mature Stable	Decline
Narrative versus Numbers	All narrative	Mostly narrative	Narrative + numbers	Numbers + narrative	Mostly numbers	All numbers
Narrative Drivers	How big is the narrative?	Plausibility of narrative	Profitability of narrative	Scalability of narrative	Sustainability of narrative	How happy is the ending?
Narrative Differences	Unconstrained & large differences	*Constraints mount as numbers build up* / *Differences across investors narrow as history deepens*				Constrained & narrow differences

In the book's fourth part, the corporate life cycle comes into play in explaining differences in investment philosophies and, in particular, the divide between growth and value investing. Value investing—at least in the form in which it is practiced today, with an emphasis on earnings and book value—will lead its followers to mature companies, while growth investing's focus will be on companies earlier in the life cycle. In fact, the life cycle provides caveats for each group regarding the risks in their respective philosophies. Growth investors risk overpaying for what they perceive as young-growth companies just before they transition to middle age, and value investors are in danger of pumping money into mature companies as they shift into decline.

In the fifth part of the book, I look at insights and extensions for managers that can come out of the corporate life cycle. I first explore what makes for a great manager and argue that the one-size-fits-all narrative of management does not work, since the skill sets needed to run a young-growth company are different from those needed in a mature company. I also look at the dreams of rebirth and reincarnation that excite managers at mature companies, and the lessons that can be learned from the few companies that have succeeded in such endeavors and the many that have failed. Finally, I examine how the shift away from manufacturing and toward technology in the global economy has altered and shortened corporate life cycles, and why much of what we accept as good business practice has not kept up with these changes.

THE CORPORATE LIFE CYCLE

The Search for a Unifying Theory

IT IS THE DREAM of many researchers and practitioners, whatever their field of study, to come up with a construct that explains all observed behavior and a template for forecasting future behavior. In the physical sciences, that search is abetted by nature, which imposes its order on observed phenomena, allowing for cleaner tests of any theory. In the social sciences, the search has been less focused, partly because human behavior does not always follow predictable patterns.

It is easy to understand why we search for universal theories that explain everything, since they offer the promise of restoring order to chaos, but that search comes with risk. The most significant risk is overreach: sensible theories get pushed to their breaking point and beyond in order to explain phenomena that they were never meant to cover. Once a theory becomes prevailing wisdom in a discipline, the temptation to use it to explain everything becomes overwhelming.

The second significant risk is bias, which takes shape as a theory's most ardent supporters become selective in their assessment of evidence, choosing to see only what they want to in the data, focusing on supportive evidence and denying evidence that contradicts their theory. Eventually, if a theory has weak links or is wrong, the weight of data or evidence contradicting it will lead to its modification or abandonment—but not before its pursuit by single-minded supporters creates damage.

The Search in Finance and Investing

Economics is a social science, but what sets it apart from the other social sciences is the easy access that its theorists have to rich economic data and, especially, market data. Researchers and many practitioners have tried, over time, to come up with economic theories or models that explain everything from how businesses make investments to financing and dividend decisions and how investors price companies. In this section, I will lay out some of the attempts over the last seventy years to build an overarching theory of finance—and explain why they have all fallen short.

Economic Theories

To the extent that finance is an offshoot of economics, it stands to reason that many of the early theories in finance came from economics, with economists' work on risk aversion and utility functions animating the search for financial theories that would explain market pricing and investor return. It can be argued that modern finance had its beginnings when Harry Markowitz, with an assist from the field of statistics, put forth his work on modern portfolio theory.* In effect, Markowitz drew on the law of large numbers to argue that investing across multiple risky assets that do not move together yields better return payoffs, for any given level of risk, than investing in an individual asset. The Markowitz efficient frontier provided an elegant way of compressing the investment process into a search for higher returns, with risk operating as a constraint.

* "Harry M. Markowitz Biographical," The Nobel Prize, accessed October 18, 2023, https://www.nobelprize.org/prizes/economic-sciences/1990/markowitz/biographical.

FIGURE 1.1 | The Markowitz Efficient Portfolio

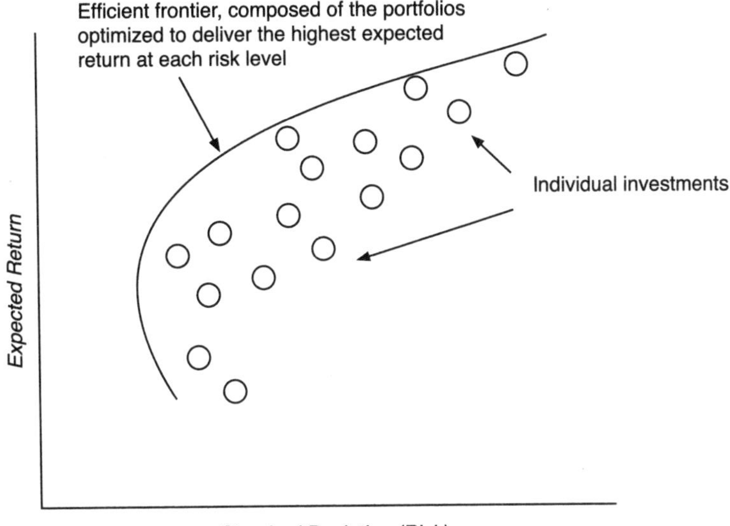

The power of Markowitz's theory went well beyond the optimized portfolios that it could be used to generate, since it upended the very notion of risk in markets, supplanting the old idea that investors should assess risk on an investment on a stand-alone basis with the idea that the risk of an individual investment comes from the risk it adds to a portfolio of investments.

By introducing a riskless asset into the Markowitz universe, John Lintner and William F. Sharpe changed and simplified the efficient frontier. They showed that for all investors, no matter their level of risk aversion, a combination of a riskless asset and a supremely diversified portfolio (labeled the *market portfolio* because it includes every traded asset in the market), held in proportion to each asset's market value, would generate a better risk/return trade-off than any portfolio composed purely of risky investments.

Figure 1.2 illustrates the effect.

FIGURE 1.2 | The Capital Asset Pricing Model

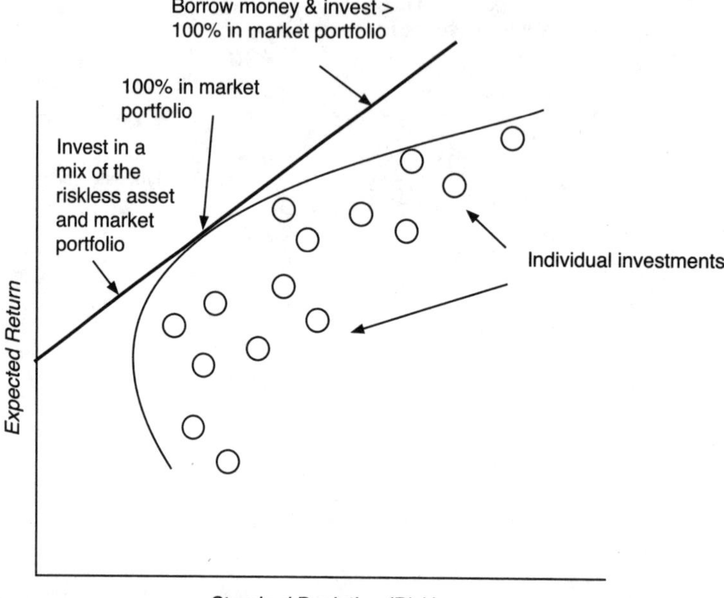

Lintner and Sharpe's capital asset pricing model ("the CAPM," as finance geeks refer to it) also had a reach that well exceeded the core application, since it allowed for a linear equation that could be used to both explain past returns and predict future ones on risky assets:

$$E(\text{Return on Investment}_j) = \text{Risk-free Rate} + \text{Beta}_i$$
$$(\text{Expected Return on the Market Portfolio} - \text{Risk-free Rate})$$

The reach of this equation, extending from businesses using it to determine their hurdle rates (for accepting or rejecting investments) to investors using it to estimate the expected returns on individual stocks and portfolios, made it one of the most widely used and studied economic models in history. Those studies, though, uncovered a painful truth: the model lacked predictive power with regard to large segments of the market.

The benefit of the grounding in theory that characterizes theory-based models—wherein you start with economic first principles and build up to models—is that the development process constrains you from fitting the data that you observe to preconceptions that you may have about how the world operates. The drawback of these models is that for them to be useful, you have to make simplifying assumptions about human behavior (ranging from how human beings derive utility to what comprises rationality), and to the extent that these assumptions are erroneous, you will end up with models that are elegant in theory but have little real-world explanatory power.

Data-Driven Models/Theories

Just as the Markowitz portfolio theory and the capital asset pricing model were being advanced as offering answers to all finance-related questions, a group of researchers centered at the University of Chicago were advancing a different approach, grounded in the belief that markets were efficient and that market prices were therefore the ultimate signals of truth. In the efficient-market world, the market response provides the tiebreaking answer to the question of whether a business decision was good or bad, with good decisions provoking positive market reactions and bad decisions resulting in negative ones. The efficient-market view of active investing, wherein investors attempt to time markets and pick the best stocks, was that it was pointless, since market prices already reflected all available information.[*]

With an abundance of data (at both market- and company-level) that has been easy to access for decades, you could argue that finance discovered big data well before the rest of the world caught on to its allure. In fact, the first model to seriously challenge the capital asset pricing model was the arbitrage pricing model, in which researchers using observed data on asset prices and related expected returns to statistical (and unnamed) factors.[†] In effect, in the arbitrage pricing model, you assume that if risky assets are priced in the market to prevent riskless profits (arbitrage), you can back out the risk factors from the pricing. These data-driven pricing attempts, which began in the late 1970s, picked up steam in the following years as access to macro- and microeconomic data widened and deepened, resulting in factor pricing models.

In 1992, Eugene Fama and Kenneth French looked at returns on all US stocks between 1962 and 1990 and noted that a significant portion of the variation in annual returns across stocks during this period could be explained by two characteristics: their market capitalizations and their book-to-market equity ratios.[‡] Specifically, they found that small-market-cap and high book-to-market (low price-to-book) stocks earned higher

[*] E. F. Fama, "Efficient Capital Markets: A Review of Theory and Empirical Work," *Journal of Finance* 25, no. 2 (May 1970): 383–417.

[†] S. A. Ross, "The Arbitrage Theory of Capital Asset Pricing," *Journal of Economic Theory* 13, no. 3 (December 1976): 341–60.

[‡] E. F. Fama and K.R. French, "The Cross-Section of Expected Stock Returns," *Journal of Finance* 47, no. 2 (June 1992): 427–65.

annual returns than large-market-cap and low book-to-market (high price-to-book stocks. They attributed the higher returns to the risks in small-market-cap and low price-to-book stocks.

In the years since, with access to more and richer data, researchers have added to the list of characteristics that explain differences in market returns, in what can broadly be categorized as factor pricing models. By 2019, there were more than 400 factors that had been identified as explaining price movements and differences in returns in major finance journals, leading some researchers to talk of a "factor zoo" and argue that most of these "market-explaining" factors are more attributable to data mining than to market behavior.*

While academics were attracted to data-driven pricing models because of their capacity to explain investor and market behavior, practitioners were drawn to these models for a much more prosaic reason: to the extent that these models can uncover market mispricing, they offer the potential for profits to those who can find those market mistakes and benefit from their correction. Jim Simons was an early adopter, and his mathematical and statistical skills allowed him to earn market-beating returns for decades.†

In more recent years, quantitative investing has drawn more players into this game and, with powerful computing added to the mix, driven down the returns available from using data to find investment opportunities. Put simply, using powerful computers to find moneymaking opportunities, as high-frequency traders did in the early part of the last decade, comes with a countdown clock for that profit making as new investors enter the market with their own computing power.

Data-driven pricing models do have an advantage over theoretical models in their capacity to explain observed behavior, but you can argue that this is an unfair test, since a data-driven model preserves the ability to add more or different variables to improve explanatory power, unconstrained by theory or even the need to provide an economic rationale for the presence of a factor. Having worked with data, and speaking as a believer in data, I understand how easy it is to manipulate data to yield the results that you would like to see, especially if you have strong priors. Put simply, access to data has proven to be a mixed blessing in finance and investing, yielding powerful results that emerge from some data analysis mixed with a great deal of sophistry that merely claims to be data driven.

* C. R. Harvey, Y. Liu, and C. H. Zhu, ". . . And the Cross-Section of Expected Returns," *Review of Financial Studies* 29, no. 1 (January 2016): 5–68.

† G. Zuckerman, *The Man Who Solved the Market: How Jim Simons Launched the Quant Revolution* (New York: Portfolio, 2019).

Behavioral Models

The failures and limitations of theory-based models, which gave rise to the data-driven models that I described in the last section, also initiated a very different movement, rooted in psychology, that has now become rich and deep enough to occupy that space called behavioral finance, a melding of psychology with finance. In the 1970s, Daniel Kahneman and Amos Tversky initiated this trend by incorporating well-established patterns in human behavior into the study of markets to provide explanations for phenomena and behavior that previously had been either deemed unexplainable or treated as anomalous.* Using their psychological insights, they proposed a new theory to explain decision-making in business and investing, called prospect theory, which conjectures that people underweigh outcomes that are probable and overweigh outcomes that are certain, leading to risk aversion in choices involving sure gains and risk seeking in choices involving sure losses.

In the decades since, behavioral finance has found its way to the heart of finance thinking, with Richard Thaler, Robert Shiller, and a host of others extending its reach to explain business and investor decision-making. Thaler adopted the idea of "bounded rationality" and extended Kahneman and Tversky's work into the pricing of assets; he also developed the theory of mental accounting, wherein people categorize money into groupings based upon the source and intended use of the money and then use different decision-making criteria for how to spend the money in each grouping. Shiller's initial work showed that stock price volatility over time could not be explained solely by fundamentals and formed the basis for his belief that there are market bubbles that can be explained by "animal spirits."†

Behavioral finance, in its weaving together of psychology and finance, is a lot more fun and more easily accessible to many investors entering the financial markets for the first time than other theories. Because it starts with a basic recognition of how humans behave and misbehave, it is grounded in reality. However, for much of its existence—albeit with exceptions—behavioral finance has had two problems. The first is that it has expended more resources in explaining past investor and business behavior than in providing prescriptive solutions for either group. The second is that as with data-driven approaches, in which data mining has led to a proliferation of conjectured market-explaining

* A. Tversky and D. Kahneman, "Judgment under Uncertainty: Heuristics and Biases," *Science* 185, no. 4157 (September 27, 1974): 1124–31.

† G. A. Akerlof and R. J. Shiller, *Animal Spirits: How Human Psychology Drives the Economy, and Why It Matters for Global Capitalism* (Princeton, NJ: Princeton University Press, 2009).

factors, the number of behavioral quirks that have been "identified" in investing and decision-making has expanded to a point where almost every action has a behavioral explanation, no matter how outlandish.

Summing Up

In sum, none of the three broad approaches (theory, data, or behavioral) that have heretofore been used in finance provides a comprehensive pathway to explaining market behavior, but each offers promise with regard to some aspect of it. One solution is to use an amalgam of these approaches where you start with theory, while being open about its limits, then test and retest with the data, and finally overlay this research with the behavioral quirks that we have learned investors exhibit to explain deviations in the results. That being said, the search for a unifying theory will not stop as a new generation of researchers enters the discipline, armed with ever more data and more powerful tools than previous generations.

The Corporate Life Cycle

I am not well-versed enough in the theory, or savvy enough with data science and psychology, to come up with a universal theory of my own to explain everything that happens in business and markets. Instead, I will borrow the notion of a corporate life cycle—a construct that has been researched and used extensively, albeit more in management/strategy than in finance—and argue that while it is neither new nor the answer to all questions in finance, it has a surprisingly comprehensive explanatory power.

The Life Cycle

The corporate life cycle is a concept that has been talked and written about for decades in management and strategy circles. Ichak Adizes, a management expert, developed a ten-stage model, depicted in figure 1.3, to describe the corporate life cycle and used it as the basis for an institute founded to advance his ideas, as well as a book on the concept.*

* I. Adizes, *Managing Corporate Lifecycles* (New York: Prentice Hall Press, 1999).

FIGURE 1.3 | The Adizes Corporate Life Cycle

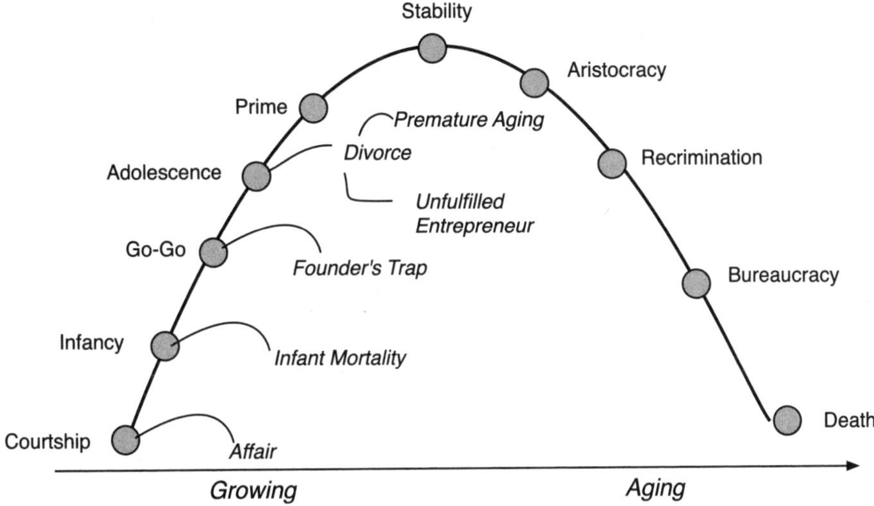

The focus in the Adizes life cycle was more on management and the strategic choices that companies must make at each stage. The financial questions were posed with the view that aging was not easily reversible but that, with superior management, it could be done. Even within management research, there seems to be no consensus on the number of stages in the corporate life cycle and the process by which companies age. In a 1984 paper, Danny Miller and Peter H. Friesen present the corporate life cycle as comprising five common stages: birth, growth, maturity, revival, and decline. This assessment is based upon a small sample population of 36 firms that they studied through 161 time periods. They concluded that the path and timing of the life cycle vary widely across companies.*

In finance, the corporate life cycle has been used more sparingly, often to explain an aspect of corporate or investor decision-making. Accounting researchers, for instance, have used the corporate life cycle to explain how accounting ratios measuring leverage and profitability change over time. They have used that evidence to provide metrics that determine where a company is in its life cycle. Corporate governance researchers have found evidence that corporate governance challenges are greater for young firms and that governance practices improve as they mature.

In valuation, I have used the corporate life cycle construct to examine why the challenges of valuation can be different for companies at different stages, and how to adapt

* D. Miller and P. H. Friesen, "A Longitudinal Study of the Corporate Life Cycle," *Management Science* 30, no. 10 (October 1984): 1161–83.

valuation models to meet these challenges.* In finance, the research is scant and has primarily been focused on how corporate financial decisions regarding investing, financing, and paying dividends vary across the life cycle.

A Standardized Version of the Life Cycle

Given the prior work across disciplines on the corporate life cycle, you may wonder what is new that I will be bringing into this book. I will draw on the research and existing literature to get started, but as I hope to show, I will use these ideas not only to dig deeper into corporate financial decisions across the life cycle but also to examine how the challenges in valuing a company can vary across its life cycle and how different investment philosophies (value investing, growth investing, information trading) can be tied to corporate life cycles.

Note that the six-phase breakdown depicted on page x is intended more to provide common structure than it is to make assertions about the number of phases in the life cycle. You may very well decide that there are five, eight, or ten stages to the life cycle instead. In fact, assigning more or fewer phases to the life cycle will have almost no effect on the conclusions that I will draw in subsequent chapters.

While I will use chapter 2 to flesh out each phase in the life cycle, here is a short summary of the core focus of each life cycle phase. In the *start-up phase*, a founder or founders have an idea for a product that they believe will meet a need in the market and attempt to turn that idea into a product. Assuming they succeed in that attempt—and many start-ups will not—the *young-growth phase* requires the creation of a business model that converts the product or service into a business, one that generates revenues and offers at least a pathway to profits in the future. For the subset of nascent companies that manage to create business models, the *scaling up or high-growth phase* is when they try to take their small business and make it larger, within the bounds of founder ambition, capital constraints, and the size of the market that their product serves. Once a company has scaled up, maintaining growth rates becomes more difficult, but companies in *mature growth* can still find ways to grow by identifying new markets for existing products or creating new products. Eventually, though, growth will fade as companies enter the *mature stable* phase, and their focus must change to playing defense as competitors and dis-

* A. Damodaran, *The Dark Side of Valuation: Valuing Young, Distressed, and Complex Businesses* (New York: Pearson FT Press, 2018).

ruptors come after their established products, especially if they are very profitable. The final phase of the life cycle is *decline*, wherein companies find revenues and margins shrinking under pressure, as their once-lucrative markets decline.

As you read this section, I am sure that you will have questions about or quibbles with this framework. For instance, how do you deal with firms that find ways (or seem to find ways) to reverse aging, allowing them to go back to being growth firms, as was the case with Apple in 2000 or Microsoft in 2013? Why do some firms (GE, GM) take decades to grow from start-up to mature, whereas others (Facebook, Google) make the transition at hyper speed? How do you explain family-owned businesses that have lasted for not just decades but centuries, generating steady growth and profits? In chapter 3, I will look at the factors that determine how quickly the life cycle unfolds for companies, how long they endure as mature companies, and how quickly they decline.

Since each phase often brings very different challenges to businesses, and there are transitions that companies must make successfully to deal with these differences, I will spend chapter 4 talking about transitions from one phase of the life cycle to the next, looking at both operating and financial transitions. As part of the latter, I will look at venture capital financing, often the pathway that start-ups use to become young-growth companies; initial public offerings, an exit choice available to some of the more successful young-growth companies; and changes in the structure and practices in both, especially in the last few decades. I will also look at buyouts—the means by which some public companies, usually later in the life cycle, are targeted by private equity investors to go private—and the motivations behind them.

Implications

The corporate life cycle is fascinating on its own, but it becomes even more so when used to explain how companies behave at different stages of the life cycle (corporate finance), how value drivers and valuation challenges vary across the life cycle (valuation), and how different investment philosophies can each claim the mantle of maximizing returns for investors despite their divergent approaches.

IN CORPORATE FINANCE

Corporate finance lays out the financial first principles that govern how to run a business, and every decision that a business makes falls under its purview. I break down these business decisions into three groups: *investment decisions*, which determine the assets or projects that a business chooses to invest in; *financing decisions*, which cover how a business raises funds (the mix of debt and equity and the type of financing used) to finance these investments; and *dividend decisions*, which determine how much cash a business returns to owners and in what form. If you are unfamiliar with corporate finance, chapter 5 provides an introduction, laying out the first principles of investing, financing, and dividends, as well as the core tools and processes I use to put them into practice.

In chapter 6, I look at investment decisions in more detail across the life cycle, examining how investment types and investment challenges vary as companies age and, as they vary, how businesses must adapt their investment techniques and decision-making rules. In chapter 7, I begin by looking at the trade-off that determines how much a business should borrow and then use that trade-off to make judgments on how the mix and type of financing changes (or should change) as companies go from growth to mature status. In chapter 8, I describe the process that can be used to determine how much cash a business can return, and then apply it to evaluate how much cash (if any) a business *should* return, given its place in the life cycle. In each of these chapters, I will also examine the consequences for businesses that choose to adopt corporate financial policies that are at odds with their age.

IN VALUATION

The value of a business is always a function of the expected cash flows investors will receive from the business and the uncertainty that they will actually receive those cash flows. That universal truth, though, can play out very differently across the life cycle. At young companies, where business models are still unformed and reinvesting for growth is paramount, expected cash flows will often be negative, at least in the near term, with substantial uncertainty not just about the level of cash flows but also about a company's survival. At more mature companies, cash flows can be positive and more predictable, but with concerns about disruption and competition affecting value. At declining companies, not only can declining revenues and shrinking margins cause expected cash flows to decline, but if the company has significant debt, even those reduced cash flows come with a chance of distress and even bankruptcy.

In chapter 9, I begin by looking at the basics of valuation, structuring a simple valuation framework to illustrate how cash flows and how growth and risk come together in the value of a business, and then follow up by contrasting this process with the basics of pricing, estimating how much to pay for a business based upon what investors are paying for similar businesses. I use these valuation and pricing principles to examine the challenges in valuing and pricing start-ups and young companies in chapter 10, high-growth companies in chapter 11, mature companies in chapter 12, and declining companies in chapter 13. As I go through these chapters and look at very different types of firms, you will notice that rather than invent new models and metrics, I use the same models and instead make my adjustments to what inputs I spend my time estimating, as well as adapt the estimation process to reflect the challenges of each life cycle stage.

IN INVESTING

Investors invest in stocks because they want to earn high returns on their investments, while protecting, as best as they can, against downside risks. That is perhaps the only thing they have in common, since investors come in with very different views on how markets work (or fail to work), leading them to target very different types of stocks in their portfolio. Classic value investors, weaned on Ben Graham's security analysis and Warren Buffett's investing nostrums, seek out companies with stable earnings, solid growth, and defensible moats. Growth investors make their bets on growth companies and on the presumption that markets are underestimating growth rates at some of these companies. Information traders try to make their money around earnings and news reports, hoping to take advantage of either their superior forecasting power or post-announcement analysis over- or underreactions. Pure traders make their money on mood and momentum, riding momentum up or down and exiting before the momentum shifts. Each of these groups claims the market high ground, purporting to have found the "right" way to invest, yet only a few players within each group emerge as consistent winners. In chapter 14, I look at these contrasting investment philosophies, with details on the assumptions, sometimes explicit and mostly implicit, that investors following each philosophy make.

At first sight, there may not seem to be a connection between these very different investment philosophies and the corporate life cycle, but in chapter 15, I look at how growth investing, both in private (venture capital) and public markets, is a play on young-growth companies and represent bets on building business models and scaling up. In chapter 16, I tie value investing to the mature phase of the life cycle; break it down into its many forms, from passive screening for cheap stocks to contrarian investing plays; and present again the ingredients for success and the potential dangers. In chapter 17, I conclude with an assessment of what it takes to win when investing or trading in declining and distressed companies. In the process, I hope to show why no one investment philosophy can claim to be the "best" one, since each one requires a different mindset and skills to be successful, as well as how your choice of investment philosophy will lead you to target firms in very different phases of the life cycle.

IN MANAGEMENT

Businesses are run by people, and I have long debated the question of what characteristics we should want to see in the top management of a business. While there is a tendency in both academia and practice to assume that there is one prototype for a great CEO, the corporate life cycle pushes back. The skills and personality traits you would like to see in the top manager(s) of a growth company will be very different from those you would look for in the top manager(s) of a mature or declining company. In chapter 18, I advance this concept by looking at the challenges that managers face at each stage of the life cycle and argue that the skill sets you need in top management will change as companies age. While a few top managers are adaptable enough to change as their businesses change, many are not, and governance challenges will ensue.

In chapter 19 of the book, I start by noting that accepting aging and adapting to it, when making business decisions, usually offers the highest odds of success for managers and owners of business. Then I examine why fighting aging is often the path more frequently taken. I look at both good news stories, of companies that manage to reverse the aging process and become young again, as well as bad news stories, wherein growing, healthy companies collapse, often overnight, and examine the fine line between success and failure. In both cases, I argue that top managers play key roles, positive ones in reincarnations and negative in collapses, and that a host of other factors, as well as luck, also make a difference. In this chapter, I also look at "sustainability," a word that has acquired a great deal of heft in business circles—in both its benign form, in which it reflects actions taken by firms to extend value creation in their growth phases, and its malignant form, in which it turns into "survival at any cost" at declining companies. I close the book by arguing, in chapter 20, that good business management and investing requires serenity, wherein you start by accepting business aging before mapping out ambitious plans to reverse or stall it.

Conclusion

It is undeniable that companies, like human beings, age, and that the challenges they face change as they move through the life cycle. That said, company life cycles are much more variegated than human life cycles and offer chances at reincarnation and rebirth that human beings don't get. As I use the corporate life cycle to illuminate why the focus and mechanics of corporate finance can change as companies age, to examine the drivers and process of valuation in each phase of the life cycle, and to evaluate fit with divergent investment philosophies, I will do so with the understanding that, as with any economic model or theory, it will come with exceptions and variations and sometimes be at odds with the data.

I

The Corporate Life Cycle: Laying the Groundwork

The Basics of the Corporate Life Cycle

IN CHAPTER 1, I introduced the corporate life cycle as a concept that has a long history in management and strategy as a useful device to explain differences across companies in corporate finance focus and practice, in valuation drivers and mechanics, and in ease of fit with different investment philosophies. In this chapter, I will begin the process of expanding on the idea, providing more description of the corporate life cycle and each of its stages, from business birth to death.

The Lead-in

While I did draw on the human life cycle as the basis for a business life cycle, I also noted that the latter has its quirks and differences that deserve attention. To examine these differences, let us start by revisiting the corporate life cycle in figure 2.1, with a focus now on the key tasks that companies face at each stage and the key risks that arise along the way.

FIGURE 2.1 | The Corporate Life Cycle in Phases

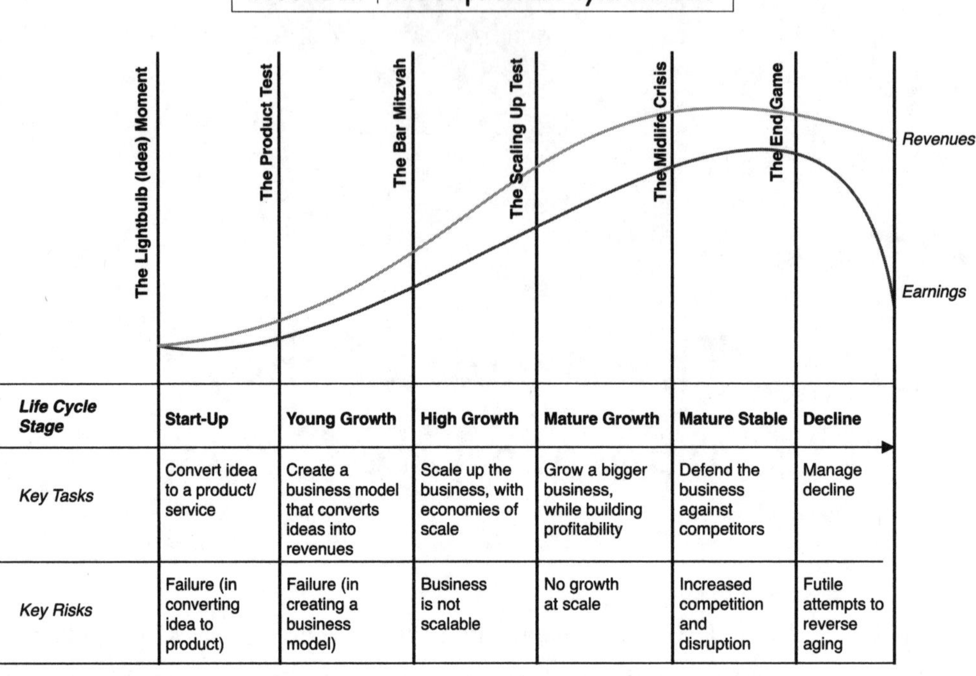

Life Cycle Stage	Start-Up	Young Growth	High Growth	Mature Growth	Mature Stable	Decline
Key Tasks	Convert idea to a product/service	Create a business model that converts ideas into revenues	Scale up the business, with economies of scale	Grow a bigger business, while building profitability	Defend the business against competitors	Manage decline
Key Risks	Failure (in converting idea to product)	Failure (in creating a business model)	Business is not scalable	No growth at scale	Increased competition and disruption	Futile attempts to reverse aging

Filling out the life cycle, as I described it in the first chapter, are six phases.

- The *start-up phase* is the period when, after a business is founded, the founder or founders try to find a way to convert a business idea into a product or service, while simultaneously raising enough capital to keep going.
- During the *young-growth phase*, the start-up works on building a business model to generate revenues and profits from the proposed product or service—with the recognition that such a model may not exist, in which case the business will not survive.
- During the *high-growth phase*, a business works on whether to scale up the revenues and profits from a new product or service and, if it does so, how much scaling can be done, given market size, competition, and capital constraints.
- During *mature growth*, the company continues to grow revenues, albeit at lower rates and on a larger scale, and works on improving profit margins, allowing earnings to grow faster than revenues.
- In *mature stability*, revenue growth will start to drop toward the growth rate of the economy, and margins will level off as the company finds some degree of constancy.

- In *decline and distress*, a company faces a combination of stagnant or shrinking revenues and profit margins under pressure, which, if accompanied by debt, will put the company into distress.

In the sections to follow, I will look at each phase, providing more detail on the business and financial challenges that companies face in that phase, while also keeping an eye on how ownership structures change as businesses age.

Phase 1: Start-up

A business is born when a person (or persons) perceives a market need that can be filled with a product or service. In many cases, this unfulfilled need exists only in the imagination of the business founder. Even if the need exists, the planned product or service may not meet the need, which explains why most business ideas are stillborn, in life cycle terms. For the few that survive this scrutiny, converting the idea into a product or service still poses logistical, capital, and management challenges.

The Numbers

The place to start a discussion of start-ups is with the numbers, by looking at how many businesses are started up each year and their industry and geographic breakdown. It is estimated that in 2021, there were 5.4 million applications to start new businesses in the United States, according to the US Census Bureau. Figure 2.2 summarizes the number of new business applications each year, as well as high-propensity applications—those to which the Census Bureau attaches a higher probability, based upon hiring and other observable variables, that an application will lead to a new business.

FIGURE 2.2 | Applications for New Businesses Filed with Census Bureau, 2005–2021

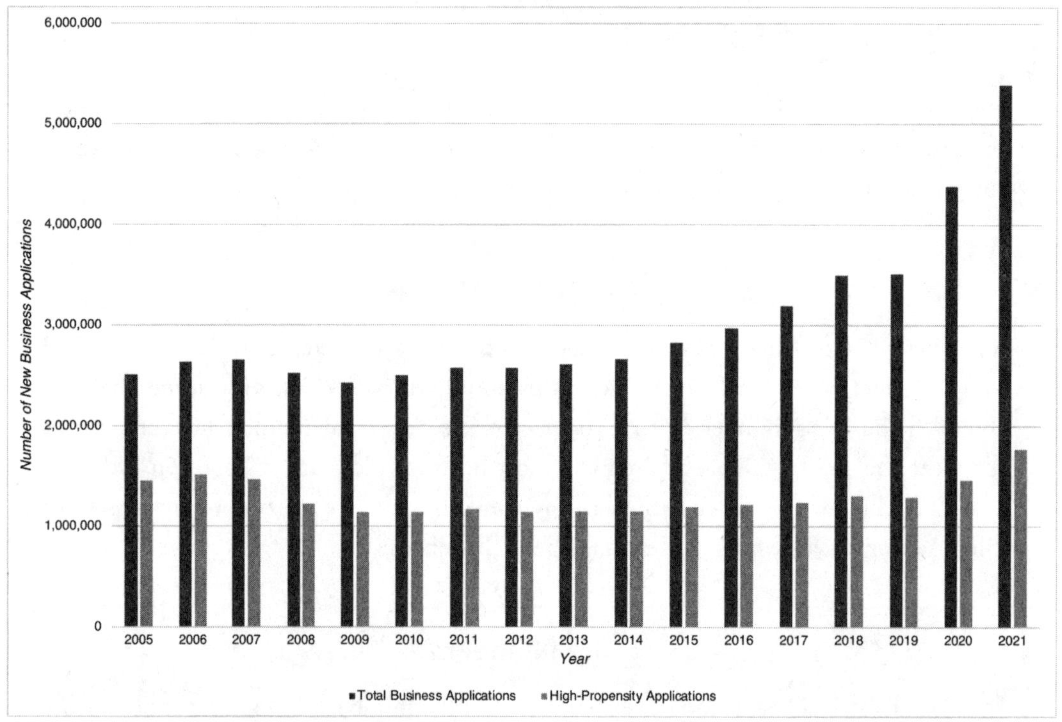

Note that many of these applications are for short-term, finite-life businesses, such as construction projects or delivering on government contracts, but the Census Bureau also keeps track of the number of applications by business grouping, and that data is summarized in figure 2.3.

FIGURE 2.3 | **New Business Applications by Industry Grouping, 2005–2021**

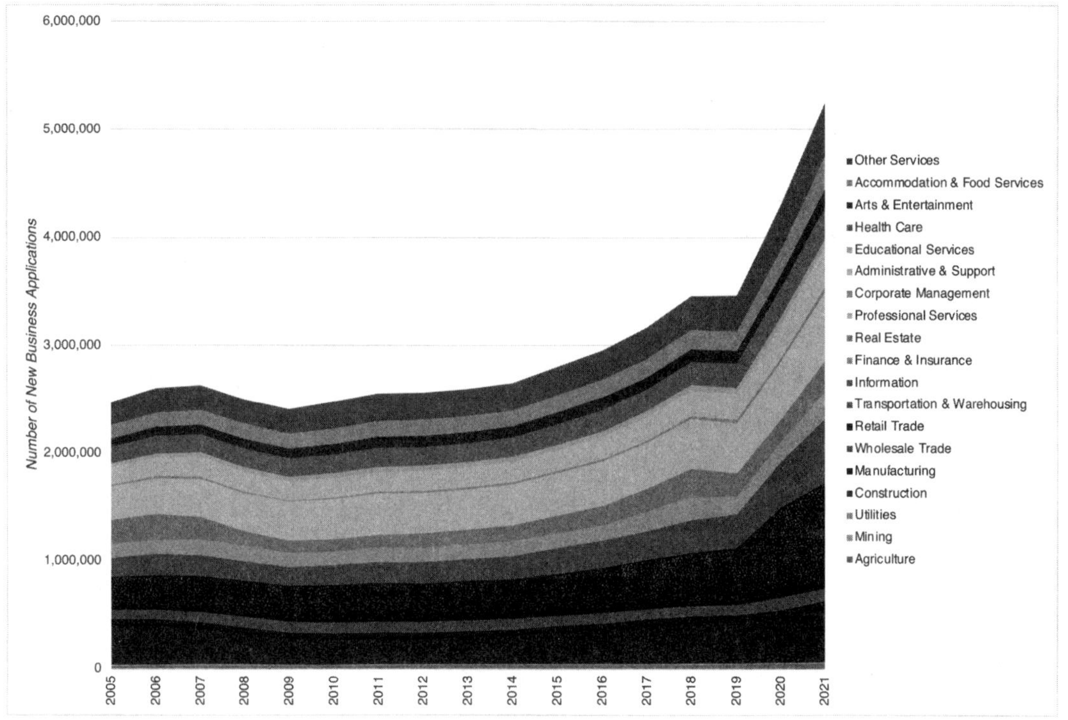

Source: US Census Bureau

You can see the surge in business applications between 2019 and 2021 and the diverse set of new businesses started in the United States. It is clear, from the sheer number, that many of these applications never became businesses or, even if they did, the founders had limited ambitions regarding how long the business would run and how big they expected it to get.

Using a narrower measure of start-ups—include only those that are incorporated and capitalized—the US continues to lead in number of start-ups, but there are signs of growth around the world. For instance, the number of start-ups, by country, in 2021 can be seen in figure 2.4.

FIGURE 2.4 | Number of Start-ups, by Country, 2021

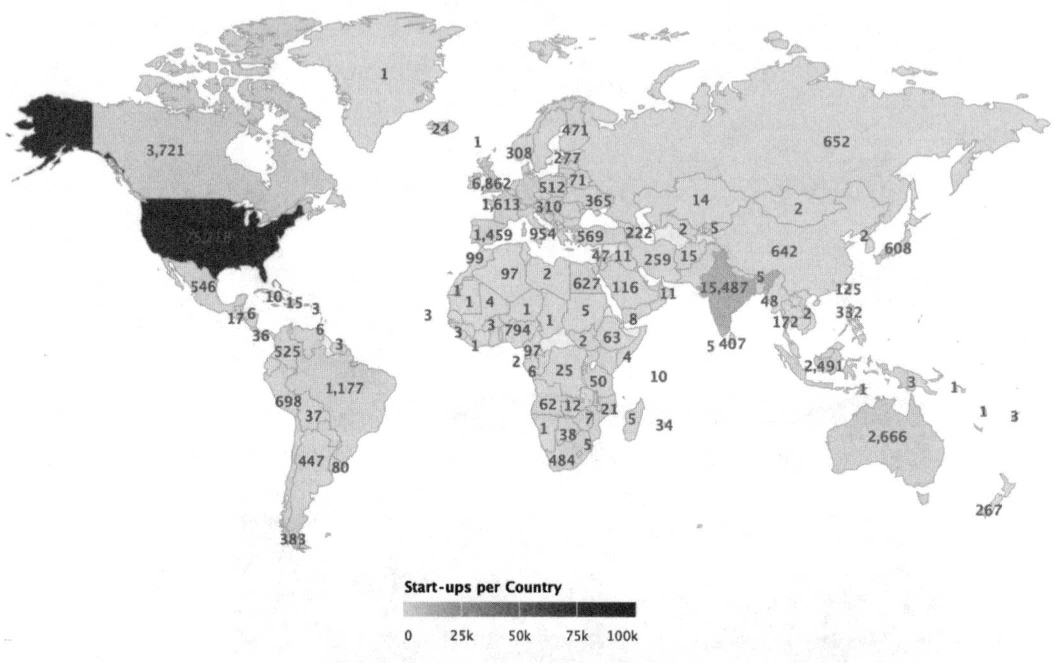

In 2021, the US had the most start-ups, at 75,218; followed by India, with 15,487 start-ups; the United Kingdom, with 6,682; Canada, with 3,721; and Australia, with 2,666. Given their weight in the global economy, Europe, China, and Japan lag in terms of new start-ups.

The Founder Effect

Businesses reflect both the strengths and weaknesses of those running them, and this is particularly true for start-ups and young-growth companies, where the founders are working on converting ideas into products and nascent business models. But there are some factors that seem to separate those (few) founders who succeed from the many who do not.

- **Age:** While it is conventional wisdom that those who found businesses are generally young, an article in the *Harvard Business Review* concluded that the average age of a successful business founder is 45, though there are wide variations (see figure 2.5).* In short, the conventional wisdom that if you are in your thirties, you have already missed your best chance to start a business is false, with a surprisingly high number of the most successful start-ups having founders who are in their fifties or even sixties.

FIGURE 2.5 | Age of Start-up Founders

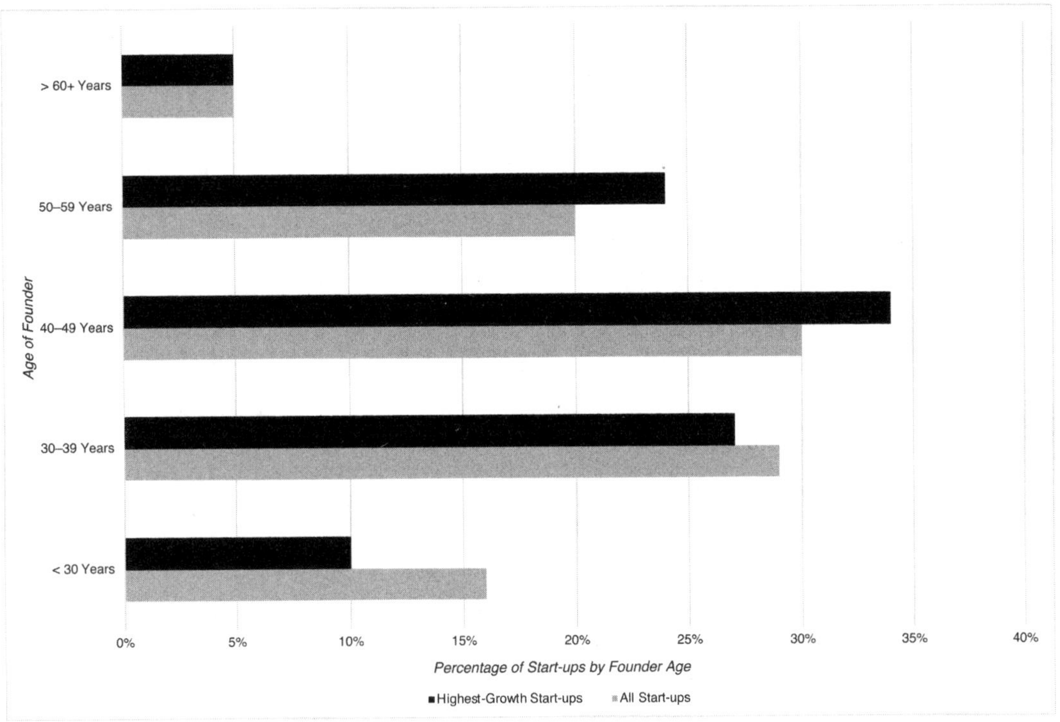

- **Personality traits:** There are some personality traits that successful founders seem to share, with the strongest ones being a higher tolerance toward risk-taking and greater self-confidence, perhaps even bordering on overconfidence. That overconfidence operates as a double-edged sword, with the positive being that it allows founders to

* P. Azoulay, B. F. Jones, J. D. Kim, and J. Miranda, "Research: The Average Age of a Successful Startup Founder Is 45," *Harvard Business Review*, July 11, 2018, https://hbr.org/2018/07/research-the-average-age-of-a-successful-startup-founder-is-45.

power through the failures that are an inevitable part of starting a business and the negative manifesting as a stubborn unwillingness to let go of a bad idea.

A review study that looked at the psychology of entrepreneurs lists what researchers have found as shared characteristics, both in entrepreneurs collectively and in those who succeed, and there seems to be little consensus.* The study does note that there are large differences in entrepreneurial makeup across countries, which it suggests may be due to cultural factors.

The Business Challenge

At inception, as businesses struggle to convert ideas into marketable products or services, the operating focus, not surprisingly, is entirely on this conversion process. That conversion will require experimentation in product design and test marketing, as well as assessing how much (if any amount) customers are willing to pay. Given all these uncertainties, it should come as no surprise that most start-ups don't even make it to the product stage. This high failure rate can be seen in another interesting data series maintained in the United States by the Bureau of Labor Statistics, which tracks survival rates for US start-ups in cumulative and marginal terms. Figure 2.6 reports on the survival rate of the 2006 cohort of start-ups over the subsequent 15 years.

* M. Frese and M. M. Gelnick, "The Psychology of Entrepreneurship," *Annual Review of Organizational Pyschology and Organizational Behavior* 1 (March 2014): 413–38.

FIGURE 2.6 | Failure Rate for Businesses over Time

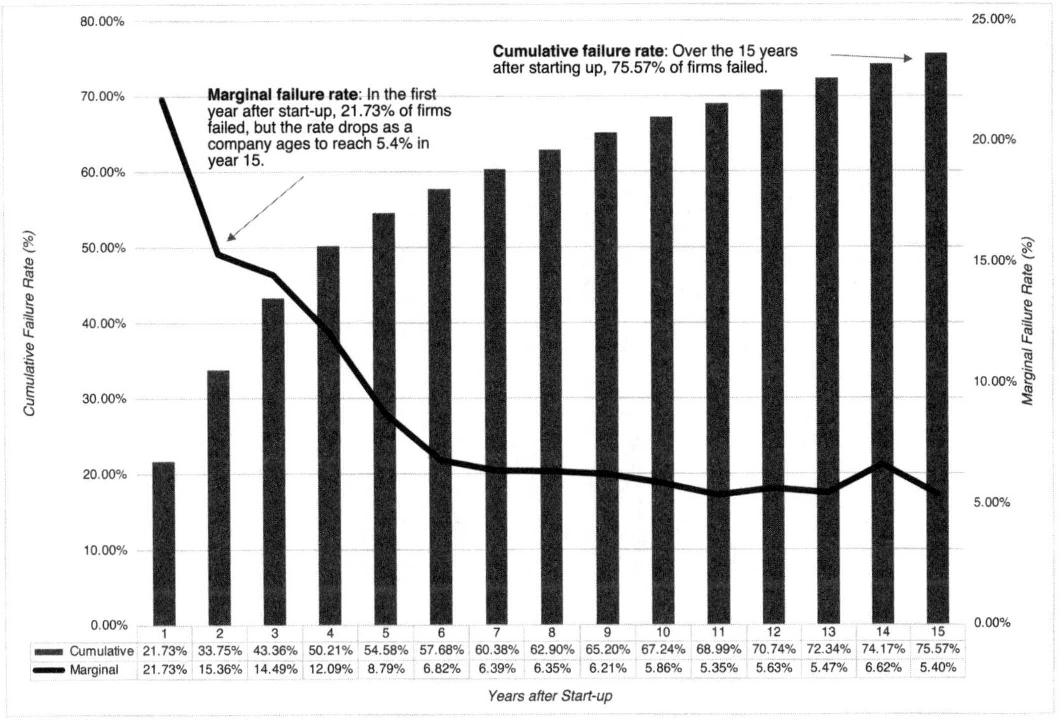

	1	2	3	4	5	6	7	8	9	10	11	12	13	14	15
Cumulative	21.73%	33.75%	43.36%	50.21%	54.58%	57.68%	60.38%	62.90%	65.20%	67.24%	68.99%	70.74%	72.34%	74.17%	75.57%
Marginal	21.73%	15.36%	14.49%	12.09%	8.79%	6.82%	6.39%	6.35%	6.21%	5.86%	5.35%	5.63%	5.47%	6.62%	5.40%

Source: Bureau of Labor Statistics

Note that about 22% of all start-ups don't make it through year 1, and almost 76% fail before year 15. The failure rate decreases, though, as businesses age, dropping to 5.4% for firms in their fifteenth year of operation.

The bureau also breaks down the failure rate by sector, and while the failure rate decreases with company age in all sectors, it remains much higher in some sectors than in others, as can be seen in figure 2.7.

FIGURE 2.7 | Failure Rates by Sector

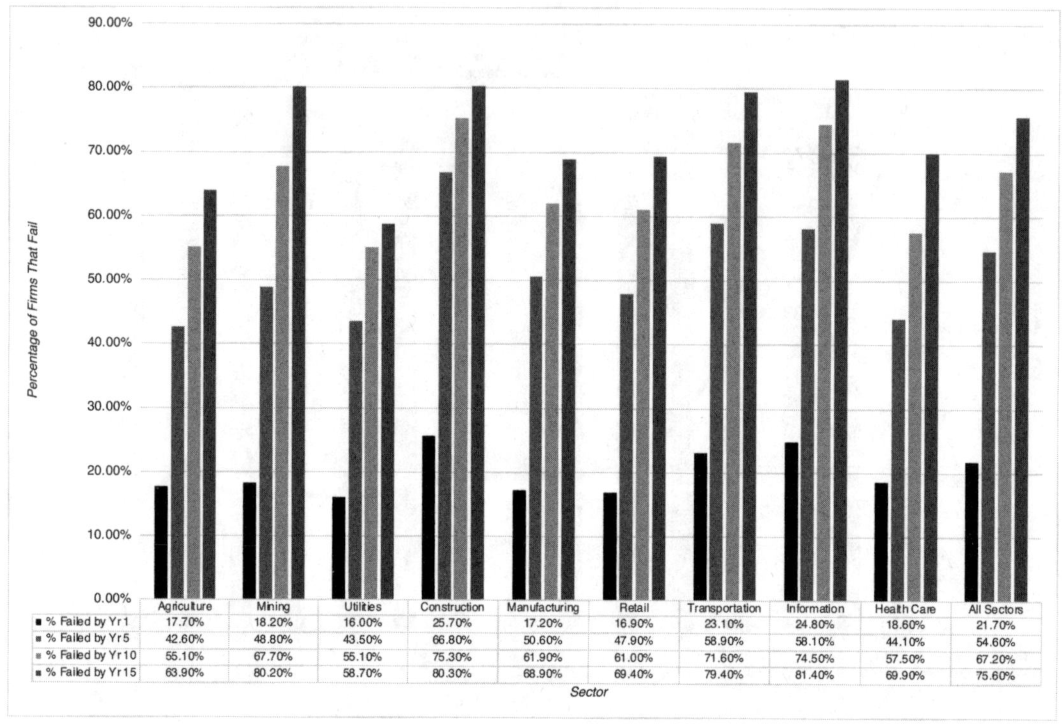

	Agriculture	Mining	Utilities	Construction	Manufacturing	Retail	Transportation	Information	Health Care	All Sectors
% Failed by Yr1	17.70%	18.20%	16.00%	25.70%	17.20%	16.90%	23.10%	24.80%	18.60%	21.70%
% Failed by Yr5	42.60%	48.80%	43.50%	66.80%	50.60%	47.90%	58.90%	58.10%	44.10%	54.60%
% Failed by Yr10	55.10%	67.70%	55.10%	75.30%	61.90%	61.00%	71.60%	74.50%	57.50%	67.20%
% Failed by Yr15	63.90%	80.20%	58.70%	80.30%	68.90%	69.40%	79.40%	81.40%	69.90%	75.60%

Source: Bureau of Labor Statistics

In the 2006 cohort, the failure rate exceeded 80% in information and construction but was less than 60% in utilities, with the overall failure rate exceeding 75% for all firms in the cohort.

The Financial Picture

Early on, absent revenues and faced with large and rising expenses in payroll, product development, and R&D, young companies will not only lose money, they will burn through cash. Start-ups and pre-revenue companies are destined to lose money, with the extent of their losses being driven by two variables. The first is market potential, with companies that see more potential being more willing to lose more money while they try to convert ideas to products. The second is founder ambition, with more ambition translating into bigger dreams, larger costs, and greater losses.

Put simply, judging a start-up by how much money it is losing or how negative its cash flows are can give you a skewed vision of the company. That said, you do want to judge whether companies are spending money on the right priorities, and at this stage in the process, the key priority *must* be converting ideas into products and services. Start-ups that get ahead of themselves, by renting upscale office space or hiring salespeople ahead of product development, can be cash-burning machines.

The Capital and Ownership Challenges

Unless founders have deep pockets, family backing, or wealthy benefactors, there will come a time when outsiders (venture capitalists and private equity investors) must be approached for the capital needed to cover the cash burn if a company intends to keep going. This "angel financing," if available, will come at a cost, as investors facing immense risk and uncertainty about founder skills and business viability will demand significant ownership stakes in return for providing capital. In short, staying with the life cycle analogy, early on, businesses resemble babies and toddlers—in constant need of care, capital, and attention—albeit with a very high mortality rate.

It stands to reason that the greater their access to venture capital, the more likely it is that you will see new businesses starting up and surviving into the next stages of the life cycle. It is this access that has historically given the United States an advantage over the rest of the world in incubating start-ups. Notwithstanding advances around the globe, you can still see a vast gap between the US and the rest of the world in figure 2.8, which looks at VC dealmaking, in the fourth quarter of 2021, by region.

FIGURE 2.8 | VC Dealmaking by Region, Fourth Quarter, 2021

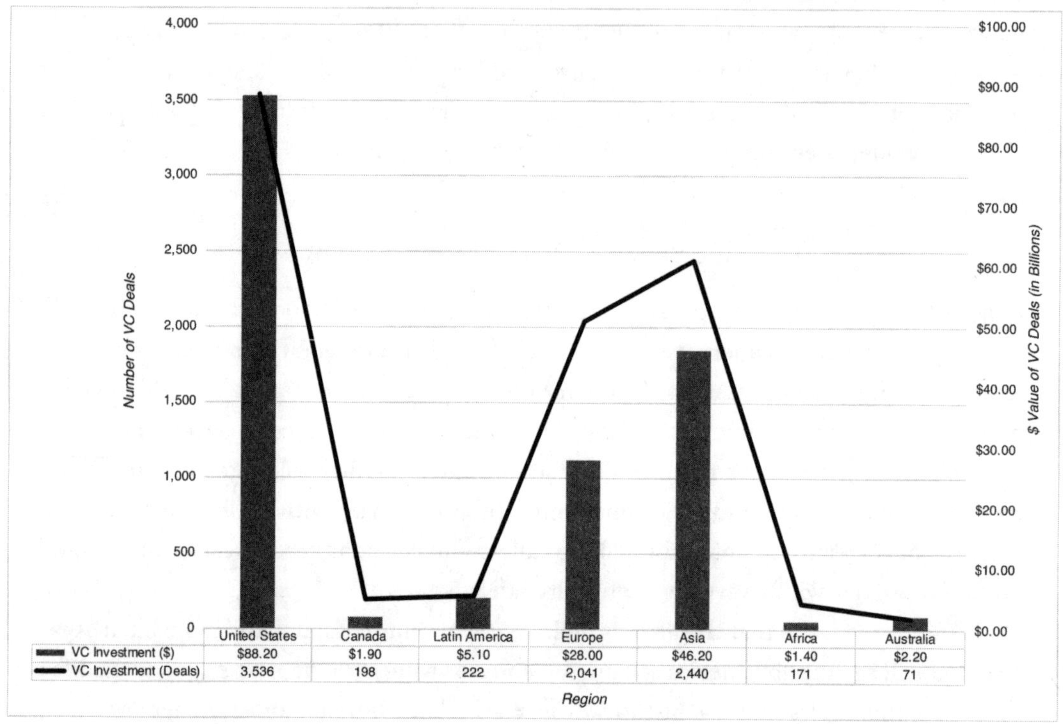

Source: KPMG VC report

Some of that advantage reflects history, since venture capital in its organized form has its deepest roots in the United States. Some of it may reflect a culture of greater risk-taking, and some may reflect the benefit a start-up gains from being close to where the action is, a networking benefit in venture capital access. Increasingly, venture capitalists seem to be willing to invest across borders, and as this process continues, I would expect start-up incubation to increase in the rest of the world.

Phase 2: Young Growth

The businesses that make it through the gauntlet of early tests have devised ways of converting their ideas into products and services that offer at least an opening for success. In the second phase of the life cycle, work must begin on constructing business models—i.e., ways of monetizing products and services and finding pathways to profitability. Note that

I did not say that young companies must make money, only that they have to find plausible ways of moving toward making money.

The Business Challenge

In terms of operating challenges, the founders/owners of the businesses will have to start working on the business basics, ranging from production choices to supply chains to marketing plans. For many founders, whose specialization may not be business-related, there will be a learning curve. A knowledgeable software engineer may have the skill set to create new and innovative software but may be a novice when it comes to hiring and keeping employees, pricing products, and generating sales.

In some cases, the investors who provide angel financing may be able to offer help on these dimensions, based upon their prior experiences with businesses that they have successfully built up. In other cases, founders may have to bring in someone from the outside with business building experience, again offering an ownership stake as an incentive. This tension between a founder's desire to maintain control and investors' wanting to change the way a business is run can lead to what Noam Wasserman has labeled the "founder's dilemma."[*] In a study, Wasserman examined 202 young companies with 5,930 months of data to examine rates of management turnover and concluded that founders are most likely to be displaced just after an idea is turned into a product, as investors seek new business building skill sets.[†]

The business model choices that are made at this stage of the life cycle require trade-offs, but once made, these business modeling decisions can become difficult to change later. Consider Spotify and Netflix and how their business models diverged early, with significant consequences for growth and profitability. Netflix chose a business model wherein it pays for content, whether rented or made by its own studio, and then signs up subscribers using that content. This makes content a fixed cost but increases the marginal revenues that Netflix gets from every additional user, increasing the value of growth. Spotify, early in its business life, decided that it would pay content providers based upon how much subscribers listened to their content, making content costs variable. That reduced the risk in the model, since content costs scale up and down with revenues, but it also reduced the value added by bringing in a new subscriber.

[*] N. Wasserman, "The Founder's Dilemma," *Harvard Business Review* 86, (February 2008): 102–19.

[†] N. Wasserman, "Founder-CEO Succession and the Paradox of Entrepreneurial Success," *Organizational Science* 14, no. 2 (March–April 2003): 149–72.

The Financial Picture

On the financial front, businesses going through young growth will see the beginnings of tangible results, with the first streams of revenues coming in and possibly even growing at high rates. Those revenues, though, will often be overwhelmed by continuing and growing expenses. In fact, even when young companies grow revenues quickly, expenses will grow even faster, partly because of the costs of business building. That will lead to increasing losses and, with rising reinvestment to generate growth, even more negative cash flows. While these aggregate numbers may look uninformative, at least in terms of what you can learn about the profitability of a business model, there are numbers under the surface that may provide clues about viability and profitability:

1. **Growth versus operating expenses:** While expenses will run ahead of revenues for most firms in this stage of the life cycle, it does matter whether those expenses are associated with the products or services that are being sold in the current period or are being driven by the company's growth ambitions. In accounting parlance, the former are operating expenses, and the latter are capital expenses, but at young companies that distinction is often difficult to make. If the distinction *can* be made, you would attach higher value to a young, money-losing business whose expenses are directed at future growth than to an otherwise similar business with expenses primarily associated with current revenues.
2. **Unit economics:** The unit economics of a business measure the marginal profitability of the extra unit that is sold, capturing the difference between revenue generated on that unit and the costs of producing that unit. The better the unit economics, measured as contribution or gross profit margins, the greater the upside of growth for young businesses. Note that a "unit" here is defined broadly, to include everything from an extra car sold by an automobile company to an extra package of software sold by Microsoft to an extra user or subscriber at a user-based company.
3. **Stock-based compensation:** Young companies have negative cash flows, and as they seek to hire and keep employees, they often can stay competitive only by offering stock-based compensation, in the form of shares or options in the underlying businesses. These expenses are often added back by young companies to compute "adjusted" income, on the dubious basis that they are non-cash, and used as the basis for reporting high profit margins. That is a nonsensical argument, since these options represent employee compensation and are real expenses, which the company is using its equity to cover.

Summing up, young growth is the phase of the life cycle where ideas become businesses and business models get built. Not surprisingly, given the losses and the cash burn, failure rates will remain high in this phase, but they should begin decreasing as the business model takes form.

The Capital and Ownership Challenges

As businesses make the transition from idea to product and try to build business models that can deliver profits, they will continue to lose money and have increasingly negative cash flows. This will necessitate capital infusions, often from venture capitalists, and therefore a dilution of founder holdings in the company. For founders who are wary of giving up control, this is the phase in which they must determine whether they would prefer to stay in control of a smaller business, with decreased growth ambitions and consequently less need for external capital, or whether they are willing to give up a significant ownership stake and even control to be able to accelerate growth and build a bigger business.

To get a sense of how founder stakes get diluted, look at the founder ownership stake in a US start-up that goes through five rounds of VC funding (seed and series A–D) in figure 2.9.

FIGURE 2.9 | Founder Ownership Stake through VC Rounds

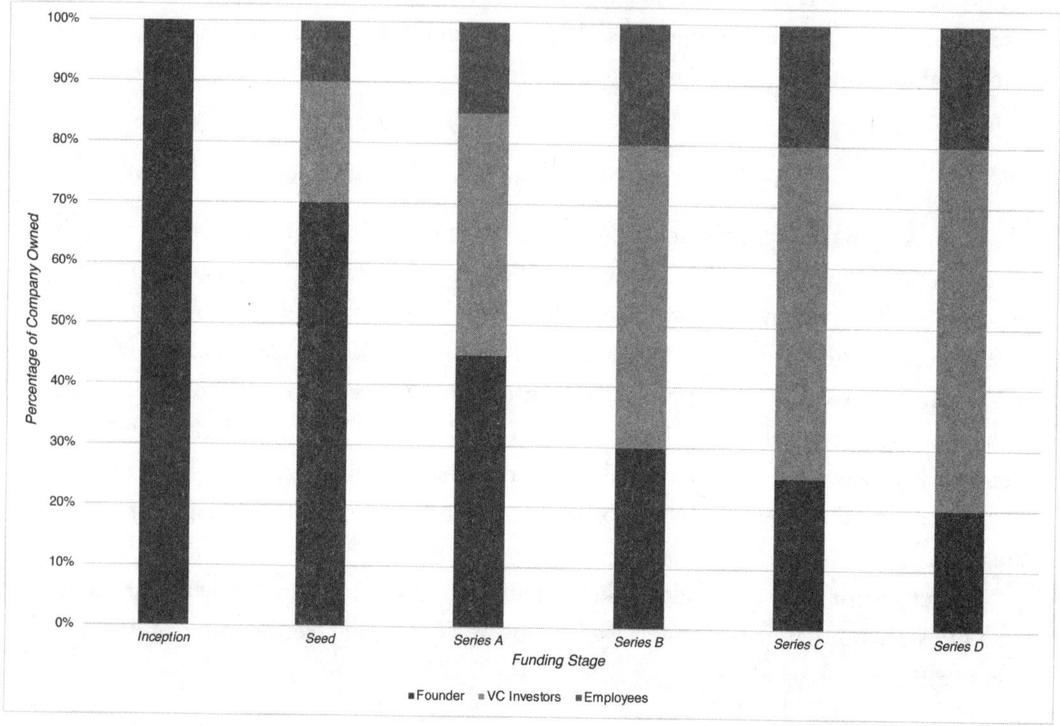

This dilution will be firm-specific and depend on a whole host of factors, but there are some general propositions that will hold. First, the more capital that a young business seeks from outside investors (venture capitalists and others), the more dilution you can expect to see in a founder's ownership stake. Second, the greater the proportion of that external capital that comes early in the process, the more significant will be the dilution in ownership. Put simply, seed capital providers will demand much larger ownership stakes, holding all else constant, than later-round venture capitalists. Third, if founders can raise capital in the form of debt (venture debt or otherwise), they will be able to reduce ownership dilution but they will also be creating enterprises with greater failure risk. Along the way, the extent of dilution created by employee stock-based compensation will depend in large part on how many and what type of employees the start-up seeks, with an increased number of employees with specialized skill sets creating more dilution.

Phase 3: High Growth

Having converted an idea to a product or service and then built a business model—albeit perhaps one that's still a work in progress—that has started delivering revenues, companies in the next phase of the life cycle face a scaling up test. Put simply, businesses that have found some success on a small or local scale will find out whether they want to grow bigger and, if they do, how much scaling up is feasible, given their circumstances.

The Business Challenge

The scaling up test has an operating component, but it also brings the trade-off between control and capital, already prevalent in the first two stages of the cycle, fully to the surface. Scaling up may require so much capital that founders who access that capital will have to give up enough of their ownership stake to outside investors so as to lose control of their business. In some cases, if the business offers enough scalability, the option of going public will be available. While researchers often pay more attention to the earlier stages in the life cycle—i.e., converting ideas to products and establishing a business model—scaling up businesses may be where much of their value is created. A 2020 McKinsey study estimated that close to two thirds of value created at new businesses comes from the scaling up phase, as can be seen in figure 2.10.

FIGURE 2.10 | Value from Build Up versus Scale Up

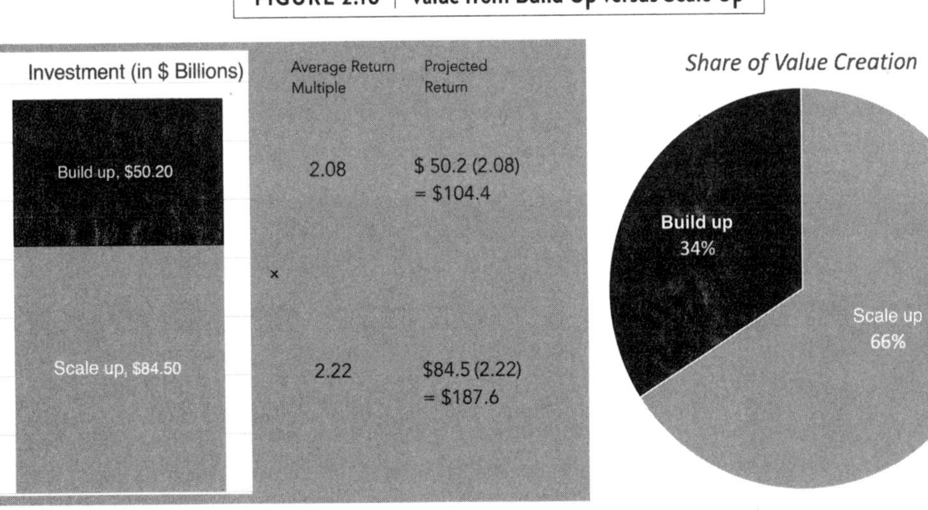

Source: McKinsey (2020)

That said, the evidence also suggests that only one in five businesses succeeds at scaling up, and the mystery of why some businesses are able to scale up while others flounder is a widely researched question with no clear answers. In some cases, the failure to scale up can be attributed to external factors, such as a product or service that is narrowly designed to serve only a small market or limits on access to capital. In many cases, though, the failure to scale up can be explained by factors within the firm, including founders who are unwilling to let go of control, flawed business models (such as reliance on production facilities and supply chains that cannot easily accommodate rapid growth), and business culture. In chapter 4, I will examine both external and internal factors that cause some businesses to stay small while allowing others to grow.

The Financial Picture

In financial terms, high growth is the phase where the company's business model will be tested and measured. If the model is successful, revenue growth will continue at high rates, while expenses will grow at lower rates (due to economies of scale), generating less negative and, in some cases, even positive profits. How quickly this will happen will depend in large part on the unit economics of the business, which I referenced in the last section. In businesses like software, where the additional unit sold has almost no cost, the company will see profits turn positive much more quickly than in businesses like auto manufacturing, where there are significant costs associated with the additional unit sold.

The bottom line is that not all successful businesses scale up, and when they fail to do so, it can be just as much because the business is not scalable as it is because its founders do not want to give up control. Businesses that choose not to scale up should not be viewed as failures, since small businesses that are self-sustaining and meet a market need represent a key part of any economy.

The Capital and Ownership Challenges

Businesses that can grow revenues and deliver profits have created business models that work, and while they can choose to stay private, their incentives to enter public markets will increase over time, especially as they scale up. One incentive is to allow founders, existing investors, and employees to cash out on their ownership holdings by selling their shares or exercising their options in more liquid, public markets. Another is that young companies that are still burning cash and need to raise capital can often do so at better terms (relative to ownership given up in exchange) in public markets than from venture capitalists. The extent of the push to go public will be greater for larger businesses, in regions of the world with liquid capital markets, and in sectors that investors see as attractive investment destinations.

When companies go public, the ownership dilution that started in earlier phases of the life cycle will continue as shares are issued in public markets, though, as I will show in chapter 4, that dilution, at least at the time of the offering, has decreased over time. In the last two decades, there has also been a movement toward dual-class shares, a system in which founders and insiders hold on to shares with more voting rights while offering lower-voting-rights shares to the public market, allowing them to maintain control, even as dilution continues.

Phase 4: Mature Growth

A business that survives its early tests, develops a business model, and then scales up is already a winner in the business sweepstakes, given the high mortality rates for young businesses and how few of those businesses that succeed are willing or able to scale up. Many businesses that arrive at this stage are content with the status quo and settle for growth, with an emphasis on improving margins. A few, though, get a second wind and find ways to keep growing, albeit at lower rates than during the high-growth phase, and improving profitability at the same time.

The Business Challenge

The operating challenge for businesses at this stage that choose to continue growth is that this growth must now occur on a much larger scale. In short, growing revenues at 25% a year is much simpler when base-year revenues are $10 million than when they are $1 billion. Companies that can pull off this unusual feat are exceptional and often get anointed as market stars. For all firms at this stage, the other key business challenge is improving operating margins, with part of that improvement coming from fine-tuning business models to make them more efficient and part from more economies of scale.

To get a sense of how growth, with scale, can create value, it is instructive to look at the FANGAM stocks (Facebook, Amazon, Netflix, Google, Apple, and Microsoft) in the decade from 2010 to 2020, when these six companies (four of which were already scaled up in 2010), at the start of the decade, continued to post double-digit annual revenue growth rates (table 2.1).

Table 2.1 • **Growth on Scale—the FANGAM Stocks, 2010–2020**

	Revenues ($Bil)		
	In 2010	In 2020	CAGR over decade
Facebook	$1.974	$117.900	50.53%
Amazon	$34.204	$469.800	29.95%
Netflix	$2.163	$29.700	29.95%
Google	$29.321	$257.600	24.27%
Apple	$65.225	$378.300	19.22%
Microsoft	$62.484	$184.900	11.46%

While it is true that Facebook and Netflix had smaller revenues at the start of the decade, and thus were able to grow off a much smaller starting scale, note that Amazon, a company with $34 billion in revenues at the end of 2010, was able to match the growth rate posted by Netflix over the same ten years. Apple and Microsoft, already among the largest firms in the world in terms of market capitalization in 2010, had compounded annual growth rates in the double digits between 2010 and 2020. In figure 2.11, I document the rewards to being able to grow, with scale, by looking at the market caps of these six stocks relative to the overall US equity market.

FIGURE 2.11 | The Market Rise of the FANGAM Stocks

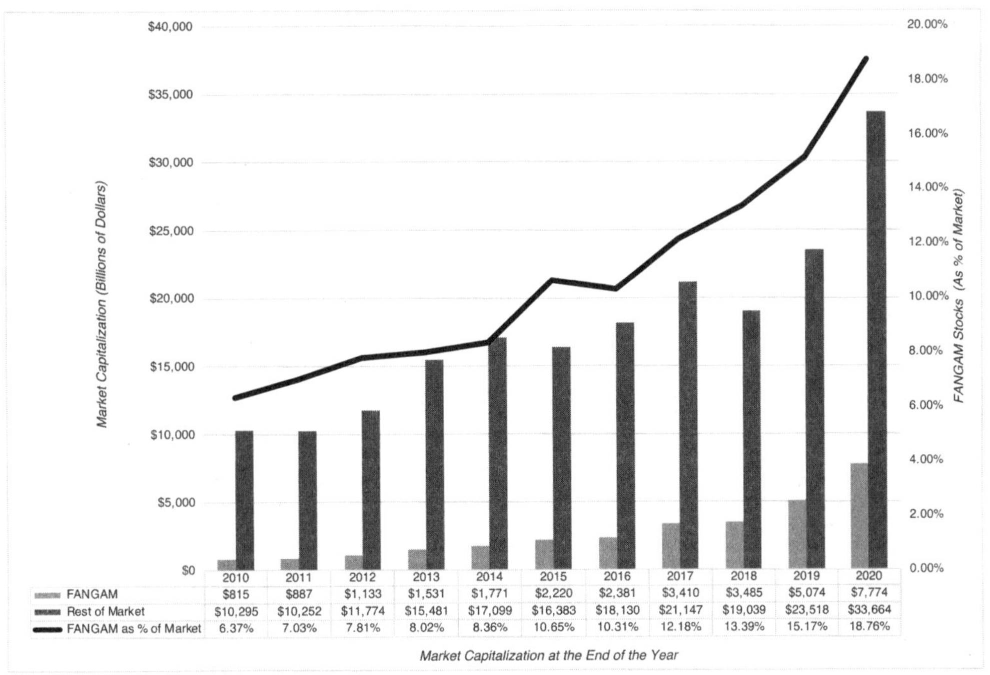

During the decade, these six companies collectively added $7 trillion in market capitalization, accounting for 24.28% of the increase in market capitalization in US equities for the decade.

The Financial Picture

With continued revenue growth and improving margins, mature-growth businesses are in the sweet spot in the life cycle where, even with a moderate revenue growth rate, earnings growth will run ahead of revenue growth. For these firms, slowing growth also yields a bonus, generating higher and more positive cash flows as reinvestment needs decrease. To the extent that these firms choose not to return cash to their owners, they are also the firms with burgeoning cash balances.

For successful businesses, this stage of the life cycle represents the best of all worlds, with the excitement of growth accompanied by the comfort of positive earnings and solid cash flows. That said, it is an adjustment phase, where young companies that have previously had to ration capital across competing investments find themselves with cash on their hands and not enough investment opportunities.

The Capital and Ownership Challenges

As growth companies mature, they become largely self-sufficient when it comes to cash flows, eliminating the need for capital raises. If these companies are publicly traded, the share of ownership in the hands of the founder and early investors in the company will decrease as they cash out on success and move on to other ventures. In many cases, the mix of public-market investors in the company will change at this stage, with institutional investors replacing individual investors and traders, and these new investors may put a different set of demands on managers. If the company's cash flows have turned positive, and/or the company is gaining the capacity to borrow money, some of these institutional investors may put pressure on the company to start borrowing and to pay dividends or initiate stock buybacks.

For founders who stay on as top managers, this is a period when they may face the downsides of being a public company. First, accounting and regulatory disclosures become more onerous in this phase, as the company's investments get more extensive and disclosure requirements ramp up. Second, founders and top managers will have to spend more time on investor relations, framing the news around earnings announcements and providing guidance. Third, they will have to deal with shareholder pressures on investing, financing, and dividend policy, though having dual-voting-class shares can reduce the need to act in response.

Phase 5: Mature Stable

Given a choice, most businesses prefer to stay as growth businesses, but as with human beings, it is inevitable that they will become middle-aged, with two caveats. The first is that the best-run businesses will be able to delay entering the mature stable phase for a lot longer than their competitors. The second is that there will be a few firms that are able to pause aging—or even reverse it, at least temporarily—by entering new businesses or markets.

The Business Challenge

The biggest challenge for mature stable businesses is a mindset shift, as they turn from playing offense, where their focus is on entering new markets or gaining market share, to playing defense, where the primary objective becomes protecting their existing market share and profit margins from competition. The capacity of a business to play defense will be determined, in large part, by its competitive advantages, or "moats." These moats can come from a variety of sources. In some cases, a company's protections against competition are legal, as is the case with patents at pharmaceutical and technology companies. In others, it is a function of brand name, often built up over time, creating customer loyalty and pricing power. No matter what the source, though, protecting these competitive advantages becomes the paramount task of managers at these businesses. In the last two decades, this task has been made more difficult by disruptors, young companies with nothing to lose and innovative business models (low capital intensity, technology driven) that can do end runs around conventional moats.

The Financial Picture

On the financial front, the combination of low growth and stable margins, at least for companies with strong moats, creates a period of stability in earnings. Stable and high earnings allow public companies to return more cash to their owners, in the form of dividends and buybacks, and allow owners to cash out of companies that are privately or family owned. In addition, to the extent that there are tax benefits to borrowing (where interest is tax deductible), this is also the phase in which a company's debt capacity is maximized, though not all mature companies choose to use it. As I will show in the chapters on corporate finance and valuation, it is with mature companies that the past is most likely to be indicative of the future. Inertia will drive corporate finance policy; companies will take investments, finance them, and pay out dividends just as they have in the past. In valuation, extrapolating historical trend lines on revenues, operating margins, and other variables can give reasonable estimates of value of these companies.

Stability in mature firms can hide inefficiencies, however, and there are times when continuing with past practices, when managing a mature business, can be value destructive, because the underlying business has changed or been disrupted. As I will show in the chapters to come, recognition of this fact can sometimes lead mature firms to restructure themselves, significantly deviating from past investing, financing, or dividend choices, either of their own volition or because of outside pressures.

The Capital and Ownership Challenges

The tension between stability and the need for change that I have shown in the financials will also play out in ownership structure and actions. Mature firms, especially if publicly traded, have a history with markets, and over time, they have collected a shareholder base that reflects their choices. Put simply, firms that have developed a practice of paying large and growing dividends will accumulate investors who prefer large and growing dividends. This phenomenon is called the clientele effect, and while it can create stability in the firm, it can become a problem if the company *must* change, either because of external challenges like disruption or new competition or due to internal decisions to adopt a different path. When a mature company changes its dividend or financing policy, even for good business reasons, it is entirely possible that the initial market reaction will be negative, as existing investors abandon the firm, and while this reaction may eventually dissipate, the company's investor base will look different after the change.

Phase 6: Decline

The final and most dreaded phase of the corporate life cycle is decline, wherein a business faces a bleak future of shrinking revenues, sometimes with pressure on profit margins, as the business economics get less attractive. Since few businesses want to be caught in this vise, it is the also the phase when many businesses try hard, and sometimes desperately, to reverse aging.

The Business Challenge

In terms of operations, the primary challenge for declining firms is dealing with a shrinking revenue base, since costs don't always scale down with revenues, resulting in lower profit margins. If your response is that such firms should find growth, it is difficult to see how they might accomplish that, while preserving at least a semblance of financial health, when there are market or macro forces aligned against them. Tobacco companies, no matter how well-run, will have a hard time finding pathways back to growth in a world where smoking is becoming rarer. That said, the high gross margin (the cost of making a cigarette is a fraction of its price) at tobacco companies has allowed their years in decline to remain lucrative, as they continue to deliver high profits. For a subset of firms, though, shrinking revenues and declining margins will conspire to cause profits to drop faster than revenues. If these firms borrowed money during their mature phase, a failure to pay down debt as revenues and earnings scale down will create moments of reckoning where bankruptcy beckons.

In many declining firms, managers will aspire to a rebirth, or at least a revamp, that would allow these firms not just to slow decline but to reverse it. While the odds against these attempts succeeding may be high, there are a few that do succeed, and that success makes them subjects of case studies that business schools and consultants pore over in the hope of replication and turns their CEOs into the folk heroes of business.

The Financial Picture

In decline, the trend lines for a company's key operating metrics will be negative, as revenues decline and operating margins come under pressure. That said, though, there are many mature firms and even some high-growth firms that can have years where revenues drop and operating margins decline, and it is a collection of circumstances that set declining firms apart from those that just had a "bad" year or years:

1. **Trend lines over time:** One year, or even two years, of revenue decline can be explained away as extraordinary, but a string that lasts five or ten years is indicative of decay in the underlying business.
2. **Macro drivers:** There are mature or even growth companies that can have extended streaks of declining revenues, if those revenues are driven by a macro variable that moves in cycles. That is the case, for example, in commodity companies, where the pricing cycle can sometimes reflect years of dropping commodity prices, leading to revenue drops at companies producing that commodity.

Companies in decline can add fuel to the fire if they carry large debt loads that stay intact even as operations deteriorate. Those companies will become distressed, which can further speed up deterioration in operations and sometimes end in bankruptcy.

The Capital and Ownership Challenge

As you look at the arc of ownership in businesses, start by looking at investors in start-ups and very young companies that are taking an active role in how the companies are run and pushing for changes in management, if needed. As companies grow, and sometimes go public, investors in companies tend to become more passive, preferring to sell their shares and move on rather than challenge incumbent managers. I noted above that with a subset of mature and stable companies, investors who see the need for change will become more activist, and that activism will increase as firms go into decline, with three groups of players. The first group, which includes private equity and activist hedge funds, will push for changes in operating and financing policy and sometimes acquire entire businesses to make that change happen, via buyouts. The second group will include investors who see more value available in the company by liquidating its assets or breaking it up than letting it continue as a going concern. The third group will focus on distressed firms and trade their securities (both equity and debt) either because they are mispriced or to exploit frictions in the legal process of unwinding operations.

The early and end stages of the corporate life cycle represent opposite ends of capital flows, with capital being raised by young firms and returned by declining firms, but they both tend to attract investors who are more likely to make their presence felt and push for changes. They are also the periods when uncertainty about the future is greatest, leading many to avoid these companies, and perhaps increasing the payoff to those who are willing to live with that same uncertainty.

Conclusion

In this chapter, I laid out the phases of the corporate life cycle, from start-up to demise, and the challenges that companies face in each phase, both in operating and financial terms. The corporate life cycle is a structure for explaining how businesses evolve over time, but it is worth emphasizing again that notwithstanding the truth that all companies grow old, the way they age can be very different. Put simply, there are many companies that never scale up but last a long time, coexisting with businesses that soar to large scale but scale down just as quickly.

3

The Corporate Life Cycle: Measures and Determinants

IN CHAPTER 2, I broke down the corporate life cycle into phases, beginning with start-up and ending with decline. In this chapter, I begin by addressing a fundamental question: measuring where a business is in the life cycle, starting with corporate age as the most simplistic tool and then looking at measures that are tied more closely to the company's operations. In the second part of the chapter, I move on to address the question of why the corporate life cycle looks different across companies, by laying out three dimensions in which life cycles vary (length, height, and slope), and I evaluate macro and micro factors that can explain deviations.

Measures of the Corporate Life Cycle

If, as the notion of the corporate life cycle posits, businesses proceed successively through the phases of the life cycle, it stands to reason that you should be able to develop measures or metrics that allow you to determine where a given business is in the life cycle. As I will show in this section, that quest does not yield easy answers, but it is worth pursuing, since insights gained in the process can be useful in the next section of the chapter, where I will try to explain differences in life cycles across businesses.

Corporate Age

If we use the analogy to the human life cycle, the most direct measure of where a business is in the corporate life cycle is its corporate age. Put simply, a business that has been around for only 5 years is more likely to be a young business, with growth opportunities and business model tests lying ahead of it, whereas one that has been around for 100 years is more likely to be aging, and perhaps even in decline. To get a sense of what corporate life spans look like, let us start by looking at the distribution of publicly traded companies, by corporate age and by region, in figure 3.1.

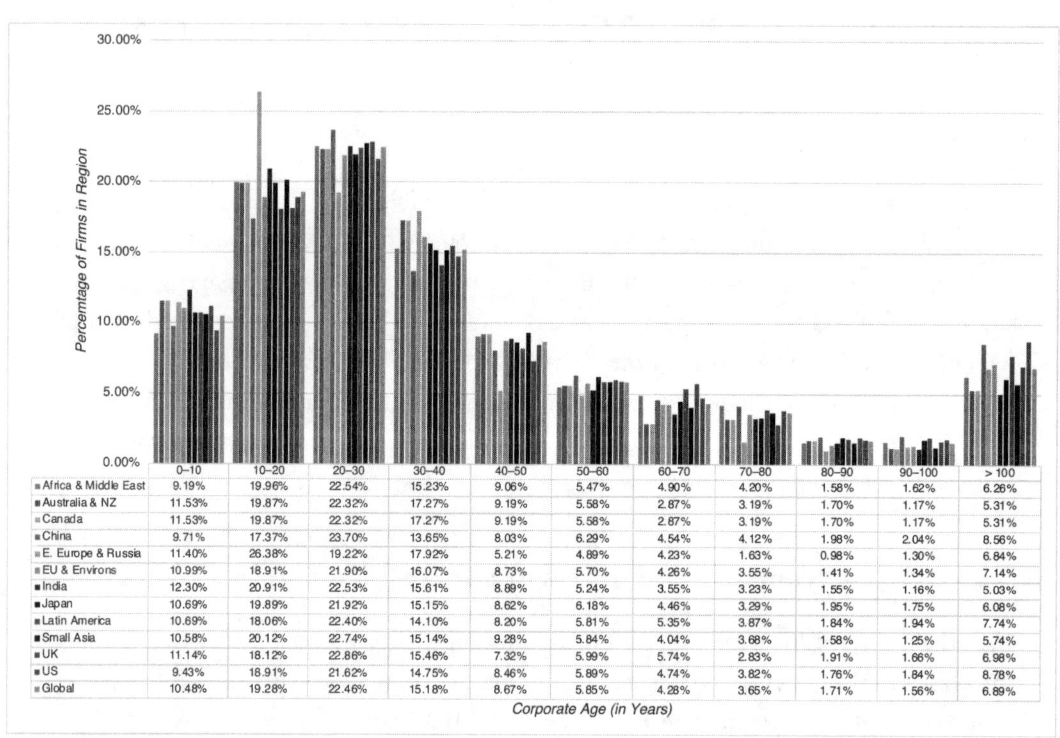

	0–10	10–20	20–30	30–40	40–50	50–60	60–70	70–80	80–90	90–100	> 100
Africa & Middle East	9.19%	19.96%	22.54%	15.23%	9.06%	5.47%	4.90%	4.20%	1.58%	1.62%	6.26%
Australia & NZ	11.53%	19.87%	22.32%	17.27%	9.19%	5.58%	2.87%	3.19%	1.70%	1.17%	5.31%
Canada	11.53%	19.87%	22.32%	17.27%	9.19%	5.58%	2.87%	3.19%	1.70%	1.17%	5.31%
China	9.71%	17.37%	23.70%	13.65%	8.03%	6.29%	4.54%	4.12%	1.98%	2.04%	8.56%
E. Europe & Russia	11.40%	26.38%	19.22%	17.92%	5.21%	4.89%	4.23%	1.63%	0.98%	1.30%	6.84%
EU & Environs	10.99%	18.91%	21.90%	16.07%	8.73%	5.70%	4.26%	3.55%	1.41%	1.34%	7.14%
India	12.30%	20.91%	22.53%	15.61%	8.89%	5.24%	3.55%	3.23%	1.55%	1.16%	5.03%
Japan	10.69%	19.89%	21.92%	15.15%	8.62%	6.18%	4.46%	3.29%	1.95%	1.75%	6.08%
Latin America	10.69%	18.06%	22.40%	14.10%	8.20%	5.81%	5.35%	3.87%	1.84%	1.94%	7.74%
Small Asia	10.58%	20.12%	22.74%	15.14%	9.28%	5.84%	4.04%	3.68%	1.58%	1.25%	5.74%
UK	11.14%	18.12%	22.86%	15.46%	7.32%	5.99%	5.74%	2.83%	1.91%	1.66%	6.98%
US	9.43%	18.91%	21.62%	14.75%	8.46%	5.89%	4.74%	3.82%	1.76%	1.84%	8.78%
Global	10.48%	19.28%	22.46%	15.18%	8.67%	5.85%	4.28%	3.65%	1.71%	1.56%	6.89%

The median age of a publicly traded company, if you look across the globe, is 29 years, and 25 years if you look only at the United States. Japan has more older companies than any other part of the world, with a median corporate age of 54 years, indicative of both its aging economy and a system that makes it difficult for newcomers to compete against the status quo. The US has the highest percentage of young companies in the world, with a first quartile of 11 years, indicating that a quarter of all US companies are less than 11 years old. (Note, though, that this analysis does not include privately owned businesses, and a reasonable argument can be made that those businesses may have shorter life spans.)

While corporate age, being easy to compute and simple to understand, is a good starting point for placing companies in the life cycle, it has limits as a tool. First, there are some businesses that seem to age faster than others, and as I will show later in this chapter, this has been particularly the case with tech companies, many of which go from having little or no substance to becoming large businesses over very short periods. Second, to the extent that the founding date of a business is used as the starting year for computing corporate age, the age of businesses that stayed small and privately owned for a long period before embarking on a growth journey may be overstated. One way of measuring how well corporate age does in capturing where a company is in its life cycle is to look at the company operating metrics, especially revenue growth and operating margins, broken down by age decile, in table 3.1.

Table 3.1 • Operating Metrics by Corporate Age Decile

		Revenue Growth Rate (CAGR over last 3 years)				Operating Margin			
Decile (Age)	# firms	First Quartile	Median	Third Quartile	% with negative growth	First Quartile	Median	Third Quartile	% with negative margins
Bottom decile	4,026	-4.86%	18.16%	72.42%	14.80%	-176.76%	-3.29%	12.22%	54.91%
2nd decile	4,164	-6.00%	13.58%	41.46%	25.55%	-53.00%	0.00%	13.77%	48.17%
3rd decile	4,930	-7.18%	8.88%	26.08%	28.86%	-15.02%	4.28%	15.61%	37.39%
4th decile	4,098	-4.55%	8.58%	21.60%	29.77%	-5.30%	4.95%	14.04%	31.63%
5th decile	4,785	-6.01%	6.19%	17.61%	32.18%	-0.48%	5.76%	14.91%	27.79%
6th decile	4,029	-7.11%	4.15%	15.51%	35.84%	0.00%	5.79%	13.98%	25.83%
7th decile	4,653	-7.04%	3.74%	14.20%	35.63%	0.00%	5.48%	13.54%	25.08%
8th decile	4,414	-6.22%	2.19%	9.87%	40.17%	0.40%	6.20%	13.42%	20.93%
9th decile	4,582	-5.24%	1.32%	8.38%	42.12%	1.21%	6.03%	12.57%	17.03%
Top decile	4,473	-3.97%	1.57%	7.33%	40.73%	0.00%	5.86%	12.37%	12.22%

As I noted in chapter 2, companies that are in the young-growth phase generally grow revenues quickly and are money-losers, mature companies have moderate or low revenue growth and solid profit margins, and declining companies have revenues that are flat or shrinking. The results in the table suggest that corporate age is a rough proxy for where companies are in the life cycle, since the youngest companies (in the lowest decile) do have high revenue growth and negative operating margins, and the oldest companies (in the highest decile) have lower revenue growth, though their margins are roughly the same as companies that fall in the middle of the corporate age distribution.

While these measures of age look at publicly traded companies, it is worth noting that some of the oldest businesses in the world are privately held and often family owned and trace their lineage back centuries, rather than decades. A joint study of the 500 largest family businesses in the world by Ernst & Young and the University of St. Gallen, in 2021, found that the median company in this group had been in existence for more than 50 years, and 9% had been operating for more than 150 years. There is of course a selection bias at work here, since these are the most successful of family businesses, and many do not make it for so long, but it does suggest that there is some aspect of being family owned that contributes to longer life for these companies. I will return and examine what that might be in the next section.

Sector

It is not uncommon for investors and analysts to use the sector in which a business operates as a proxy for where the business falls in the life cycle. Thus, technology companies are habitually categorized as young- and high-growth just because they are technology companies, and utilities as old and mature just because they are utilities. In figure 3.2, I start by looking at the breakdown of publicly traded companies, by sector, across global markets.

FIGURE 3.2 | Company Breakdown by Sector

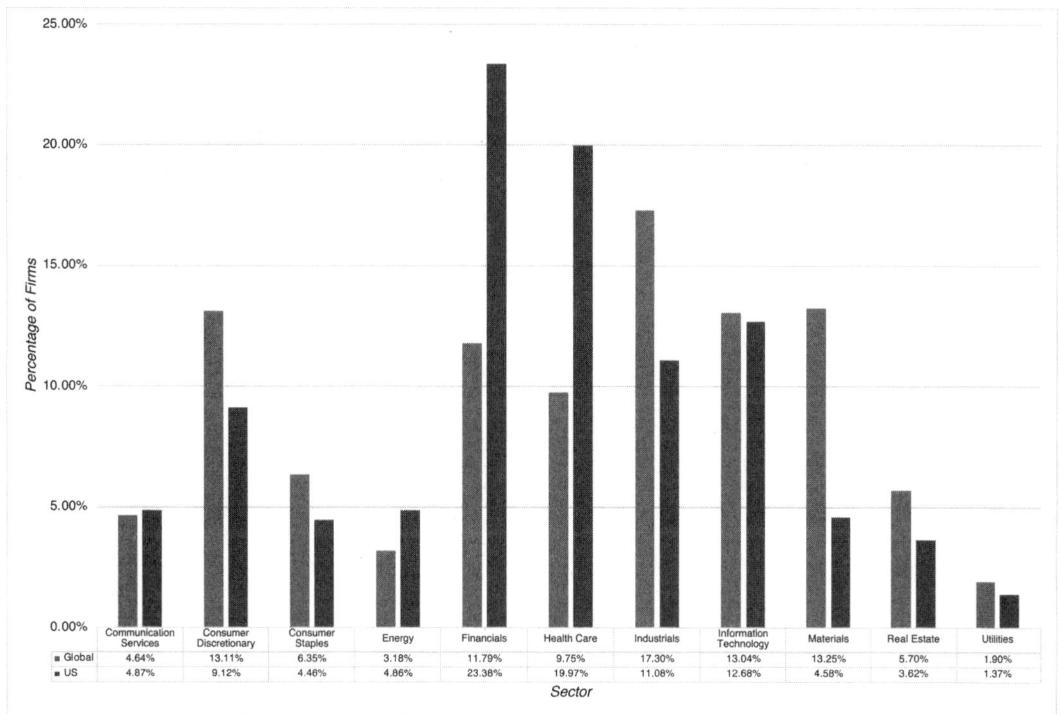

	Communication Services	Consumer Discretionary	Consumer Staples	Energy	Financials	Health Care	Industrials	Information Technology	Materials	Real Estate	Utilities
Global	4.64%	13.11%	6.35%	3.18%	11.79%	9.75%	17.30%	13.04%	13.25%	5.70%	1.90%
US	4.87%	9.12%	4.46%	4.86%	23.38%	19.97%	11.08%	12.68%	4.58%	3.62%	1.37%

In July 2022, there were 6,246 (913) publicly traded technology companies that were listed globally (in the US). If the sector shorthand for life cycle phase is used, these would all be young-growth companies, and the 1,522 (350) publicly traded energy companies that were listed globally (in the US) would all be mature or even declining businesses.

Using sector as a proxy for standing in the life cycle is as problematic as—perhaps more so than—using corporate age. First, as sectors age and become more diverse, it becomes more difficult to put all companies in that sector into the same phase of the corporate life cycle. With the technology sector, the notion that tech companies are all young- and high-growth started in the 1980s, when the entire tech sector was starting its growth climb and most tech companies were young and growing. In 2022, when the technology sector is home to some of the most valuable companies in the market and accounts for the largest slice of overall market capitalization, the companies that fall into this sector are diverse, including a mix of growth, mature, and even declining businesses.

Again, to get a sense of how well sector categories work as proxies for the corporate life cycle, I looked at revenue growth and operating margin statistics, broken down by sector, and also estimated the distribution of corporate age across the sector, in table 3.2:

Table 3.2 • Operating Metrics and Age, by Sector—Global Firms, July 2022

Primary Sector	# firms	Median Age	First Quartile	Median	Third Quartile	% with negative growth	First Quartile	Median	Third Quartile	% with negative margins
Communication Services	2,223	23	-10.76%	1.92%	16.98%	40.40%	-13.06%	4.68%	14.59%	37.22%
Consumer Discretionary	6,277	34	-11.29%	0.37%	11.37%	45.45%	-3.68%	4.16%	10.10%	32.10%
Consumer Staples	3,041	38	-3.99%	3.93%	12.66%	32.65%	0.39%	4.87%	11.03%	23.54%
Energy	1,522	25	-12.03%	0.18%	14.34%	40.47%	-10.34%	4.19%	22.19%	34.64%
Financials	5,646	28	-3.29%	6.90%	18.74%	24.35%	0.00%	0.00%	10.27%	21.94%
Health Care	4,670	21	-1.74%	10.42%	34.55%	22.36%	-209.09%	-0.64%	13.89%	50.52%
Industrials	8,288	35	-5.97%	2.98%	14.45%	37.52%	0.27%	5.57%	11.63%	24.21%
Information Technology	6,246	25	-1.87%	8.47%	22.19%	26.48%	-6.52%	4.96%	12.66%	32.33%
Materials	6,345	29	-3.81%	5.25%	16.24%	24.37%	1.34%	7.69%	14.55%	22.21%
Real Estate	2,728	28	-12.02%	1.81%	16.06%	41.39%	5.47%	22.69%	52.20%	19.14%
Utilities	910	27	-2.13%	4.22%	14.44%	30.66%	4.64%	14.96%	27.90%	15.16%
Total	47,907	29	-5.75%	4.44%	17.04%	32.35%	-1.79%	5.07%	13.74%	29.29%

The two sectors that have the highest revenue growth rates are technology and health care, but both sectors also have above-average margins. To add to the confusion, the health care sector has the highest percentage of firms that are money losing, with 50.5% of all companies in the group posting operating losses. Looking at the median age of companies, the health care sector has the youngest companies, with a median corporate age of 21 years, whereas the oldest companies are in consumer staples. In sum, the numbers that emerge from a sector analysis yield, at best, a tenuous link to the corporate life cycle, with the only solid conclusion being that the sector that is most likely to contain young-growth companies in July 2022 is health care, and the sectors that look as if they contain the most declining companies are energy and consumer discretionary.

Does this imply that you should never use sector as a proxy for where companies stand in the life cycle? Not necessarily! First, sector breakdowns may be too broad to use as proxies, but *industry*-level breakdowns may sometimes help. For instance, while the technology sector collectively does not diverge dramatically from the rest of the market, internet software companies have much higher revenue growth and much more negative operating margins than the rest of the market, consistent with many or most of the companies in the sector being young-growth companies. Similarly, breaking out just biotech companies from the health care sector generates industry-level numbers with higher revenue growth and more negative margins than the rest of the market. Breaking the market down into 93 industries, I find that five industries had the highest revenue growth, depicted in table 3.3:

Table 3.3 • Industries with Highest Revenue Growth, July 2022

			Revenue Growth Rate (CAGR over last 3 years)				Operating Margin			
Industry Group	# firms	Median Age	First Quartile	Median	Third Quartile	% with negative growth	First Quartile	Median	Third Quartile	% with negative margins
Heathcare Information and Technology	447	20	2.91%	17.08%	40.44%	17.90%	-80.78%	-1.26%	14.78%	50.51%
Retail (Online)	381	17	-0.68%	14.90%	38.34%	23.62%	-16.93%	-0.21%	5.54%	50.86%
Software (Internet)	152	21	1.32%	13.41%	36.96%	21.71%	-22.93%	2.16%	11.26%	43.80%
Drugs (Biotechnology)	1,293	15	-23.51%	13.33%	59.02%	25.29%	-1439.25%	-267.69%	-15.53%	79.66%
Software (System & Application)	1,625	21	-1.18%	12.74%	31.93%	23.38%	-44.89%	-0.23%	11.99%	50.24%

These five industry groups do contain a disproportionately large number of young-growth companies, since revenue growth is accompanied at many of these companies with negative operating margins. In short, it is not unreasonable to start with the presumption that a system software or biotech firm is likely to be a young-growth company.

At the other end of the spectrum, the industry groups with the lowest revenue growth rates are listed in table 3.4.

Table 3.4 • Industries with Lowest Revenue Growth, July 2022

			Revenue Growth Rate (CAGR over last 3 years)				Operating Margin			
Industry Group	**# firms**	**Median Age**	**First Quartile**	**Median**	**Third Quartile**	**% with negative growth**	**First Quartile**	**Median**	**Third Quartile**	**% with negative margins**
Air Transport	154	31	-27.38%	-17.35%	-7.62%	79.87%	-39.77%	-12.28%	5.20%	65.25%
Hotels/Gaming	644	32	-31.62%	-16.85%	-1.65%	71.74%	-48.83%	-10.09%	8.79%	62.29%
Transportation (Railroads)	51	47	-10.74%	-5.69%	2.59%	66.67%	-0.47%	4.55%	21.18%	26.00%
Restaurants/ Dining	382	31	-15.49%	-5.20%	5.07%	60.47%	-11.54%	-0.49%	6.42%	51.82%
Publishing & Newspapers	334	38	-10.76%	-2.77%	7.27%	53.59%	-0.53%	5.03%	10.71%	26.86%

There should be no surprises in this listing: it includes five industries where revenue growth is negative for the median company, and three of the five industry groups also have negative operating margins. That's a toxic combination for any ongoing business, and clearly indicates that these industry groups include a disproportionately large number of declining companies.

Operating Metrics

As the last two sections should make clear, the ultimate measures of where a company falls in the life cycle are rooted not in its age or even in what sector or industry grouping it belongs to but in its operations. Using revenue growth and operating margins as the key metrics, table 3.5 summarizes what you should expect to see for companies at each stage of the life cycle.

Table 3.5 • Operating Metrics across the Life Cycle

Life cycle stage	Start-up	Young Growth	High Growth	Mature Growth	Mature Stable	Decline
Revenue Growth	N/A at pre-revenue; very high for initial revenues	Very high	High	Moderate	Low	Close to zero or negative
Operating Margin	Very negative	Negative, perhaps becoming more so over time	Negative, but becoming less so over time	Positive, and becoming more so over time	Stable and predictable	Positive, but declining
Reinvestment	High	Very high	High, but stable relative to revenues	High, but declining relative to revenues	Low, and a function of revenues	Divestment and shrinkage
Free cash flows (cash available after taxes and reinvestment)	Very negative	Very negative, perhaps becoming more so over time	Negative, but becoming less so over time	Positive, and growing faster than revenues and earnings	Positive and stable	More positive than earnings

In short, the best indicator for where a company is in the life cycle will be in the company's financial statements. Zeroing in just on revenue growth and operating margin, I broke companies into deciles on each dimension and then created a cross table, looking at the number of firms that fall into each cell, in figure 3.3.

FIGURE 3.3 | Revenue Growth and Operating Margins

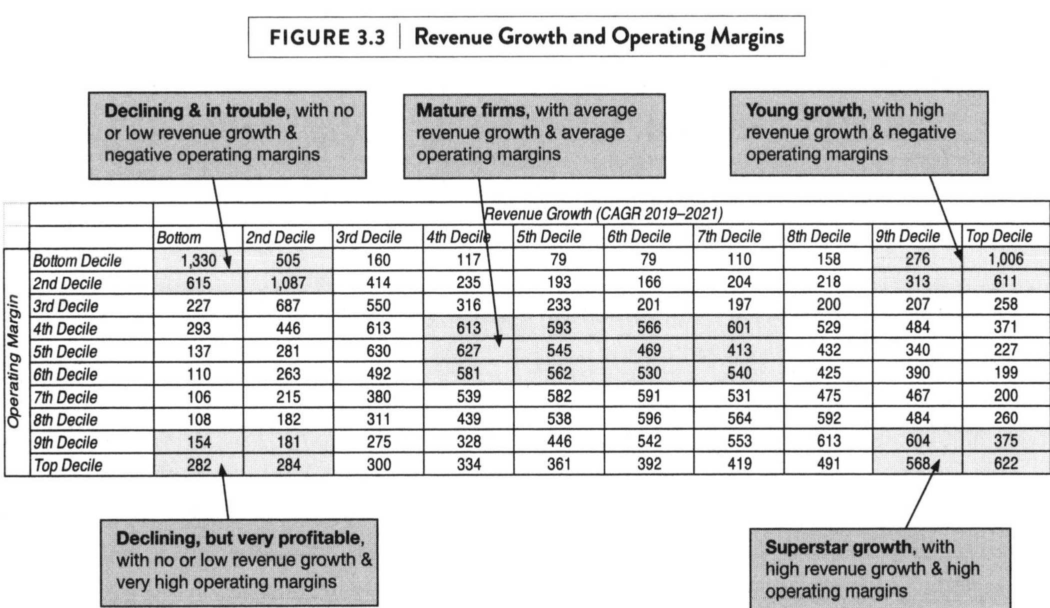

Operating Margin	Revenue Growth (CAGR 2019–2021)									
	Bottom	2nd Decile	3rd Decile	4th Decile	5th Decile	6th Decile	7th Decile	8th Decile	9th Decile	Top Decile
Bottom Decile	1,330	505	160	117	79	79	110	158	276	1,006
2nd Decile	615	1,087	414	235	193	166	204	218	313	611
3rd Decile	227	687	550	316	233	201	197	200	207	258
4th Decile	293	446	613	613	593	566	601	529	484	371
5th Decile	137	281	630	627	545	469	413	432	340	227
6th Decile	110	263	492	581	562	530	540	425	390	199
7th Decile	106	215	380	539	582	591	531	475	467	200
8th Decile	108	182	311	439	538	596	564	592	484	260
9th Decile	154	181	275	328	446	542	553	613	604	375
Top Decile	282	284	300	334	361	392	419	491	568	622

As you can see, the mix of revenue growth and operating margins that you see at companies varies widely. The bottom line is that no matter what phase of the life cycle you look at, there are hundreds of firms, sometimes thousands, that fall into that grouping when you look across global companies.

Other Proxies

There are other proxies that can be used to categorize companies in the corporate life cycle, but most of them are fatally flawed. Some thinkers argue that company size, measured in operating terms (revenues), should be a good proxy, with smaller companies more likely to be in the growth phase and larger companies in the mature phase. There may be some truth to this argument, but crucially, there seems to be little correlation between company size and operating metrics (revenue growth and operating margins). There are others who believe that a market metric is better than an operating one, since markets have the capacity to incorporate what they expect to happen in the future. Here again, though, the claim does not hold up to the data, since small cap companies don't seem to have higher expected growth than large cap companies.

In sum, I believe that corporate age and industry grouping offer information that can be used to assess where a company is in its life cycle, but the best indicators of corporate life cycle phase are in the financial statements of the company, with revenue growth and operating margins being the key indicators.

Dimensions and Determinants of the Life Cycle

Every business will go through a life cycle, but some complete it quickly, while others climb higher (scale up) and still others settle for less. In this section, I will look at the dimensions that characterize a corporate life cycle and the reasons for life cycle differences across companies.

Dimensions

At the risk of oversimplifying, the shape of a corporate life cycle can be captured in four dimensions. The first is the length of the life cycle—the period over which a business exists, with some businesses lasting a lot longer than others. The second is the height of the life cycle, characterizing the peak of the business—how big it is at its biggest. The third dimension is the steepness of the slope of the life cycle curve, reflecting how quickly a founder or business novice is able to scale up a company's size, as well as how quickly it scales down. The final dimension is the *flattening part of the life cycle*, a measure of how long a business is able to stay at the top once it becomes mature.

Length of Life Cycle

The length of the life cycle looks at the length of time it takes for a company to go from being a start-up to its demise. The world's oldest company, Kongo Gumi, founded in 578 and acquired in 2006, kept its business of constructing temples and shrines in Japan for almost 1,500 years. The oldest publicly traded company in US equity markets is Consolidated Edison, which started life as New York Gas Light in 1824, and GE and Exxon Mobil are both well over a hundred years old. However, these long-lived companies are much more the exception than the rule, since the median US company is estimated to have a life span of just over ten years before it fails, is acquired, or goes out of business. The factors that determine the length of a corporate life cycle are listed below:

a. **Type of business:** There are some businesses that have more staying power than others because the products and services they offer enjoy durable demand. A general retailer will likely have a longer life than a specialty retailer, especially one that offers a niche product.
b. **Time to build business:** Businesses that take time to establish are more likely to have long lives than those that can ramp up production and be in business quickly. It should therefore come as no surprise that infrastructure companies that may require years, or even decades, to get their operations started have far longer lives than a software firm that can start generating revenues without spending long time periods on production facilities or construction.
c. **Competitive barriers to entry:** The decline and demise of businesses often comes from new players entering the market, and having strong and long-standing barriers to entry can allow companies to stay in business far longer than if they operate in free-for-all settings.
d. **Macroeconomic conditions:** A business that operates in a more volatile macroeconomic environment will face more risks that could potentially shorten its life than an otherwise similar business in a stable environment. Thus, you would expect businesses in emerging markets to have shorter lives, on average, than those in developed markets.
e. **Ownership structure and governance:** For a business to keep going, it needs management continuity. A business that is dependent on a key person or persons for its

continued operation will have a shorter life than one that has a management team and well-established succession plans. At first sight, this should imply that publicly traded companies should have longer life spans than privately owned businesses, but while that may be true in the aggregate, it is worth noting that some of the longest-lived businesses in the world are family-owned companies where the family has developed a structure for smoothly passing the management reins to the next generation.

f. **Time horizon:** One reason why a successful family business may have a much longer life than a successful publicly traded company is the incentive structure of the decision-makers who build the business and how it may affect business life span. In a family-owned business, where the owners get the residual claim in the business and expect the business to stay in family hands for the long term, you would expect decisions that extend business life span to be taken over decisions that generate higher earnings in the short term at the cost of longevity. In contrast, the top management of a publicly traded firm may see more reward in delivering higher stock prices for investors and cashing out on stock-based compensation, even if that decision comes with the cost of shortening corporate life span.

Japan offers a laboratory for researching long-lived businesses, with more than 20,000 businesses that have lasted more than 100 years, and the Japanese have coined a word, *shinise*, to describe a business with this longevity. Most of these businesses are small and family-owned, suggesting that there is a trade-off, which I will examine more closely in the next section, between wanting a longer life for a business and seeking to scale up that same business, with scaling up more shortening business life.

Height of Life Cycle

The height of the life cycle references how large a company becomes after its scaling up phase. In effect, it is a measure of revenues at their peak, and even through casual empiricism you can see that some companies climb much higher than others. There is a mix of internal and external factors that determine peak revenue differences across companies. The external factors include:

a. **Potential market for product or service:** The choices made by a business regarding whether to offer a product or service to a niche market or a mass market can determine how much it can scale up. A luxury automaker like Ferrari can never generate as much revenue as a mass-market auto company like Volkswagen—but, let us hasten to add, the former will be able to generate much higher margins on its smaller revenue base.

b. **Geographic reach:** In the last three decades, companies all over the world have learned to look past their local markets for growth. This has allowed companies that would have been historically constrained to be small, because they operated in small domestic markets, to expand into foreign markets and increase their size.

c. **Technological and economic innovation:** There have been innovations in history that have opened the door for firms to expand to levels they could not attain prior to those innovations. Almost three centuries ago, the industrial revolution allowed companies to expand production, using factories, to levels that would have been unreachable with a manual workforce. At the start of the last century, the introduction of assembly lines provided a boost to potential production, allowing its most successful practitioners to produce and sell far more than they could have in prior years. In the 1990s, the development of the internet opened the door to e-commerce, allowing online businesses to reach larger markets. In this century, the invention of the smartphone and its ubiquity has allowed businesses to use its easy access as a way of building businesses that not only are easy to scale but have much higher ceilings, if successful. After all, without the reach and convenience of the smartphone, it is unlikely that Uber would have upended the car service business and have been able to scale up as much as it did.

d. **Networking benefits:** One feature of the tech revolution has been a competitive advantage that accrues to companies that are able to establish early dominance in a market. These companies find that their dominance makes it easier for them to attract customers and resources as they get bigger—i.e., networking benefits. In this winner-take-all environment, you can end up with two or three very large players in a market, with each of these players capable of delivering much higher than average revenues. The advertising market provides a good illustration: Two big players, Google and Facebook, have increased their market share each year, at the expense of the newspapers, billboards, and television/radio stations that comprised the market prior to their entry. As their market share has gone up, they have become more attractive destinations for advertisers.

e. **Regulatory constraints:** The potential for a company to grow can be restricted by laws that crack down on oligopolies and natural monopolies, putting caps on market share and growth for larger companies.

In addition to these macro factors, there are business-level factors that can also create ceilings on growth. A key one is the tension between growth ambitions and control, since scaling up more may require company founders to give up control to those who supply the capital that makes scaling up feasible. Thus, businesses where the owners (founders or family) are unwilling to cede control to outsiders may find their revenues plateauing far sooner than businesses where founders are willing to give up a portion of their control in return for larger capital infusions.

Slope of Life Cycle

The slope of the corporate life cycle measures the rate at which a business climbs the life cycle curve, with some companies taking decades to scale up and others accomplishing the same in a few years. To explain these differences, I would look at the following factors:

a. **Capital intensity:** It takes more time to build a business and start generating positive cash flows in capital-intensive industries than in capital-light settings. The telecommunications and cable businesses that endured for decades through the last century required long periods of up-front investment before beginning operations. That said, some of the more successful businesses of the last decade have been start-ups that created capital-light models to enter and upend capital-intensive industries. Take the hospitality business, where the conventional approach to growth for hotel companies was painstaking and time-consuming, requiring the construction of hotels in different parts of the world or, more expensive, acquiring established hotels from others. Airbnb, a company started in 2009, has acquired a significant stake in the business, larger than that of any established hotel company, by acting as an intermediary between hosts (people with excess housing) and customers (people who wanted to use that housing on a temporary basis), a business model that requires little capital and scales up quickly.
b. **Capital access:** Even for capital-light businesses like Airbnb and Uber, access to capital to fund investments critical for rapid growth. When capital is freely accessible and available in large quantities, companies can accelerate through the life cycle quicker than when they have limited or no capital access. For decades, one of the reasons start-ups in the United States were able to grow faster than start-ups in much of the rest of the world was the existence of a vibrant venture capital base in the country. At the other end of the spectrum, the absence of capital markets in Asia and Latin America created economies dominated by family-owned businesses, many

of which never scaled up. Even as venture capital has globalized, access to it can ebb and flow over time, as I will show in the next chapter, and start-ups that are fortunate enough to begin their lives when capital is plentiful will be able to grow more quickly than start-ups that begin their lives when venture capital is scarcer.

c. **Customer inertia:** In marketing, customer inertia refers to the phenomenon of customers remaining attached to offerings from the status quo (existing businesses that dominate the market), reluctant to try products or services from newcomers. What sets customer inertia apart from customer loyalty is that this attachment to existing offerings is rooted less in their meeting customer needs and more in a fear of trying something new. That said, customer inertia varies across businesses, sometimes across cultures and, perhaps, across age groups. A business that offers critical products to an older audience—say, health care—generally faces more customer inertia than one that offers more discretionary products to a younger audience, such as fashion apparel. Uber's initial success in ride sharing came from younger customers, who found its smartphone-based approach to summoning rides more intuitive and appealing than hailing a cab, and its early growth was sufficient for it to eventually draw in older customers, who came for reduced costs and increased convenience.

d. **Regulatory restrictions:** Start-ups in businesses that require licensing or regulatory approval to expand are, by their very nature, constrained in how quickly they can start showing operating success. Consider the biotech business, where even the most promising entrants must go through a time-consuming process of having their products tested before approval for their sale is granted, resulting in long runways before these businesses can take off. A controversial aspect of both the Uber and Airbnb models is that they chose to grow first in many new geographies and to seek regulatory approval later, leading to legal costs and outright bans, at least in some parts of the world.

There is one final point about life cycle slope that is worth making. The same forces that determine how quickly a company climbs up the life cycle will often determine how quickly it is forced to climb down. Thus, a company in a capital-light business will scale up much faster but will also generally scale down much faster as well.

Stay at the Top

The final dimension of the life cycle measures how long a business, once mature, can stay as a mature company, harvesting the benefits of having arrived there. The variability here lies in the competitive advantages that the business has nurtured, as it built up to maturity, and how defensible those advantages are from competitive onslaughts. Companies that are able to build strong and sustainable competitive advantages should have longer and more lucrative stays at the top than companies that don't manage to do so.

I am not a strategist, and rather than bore you with a list of possible competitive advantages, I will borrow Morningstar's solid, albeit dated, assessment of these advantages, with examples, from strong to weak, in table 3.6:

Table 3.6 • Morningstar's Moat Assessment

	Brand Name	Switching Costs	Network Effect	Cost Advantages	Efficient Scale
Wide	**Coca-Cola:** Just sugar water, but consumers pay a premium	**Oracle:** Ties to integrated databases make switching very expensive	**Chicago Mercantile Exchange:** Clearinghouse function creates captive volume.	**UPS**: Past logistics investments result in low marginal costs of delivery	**International Speedway:** Owns the one NASCAR track that each metro area can support
Narrow	**Snapple:** Solid brand, but with less pricing power	**Salesforce:** Popular, but weaker costs to switching	**NYSE Euronext:** Leader in market, but leadership does not create as much of a network effect	**FedEx:** Higher fixed costs from air express segment create smaller cost advantages	**Southern Company:** Natural geographic monopoly, backed by regulators
No Moat	**Cott:** Generic player with no brand loyalty or pricing power	**TIBCO:** High-end software but low or no costs to switching to competitors	**Knight Capital:** An order-taker/market maker, with little in networking benefits	**Con-way:** Trucking company, but fragmented business with few cost advantages	**Valero:** Refiner that has to be a price-taker in a commodity business

Source: Morningstar

There is much to debate with the Morningstar choice of companies for the various cells in the table, and I disagree with the moat assessments of some of the companies picked, but the process that Morningstar followed in making these assessments is a healthy one. Rather than create a long list of competitive advantages, mixing in strong, weak, and nonexistent advantages, Morningstar is drawing a contrast between the advantages that are strong and long-standing and those that are weak and fleeting.

Assessing how strong a company's moats are remains as much art as craft, but Michael J. Mauboussin has done some yeoman's work on providing structure to this analysis, using accounting disclosures, and a return on capital, to measure the height of a moat and competitive advantage periods, based upon market pricing, to measure its sustainability.* As you consider the moat advantages of a business, it is worth noting that even

* M. J. Mauboussin, D. Callahan, and D. Majd, "Measuring the Moat," Credit Suisse, 2016.

the widest moats can erode over time, and that a business that was considered impregnable in one period can become vulnerable in another.

Contrasting Life Cycles

As you can see, there are multiple factors that determine why life cycles vary across businesses, with some of these factors, like capital access, playing a role in both how long a business lasts and how quickly it grows. That said, it is also clear that some of these factors are not within the control of start-up businesses, and a start-up that is born in an environment where regulation is rife and capital is difficult to raise is already at a disadvantage relative to a start-up in a business where scaling up is easy, capital is accessible, and there is little customer inertia. In figure 3.4, I bring all of these factors together in explaining life cycle dimensions (length, height, slope, and flatness).

FIGURE 3.4 | Corporate Life Cycle Dimensions

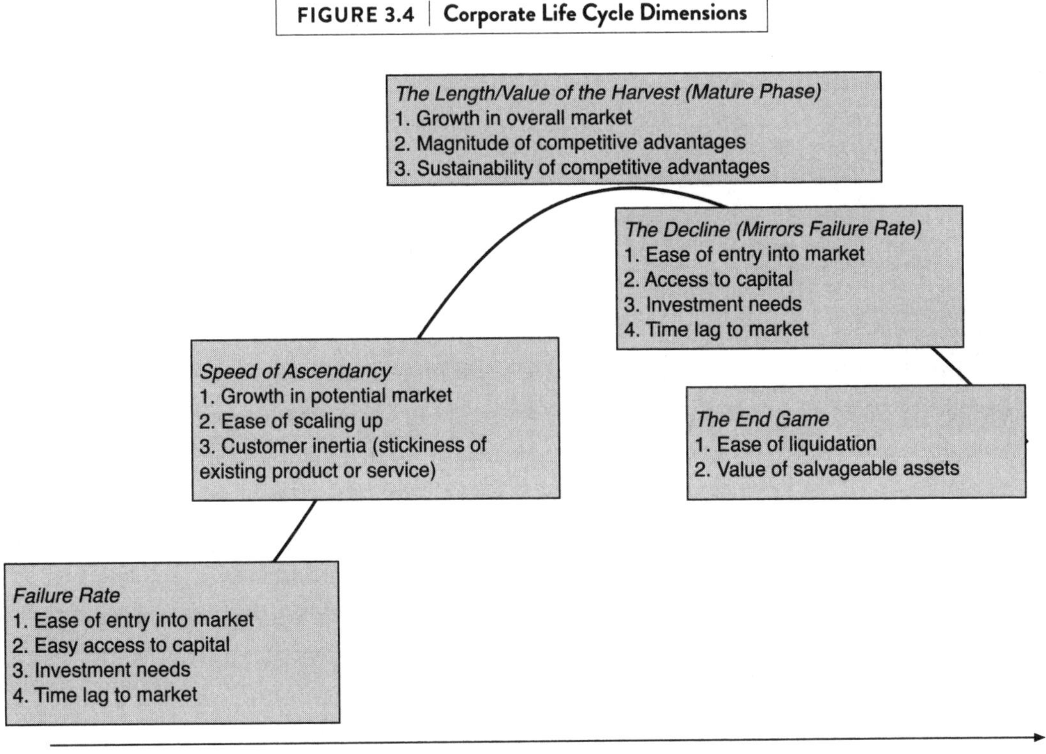

As a result of the differences across businesses, it should come as no surprise that the corporate life cycle can take many different forms. In figure 3.5, I illustrate just three of those forms:

FIGURE 3.5 | Corporate Life Cycle—Three Common Variations

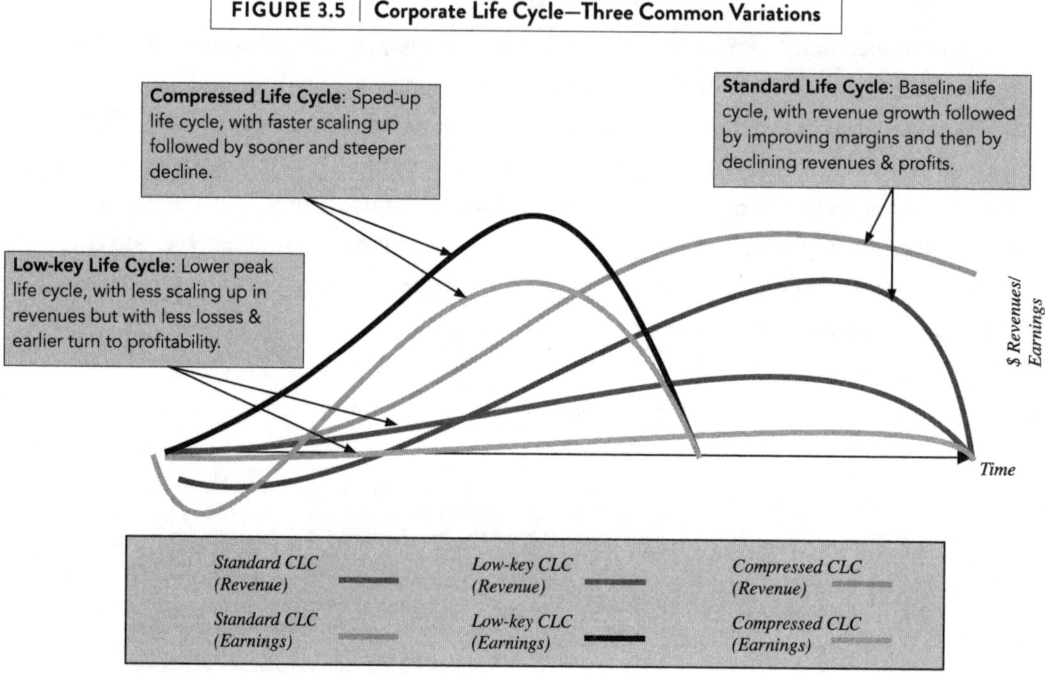

Put simply, the base or standard life cycle illustration that I have been using so far in this book as the lead-in to discussion may very well be the exception, since only a few firms follow its path of a gradual buildup as a growth business, an extended stay as a mature business, and a gradual decline. Some firms find ways to build up more quickly, but then stay mature for a shorter periods before embarking on a rapid decline, thus exhibiting a compressed life cycle. Many firms, even if successful, never scale up, constrained by either an absence of capital, a lack of ambition, or a small target market, and so have low-key life cycles that can extend for very long periods.

Life Cycle Twists, Trends, and Changes

The influx of technology companies has changed both markets and economies. In this section, I would like to use the corporate life cycle construct to discuss two changes that technology has brought to the market, with significant consequences for both business and investing.

Tech versus Non-tech Life Cycles

The great companies of the twentieth century, from the railroad, oil, and steel companies that dominated the economy in the earlier decades to the automobile manufacturing firms that represented the heart of the economy and the market in the middle of the century, shared common features. They required large investments in production resources, in periods when capital was not always easily accessible, and it took decades for these companies to scale up. However, once they reached maturity, these firms were able to use the same factors that slowed their climb up the life cycle curve to fend off competition and stay mature for decades. The auto business is a good illustration: the big three automakers (GM, Ford, and Chrysler) essentially had the US auto market to themselves until the oil crisis in the 1970s and the rise of Japanese competitors. It is undeniable that automakers have faced challenges, and perhaps even decline, in recent decades, but that decline has been slow and has taken place in fits and starts.

In contrast, consider Yahoo!, a company founded in the 1990s, but one I would consider a prototype for a typical twenty-first-century company. Its search engine started delivering revenues quickly, albeit with losses, and the company's market capitalization breached $100 billion in 1999, less than a decade after it was founded. That type of rapid growth has played out in many other companies in the last two decades as they have climbed the market-cap rankings to displace their traditional competitors. While the status quo companies have watched these rapid scaling up stories with envy, there is a dark side to the rapid growth at tech companies, since the same forces that allow them to scale up often become an impediment when they become mature and accelerate decline once it starts. Yahoo!'s stay at the top as a search engine, with the concurrent online advertising revenues, lasted five years before Google moved in and displaced it as the market leader, and once Yahoo! started to decline, its unraveling was rapid and devastating over the next decade. In figure 3.6, I illustrate the tech life cycle and contrast it with the non-tech life cycle, and you can see why I describe tech companies as aging in "dog years."

FIGURE 3.6 | Tech versus Non-tech Life Cycle

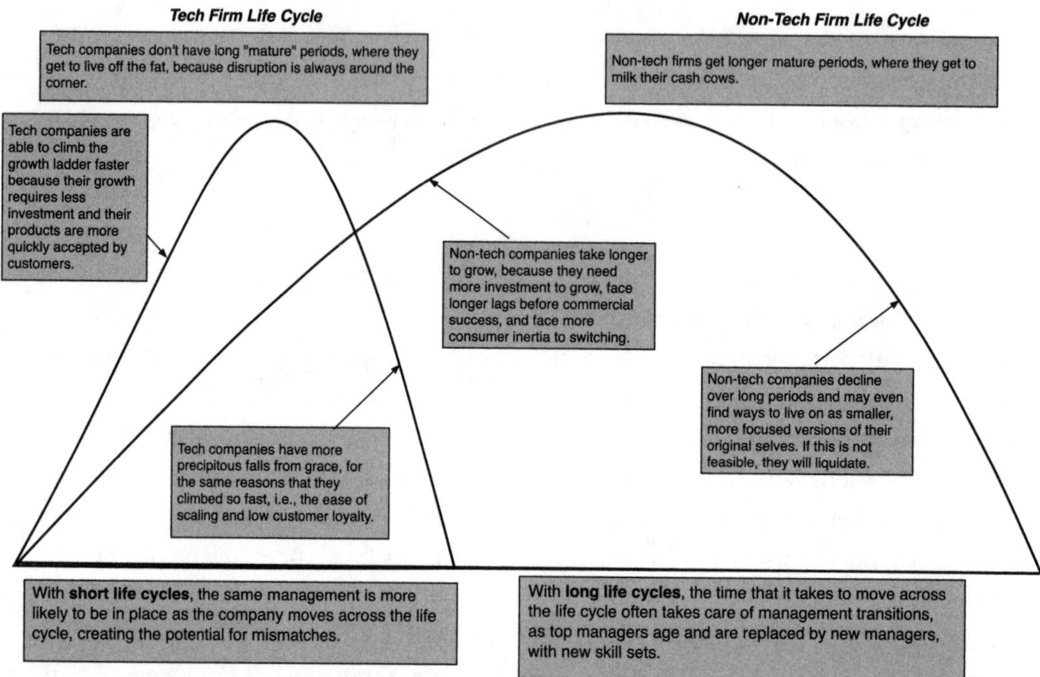

To the extent that the center of gravity, in the economy and markets, has shifted toward companies with much shorter life cycles, running a successful company today requires a rethinking of business management and investing. Much of the wisdom I read in business books and use in business models was developed in the twentieth century for the long-life-cycle company, and applying it to a compressed-life-cycle company can be disastrous. To provide one concrete example, when valuing a company using a discounted cash flow model, the conventional practice to apply closure is to estimate a terminal value for a business at the end of the forecast period, generally obtained by assuming that the business will continue in perpetuity. The perpetuity assumption is made for convenience, since the value you obtain with it is very close to the value that you would get by assuming that the business will continue for 50, 60, or 80 years, a defensible assumption for the long-life-cycle company. When valuing a company with a 25-year life cycle, using a perpetuity assumption at the end of 10 years, when it likely only has 15 years of life left, will yield a distorted terminal value.

Conglomerates and Holding Companies

There is one final point that must be made, at least for purposes of understanding the corporate life cycle: the distinction between a company and a business. While much of the discussion above has been about the life cycle of a business, it is possible to create a company that outlasts individual businesses. To see why, reflect that a company can be in multiple businesses, effectively creating a portfolio of businesses, some of which are young, some mature, and some declining. A conglomerate clearly fits the bill—but putting high-growth, mature, and declining businesses under one corporate umbrella risks opening the door to cross subsidization (cash-rich businesses) and inefficiency in management. In short, the good businesses in the conglomerate portfolio can fund growth in the bad ones, with disastrous consequences for value.

A holding company is a better fit, since not only can its holdings be in different stages of the life cycle, it can add new businesses and shed old ones to keep the life cycle in balance. There are family-controlled holding entities in Europe, Asia, and Latin America that do exactly this, and to the extent that they can do it well, these entities will have much longer lifetimes than publicly traded firms that operate in only one or two businesses and are held by institutional investors. Consider, for instance, the Tata Group, one of India's oldest and best-regarded family holding groups. Founded in 1868, when Jamsetji Tata bought a bankrupt oil mill that he converted into a cotton mill, it now includes more than a hundred companies under its holding company umbrella, sprawling across multiple businesses, as can be seen in figure 3.7 for a subset of companies in the group.

FIGURE 3.7 | The Tata Group—Business Breakdown

In 1868	Tata Group in 2021	
	Sector	*Tata Companies*
Jamsetji Tata founded a trading company that bought a bankrupt oil mill in Chinchpokli in Mumbai and converted it into a cotton mill.	Metals	Tata Steel, Tata Metaliks
	Technology	Tata Elxsi, Tata Consultancy Services
	Financial	Tata Capital, Tata AIG, Tata AIA
	Automotive	Tata Motors, Tata AutoComp, JLR
	Retail	Tata Starbucks, Tata CLiQ, Tata Tanishq
	Infrastructure	Tata Power, Tata Projects
	Telecom	Tata Sky, Tata Communications, Tata Teleservices
	Tourism	Taj & Ginger Hotels, Vivanta, Vistara, AirAsia
	Aerospace and Defense	Tata Advanced Systems
	Agriculture & Food	Tata Tea, Tetley, Tata Agrico
	Consumer Products	Titan, Voltas
	Housing	Tata Housing

In the last two decades, as tech companies soared in market cap and earnings, many family-owned businesses added tech subsidiaries, albeit with different amounts of capital invested and different degrees of separation from the family-owned parent. The largest single slice of the Tata Group is Tata Consultancy Services, a technology company, but in the last decade, the group has invested in multiple technology start-ups. Not all these undertakings succeed, and the extent to which they can extend the life of a company will vary across companies.

Note that the longer lives of family group holding companies do not necessarily make them more valuable or productive than stand-alone companies. In fact, there is evidence that investors in these holding companies discount their value for potential conflicts of interests, wherein family interests are put ahead of shareholder interests, as well as inefficiencies that can proliferate across group companies. Family culture can also cut both ways, helping at some family group companies and hurting at others. Even at the Tata Group, there are shareholders who have taken issue with corporate governance at individual companies and raised questions about whether Tata Consultancy Services, with its immense profitability and value, is carrying other companies in the group on its back.

The Disruptor Effect

Disruption has always been part of business, as newcomers seek out ways to enter an existing business with a new product or business model and shake up the status quo. However, the pace and reach of disruption seems to have become greater in the last two decades, partly because of developments in technology and partly because of greater access to capital, not only from the traditional sources (like venture capital) but also from public-market investors. Businesses that were considered impervious to disruption just a few decades ago, such as telecommunications, energy, and automobiles, have been upended by newcomers.

While much of the debate around disruption has focused on the disruptors, it is worth focusing just as much attention on the disrupted. Amazon's devastating effects on brick-and-mortar retailing in the United States are well documented, and Netflix, with its subscriber-growth-based model and large investments, has made the entertainment business much risker and less profitable for traditional entertainment companies. Global ride-sharing companies have laid waste to smaller and localized taxicab companies, and Google and Facebook have decimated traditional advertising businesses.

From a practical standpoint, you could argue that there is now a far greater chance of being disrupted today, for companies in almost every business, than just a few years ago, and that threat must show up in business and investment practices. First, the assumption of mean reversion that is at the heart of how many analysts run and evaluate businesses must be reexamined—i.e., a decline in margins at a company with a long history of earning high margins may not be temporary, if there is a chance of disruption, and the assumption that there will be a bounce back to historical margins may not be merited. Second, even companies with strong competitive advantages (brand name, licensing, economies of scale) should have contingency plans, since change from disruption, when it happens, will be abrupt and damaging. Inertia, whereby companies continue to do what they have done in the past because it has worked well before, can lead these companies to be unprepared for the changes that disruptors can bring to their businesses. Third, regulators and lawmakers must consider the possibilities that the rules and laws that they write to keep existing companies in check, often with the best of intentions (increase competition, protect customers), can handicap them when disruptors enter the game. Taxicab operators were undoubtedly put at a disadvantage by rules imposed on them by regulators that Uber had no qualms about ignoring, and a portion of the growth in fintech companies can be attributed to the fact that they are able to provide products and services in the financial services business that the traditional players (banks, insurance companies) are prohibited from providing, without facing the same regulatory constraints.

Conclusion

The corporate life cycle can take very different forms at different businesses, with variations in length, height, and duration of the stable phase (flatness). In this chapter, I looked at the factors that can explain these variations and argued that while some are out of the control of a business, others are within its control. A start-up whose founder refuses to give up control will grow slower than one whose founder is more willing to trade off control for capital, and there are companies, like Uber and Airbnb, that have found ways of overcoming conventional barriers to growth in their businesses, sometimes by cutting corners and breaking rules. If there is an overriding message, though, it is that every approach carries trade-offs, since the choices you make as a business that allow you to scale up quickly may impede you when you try to create a sustainable and profitable business model.

The Corporate Life Cycle: Transitions

IN THE CHAPTERS LEADING to this one, I looked at the phases that comprise the corporate life cycle and discussed why the life cycle takes different forms in different businesses. In this chapter, I would like to take a closer look at the transitions, in ownership, operating, and financing, that are needed to get from one phase to another. These transitions are significant for two reasons. The first is that transitions always involve change, and not all businesses (or their founders) do well with change, with success in business most often coming to those that can navigate the transitions most smoothly. The second is that there are macro changes occurring in each of the transitions that are worth examining, because they have implications for businesses that are approaching these transitions.

Corporate Life Cycle Transitions

As a business moves through the life cycle, it will face tests that it must overcome to get to the next stage. These tests can sometimes occur at a given point in time, but they are more likely to happen over a longer period, and there are times when a business that has previously passed a test will find itself retested. With all those caveats, I will begin by classifying these transitions into three groupings:

- The first group are *operating transitions*, with start-ups facing a test of how to convert an idea into a product, young-growth companies trying to journey from having a product to developing a viable business model, high-growth companies attempting to unlock the challenge of scaling up a small to a large business, mature-growth companies seeking to maintain high growth on a much larger scale, mature stable companies figuring out how to keep competitors and disruptors from upending their businesses, and declining companies confronting the problems that come with a shrinking market.
- The second group are *financial transitions*. With start-ups, this transition will almost always require looking for external financing from venture capitalists and other risk capital providers who are willing to make a bet on unproven ideas. With young-growth companies, the need for capital will pick up further, as a combination of nascent business models and investments needed for growth will create negative cash flows, and new rounds of venture capital funding will ensue. With high-growth companies, the option to enter public markets may be available at least for the most successful ones, as venture capitalists plot exit strategies and public-market investors enter the game. With mature-growth companies, operating success will bring the benefits of internal financing, sometimes augmented by financing from public markets, in the form of debt or equity. With mature stable companies, profitable operations and stable growth will combine to create large, positive cash flows, allowing them to consider borrowing money (debt) and returning cash to owners (dividends and buybacks). In declining companies, the key financial challenge is to reduce debt (by retiring existing debt as it comes due) and shrink equity (through liquidating dividends) as the company scales down.
- As a company goes through these operating and financial transitions, there will be *governance transitions* that occur at each phase, and these transitions can sometimes be difficult for founders to deal with. In the start-up phase, bringing in external capital providers (venture capitalists) will require founders to share ownership of their business with individuals who may have very different views on how the business should evolve. In the young-growth phase, the challenges of building a business may test founders on whether they are willing to take advice on business building from others, a sharing of operating power with outsiders that can be stressful. In the high-growth phase, especially at businesses that can scale up, the capacity to build management teams and delegate responsibility can make the difference between success and failure. In the mature-growth phase—again especially among those companies that go public—those running the firm will face the challenge of balancing insider (founder)

interests with public-market investor interests, with the latter being disproportionately growth investors who prize growth over cash return. As companies become mature, stable businesses, the shift toward public-market investors driving decisions will continue, but the composition of public-market investors is likely to change, with value investors, who are focused less on growth and more on cash returns, taking over. In decline, if the company stays public, it is likely to face pressure from activist investors to spin off or divest assets and return more cash, and in some cases, investors may take it private again, with the intent of liquidating large portions and cashing out. In figure 4.1, I summarize these transitions.

FIGURE 4.1 | Corporate Life Cycle Transitions

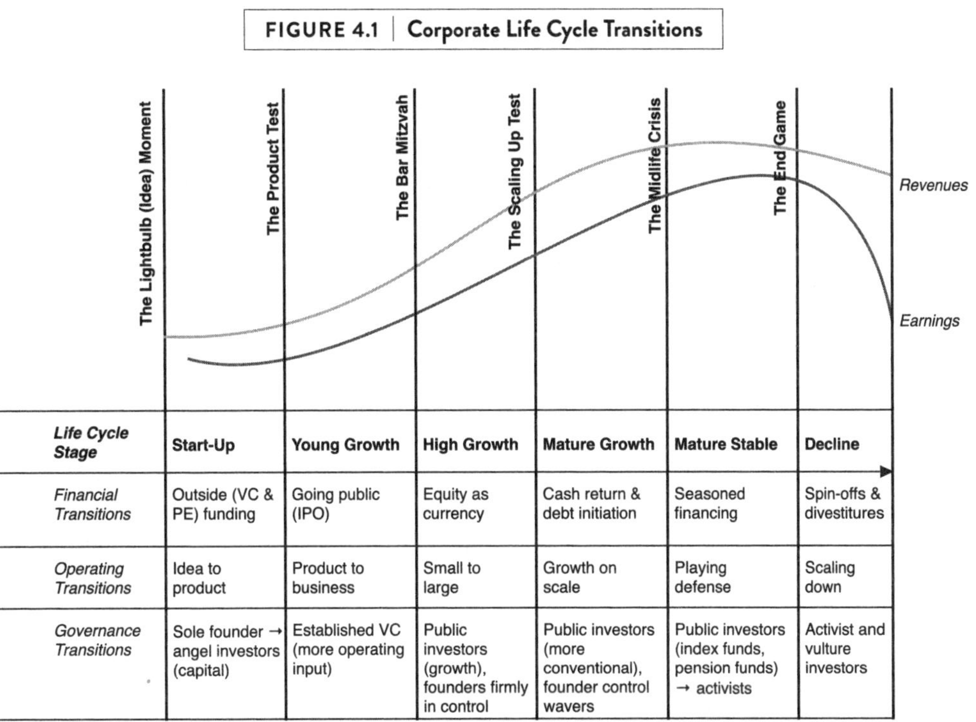

Life Cycle Stage	Start-Up	Young Growth	High Growth	Mature Growth	Mature Stable	Decline
Financial Transitions	Outside (VC & PE) funding	Going public (IPO)	Equity as currency	Cash return & debt initiation	Seasoned financing	Spin-offs & divestitures
Operating Transitions	Idea to product	Product to business	Small to large	Growth on scale	Playing defense	Scaling down
Governance Transitions	Sole founder → angel investors (capital)	Established VC (more operating input)	Public investors (growth), founders firmly in control	Public investors (more conventional), founder control wavers	Public investors (index funds, pension funds) → activists	Activist and vulture investors

In chapter 2, I talked about operating transitions and why so few ideas become products, as well as why only a subset of these products become businesses, and yet a smaller fraction of these scale up. In the rest of this chapter, I will focus on the players who enter as businesses transition, starting with the venture capitalists and others who provide the capital for very young companies, moving to public-market investors, both at the time a company goes public and in the years after, and closing with the activist and private equity investors who do the mopping up in declining companies.

Young Company Financing

Young businesses need capital to survive their early years, and through history, that capital has come from investors willing to live with the risk of failure that is part and parcel of these companies. In this section, I will begin by looking at venture capital as a primary source of funding to young companies, starting with its history and then examining the VC funding process, as well as the ebbs and flows of venture capital over time. I will then move on to how young company financing has widened to include corporate venture capital arms, crowdfunding, and public-market investors, and how this expansion has created a gray market at the nexus of private and public-market investing, where large private companies can continue to stay private while enjoying the access to capital that used to be available only to public companies.

Venture Capital

While I assume that venture capital has always existed as a source of capital infusions to private businesses, venture capital in its current, structured form is of more recent origin and was primarily US-based for the early part of its existence. This section begins with an examination of the venture capital funding process and continues with a history of the ebbs and flows of venture capital over time.

A SHORT HISTORY

Young companies have always drawn on capital providers, and the earliest suppliers of this capital date back centuries. To illustrate the early attempts at venture capital investing, Tom Nicholas, in his examination of the history of venture capital, goes back to nineteenth-century whaling ventures in the United States—highly lucrative if successful, but with a high likelihood of failure.* The laying of the railroads in the late nineteenth and early twentieth century required immense amounts of capital, but that capital was provided by bankers, with Andrew Mellon and J. P. Morgan among the key figures.

Venture capital, as an organized source of capital, can trace its history back to American Research and Development (ARD) Corporation, founded in 1946 by Georges Doriot, a Harvard Business School professor who raised funds from foundations, endowments, and pension funds to invest in young companies. One of its biggest successes was the investment of $70,000 that it made, in 1957, in Digital Equipment Corporation,

* T. Nicholas, *VC: An American History* (Cambridge, MA: Harvard University Press, 2019).

which delivered a value of $52 million a few years later. A precipitating factor in the growth of the venture capital business was the Small Business Investment Companies (SBIC) program, enacted by Congress in the 1950s with the intent of providing government funding for start-ups. While the government funding itself was underwhelming in its impact, it opened the door for venture capital firms, with Sutter Hill Ventures, a Palo Alto VC firm founded by William Draper and Paul Wythes in 1964, being an early standout. In the years since, Silicon Valley has remained a central hub for venture capital. With a few long-term winners—and a lot of entry and exit, as venture capital funds have ebbed and flowed over time—not only has its reach has expanded across the US (Boston, New York, Austin, and Miami), it now has a global footprint. Between 2010 and 2020, venture capital not only multiplied its size (in capital), it also exerted an outsized influence in public markets, as the companies that it built and brought to market were among the biggest public-market winners.

THE VC PROCESS

When a start-up or young company decides to seek out venture capital, there is a process, albeit with wide variations across firms, that it must go through. The very first rounds of venture capital, called pre-seed or seed funding, are provided by venture capitalists who are willing to invest in the riskiest of businesses and to accept high failure rates. The businesses that accept that seed capital, and thereby can move on to the next stage of the life cycle, will seek out more venture capital in subsequent rounds, with each round requiring some sacrifice of ownership, in return for capital provided, as can be seen in figure 4.2.

FIGURE 4.2 | The Venture Capital Process

Pre-Seed & Seed
This is usually the first capital raised by a start-up, as it works on converting idea to product.

Series A
Funding of a much greater magnitude than seed money for firms further along the idea-to-product transition.

Series B
Funding for businesses that are generally working on developing business models and have user/customer activity.

Series C
Funding for businesses that have business models that are producing results but want to scale up.

VC Terms
In return for providing capital, VCs get a share of ownership of the firm, based on pricing.

VC Pricing
VCs price young firms based on activity metrics (users, downloads, subscribers), or multiples of forward revenues or earnings.

VC Rounds
A growing firm can have multiple rounds of financing from VCs at each stage, with each round commanding a different pricing.

VC Up & Down Rounds
A new round that occurs at a higher (lower) price than a prior one is an up (down) round. Up and down rounds can sometimes alter the terms of prior rounds.

There is a misconception among many, including a few venture capitalists, that venture capitalists value companies by making a judgment on how much ownership they will demand in return for capital provided. The truth is that venture capitalists price companies based upon what other venture capitalists are paying for businesses and scaling that price to an observable metric. Thus, a VC looking at a young start-up with little in revenues, large losses, and a million subscribers will price the company on its subscriber count and what other VCs are paying per subscriber at the companies they invest in. As a business starts to show tangible revenues, with the promise of a turnaround in earnings in a few years, the pricing may shift to forward revenues, or earnings, and a pricing multiple based upon those metrics, with a target discount rate operating partly as a mechanism to reflect risk and time value and partly as a negotiating tool.

FIGURE 4.3 | VC Forward Pricing

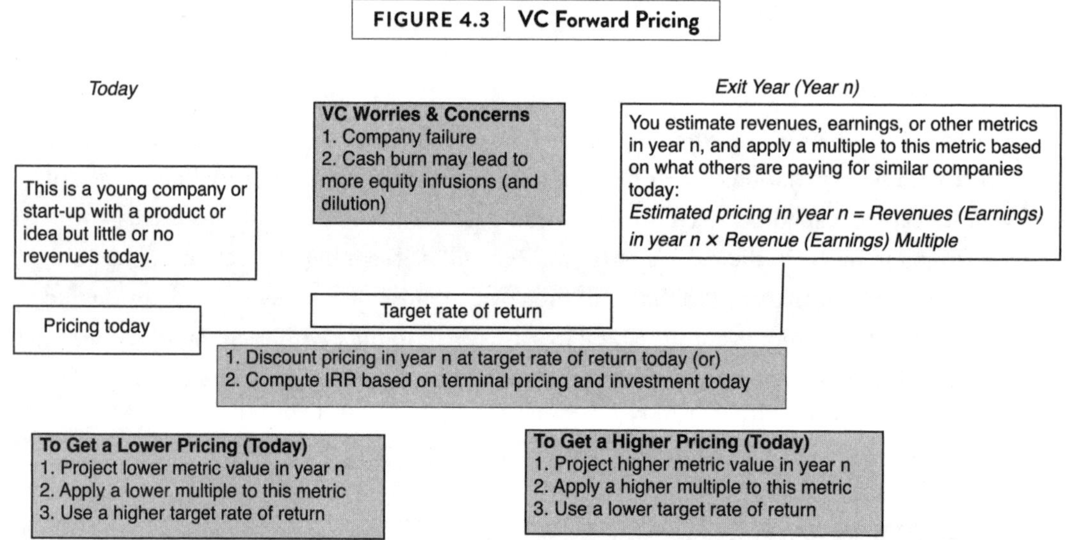

To provide a very simple example, assume that you are a VC evaluating a company that is expected to have \$50 million in revenues in year 4 of operation, that other VCs are paying five times revenues for similar companies, and that your target rate of return is 40%. Your estimate of the pricing of the company today is:

$$\text{Pricing for company in year 4} = \$50 \text{ million} \times 5 = \$250 \text{ million}$$

$$\text{Pricing today} = \frac{\$250 \text{ million}}{(1.40)^4} = \$65.08 \text{ million}$$

Since there is a pricing, pure and simple, that is only loosely moored in business fundamentals, the process becomes one of negotiation, with the venture capitalists pushing for lower revenues in year 4, a lower multiple to be applied to those revenues, and a higher target rate of return, and the founder pushing back with the opposite. For those who are familiar with intrinsic valuation, the target rate of return may look like a discount rate, but it is not, since it is, in a sense, made up. In July 2022, for instance, venture capitalists providing seed financing were targeting returns more than 50% when pricing the businesses seeking out the financing. While that target return may sound outlandishly high, as an annual return, looking at long-term averages, the actual return earned by venture capitalists on seed financing investments was closer to 20%.

There are two other aspects of venture capital that make it unique, and understanding what they are and why they exist is central to accessing or investing venture capital.

a. **Pre-money versus post-money value:** Venture capitalists often draw a distinction between pre-money valuation of a business (the value prior to the venture capitalist investing) and a post-money valuation of the same business (after the venture capital infusion). There is an element of judgment involved here, leading to different approaches to differentiating between the two estimates. If you are working with an existing pricing of a business, the post-money pricing is estimated by adding the capital infusion to the pricing. Alternatively, the venture capital pricing described in the last section is considered a post-money pricing, and netting out the capital provided from it yields the pre-money pricing.
b. **VC protections:** When venture capitalists invest in a young business, they are hoping for upside, but they are also concerned about the downside. If a young business that a VC invests in is priced at $100 million, a $20 million capital infusion gives the VC a 20% share of that business. However, if that business drops in value to $50 million, and it then seeks out a fresh venture capital infusion of $10 million, that investment will also give its provider a 20% share of the business, leaving the first provider worse off with each subsequent "down round." Many venture capital investments provide protection against this ownership loss by adjusting the ownership shares of existing venture capitalists to reflect the lower business value on the down round. Figure 4.4 provides a sense of how the downside protection works in a hypothetical VC investment, where the VC invests $100 million to get a 10% share of a company with an estimated value of $1 billion but gets full protection if the company's value drops to less than $1 billion. If you are wondering why you should care, the answer is that the presence of downside protections makes the common practice of extrapolating

the overall pricing of a company from a round of VC funding dicey. Thus, when a VC invests $50 million in a company for a 5% share, the assumption that the company must be worth $1 billion ($50 million/.05) does not hold if the VC received significant downside protection in the investment. That downside protection has value, and if that value is incorporated into the price paid, the true value of the company will be much lower than $1 billion.*

FIGURE 4.4 | VC Protection Clauses and Payoffs

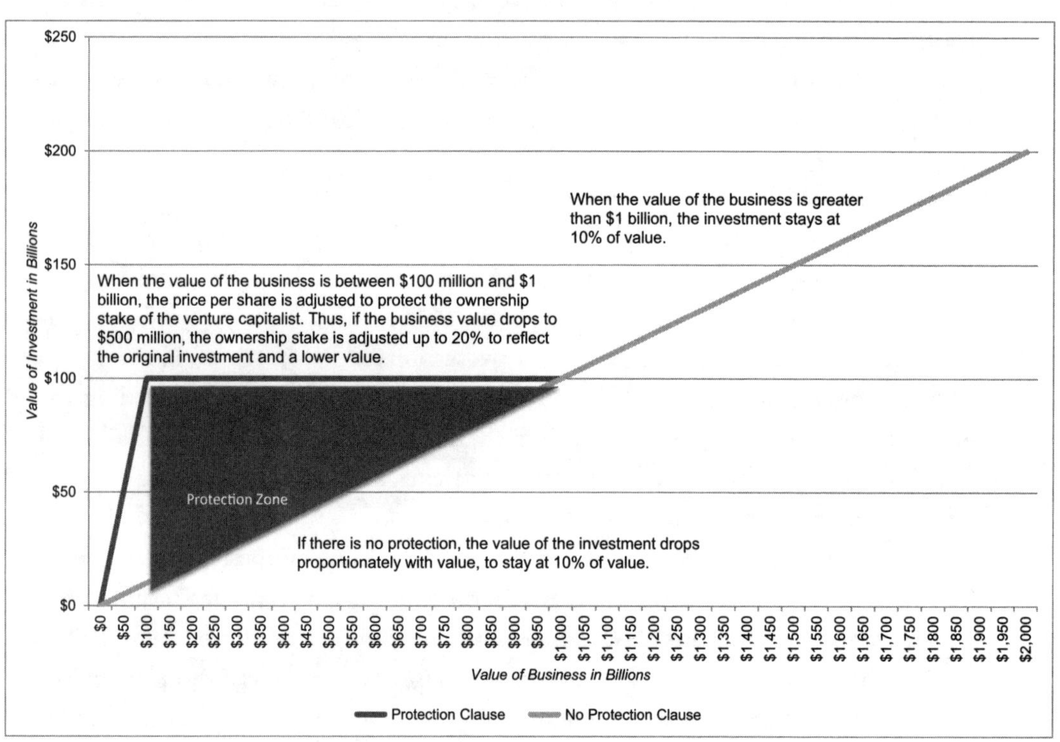

THE EBBS AND FLOWS OF VC

Young and start-up companies are dependent on venture capital not just to meet their reinvestment needs to grow, but also to survive. The availability of venture capital, though, can vary over time and reflects the willingness on the part of investors to accept risk. In

* In effect, venture capitalists are receiving put options with their investment, and if that put option has a value of $15 million, the VC is investing $35 million ($50 million - $15 million) for 5% of the company, making the company's value only $700 million.

figure 4.5, I look at the ebbs and flows of venture capital between 1985 and 2021 in the United States.

FIGURE 4.5 | The Ebbs and Flows of Venture Capital over Time

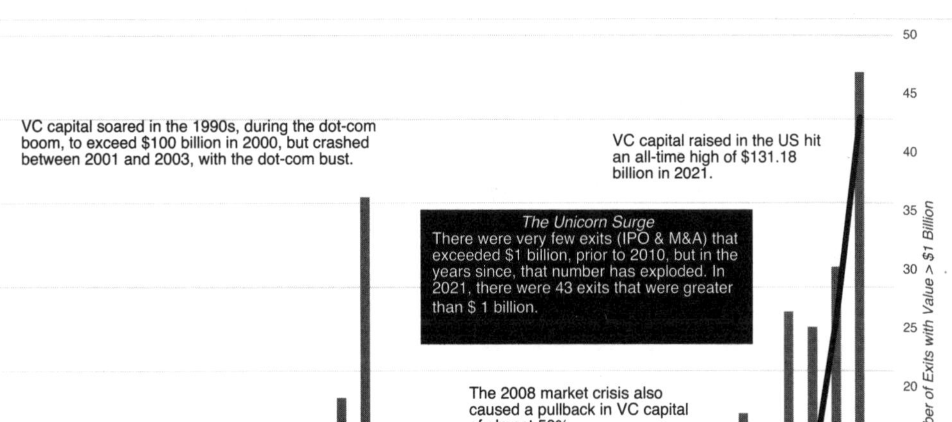

In the last forty years, there have been periods of plenty (the 1990s, 2011–2020), interspersed with periods of scarcity (2002–2004, 2009–10), and these different fields of play have predictable consequences for young companies seeking capital. When venture capital is plentiful and accessible, young companies are able not only to raise the capital they want but also to get better terms (giving up less ownership in return). When venture capital becomes scarce, these same companies are likely to face down rounds and failure.

Trends in Young Company Funding

Looking back at the last few decades demonstrates that the business of funding young companies has changed, drawing new types of investors into the fold, often with creative variations on the traditional VC structure.

1. **Globalization:** For much of the last century, venture capital, at least in its structured form, was primarily US-focused, as young companies in the rest of the world made do with government grants and bank funding to get by, putting them at a disadvantage relative to their established domestic competitors. That changed as access to venture capital started to globalize during the 1990s, in the dot-com era, and continued to do so in the last decade, especially in Asia. In the second quarter of 2022, while the US continued to lead the VC race, with $52.9 billion invested in 2,698 deals, there was $27 billion invested in Asia in 2,630 deals, and $22.7 billion in Europe in 1,705 deals. While Latin America ($2.3 billion), Africa ($0.88 billion), Australia ($0.7 billion), and Canada ($2 billion) lagged in this period, there is life now in the VC business globally, evening the playing field for start-ups around the world.
2. **Investor makeup:** In its original form, venture capital was marketed as an alternative investment to institutional investors (endowment funds, pension funds) and to very wealthy investors. In the last decade, with innovations made possible by technology, the game has opened up to individual and retail investors. Crowdfunding, for instance, has allowed some young companies to raise capital from customers and small investors who see promise in their products, with $13.6 billion raised in the global crowdfunding market in 2021. As work is done to provide more protections and expanded corporate governance rights to investors in crowdfunded ventures, the crowdfunding market will grow and draw more investors into its fold. In the last decade, I have also seen public equity funds (like Fidelity and T. Rowe Price) dip their toes into the young company funding business, supplying billions of dollars in capital to private businesses.
3. **Corporate venture capital:** Some of the capital invested in young companies has always come from mature companies that have excess cash and relatively few organic investments, or from companies seeking to make strategic investments in start-ups that may provide technology or support to their businesses. The flows from corporate venture capital have increased in the last two decades because of two developments. The first is the growth in the health care and technology businesses, where mature companies have discovered that the most efficient way for them to grow is to put their capital into young companies with promising technologies, rather than spend the same money on internal R&D. The second is that the winners in these businesses have also accumulated unprecedented amounts of cash on their balance sheets, giving them capital to invest in a multitude of businesses. Thus, companies like Google, Microsoft, and Apple, each of which has $100 billion in cash or more to invest, have venture capital funds that they run.

As access to capital has widened for young, growth companies, it has changed the calculus of when these companies choose to go public and even how they grow. Companies that would have outgrown their venture capital funding and had to go public a few decades ago can now choose to stay private, accessing corporate, retail, and public equity funds. A good example is Uber, a company that raised and spent tens of billions of dollars as a private company before going public, in 2019, at a $60 billion valuation.

Public Equity

Of the many young businesses that convert ideas into products and then develop business models that succeed, only a few become publicly traded companies. For some businesses, the reason is scale; even with scaling up, they never reach the critical mass of size needed to be a publicly traded company. For others, it is a choice made by founders and capital providers to stay private, largely because they do not want the scrutiny that comes with being publicly traded. In this section, I will focus on the subset of companies that choose to go the public equity route, by first looking at the process of going public and then at subsequent access to financing as a publicly traded firm.

Initial Public Offerings (IPOs)

In this section, I will begin by looking at the trade-off of the decision that some businesses face between staying private and going public, before describing the process of going public. With the latter description, I will draw attention to the way in which companies have gone public in the United States for much of the last century, as well as alternatives that have emerged in the last decade.

THE TRADE-OFF OF GOING PUBLIC

In the section on venture capital, I highlighted the pros and cons of venture capital for privately owned businesses, with founder-owners offering ownership stakes in their businesses in exchange for capital infusions. For some ambitious firms with big growth plans, there may come a point where venture capitalists are either unable to provide capital in the amounts needed and/or require disproportionately large ownership stakes in return. It is at that point that the option to go public becomes a consideration, at least for those firms where public equity markets are offering better pricing terms and higher liquidity. The better pricing terms arise because public equity investors have more diversified portfolios than most venture capitalists and are thus much more willing to let some risks pass through without demanding higher returns in exchange. The greater liquidity in public markets is driven by first standardizing equity ownership (with one or two classes of shares) and then breaking share ownership into smaller-sized bites that are more tradeable. That greater liquidity allows existing owners (founders, venture capitalists) to cash out on at least a portion of their ownership as well as enabling employees of the firm, many of whom have been paid in stock or options, to also monetize these benefits.

There are at least two costs to going public that must be weighed into the decision. The first is that the information disclosure requirements for firms in public markets tend to be more onerous than for those in private businesses, and to the extent that this disclosure is costly and/or reveals information about the business that may be useful to competitors, it may be undesirable. The second is that the pressure on the firm to match or beat investor expectations on a short-term (quarterly, semi-annual) basis on metrics (user numbers, revenues, earnings) can not only add to the stresses of managing a firm but can, at least in some cases, lead to decisions that are damaging to the firm in the long term. The trade-off of going public, in conjunction with the increased access to private capital that young companies have had for the last decade, has caused many of them to delay going public, but it has not stopped the process.

THE GOING-PUBLIC PROCESS

For decades, the standard operating procedure for a company going public has been to use a banker or a banking syndicate to market itself to public investors at a "guaranteed" price, in return for a sizeable fee. That process has developed warts along the way, but it has remained surprisingly unchanged, even as the investing world has changed dramatically. The process begins with the young company that plans to go public approaching a banker or bankers about its plans. The bankers analyze the company's financials, help in filing the documents (prospectus) required by regulatory authorities, price the company by assessing demand for its shares, and then set an offering price that is guaranteed. The guarantee effectively requires the investment bank to deliver the offering price even if, in hindsight, the demand does not exist to deliver that price—and while that sounds like a good deal, it comes with a catch that I will explore next. Figure 4.6 describes the standard going-public process.

FIGURE 4.6 | A Banker-Led Initial Public Offering

Issuing Company	Banker's Role
Private company chooses to go public.	**Timing** Help in finding timing window and location for public offering. Also help in crafting company's narrative and getting financials in order for offering.
Company picks a lead investment banker to manage the process, who creates a syndicate of other banks to help market and distribute.	
Issuing company files a prospectus and specifies how much it plans to raise in the issuance and how it plans to use the proceeds.	**Filing & Offering Details** Assist in the writing of the prospectus and in offering size.
Bankers set a preliminary price and test out the price with prospective investors.	**Pricing** Frame the pricing (metric and peer group), gauge demand for the shares, and fine-tune the pricing to keep issuing company and investors "happy."
Bankers decide on final offering price and number of shares that will be offered.	
Bankers and company managers do a road show for investors.	**Selling/Marketing** With company's help, inform and excite potential investors.
On offering date, shares start trading, with market setting a clearing price.	**Price Guarantee** If market opens at below "offer" price, deliver the guaranteed price.
Post-offering, bankers provide support for the issuing company's shares, allowing for a smooth transition to owners cashing out.	**After-Market Support** Provide both explicit support, by buying shares if needed, and implicit support, with favorable research and recommendations.

While this process has held its own for almost a century, its effectiveness is being questioned on many fronts. First, the notion that a young company, unknown to investors and untested, needs a seal of approval from an investment bank is fraying, as the companies going public acquire higher profiles and investment banking reputations dwindle. In the Facebook IPO, for instance, there is reason to believe that more people had heard about Facebook at the time of its offering than had heard of Morgan Stanley. Second, the marketing and pricing services offered by bankers have lost value as alternatives emerge, and the investment banking guarantee is rendered almost worthless by the fact that bankers discount the offering price so much. The evidence for the last contention is in what happens in the market on the first trading day, where companies see their stocks jump 20%, 30%, or even 50% from the offering price.

As company founders and venture capitalists confront these realities and wonder why they should be paying bankers 5 to 6% of the proceeds for nonexistent benefits, there are a few that have suggested an alternative approach to going public, wherein private companies would list directly in the market and let the market determine the right pricing for the company. Not only does this eliminate the windfall profits to investment banking clients who were lucky or privileged enough to get shares at the offering price, it significantly reduces the cost of going public. The steps in the direct listing process are described in figure 4.7, along with the limitations that come with this alternative.

FIGURE 4.7 | A Direct-Listing Initial Public Offering

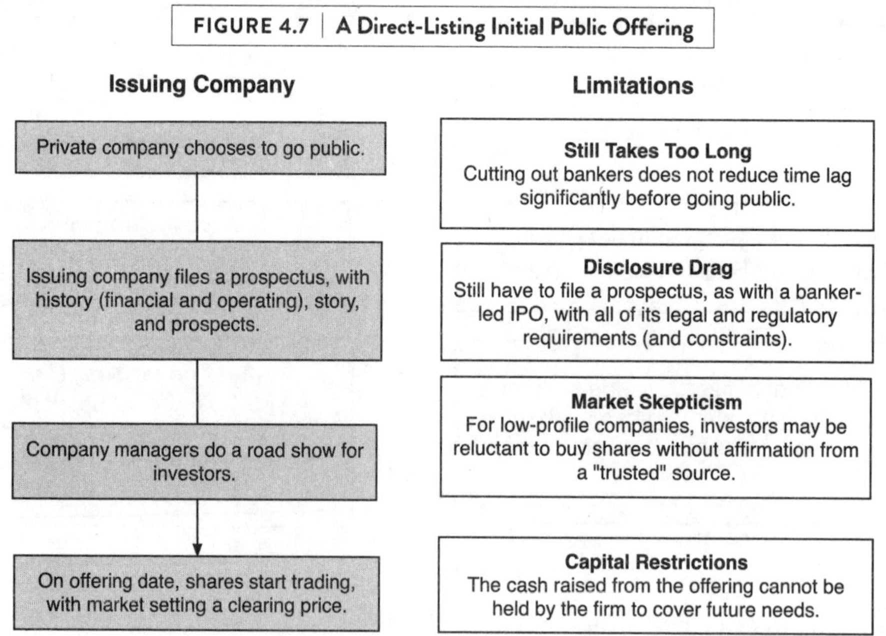

The biggest drawback for young firms considering direct listing is the constraint that funds raised in a direct listing offering *must* be cashed out by owners and not held in the firm to cover future investing needs. While there are pragmatic ways of overcoming this constraint, it has still restricted the use of direct listings.

In the last few years, a third alternative has emerged for some companies planning to go public, wherein a high-profile investor or investors raise funds from retail investors in a special purpose acquisition company (SPAC) to take a company public, but do so ahead of the offering and before the terms have been finalized. Figure 4.8 describes the SPAC process, again with its limitations.

FIGURE 4.8 | A SPAC-Led Initial Public Offering

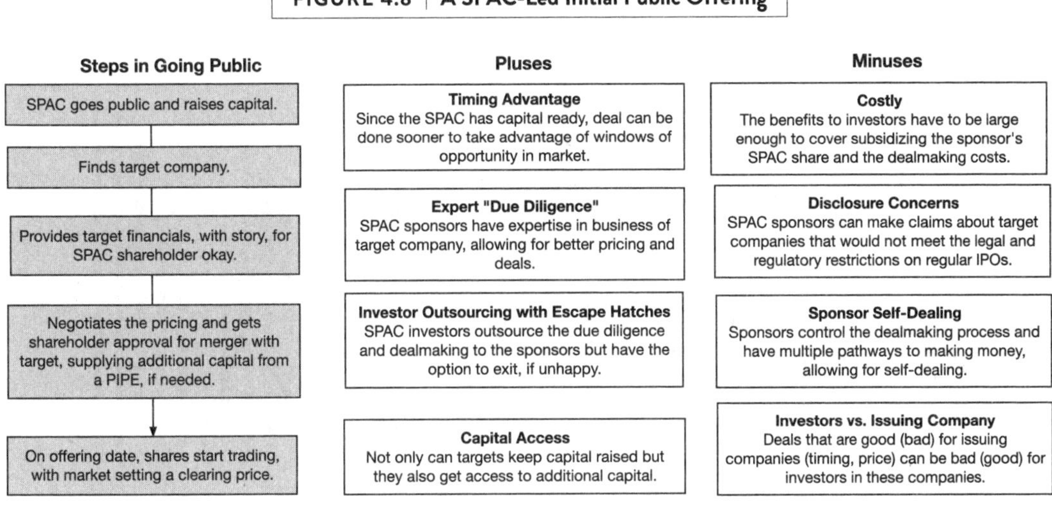

In effect, retail investors are putting their trust in the SPAC's promoters not only to pick the right private company to merge with but also to get the best terms on that deal. While that, by itself, may not worry you, the fact that SPAC promoters usually take 20% of the funds raised as their compensation should, since you, as the retail investor, will have to make that money back on the IPO.

It is ironic that the IPO process, which is what many of the disruptors of traditional businesses have used to access capital, is now itself being disrupted. I believe that change is coming to the IPO process, and that none of the existing alternatives, at least now, is a clear front runner. For the foreseeable future, there will be firms that continue with the banker-led status quo, but there will be others that explore more efficient and less costly approaches to going public.

TRENDS IN IPO MARKETS

As with venture capital, the IPO markets go through hot periods, when dozens or even hundreds of companies go public, and cold periods, when the number of public offerings drops off. In figure 4.9, I use data maintained by Jay Ritter on initial public offerings to list the number of IPOs and IPO proceeds, by year, from 1980 to 2021.

FIGURE 4.9 | Number and $ Value of IPOs in the United States, 1980–2021

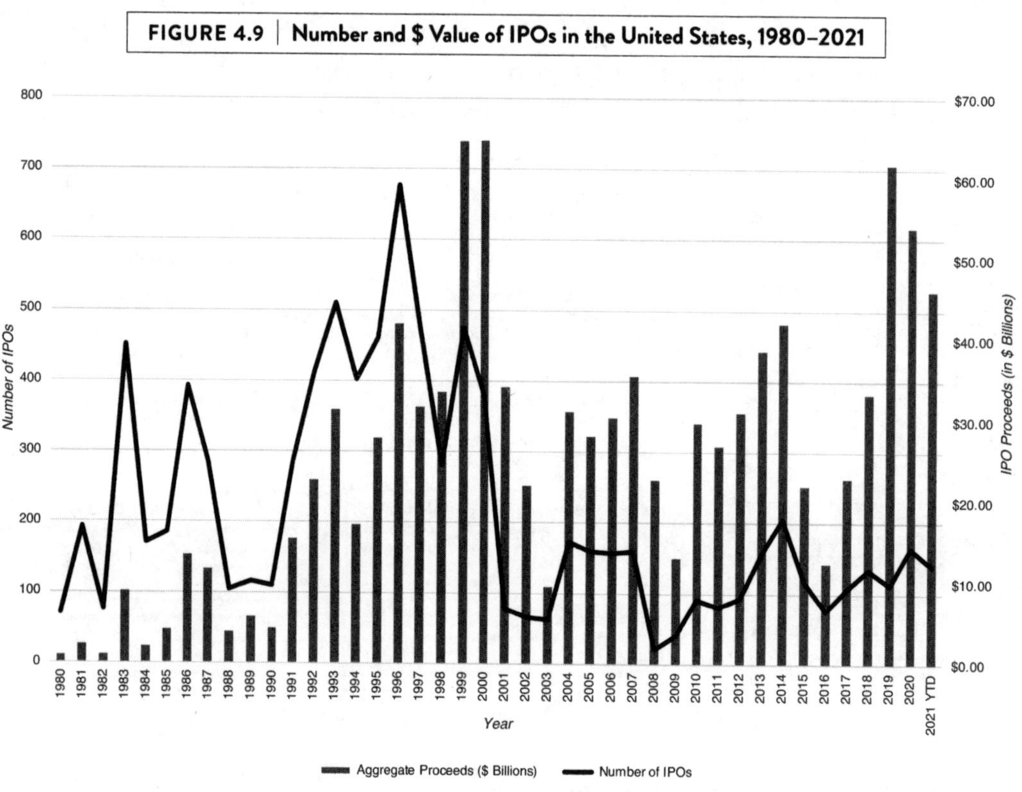

Note again the rise in IPOs in the 1990s, the drop-off in the years after, and the rise, at least in offering proceeds, in IPOs in the last decade. In fact, comparing this graph to the one where I looked at VC capital flows (figure 4.5), you will notice that the ebbs and flows in VC capital match the hot and cold periods for IPO markets.

It is not only the number of initial public offerings that has varied over time but also the types of companies going public. As I noted in the venture capital section, the rise of a gray market, where private companies may be able to access more capital at better terms, has led to changes in when private companies go public and what they look like at the time of their offering. In figure 4.10, I graph out the dollar revenues of companies going public each year, as well as the percentage of these companies that are money losing.

FIGURE 4.10 | IPO Company Characteristics

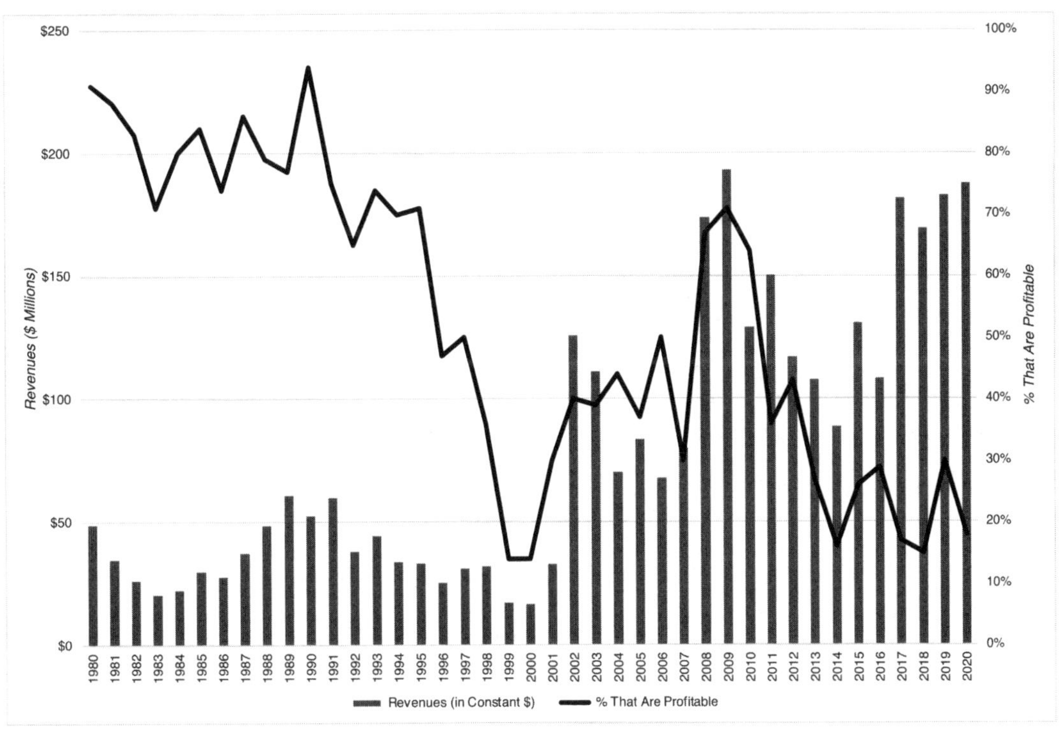

In sum, companies going public in the last decade have been much bigger (in terms of revenues) while having less formed business models than the companies that were going public two or three decades ago. For private companies, free access to capital for longer periods has led to less discipline at these companies, at least on average, in building business models—and that is worrisome.

Secondary Financing

Once a company becomes public, its access to capital widens, as equity and debt markets open up for offerings. In this section, I will look at financing patterns of public companies and note that while they may continue to access equity markets, at least in the early years of growth, their primary source of equity investing becomes internal—i.e., retained earnings from operations—and that if there is need for external capital, it is more likely to be raised via debt than equity.

THE CHOICES

Ultimately, there are only two sources of funding for any business: owners' funds (equity) or borrowed money (debt). With publicly traded companies, equity funding comes from two sources, the first being equity raised by issuing shares in the market, and the second being retained earnings, i.e., the portion of earnings that is reinvested in the company. Figure 4.11 provides a breakdown of how much publicly traded companies in the United States have used each source of financing between 1975 and 2020.

FIGURE 4.11 | Financing Sources for US Companies

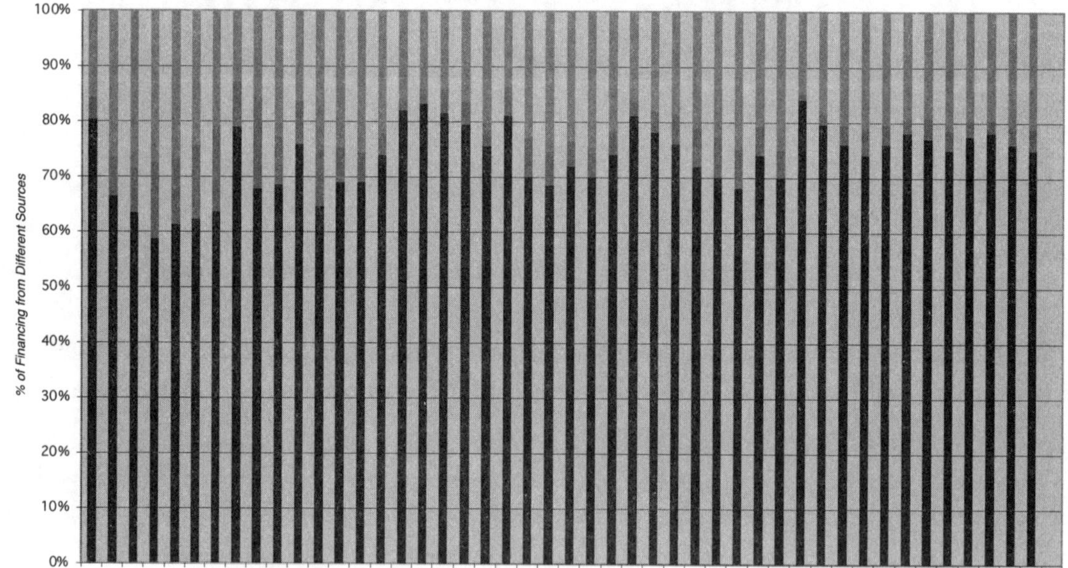

As you can see, once companies go public, they rely on internal financing (from retained earnings) more than any other source to fund themselves. When they do raise external financing, it is far more likely to be in the form of debt or bond issuances than in equity issuances.

There is one caveat to add to this financing discussion. As companies make the transition from young to mature growth, they still need capital to grow, and often they are not ready for debt financing, because they are still risky and often are not making much money. That leaves them dependent on equity—but rather than issue equity to the market and get cash proceeds that they can spend to meet their needs, these companies use their shares as currency to pay employees and acquire companies.

THE PROCESS

The process of raising secondary financing, in either equity or debt form, usually starts with a registration statement and prospectus filed with regulators, specifying how much capital will be raised and in what form. While companies used to file registrations for each individual financing round, the process has been streamlined through shelf registrations, wherein companies can now register to raise financing in future periods without going through the sequence of filing a prospectus in each round.

To raise the funding, companies still tend to rely on bankers, just as they did in the IPO process, but there is far less activity needed on the part of the banker, since the stock is already traded (and has a price) and investors are familiar with the company. That does not mean that issuance costs are nonexistent, but they are lower than with an IPO and tend to decrease with the size of the issuance (see figure 4.12).

FIGURE 4.12 | Issuance Costs by Financing Type

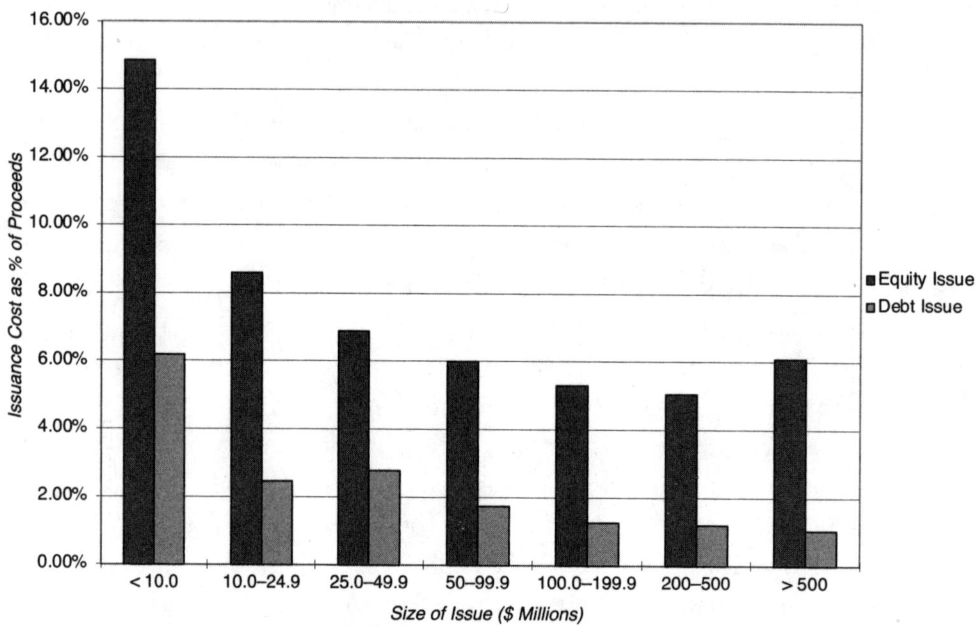

It is also undeniably less costly, from an issuance cost perspective, for publicly traded companies to raise debt financing than equity financing, which might explain why new equity issuances are so much more infrequent than debt issuances.

With equity issuances, there is an available variation that offers the promise of lower costs, and that is to make a rights issuance, wherein existing equity investors are given the right to buy additional shares at a discounted price. Since everyone gets the right, and those who do not want to use the right can sell it, the lower stock price after the rights issuance will not hurt shareholders: they will all have either more shares, to compensate, or cash in their pocket from selling rights. The advantage of rights issuances, relative to general subscription offerings, is that the issuance cost is far lower (see figure 4.13).

FIGURE 4.13 | Issuance Costs by Issuance Type

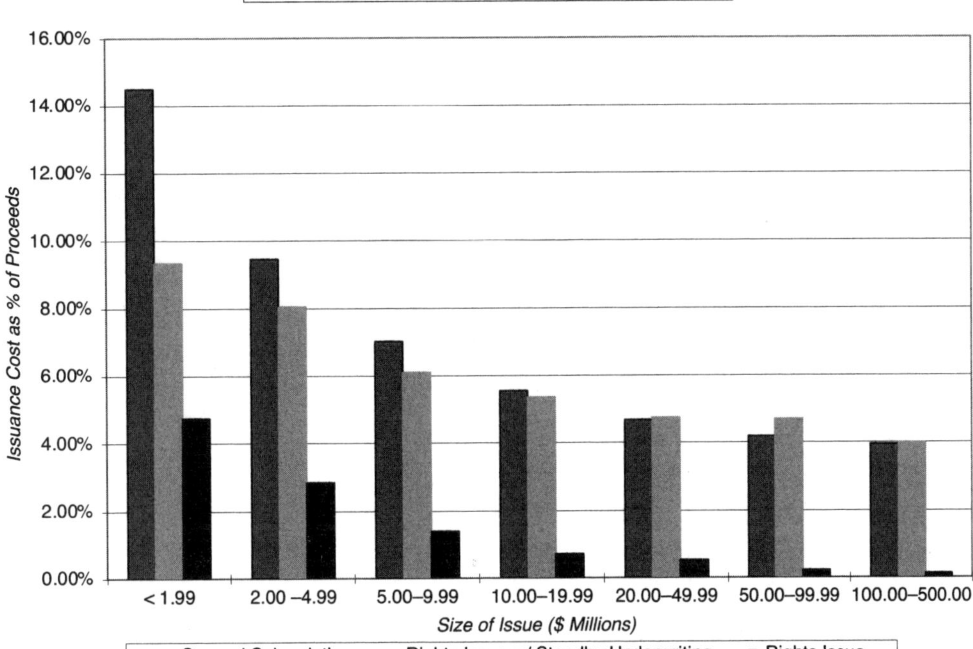

Notwithstanding the lower costs, US companies, terrified of the stock "dilution" (the increase in share count and resulting decrease in per-share earnings) that will occur from rights issuances, have been much less willing to use that option than European companies.

Private Equity

Young companies seek out venture capital to get their businesses off the ground and running, and some of them later make the transition to public equity, starting with initial public offerings and moving on to secondary financing. As companies mature and approach decline, there is a third player in capital markets that enters the fray: private equity. Note that "private equity" as a category can be used expansively, to also include venture capital, which is also equity provided by private sources. The private equity that I will talk about in this section is a subset of the capital that is directed at public companies, often with the intent of taking them private, "fixing" their problems, and then taking them public again.

The Process

As noted in the last section, the private equity I am referencing in this section refers to the private equity (PE) firms that are focused on buying out public companies and converting them into private businesses, at least for the near term. While this may strike some readers as a reversal of the normal sequence of events in a company's life, recognize that the benefits of being a public company decrease as a company ages and approaches decline. Since it has no need for reinvestment, its access to capital markets is not a plus, and the scrutiny that comes with being a public business may make it more difficult to make the changes that declining companies have to make, in the form of divestitures and layoffs, to survive.

The PE space is diverse, with big players like KKR and Blackstone coexisting with small PE firms that are often focused on a geography or a sector, but all PE firms follow the VC script of raising funds from investors (endowment funds, pension funds, wealthy investors) and then investing that money in companies. What makes them different from VCs is the types of companies that they target. Rather than looking for young-growth companies with lots of potential, private equity investors frequently target older companies whose best days are behind them. These companies often have solid earnings power but are underperforming their peer group in profitability, and many of them are at a point in their life cycle where they have trouble generating returns on their businesses that exceed their cost of capital. If you add governance problems—common at older firms, as managers often have little or no shareholding in the company—you can see the potential for PE investors to turn the company around. A study of thousands of target firms that were bought out between 1992 and 2014 found that smaller companies with lagging profitability and low debt are more likely to be targeted in acquisitions, as can be seen in figure 4.14.*

* "Attractive M&A Targets: Part 1: What do buyers look for?" Cass Business School, City University London, and Intralinks, September 2016, https://www.mergermarket.com/assets/Attractive_M&A_Targets_PART%201_v2.pdf.

FIGURE 4.14 | The Characteristics of Companies Targeted by PE Firms

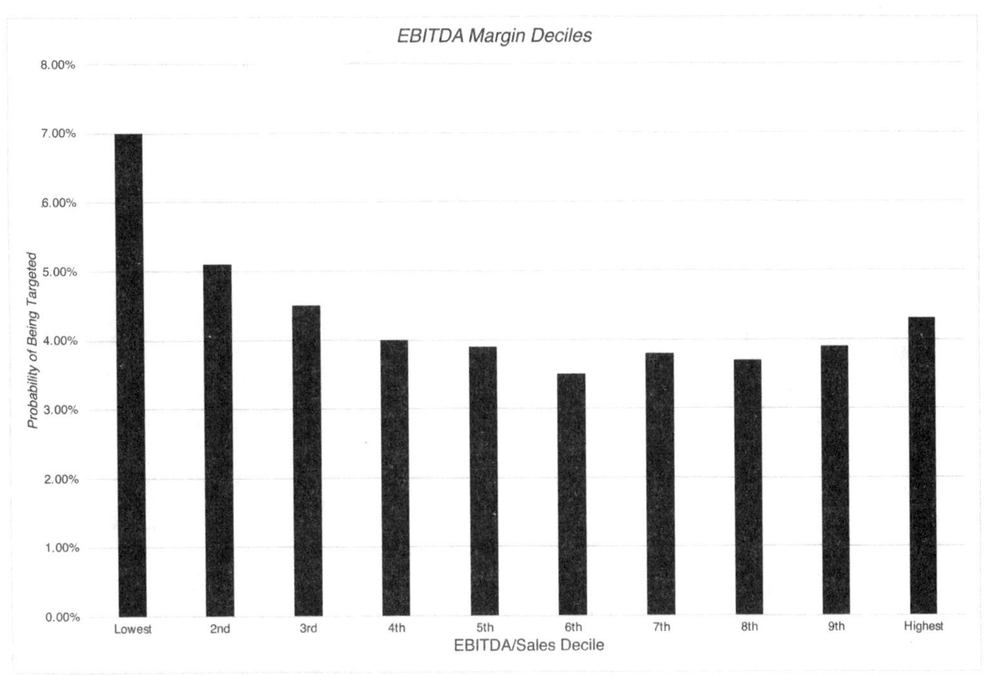

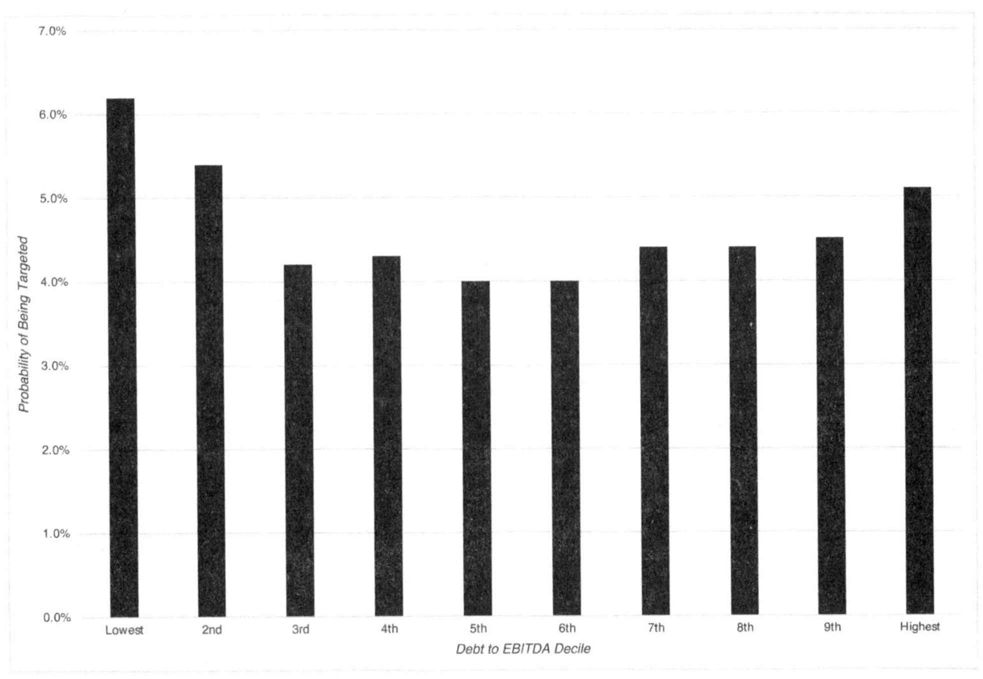

In a typical PE buyout, the PE firm approaches insiders/managers at the firm and gets them to buy in as equity investors in the privatized firm, while raising funding from limited partners and from debt to buy out the public shareholders in the firm. Figure 4.15 describes this process in a typical leveraged buyout.

FIGURE 4.15 | Ownership Shift in LBO

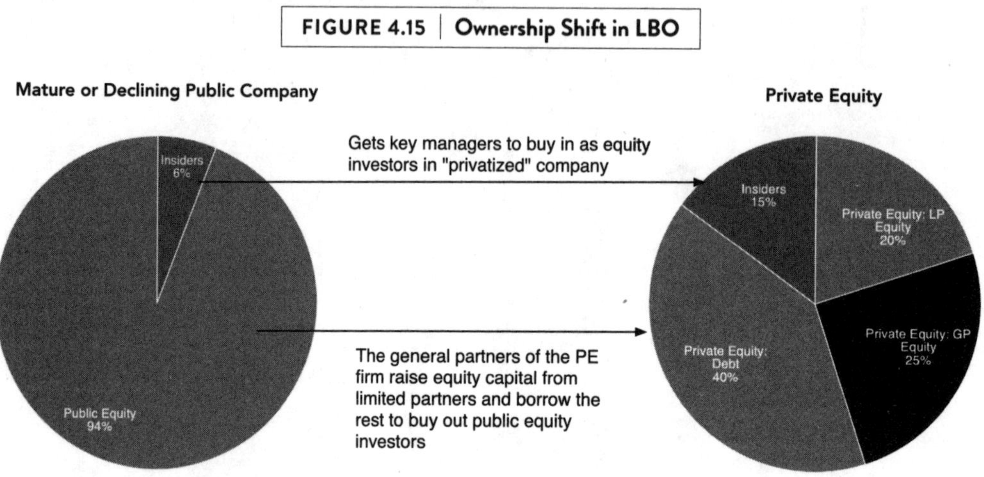

The percentage of the deal that is funded with debt will vary across deals, with some deals being far more levered and some far less, but the structure will hold. If the debt used to get the deal done represents a substantive part of the new financing, the buyout becomes a leveraged buyout.

Once the company is privatized, the PE firm's real work begins, as it tries to fix what it perceives to be the fixable problems at the target firm, with the intent of improving profitability and perhaps even finding a semblance of growth. Along the way, the PE firm may divest assets or divisions that don't fit into the corporate storyline. As I will show in more detail in chapter 17, there is some evidence, albeit mixed, that PE firms do succeed at improving operating metrics at their targets. If the PE firm succeeds in slimming down the target firm and improving its profitability—and there is no guarantee it will—the returns on the deal come from exiting, by either taking the company public again, presumably at a much higher price than was paid to buy it, or by selling the company to an acquirer. Figure 4.16 provides the timeline for a successful private equity deal, along with the caveats regarding what can go wrong at each stage.

FIGURE 4.16 | The Timeline for Private Equity

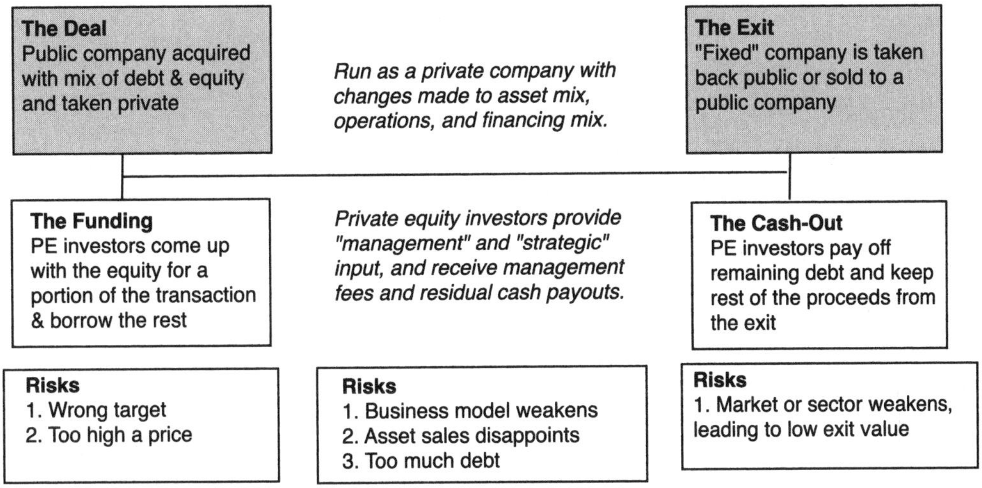

The Deal
Public company acquired with mix of debt & equity and taken private

Run as a private company with changes made to asset mix, operations, and financing mix.

The Exit
"Fixed" company is taken back public or sold to a public company

The Funding
PE investors come up with the equity for a portion of the transaction & borrow the rest

Private equity investors provide "management" and "strategic" input, and receive management fees and residual cash payouts.

The Cash-Out
PE investors pay off remaining debt and keep rest of the proceeds from the exit

Risks
1. Wrong target
2. Too high a price

Risks
1. Business model weakens
2. Asset sales disappoints
3. Too much debt

Risks
1. Market or sector weakens, leading to low exit value

As to the question of whether private equity investors emerge as winners or losers, I will hold off until later in this book to discuss the determinants.

Trends

Earlier in this chapter, I noted the ebbs and flows in both venture capital and IPOs over time. Not surprisingly, PE dealmaking also has its up and down years. Figure 4.17 graphs out PE deal numbers by year.

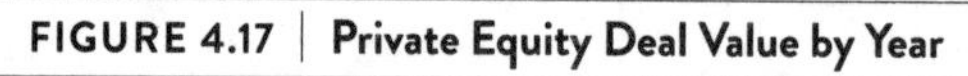

FIGURE 4.17 | Private Equity Deal Value by Year

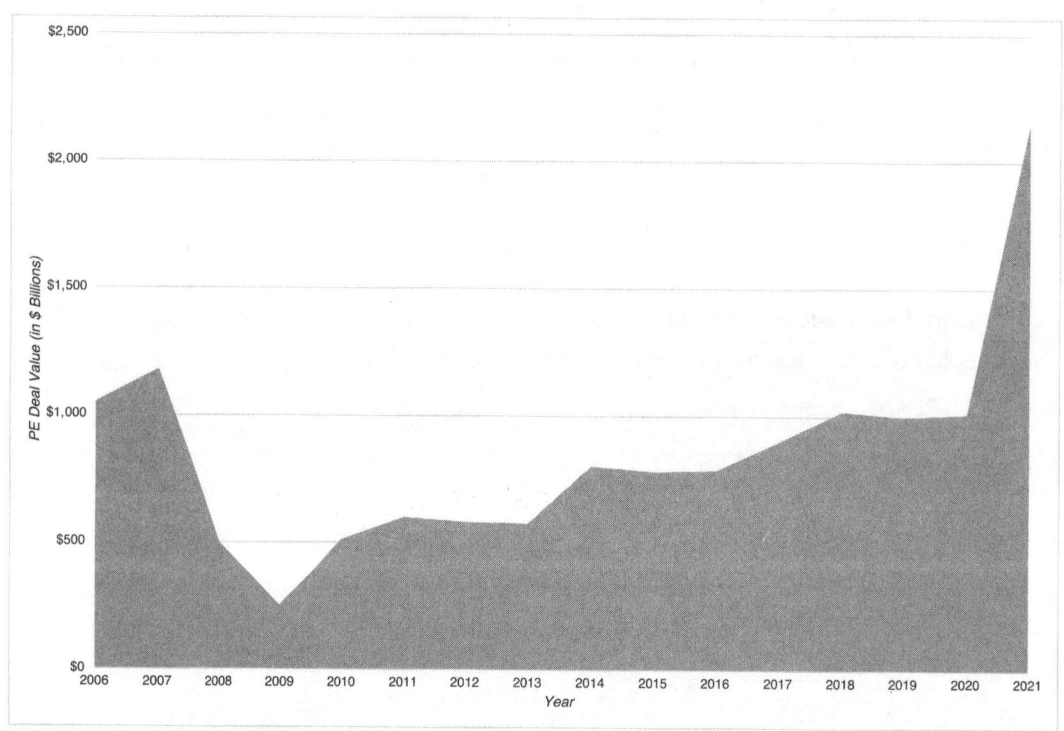

Note that PE dealmaking is not closely tied to the year-by-year movements in venture capital and IPOs, perhaps because it is focused on companies in a different stage of the life cycle and requires a different set of macro variables to succeed.

Looking at trends over time, the nature of PE dealmaking has changed, reflecting the following shifts:

1. **Bigger deals:** As the amount of capital flowing into private equity has increased, so has its capacity to do big deals. In 2021, Carlyle acquired Medline for $34 billion, and the number of deals that year that exceeded a $10 billion value set a record.

2. **Globalization:** As with venture capital and initial public offerings, private equity has evolved from a primarily US phenomenon to a more global practice. It is thus not uncommon now to see activist investors targeting mature European and Asian firms, with the intent of challenging corporate governance norms and operating practices. In fact, the largest PE deal in 2021 was a KKR buyout of Telecom Italia for $37 billion.
3. **Flexibility on leverage:** In the early years, almost every PE buyout was accompanied by leverage, giving rise to the "LBO" acronym. That, thankfully, has started to change, as there are more variations in financing mixes used in buyouts, with some PE firms depending more on equity for their dealmaking. That is healthy, since a leveraged buyout, no matter how well structured, is a bet on the economy staying healthy, with a recession right after the deal often representing a death knell for the deal.

In many ways, the emergence of private equity completes the capital cycle to accommodate every stage in the corporate life cycle, with its focus on finding the best pathways for mature and declining companies to age gracefully.

Conclusion

In this chapter, I looked at the transitions that businesses have to make to get through the corporate life cycle, using a financing lens. For start-ups and young companies, it is venture capital that changes not just the financing constraints of the firm but its ownership and governance structure. For a subset of these firms—usually the ones that have the most potential for scaling up—the next financing transition is to public equity markets, first through an initial public offering, and then by accessing equity and debt as a seasoned company. Mature and declining firms turn to private equity again, but this time through the involvement of private equity firms that buy out such companies, fix them while they are under private ownership, and then take them back public again or sell them.

In a healthy capital market, you need to have all three sources of capital (venture capital, public equity, and private equity) and balance across the sources. Over time, there will be ebbs and flows in all three capital sources, and prudent businesses that wish to access this capital will plan for the downturns that will occur in each.

Corporate Finance across the Life Cycle

5

Corporate Finance 101: A Life Cycle Overview

CORPORATE FINANCE IS THE ultimate big-picture discipline, covering the financial first principles that govern how to run a business. Since "corporate finance" covers any decision made by a business that involves the use of money, every business decision is ultimately a corporate finance decision, and all business decisions can be categorized as investing, financing, or dividend decisions. In this chapter, I will start by laying out the big picture of corporate finance and then spend the rest of the chapter expanding on the investment, financing, and dividend principles.

The Big Picture

If corporate finance covers, as I contend, the first principles that govern how to run a business, it follows that everything that businesses do falls under its purview. Broadly speaking, all decisions made by a business can be put into one of three groupings:

- **Investment decisions:** These are decisions regarding the assets or projects that a business chooses to allocate its resources to, and consequently, the category covers a broad range of investments, from small to large and from cost saving to revenue generating. Thus, a decision as to how much and what inventory to carry is just as much an investment decision as is a decision to acquire another company.

- **Financing decisions:** All businesses need funding to operate, and this funding can come from either owner funds (equity) or borrowed money (debt). Financing decisions include those that affect the mix of financing used, as well as the types of instruments used to raise that financing. A decision to use $100 million in debt to take on a new project is a financing decision, as are the choices of whether that debt should be a bank loan or a corporate bond and whether it should be fixed rate or floating rate.
- **Dividend decisions:** Through a combination of improved earnings power and less need for reinvestment, mature businesses will face a surplus of cash. While some will use this cash in a mostly futile attempt to become young again, through acquisitions and over-the-top investments, many others will decide to return some or all of the cash to the owners. With public companies, where the owners are shareholders, the cash can be returned either as dividends or as stock buybacks, and the question of how much cash to return and in what form becomes the heart of the dividend decision.

In charting a company's course, decision-makers need an end-game objective, and in classical corporate finance, that objective is maximizing the value of the business and, in many cases, the value to the owners (shareholders) in the business. In figure 5.1, I summarize the first principles that govern the investing, financing, and dividend decisions that emerge from this end game.

FIGURE 5.1 | The Big Picture of Corporate Finance

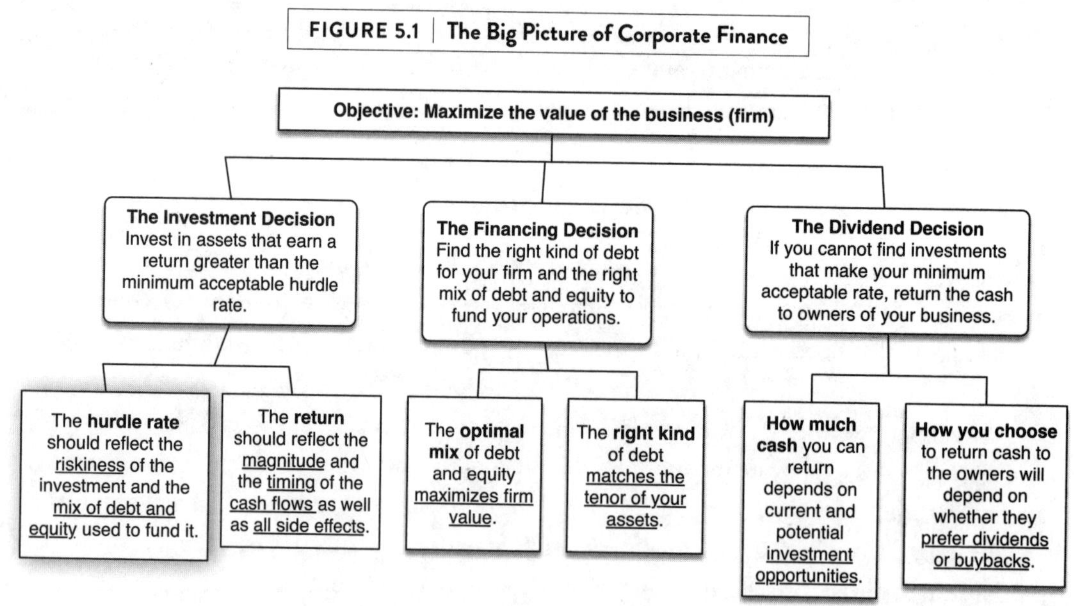

In short, in classical corporate finance, choosing value maximization as an objective allows for focus, since a good decision then becomes one that increases value and a bad decision one that reduces value, thereby yielding rules for making investing, financing, and dividend decisions. However, if you do not agree with the end game of maximizing value, the resultant decision rules also become questionable, and it is for this reason that I will start this chapter by looking at alternatives that have been offered to value maximization, along with the benefits and drawbacks to each.

The End Game in Business

To understand why there is so much debate about the end game in running a business, it is instructive to begin with a look at all the stakeholders in a business, starting with the equity investors and lenders who provide capital to the business, but then extending to also include the employees of the business, its customers and suppliers, and even society. Figure 5.2 provides a picture of the stakeholders in a business.

FIGURE 5.2 | The Stakeholders in a Business

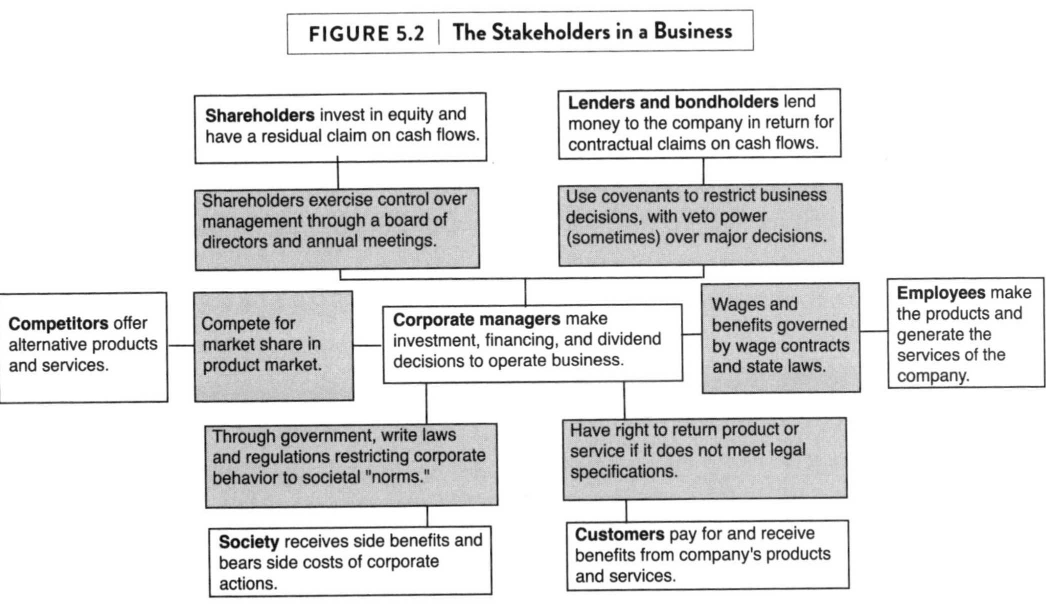

It is undeniable that for a business to be successful, it needs all of these stakeholders, and thus it seems unfair that classical corporate finance focuses on just one of them—i.e., the shareholders. The reason for that focus, though, is simple. Every other stakeholder in a business has a contractual claim against the business, with lenders setting interest rates and imposing loan covenants; employees structuring agreements specifying wages, benefits, and protections; and customers deciding whether the firm's products or services are worth the prices that they are being charged. Even society, in the form of government (elected, in some cases), writes laws and regulations that govern businesses and collects taxes from them. Shareholders, though, have only a residual claim—they get whatever is left over after all other stakeholders' contractual claims have been met—and without the primacy offered them by corporate finance, they have little incentive to partake in this endeavor.

In the last two decades, the primary challenge to the objective of shareholder value maximization has come from those who argue that businesses should maximize *stakeholder* value, and their argument has found buy-in from some corporate CEOs and institutional investors. While the notion that a business should consider the interests of all of its different stakeholders is unexceptional, it fails, in my view, for two reasons:

- **It leaves businesses rudderless:** While all stakeholders provide key ingredients for a business to succeed, they do have very different interests in the firm, and those interests will often collide. For instance, customers benefit from lower prices being charged for products and services, but these come at the expense of profits to shareholders and perhaps even wages for employees. Without a road map on how to balance these competing interests, decision-makers will either end up making their own subjective judgments or, worse, end up with decision paralysis. In practical terms, if you want a functional business, you need to give primacy to one stakeholder group, while also setting constraints that protect other stakeholder groups from being exploited. Classical corporate finance does so by elevating shareholders, since they have no contractual protection, to the top, but in most settings, shareholder value maximization is constrained by both market competition and regulation.
- **It leaves managers unaccountable:** If decision-makers in a business are accountable to all stakeholders, I would argue that they are effectively accountable to none of them. That may sound counterintuitive, but stakeholder value maximization allows managers, when challenged by any stakeholder group on any failure, the easy excuse that it was catering to other stakeholders that caused the shortcoming. Thus, for example, a top management team, when asked by employees why their wages are lagging, can argue that it was because products and services had to be priced at more affordable levels for customers.

Shareholder value maximization is not a perfect objective, by any stretch of the imagination, but the notion that it is inimical to the well-being of the other stakeholders in a business is neither logical nor backed by data. I would argue that businesses that do well for their shareholders are in a much better position, because of their profitability, to pay their employees more and provide additional services to their customers, and empirically, that turns out to be true. That said, there will always be some businesses that deliver higher value for shareholders by charging unconscionably high prices for their products and services and/or treating their employees unfairly, and the question of where you will come down in this debate depends on whether you view these businesses as the exception or the rule.

While the objective of maximizing shareholder value applies for any business, you can see why it is more of a struggle in young businesses than in more mature firms. Not only are young businesses less likely to be publicly traded, such that they have no market prices for their shares—a flawed but still easily observable measure of shareholder value—much of their value comes from what they will they do in the future, rather than what they have done in the past. Consequently, questions about whether a decision will increase or decrease the business's value are more difficult to answer in young businesses than in mature ones, and I will explore how this reality plays out in differences in corporate financial policy across these firms.

The Investment Principle

The investment principle covers whether and how much a business should invest in an asset or a project, but "projects," in this formulation, can span the spectrum from small to large and cost cutting to revenue generating. The question of what health benefits to provide to employees or whether to offer credit to customers is just as much a project, entailing an investment decision, as a plan to enter a new business or acquire another company. If you believe that maximizing value is the end game for a business, it follows that it should invest in a project or an asset or an acquisition only if the expected return on that investment exceeds a minimum acceptable hurdle rate. In figure 5.3, I lay out the comparison between the hurdle rate and return on investment, along with the drivers and determinants of each.

FIGURE 5.3 | The Investment Principle—Hurdle Rate and Return on Investment

The Hurdle Rate for an Investment
Should reflect the risk of the investment, not the entity taking the investment. Should use a debt ratio that is reflective of the investment's cash flows.

The Return on an Investment
Should reflect the cash flows that you will get from the investment. Should be time weighted, reflecting when you will get those cash flows.

In this section, I will begin by providing a broad structure for thinking about hurdle rates and investment returns, but I will return to add more detail on the topic in the next chapter.

The Hurdle Rate

The idea that hurdle rates should reflect the riskiness of an investment is a common-sense one, but for it to have practical impact, you need a framework for thinking about risk, and at least the beginnings of one regarding how to convert risk measures into required rates of return. To start, I will define "risk" as the likelihood that what I observe, as the result of an investment, will be different from what I expected to observe. Note that with this definition of risk, risk can manifest as either a negative (I earn or receive less than I expected to on an investment) *or* positive outcome (I generate more return than I expected to on the same investment). Unlike some economists, who use measurability as a dividing line, I do not draw a distinction between risk and uncertainty, and I will use the words interchangeably.

When running a business, you are undeniably exposed to uncertainty on almost every front, and to understand and deal with that uncertainty, you should consider categorizing and breaking it down into components. Table 5.1 provides a breakdown of business uncertainties/risks on three dimensions:

Table 5.1 • Breaking Down Business Uncertainties/Risks

Type of Uncertainty/Risk	The Difference	Why We Care in Corporate Finance
Estimation versus Economic	*Economic uncertainty* refers to the unexpected changes doled out by fate that no amount of research or information is going to give us insight into. *Estimation uncertainty* relates to judgments in investing and valuation that can be improved by collecting more information and using it better.	Businesses must make decisions in the face of uncertainty, and while more due diligence and research will reduce estimation uncertainty, they will have no effect on economic uncertainty.
Micro versus Macro	*Micro uncertainty* occurs at the company level and comes from management decisions, legal entanglements, and even from immediate competitors. *Macro uncertainty* can be traced back to larger forces, i.e., the swings in fortune caused by changes in inflation, interest rates, and economic cycles.	The managers of a business can affect only the micro component, with better decisions translating into better payoffs. They cannot control the macro component, which comes from overall economic or country risk.
Discrete versus Continuous	*Continuous risk* is risk that you are exposed to on a continuous basis, though the moment-to-moment risks will tend to be small. *Discrete risk* is risk that is uncommon but potentially catastrophic.	Risk management systems often are built to manage continuous risk, partly because you get constant reminders of its presence, and ignore or underplay discrete risks.

While every business is exposed to each of these uncertainties, the type and magnitude of uncertainty that a business is exposed to will vary as the business ages. Figure 5.4 captures the evolution of uncertainty over the corporate life cycle.

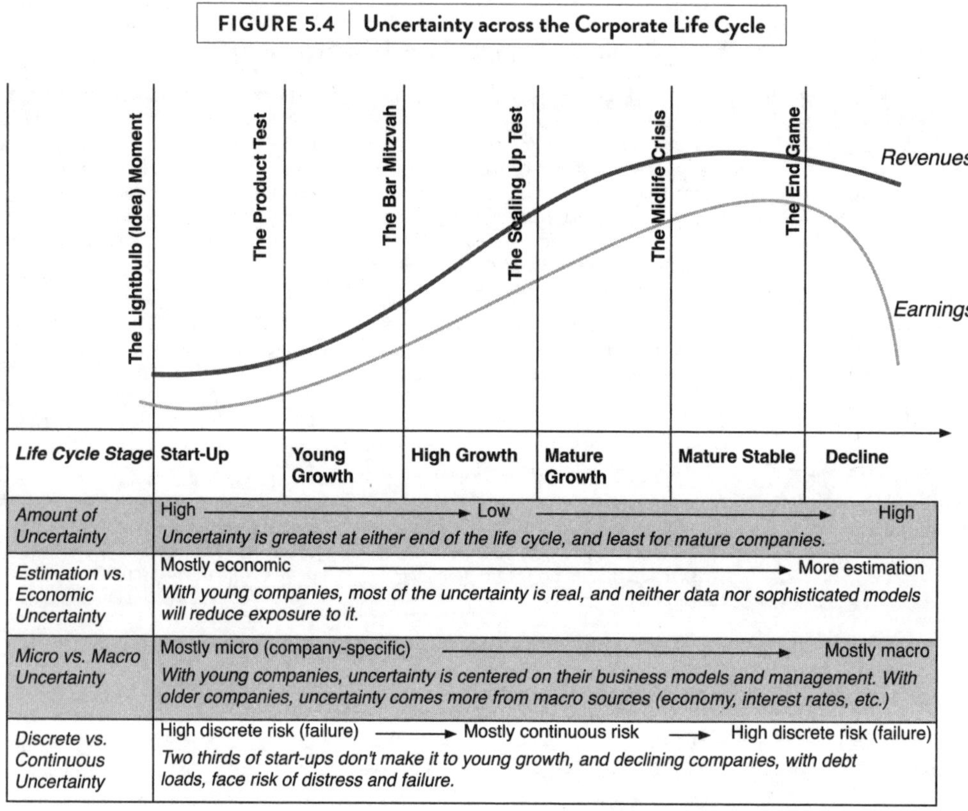

Life Cycle Stage	Start-Up	Young Growth	High Growth	Mature Growth	Mature Stable	Decline
Amount of Uncertainty	High → Low → High Uncertainty is greatest at either end of the life cycle, and least for mature companies.					
Estimation vs. Economic Uncertainty	Mostly economic → More estimation With young companies, most of the uncertainty is real, and neither data nor sophisticated models will reduce exposure to it.					
Micro vs. Macro Uncertainty	Mostly micro (company-specific) → Mostly macro With young companies, uncertainty is centered on their business models and management. With older companies, uncertainty comes more from macro sources (economy, interest rates, etc.)					
Discrete vs. Continuous Uncertainty	High discrete risk (failure) → Mostly continuous risk → High discrete risk (failure) Two thirds of start-ups don't make it to young growth, and declining companies, with debt loads, face risk of distress and failure.					

FIGURE 5.4 | **Uncertainty across the Corporate Life Cycle**

Faced with a myriad of uncertainties, it is easy to see why business managers get overwhelmed, but bringing in a risk distinction based upon how investors in the business perceive risk can restore some order. If you invest all your wealth in a single business, you are exposed to *all* its risk: estimation and economic, micro together with macro, continuous and discrete. However, if you spread your wealth across multiple businesses—i.e., you diversify—you find that some risks will become less visible or even disappear in your portfolio. That may sound magical, but it is just a simple extension of the fact that if the risk that you are exposed to in a business is specific to that business, for every firm that underperforms expectations on that risk, there should be another firm that outperforms them, resulting in an averaging out across your many holdings. Figure 5.5 provides a breakdown of risks on this dimension, with an explanation of how the needed diversification can sometimes be accomplished by the business, and sometimes by investors in it.

FIGURE 5.5 | Diversifiable versus Undiversifiable Risk

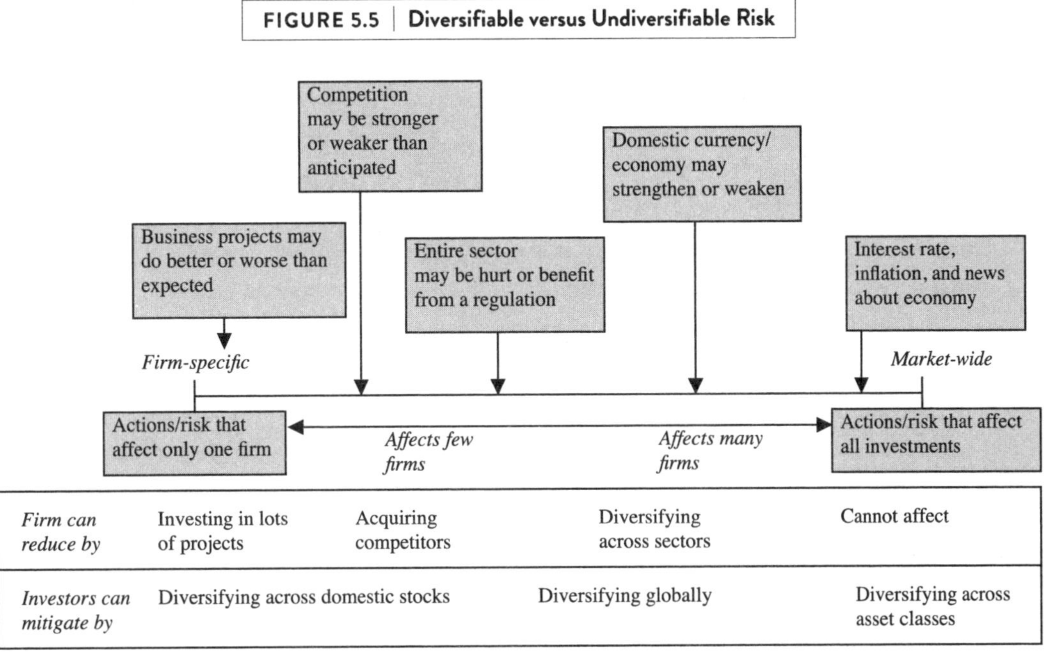

Firm can reduce by	Investing in lots of projects	Acquiring competitors	Diversifying across sectors	Cannot affect
Investors can mitigate by	Diversifying across domestic stocks		Diversifying globally	Diversifying across asset classes

Businesses can try to reduce or even eliminate exposure to some risks on their own—as is the case when a retailer opens multiple stores or when a consumer products company creates many different brands—but it becomes increasingly difficult to do so as the risks become more sector- or country-level concerns. Investors can often still reduce their exposure to these risks by diversifying, and often at a much lower cost than businesses can, especially if the business is publicly traded.

If you are wondering why you should care about the risk perspective of investors, I would argue that the minimum acceptable hurdle rate for an investment should reflect the risk that marginal investors—i.e., the investors who hold large stakes in the business and dominate trading—see in it, not the perspective of the business itself. Again, you can see why this can have consequences for a business based upon where it is in the life cycle: many young businesses are held by founders (who are not diversified) and venture capitalists (who are only partially diversified), whereas more mature businesses tend to be publicly traded, with institutional investors accounting for the bulk of trading. It stands to reason, then, that the minimum acceptable hurdle rates for young businesses may reflect some or a great deal of firm-specific risk, while for more mature businesses, the only risks that get priced in are macroeconomic risks.

In this discussion, I have studiously avoided the metrics I use to measure risk and the specifics of converting those risk metrics into hurdle rates. I will address those questions in chapter 6.

Investment Returns

When looking at an investment, small or large, businesses must forecast what that investment will deliver as a payoff for the business in future years. Since investments can have very diverse time horizons, this may be less work for a three-year investment than for a ten-year or fifty-year one, but no matter what the time horizon, businesses face a choice of estimating the payoff in terms of accounting earnings or in terms of cash flows. Estimates of the former kind, accounting earnings, are determined by accounting rules on revenues and expenses, and while they meld more closely to the proverbial bottom line in income statements, they can offer a distorted view of reality. The latter estimate category, cash flows, are purely a function of the cash inflows and outflows on a project and are more difficult to manipulate or skew.

The second big choice that businesses face in converting either earnings or cash flows to investment returns relates to timing. It does not require elaborate financial logic to understand that earnings or cash flows that you receive earlier in time are worth more than the same received in a later year. One reason for that is the time value of money, which reflects the effects of inflation on a currency as well as the well-established preferences of human beings for current over future consumption. The other reason is risk or uncertainty, since any risk that you face in a business compounds over time, making a cash flow in year 5 more uncertain, on a cumulated basis, than a cash flow in year 1.

Broadly speaking, the approaches to estimating investment return reflect these choices that businesses make. At one end of the spectrum stand accounting returns, a method where you simply divide accounting earnings by some measure of what the business has invested in a project; a project that requires a $100 million investment and delivers $20 million in after-tax earnings has a return on investment of 20%. As I will show in the next chapter, these accounting returns can be computed from the perspective of only equity investors, as a return on equity, or from the perspective of all capital providers, as a return on invested capital. At the other end of the spectrum are time-weighted cash flow returns, a method where the returns not only are computed based on the cash flows generated by a project but also weight earlier cash flows more than equivalent later cash flows, by discounting them. These time-weighted returns can be computed in dollar value terms (net present value, or NPV) or in percentage terms (internal rate of return, or IRR). Figure 5.6 captures these choices.

FIGURE 5.6 | Investment Return Approaches

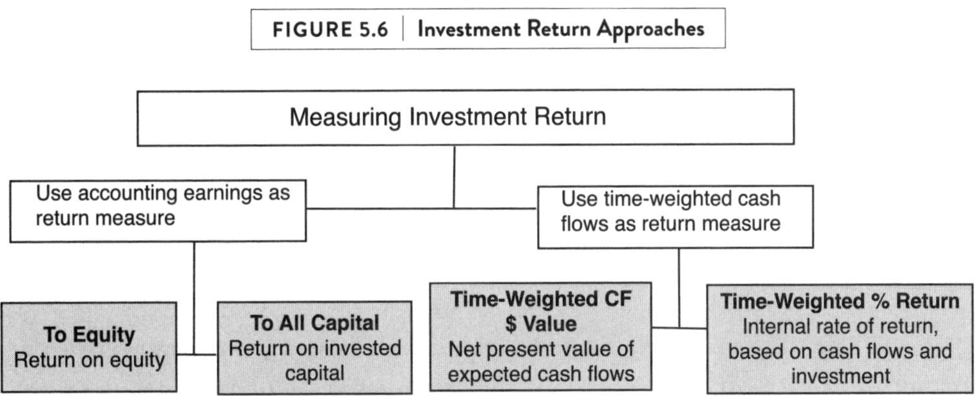

While net present value already incorporates your hurdle rate as a discount rate, and thus yields a measure of surplus value, the accounting return approach and the internal rate of return require an additional step before an investment is deemed to be good or bad. With these estimating methods, the return on equity (capital) must be higher than the cost of equity (capital) for an investment to be a good investment.

There are clearly estimation questions that I have left unanswered here, including how best to measure invested capital or equity and how to estimate cash flows, but I will return to those details in chapter 6. In the process, I hope to also address the question of whether the investment return approach a business uses will or should change as it goes from being a young-growth to a mature business.

The Financing Principle

As financing choices proliferate and balance sheets get more complicated, it is easy to lose sight of a fundamental truth in business: ultimately, all capital raised by a business must come from either its owners, as equity, or lenders, as debt. This is true whether a business is privately owned, with a sole owner providing equity and a bank loan representing debt, or publicly traded, with common shares representing public equity, and corporate bonds as debt. In fact, you can describe *any* business with a financial balance sheet, as shown in figure 5.7.

FIGURE 5.7 | A Financial Balance Sheet

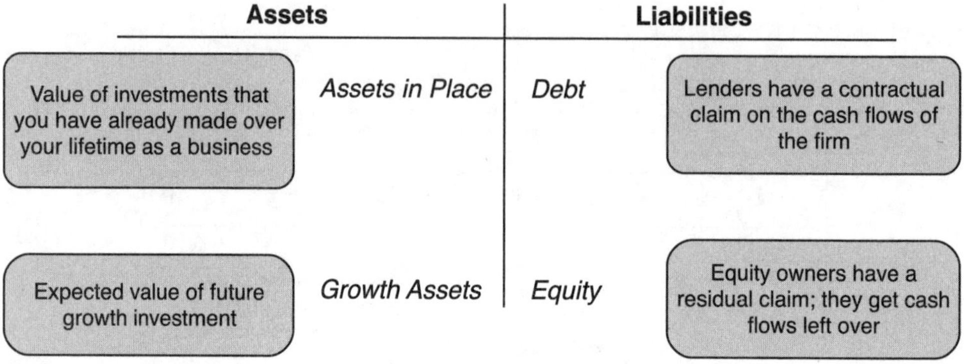

Notwithstanding the resemblance in its headings (assets and liabilities) to an accounting balance sheet, the financial balance sheet provides a forward-looking perspective on a business, where value not only comes from the existing investments made by the business (assets in place) but also incorporates the value added by expected future growth and investments (growth assets). In the vernacular of the corporate life cycle, businesses that are young- and high-growth will derive most of their value from growth assets, whereas the balance will shift toward assets in place at mature firms. On the other side of the financial balance sheet are equity and debt, with both terms defined broadly so as to cover both private and publicly traded businesses.

Financing Mix

The core financing question that corporate finance tries to answer is whether businesses should borrow and, if yes, how much of their funding should come from debt. If you follow the proposition that in corporate finance, good decisions increase value, the question of whether a firm should borrow money can be answered by looking at whether taking on debt will increase or decrease its value. That will require bringing in the costs and benefits of using debt, as opposed to equity, to finance investments. While the full trade-off discussion must wait until chapter 7, I will address the most substantive elements in this section.

On the plus side, the biggest and often the sole benefit to using debt instead of equity to finance investments is that tax codes in much of the world are tilted toward borrowing, allowing businesses to claim tax deductions for interest expenses on debt, while cash returned to equity investors, as dividends or buybacks, has to come out of after-tax cash flows. On the minus side, the greatest danger of borrowing is that it increases the risk that the business may not be able to make its contractual payments (interest and principal), leading to bankruptcy and truncating its life. Figure 5.8 captures these key trade-off factors.

FIGURE 5.8 | Debt versus Equity—Biggest Plus and the Biggest Minus

The Biggest Plus	*The Biggest Minus*
Tax Benefit: Debt gives rise to interest payments, which are tax deductible and thus lower the taxes due. Equity receives cash from dividends or buybacks, and neither is tax deductible.	**Bankruptcy or Default Risk:** Debt creates contractual obligations in the form of interest and principal payments, which if not met can result in either bankruptcy or loss of control (to lenders) of the business.

Financing Mix Follow-Up: Firms that receive large (small) tax benefits from debt while facing little (lots of) risk of default should choose to use more (less) debt, as opposed to equity.

While a fuller accounting of the debt-equity trade-off must wait until chapter 7, where I will also address what I deem the illusory benefits that some businesses believe come from using debt, the broad outlines of how the trade-off will play out across the life cycle should already be starting to take form here. Young, growth firms that are money losing or barely moneymaking will get no or smaller tax benefits from borrowing, since without taxable income, the interest tax deduction becomes worthless. If you incorporate the risk that comes from bankruptcy, where growth assets are put at risk, it stands to reason that the bulk of financing for young companies should come from equity. As businesses age, and their earnings become larger and more sustainable, the capacity of a business to borrow money will expand, albeit at different rates in different types of businesses.

Financing Type

There is a secondary component to the financing principle that often gets short shrift at businesses, and it relates to the type of financing that a business should use to fund itself. More specifically, this part of the financing principle addresses the questions of whether a firm that borrows money should use corporate bonds or bank debt, borrow long-term or short-term, in dollars or euros, and try for floating-rate or fixed-rate debt. While I could write extended and complicated theses on each of those choices, if value maximization is your goal, you should start with the presumption that the best financing for a business will be the one that mirrors its typical project or asset characteristics. In fact, in a perfect financing environment, the cash flows on a business's financing will ebb and flow in conjunction with the cash flows from its operations, as can be seen in figure 5.9.

FIGURE 5.9 | Firm and Equity Value with Matched Debt

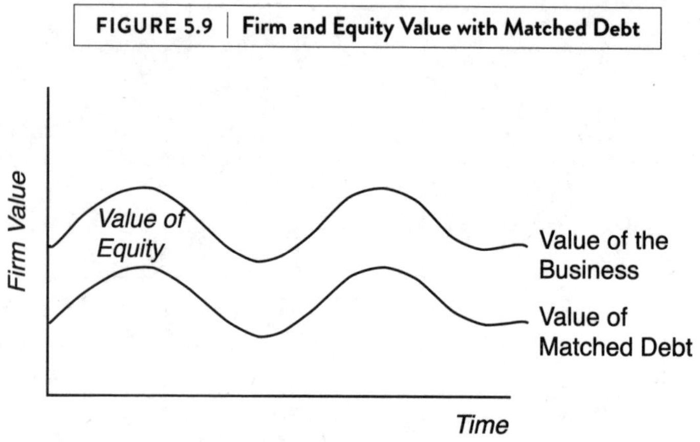

In this figure, the value of the business is volatile, rising and falling over time, but since its debt moves concurrently, increasing as business value increases and decreasing as it falls, the firm's equity value stays intact.

If this firm had used mismatched debt, the value of its debt would move independently of the value of its equity, leaving the firm facing default in periods when its operating asset value is low, as can be seen in figure 5.10.

FIGURE 5.10 | Firm and Equity Value with Mismatched Debt

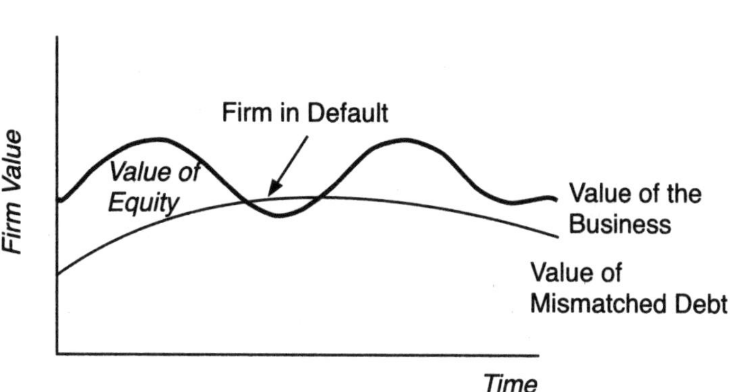

In chapter 7, I will return to this concept of matching up debt to assets and examine how the type of financing used by a business should change as it moves through the life cycle.

The Dividend Principle

A business that is successful will eventually be able to return cash to its investors (owners), and the dividend principle in corporate finance addresses questions of how much cash to return and, if the company is a publicly traded firm, in what form. Returning to figure 5.1, where I laid out the first principles of corporate finance, a business that is focused on maximizing value should return cash to its investors if it cannot find investments that generate returns that exceed the hurdle rate.

Cash Return: How Much?

To determine how much cash a company can return to shareholders, it is worth emphasizing that that decision should be the last step in a sequence that incorporates the investing and financing decisions of the business. Figure 5.11 outlines how cash return should work in a firm run in accordance with financial first principles.

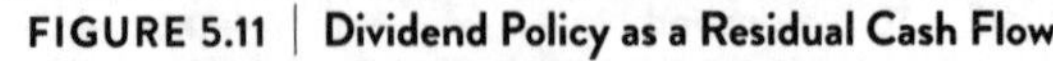
FIGURE 5.11 | Dividend Policy as a Residual Cash Flow

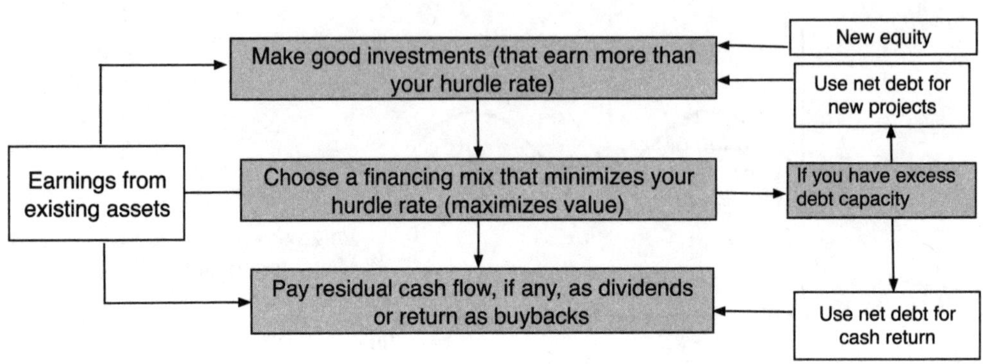

Thus, the cash available for return will be the cash left over after equity investors have decided how much money, if any, to reinvest in new projects or acquisitions, in the attempt to generate growth in the future, as well as in receivables or inventory, to support these growth investments. It will also reflect the effects of debt financing, with the decision to borrow new money creating a cash inflow, and that to retire old debt causing cash outflows. In figure 5.12, I trace out the cash available to a business for return or potential dividends by incorporating these effects.

FIGURE 5.12 | Potential Dividends (Free Cash Flows to Equity)

Potential Dividends (The Logic)	Potential Dividends (Calculation)
Start with the income available for equity investors	Net Income
Net out	*minus*
Cash invested in long-term assets to generate future growth	CapEx – Depreciation & Amortization
Net out	*minus*
Cash invested in short-term assets to generate future growth	Change in Non-cash Working Capital
Add back or net out	*plus*
Add back cash inflows from new borrowing and net out cash outflows from paying off debt	(New Borrowings – Debt Repaid)
Yields	*equals*
Free Cash Flow to Equity	Free Cash Flow to Equity

Even with this preliminary figure of cash return, you can see a link to the corporate life cycle. Young, growth firms that generate little or no net income will have negative free cash flows to equity, after factoring in reinvestment needs, and may need equity infusions to cover those cash flows. As businesses mature, a combination of rising, positive earnings and declining reinvestment needs, as growth subsides, will cause free cash flows to equity to turn positive and give these businesses at least the capacity to return cash. If they choose not to, they will experience a buildup of cash balances over time. In decline, net income will drop, but a shrinking business may be able to augment its cash flows to equity through divestitures and return far more in cash than it reports in net income.

Cash Return: In What Form?

If a business stays privately owned, there are multiple pathways that owners can use to extract cash from the business, from paying themselves large dividends to increasing their salaries. If it is publicly traded, the only way for most firms to return cash, until a few decades ago, was to pay dividends to their shareholders. Those dividends were structured like coupons on bonds, paid at regular intervals (ranging from quarterly to annual)—but unlike coupons on bonds, they often grew over time and were not contractual claims. Starting in the 1980s, in the United States, dividends were supplemented and, in many firms, increasingly supplanted by stock buybacks, where companies used the cash that they had been planning to return to buy back shares from investors who chose to sell their holdings back. Unlike dividends, which are timed and sticky—i.e., do not change from period to period, or change in a predictable way—buybacks are irregular and flexible, giving companies a chance to return cash without creating a commitment to continue returning cash in future periods. Figure 5.13 lays out the differences, from the perspective of the business, between paying dividends and buying back stock.

FIGURE 5.13 | Dividends versus Buybacks

Dividends	*Stock Buybacks*
Sticky: Dividends, once set, are slow to change, more likely to increase than decrease.	**Flexible:** Buybacks are flexible and, even if announced, can be reversed with little or no consequence.
Timed: Dividends are paid out at regular intervals of time (quarterly, annually).	**Opportunistic:** Buybacks do not follow a time pattern and can be done at any time (of the company's choosing).
General: Dividends are paid to all shareholders in the firm, whether they need or want the cash.	**Selective:** Cash is returned to shareholders, but only to those who choose to sell their shares back.

Dividends vs. Buybacks: Firms that have large (small) and stable (volatile) earnings and shareholders who like (don't need) regular, predictable cash flows will return cash as dividends (in stock buybacks).

While there are many academics and practitioners who view buybacks with disdain or worse, I believe that they offer some businesses an alternative, and often healthier, route to returning cash than paying dividends.

Again, tying into the framework of the life cycle, I will argue that when young businesses first find themselves with excess cash flows, those flows will be unpredictable and volatile, making buybacks a better initial approach to returning cash. As these businesses become more mature, that reality may change, and they may choose to replace buybacks with dividends.

Corporate Finance across the Life Cycle

In the big picture of corporate finance, all business decisions can be broken down into investing, financing, and dividend components. That may suggest that these decisions are all of equal importance for every business, but that presumption is false. The primary corporate focus of a business will change as the business moves through the life cycle. For a start-up or a very young firm, early in the life cycle, it is the investment decision that will make or break them, as there is no point in optimizing financing mix (since these firms cannot afford to borrow money) or dividend policy (since they have no cash to return). For young-growth firms, the investment principle will still dominate, since at peak project returns, the payoff to making better investments vastly exceeds any benefit from finding a better mix of financing or playing dividend-policy games. It is as businesses mature that you will see the focus shift to the financing principle, driven partly by declining returns on new investments as competition picks up and scaling works against the firm. Not surprisingly, it is mature firms that tend to be most active in recapitalizations, where new debt is raised and used to buy back stocks or pay dividends. As firms decline, there is little or no point in fine-tuning investment policy, since there are few or no new projects that will pass muster, and the emphasis will move to returning cash to shareholders, sometimes by divesting portions of the business that no longer can sustain themselves. Figure 5.14 shows the shifts in corporate finance emphasis as you move through the life cycle.

FIGURE 5.14 | Corporate Financial Emphasis across the Life Cycle

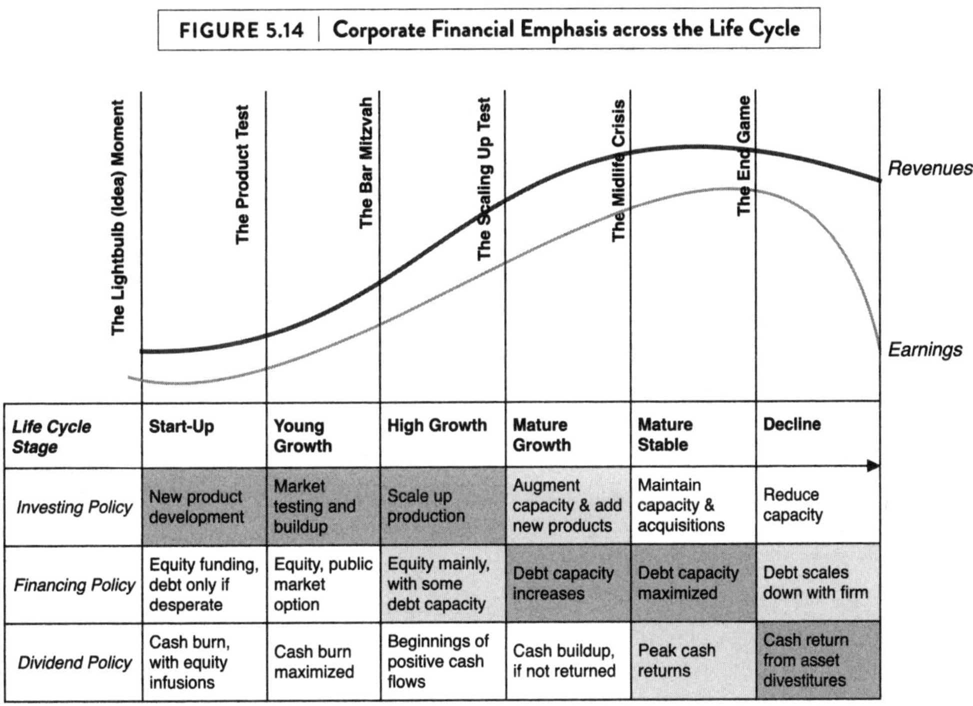

Life Cycle Stage	Start-Up	Young Growth	High Growth	Mature Growth	Mature Stable	Decline
Investing Policy	New product development	Market testing and buildup	Scale up production	Augment capacity & add new products	Maintain capacity & acquisitions	Reduce capacity
Financing Policy	Equity funding, debt only if desperate	Equity, public market option	Equity mainly, with some debt capacity	Debt capacity increases	Debt capacity maximized	Debt scales down with firm
Dividend Policy	Cash burn, with equity infusions	Cash burn maximized	Beginnings of positive cash flows	Cash buildup, if not returned	Peak cash returns	Cash return from asset divestitures

Note that the fact that the focus shifts over the corporate life cycle does not imply that a business can be casual about first principles on the aspects of corporate finance that it is not focused upon. As I will show in the next three chapters, some firms refuse to act their age and adopt corporate financing policies that are unsuited to where they stand in the life cycle. A young-growth firm that chooses to borrow money, even though it has the option of raising fresh equity, or a mature firm that refuses to return cash, even as its existing operations become more profitable and its investment opportunities dry up, is choosing to go against first principles, and there will be a price to be paid, sooner or later.

Conclusion

Corporate finance provides a set of principles that can govern how to run a business, but as I noted early in the chapter, the first principles that emerge from classical corporate finance reflect its choice of maximizing shareholder value as the end game for all business. The debate about whether that is the right end game for a business or whether it should be replaced with an objective that focuses on a different stakeholder group (like employees or customers) or with one that looks at all stakeholders is a healthy one, and while I believe that shareholder value is the best of the available objectives, it remains imperfect.

Staying within the constructs of corporate finance, I introduced the investment, financing, and dividend principles, at least in their most general forms, in this chapter, and noted the differences in how they play out for companies at different stages in the life cycle. In the next three chapters, I will take up each of these principles and explore its details.

6

Investing across the Life Cycle

IN THE LAST CHAPTER, I looked at the investment principle as the first of the three corporate finance principles, and at first sight, it seems simple. After all, if a good investment is one that earns a return that exceeds the hurdle rate, reflective of the risk in the investment and the financing mix used to fund the investment, how difficult can it be to measure those components? The answer lies in practice, where you see a range of approaches used to measure both components playing out as different investment decision rules. I will start this chapter with a deeper assessment of hurdle rates and how they vary across the life cycle, and then look at why the choice of an investment decision rule may depend on where a business is in the life cycle.

The Hurdle Rate

In chapter 5, I argued that the hurdle rate for an investment should incorporate the risk in that investment, but then noted that risk should be measured from the perspective of the marginal investors in the business, not the business itself. In this section, I will look at the process of measuring this risk and converting the risk measures that emerge into hurdle rates.

The Cost of Capital as the Hurdle Rate

To get from generalizations about hurdle rates to specifics, I will reframe the hurdle rate as the cost of funding an investment, i.e., a cost of capital. Since, as I noted in the last chapter, there are only two sources of funding, owner's funds (equity) and borrowed money (debt), the cost of capital can be computed as a weighted average of the costs of raising equity and debt, with the weights based upon how much of each is used in the mix. Figure 6.1 uses the financial balance sheet that I introduced in the last chapter to capture the essence of what the costs of debt and equity measure.

FIGURE 6.1 | Cost of Capital—A Balance Sheet Perspective

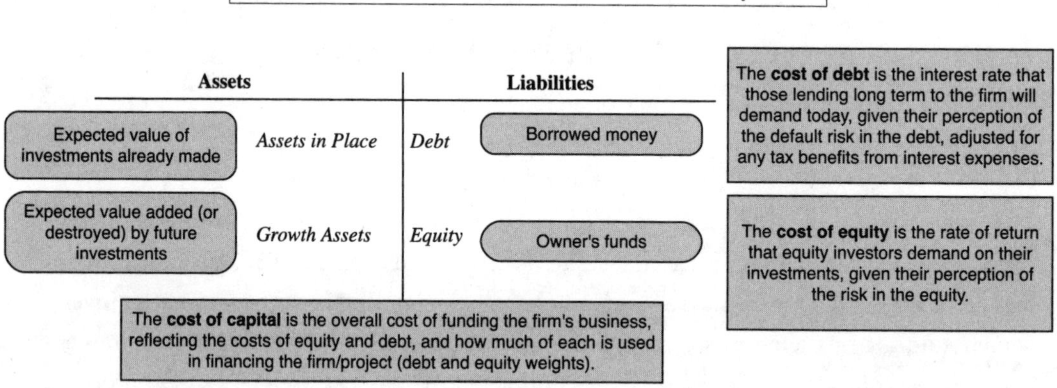

The cost of debt is usually the easier of the two costs to estimate, since it is a long-term borrowing cost and needs only two components. The first is the credit or default spread that lenders will charge, based upon the likelihood of default that they perceive in the business, with businesses perceived as bigger credit risks carrying higher default spreads. The second is the effect of the tax code tilt toward debt, manifested as a tax adjustment that makes the after-tax cost of debt lower than the actual borrowing rate. Both effects can be seen in figure 6.2.

FIGURE 6.2 | Cost of Debt (Pre-tax and After-tax)

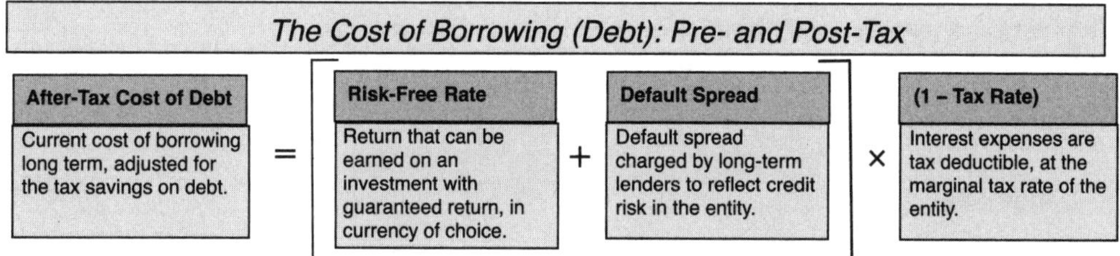

The cost of equity is a tougher number to estimate because, unlike the interest rate on a loan, the cost of equity *drives* the price you pay for equity, but it is unstated and requires making judgments about what types of investors (individual, institutional, etc.) are the business's marginal investors.* Without entangling ourselves in the labyrinth of risk and return models in finance, the cost of equity for a project can also be broken down into three components, as can be seen in figure 6.3.

FIGURE 6.3 | The Cost of Equity

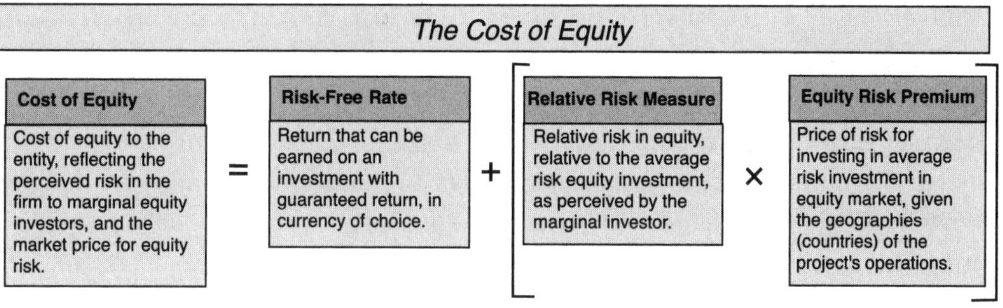

If you compare the cost of equity to the cost of debt, you will notice that the price of risk in the debt market, i.e., the default spread, is replaced with the price of risk for the average risk investment in the equity market, i.e., the equity risk premium. This premium is multiplied by a relative risk measure, which reflects how risky an equity investment is relative to the average risk investment.

* Even though the cost of equity may not be explicitly stated, the price you pay per share of equity will reflect your expectations of risk and required return on that equity. Holding expected cash flows constant, as your cost of equity rises, the price you will pay for equity will decrease.

Inputs to the Cost of Capital

In practical terms, the estimation of costs of debt and equity requires us to estimate a risk-free rate and risk premiums in the form of default spreads, for debt, and relative risk measures and equity risk premiums, for equity.

THE RISK-FREE RATE

While there are some who operate on the presumption that there is a global risk-free rate, or that it is a constant that does not change over time, the truth is that risk-free rates will vary across currencies at a point in time, and in the same currency across time. There are treatises you could write about why this happens, but the key driver of the differences, both across currencies and across time, is expected inflation. Currencies with high expected inflation will have higher risk-free rates than currencies with low expected inflation, and deflationary currencies could have negative risk-free rates.

Practitioners often use the local-currency government bonds rate as the risk-free rate on a currency, with the rationale that a government should never default on its local-currency bonds, no matter how badly it manages its finances, because of its power to print currency. Empirically, though, it is worth noting that about a third to a half of all sovereign (government) defaults in the last three decades have been in local-currency bonds, suggesting that government bond rates in currencies, where there is perceived default risk, are not in fact risk-free rates. In figure 6.4, I estimate risk-free rates in about four dozen currencies, using the government bond rate as the risk-free in currencies where the sovereign is at the highest rating (AAA, with S&P, or Aaa, with Moody's), and starting with the government bond rate and netting out a default spread based upon the sovereign rating for a government for countries with lower ratings.

FIGURE 6.4 | Interest Rates by Currency

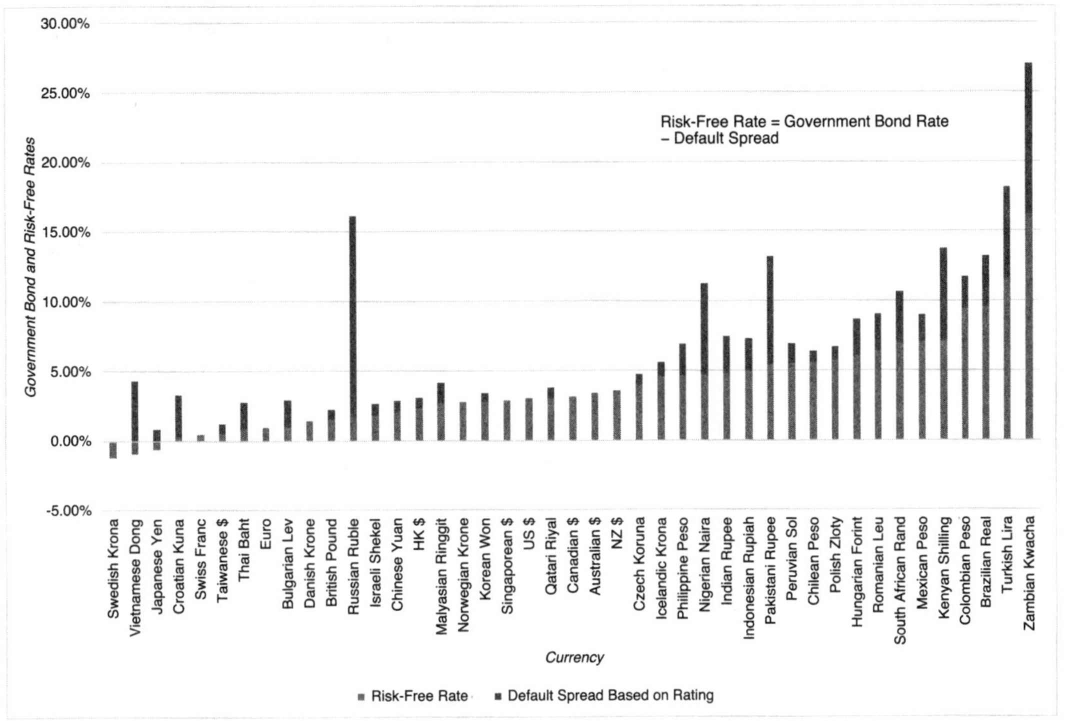

Note that since the key driver of differences in risk-free rates is expected inflation, using a higher-inflation currency for your analysis will result in higher hurdle rates and, if inflation can be passed through into earnings, higher earnings and returns in that currency as well.

DEFAULT SPREADS FOR DEBT

The default spreads for debt represent the price that lenders and bondholders charge when lending money to businesses with credit risk. Not surprisingly, these prices will change over time, as investors increase default spreads in times of fear (recessions, crises) and reduce them in good times. As a proxy for the level of credit risk, I will use bond ratings, assigned by ratings agencies to companies that borrow, and based upon a combination of financial and qualitative factors. In figure 6.5, I look at the evolution of default spreads on bond ratings classes from AAA to high yield from the start of 2015 to the start of 2022.

FIGURE 6.5 | Default Spreads by Bond Ratings Class

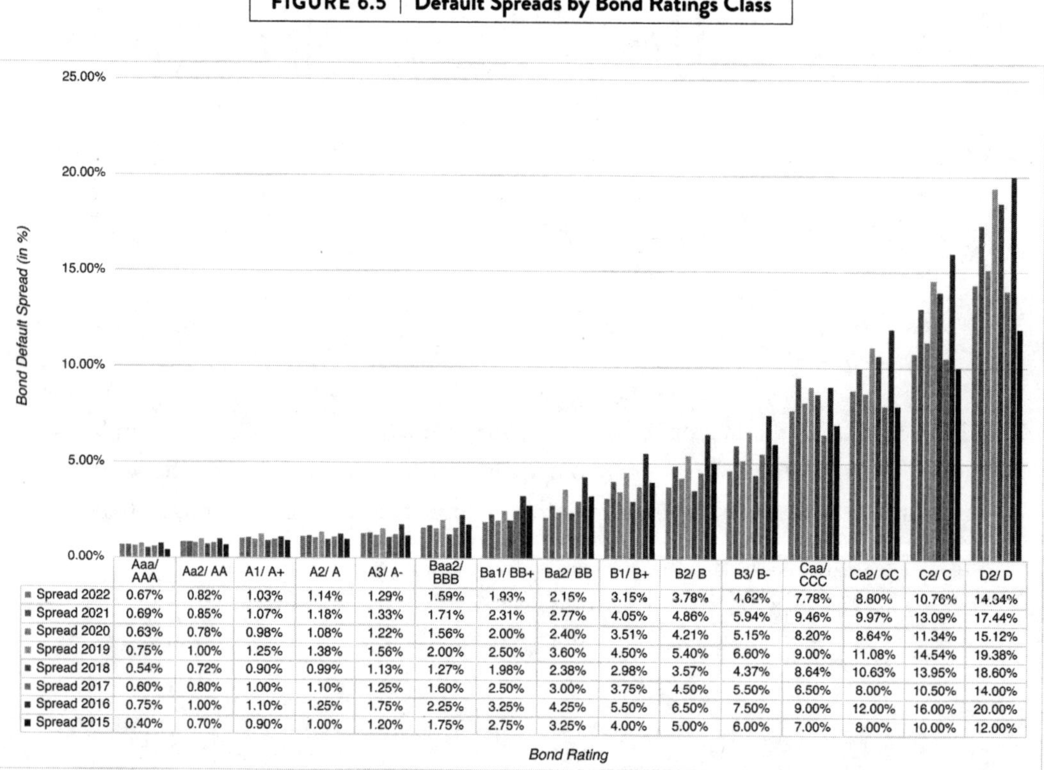

	Aaa/ AAA	Aa2/ AA	A1/ A+	A2/ A	A3/ A-	Baa2/ BBB	Ba1/ BB+	Ba2/ BB	B1/ B+	B2/ B	B3/ B-	Caa/ CCC	Ca2/ CC	C2/ C	D2/ D
Spread 2022	0.67%	0.82%	1.03%	1.14%	1.29%	1.59%	1.93%	2.15%	3.15%	3.78%	4.62%	7.78%	8.80%	10.76%	14.34%
Spread 2021	0.69%	0.85%	1.07%	1.18%	1.33%	1.71%	2.31%	2.77%	4.05%	4.86%	5.94%	9.46%	9.97%	13.09%	17.44%
Spread 2020	0.63%	0.78%	0.98%	1.08%	1.22%	1.56%	2.00%	2.40%	3.51%	4.21%	5.15%	8.20%	8.64%	11.34%	15.12%
Spread 2019	0.75%	1.00%	1.25%	1.38%	1.56%	2.00%	2.50%	3.60%	4.50%	5.40%	6.60%	9.00%	11.08%	14.54%	19.38%
Spread 2018	0.54%	0.72%	0.90%	0.99%	1.13%	1.27%	1.98%	2.38%	2.98%	3.57%	4.37%	8.64%	10.63%	13.95%	18.60%
Spread 2017	0.60%	0.80%	1.00%	1.10%	1.25%	1.60%	2.50%	3.00%	3.75%	4.50%	5.50%	6.50%	8.00%	10.50%	14.00%
Spread 2016	0.75%	1.00%	1.10%	1.25%	1.75%	2.25%	3.25%	4.25%	5.50%	6.50%	7.50%	9.00%	12.00%	16.00%	20.00%
Spread 2015	0.40%	0.70%	0.90%	1.00%	1.20%	1.75%	2.75%	3.25%	4.00%	5.00%	6.00%	7.00%	8.00%	10.00%	12.00%

As the data shows, default spreads change significantly over time, for every ratings class, with wider swings in the lower ratings.

EQUITY RISK PREMIUM

The equity risk premium is the price of risk in the equity markets—but unlike default spreads, which can be easily observed in the bond market, the equity risk premium (ERP) is implicit, built into what investors pay for equities, rather than a rate. While some estimate ERPs by looking at the past and the historical premiums that stocks have earned over riskless securities over long periods, I prefer a forward-looking and more dynamic approach, where I back out of stock prices, which are observable, and expected cash flows from investing in stocks, which are estimated, the internal rate of return that investors can expect to make on stocks. Netting out the risk-free rate from that internal rate of return generates an implied equity risk premium, and figure 6.6 looks at its ups and downs, for US equities, from 1960 to July 2022.

FIGURE 6.6 | Equity Risk Premium (Implied) for US Equities, 1960 to July 2022

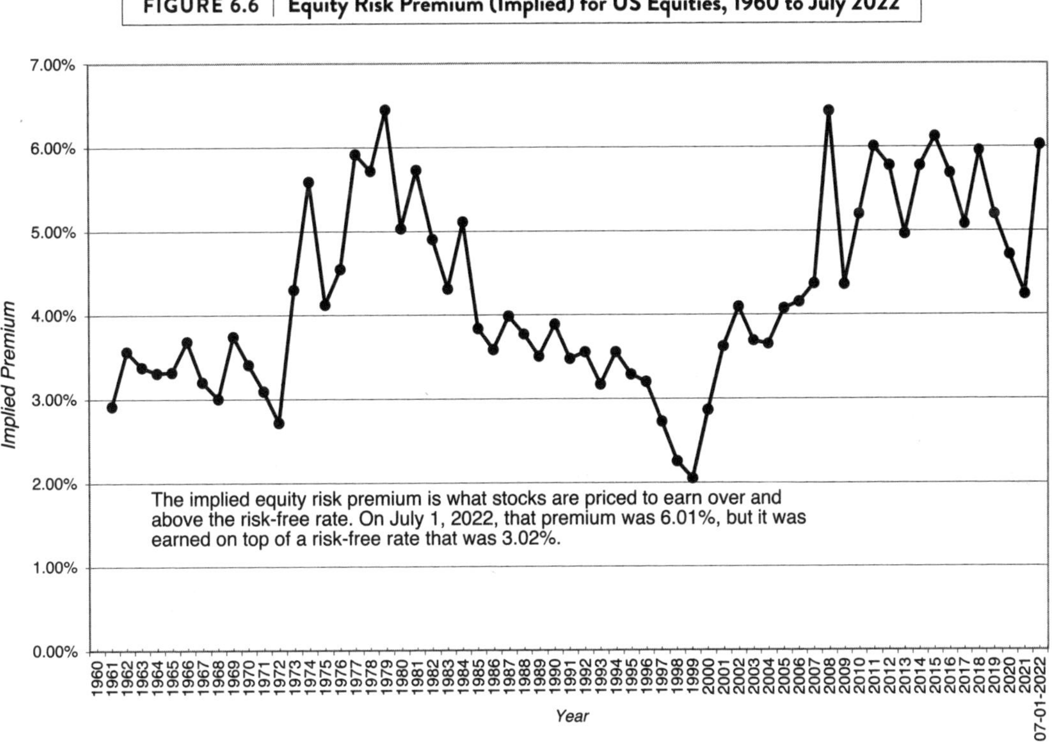

As is the case with default spreads, equity risk premiums reflect the fears and hopes of investors, falling in good times, when investors feel more secure about the future, and rising when investors become fearful. On July 1, 2022, the implied equity risk premium for US stocks was approximately 6.00%.

If I consider the US a mature market, it follows that equity risk premiums should be higher in other parts of the world, where political and economic risk are greater. In figure 6.7, I estimate these equity risk premiums, starting with the US ERP as a base and adding a country risk premium, which is a function of the default risk of a country.

FIGURE 6.7 | Equity Risk Premium, by Country, July 2022

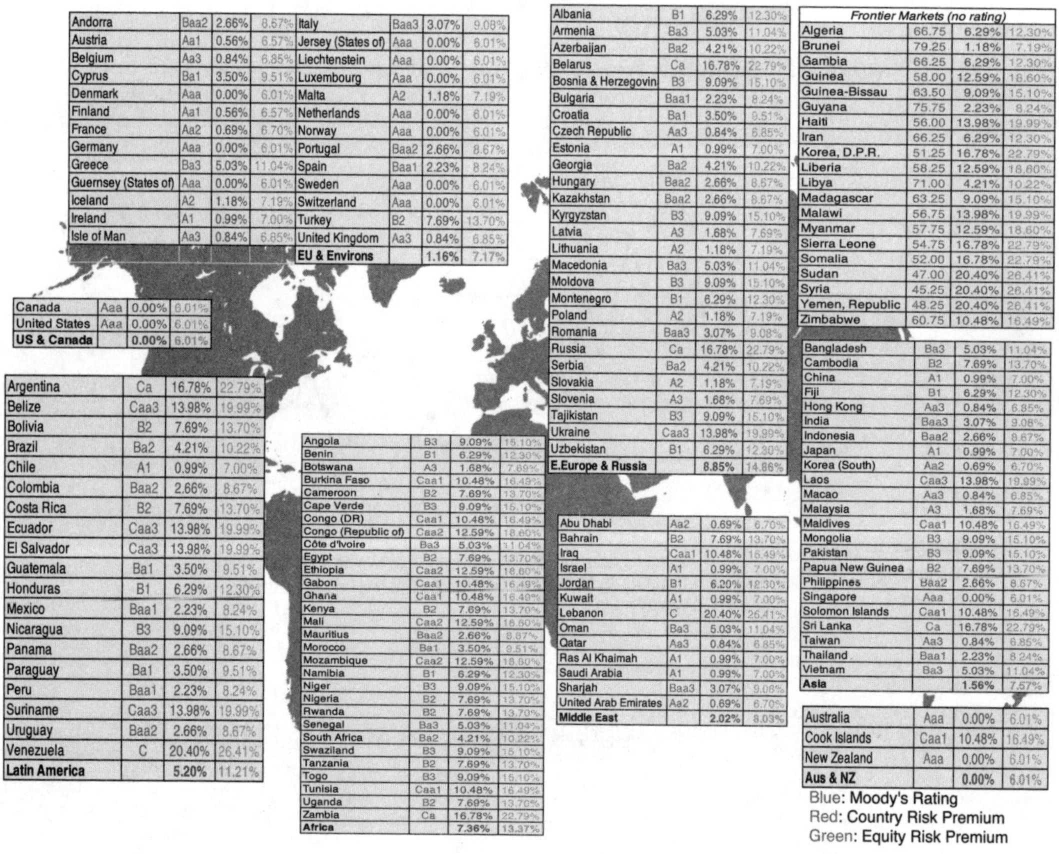

Country	Rating	CRP	ERP	Country	Rating	CRP	ERP
Andorra	Baa2	2.66%	8.67%	Italy	Baa3	3.07%	9.08%
Austria	Aa1	0.56%	6.57%	Jersey (States of)	Aaa	0.00%	6.01%
Belgium	Aa3	0.84%	6.85%	Liechtenstein	Aaa	0.00%	6.01%
Cyprus	Ba1	3.50%	9.51%	Luxembourg	Aaa	0.00%	6.01%
Denmark	Aaa	0.00%	6.01%	Malta	A2	1.18%	7.19%
Finland	Aa1	0.56%	6.57%	Netherlands	Aaa	0.00%	6.01%
France	Aa2	0.69%	6.70%	Norway	Aaa	0.00%	6.01%
Germany	Aaa	0.00%	6.01%	Portugal	Baa2	2.66%	8.67%
Greece	Ba3	5.03%	11.04%	Spain	Baa1	2.23%	8.24%
Guernsey (States of)	Aaa	0.00%	6.01%	Sweden	Aaa	0.00%	6.01%
Iceland	A2	1.18%	7.19%	Switzerland	Aaa	0.00%	6.01%
Ireland	A1	0.99%	7.00%	Turkey	B2	7.69%	13.70%
Isle of Man	Aa3	0.84%	6.85%	United Kingdom	Aa3	0.84%	6.85%
				EU & Environs		**1.16%**	7.17%

Country	Rating	CRP	ERP
Canada	Aaa	0.00%	6.01%
United States	Aaa	0.00%	6.01%
US & Canada		**0.00%**	6.01%

Country	Rating	CRP	ERP
Argentina	Ca	16.78%	22.79%
Belize	Caa3	13.98%	19.99%
Bolivia	B2	7.69%	13.70%
Brazil	Ba2	4.21%	10.22%
Chile	A1	0.99%	7.00%
Colombia	Baa2	2.66%	8.67%
Costa Rica	B2	7.69%	13.70%
Ecuador	Caa3	13.98%	19.99%
El Salvador	Caa3	13.98%	19.99%
Guatemala	Ba1	3.50%	9.51%
Honduras	B1	6.29%	12.30%
Mexico	Baa1	2.23%	8.24%
Nicaragua	B3	9.09%	15.10%
Panama	Baa2	2.66%	8.67%
Paraguay	Ba1	3.50%	9.51%
Peru	Baa1	2.23%	8.24%
Suriname	Caa3	13.98%	19.99%
Uruguay	Baa2	2.66%	8.67%
Venezuela	C	20.40%	26.41%
Latin America		**5.20%**	11.21%

Country	Rating	CRP	ERP
Angola	B3	9.09%	15.10%
Benin	B1	6.29%	12.30%
Botswana	A3	1.68%	7.69%
Burkina Faso	Caa1	10.48%	16.49%
Cameroon	B2	7.69%	13.70%
Cape Verde	B3	9.09%	15.10%
Congo (DR)	Caa1	10.48%	16.49%
Congo (Republic of)	Caa2	12.59%	18.60%
Côte d'Ivoire	Ba3	5.03%	11.04%
Egypt	B2	7.69%	13.70%
Ethiopia	Caa2	12.59%	18.60%
Gabon	Caa1	10.48%	16.49%
Ghana	Caa1	10.48%	16.49%
Kenya	B2	7.69%	13.70%
Mali	Caa2	12.59%	18.60%
Mauritius	Baa2	2.66%	8.67%
Morocco	Ba1	3.50%	9.51%
Mozambique	Caa2	12.59%	18.60%
Namibia	B1	6.29%	12.30%
Niger	B3	9.09%	15.10%
Nigeria	B2	7.69%	13.70%
Rwanda	B2	7.69%	13.70%
Senegal	Ba3	5.03%	11.04%
South Africa	Ba2	4.21%	10.22%
Swaziland	B3	9.09%	15.10%
Tanzania	B2	7.69%	13.70%
Togo	B3	9.09%	15.10%
Tunisia	Caa1	10.48%	16.49%
Uganda	B2	7.69%	13.70%
Zambia	Ca	16.78%	22.79%
Africa		**7.36%**	13.37%

Country	Rating	CRP	ERP
Albania	B1	6.29%	12.30%
Armenia	Ba3	5.03%	11.04%
Azerbaijan	Ba2	4.21%	10.22%
Belarus	Ca	16.78%	22.79%
Bosnia & Herzegovina	B3	9.09%	15.10%
Bulgaria	Baa1	2.23%	8.24%
Croatia	Ba1	3.50%	9.51%
Czech Republic	Aa3	0.84%	6.85%
Estonia	A1	0.99%	7.00%
Georgia	Ba2	4.21%	10.22%
Hungary	Baa2	2.66%	8.67%
Kazakhstan	Baa2	2.66%	8.67%
Kyrgyzstan	B3	9.09%	15.10%
Latvia	A3	1.68%	7.69%
Lithuania	A2	1.18%	7.19%
Macedonia	Ba3	5.03%	11.04%
Moldova	B3	9.09%	15.10%
Montenegro	B1	6.29%	12.30%
Poland	A2	1.18%	7.19%
Romania	Baa3	3.07%	9.08%
Russia	Ca	16.78%	22.79%
Serbia	Ba2	4.21%	10.22%
Slovakia	A2	1.18%	7.19%
Slovenia	A3	1.68%	7.69%
Tajikistan	B3	9.09%	15.10%
Ukraine	Caa3	13.98%	19.99%
Uzbekistan	B1	6.29%	12.30%
E.Europe & Russia		8.85%	14.86%

Country	Rating	CRP	ERP
Abu Dhabi	Aa2	0.69%	6.70%
Bahrain	B2	7.69%	13.70%
Iraq	Caa1	10.48%	16.49%
Israel	A1	0.99%	7.00%
Jordan	B1	6.29%	12.30%
Kuwait	A1	0.99%	7.00%
Lebanon	C	20.40%	26.41%
Oman	Ba3	5.03%	11.04%
Qatar	Aa3	0.84%	6.85%
Ras Al Khaimah	A1	0.99%	7.00%
Saudi Arabia	A1	0.99%	7.00%
Sharjah	Baa3	3.07%	9.08%
United Arab Emirates	Aa2	0.69%	6.70%
Middle East		**2.02%**	8.03%

Frontier Markets (no rating)			
Algeria	66.75	6.29%	12.30%
Brunei	79.25	1.18%	7.19%
Gambia	66.25	6.29%	12.30%
Guinea	58.00	12.59%	18.60%
Guinea-Bissau	63.50	9.09%	15.10%
Guyana	75.75	2.23%	8.24%
Haiti	56.00	13.98%	19.99%
Iran	66.25	6.29%	12.30%
Korea, D.P.R.	51.25	16.78%	22.79%
Liberia	58.25	12.59%	18.60%
Libya	71.00	4.21%	10.22%
Madagascar	63.25	9.09%	15.10%
Malawi	56.75	13.98%	19.99%
Myanmar	57.75	12.59%	18.60%
Sierra Leone	54.75	16.78%	22.79%
Somalia	52.00	16.78%	22.79%
Sudan	47.00	20.40%	26.41%
Syria	45.25	20.40%	26.41%
Yemen, Republic	48.25	20.40%	26.41%
Zimbabwe	60.75	10.48%	16.49%

Country	Rating	CRP	ERP
Bangladesh	Ba3	5.03%	11.04%
Cambodia	B2	7.69%	13.70%
China	A1	0.99%	7.00%
Fiji	B1	6.29%	12.30%
Hong Kong	Aa3	0.84%	6.85%
India	Baa3	3.07%	9.08%
Indonesia	Baa2	2.66%	8.67%
Japan	A1	0.99%	7.00%
Korea (South)	Aa2	0.69%	6.70%
Laos	Caa3	13.98%	19.99%
Macao	Aa3	0.84%	6.85%
Malaysia	A3	1.68%	7.69%
Maldives	Caa1	10.48%	16.49%
Mongolia	B3	9.09%	15.10%
Pakistan	B3	9.09%	15.10%
Papua New Guinea	B2	7.69%	13.70%
Philippines	Baa2	2.66%	8.67%
Singapore	Aaa	0.00%	6.01%
Solomon Islands	Caa1	10.48%	16.49%
Sri Lanka	Ca	16.78%	22.79%
Taiwan	Aa3	0.84%	6.85%
Thailand	Baa1	2.23%	8.24%
Vietnam	Ba3	5.03%	11.04%
Asia		1.56%	7.57%

Country	Rating	CRP	ERP
Australia	Aaa	0.00%	6.01%
Cook Islands	Caa1	10.48%	16.49%
New Zealand	Aaa	0.00%	6.01%
Aus & NZ		**0.00%**	6.01%

Blue: Moody's Rating
Red: Country Risk Premium
Green: Equity Risk Premium

The cost of capital for a project should reflect where its operations are located, in terms of both production and revenue, rather than the country that the project-taking company is incorporated in. Thus, a US company that is considering a project in India should be using an ERP of 9.08% in estimating the cost of equity for that project.

RELATIVE EQUITY RISK MEASURE (BETA)

The final piece of the cost-of-equity puzzle requires an assessment of relative risk, i.e., how risky a business is relative to the average risk investment in the market. Financial analysts often use a beta to measure that risk, and rather than go through its derivation or debate its usage, it is simpler to think of it as a relative risk measure, with a beta of one representing an average risk equity investment and betas greater or less than one indicating above- or below-average risk, respectively.

The fundamentals that determine the relative risk exposure of a business or project come from business choices, ranging from how discretionary the products or services that a project offers are to the fixed-cost structure of the project, with higher fixed costs increasing relative risk, and how much debt the project or business will carry, with more debt pushing up relative risk. Figure 6.8 summarizes these determinants.

FIGURE 6.8 | Determinants of Relative Risk (Beta)

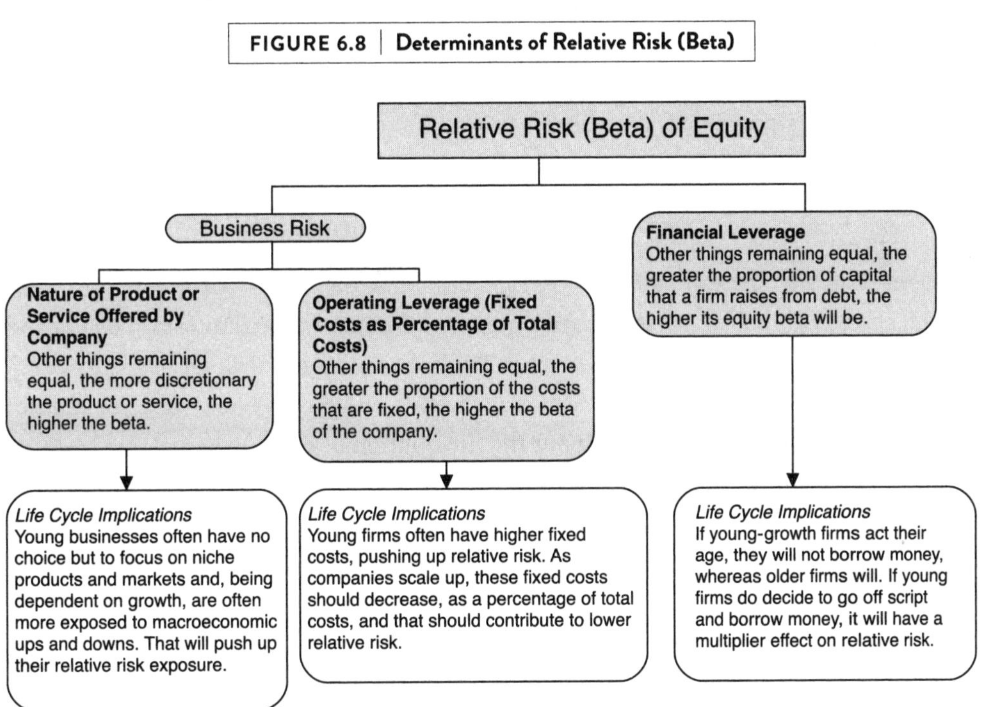

Looking at the determinants of relative risk, you can see why young-growth firms are more exposed to business risk, though mature firms may use financial leverage that results in high relative risk, from an equity perspective.

To measure relative risk exposure, you must use historical data on either fundamentals (revenues, earnings) or market prices (if the company is publicly traded) over time. Since the former are measured infrequently (quarterly or annually) and are subject to accounting smoothing, most analysts use market prices to estimate relative risk, and that gives rise to three problems. The first is that the approach is a nonstarter for private businesses that are not publicly traded, and thus have no market price. The second is that even for publicly traded businesses, you can estimate only a single beta or relative risk measure for the entire business, and applying that beta to individual projects that vary in risk can yield skewed estimates of hurdle rates. The third is that an estimate of risk based upon past prices will be noisy, i.e., you will get a range of values for the estimate, not a single value. The solution to all three problems is to use the average relative risk (beta) measure for all publicly traded companies in a business as the relative risk measure for a given project or company in that business. Thus, a technology company making an investment in an entertainment software project can use the average beta of publicly traded entertainment companies. This approach can likewise be used to estimate risk measures for private businesses and projects and has the added advantage of yielding better estimates, since an average of many flawed relative risk measures will yield an estimate with a much narrower range and greater precision.

Cost of Capital across the Life Cycle

Bringing together the estimates of risk-free rates, risk premiums (ERP for equity and default spreads for debt), and relative risk measures, I can estimate the costs of equity and debt for any business. Weighting these costs by the proportions in which they are used in funding, where those proportions reflect market value rather than book value, the costs of capital emerge. In figure 6.9, I graph out the distribution of costs of capital, in US dollar terms, for global firms in July 2022.

FIGURE 6.9 | **Cost of Capital (US $) Distribution—Global Firms, July 2022**

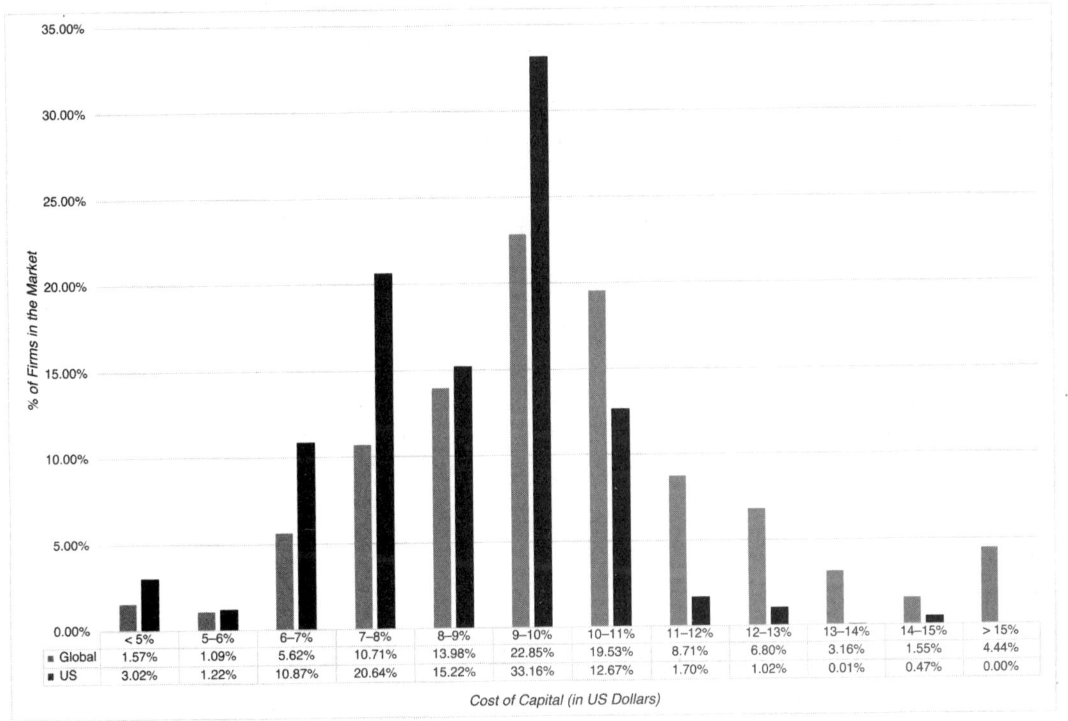

These dollar costs of capital reflect the risk-free rate of 3.02% in US dollars on July 1, 2022, and the equity risk premiums as of that date, as shown in figure 6.6 and figure 6.7. The median US dollar cost of capital for a US (global) firm in July 2022 was 8.97% (9.70%), and the range in values is surprisingly small, with 80% of US (global) companies having costs of capital between 6.76% and 10.24% (7.20%—12.84%). (The wider range in costs of capital for global firms comes from more exposure to risky markets.)

Should the cost of capital be different for firms across the life cycle? At first sight, the answer may seem obvious. As I noted in our earlier discussion of uncertainty across the life cycle, young firms are exposed to more risk than more mature firms, and it seems to stand to reason that costs of capital should reflect this risk difference. The reason for caution, though, comes from the recognition that costs of capital, at least as computed in the figure above, reflect only the risk that is perceived by diversified investors, and if much of the risk in young companies is firm-specific, the cost of capital may not fully reflect that risk, if investors in young companies tend to less diversified. In table 6.1, I estimate costs of capital for just US companies (to reduce country risk effects), classified by corporate age, one of the measures for country risk that I introduced in chapter 3:

Table 6.1 • Costs of Capital (US $), by Age Decile, for US Firms

		Cost of Capital in US $		
Age Decile	**Average Age**	**Lowest Quartile**	**Median**	**Highest Quartile**
Youngest	5.04	8.73%	9.27%	9.64%
2nd decile	9.43	8.58%	9.20%	9.64%
3rd decile	13.58	8.19%	9.19%	9.77%
4th decile	18.12	8.13%	9.15%	9.78%
5th decile	23.49	7.64%	9.12%	9.81%
6th decile	29.49	8.10%	9.15%	9.70%
7th decile	38.19	7.81%	9.05%	9.68%
8th decile	52.48	7.53%	8.94%	9.67%
9th decile	86.88	6.91%	8.59%	9.24%
Oldest	140.22	6.66%	7.03%	8.88%

If there is a conclusion to be drawn from this table, it is that the oldest firms have much lower costs of capital than younger firms, with the companies in the top decile having a cost of capital of 7.03%, well below the median. The youngest firms do have the highest cost of capital, at 9.27%, but that number does not decrease by much until you get to the 9th decile of companies.

It is worth noting that most young firms are not publicly traded, and that the conclusions from table 6.1 may not carry over where that is the case. To the extent that the owners of young, private businesses are either undiversified, which is often the case with founders, or only partially diversified, as is true for many venture capitalists, the costs of capital will rise to incorporate company-specific risks. Just as an exercise, to show the difference that comes from risk perspective, I computed the relative risk measures of companies using total risk, instead of just undiversifiable risk, and estimated the costs of capital for public companies, based on age decile, in table 6.2.

Table 6.2 • Total Risk Costs of Capital (US $), by Age Decile, for US Firms

			Total Cost of Capital		
Age Decile	Number of Firms	Correlation with Market	First Quartile	Median	Third Quartile
Youngest	483	28.31%	20.86%	25.31%	28.73%
2nd decile	674	28.61%	20.64%	25.25%	27.96%
3rd decile	442	29.11%	19.52%	24.15%	27.75%
4th decile	731	29.11%	19.39%	24.01%	27.59%
5th decile	611	29.11%	17.85%	23.92%	27.45%
6th decile	560	29.28%	18.02%	23.33%	26.93%
7th decile	592	29.60%	17.84%	22.25%	26.36%
8th decile	621	30.97%	16.89%	20.63%	24.43%
9th decile	584	31.77%	12.70%	20.08%	23.01%
Oldest	595	33.52%	12.02%	12.70%	21.10%

As you can see, the total risk cost of capital is much higher, across the board, for all companies, but assessed this way, the divergence in risk between the youngest and oldest companies is much larger.

Investment Decision Rules

In the last chapter, I noted that while investment decisions can be based simply on accounting earnings or cash flows, a good measure of investment returns should be based not just upon cash flows but also on the *timing* of those cash flows. I will begin this section by looking at accounting returns and explain why, in spite of their limitations, they still have staying power in investment analysis. Then I will move on to discuss the two most used time-weighted cash flow return approaches, net present value and internal rate of return, and why the right choice between the two will depend upon where a firm is in the life cycle. I will conclude with a real options approach, where I provide a rationale, sometimes misapplied, that young firms use for overriding traditional investment decision rules.

Accounting Returns

The accounting return on a project or a business is determined by scaling earnings—the accounting measure of the success of a project—by the capital invested in a project, again defined with an accounting perspective. As with other aspects of a business, the accounting return can be measured through the eyes of only the equity investors in the business, as a return on equity, or of capital providers, as a return on invested capital. Using the balance sheet perspective that I introduced in discussing hurdle rates, you can contrast the two measures of return in figure 6.10.

FIGURE 6.10 | Accounting Returns—Equity versus All Capital

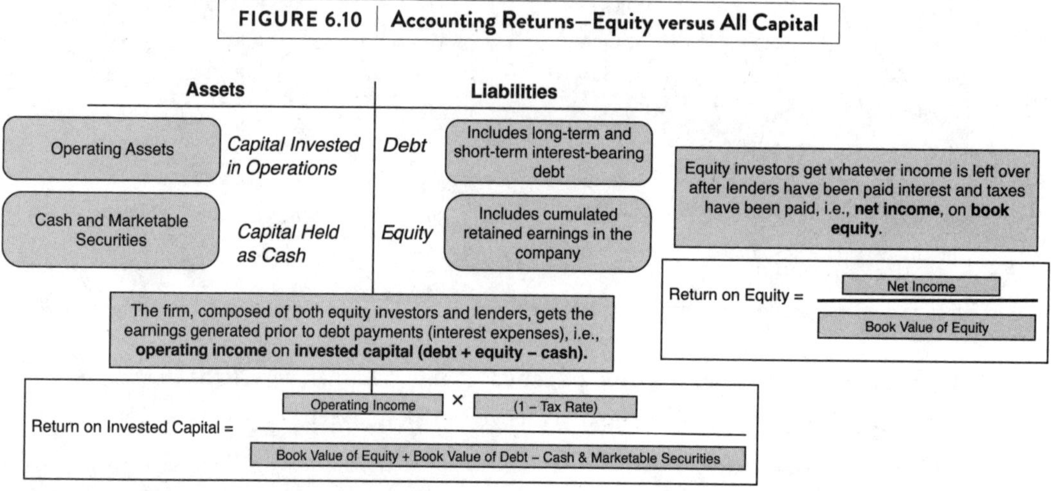

Intuitively, the return on invested capital is a measure of the quality of returns that a business makes, but the return on equity is augmented, to incorporate the effects of borrowing money. A business with projects that have moderate returns on capital can have high returns on equity if it is using more debt to finance its projects.

MEASUREMENT ISSUES

While the accounting return (return on equity or capital) is easy to compute and reflects data that should be easily available for any business in its financial statements (earnings and book value), its weaknesses lie in its accounting roots.

- The accounting earnings on a project or business reflect the difference between revenues, as recorded by accountants, and earnings, reflecting accounting classifications of expenses into operating, financing, and capital components. When accountants misclassify expenses—as they did in treating lease expenses, which are financing expenses, as operating expenses until 2019, and as they continue to do with R&D expenses, a capital expense if you follow first principles but one that is treated as an operating expense—the accounting earnings can be skewed significantly.

- The invested capital in a project is usually estimated from the book value that accountants attach to investments made in the project. While that may not be a bad assumption to make for a project at its start, it can still be skewed by the miscategorization of expenses like leases and R&D that I referenced above, and it increasingly loses its relevance as a project's assets age and book value deviates from current value.
- Finally, in its conventional form, the return on capital *does not incorporate the time value of money*, since earnings in future years (and the returns that they represent) are weighted the same as earnings in the next year.

Accounting Returns across the Life Cycle

In short, the computed return on invested capital or return on equity for a project or business may not bear close resemblance to its actual returns. To see how that divergence relates to the corporate life cycle, I computed returns on equity and capital for publicly traded US companies in 2022, classified into deciles by age, in table 6.3.

Table 6.3 • Accounting Returns at US Companies, Classified by Age, 2022

		Return on Capital			Return on Equity		
Age Decile	Average Age	Median	Aggregate	% Negative	Median	Aggregate	% Negative
Youngest	5.04	-74.99%	7.28%	47.41%	-15.50%	0.43%	73.91%
2nd decile	9.43	-57.06%	4.14%	43.92%	-15.96%	-4.21%	67.66%
3rd decile	13.58	-27.77%	-5.18%	42.08%	-9.40%	-8.74%	57.01%
4th decile	18.12	-7.40%	11.84%	36.94%	-4.84%	12.42%	51.03%
5th decile	23.49	0.10%	13.64%	28.81%	5.79%	18.23%	37.48%
6th decile	29.49	4.65%	11.38%	27.14%	6.83%	22.74%	34.11%
7th decile	38.19	6.26%	17.81%	24.32%	9.90%	18.64%	28.72%
8th decile	52.48	9.30%	10.24%	19.32%	12.65%	31.45%	19.16%
9th decile	86.88	10.22%	4.72%	18.15%	12.66%	22.04%	16.95%
Oldest	140.22	5.18%	7.83%	22.69%	11.84%	15.10%	8.57%

Within each decile, I computed the median company's returns, as well an aggregated measure of this return, where I divided the total earnings generated by all companies in a group by the total capital invested by those companies. In effect, the latter is closer to a weighted average, with larger companies in a group weighted more than smaller companies. Note the high percentage of young firms that report negative returns on capital (47.41%) and negative returns on equity (73.91%). Before you jump to the conclusion that these firms are taking bad investments, it is worth noting that the accounting returns are computed using earnings in the most recent twelve months and that early in a company's life cycle, you should expect to see negative earnings. As businesses mature, you do see improvements in the accounting returns, and a smaller percentage of firms report negative accounting returns. It is also interesting that while relatively few of the oldest firms (in the top decile) lose money, their returns on capital decline, perhaps as their businesses lose their luster.

I realize that for some analysts, especially those with accounting backgrounds, the return on capital (or equity) is considered a measure of company (and management) quality. While that may be the case for older, more mature firms, it has little utility with firms earlier in the life cycle, where low or even negative accounting returns are more a reflection of corporate age than quality. Later in this book, I will argue that value investors who screen companies using accounting returns—i.e., who invest only in companies that earn high returns on equity—will screen out most younger firms from their investing universe.

Discounted Cash Flow Measures

At the other end of the investment return spectrum are measures that are based upon cash flows and reflect the timing of these cash flows by discounting cash flows to the present. The two most widely used discounted cash flow measures are the net present value (NPV) and internal rate of return (IRR).

- The net present value of a project is the sum of the present values of the expected cash flows on the project over its lifetime, discounted back at the hurdle rate, i.e., the cost of equity or capital. Since the investments needed, now or in the future, to start and keep the project going are shown as negative cash flows, the net present value investment rule is simple: if the NPV is greater (less) than zero, the project is generating a return that exceeds (trails) its hurdle rate and is a good (bad) investment.
- The internal rate of return is the discount rate that makes the aggregated present value of all cash flows on the project equal to zero. That internal rate of return can be compared to the hurdle rate for the project, and if it exceeds (falls below) the hurdle rate, the project is a good (bad) investment.

While both approaches are built on the same principle, that of focusing on cash flows and adjusting them for time, there are key differences:

1. **Percentage versus absolute value:** The first difference is that the NPV for a project is an absolute value—i.e., with expected dollar cash flows, the NPV will be a dollar value—and a project with higher net present value is more value-additive than a project with lower net present value, even if it requires five or ten times the initial investment. The internal rate of return, as a percentage value, is likely to skew toward projects that require less capital over those that need more and can yield rankings that diverge from the NPV rule.
2. **Unique versus multiple values:** There can be only one net present value for a project, but if a project has cash flows that change sign more than once, going from negative to positive and then back to negative, over time, there can be more than one internal rate of return for the project. With multiple IRRs, decision-makers may find themselves in a quandary if one IRR for a project exceeds the hurdle rate (making it a good investment) and one is lower than the hurdle rate (making it a bad investment).
3. **Reinvestment of intermediate cash flows:** While both NPV and IRR are time-weighted cash returns, there is a subtle difference in what each approach assumes about the cash flows that occur in intermediate years—i.e., the cash flows in years 1 through 4 of a five-year project. The NPV rule assumes that these intermediate cash flows are reinvested at the hurdle rate, a safe assumption if these hurdle rates represent what investors can earn in the market right now on investments of equivalent risk. The IRR rule assumes that intermediate cash flows are reinvested at the computed IRR for the project, an implicit assumption that, in the future, the business will continue to have new projects very similar in quality and returns to the one that is being assessed.

While many corporate finance textbooks are dogmatic in their contention that the net present value rule is best, bringing the corporate life cycle into the discussion adds layers of ambiguity. For young-growth firms, often faced with far more investment opportunities than they have available capital, the internal rate of return rule makes more sense, because you want to maximize the value added given the capital constraint. As firms mature and have more than enough capital to take on available projects, it makes more sense to shift to the net present value rule.

Real Options

There is a third way of assessing investment projects—one that remains controversial, because it requires overriding traditional investment decision rules, but that can provide new perspective and alter investment decision-making in some cases. In this approach, you start with a conventional investment analysis, computing either the NPV or IRR for a project—but you then bring into consideration the possibility that making an investment, even if it has a negative NPV, may allow you to expand into new businesses or markets in the future. In effect, taking that first, negative net present value investment gives you the option to take other, potentially lucrative investments in the future. Figure 6.11 provides a cash flow payoff diagram that illustrates the structure of this option.

FIGURE 6.11 | A Real Options Payoff Diagram

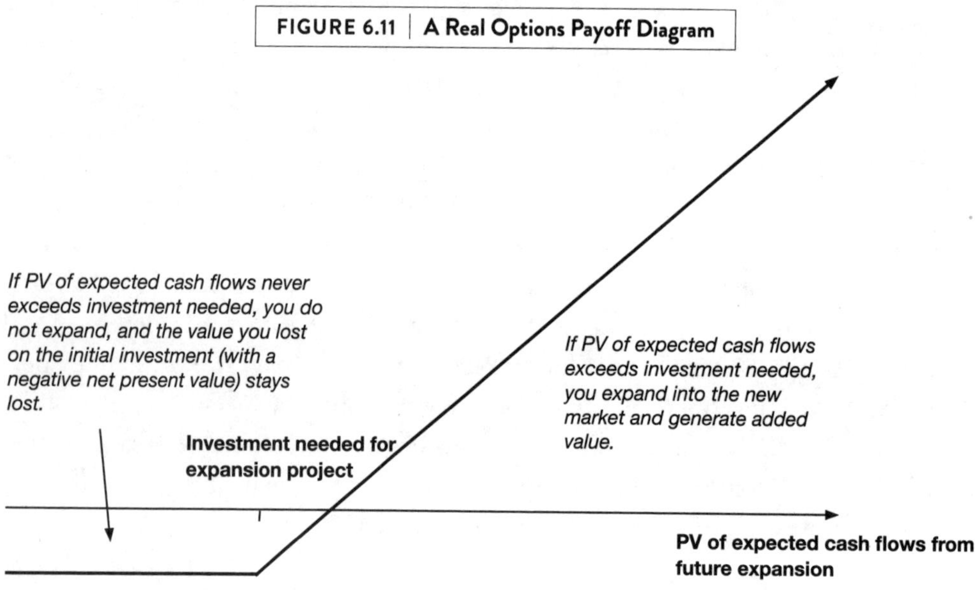

Real options are notoriously difficult to value, since the option pricing models that I use to value listed options do not adapt well to valuing project options, where the underlying asset is not traded, the options are long-term, and early exercise is more the rule than the exception. However, recognizing that there is a real option embedded in a project can yield valuable insights and alter decision-making. Thus, even without attaching a value to the option, I know that options to expand have the most value when the market you plan to expand into is a big one, and when you are most uncertain about its size and whether you will be able to enter it. While businesses across the life cycle can and often do make real options arguments for investing in projects that don't pass financial muster (NPV is less than zero, or return on capital is less than the cost of capital), you can see the appeal to young firms, especially those entering large markets, since they often face the most uncertainty about the future.

If you have worked at a young company and have never heard the term "real option" used in the firm's investment decision-making, recognize that there are other terms that are close relatives. A young firm that takes an investment that does not pass muster on the number, but does so because there are "strategic imperatives" involved, is making a real options argument. In the last decade, corporate managers and investors who have spent billions on building or acquiring platforms (of users and subscribers) have done so with the implicit argument that the users on these platforms could be the basis for lucrative businesses in the future—also an options argument.

Investment Decision-Making across the Life Cycle

The principle that a business should invest in assets, projects, or acquisitions only if it expects to earn a return higher than its hurdle rate remains true across the life cycle, but as I have shown in the discussion so far, the challenges that businesses face while making investments, the way in which the principle is applied, and the types of errors they make can change as companies go through the life cycle.

I will begin with the challenges businesses face, and the mistakes they often make, based upon where they are in the life cycle.

- For start-ups and toddler firms, the biggest challenge in investment analysis is that, without any historical experience and a market-tested product or service, every aspect of determining what an investment will bring as returns becomes filled with uncertainty, starting with the life of the project and its earnings and cash flows during that life. If you add the concern that each project being considered is likely to be large enough to make or break the firm, it is easy to see why firms in this phase often go into denial. Rather than confront uncertainty and make their best estimates, they often rely on gut feeling and surface metrics (adding users, increasing downloads) to determine whether to invest, and use real options arguments (large markets, lots of uncertainty) without any rigor.
- As firms enter their youth and start developing working business models and learning more about what does and does not work in markets, you see the beginnings of a formalized investment process. That said, there will still be significant uncertainty in

estimating cash flows and arriving at hurdle rates, especially if a firm has accessed venture capital. If you add to this the view, which is held in some young firms, that forecasting cash flows and doing financial analysis is somehow a threat to business creativity, it is easy to see why investing remains ad hoc and disorganized in this phase. Among those young firms that choose to do investment analysis, the scarcity of capital, relative to investment opportunities, will push the internal rate of return to the forefront, with a bias toward shorter-term projects over longer-term ones (because of concern around tying up large chunks of capital for long periods and generalized uncertainty about the long term).

- For those firms that successfully make it to high growth, there must be a recognition not only that success will increase the number of projects that need to be assessed, but also that these projects will be on a larger scale than the projects assessed in the past. It is important, therefore, to also understand that as projects scale up, the percentage returns on these projects will be lower; it is easier to earn 50% on a $1 million project than on one that requires an investment of $100 million. A subset of high-growth firms that continues to demand that these new, larger projects earn the same percentage returns as their much smaller projects earned, as internal rates of return, in the past is destined to stay small and turn away good investments.
- In mature growth, businesses have the comfort of drawing on history when making forecasts for projects, partly because they have taken similar projects in the past. However, maintaining high growth, as larger businesses, will require being opportunistic in pursing growth in new markets and geographies, and rigidity in investment analysis (either as process or in rules of thumb) can be an impediment in this pursuit. With fewer investment opportunities, and cash flows building up, the focus at these firms is likely to shift from percentage returns to dollar value added (net present value). One peril that managers face at this stage is that they are so focused on delivering growth and scaling up that they overinvest to reach their growth targets, often at the expense of profitability.
- For mature stable firms, estimating cash flows on internal projects is driven by historical experience, but to the extent that these firms still want to grow, they often turn to acquisitions. The nature of investment analysis in acquisitions is that you are estimating cash flows for a business that you are acquiring, not a project, and there can be side costs and side benefits (synergies) that must be incorporated into the analysis. When these acquisitions are of large, publicly traded companies, the history of dealmaking suggests that you are more likely to pay too much than too little, and while you may

be able to buy growth, it will be at too high a price. This is the stage where businesses must worry the most about using one "corporate hurdle rate" while assessing investments in businesses with different risk profiles, leading to safe businesses subsidizing riskier ones. Differences between accounting earnings and cash flows will also tend to get smaller, book value may have a fighting chance of capturing invested capital, and accounting returns can convey information about project quality. Not surprisingly, these are the firms where accounting returns have been entrenched the longest as an assessment tool and are still used in investment analysis. In addition to these challenges, mature businesses must keep a wary eye on newcomers, often with little or nothing to lose, that are intent on disrupting the business.

- For declining firms, the absence of growth assets (going back to our breakdown of a business into assets in place and growth assets) is often accompanied by a deterioration in returns on existing projects/assets. Consequently, the investment process gets upended: rather than invest up front in a new project or business and expect to generate cash flows in the future, these firms may have to consider divesting some of their existing businesses, if there are buyers willing to pay more than what those businesses will deliver as value on a continuing basis. Logically, this is not difficult to do, since assessing a divestiture just flips the normal sequence of cash flows, with a positive cash flow up front (from the divestiture) being weighed against the loss of cash flows from continuing with a project. That said, many businesses struggle with decline, as managers have been programmed to believe that growth is good and that shrinking a business is weakness. In fact, for these managers, the challenge is in fending off the many sellers of magic remedies that claim to reverse aging effortlessly and at a low cost.

In sum, the investment process across the life cycle is captured in figure 6.12, where I look at how investment types and techniques vary across time.

FIGURE 6.12 | The Investment Principle across the Life Cycle

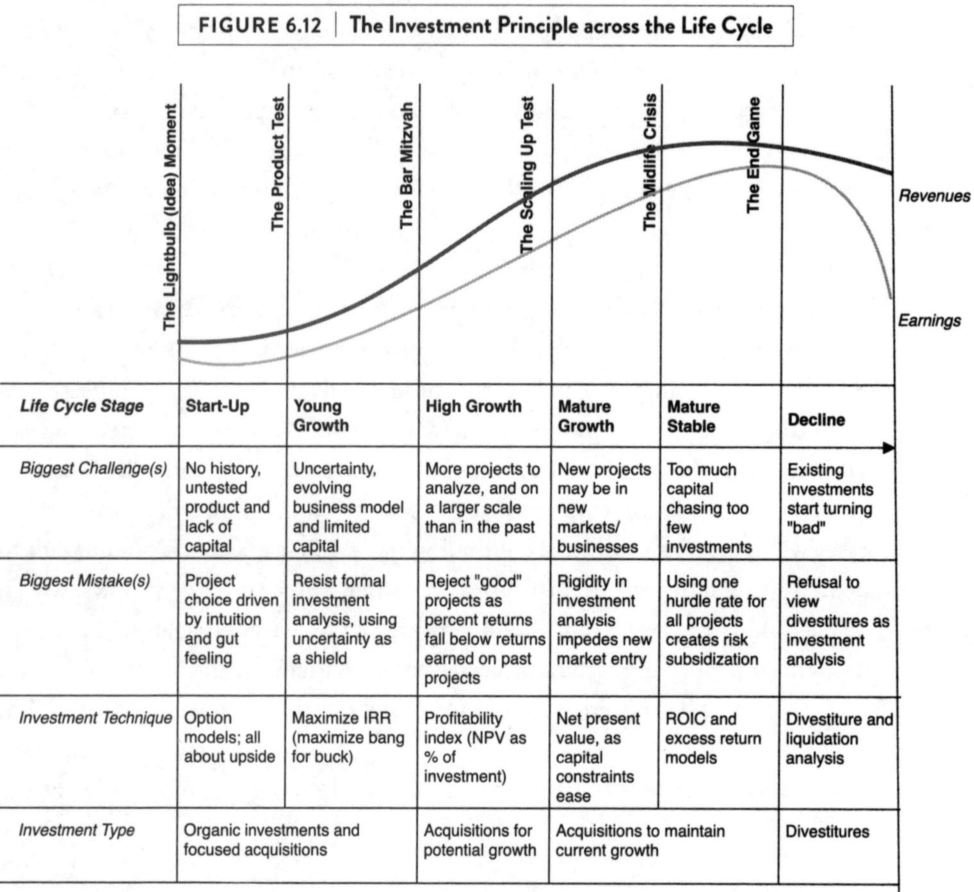

Life Cycle Stage	Start-Up	Young Growth	High Growth	Mature Growth	Mature Stable	Decline
Biggest Challenge(s)	No history, untested product and lack of capital	Uncertainty, evolving business model and limited capital	More projects to analyze, and on a larger scale than in the past	New projects may be in new markets/ businesses	Too much capital chasing too few investments	Existing investments start turning "bad"
Biggest Mistake(s)	Project choice driven by intuition and gut feeling	Resist formal investment analysis, using uncertainty as a shield	Reject "good" projects as percent returns fall below returns earned on past projects	Rigidity in investment analysis impedes new market entry	Using one hurdle rate for all projects creates risk subsidization	Refusal to view divestitures as investment analysis
Investment Technique	Option models; all about upside	Maximize IRR (maximize bang for buck)	Profitability index (NPV as % of investment)	Net present value, as capital constraints ease	ROIC and excess return models	Divestiture and liquidation analysis
Investment Type	Organic investments and focused acquisitions		Acquisitions for potential growth	Acquisitions to maintain current growth		Divestitures

Note that while it is true, in general, that young firms are more likely to depend on internal or organic investments for growth and that more mature firms shift toward acquisitions, there are many exceptions to the rule. Apple, the company with the largest market cap in the world in July 2022, has been a mature company for much of the last decade but has avoided falling into the "big acquisition" trap. Conversely, Zomato, a young food-delivery firm in India, with a business model still a work in progress, has made dozens of acquisitions, mostly of small, privately owned technology companies, in its first few years of existence.

Conclusion

"Invest only in projects or assets that earn a return that exceeds a minimum acceptable hurdle rate" is advice that is more easily dished out than accepted. The hurdle rate is a vehicle for reflecting the risk in an investment, but as I showed in this chapter, determining the marginal investor, whose risk perspective should drive risk measurement, or estimating that risk measure is not easy to do. That said, you should expect young business to have higher hurdle rates, when assessing whether to invest in new projects, than older businesses. In measuring the expected return on an investment, doing the analysis properly requires us to forecast earnings and cash flows over the life of the investment, and then time-weight these cash flows by discounting at the hurdle rate. To make matters even more unbalanced, I also offered a pathway to override the investment principle and take investments that generate returns that are less than the hurdle rate, especially if these investments offer an entrée into big markets and there is substantial uncertainty about the future.

7

Financing across the Life Cycle

TO FUND A BUSINESS, its owners can use their own money (equity) or they can borrow money (debt). As a business expands and perhaps goes public, the available sources of equity and debt will multiply, with venture capital and public equity supplementing owner savings, as equity, and corporate bonds augmenting bank loans, as debt. So will the available choices regarding how to structure the borrowing, in terms of maturity, interest payments (fixed versus floating rate), conversion options, and currency. The financing principle looks at the trade-off that determines how much of an investment's funding, if any, should come from debt, as well as the choice of the type of financing that will best match the business.

The Debt versus Equity Trade-off

If the choice that businesses face is between using equity and debt, the way to determine which funding source will benefit them more is to weigh the costs and benefits of borrowing money, relative to using equity. I will start by arguing that many businesses are drawn to debt for what I will term *illusory reasons*, i.e., these reasons for borrowing that look compelling but fall apart under scrutiny. I will then move to the other end of the spectrum and consider solely the financial trade-offs—i.e., the fundamental costs and benefits of borrowing—and why they change over the course of the corporate life cycle. I will end by looking at market frictions, mispricing, and distortions that can lead some businesses to borrow more or less than they should, given fundamentals, and how these deviations vary across the life cycle.

Debt and Equity: The Illusory Reasons

Since the decision to borrow (or not borrow) money is a consequential one, you would think that it would be based upon the fundamental factors that drive value. While that may be true for some businesses, the choice of borrowing money or using equity in many businesses is still driven by what I label as illusory reasons, some in debt's favor and some against it.

- On the side that favors debt, one of the most common illusory reasons is that debt is cheaper than equity, even without considering tax benefits, with this judgment being made by comparing interest rates on debt to costs of equity. Technically, it is true that debt will almost always look cheaper than equity, but since the risk in a project or business must be borne by one of the capital providers, the benefits of replacing more expensive equity with cheaper debt will be offset by equity becoming riskier and commanding a higher cost.
- A second illusory reason for borrowing more is that it allows equity investors to earn a higher return on equity on their investment—but that is true only if the project return is higher than the interest rate paid on debt; borrowing money at 6% to invest in a project that makes only 5% will reduce the return on equity. Even if a company can borrow money at a rate lower than what it earns on its projects, the higher return on equity will now be accompanied by a higher cost of equity, effectively negating much or all of the benefit of borrowing.
- On the side against debt, there are some businesses that refuse to borrow money because borrowing more will create interest expenses that reduce the income available to equity investors. They argue that this will make investors worse off, ignoring the fact that since equity investors need therefore contribute less equity to the business, they may not share that view. In public companies, with shares outstanding, borrowing money will translate into fewer shares outstanding and higher per-share earnings.
- A second illusory reason for not borrowing money is that some businesses even believe that equity is cheaper than debt, viewing the dividends paid on equity as their cost, thereby effectively making equity free to any non-dividend-paying entity—and ignoring the reality that the cost of equity also includes an expected price appreciation.

In figure 7.1, I capture both these benefits and costs of borrowing, with explanations as to why they are illusory.

FIGURE 7.1 | Debt versus Equity—The Illusory Reasons

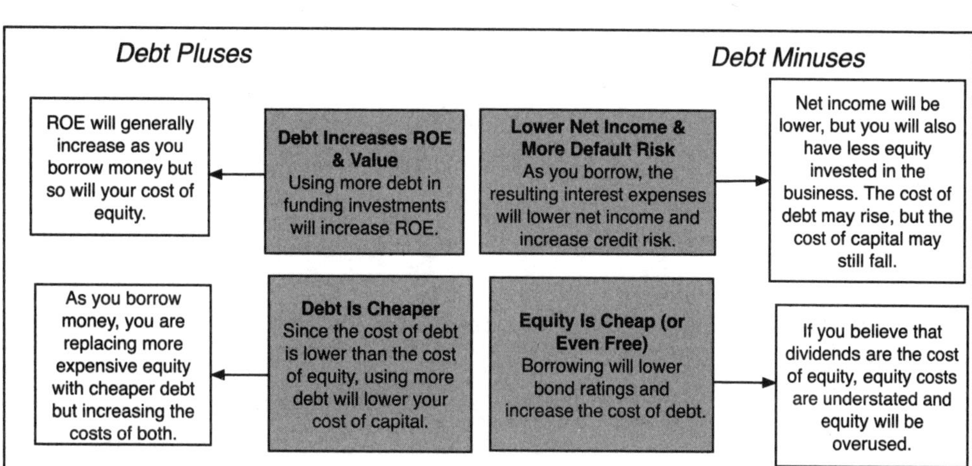

These illusory reasons are used by firms across the life cycle and often explain seemingly inexplicable choices made by firms at each stage.

- There are young firms, clearly unsuited to debt, that choose to borrow money because the interest rate that they pay on the debt looks lower than the target rates demanded by venture capitalists. This illusion is fed by the inclusion of equity components in debt, as is the case with convertible debt or venture debt paired with equity warrants that lower the interest rate on the debt. In short, first impressions notwithstanding, convertible or venture debt at 8% may be much more expensive to firms than venture equity that demands 20%.
- At the other end of the spectrum, there are mature firms that are family-run that view equity as a free or very cheap source of capital and so choose to borrow very little or no money and take investments that barely make money, because of their misconceptions about funding costs. At the heart of this illusion is the belief that dividends are the only cost of equity, reflecting a failure to incorporate the price appreciation that equity investors build into their expectations.

Debt and Equity: The Financial Trade-offs

In chapter 6, I listed the primary benefit of borrowing money as a tax benefit and the dominant cost as a bankruptcy or default cost. The tax benefit of debt, which flows from the fact that companies are allowed to claim interest expenses as a tax deduction, is entirely driven by the tax code and, if governments chose to do so, could be restricted or even eliminated. With the prevailing tax codes in much of the world, though, not only does the tax benefit persist, it becomes greater as the marginal corporate tax rate rises. Put simply, an Irish company that borrows money will get a far smaller benefit from borrowing than a German company that does the same, because the marginal corporate tax rate is 12% in Ireland and 29.5% in Germany. Using the same logic, a firm in the United States that borrowed money in 2016, when the marginal corporate tax rate in the US was 35% at the federal level (close to 40% after state and local taxes), would have received less tax benefit from debt in 2018, after a tax code change that lowered the marginal tax rate in the US to 21% at the federal level (close to 25% including state and local taxes). The expected bankruptcy cost is a function of the probability that a business will be unable to meet its contractual obligations (to lenders) and the cost of bankruptcy, deriving from the actual deadweight and legal costs of going bankrupt and the indirect costs of being perceived to be headed toward that outcome. When a business is viewed as being on the precipice, customers will stop buying its products, employees will abandon it, and suppliers will impose onerous terms, and the lost sales and earnings that arise from these conditions can have a significant impact on value.

In addition to these primary factors, there are secondary benefits and costs of using debt instead of equity. On the plus side, there are some businesses in which borrowing money can make decision-makers or managers more disciplined in their project selection, especially when they are investing other people's money. Specifically, if they persist in taking poor investments (those that lose money or earn less than the hurdle rate), more debt will increase the likelihood that the firm will fail, and the managers will lose their jobs. On the minus side, the interests of equity investors and lenders will often diverge, with the former drawn more toward projects with more upside, even if they are riskier, and the latter toward safety. That divergence will play out as debt covenants and restrictions, which impose costs on businesses that value flexibility. Figure 7.2 summarizes the full financial trade-off of debt versus equity.

FIGURE 7.2 | **Debt versus Equity—The Financial Trade-offs**

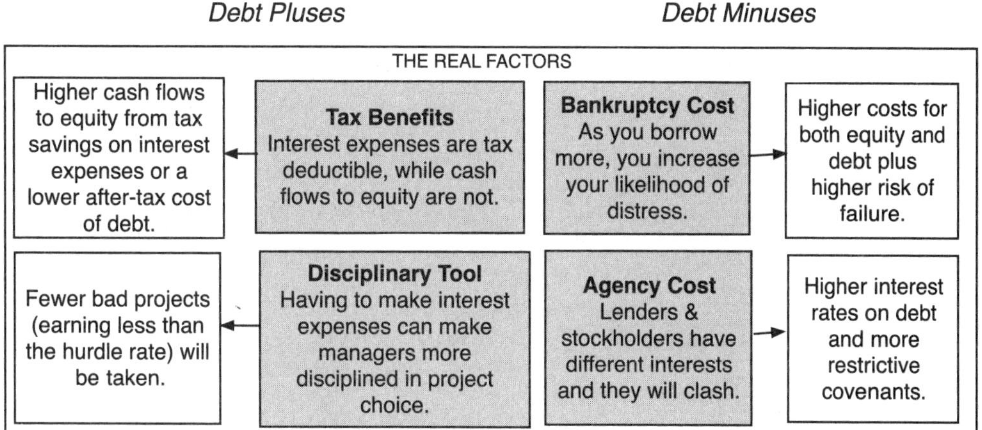

In the sections that follow, I will highlight each of these factors and examine how they might vary across the life cycle.

THE TAX BENEFIT

At first sight, the benefits of debt look as though they should accrue to businesses across the life cycle, but that conclusion misses an obvious point: to get the tax benefit of debt—i.e., for interest expenses to deliver tax savings—a business must have taxable income. As I noted in the lead-in chapters on the corporate life cycle, young businesses are more likely than mature businesses to be money losing, as they struggle to get a handle on markets, have unformed business models, and are often too small to benefit from economies of scale.

To back up this assertion, I looked at publicly traded US firms, classified into age deciles, and estimated the percentage of companies within each group that is money losing and the average effective tax rate paid by companies in that group. The results are in figure 7.3.

FIGURE 7.3 | Effective Tax Rates across Corporate Age Classes—US companies

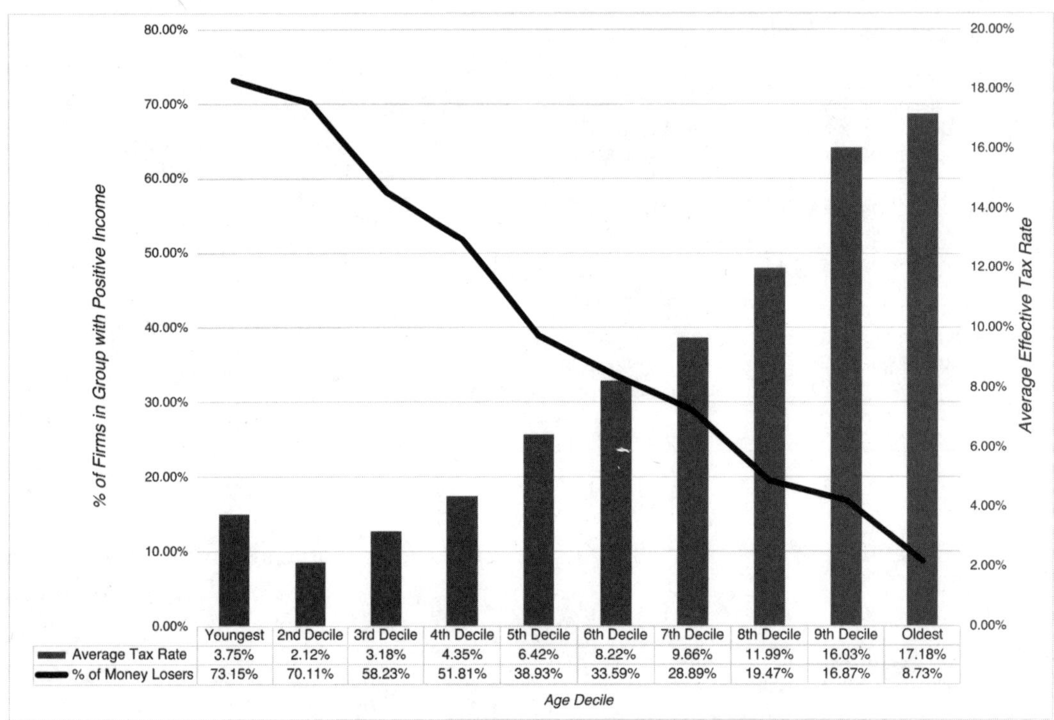

	Youngest	2nd Decile	3rd Decile	4th Decile	5th Decile	6th Decile	7th Decile	8th Decile	9th Decile	Oldest
Average Tax Rate	3.75%	2.12%	3.18%	4.35%	6.42%	8.22%	9.66%	11.99%	16.03%	17.18%
% of Money Losers	73.15%	70.11%	58.23%	51.81%	38.93%	33.59%	28.89%	19.47%	16.87%	8.73%

As you can see, almost three quarters (73.15%) of the firms in the youngest decile reported losses in the most recent year. On average, these companies paid an effective tax rate of 3.75%. As companies age, both the percentage of moneymaking firms and their effective tax rates increase, a rough indicator that they are better positioned to benefit from borrowing money. If you add in the capacity to carry accumulated losses forward—a feature of the tax code in most countries—the capacity to generate tax benefits from debt will continue to be limited even during the first few years that a company makes money.

ADDED DISCIPLINE

The idea that borrowing money can make decision-makers more disciplined in project choice is not a new one and was used in the 1980s by Michael Jensen to explain why some companies increased their debt ratios substantially, and often over short periods. That said, the argument makes sense only if the decision-makers in a business have interests and incentives that diverge from those of the owners (shareholders, equity investors) in that business. In the context of the corporate life cycle—and this may be a generalization—young businesses are frequently run by their founder/owners, with venture capitalists looking over their shoulder, and consequently, there should be little need for debt to add discipline. As businesses age—and especially if they go public—founder stakes are diluted, and in mature businesses, there can be far greater separation between managers and shareholders, creating the conditions for debt as a disciplinary tool. In table 7.1, I assess how owner holdings shift, as businesses age, by looking at publicly traded US companies, broken down into age deciles:

Table 7.1 • Insider and CEO Holdings, by Corporate Age Class

			Institutional Holding			Insider Holding		
Age Class	Number	Average Age	1st Quartile	Median	Average	1st Quartile	Median	Average
Youngest	499	5.04	10.12%	27.18%	50.27%	1.53%	6.32%	20.85%
2nd decile	522	9.43	10.60%	28.77%	59.74%	2.10%	7.18%	20.50%
3rd decile	577	13.58	8.48%	29.27%	64.36%	1.90%	6.41%	19.51%
4th decile	718	18.12	8.40%	32.08%	69.69%	1.98%	6.03%	18.16%
5th decile	488	23.49	11.57%	42.56%	80.69%	1.55%	5.79%	16.44%
6th decile	652	29.49	16.58%	48.95%	86.52%	1.37%	4.23%	17.73%
7th decile	578	38.19	17.92%	54.75%	85.35%	1.45%	4.86%	17.82%
8th decile	606	52.48	30.66%	68.83%	89.27%	1.07%	4.28%	15.52%
9th decile	581	86.88	31.49%	70.94%	87.95%	0.88%	2.87%	10.36%
Oldest	584	140.22	28.30%	67.18%	84.45%	0.67%	2.19%	6.66%
All firms	6,542	42.24	13.13%	43.94%	79.80%	1.30%	4.96%	16.55%

Insiders—defined by the Securities and Exchange Commission to include managers, founders, and shareholders who own more than 5% stakes—do hold slightly larger percentages of younger firms than older ones, but the real difference is in institutional holdings, which are more than two and a half times higher at older businesses than younger ones. While there are a handful of institutional shareholders who try to oversee managers and push back on bad management decisions, evidence suggests that most of them prefer to vote with their feet, selling shares in companies that they do not like rather than confronting management. It should come as no surprise that debt as a disciplinary tool is more needed and more used in mature businesses, which are primarily institutionally held, than at younger businesses.

BANKRUPTCY COSTS

It is true that any business that borrows money increases its likelihood of default, and that in doing so it faces both direct costs (the legal costs of defaulting) and indirect costs (resulting from customers, suppliers, and employees reacting to the risk that it might default). However, this expected bankruptcy cost will be higher at some firms than others, driven partly by more volatile income streams and partly by indirect bankruptcy costs being higher at firms that sell products that need long-term service and maintenance.

Connecting expected bankruptcy costs to where a business is in the life cycle, I would argue that income is likely to be more volatile at younger, rather than older, businesses and that worries about long-term survival can have much wider ripple effects at businesses that are dependent on growth for value. In table 7.2, I look at the volatility in earnings (measured by dividing the standard deviation in operating income in the past by the average operating income) and the safety buffer in earnings (measured as the ratio of operating income to interest expenses) at publicly traded US companies across age deciles:

Table 7.2 • Operating Income Variability and Interest Coverage Ratios

			Variability in Operating Income			Interest Coverage		
	Number	Average Age	1st Quartile	Median	Average	1st Quartile	Median	Average
Youngest	499	5.04	0.33	0.78	0.95	1.58	3.34	7.37
2nd decile	522	9.43	0.64	0.97	1.28	1.25	4.13	10.89
3rd decile	577	13.58	0.66	0.96	1.35	1.85	4.68	21.27
4th decile	718	18.12	0.55	0.85	1.17	1.66	3.89	17.68
5th decile	488	23.49	0.48	0.76	1.17	1.71	6.40	17.38
6th decile	652	29.49	0.38	0.66	1.10	2.71	7.01	30.91
7th decile	578	38.19	0.40	0.70	1.13	2.79	7.93	22.92
8th decile	606	52.48	0.32	0.57	0.99	2.90	8.69	23.10
9th decile	581	86.88	0.25	0.44	0.84	4.15	9.40	22.08
Oldest	584	140.22	0.19	0.31	0.57	3.09	6.90	12.79
All firms	6,542	42.24	0.36	0.66	1.08	2.62	6.73	18.59

Young firms have more volatile earnings than older firms, and they have less of a safety buffer in earnings, with lower interest coverage ratios. If you add to these facts the concern that borrowing money can put your growth assets at risk in the event of default, you can see why younger firms face higher expected bankruptcy costs than older ones and should therefore use debt less.

AGENCY COSTS

When you lend money to a business, the two biggest factors determining how concerned you are about equity investors putting your interests at risk relate to the composition of your assets and your capacity to monitor how equity investors are using the capital you provide them.

- On the first count, lenders seem to feel less concerned about this agency problem when they lend based on tangible assets, such as real estate or physical plant, than based on intangible assets. With young businesses, where the bulk of value comes from growth assets—i.e., investments that they make in the future—you can understand why lenders are leerier about giving equity investors free play with their capital.
- In addition, as young businesses experiment with different business models and try to gauge market size, lenders also often find themselves unable to monitor how money is being spent in a business, and this fear gets worse in evolving sectors such as technology, where they know far less about the business than the founders/equity investors do.

To induce a lender to lend money to a young company, not only do interest rates have to be set much higher and covenants made more restrictive, but lenders also generally must be offered a share of the upside, in the form of an equity stake, to commit. As I will show in the next section, this explains why debt, to young businesses, is more likely to be convertible into equity.

Debt Choices across the Life Cycle

Summing up, young companies get less tax benefit from debt, since so many of them are money losing, and need debt less as a disciplinary tool, since the companies' owners (founders and insiders) are often in charge of running them. They face higher expected bankruptcy costs, with more volatile income increasing their risk of default, and more agency problems, as lenders charge higher interest rates and/or add more restrictive covenants to debt agreements to protect themselves. If debt has less benefit and more damaging consequences, you should expect young businesses to borrow far less than mature businesses.

To test whether this is true, I look at how much debt was carried by publicly traded US companies, broken down by age class, at the start of 2022, relative to their market value as companies (market value of debt plus equity) and their accounting book value (book value of equity plus debt), in table 7.3.

Table 7.3 • **Debt Mix by Corporate Age Class—US Companies, 2022**

		Median		Debt-to-Capital (Market)			Debt-to-Capital (Book)		
	Number	Average Age	Revenue Growth	1st Quartile	Median	3rd Quartile	1st Quartile	Median	3rd Quartile
Youngest	499	5.04	26.90%	0.33%	3.66%	20.43%	1.34%	9.92%	37.14%
2nd decile	522	9.43	27.40%	0.23%	4.93%	20.47%	2.72%	18.49%	46.31%
3rd decile	577	13.58	23.80%	0.17%	3.54%	25.18%	4.84%	23.99%	52.83%
4th decile	718	18.12	21.50%	0.07%	5.03%	21.72%	3.61%	21.47%	46.87%
5th decile	488	23.49	16.20%	0.00%	5.88%	22.77%	7.96%	27.97%	51.90%
6th decile	652	29.49	13.40%	0.22%	6.03%	23.25%	7.02%	27.01%	54.55%
7th decile	578	38.19	12.50%	1.19%	11.55%	32.42%	10.50%	32.04%	55.61%
8th decile	606	52.48	10.30%	2.63%	16.31%	34.64%	14.11%	38.16%	57.96%
9th decile	581	86.88	9.27%	7.59%	18.66%	35.05%	18.92%	35.87%	51.81%
Oldest	584	140.22	6.89%	11.36%	22.81%	38.35%	22.27%	37.52%	56.07%
All firms	6,542	42.24	12.90%	0.29%	8.50%	27.85%	7.57%	28.90%	51.58%

At least in the aggregate, the data backs up what you would expect to see, given the trade-off involved. Younger firms carry far less debt, relative to both book and market value, than older firms, with the firms in the lowest decile for age having a median debt-to-capital ratio of 3.66% (9.92%), in 2022, and the firms in the highest decile having a median debt-to-capital ratio of 22.81% (37.52%).

Debt and Equity: The Frictional Trade-offs

Much of the discussion of how much businesses should borrow, at least in classical corporate finance, is premised on the assumptions that markets are efficient and that debt and equity not only are fairly priced but are always accessible. In the real world, governments and regulators can sometimes tilt the scales toward or away from debt, markets can make mistakes in their pricing of debt and equity, and owners can put high value on control and flexibility.

- **Government/regulatory actions:** To see the effect of regulatory/government actions that can alter the debt versus equity trade-off, let's start with the simplest such action, which is providing access to subsidized debt. Frequently, governments will lend money at below-market rates to companies in segments of the economy that the government views as critical. In the United States, those favored segments have changed over time, from defense companies during the Cold War to green-energy companies in recent years. In many emerging markets, the benefits of subsidized debt are offered to companies that provide employment or are viewed as national symbols. In Brazil, for instance, Petrobras and Vale, two natural-resource companies with long histories, had access to subsidized debt, at least in their first few decades of growth. Even if they do not subsidize debt, governments can induce companies to borrow more than they "should," given fundamentals, by bailing out these businesses if they are unable to pay off their debt, often because they are "too big to fail" or because there may be social costs. On the other side of the ledger, companies may borrow less than they "should"—again, given fundamentals—if regulators restrict borrowing, often by using arbitrary constraints on book debt or interest coverage ratios.

- **Mispricing in markets:** Markets can also play a role in skewing debt choices, increasing the use of debt by either overpricing debt (lending money to companies, or pricing bonds, at interest rates that are too low given default risk) or underpricing equity, with overly pessimistic growth and earnings expectations. Conversely, if markets underprice debt (setting interest rates higher than justified given default risk) or overprice equity (exaggerating growth and profit potential), firms will overuse equity and underutilize debt.
- **Internal factors/constraints:** In addition to these external factors, there are two internal factors that can play a role in driving the debt decision. The first is the desire on the part of founders or insiders to maintain control, making them reluctant to raise equity and thereby dilute their ownership. The second is the desire on the part of businesses to preserve flexibility, which will push them away from debt, since it usually comes with restrictions and covenants.

In figure 7.4, I summarize these frictional trade-offs, which can contribute to pushing businesses away from the debt mix that a purely financial trade-off would have led them to.

FIGURE 7.4 | **Debt versus Equity—The Frictional Trade-offs**

Debt Pluses

If the tax benefits of debt persist and bankruptcy costs are alleviated, you will borrow more. ← **Bankruptcy Protection** Firms may be protected from default with bailouts and other protections.

With subsidized debt, you are getting an added benefit from borrowing money that you will not get with equity. ← **Subsidized Debt** The cost of debt may be set at below "market" rates, because of government or bank subsidies.

Borrow money, even if it comes at a high cost and puts survival at risk, in order to maintain control of business. ← **Retain Control** Issuing new equity can dilute ownership of a business and put control (by founders and insiders) at risk.

Debt Minuses

Debt Covenants Lenders add restrictive covenants to debt agreeements, and borrowers have little choice but to accept them. → Firms that value flexibility and do not want to give lenders veto power over decisions will refuse to borrow money.

Overpriced Equity Equity is overpriced by providers (VCs and public market investors), making it cheaper. → Firms will take advantage by using more equity to fund their operations.

Regulatory Constraints Equity issuances may be required to meet regulatory restrictions on minimum (book) equity. → Firms that are close to regulatory minimums may have to raise more equity to continue operations.

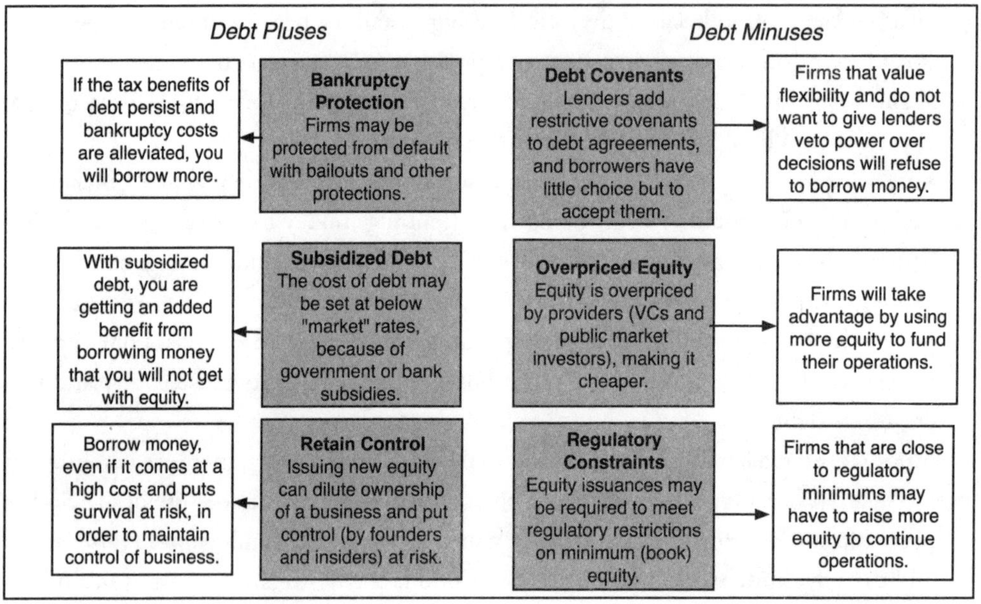

These frictions, externally or internally imposed, can often explain why businesses sometimes choose debt mixes that are at odds with their fundamentals. In young businesses, the desire for control on the part of founders and owners and/or the existence of subsidized debt can lead to the use of debt, even though it brings little in tax benefits and creates significant risk to growth assets. Mature businesses may refuse to borrow money, even though their cash flows can support debt and they can lower their costs of capital by borrowing, if they value flexibility and/or are constrained from borrowing by regulators. The frictions also explain why the use of debt can vary across time, with too little debt in stock market booms as equity becomes overpriced, and too much debt during extended stock market declines.

The Debt Mix: Optimizing Tools

Looking at the costs and benefits of using debt instead of equity, whether in illusory, financial, or frictional terms, provides a powerful framework for explaining why some companies borrow less than others, but the trade-offs cannot be used to arrive at a specific debt ratio as the optimal one for an individual company. In other words, companies that face high marginal tax rates and face low bankruptcy risk should borrow more money—but does that translate into an optimal debt ratio of 40%, or 60%? In this section, I will introduce a few tools that can be used to estimate the optimal debt ratio for a business, in more specific terms, and try out these tools on real companies across the life cycle.

The Cost-of-Capital Approach

A key component of corporate finance is identifying a financing mix that optimizes business value. Of course, you could make the argument that debt is of little consequence to value, but that view is indefensible in a world with taxes and default risk.* Put differently, if you accept the argument that some firms can borrow too much and others too little, it follows that there is an optimal mix of debt and equity for a business, and the only question is how you determine that optimal mix. Here, the cost of capital can operate as an optimizing tool, where the mix of debt and equity that minimizes cost of capital is the one that the business should aspire to use, since, in effect, it maximizes the value of the business. Figure 7.5 provides an illustration of the process for a hypothetical firm.

* Merton Miller and Franco Modigliani argued convincingly that the value of a business is independent of its debt choices, but only in a world with no taxes or default risk. Introducing one or both of these considerations upends the conclusions.

FIGURE 7.5 | **Debt Ratio and Cost of Capital**

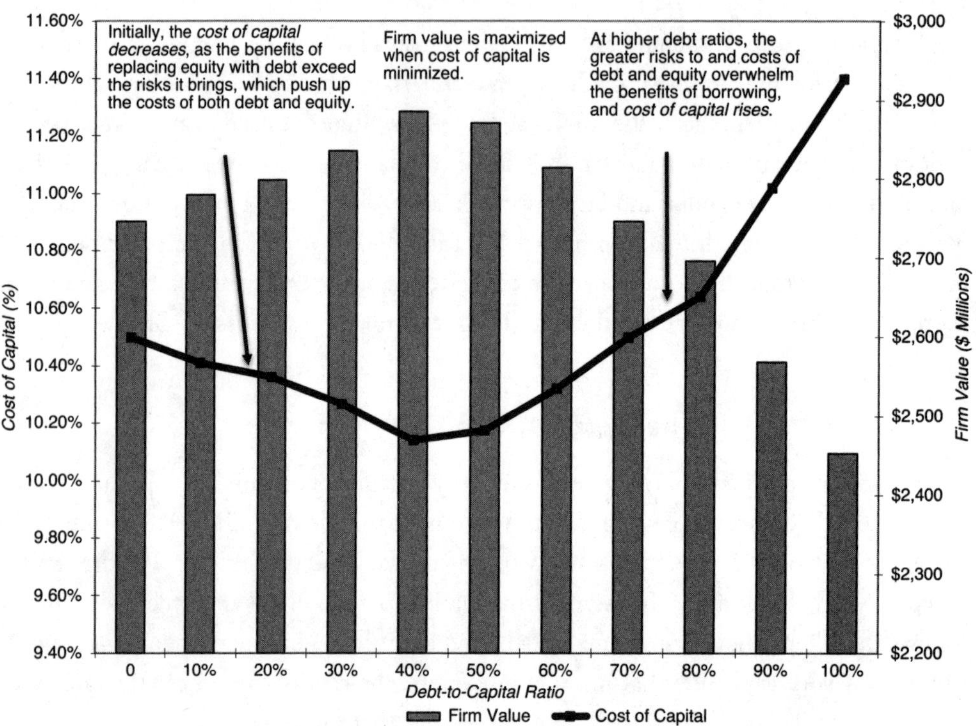

To use the cost of capital as an optimizing tool, though, you have to be able to incorporate the effects of borrowing more into both your cost of equity and your cost of debt, since both are likely to increase as the debt ratio goes up—the former because equity investors will be exposed to more volatile equity earnings, after interest payments, and the latter because default risk will increase with the debt. Figure 7.6 includes these effects.

FIGURE 7.6 | Cost of Capital as an Optimizing Tool

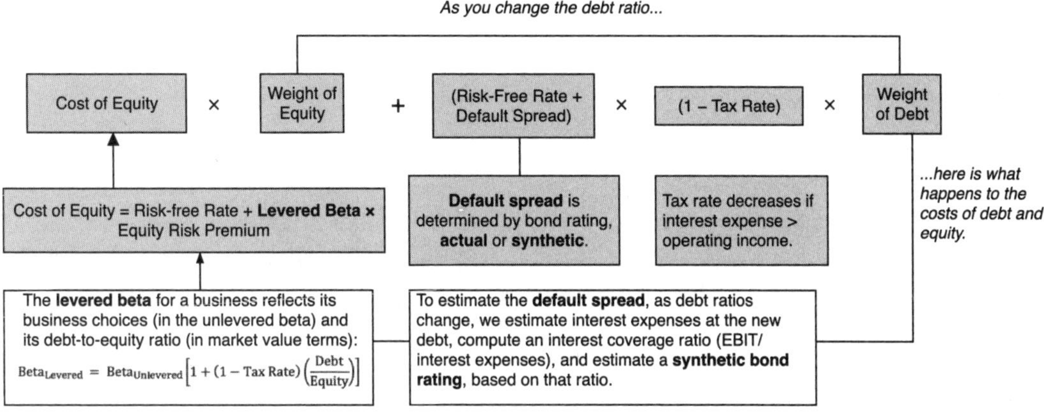

While the conventional cost-of-capital approach is built around the assumption that the operating income of a company is unaffected by its debt policy, a simple extension would allow the operating income to change (dropping as a company's default risk increases), and the optimal debt ratio then would be the one that maximizes firm value (rather than minimizes cost of capital).

COST-OF-CAPITAL OPTIMIZATION: EXAMPLES ACROSS THE LIFE CYCLE

To apply the cost-of-capital approach in practice, I do have to be pragmatic in estimating costs of debt and equity at different debt ratios, but if I am willing to accept approximations, the approach can be used to compute the costs of capital for companies across the life cycle. In this section, I will first describe the processes that I will adopt in estimation and then apply these processes to estimate costs of capital for three companies: Airbnb, a young company that went public in 2020, with significant growth potential and a business model that is still a work in progress; Adobe, a high-growth company that has shown the capacity to earn money consistently while scaling up; and Kraft Heinz, a mature company with a storied history of growth and success.

THE ESTIMATION PROCESS

To estimate the cost of capital at different debt ratios, you need a process for estimating the costs of equity and debt, not just at current levels of borrowing but also at each of the hypothetical debt ratios.

- To estimate the cost of equity, I go back to our measure of relative risk (beta) and break it down into its operating component (based upon the business or businesses that a company operates in) and financial component (determined by how much debt a company has, relative to equity).

$$\text{Beta}_{\text{Levered}} = \text{Beta}_{\text{Unlevered}}\left[1 + (1 - \text{tax rate})\left(\frac{\text{Debt}}{\text{Equity}}\right)\right]$$

  The unlevered beta captures the business risk, and the levered beta incorporates the additional risk created by debt. As a company borrows more money, keeping its business mix unchanged, its levered, or equity, beta will rise.
- To estimate the cost of debt, in both pre-tax and after-tax terms, I start with the dollar debt that a business will have at a specified debt ratio, estimate the interest expense that would accrue at that debt level, then compute an interest coverage ratio (operating income divided by the interest expense) and convert that coverage ratio into a bond rating and a default spread. If the interest expense is less than the operating income, I use the marginal tax rate to compute the after-tax cost of debt, but if the interest expense rises above the operating income, I reduce the tax rate to reflect the inability to obtain tax savings on the surplus interest expense.

Figure 7.7 captures the steps in the process.

FIGURE 7.7 | Cost of Capital at Different Debt Ratios—Estimation Process

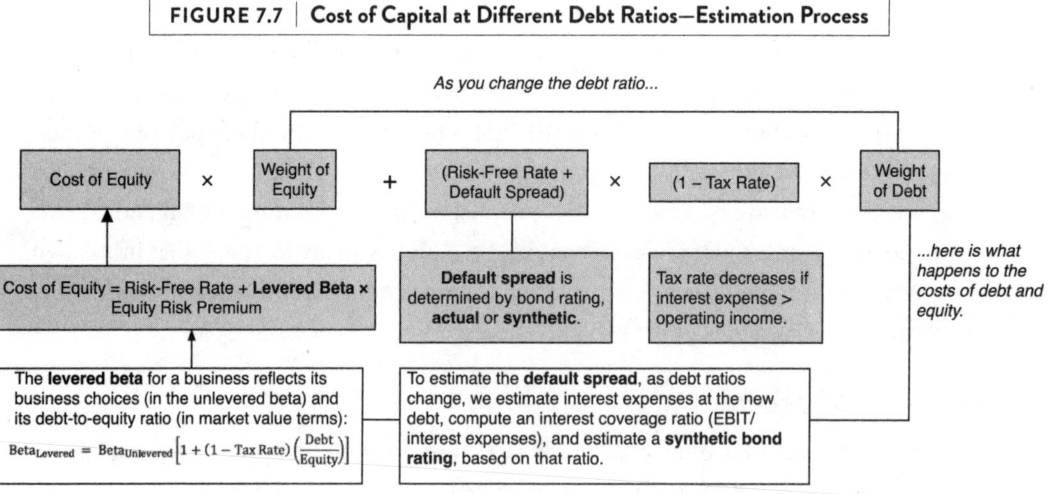

The approaches that I use to estimate costs of equity and debt are simplistic, and there are variations on the levered beta calculation and augmentations of the ratings estimation process that you can use if you want to finesse this calculation.

OPTIMAL DEBT MIX: AIRBNB, ADOBE, AND KRAFT HEINZ

I will now apply the cost-of-capital approach described above to estimate the optimal mix of debt and equity at three firms: Airbnb, Adobe, and Kraft Heinz. To illustrate the differences across these firms, as they relate to their standing in the corporate life cycle, I estimated the age, revenue growth rate, and operating income at each firm in the most recent fiscal year in table 7.4:

Table 7.4 • The Tale of the Tape—Airbnb, Adobe, and Kraft Heinz

	Airbnb	Adobe	Kraft Heinz
Corporate Age	15	40	153
Revenue Growth (last 3 years)	64.07%	20.50%	0.80%
Expected Revenue Growth (next 2 years)	47.20%	14.30%	-2.96%
Operating Income in 2021 ($ Mil)	$429	$5,802	$5,222
Operating Income in 2019 ($ Mil)	$(501)	$3,268	$5,077

Clearly, Airbnb qualifies as a young firm, not only in terms of age (15 years) but also in terms of its high revenue growth, and it earned a positive operating profit for the first time in its history in 2021. Kraft Heinz, at the other extreme, is ancient in terms of age (153 years old); its revenue growth is minimal (and expected to go negative) and it has stagnant operating income. Adobe falls in the middle, with a corporate age of 40 years but with impressive revenue growth, notwithstanding its scale, and the capacity to generate significant and growing operating profits.

Using the approach described in figure 7.7, I estimated the costs of capital for each firm for debt ratios ranging from 0% (no debt) to 90% of overall firm value (again, defined in terms of market value), in figure 7.8.

FIGURE 7.8 | Optimal Debt Mix—Airbnb, Adobe, and Kraft Heinz

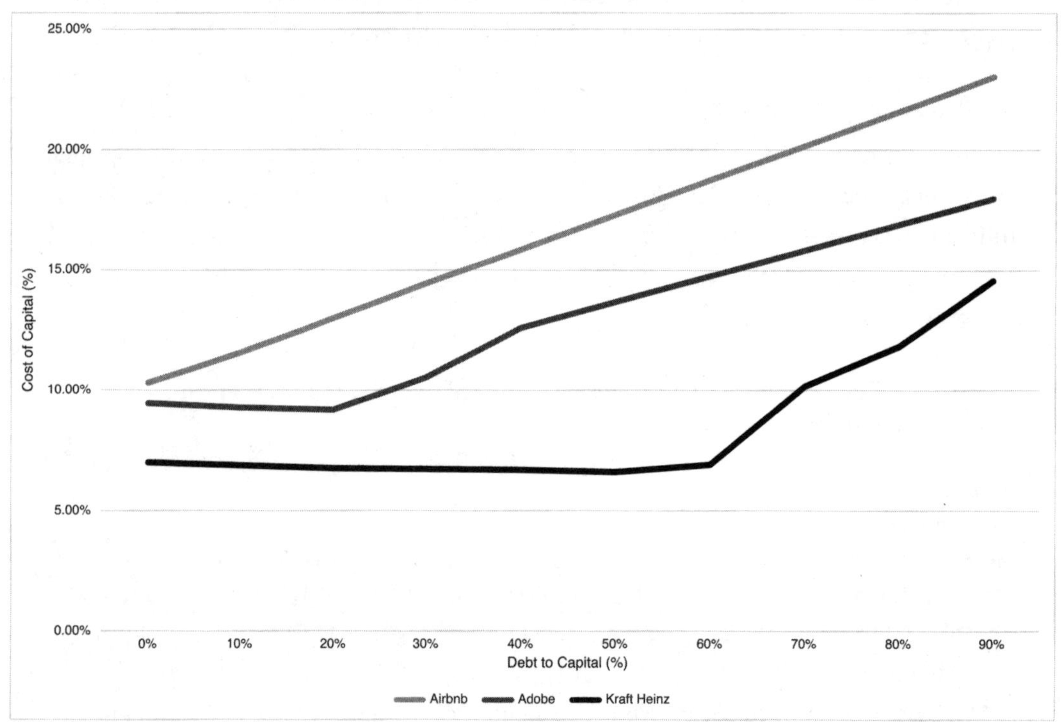

The optimal debt ratios are highlighted as the debt ratios at which costs of capital are lowest, and as you can see, Airbnb's cost of capital is minimized at no debt, with its cost of capital climbing as the debt ratio goes up. Adobe does have debt capacity, with its cost of capital declining initially, as debt is taken, but increasing if the debt ratio rises above 20%. For Kraft Heinz, though, the cost of capital continues to decline, with added debt, until the debt ratio reaches 50%, before starting to go up. Figure 7.8 also highlights the actual debt ratio at all three firms, with Airbnb and Adobe barely using debt (each has a debt ratio of about 3%) and Kraft Heinz indicating a much heavier debt load, at 31.69% of firm value.

EXPLANATION AND IMPLICATIONS

To understand why optimal debt mixes vary across companies and have a link to the corporate life cycle, I looked at three variables for Airbnb, Adobe, and Kraft Heinz. The least interesting is their marginal tax rate since, as money-making US companies, they all face roughly the same marginal tax rate of 25%. The most compelling difference is in how much each firm earns as operating income, relative to its overall enterprise value, with Airbnb's operating income barely registering, at 0.64% of enterprise value, and Kraft Heinz reporting operating income at almost 8.00% of enterprise value. Put simply, Airbnb is making money, but so little that even going to a 10% debt ratio risks putting the company into default. I also looked at the variability of operating income, using the coefficient of variation in operating income over the last decade, and while Airbnb's short history and mostly negative operating income made the variation impossible to compute, Kraft Heinz has more stable income than Adobe. Table 7.5 summarizes the results:

Table 7.5 • Explanatory Variable for Optimal Debt Ratio

	Airbnb	Adobe	Kraft Heinz
Operating Income ($ Mil)	$429	$5,802	$5,222
Enterprise Value ($ Mil)	$67,045	$173,818	$65,356
EBIT/Enterprise Value	0.64%	3.34%	7.99%
Marginal Tax Rate	25%	25%	25%
Variability in Operating Income	NA	0.70	0.54

In general, the optimal debt ratio for a business will increase as its earnings power increases, relative to its value, and as its earnings become more stable and predictable. Those two forces contribute to increasing debt capacity as businesses age. Superimposed on these forces is the marginal tax rate, and if it is set to zero—as is the case in some parts of the world—the optimal debt ratio for all firms, across the life cycle, will converge on zero.

Peer Group Assessment

For many firms, finding the right mix of debt and equity does not come from the capacity of the firms to generate tax benefits from debt or weighing this benefit against expected bankruptcy costs but from looking at what other companies in their peer group are choosing to borrow. Put simply, if you are managing a company in the software business, where peer-group companies have little or no debt, you will tend to either not borrow money or borrow very little, even if your fundamentals suggest that you should. Conversely, if you are an infrastructure company, and companies in your peer group tend to carry large debt loads, you will as well, even if you are receiving little in tax benefits from that debt, while also exposing yourself to bankruptcy risk.

The roots of *me-too finance*, which is my descriptor for making major corporate finance decisions (borrowing, dividend policy, and even investing) based upon what other companies in the sector are doing, lie in the belief that making mistakes, as a manager, becomes easier to defend when you have others making the same mistakes. The infrastructure company that becomes distressed because it borrowed too much can defend itself by pointing to the high debt loads of peer-group companies, just as the software company can explain its unwillingness to use debt.

The perils of peer-group-driven debt decisions lie in the choices that managers must make in picking companies that will comprise their peer group and coming up with a metric that measures debt load. For instance, you can define Adobe's peer group as all software companies or as only large-market-cap software companies; but the companies in the former group generally have much lower debt ratios than those in the latter. In terms of measuring debt loads, managers can measure the peer group's debt-to-capital ratios in book or market terms, or even scale to earnings or cash flows (debt to EBITDA is a common metric).

Financing Type

In chapter 5, when introducing the financing principle, I posited that the right financing type for a business is one that matches its assets, and that this matching increases the value of the business. In this section, I will examine this financing matching principle in more detail and explain why it can lead to different choices at different stages of the corporate life cycle.

The Matching Principle

To put the matching principle into practice, a business must look at its investments/projects and establish the key characteristics that identify these investments, and then try to incorporate these characteristics into the financing used by the business. In designing financing, there are five key components to a project that are worth focusing on, including the following:

1. **Project duration:** The most obvious place to start is with typical project duration, with long-term debt representing a better choice if projects are long-term. Thus, in an infrastructure business, where projects can take years to get off the ground and last decades, debt should be long-term as well. In contrast, a software business, where a

typical product takes a few months to develop and has a shelf life of only two or three years, is better off with short-term debt.

2. **Currency/ies of cash flows:** As businesses globalize, it is more common than not for a business to have both costs and revenues in multiple currencies, with the former being driven by where the company produces its products or services and the latter by where it sells them. In general, the currency makeup of financing should be reflective of the currency makeup of a project's cash flows, with a project with euro cash flows being funded with euro debt and a project with Thai baht cash flows financed with Thai baht debt.
3. **Inflation sensitivity of cash flows:** Inflation is a factor that affects all businesses and can vary over time, but the extent of its effect on earnings and cash flows will depend on how well a business can pass through unexpected inflation. To generalize, businesses with pricing power should be better positioned to have cash flows that move with inflation, rising (falling) with higher (lower) inflation, and these businesses are therefore better candidates for floating-rate debt, since interest rates on debt will tend to increase (decrease) with higher (lower) inflation. Businesses without pricing power will find themselves squeezed when inflation is higher than expected, since their costs will increase but they are unable to increase prices in response. These businesses should be cautious about how much they borrow and, if they do, should not use floating-rate debt.
4. **Expected growth in cash flows:** Some projects are quick to ramp up and, once ramped up, deliver stable cash flows over their lifetimes. Other projects are slower to develop, often starting with low or even negative cash flows and growing more positive over time. This cash flow pattern makes them better suited to convertible debt, wherein the conversion option keeps coupon rates low early in the project's life but, as the project ages, the debt gets converted and can be replaced with straight debt.
5. **Other factors determining cash flows:** To the extent that the cash flows on a project are affected by other factors, incorporating these factors into matching financing can reduce risk to the business. For an oil company, for example, oil prices are a key driver of earnings and cash flows, and tying the coupon rate on debt to oil prices, with higher (lower) coupons when oil prices are high (low), can reduce the likelihood of default.

Figure 7.9 summarizes project characteristics and how they play out in financing characteristics.

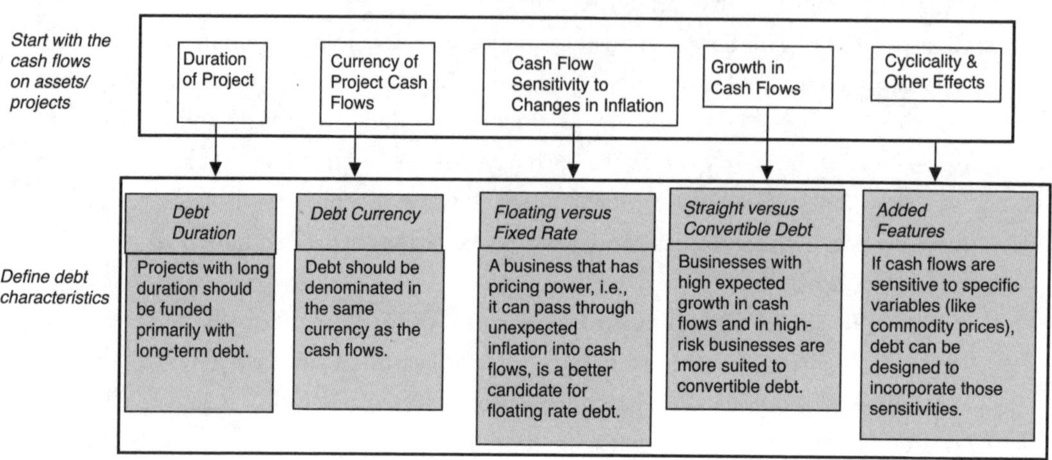

To see how the matching principle plays out across the corporate life cycle and leads to different financing choices, it is worth recognizing that early in the life of a business, it is individual projects that are being funded, but as a business matures and scales up, it accumulates a portfolio of projects that need financing. As a simple example, a young biotechnology company is often funding a single drug that is working its way through the approval pipeline, whereas a more mature biotechnology or pharmaceutical company has a portfolio of drugs, often at different stages in the pipeline. Both businesses may borrow money, but the young biotech firm, with a single product, is more likely to use convertible debt, while the more mature drug company, with a portfolio of products, is better suited to straight debt.

In effect, matching financing characteristics to project features allows businesses to share risk with their capital providers. It is clearly not a free lunch, since the capital providers are compensated for bearing risk with conversion options, on convertible bonds, or with higher interest rates, on commodity-price-linked bonds. For young firms, where risk represents a clear and present danger to survival, this risk sharing can make the difference between failure and success, but for more mature firms, with a more diversified investor base, the benefits are smaller, though there will still be a payoff in terms of lower default risk.

Financing across the Life Cycle

Figure 7.10 brings together the discussion on financing mix and type in this chapter and relates it to where a business is in the corporate life cycle.

FIGURE 7.10 | The Financing Principle across the Corporate Life Cycle

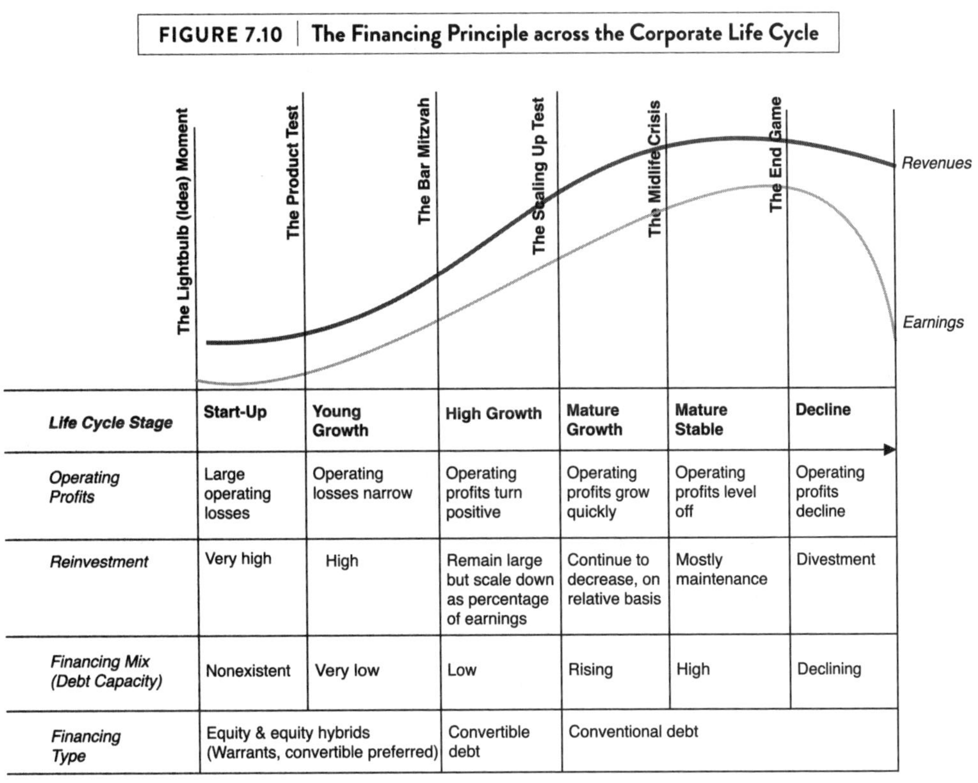

Life Cycle Stage	Start-Up	Young Growth	High Growth	Mature Growth	Mature Stable	Decline
Operating Profits	Large operating losses	Operating losses narrow	Operating profits turn positive	Operating profits grow quickly	Operating profits level off	Operating profits decline
Reinvestment	Very high	High	Remain large but scale down as percentage of earnings	Continue to decrease, on relative basis	Mostly maintenance	Divestment
Financing Mix (Debt Capacity)	Nonexistent	Very low	Low	Rising	High	Declining
Financing Type	Equity & equity hybrids (Warrants, convertible preferred)		Convertible debt	Conventional debt		

During their youth, businesses should borrow nothing or very little, as a combination of negative earnings and high reinvestment eliminates both their motivation and their capacity for borrowing money. As these businesses mature, a combination of positive earnings (creating the conditions for the tax benefit of debt) and reduced need for reinvestment will create a capacity to borrow money that will only increase as the company ages. In decline, absolute borrowing will have to scale down as the business shrinks, but on a relative basis, debt as a percentage of capital will remain high.

While young, money-losing companies should be funded primarily or entirely with equity, some do choose to borrow money, and if they do, they must find ways to keep interest payments on that debt low, at least for the early years, and tie the payments, if possible, to success in operations. Adding conversion features to financing that involve payment commitments (like debt and preferred stock) allows them to accomplish this objective. As businesses age, their borrowing will transition from convertible to straight issues (of debt and preferred stock), but the choice between fixed and floating-rate debt will remain a function of how much pricing power they have.

Conclusion

Every business—small or large, private or public, young or old—has to decide how it will fund itself, with two broad choices. The first choice is equity, wherein capital providers settle for residual cash flows in exchange for an ownership stake in the business, and the second is debt, wherein capital providers have contractual claims on the cash flows, for interest and principal payments, but limited or no say in how the business is run.

The judgment on how much to borrow, at many firms, comes from what I have termed illusory reasons, such as "debt is cheaper than equity"—compelling on the surface, but not if you dig deeper. On a fundamental basis, answering the question of how much to borrow will rest on calculating the benefits of debt, in the form of tax savings arising from interest payments and added discipline in project assessment, against the costs of debt, captured in higher risks and expected costs of bankruptcy and the costs of reconciling the competing interests of lenders and shareholders. In general, young businesses, which are often money losing, will get less in tax benefits from borrowing and face much higher bankruptcy and agency costs, and should be expected to borrow much less than more mature businesses. It is possible, though, that frictions in the market or economy, such as subsidized debt and/or market mispricing, can alter this trade-off.

On the question of the right type of debt for a business, I start with the principle that matching debt to assets, with long-term (short-term) debt funding long-term (short-term) assets and debt in a given currency funding assets that generate cash flows in that same currency, reduces default risk.

8

Dividend Policy across the Life Cycle

THE END GAME FOR a successful business—if it has found a product that meets a market need, built a business around it, and scaled up as much as it can—is to return some or all of the cash flows that accrue from this success to its owner. This return of cash, which at publicly traded firms took the form of dividends until a few decades ago, has now expanded to include more flexible cash-return policies like stock buybacks. In this chapter, I will explore how the capacity to return cash, as well as the form that this cash return takes, varies across the corporate life cycle.

Cash Return: Measuring Potential Dividends

It is common sense that the cash that a business can return to its equity owners will be the cash left over after every other claimholder's needs are met. That said, there is a surprising amount of confusion over how to measure this potential dividend and what happens when a business chooses to return more or less than this potential dividend. In this section, I will look at the answers to both questions.

Measuring Potential Cash Return

To assess how much cash can be returned to the owners of a business, let us first dispense with how it should not be measured. Contrary to the belief of some, the earnings or net income that a business generates is *not* the potential dividend—first, because earnings are not cash flows, and second, because even if they were, earnings are prior to reinvestment needs, i.e., investments needed to deliver on expected future growth. To estimate potential dividends or cash return, I follow a sequence of steps:

1. I start with accounting earnings to equity investors—i.e., net income—and recognize that these earnings are already after taxes and interest expenses.
2. To get to cash flows, I subtract out the change in non-cash working capital and then add back non-cash accounting expenses including, but not restricted to, depreciation and amortization. The first adjustment is designed to convert accrual earnings to cash earnings, since receivables, inventory, and payables (all working capital ingredients) reflect gaps between revenues and expenses recorded by accountants and their cash analogs. The second adjustment, adding back depreciation and amortization, reverses a non-cash expense that lowered earnings but did not affect cash flows.
3. While accountants do not consider capital expenditures—i.e., expenditures in what accountants classify as capital assets (land, buildings, equipment)—to be expenses for purposes of computing net income, they still represent cash outflows, and I have to subtract them. In doing so, I also treat cash acquisitions as large capital expenditures and reduce cash flows accordingly.
4. As a final step, I incorporate the cash flows from and to debt. If you are mystified as to why, note that borrowing money to pay for some or a large portion of capital expenditures will bring in cash flows to equity investors, and paying off debt that is coming due will cause cash outflows. The net debt figure, representing debt issues minus debt repaid, thus is added to the cash flows to arrive at the final residual cash flow.

These steps are illustrated in figure 8.1. The final residual cash flow, after taxes, reinvestment, and debt cash flows are considered, is called the free cash flows to equity (FCFE), but it could also be called potential dividend, and it represents cash that is available for return to shareholders, in a public company, or equity owners, in a private business.

FIGURE 8.1 | Estimating Potential Dividends (FCFE)

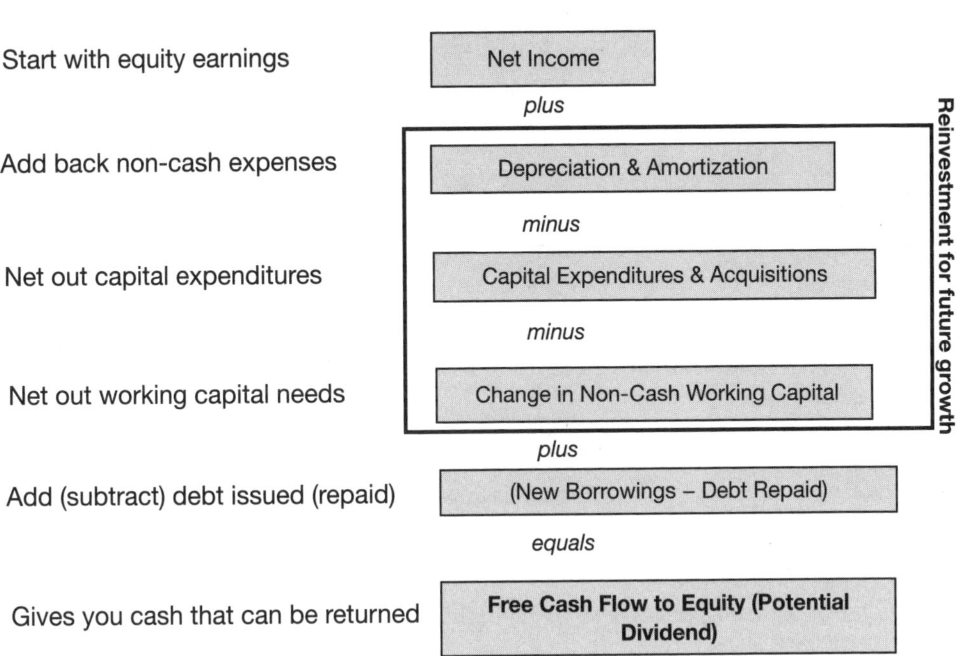

As you assess this measure of potential dividends, it is worth noting that it can be negative, because a company may be a money-losing business and/or because a company may have capital expenditure and investment needs that overwhelm even positive earnings.

Consider again Airbnb, Adobe, and Kraft Heinz, the three companies that I used to illustrate the financing choices of firms across the life cycle in chapter 7. I have calculated the FCFE for all three firms, using the approach described above, in table 8.1.

Table 8.1 • FCFE ($ Millions) at Airbnb, Adobe, and Kraft Heinz, 2021

	Airbnb	Adobe	Kraft Heinz
Net Income	-$352	$4,822	$1,012
+ Depreciation	$147	$788	$910
- Cap Expenditures	$25	$3,030	$905
+ Divestitures	$0	$0	$5,014
- Change in non-cash WC	-$138	-$742	-$406
FCFE before debt	-$93	$3,322	$6,437
+ New Debt Raised	$1,979	$0	$3,772
- Debt Repaid	$1,995	$0	$1,960
FCFE	-$109	$3,322	$3,235

Airbnb had an operating loss of $352 million during 2021, and even though its capital expenditures were muted and its non-cash working capital decreased during the year, its free cash flows to equity was negative for the year, both before and after incorporating debt cash flows. Adobe and Kraft Heinz both posted large, positive FCFE for 2021, with one difference reflecting their respective standings in the life cycle: a large chunk of Kraft Heinz's FCFE for 2021 came from divestitures, as the company scaled down. Given these FCFE, I would not expect Airbnb to pay dividends or buy back stock, but both Adobe and Kraft Heinz can return large amounts to shareholders. Kraft Heinz paid dividends of $1.96 billion during the year, but Adobe chose to buy back almost $4.7 billion in stock and paid no dividends.

To get a sense of how the free cash flows to equity for a firm change as it ages, I looked at the short but eventful history of Tesla, a company that has gone from start-up to market giant in the space of less than 20 years. Figure 8.2 charts Tesla's net income and FCFE, by year, from 2006 to 2021.

FIGURE 8.2 | Net Income and FCFE at Tesla, by year, 2006–2021

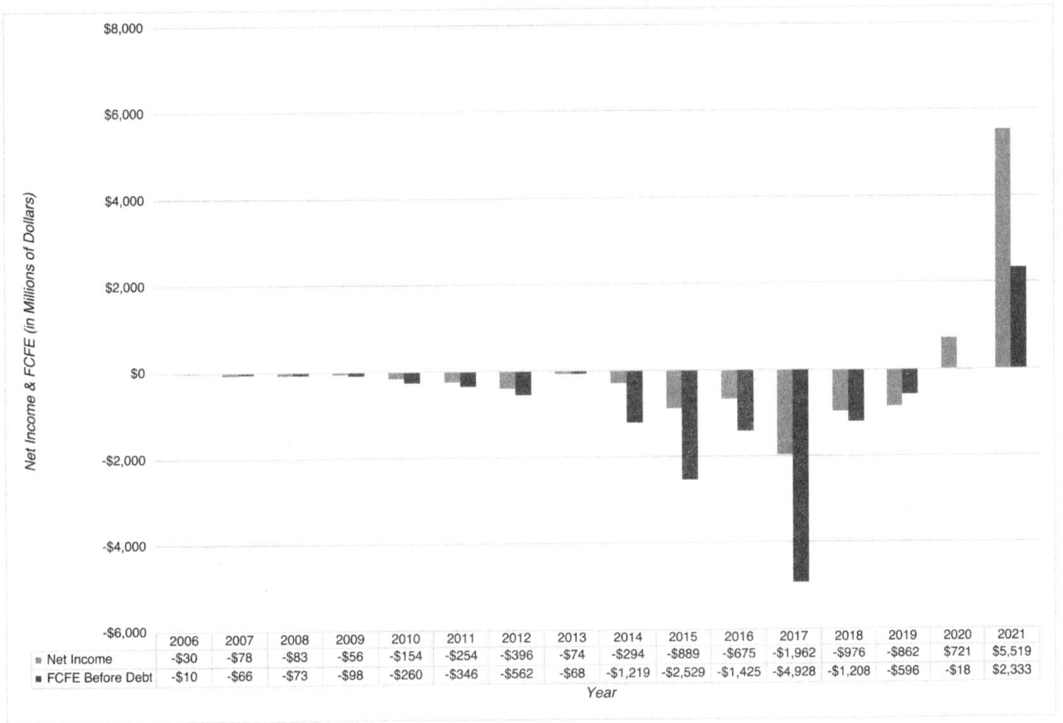

	2006	2007	2008	2009	2010	2011	2012	2013	2014	2015	2016	2017	2018	2019	2020	2021
Net Income	-$30	-$78	-$83	-$56	-$154	-$254	-$396	-$74	-$294	-$889	-$675	-$1,962	-$976	-$862	$721	$5,519
FCFE Before Debt	-$10	-$66	-$73	-$98	-$260	-$346	-$562	-$68	-$1,219	-$2,529	-$1,425	-$4,928	-$1,208	-$596	-$18	$2,333

Not surprisingly, the company reported losses through from 2006 to 2019 before reporting profits in 2020, though its reinvestment needs kept free cash flows to equity negative in that year. In 2021, a surge in profitability finally allowed the company to become FCFE positive. (Note that these FCFE are prior to cash flows from debt, and Tesla has raised far more debt than it has repaid in the last five years. Incorporating those cash flows, Tesla's FCFE turned positive in 2019.)

Potential Dividends across the Corporate Life Cycle

As businesses age, their capacity to return cash will change, as will their ability to accumulate or burn through cash. In this section, I will use the definition of potential dividends (FCFE) that I developed in the last section to examine how these numbers change as a company ages and examine the consequences for cash balances at each stage.

To assess how free cash flows to equity change over the life cycle, I will break down the estimate into three constituent parts.

a. **Net income:** While earnings are not cash flows, it helps to start with positive earnings, and companies that are money losers are clearly less capable of returning cash to owners than those that are moneymakers. In table 8.2, I look at net income at all publicly traded US firms, broken down by corporate age.

Table 8.2 • Net Income at US Firms, by Corporate Age Decile (in 2021)

			Net Income		Absolute Values			Relative Values	
Age Decile	# Firms	Average Age	% Positive	% Negative	Net Income ($ Mil)	Market Cap ($ Mil)	Revenues ($ Mil)	As % of Market Cap	As % of Revenues
Youngest	499	5.04	26.85%	73.15%	$(55)	$1,126,924	$319,900	0.00%	-0.02%
2nd decile	522	9.43	29.89%	70.11%	$(7,107)	$1,411,921	$234,351	-0.50%	-3.03%
3rd decile	577	13.58	41.77%	58.23%	$(13,783)	$1,676,741	$285,956	-0.82%	-4.82%
4th decile	718	18.12	48.19%	51.81%	$45,637	$3,648,970	$698,047	1.25%	6.54%
5th decile	488	23.49	61.07%	38.93%	$237,085	$5,335,170	$1,124,673	4.44%	21.08%
6th decile	652	29.49	66.41%	33.59%	$141,129	$5,200,863	$1,379,075	2.71%	10.23%
7th decile	578	38.19	71.11%	28.89%	$168,379	$4,306,529	$1,883,320	3.91%	8.94%
8th decile	606	52.48	80.53%	19.47%	$441,970	$12,785,577	$3,675,083	3.46%	12.03%
9th decile	581	86.88	83.13%	16.87%	$272,575	$6,338,688	$3,392,256	4.30%	8.04%
Oldest	584	140.22	91.27%	8.73%	$443,447	$8,875,169	$4,619,250	5.00%	9.60%
All firms	6,542	42.24	60.27%	39.73%	$1,746,044	$51,632,631	$18,010,220	3.38%	9.69%

As you can see, there are far more money losers among the youngest firms than among older firms, and the net income generated is smaller, relative to both market capitalization and revenues, at these firms.

b. **Reinvestment:** The need for reinvestment is driven by expectations of growth and, not surprisingly, young businesses have a much greater need for reinvestment than more mature businesses. In table 8.3, I report on reinvestment at publicly traded US firms, broken down by corporate age:

Table 8.3 • Reinvestment at US Firms, by Corporate Age Decile (in 2021)

			Reinvestment (in $ Mil)			Reinvestment as % of Revenues		
Age Decile	# Firms	Average Age	Net Cap Ex	Change in non-cash WC	Reinvestment	Net Cap Ex	Change in Non-Cash WC	Reinvestment
Youngest	499	5.04	$23,630	$8,058	$31,688	7.39%	2.52%	9.91%
2nd decile	522	9.43	$13,198	$9,176	$22,373	5.63%	3.92%	9.55%
3rd decile	577	13.58	$16,247	$8,671	$24,918	5.68%	3.03%	8.71%
4th decile	718	18.12	$62,010	$8,105	$70,116	8.88%	1.16%	10.04%
5th decile	488	23.49	$90,396	$19,875	$110,271	8.04%	1.77%	9.80%
6th decile	652	29.49	$97,602	$30,451	$128,053	7.08%	2.21%	9.29%
7th decile	578	38.19	$109,105	$24,922	$134,027	5.79%	1.32%	7.12%
8th decile	606	52.48	$151,139	$51,906	$203,044	4.11%	1.41%	5.52%
9th decile	581	86.88	$135,034	$7,848	$142,882	3.98%	0.23%	4.21%
Oldest	584	140.22	$196,861	$14,437	$211,298	4.26%	0.31%	4.57%
All firms	6,542	42.24	$908,805	$189,037	$1,097,842	5.05%	1.05%	6.10%

The dollar reinvestment is much larger, in dollar terms, at older companies than in younger ones, but one reason for that is that older companies are larger. Scaled to revenues, reinvestment is about 10% of revenues, for the five younger deciles, and lower for the top three deciles.

c. **Debt cash flows:** As I noted in the last section, borrowing money brings in cash flows to equity investors, and repaying debt creates cash outflows. In table 8.4, I examine debt issuances and repayments at publicly traded US firms, broken down by corporate age:

Table 8.4 • Debt Cash Flows at US Firms, by Corporate Age Decile (in 2021)

			Debt Cash Flows (in $ Mil)			Debt Cash Flows (as % of Mkt Cap)		
Age Decile	# Firms	Average Age	Debt Raised	Debt Repaid	Debt Raised - Debt Repaid	Debt Raised	Debt Repaid	Debt Raised - Debt Repaid
Youngest	499	5.04	$84,557	$81,784	$2,773	7.50%	7.26%	0.25%
2nd decile	522	9.43	$440,923	$407,614	$33,309	31.23%	28.87%	2.36%
3rd decile	577	13.58	$3,047,999	$3,029,136	$18,863	181.78%	180.66%	1.13%
4th decile	718	18.12	$139,534	$129,418	$10,115	3.82%	3.55%	0.28%
5th decile	488	23.49	$253,522	$198,831	$54,691	4.75%	3.73%	1.03%
6th decile	652	29.49	$2,579,024	$2,532,428	$46,597	49.59%	48.69%	0.90%
7th decile	578	38.19	$409,397	$359,079	$50,318	9.51%	8.34%	1.17%
8th decile	606	52.48	$1,541,161	$1,500,417	$40,744	12.05%	11.74%	0.32%
9th decile	581	86.88	$1,969,257	$2,067,172	$(97,915)	31.07%	32.61%	-1.54%
Oldest	584	140.22	$772,170	$932,487	$(160,317)	8.70%	10.51%	-1.81%
All firms	6,542	42.24	$11,320,471	$11,321,542	$(1,071)	21.93%	21.93%	0.00%

Companies in the top eight age deciles all raise more debt than they repay, making them net sources of cash inflows, but the companies in the top two (oldest) deciles repay more debt than they raise, making them net sources of cash outflows. As a percentage of market capitalization, there is no discernible pattern on debt cash flows, and younger firms use less debt overall.

To bring all three components into the calculation of potential dividends: The combination of losses, or very small earnings, at young firms, with their large reinvestment needs and limited use of debt, leads to negative free cash flows to equity at these firms. As businesses mature, improved earnings power, together with lower reinvestment needs (relative to earnings) and expanding debt capacity, leads to positive and rising free cash flows to equity. In table 8.5, I look at free cash flows to equity, scaled to market capitalization and revenues, for publicly traded US companies, classified by corporate age:

Table 8.5 • Free Cash Flows to Equity for US Companies, by Corporate Age Decile (in 2021)

			Free Cash Flows to Equity (Pre-debt)			Free Cash Flows to Equity (Post-debt)		
Age Decile	**# firms**	**Average Age**	**Value ($ Mil)**	**% Negative**	**As % of Revenues**	**Value ($ Mil)**	**% Negative**	**As % of Revenues**
Youngest	499	5.04	$(31,743)	76.15%	-9.92%	$(28,970)	75.75%	-9.06%
2nd decile	522	9.43	$(29,480)	72.99%	-12.58%	$3,828	70.11%	1.63%
3rd decile	577	13.58	$(38,702)	61.53%	-13.53%	$(19,839)	62.74%	-6.94%
4th decile	718	18.12	$(24,478)	55.99%	-3.51%	$(14,363)	56.96%	-2.06%
5th decile	488	23.49	$126,814	45.08%	11.28%	$181,504	48.77%	16.14%
6th decile	652	29.49	$13,077	43.87%	0.95%	$59,673	45.55%	4.33%
7th decile	578	38.19	$34,352	44.64%	1.82%	$84,670	46.89%	4.50%
8th decile	606	52.48	$238,926	37.95%	6.50%	$279,670	45.38%	7.61%
9th decile	581	86.88	$129,693	35.46%	3.82%	$31,778	44.75%	0.94%
Oldest	584	140.22	$232,149	27.05%	5.03%	$71,832	42.47%	1.56%
All firms	6,542	42.24	$648,201	48.98%	3.60%	$647,130	52.37%	3.59%

Note that a far higher percentage of young firms than older firms has negative free cash flows to equity, and that, in the aggregate, the free cash flows to equity are negative for the youngest four deciles and peak in the middle of the distribution. While FCFE is positive for the older firms, there is no pattern across the age deciles.

Cash Return: Practices and Consequences

For much of the history of public equity markets, companies that chose to return cash to owners did so by paying dividends. As a result, over time, there are practices in paying dividends that have become deeply ingrained, and I will begin this section with a description of these practices. Over the last five decades, though, as companies have discovered stock buybacks as an alternate form of cash return, they have shifted significantly from dividends to buybacks, and I will also examine why. In the final part of this section, I will explore how the amount and form of cash return changes as companies age.

Dividend Practices

The practice of returning cash to shareholders in the form of dividends is an old one and can be traced back to the beginnings of public equity markets. The original intent may have been a return of residual cash flows to owners, but over time, conventional dividends have become sticky—i.e., companies that start paying dividends find it difficult to reduce or suspend dividends and often pay, as dividends, whatever they did in prior periods. You can see this in figure 8.3, where I compare dividends per share in a year to dividends per share in the prior year and look at the percentage of US companies that paid the same, higher, or lower annual dividends than they did in the prior year, from 1988 to 2021.

FIGURE 8.3 | Dividend Changes at US companies, 1988–2021

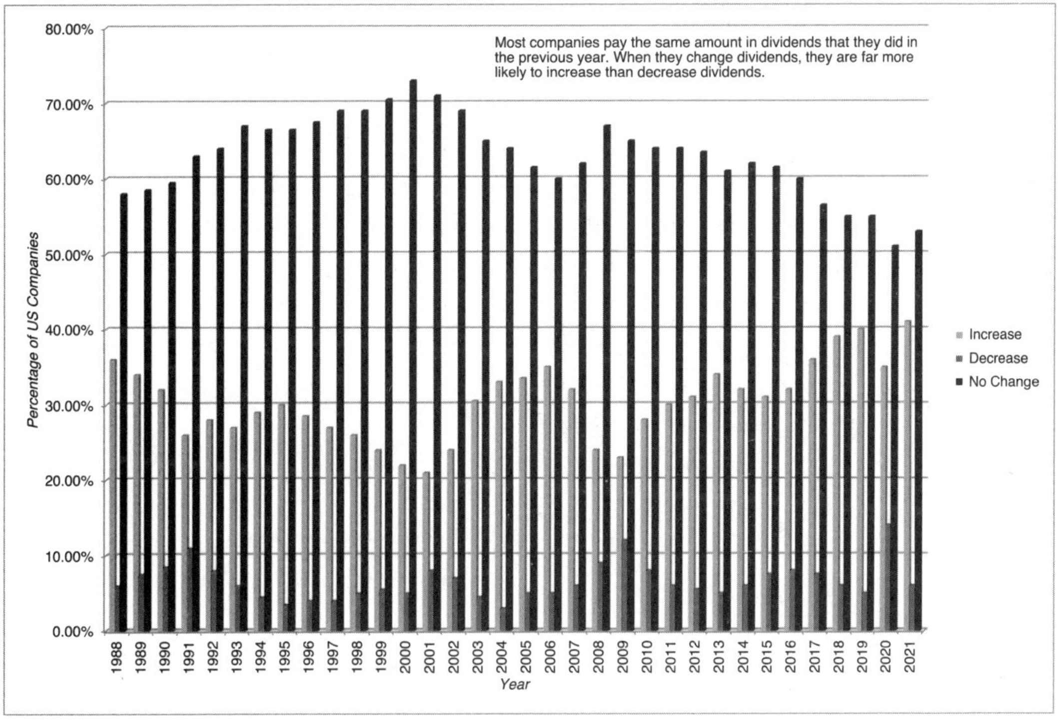

Source: S&P Capital IQ

In every year, the proportion of companies that left dividends per share unchanged outnumbered companies that increased or decreased dividends, and among the companies that changed dividends, increases outnumbered decreases by a hefty margin. Looking at global equities, I find that dividends are sticky in every part of the world, though there are differences in dimension. In Latin America, for instance, it is the payout ratio—i.e., the proportion of earnings that gets paid out as dividends—that is sticky, rather than the dollar dividends per share.

The stickiness of dividends may strike you as odd, given that free cash flows to equity are volatile over time, but there are two explanations. First, companies, knowing that free cash flows to equity go up and down, pay dividends that represent a smoothed-out value. Thus, they pay less than they can afford to in years of plenty, saving the buffered cash flows to pay dividends in years when earnings and cash flows are low. Second, there *are* investors who prefer the stability of sticky dividends and are sometimes willing to pay a premium for that stability, and if a company's shareholders are drawn disproportionately from this group, it will have an incentive to preserve stable dividends.

Dividends versus Buybacks: The Trade-off

From the perspective of a business, a dividend and a stock buyback both return cash to owners and have the same effect on the company's overall value. The cash paid out reduces the company's value by the payout, and to the extent that debt is used to fund the dividend or buyback, it can affect the debt mix and cost of capital for a business. If a business returns more cash than it can afford, in either dividends or buybacks, it may find itself rejecting investments it could have taken with the cash. Figure 8.4 shows that dividends and buybacks have equivalent effects on a business.

FIGURE 8.4 | The Value Effects of Dividends and Buybacks

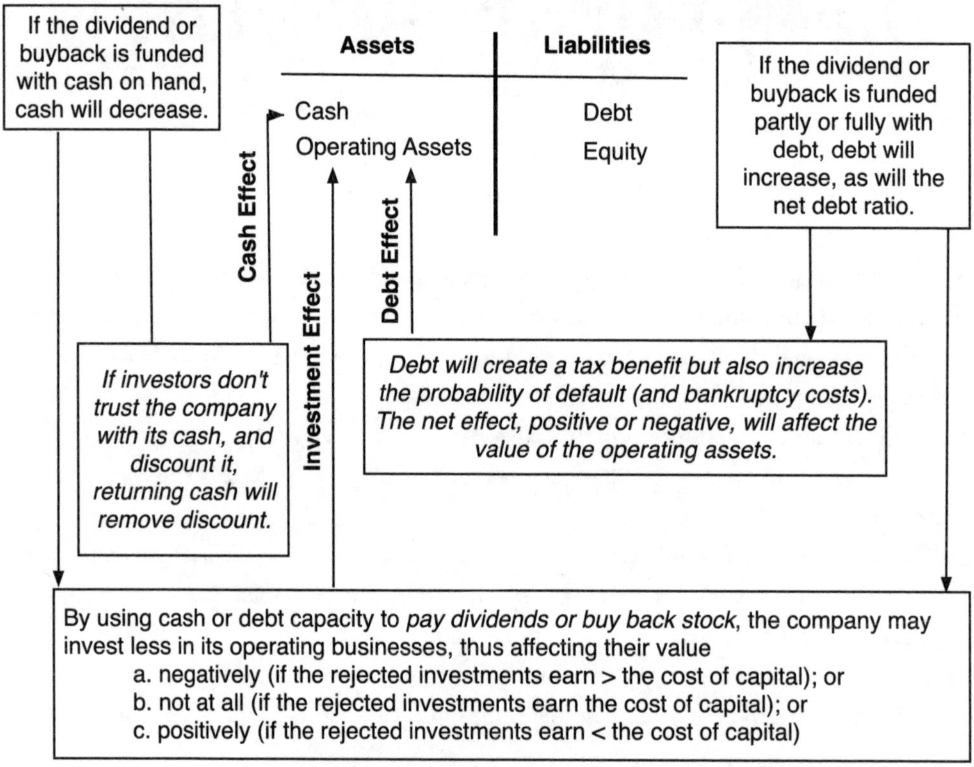

The biggest difference between dividends and buybacks, from a company's perspective, is in the flexibility that it offers them on cash return. Unlike dividends—which, once committed to, are sticky—buybacks can be reversed, even after they have been announced. The stickiness of dividends and the flexibility offered by buybacks create a side effect that can influence companies on dividend policy: Since investors are aware that companies do not like to reduce dividends, they may view a company that initiates or increases its dividend as one that is confident enough in its prospects to be able to make this commitment and respond to this positive signal by raising the stock price. Conversely, given the reluctance to cut dividends, investors may view a dividend reduction or suspension as a negative signal and reduce stock prices.*

From the perspective of the shareholders of a business, dividends and stock buybacks can have different consequences. With dividends, all shareholders receive an amount that reflects their proportional ownership, while with stock buybacks, the cash is returned only to those shareholders who sell their shares back to the company and not to those who choose to remain as shareholders, with tax and control effects. Investors who do not need the cash in current periods, and who are taxed at high rates on investment income, will prefer stock buybacks to dividends, whereas investors who are reliant on continuing cash flows from their investments will tilt toward preferring dividends.

There is a final factor that comes into play in the dividends versus buybacks debate, and that is the company's current stock price. Since buybacks are made at the current price, or even at a premium over that price, buying back stock in a company with overpriced shares will transfer wealth to investors who sell their shares back from investors who do not. When a stock buyback is underpriced, the wealth transfer will occur in the opposite direction, with investors who keep their holdings in the firm gaining at the expense of those who sell their shares back.

The Growth of Buybacks

In 1981, almost all the cash returned to shareholders at US companies took the form of dividends, and share buybacks were rare. Through the 1980s, businesses began buying back stock, and that trend has not let up, as can be seen in figure 8.5, where I graph aggregate dividends and buybacks at US companies from 1988 to 2021.

* There is evidence that is supportive of this proposition. On average, the announcements of dividend increases (decreases) are accompanied by stock price increases (decreases), but the signaling effect of dividends seems to have weakened over the last few decades.

FIGURE 8.5 | Dividends and Buybacks at US Firms, 1988–2021

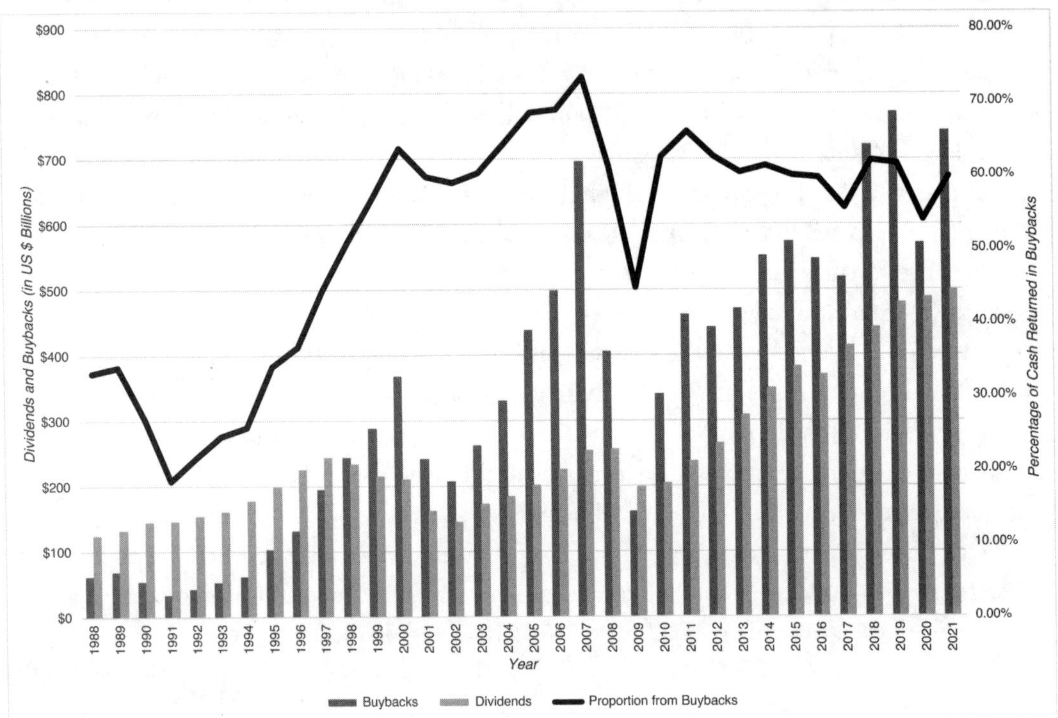

In 2021, US companies collectively returned almost $750 billion in stock buybacks, significantly more than the $500 billion that they paid out in dividends. The statistic that best captures the shift to buybacks is the percentage of cash returned in the form of buybacks, which has risen from less than 35% to almost 60% of total cash returned.

While the shift from dividends to buybacks has been most pronounced in the United States, it is a global phenomenon, and you can see the results when cash return is broken down into dividends and buybacks by region, in table 8.6.

Table 8.6 • Dividends and Buybacks, by Global Region (in 2021)

Sub Region	Number of Firms	Market Cap ($ Mil)	Net Income ($ Mil)	Dividends ($ Mil)	Buybacks ($ Mil)	Dividend Payout	% of Cash Return from Buybacks	Cash Payout Ratio
Africa and Middle East	2,356	$4,698,102	$260,259	$138,928	$12,275	53.38%	8.12%	58.10%
Australia & NZ	1,878	$1,930,982	$77,123	$45,034	$6,579	58.39%	12.75%	66.92%
Canada	2,937	$3,129,490	$162,432	$65,382	$34,781	40.25%	34.72%	61.66%
China	7,043	$19,024,215	$1,001,151	$471,821	$50,414	47.13%	9.65%	52.16%
Eastern Europe & Russia	528	$649,262	$99,799	$33,562	$6,155	33.63%	15.50%	39.80%
EU & Environs	6,000	$17,098,249	$868,662	$332,208	$132,019	38.24%	28.44%	53.44%
India	3,982	$3,572,361	$120,717	$35,772	$8,540	29.63%	19.27%	36.71%
Japan	3,947	$6,510,572	$448,920	$127,328	$58,088	28.36%	31.33%	41.30%
Latin America & Caribbean	1,043	$1,724,743	$122,751	$61,399	$17,401	50.02%	22.08%	64.19%
Small Asia	9,408	$7,205,112	$426,861	$160,991	$10,953	37.72%	6.37%	40.28%
United Kingdom	1,255	$3,599,149	$193,457	$86,628	$18,861	44.78%	17.88%	54.53%
United States	7,229	$52,446,672	$1,789,714	$591,709	$842,300	33.06%	58.74%	80.12%
Global	47,607	$121,588,908	$5,571,847	$2,150,763	$1,198,364	38.60%	35.78%	60.11%

You can see the global shift from dividends to buybacks taking form in the rest of the world, with Japanese and Canadian firms returning close to a third of their cash in buybacks, and European firms close behind, returning just over 28% of cash in the form of buybacks. Even emerging-market companies are joining in, with cash returned in buybacks standing at 22.08% at Latin American companies and 19.27% in Indian companies.

Choices across the Life Cycle

If dividends and buybacks are the mechanisms available for a company to return cash to its shareholders, and its choice will depend largely on how much it values the flexibility that is offered by buybacks and how much its shareholders like or dislike dividends, you would expect to see differences in their usage across the life cycle.

- Early in the life cycle, when a business has less cash available to return to shareholders and there is more volatility in that cash balance, you would expect companies to be less likely to initiate and pay dividends.
- As businesses age, there are two forces that would push them toward returning cash in the form of dividends. The first is that mature businesses generally have more stable and predictable earnings and cash flows, and thus can afford to return more cash in the form of dividends. The second is that institutional investors own a larger share of the outstanding equity at mature firms, and some of them (such as pension funds) prefer predictable dividends.

To see if there are differences in cash return across the life cycle, in table 8.7 I classified publicly traded US firms into age deciles and looked at whether they returned cash to shareholders in 2021 and, if so, whether they paid dividends or bought back stock.

Table 8.7 • Cash Return, by Age Decile, for Publicly Traded US Firms, in 2021

			Cash Returners		Dividend Payers		Stock Buybacks	
Age Decile	# Firms	Average Age	% Returning Cash	% Not Returning Cash	% of Dividend Payers	% of Non-dividend Payers	% Buying Back	% Not Buying Back
Youngest	499	5.04	30.66%	69.34%	15.03%	84.97%	23.05%	76.95%
2nd decile	522	9.43	30.27%	69.73%	11.49%	88.51%	26.44%	73.56%
3rd decile	577	13.58	30.85%	69.15%	12.31%	87.69%	27.38%	72.62%
4th decile	718	18.12	32.31%	67.69%	11.56%	88.44%	28.41%	71.59%
5th decile	488	23.49	43.24%	56.76%	15.98%	84.02%	38.52%	61.48%
6th decile	652	29.49	48.16%	51.84%	22.39%	77.61%	41.87%	58.13%
7th decile	578	38.19	56.92%	43.08%	25.61%	74.39%	49.13%	50.87%
8th decile	606	52.48	68.15%	31.85%	42.74%	57.26%	57.92%	42.08%
9th decile	581	86.88	79.69%	20.31%	62.13%	37.87%	63.86%	36.14%
Oldest	584	140.22	84.42%	15.58%	74.83%	25.17%	64.38%	35.62%
All firms	6,542	42.24	46.90%	53.10%	27.10%	72.90%	39.15%	60.85%

Younger firms are far less likely to return cash to owners than older firms, with more than 69% of firms in the youngest decile returning no cash and only 15.58% of older firms not returning cash. The same patterns apply for both dividends and buybacks, with fewer young firms returning cash in either form. These results make sense in light of what I found when I looked at free cash flows to equity by corporate age class, in table 8.5, since younger firms are also more likely to have negative FCFE, indicating an incapacity to return cash to shareholders.

Dividend Dysfunction and Consequences

I started this chapter by measuring potential dividends as the cash flow to a business left over after all other claims have been met, including reinvestment for future growth, and then considered actual cash returned in the form of dividends and stock buybacks. In this section, I will look at the root causes of why the latter can deviate from the former, even over long periods, and the consequences of that deviation to the business.

Dysfunctional Dividend Policy

In classical corporate finance, dividends are paid out of residual cash flows, i.e., cash flows left over after taxes, reinvestment needs, and debt payments have been met. However, there are companies that seem to view dividends as a commitment to be paid *before* looking at projects to take and debt to be serviced. In figure 8.6, I provide a contrast between dividends as a residual cash flow—the classical corporate finance view—and dividends as the leading cash flow, in the world of dysfunctional dividends.

FIGURE 8.6 | **Residual versus Dysfunctional Dividends**

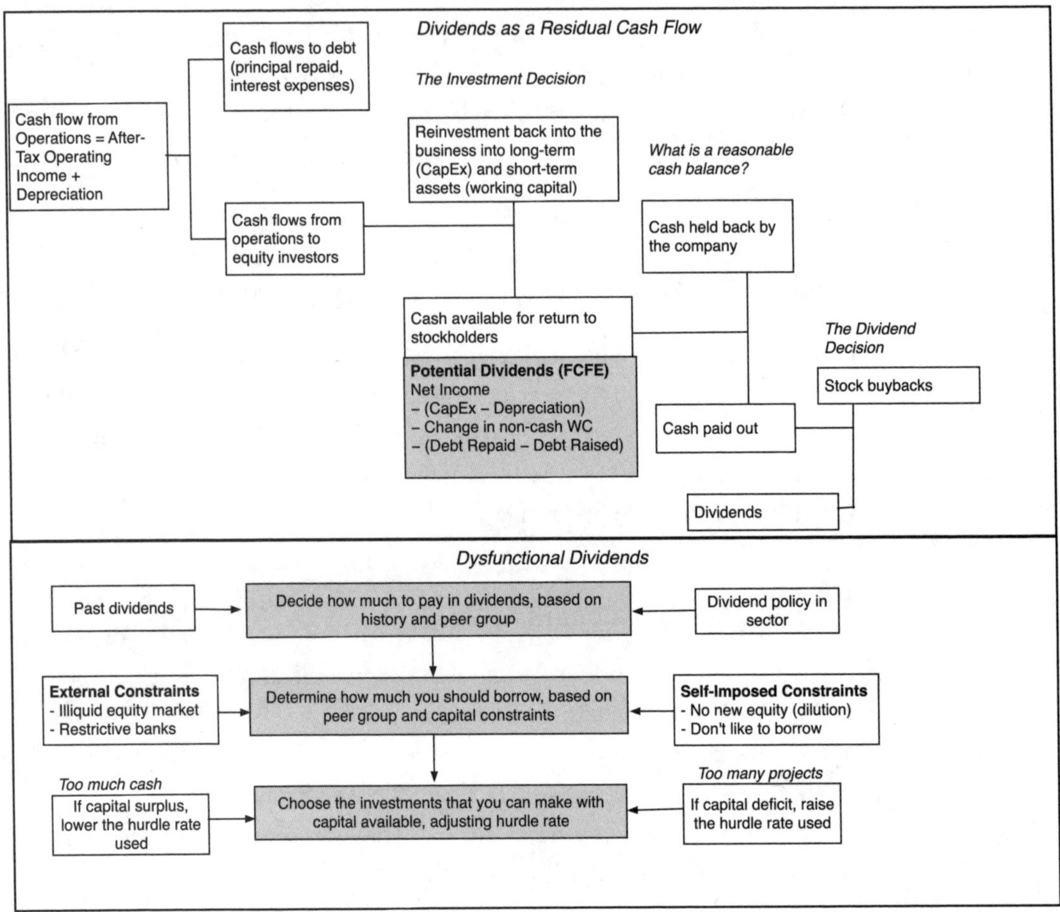

The consequences of a dysfunctional dividend policy, wherein dividends drive investment and financing decisions, are predictably catastrophic for some businesses. A firm that gets locked into dividends that it cannot afford to pay out, based upon either historic dividends or peer-group practice, may find itself borrowing well beyond its capacity to pay these dividends, while rejecting good investments along the way.

The nature of dividend dysfunction can vary across the life cycle. Early in the life cycle, with young and growing firms, it can take the form of dividends or share buybacks in the face of negative free cash flows to equity. These companies, already in a cash flow hole, dig themselves deeper into that hole and must raise fresh capital, either from new debt (which puts their survival at risk) or from new equity. As firms start to mature, dividend dysfunction can take the form of refusing to pay dividends, even as free cash flows to equity turn positive and grow. That refusal can stem from a denial of aging, as growth firms try to put off middle age, or from a peer-group comparison where other companies in the sector also do not return cash. For mature firms, there is the risk, for some, of getting locked into a policy where too much cash is being returned, either because of having committed to dividends in good years that cannot be sustained or due to a reliance on buybacks in the hope that they can sustain stock prices. For declining firms, where the business is shrinking, there can be an unwillingness to adopt a dividend policy that reflects that reality.

To provide a snapshot of the divergence between potential and actual cash return, I broke down all publicly traded firms worldwide into groupings based upon their FCFE and cash return (in dividends and buybacks) in figure 8.7.

FIGURE 8.7 | Cash Returns versus FCFE—Global Firms, in 2021

Returning no cash when a firm has positive FCFE or returning less cash than is available as FCFE adds to cash balances.

Returning cash when a firm has negative FCFE or returning more cash than is available as FCFE will burn through cash.

	Positive FCFE, No cash returned	*Cash returned, FCFE > Dividends + Buybacks*	*Cash Accumulators*	*FCFE < 0, No Cash Return*	*Cash returned, FCFE < (Dividends + Buybacks)*	*FCFE Negative, Cash Returned*	*Cash Burners*
Australia, New Zealand, and Canada	9.45%	9.19%	18.64%	67.71%	3.92%	9.74%	81.37%
Developed Europe	18.01%	22.12%	40.13%	33.30%	7.46%	19.10%	59.86%
Emerging Markets	14.66%	24.29%	38.95%	24.62%	8.25%	28.18%	61.05%
Japan	13.93%	36.89%	50.82%	13.59%	7.61%	27.98%	49.18%
United States	10.88%	18.47%	29.35%	35.11%	8.10%	27.44%	70.65%
Global	14.06%	22.77%	36.83%	30.75%	7.61%	24.82%	63.18%

In a sample of 47,606 publicly traded firms, listed globally, 36.83% returned less cash than they had available as FCFE, in 2021, and 63.18% returned more in cash than they had available as FCFE.

Clearly, there are few firms that follow a purely residual dividend policy, returning their FCFE to shareholders every year. At least in 2021, more companies were returning too much cash, relative to FCFE, than were returning too little cash.

Cash Return and Cash Balances

The potential dividend or free cash flows to equity of a business is the cash it has left over after taxes, reinvestment, and debt servicing—but businesses are not obligated to return this cash to owners. If they do, the cash balance of the business will remain unchanged. If a business chooses to return more in cash to owners than it has available as free cash flows to equity, it will be dipping into its cash balance, causing a decline in cash held in the period. If a business chooses not to return cash or returns less cash to owners than it has in free cash flows to equity, its cash balance will be augmented by the difference. Figure 8.8 summarizes this dynamic.

FIGURE 8.8 | **FCFE, Cash Return, and Cash Balances**

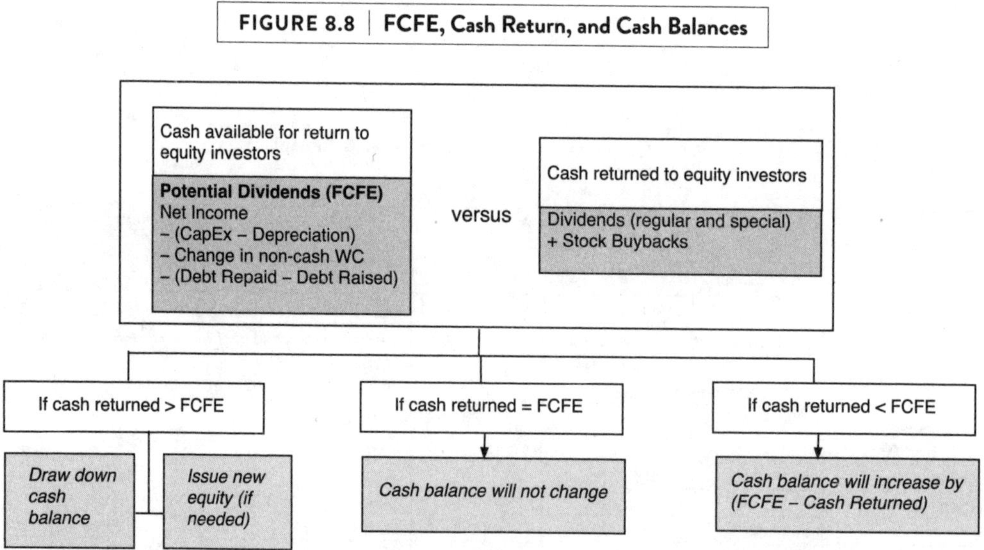

Note that if a business has negative FCFE, it is in the group of companies that returns more cash (zero) than it should return (negative), and the difference has to be covered either by drawing down an existing cash balance or by raising new equity (from venture capitalists or public-market equity investors). If you follow this logic, you can see why companies that choose not to return cash over long periods, in the face of large and positive free cash flows to equity, will accumulate large cash balances.

Is cash accumulation in a company damaging to shareholders? In the most benign scenario, shareholders in a business with a large cash balance own a share of that cash balance, and that should show up as a higher equity value or stock price. In a malignant version, shareholders in businesses with large cash balances may be concerned that managers will waste that cash on a bad investment (a bad project, or overpayment on an acquisition) and discount the cash in the hands of these firms. There is a third and positive outcome, wherein a business with significant constraints on raising capital and worries about failure risk that accumulates cash will be rewarded with a premium on that cash balance, because it reduces failure risk and alleviates capital constraints. In sum, you can see very different market reactions to cash being accumulated at companies, depending on where these companies stand in terms of investment opportunities and how much shareholders trust management to deliver on these prospects. In figure 8.9, I summarize the results from a study of cash balances at US companies, with a focus on how much markets valued a dollar in cash at each company.*

FIGURE 8.9 | Market Value of a Dollar in Cash Balance at US companies

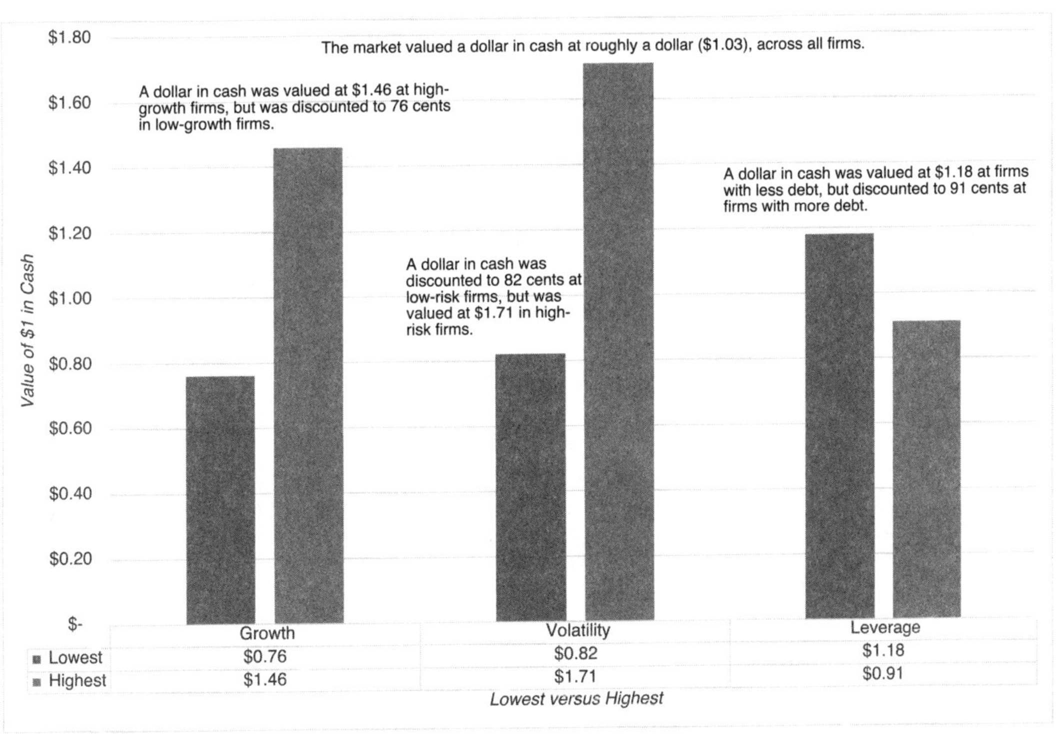

	Growth	Volatility	Leverage
Lowest	$0.76	$0.82	$1.18
Highest	$1.46	$1.71	$0.91

* L. Pinkowitz and R. Williamson, "What Is the Market Value of a Dollar of Corporate Cash?" *Journal of Applied Corporate Finance* 19, no. 3 (September 10, 2007): 74–81.

Looking at how this process will play out across the life cycle, we can conclude that young firms with negative free cash flows to equity are likely to burn through cash and be in constant need of equity infusions. That said, since these firms have good growth prospects and are risky, markets are more likely to view cash balances at such companies positively and attach a premium to them. As firms mature, their free cash flows to equity will turn positive, and to the extent that these firms choose not to return cash, cash balances will build up. If firms choose to stay with their policies of not returning cash, as growth levels off and earnings power improves, that increase in cash balances will continue and gather momentum. Along the way, markets will shift to first viewing these cash balances neutrally, valuing a dollar in cash at roughly a dollar—but as growth opportunities become scarcer, you may start to see the market discounting these cash balances. This will create opportunities for activist investors to pressure companies to return cash, and if and when they do, their cash balances will level off and perhaps even decline, if cash return exceeds the free cash flows to equity.

Dividend Policy across the Life Cycle: Summing Up

Over the course of this chapter, I have looked at how the amount of cash that businesses have to return will vary over the corporate life cycle, with young firms less likely to have cash to return than older firms, and provided evidence to back up that view. In addition, I looked at the trade-off between paying dividends and buying back stock and argued that young firms are less likely to commit to paying dividends and more likely to use stock buybacks as a way of returning cash to shareholders. Figure 8.10 summarizes both aspects of dividend policy across the corporate life cycle.

FIGURE 8.10 | Cash Return across the Corporate Life Cycle

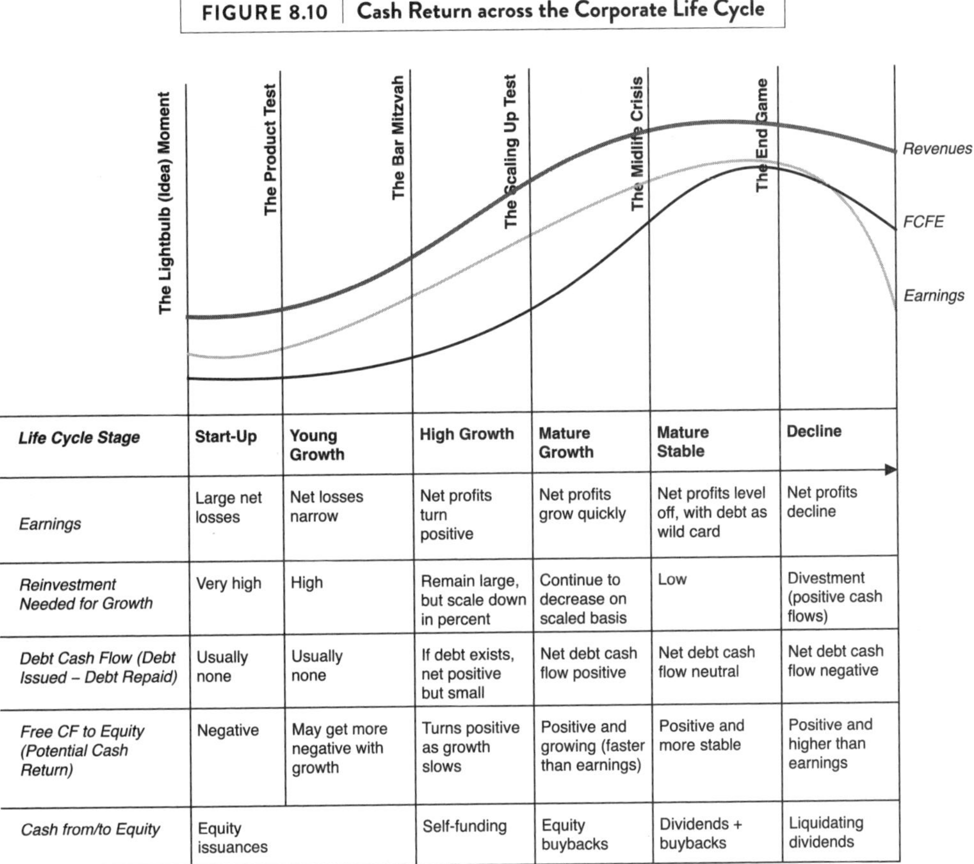

Life Cycle Stage	Start-Up	Young Growth	High Growth	Mature Growth	Mature Stable	Decline
Earnings	Large net losses	Net losses narrow	Net profits turn positive	Net profits grow quickly	Net profits level off, with debt as wild card	Net profits decline
Reinvestment Needed for Growth	Very high	High	Remain large, but scale down in percent	Continue to decrease on scaled basis	Low	Divestment (positive cash flows)
Debt Cash Flow (Debt Issued – Debt Repaid)	Usually none	Usually none	If debt exists, net positive but small	Net debt cash flow positive	Net debt cash flow neutral	Net debt cash flow negative
Free CF to Equity (Potential Cash Return)	Negative	May get more negative with growth	Turns positive as growth slows	Positive and growing (faster than earnings)	Positive and more stable	Positive and higher than earnings
Cash from/to Equity	Equity issuances		Self-funding	Equity buybacks	Dividends + buybacks	Liquidating dividends

Looking at dividend policy differences across the life cycle, in conjunction with investment and financing policy differences that I noted in the last two chapters, you can see how following first principles in corporate finance can play out in very different ways at young companies as opposed to older ones.

Recognizing that how much cash a business should return to its shareholders and in what form will vary across the life cycle is critical in understanding why blanket judgments, or regulations, on dividend policy are likely to hurt more than help. A regulation requiring every company to pay a portion of its earnings as dividends will have little effect on value at an older firm but can be devastating for a younger firm, where FCFE can be negative even with positive earnings. At the other extreme, arguing that stock buybacks are bad for business, and that firms should be reinvesting that cash back into their operations, makes little sense at mature or declining firms, with relatively few investment opportunities.

Conclusion

Dividend policy is the last of the three principles that comprise corporate finance, and in a rational universe, a business should decide how much to return to its shareholders only after making judgments on how much to invest back into the business (investment policy) and whether borrowing makes sense (financing policy). This notion of dividends being a residual cash flow is a sensible one, but it is ignored frequently at companies, which are sometimes tempted to make the decision of how much cash to return first, based upon history or peer-group behavior, and then adjust investing and financing decisions to reflect the dividend decision. As a consequence, dividend policy can take dysfunctional forms, with firms paying out dividends with debt that they cannot afford to take on and putting their survival at risk.

Dividend policy should vary across the life cycle, with young firms returning less cash than more mature firms and choosing more flexible cash-return policies (like buybacks) over rigid ones (like dividends). While there is evidence that companies do follow this principle, in the aggregate, there are clearly cases of firms that do not.

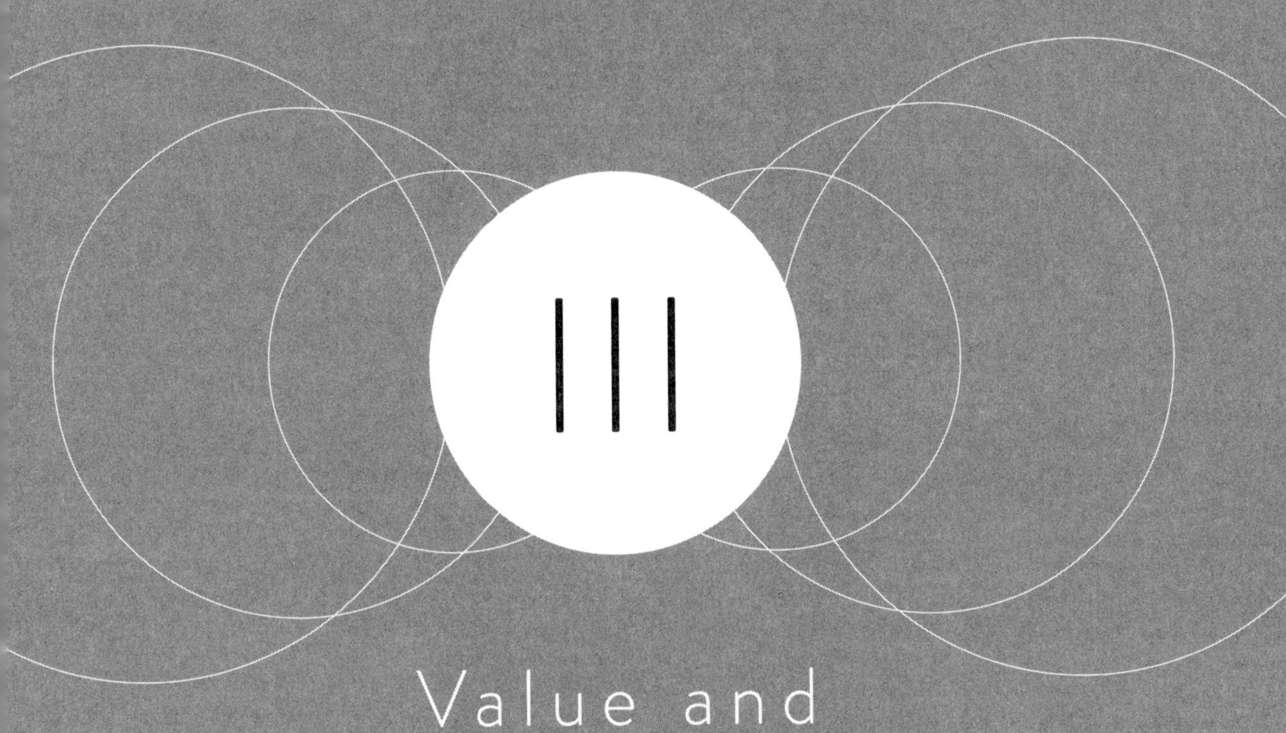

III

Value and Price across the Life Cycle

9

Valuation and Pricing 101: A Life Cycle Overview

CORPORATE FINANCE BREAKS DOWN business decisions into investing, financing, and dividend decisions, but the composite effect of these decisions is in the value of the business and, if it is publicly traded, in its market price. In this chapter, I will begin by looking at the mechanics of intrinsic value, and then reframe these mechanics in terms of fundamental questions that need to be answered to estimate value. In the process, I will trace the value of a business back to its key drivers and argue that to estimate these drivers, you need a narrative about the business. In the second part of the chapter, I will examine pricing and the process by which investors price companies, noting that the drivers of price not only are different from value drivers but can yield different outcomes. Along the way, I will look at how both the value and pricing processes change as businesses age and move through the life cycle.

Valuation 101

In intrinsic valuation, I begin with a simple proposition: the value of an asset is not what someone perceives it to be worth but a function of the expected cash flows on that asset. Put simply, assets with high and predictable cash flows should have higher values than assets with low and volatile cash flows.

Value Mechanics

Putting intrinsic valuation into practice requires grappling not only with how to define cash flows and incorporate risk into value but also with how to factor in the time value of money. Figure 9.1 captures the essence of valuation in an equation.

FIGURE 9.1 | The Intrinsic Value of an Asset

Expected cash flows in time period

$$Value = \frac{E(CF_1)}{(1+r)^1} + \frac{E(CF_2)}{(1+r)^2} + \cdots + \frac{E(CF_n)}{(1+r)^n}$$

Risk-adjusted discount rate

For an asset with a limited life—say, ten years—I would estimate the expected cash flows on that asset for ten years and then discount back these cash flows at a discount rate that reflected the riskiness of the cash flows.

Applying this principle to valuing an ongoing business, in general, and a publicly traded company, specifically, requires that I grapple with two other issues.

- **Equity versus firm:** The first issue is that with a business, you have a choice between valuing only the owner's stake (equity) or valuing the entire business. For the former, I estimate the free cash flows to equity—i.e., the cash flows left over after all other claims on the cash flows have been met—and discount these cash flows back at the cost of equity. In a publicly traded firm, you could use dividends as a measure of equity cash flows, or use free cash flows to equity, the potential dividends that I described in chapter 8. When valuing the entire business, I discount back the cash flows that both equity investors and lenders receive from the business—the former in free cash flows to equity and the latter in interest and principal payments—and discount these pre-debt cash flows back at the cost of capital. Figure 9.2 contrasts the value of equity in a business to the value of an entire business.

FIGURE 9.2 | Value of Equity versus Value of Business

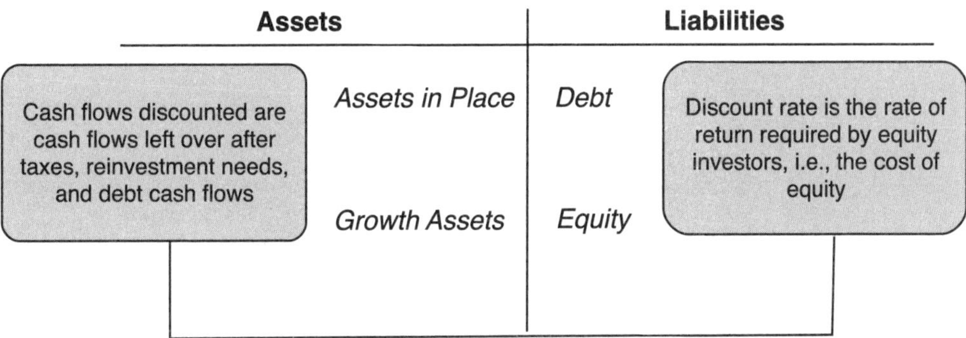

Present value of cash flows to equity, discounted back at the cost of equity, is the value of equity.

Firm/Business Valuation

Assets | **Liabilities**

Cash flows discounted are cash flows left over after taxes and reinvestment needs but before debt cash flows

Assets in Place

Growth Assets

Debt

Equity

Discount rate is the weighted average of the required returns for equity investors and lenders

Present value of cash flows to firm, discounted back at the cost of capital, is the value of the entire firm (business).

- **Life of business:** A business has the capacity to renew itself by investing in new assets, making it difficult to pin down its life span. In theory, a publicly traded company can continue as a going concern for decades or even centuries. Since I cannot estimate cash flows each year for these long periods, I must find a way to impose closure on the exercise, and one practice that valuation analysts use is to assume that cash flows beyond a point in time in the future will grow at a constant rate forever. That assumption allows us to capture the present value of all cash flows beyond with a "terminal value" and to break down, as in figure 9.3, the value of a business into two parts: the present value of cash flows during the explicit forecasting period and the present value of the terminal value at the end of the period.

FIGURE 9.3 | Value of a Business

$$Value\ of\ Business = \frac{E(Cash\ Flow_1)}{(1+r)^1} + \frac{E(Cash\ Flow_2)}{(1+r)^2} + \cdots + \frac{E(Cash\ Flow_{n+1})}{(r-g_n)(1+r)^n}$$

Value of business today

Present value of expected cash flows in explicit forecast period (n years)

Present value of terminal value, i.e., the value at the end of year n, assuming a constant growth rate forever after year n

At first sight, it seems unreasonable to assume that any business, no matter how successful, can last forever, but in defense of the perpetual-growth assumption, it should be noted that it yields roughly the same value that I would have arrived at if I had assumed that the business would last for decades, rather than forever. In other words, if I expect a business to last a long time, the perpetuity assumption will yield a reasonable value. When valuing a business with a shorter life, I can and should abandon this assumption and estimate the terminal value for a finite period instead.

If I accept the proposition that I should value a business based upon its expected cash flows, factoring in risk, expected growth, and timing, I can break down the valuation of a business, in purely mechanical terms, into three sets of inputs. The first are the expected cash flows from the business, estimated after taxes and the reinvestment needed to sustain the growth that is being incorporated into the cash flows. The second is the discount rate that reflects the risk in the cash flows and the market rates at the time of the valuation. The third is the terminal value, if any, that I should be attaching to the business at the end of the forecasting period.

Value Drivers

The mechanics of valuation can sometimes obscure the reality that the inputs into valuation should reflect the economics of the business that is being valued. To understand a business well enough to value it, I need to estimate four basic sets of inputs.

- The first, and perhaps most straightforward, set of inputs estimates the cash flows that the business derives from its existing investments, usually from the current financial statements of the business.
- The second, and most difficult, set of inputs looks at the effects of growth in the cash flows to the business and evaluates how much value will be added or destroyed by growth. To understand why growth is not always a positive for value, recognize that while growth allows revenues and earnings to increase over time, it also comes at a cost, since that growth will require reinvestment, and the latter can, and often does, overwhelm the former.
- The third set of inputs relates to risk—how to measure it and bring it into the discount rate, leaving open the possibility that risk can change over time in a business and so allowing for discount rates to change as well.
- The final set of inputs deals with closure. Since the conventional terminal value calculation requires cash flows to grow at a constant rate, it is best used when a business becomes mature—i.e., when a business grows at a rate less than or equal to the growth rate of the economy in which it operates. For businesses where the assumption of long lives is untenable, you can either estimate a liquidation value for the assets or a terminal value based upon a finite life for the cash flows.

Figure 9.4 summarizes the questions that underpin the valuation of a business.

FIGURE 9.4 | Key Questions in the Valuation of a Business

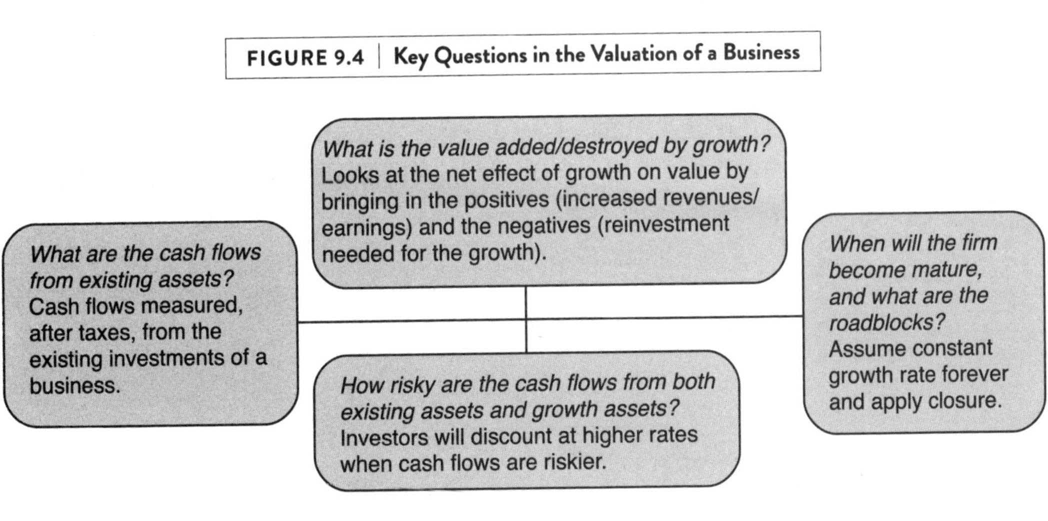

To make explicit the link between these questions and the intrinsic value equation that I laid out in the last section, I examine the connections between the two in figure 9.5.

FIGURE 9.5 | Intrinsic Value—Questions and Equation Inputs

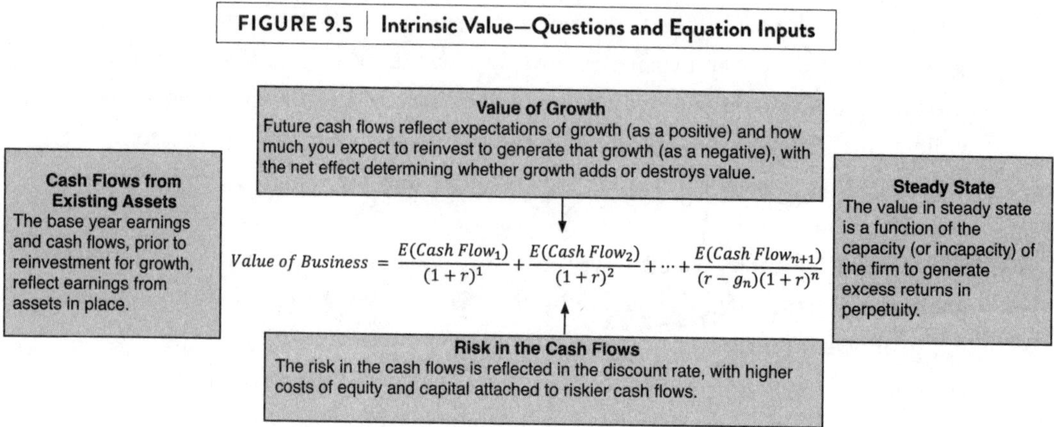

As you can see, the inputs into valuation reflect your assessment of the quality of a business and its risk. In the next section, I will build on this theme.

Value = Story + Numbers

In the last four decades, alongside an explosion in access to data and more powerful tools to analyze that data, I have also seen many analysts lose sight of a simple truth of valuation. Every business valuation, no matter how number laden and complex, is implicitly telling a story about the business, and making that story explicit is a big step toward more defensible and consistent valuations. In figure 9.6, I begin by describing a good valuation as a bridge between stories and numbers.

FIGURE 9.6 | Valuation as a Bridge between Stories and Numbers

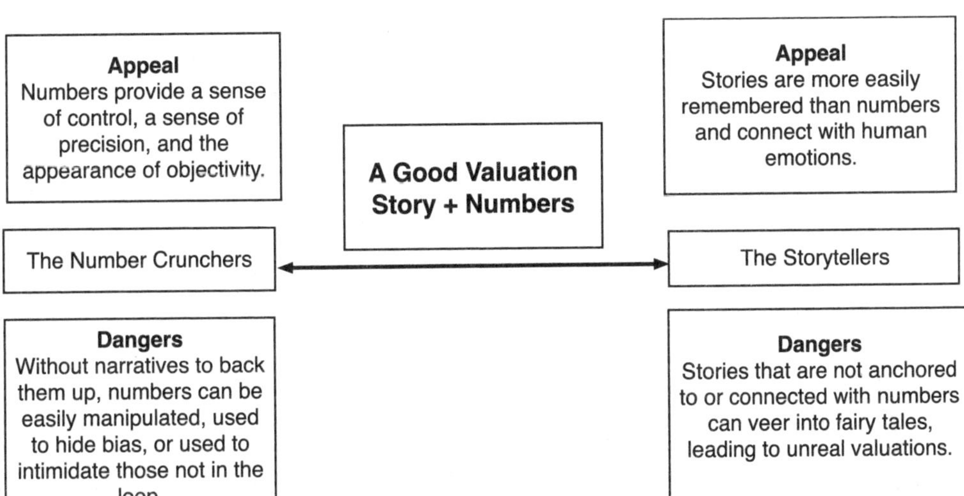

The figure also spells out the dangers of a valuation that is entirely number driven or completely story focused. With a purely number-driven valuation, it is easy to create magical businesses, with characteristics of growth, cash flows, and risk that no real business could replicate. In fact, numbers can be manipulated to yield values that reflect one's predispositions and biases about the business and then used to intimidate non–"numbers people." With a purely story-driven valuation, the line between reality and fantasy is similarly easy to cross, especially if the market that a company is going after is a big one and there are macro trends working in its favor. By connecting stories to numbers, you introduce discipline on both fronts, by forcing numbers people to come up with business stories that back up their numerical inputs and inducing story people to explain how their stories play out in the numbers.

That brings us to another side cost of increased data access and more powerful tools, which is the ease with which analysts can now overload valuation models with detail, with the complexity often making it difficult to make story connections. In my experience, the best valuations are parsimonious, relying on a few key inputs. In fact, for most non–financial service companies, the value of the business can be captured in five inputs. The first three are revenue growth, operating margins, and reinvestment efficiency (generally estimated as dollars of revenue per dollars of capital invested); with these three inputs, you can convert a business model into expected cash flows. The other two inputs are risk measures: a risk-adjusted discount rate that incorporates the effect of operating risk into value, and a failure probability that reflects the likelihood that the business will not survive as a going concern. Figure 9.7 summarizes these inputs.

FIGURE 9.7 | The Drivers of Value

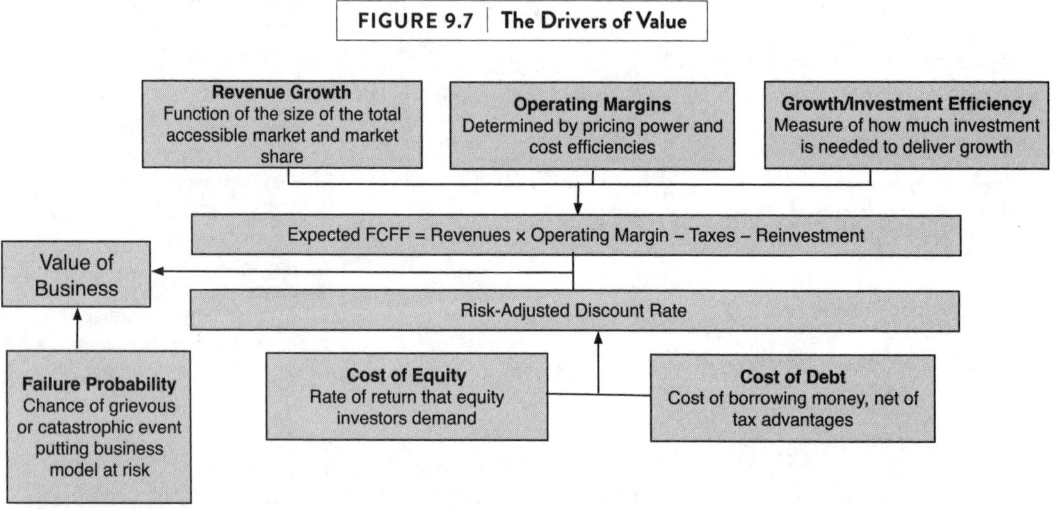

Financial service companies, including banks, insurance companies, and payment processors, have a different set of drivers, but they too can be valued with models that require fewer, rather than more, inputs.

One of the benefits of using simpler valuation models is that the work of converting stories into valuation inputs becomes simpler. In figure 9.8, I summarize the inputs through which different valuation stories that are told about companies play out in value.

FIGURE 9.8 | Valuation Stories and Inputs

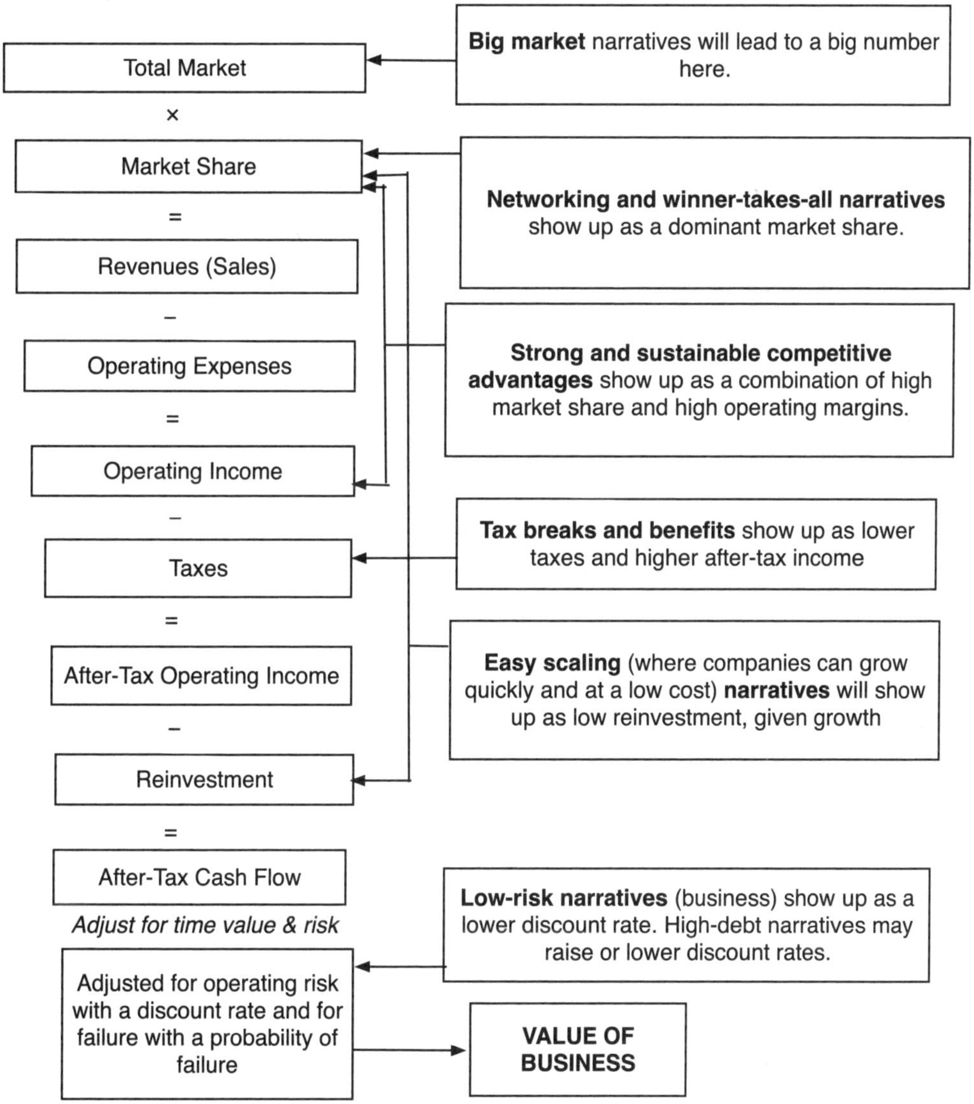

Total Market

×

Market Share

=

Revenues (Sales)

–

Operating Expenses

=

Operating Income

–

Taxes

=

After-Tax Operating Income

–

Reinvestment

=

After-Tax Cash Flow

Adjust for time value & risk

Adjusted for operating risk with a discount rate and for failure with a probability of failure

VALUE OF BUSINESS

Big market narratives will lead to a big number here.

Networking and winner-takes-all narratives show up as a dominant market share.

Strong and sustainable competitive advantages show up as a combination of high market share and high operating margins.

Tax breaks and benefits show up as lower taxes and higher after-tax income

Easy scaling (where companies can grow quickly and at a low cost) **narratives** will show up as low reinvestment, given growth

Low-risk narratives (business) show up as a lower discount rate. High-debt narratives may raise or lower discount rates.

In sum, while a completed valuation may look as if it is all about numbers, recognizing that the numbers are telling a story about a business and asking commonsense questions about the story is integral to good valuation.

Valuation across the Corporate Life Cycle

With that long lead-in, let us talk about how the valuation process changes, or does not change, as a company moves through the life cycle.

- **Intrinsic value is a constant:** The notion of the intrinsic value of a business as the present value of the expected cash flows from that business, over time, applies for companies across the life cycle.
- **Different cash flow paths:** With young companies, which are struggling with building business models, the cash flows will be negative in the early years, turn positive only as they approach high growth, and then grow rapidly before settling into stability. With mature companies, you are far more likely to see positive cash flows immediately, but with far less growth in future years. With declining companies, you may see shrinkage in the cash flows over time, as businesses get smaller.
- **Changing dependence on terminal value:** Earlier in this chapter, I noted that the value of a business today will be the sum of the present value of its expected cash flows in the forecast period and the present value of its terminal value, capturing cash flows beyond the forecast period. Young companies, with negative cash flows in their early years and positive and growing cash flows only later, will get a much large proportion of their value from the cash flows in the later years and the terminal value than will more mature companies.

It is true that the estimation challenges that a company faces will change as a company ages, and in the next four chapters, I will focus on these challenges, starting with young-growth companies in chapter 10; moving on to high-growth companies in chapter 11; mature companies in chapter 12; and concluding with declining companies, in chapter 13.

Staying with the theme that a good valuation is a bridge between stories and numbers, I will argue that the question of which one (story or numbers) should be given priority and dominate the business valuation will also shift over the life cycle. Early in the life cycle, with little historical data available on a company and big questions about business models still unanswered, it is the story that dominates the valuation, driving the inputs and the numbers. As a company ages, data will accumulate on the successes and failures of its business model, and the resulting numbers on revenue growth, margins, and reinvestment will move to the forefront, with the stories retreating to the background. In figure 9.9, I capture this shift from narrative to numbers, with key narrative drivers, at each stage in the life cycle.

FIGURE 9.9 | Narrative versus Numbers across the Corporate Life Cycle

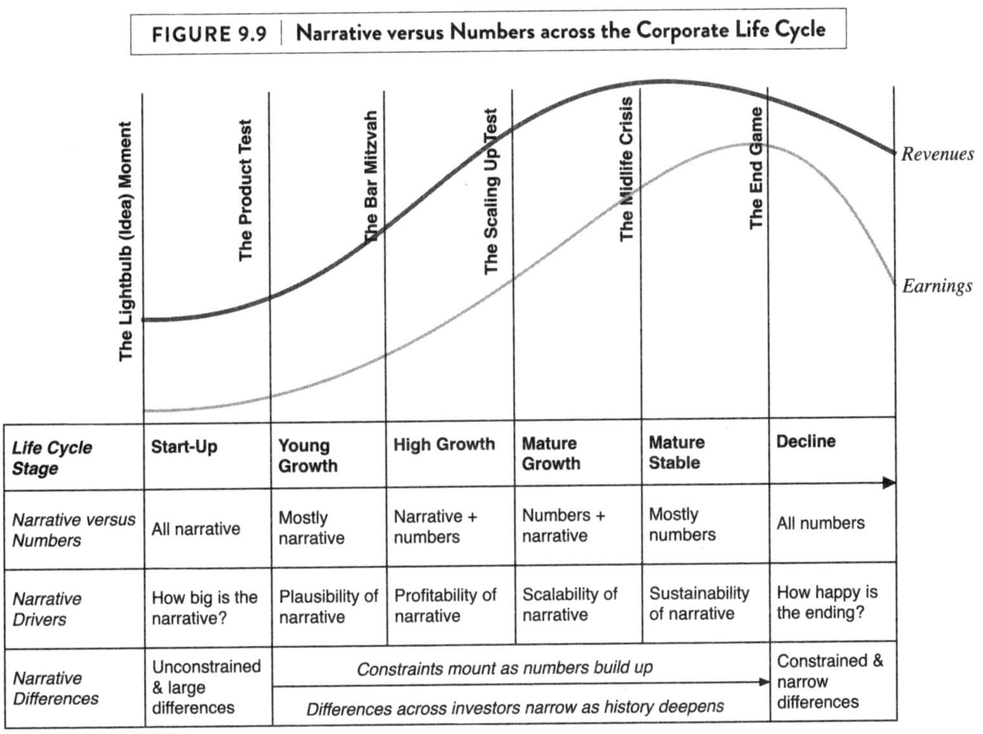

Life Cycle Stage	Start-Up	Young Growth	High Growth	Mature Growth	Mature Stable	Decline
Narrative versus Numbers	All narrative	Mostly narrative	Narrative + numbers	Numbers + narrative	Mostly numbers	All numbers
Narrative Drivers	How big is the narrative?	Plausibility of narrative	Profitability of narrative	Scalability of narrative	Sustainability of narrative	How happy is the ending?
Narrative Differences	Unconstrained & large differences	*Constraints mount as numbers build up* → *Differences across investors narrow as history deepens*				Constrained & narrow differences

It is worth noting also that when it is the story that drives valuation, as is often the case with young companies, you will find wide divergences in stories and valuation across investors, and when the numbers are dominant, those divergences will narrow, leading to more convergence on value. That is a partial explanation for why, even if markets are rational and efficient, you should expect to see far more volatility in stock prices at younger companies than at more mature ones.

Pricing 101

In intrinsic valuation, the objective is to find the value of an asset, given its cash flow, growth, and risk characteristics. In pricing, I determine how much to *pay* for an asset by looking at what other investors are paying for similar or identical assets. The tricky part of this process is finding similar or identical assets and controlling for differences that exist across assets.

Pricing versus Value

To draw a contrast between intrinsic valuation and pricing, you have to begin by understanding the differences between the processes that determine value and price. Value, as I showed in the last section, is determined by cash flows, growth, and risk, and the discounted-cash-flow approach tries to bring these determinants into an estimate of the value of the business today. Price is determined by demand and supply, and while the fundamentals (cash flows, growth, and risk) may be drivers of price, mood, momentum, and liquidity, all play key roles in the pricing process. As I will show you in the sections to follow, the pricing of an asset will be based on what other investors are paying for similar assets. Figure 9.10 summarizes the value versus price divide.

FIGURE 9.10 | Value versus Price

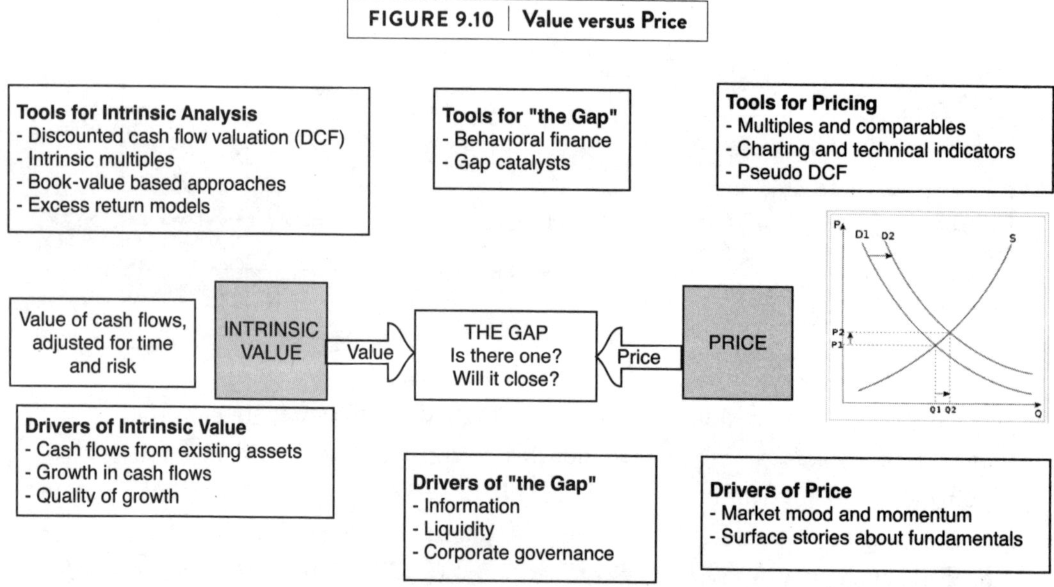

If the value process is driven by fundamentals, and the pricing process is additionally influenced by mood, momentum, and behavioral forces, will they yield the same number for an asset or a business? For believers in efficient markets, the answer is yes, since, in their view, the behavioral forces will cancel out in markets, creating deviations from value that are random and unpredictable. Investors who actively seek to beat the market believe that there can be a gap between value and price that can be exploited—though they may disagree, based upon their investment philosophies, on what types of companies are most likely to have such gaps and how best to exploit them. I will examine these differences across investment philosophies later in the book and examine how they play out across the corporate life cycle.

Price Drivers

To understand why the pricing process can yield a number that is very different from the valuation process, I look at price drivers, the forces that can make prices move even in the absence of any change in fundamentals.

1. **Mood and momentum:** The first and strongest force behind pricing moves is mood and momentum. What has happened to prices in the past exercises influence over what will happen to them in the future. Looking at price movements on stocks, there is evidence of positive momentum in the short term (minutes, hours, days, and even weeks), where stocks that have done well (badly) in the past continue to do well (badly). Traders often use this momentum to book "easy" profits—but the catch is that there is also significant evidence of reversals, wherein momentum can shift, often unpredictably and violently, as you extend your time horizon. Put simply, the easy profits earned on momentum, over weeks or months, can be wiped out in a few days in a reversal.
2. **Incremental information:** The price of an asset or business can also be affected significantly by news stories that have little or almost no effect on the fundamentals that drive value. You see this phenomenon at play sometimes during earnings reports, where the announcement by a company that it beat or fell short of expectations by a trivial amount can trigger substantial buying or selling, resulting in large price movements.
3. **Groupthink:** If you want to put a rationale on the momentum story, it is that there is herd behavior in markets—not only do traders behave irrationally, they do so in concert. Thus, instead of averaging out, as is the case in efficient markets, crowd irrationality can cause prices to move further away from value.
4. **Liquidity and trading ease:** Pricing is driven by trading, and traders, not surprisingly, worry about being able to open and close out positions easily and at low cost. Thus, liquidity plays a much more significant role in the pricing process than it does in valuation, where, at best, it can affect discount rates, with higher discount rates for less liquid assets. Liquidity also is related to momentum, since in its absence, the forces of momentum usually get stronger, with surges of buying (selling) having a much greater impact on prices of less liquid assets.

Figure 9.11 summarizes the drivers of price.

FIGURE 9.11 | The Drivers of Price

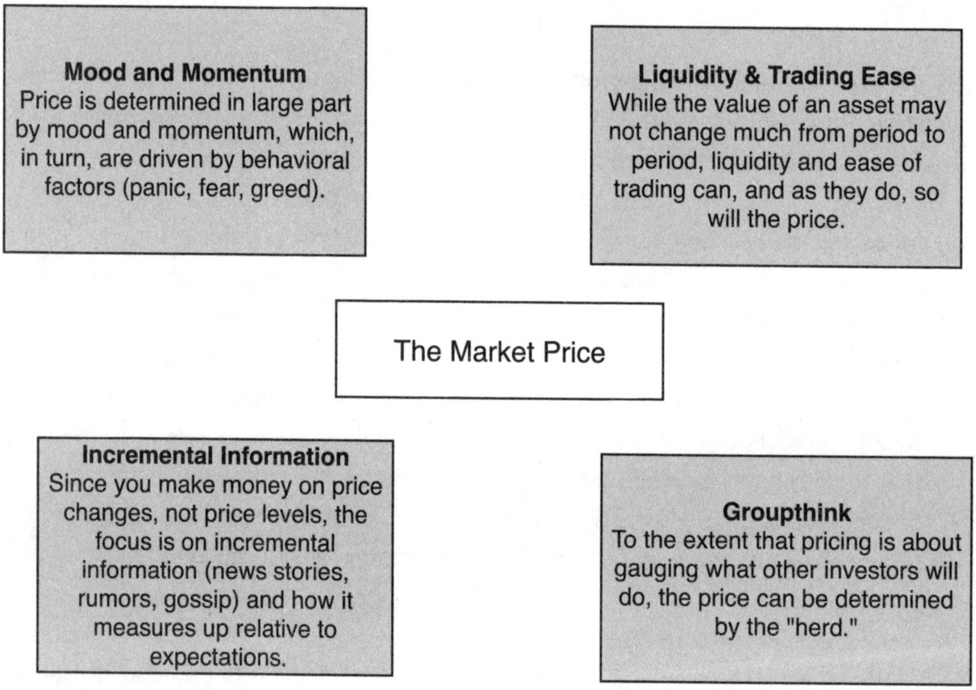

Mood and Momentum
Price is determined in large part by mood and momentum, which, in turn, are driven by behavioral factors (panic, fear, greed).

Liquidity & Trading Ease
While the value of an asset may not change much from period to period, liquidity and ease of trading can, and as they do, so will the price.

The Market Price

Incremental Information
Since you make money on price changes, not price levels, the focus is on incremental information (news stories, rumors, gossip) and how it measures up relative to expectations.

Groupthink
To the extent that pricing is about gauging what other investors will do, the price can be determined by the "herd."

Over the last five decades, finance has been enriched by insights from psychology, with the melding of the two creating what is called behavioral finance. The greatest contribution of this field to financial understanding is the acceptance that demand and supply, the forces that drive pricing, are determined by human beings, and their behavioral quirks can, and often do, lead to price deviating from value.

Pricing Mechanics

Unlike in intrinsic valuation, you price an asset based upon how similar assets are priced in the market. A prospective homebuyer decides how much to pay for a house by looking at the prices paid for similar properties in the neighborhood. In the same vein, a potential investor in Porsche's IPO, in 2022, could have estimated its price by looking at the market pricing of other luxury automobile companies. Embedded in this description are the three essential steps in relative valuation:

1. **Find comparable assets that are priced by the market,** a task that is easier to accomplish with real assets, like baseball cards and houses, than it is with stocks.
2. **Scale the market prices to a common variable** to generate standardized prices that are comparable. Other things remaining equal, a smaller house or apartment should sell at a lower price than a larger residence. In the context of stocks, this equalization usually requires converting the market values into multiples of revenues, earnings, book value, or revenues.
3. **Adjust for differences across assets** when comparing their standardized values. Again, using the example of a house, a newer house with more updated amenities should be priced higher than a similar-sized older house that needs renovation. With stocks, differences in pricing can be attributed to all of the fundamentals that I talked about in the section on discounted cash flow valuation. Higher-growth companies, for instance, should trade at higher multiples than lower-growth companies in the same sector.

Most assets are priced, not valued, not only because pricing often requires less information and can be done more quickly than intrinsic valuation but also because pricing differences, if they exist, are far more likely to be corrected quickly.

Comparing assets that are not especially similar can be a challenge. If you compare the prices of two buildings of different sizes in the same location, the smaller building will look cheaper unless you control for the size difference by computing the price per square foot. When comparing publicly traded stocks across companies, the price per share of a stock is a function of both the value of the equity in a company and the number of shares outstanding in the firm. To compare "similar" firms in the market, their value can be standardized relative to how much the company earns, to its accounting book value, to revenue generated, or to a measure specific to a firm or sector (number of customers, subscribers, units, etc.). In addition, you have to make judgments on timing (current or a future year's numbers) and a peer group for the comparison. The entire process is captured in figure 9.12.

FIGURE 9.12 | The Pricing Process

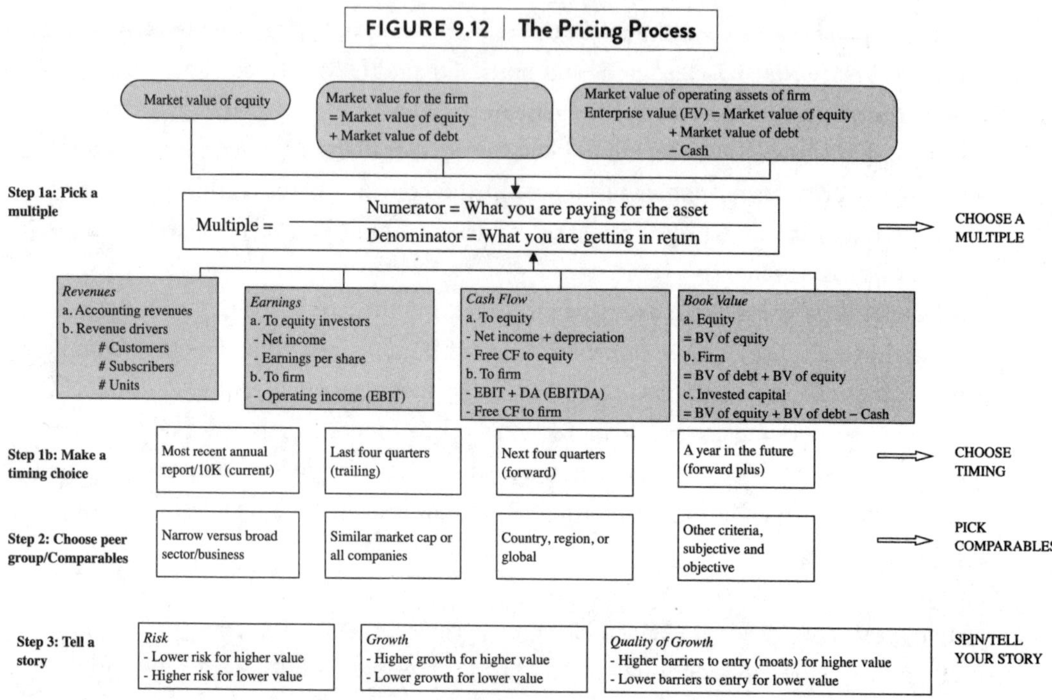

Again, when measuring earnings and book value, you measure them from the perspective of just equity investors or both debt and equity (firm). Thus, earnings per share and net income are earnings to equity, whereas operating income measures earnings to the firm; the shareholders' equity on a balance sheet is book value of equity, whereas the book value of the entire business includes debt, and the book value of invested capital is that same book value, net of cash. You can divide the market value of equity by the net income to estimate the price-earning ratio (measuring how much equity investors are paying per dollar of earnings), or the enterprise value by EBITDA to get a sense of the market value of operating assets relative to operating cash flows. The central reason for standardizing, though, does not change: you will want to compare these numbers across companies.

Pricing across the Corporate Life Cycle

As with valuation, the pricing process follows the same steps for companies no matter where they are in the life cycle. However, the pricing issues that you will confront at young companies can be different from those of more mature companies and challenges can occur at each stage of the process:

a. **Scaling metric:** The first step in pricing, at least in the context of businesses, is scaling the pricing to metrics, with the choices ranging from revenues to earnings to book value to cash flows. However, for a metric to work as a scalar, it must be positive, and for young companies, which often are money losing and cash burning, that reduces the choices that you have, commonly eliminating earnings and cash flow from the mix. Since book value is primarily a reflection of existing investments, it can be trivial at young companies, making it a shaky base for pricing. Not surprisingly, revenue becomes the scaling metric at many young companies, and for some that are pre-revenue, the scalar can even be something that you believe will be correlated with revenues in the future, such as number of users or subscribers. As companies mature and start making money, you are more likely to see earnings become the scalar (leading to price-earnings ratios to EBITDA), with growth brought into the scalar with high-growth companies (PEG ratios). In decline, where investors and traders start to look at asset divestitures and liquidations, you will see book value used more frequently (price to book and EV to invested capital ratios) as the scaling variable.
b. **Timing choice:** When computing pricing multiples, you can scale prices to a current year's value, a normalized value (usually computed by looking at the average value over a period of many years), or a future value. For example, with price-earnings ratios, the market price can be divided by the current year's earnings per share (current PE), average earnings per share over the last five years (normalized PE), expected earnings per year next year (forward PE), or even expected earnings per share five years from now. With mature companies, any of these choices may work, but you are likely to see a dependence on current values or near-term forward values (next year's revenues or earnings). With young companies, especially those with small revenues and big losses in the most recent year, you are far more likely to see forward values projected for five or even ten years from now being used to create multiples, just to get substance on the values.
c. **Peer group creation:** To price a company, you will need to find other companies like it that are also priced. That is true for all companies, but in general, it is more difficult to do for young companies, for two reasons. The first is that many young companies are not publicly traded, and while you can use their pricing from venture capital rounds, the resulting numbers are less frequently updated and more subject to estimation error. As companies mature, finding similar companies that are priced becomes easier, since more such companies list on markets, though in the growth phase, many will still struggle with finding companies with similar growth and risk. With

stable and declining companies, finding peer groups remains relatively easy, since you can sometimes bring companies in other sectors into the comparison.

d. Controlling for differences: The final step in pricing is controlling for differences in fundamentals (growth, risk, and reinvestment efficiency) across the companies in the peer group. That task, again, is more difficult at young companies, where vast differences can persist in every dimension across the peer group, than at more mature businesses, where growth rate and risk differences tend to narrow.

Figure 9.13 summarizes the differences in the pricing process across the corporate life cycle.

FIGURE 9.13 | The Pricing Process across the Life Cycle

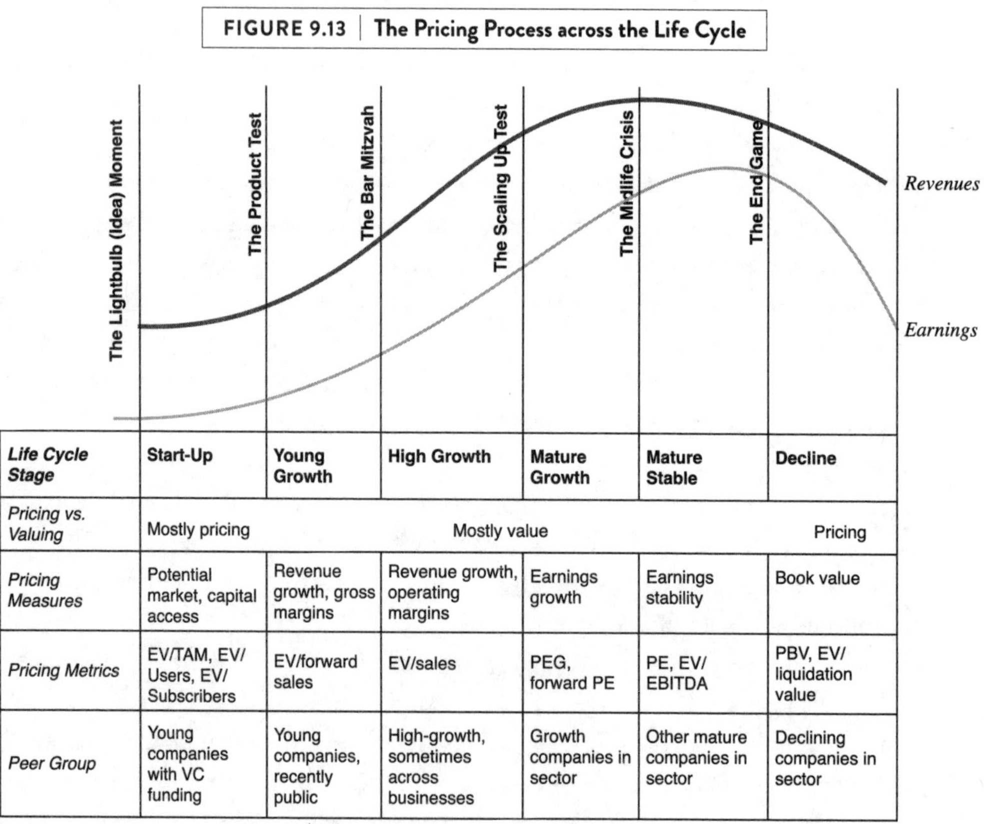

Life Cycle Stage	Start-Up	Young Growth	High Growth	Mature Growth	Mature Stable	Decline
Pricing vs. Valuing	Mostly pricing		Mostly value			Pricing
Pricing Measures	Potential market, capital access	Revenue growth, gross margins	Revenue growth, operating margins	Earnings growth	Earnings stability	Book value
Pricing Metrics	EV/TAM, EV/Users, EV/Subscribers	EV/forward sales	EV/sales	PEG, forward PE	PE, EV/EBITDA	PBV, EV/liquidation value
Peer Group	Young companies with VC funding	Young companies, recently public	High-growth, sometimes across businesses	Growth companies in sector	Other mature companies in sector	Declining companies in sector

In sum, pricing is more difficult at young businesses than at more mature companies. Consequently, for young companies, the pricing process will play a much bigger role in determining what a business trades at than for older ones—an insight that I will use in the subsequent chapters to explain why traders are drawn to young companies and investors to more mature ones.

Conclusion

The value of every business, no matter where it is in the life cycle, is a function of its cash flows, growth, and risk, but the estimation challenges that you face when valuing young companies, with their untested business models and limited history, are greater than those that you face at more mature companies. If you view valuation as a bridge between stories and numbers, valuations are more story-driven at young businesses and more numbers-driven at more mature businesses.

In contrast to its valuation, the *price* of every business is determined by demand and supply, with mood, momentum, and a host of behavioral forces causing price and value to diverge. To price a business, I first standardize it by scaling it to a metric (revenues, earnings, cash flows, book value), finding a peer group of similar companies that are priced, and then controlling for differences in fundamentals. Again, the pricing process is more difficult to apply at young companies, with fewer viable scaling options and comparable firms, than at more mature ones.

In the chapters to come, I will begin by discussing how to value and price young and growth companies, notwithstanding the difficulties, and then move on to mature companies, growth and stable, before concluding with a discussion of how best to value and price declining companies.

10

Valuation and Pricing: Start-up and Young-Growth Businesses

IT IS UNDENIABLE THAT valuing or pricing young businesses is more challenging than valuing or pricing mature businesses. I believe that the valuation and pricing models I described in chapter 9 are versatile enough to work for companies in the nascent stages of the life cycle and that the challenges are primarily in the estimation process. In this chapter, I will develop ways of dealing with the uncertainty that is inherent in valuing young businesses and argue that the payoff to doing valuation is greatest for these businesses.

Valuation

In the last chapter, I argued that while the valuation process is unchanged for young companies compared to older ones, with value coming from their expected cash flows, growth, and risk, there are estimation challenges unique to these companies. There are many investors in start-up and young companies who have abandoned valuation, arguing that the uncertainties about market size and business model viability are so large that valuations become more guesswork than analysis. I agree that uncertainties abound with companies at this stage in the life cycle, but I disagree that this makes valuation pointless. In this section, I will look at ways to respond to the estimation challenges, as well as add-ons and augmentations that can enrich young-company valuations.

The Challenges

To understand the challenges in valuing young companies, I go back to the four questions that I argued, in chapter 9, determine the value of a business and look at what makes those questions difficult to answer when valuing young companies.

- On the question of cash flows from existing investments, young companies often have little to show, since their revenues are small or nonexistent, and their investments usually have not started paying off yet. Since these companies still have expenses that they incur to stay in operation, they often come into the valuation process losing money.
- On the question of the value added or destroyed by future growth, much or all of a young company's value will come from this component—but there is little to use in terms of data to make judgments on key drivers of the value of growth.
- On the issue of risk measurement, it is generally the case that young companies are risky, but with limited or no price and earnings history, the conventional processes for estimating risk parameters often do not work.
- Finally, on the questions of when a young business will become mature and what its fundamentals will look like at that stage, the high mortality rate for young businesses implies that many of them will never become mature. In figure 10.1, I summarize the key valuation questions and challenges faced by young companies.

FIGURE 10.1 | Valuation Challenges—Young Businesses

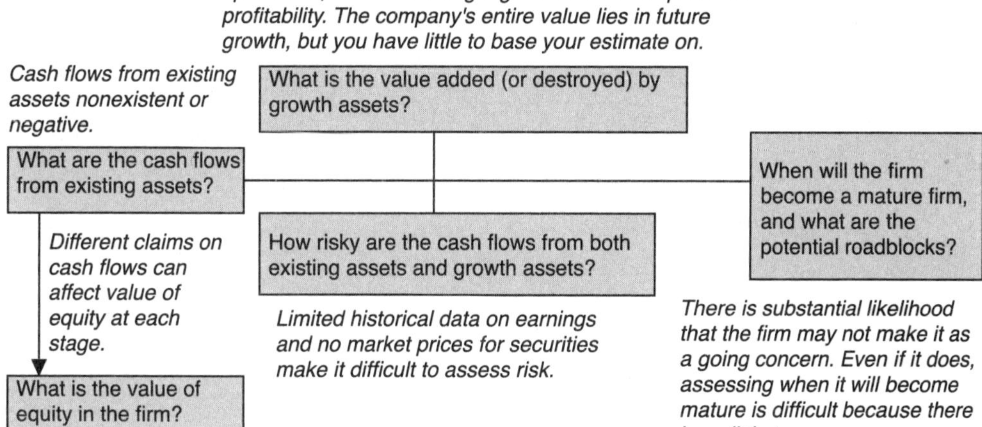

In summary, an untested business model, the absence of a track record, and worries about failure conspire to make young-company valuation difficult.

The Responses

How should we deal with the uncertainty endemic to young companies when valuing them? In this section, I will begin by looking at how venture capitalists try to navigate these shoals when assessing how much the young companies that seek capital from them are worth. The flaws in the VC approach will lead us back to a more conventional valuation approach, modified to reflect the uncertainties inherent in young-company valuation.

THE VENTURE CAPITAL APPROACH

Of all investor groups, venture capitalists have the most exposure to young companies, and they have developed approaches to assess value at these companies that seem, at least at first sight, to address the challenges in valuing these companies. In chapter 4, I described the steps in the VC assessment process, starting with an estimate of expected earnings and revenues in a future year, followed by the use of a pricing multiple (PE or EV to sales) to estimate a pricing in that future year and then the discounting back of that future pricing at a target rate of return. I captured these steps in figure 4.3 and reproduce a compressed version of it here, in figure 10.2.

FIGURE 10.2 | VC Forward Pricing—Compressed Picture

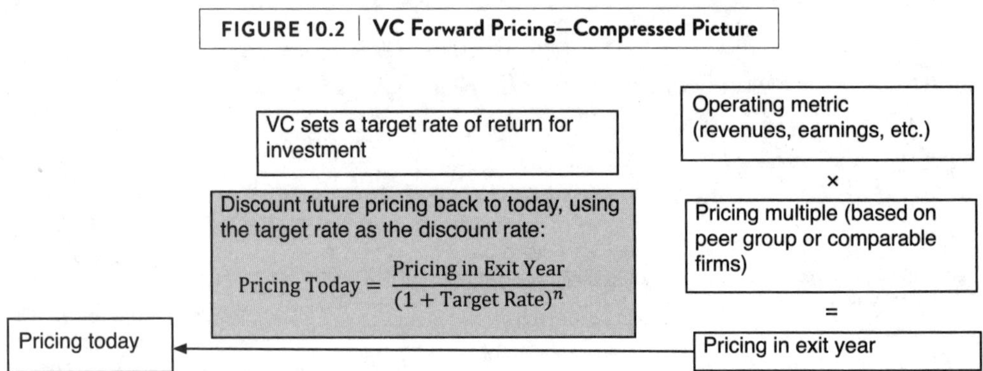

I also noted that while the target rate of return operates as a discount rate in the VC process, it is effectively a made-up number, designed more for negotiation than as a reflection of operating or failure risk. Table 10.1 summarizes typical target rates of return demanded by venture capitalists, categorized by how far along a firm is in the life cycle.

Table 10.1 • VC Target Return Rates, by Development Stage

Stage of Development	Typical Target Rate of Return
Start-up	50% to 70%
First stage	40% to 60%
Second stage	35% to 50%
Bridge/IPO	25% to 35%

How do we know that these rates of return have survival risk built into them? In addition to the intuitive rationale that they decrease as firms move through the life cycle and the chance of failure drops off, we know because the actual returns earned by venture capitalists at every stage of the process are much more modest. In short, venture capitalists who invest in start-ups earn closer to 15% to 20% on an annual basis across their portfolios, even during good times, than 50% to 70%.

The venture capital approach has several problems. First, venture capital valuations try to avoid the serious challenges of estimating operating details for the long term by cutting off the estimates prematurely, with a short forecast period, and using a multiple that is usually based on what comparable companies are currently trading at. However, the multiple of earnings or revenues that a business will trade at three years from now will be a function of the cash flows after that point, and using that multiple to arrive at a value makes it more a pricing than a valuation. Second, there is a degree of sloppiness associated with the use of a target rate of return to discount the firm's future value. While the target rate is supposed to include both operating and failure risk, it is not clear how these factors are incorporated into the stated rate. In short, a venture capital valuation is more accurately a forward pricing, discounted back at an arbitrarily high discount rate that has no connection to the actual risk in a business.

INTRINSIC VALUATION

To value a start-up or young company, I need to start with accepting that uncertainty in valuing these companies is not something that can be wished away or denied. Rather than stop after a short and arbitrary period and apply a pricing, as the VC approach does, I stay with the full horizon that is necessary for a complete valuation and make my best estimate of cash flows over the entire period.

Step 1: Tell a Story

To find a way to make estimates in the face of uncertainty, I suggest starting with a story that is grounded in everything you know about the company, including what need is filled by its product or service, the market that it is aspiring to take a share of, and the capabilities of its founders. Figure 10.3 summarizes some of the background information that can be helpful in framing a business's valuation story.

FIGURE 10.3 | Background for Valuation Story

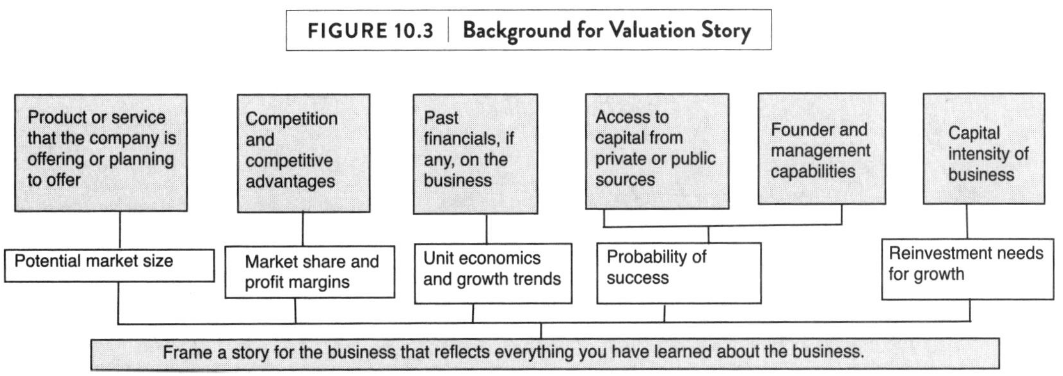

Note that while your first instinct may be to reach for past financial statements, since that is what you are conditioned to do in valuation, you should not be surprised to see a very short history, and one filled with small, albeit growing, revenues and large losses. There are still things you can learn about the unit economics and reinvestment pathways for the business that can be useful in framing your story. In general, you will find yourself relying more on information about the total market, the competition, and the history of other companies that have followed the same path as the one you are valuing.

Step 2: Run the 3P Test (Possible? Plausible? Probable?)

Before you convert this story into valuation inputs, you should stop and assess whether the story passes the *3P test*, wherein we check to make sure that it is *possible* (not a fairy tale), it is *plausible* (that someone else has done something similar, in the past, to what the company is aspiring to do), and it is *probable* (that the company can provide some tangible evidence that its business model works, at least on a limited scale). Figure 10.4 illustrates these tests.

FIGURE 10.4 | The 3P Test for Business Stories

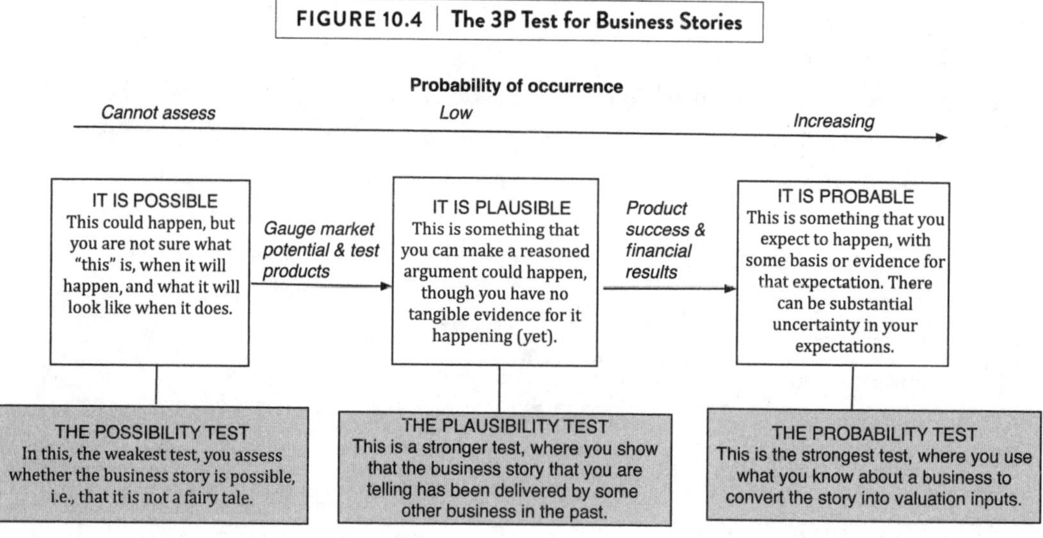

As you pass a business story through these tests, keep tabs on the biases that you bring into the assessment. In short, if you fall in love with a business story before assessing its credibility, you can delude yourself into believing that fairy tales are probable.

Step 3: Convert the Valuation Story into Valuation Model Inputs

Once you have a valuation story for a company, the next task is converting that story to inputs into a valuation model. In making this connection, you will benefit by staying with the parsimonious version of the model that I described in chapter 9, wherein expected earnings are estimated from projected revenues and margins, reinvestment is estimated as a consolidated value relative to revenues, and risk is captured in a cost of capital, for operating risk, as well as in a failure risk probability, to bring in the likelihood that the business will not make it as a going concern.

a. **Growth:** The first and perhaps most daunting part of valuing young companies is forecasting future revenues, and there are two pathways that you can use to get these forecasts.
   - In the first pathway, the *top-down approach*, you begin with a forecast of the total market that the company is going after, with consideration given to the appeal of its products or services and whether the business plans to stay localized or go bigger; this is the total addressable market (TAM) that has taken a central place in valuation narratives, especially with young technology companies. You then estimate the market share that you expect the company to acquire over time, again factoring in the economics of the business and the competition. The product of the two inputs (total market × market share) yields revenues.
   - In the second pathway, *the bottom-up approach*, you start with existing revenues and estimate annual growth rates in those revenues, incorporating founder ambitions and access to capital in your estimates. While both approaches result in expected revenues, your choice of which approach to use will depend on the company that you are valuing. For companies with little or no revenue but significant growth ambitions, the top-down approach is the often the only option, but for companies that have tangible revenues and more established business models, the bottom-up approach will also work.

b. **Profitability:** For a business to become valuable, it has to find a pathway to profitability, and the answer to the question of how lucrative the payoff will be depends in large part on how the company's operating margins evolve as it grows and approaches stability. To estimate this target margin, you should start with the unit economics in the business, defined as the profit made on the additional or marginal unit sold. Businesses like software that have a low cost of goods sold, or direct costs, relative to revenues can earn higher operating margins in steady state than businesses like steel or auto manufacture that face significant production costs. The notion of unit economics can be adapted to accommodate different unit measures: With a subscriber-based company like Netflix, the unit economics can be the difference between the value of adding a new subscriber and the cost of acquiring that subscriber. For a user-based company like Uber, it can be the difference between the value of a new rider and the cost of acquiring that rider. The other driver of expected margins over time will be the economies of scale that you expect to observe in other costs, including selling and administrative expenses, with greater economies of scale translating into higher operating margins in the long term.

c. **Reinvestment:** Left unrestrained, businesses will often push for the highest growth rates that they can, hoping to get rewarded for scaling up, but that growth will need reinvestment—in equipment and factories, for manufacturing companies; in R&D, for pharmaceutical companies; and in acquisitions, for technology companies.* To keep valuations internally consistent, you should tie reinvestment to sales forecasts, with higher growth in sales requiring more reinvestment. Companies that can deliver growth more efficiently, i.e., deliver more revenues for each dollar of capital invested, should be worth more than companies that are not as efficient.

d. **Risk:** Businesses face operating risk as going concerns—wherein macroeconomic forces (economy, interest rates, inflation) will cause revenues and operating income to deviate from expectations—and this risk is captured in the cost of capital that you use in the valuation. Young businesses also face failure risk, and this risk must be assessed separately.

Figure 10.4 captures the key steps in this process.

* If you are familiar with valuation terminology, a company's reinvestment is broken down into "net capital expenditures" (capital expenditures minus depreciation) and change in working capital. The reinvestment number that I estimate is a consolidation of these two items and includes acquisitions, R&D, and even customer acquisition costs.

FIGURE 10.4 | Story to Valuation Inputs

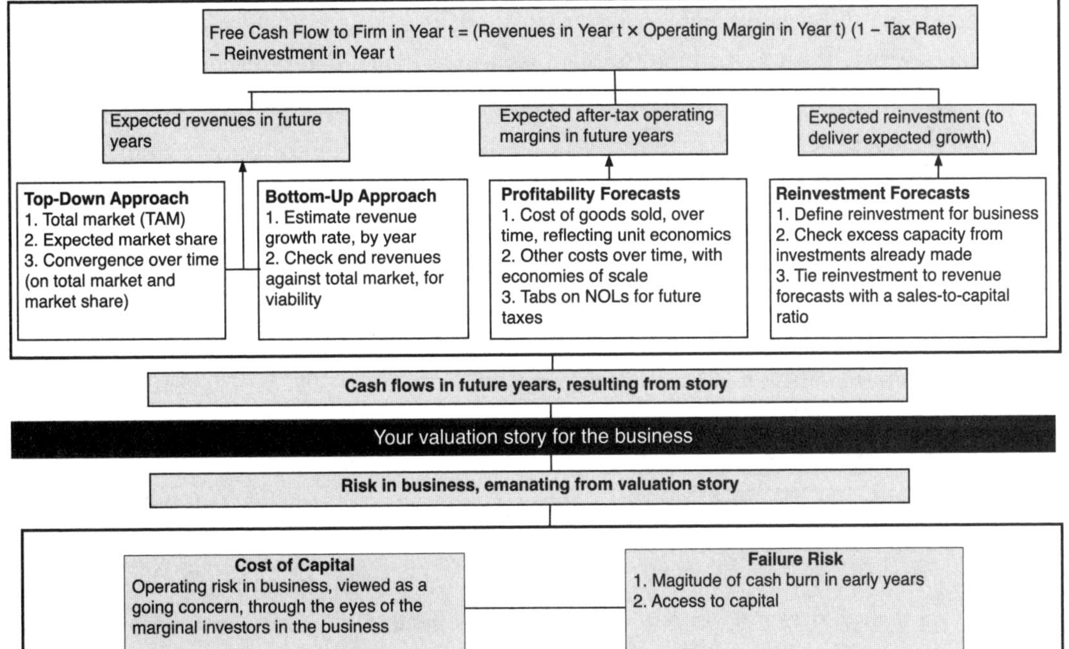

Step 4: Value the Business

Once a story has been converted to valuation inputs, the cash flows and risk adjustments from the story flow into a valuation, and the value of the business should result. There are times, though, when your valuation numbers can signal issues in your valuation story. Here are a few indicators to watch for:

- **Cash flow patterns:** The expected cash flows that underpin your valuation will reflect assumptions made about revenue growth, operating margins, and reinvestment. Specifically, businesses with high revenue growth and negative margins that are slow to turn positive will be saddled with negative earnings in the early years, and incorporating the reinvestment needed to deliver their revenue growth will make cash flows more negative. If the negative cash flows last long enough, and the operating margins in steady state are low (because of weak unit economics and limited economies of scale), you can end up with a current valuation for the asset that is either negative or less than the debt due, leading to equity being worthless. This is a signal of a bad business model, for which failure rates should be set higher. For businesses where there is significant cash burn in the early years but a decisive move to positive cash flows late in the forecast period, the present value of the cash flows during the forecast period may be negative, but it will be more than offset by a terminal value that is large and positive. This too is an indication of a business model that needs time and capital to get going, and access to capital can play a significant role in whether the business survives to deliver the terminal value.

- **Discount rate check:** Separating the total risk in a young business into operating and failure risks, I estimate a cost of capital to reflect only the former. Thus, you should not be surprised to see costs of capital in young-company valuation that are much lower than the target rates that venture capitalists concoct and more reflective of costs of capital of established companies in public markets, where investors are diversified. In fact, if much of the risk in a young company is firm-specific, as is the case with a start-up biotech or pharma company, its cost of capital can resemble that of a mature biotech or pharma company.
- **Failure risk:** The failure risk is the input that reflects the likelihood that many young businesses will not make it, either because they run out of cash and lose access to fresh capital or because their business models never turn to profitability. While there is no crystal ball that can be used to estimate the probability of failure, you can draw on some of the statistics that I presented earlier in this book on failure rates in different sectors, broken down by company age, to make your best estimates.
- **Equity valuation loose ends:** Getting from the value of a business, estimated by discounting the free cash flows at the cost of capital, to the value of equity, especially on a per-share basis, requires attention to detail. In addition to adding on the company's current cash balance[*] and netting out the debt due, you also must adjust the resulting value of equity[†] for the value of equity options granted either to venture capitalists (in private businesses) or to employees in publicly traded firms. For firms where restricted stock is the preferred device for stock-based compensation, the adjustment is easier, since you can add on the restricted share units to outstanding shares in computing the value of equity per share.

[*] While many analysts draw a distinction between operating and excess cash at companies, with only excess cash being added to value, I would suggest that the distinction should be between wasting and non-wasting cash, with the latter invested in marketable securities (like treasuries and commercial paper) and earning a fair rate of return. It is the latter that should be added to get to value, and since, for most firms, the bulk of cash is invested in marketable securities, I would recommend adding the entire cash balance.

[†] To value the options, you have to use option pricing models. There are many in use, and the resulting value will reflect the likelihood that the options will be exercised in the future and will have a time premium over what you would get as cash flows if you exercised the options today.

In figure 10.5, I summarize the steps involved in getting from business value to equity value per share, and the corrections for failure risk and stock-based compensation.

FIGURE 10.5 | **From Business Value to Equity Value Per Share**

Discount estimated free cash flows during the forecast period at the discount rates that you estimated for the business. Estimate the value at the end of the forecast period, assuming constant growth forever or for a finite period, and discount the terminal value back to today.	**Value of business as going concern** = PV of cash flows during forecast period + PV of terminal value at the end of forecast period
Adjust the value for the likelihood of failure by estimating the probability of failure and the value of the business upon failure.	**Value of business adjusted for failure** = Going concern value × (probability of staying a going concern) + failure value × (probability of failure)
Add cash, marketable securities, and the value of minority holdings in other businesses, if any.	**Value of business, with cash & non-operating assets** = Value of business adjusted for failure + cash + value of cross holdings (if any)
Subtract out debt, including lease and other contractual commitments, and minority interests in consolidated entities (if using consolidated financials).	**Value of equity in business** = Value of business with cash & cross holdings – debt commitments – minority interest in consolidated entities
Value all equity options due, using an option pricing model, and net the value of the options from equity value.	**Value of equity in common shares** = Value of equity in business – value of extant equity options
Adjust share count for restricted shares, if any, and for vesting probability, if unvested.	**Value of equity per share** = Value of Equity in common shares / number of shares outstanding

Step 5: Keep the Feedback Loop Open

When building a valuation story and converting that story into inputs and a value, especially with a young-growth business or start-up, it is often easy to develop blind spots and get attached to your own stories. As a final step in the process, I would recommend keeping the feedback loop open, seeking out feedback from people who think least like you and sometimes are better versed in the business details of the company you are valuing. Thus, when valuing Airbnb for its IPO in 2020, I sought out friends who were Airbnb hosts, as well as frequent guests, to see if there were rough spots in the Airbnb story and cost structure that I was missing. In addition, as you value a business, you will find that news stories about the business or its immediate competition come out during your valuation, and this news can sometimes alter your storyline for the company. When

I was valuing Uber in 2016, a California Supreme Court decision requiring the company to treat its drivers as employees changed the cost structure and legal liabilities for the company enough to require a rethinking of the valuation. In some cases, a macro or political development can alter the storyline for a company and the resulting valuation: the 2008 global banking crisis that caused risk capital (venture capital and private equity) to flee the market increased the failure risk for all cash-burning young companies, and the Russian invasion of Ukraine in 2022 upended the stories told about energy companies.

CASE STUDY—PART 1: VALUING ZOMATO, A YOUNG COMPANY, FOR AN IPO, JULY 2021

Background

Zomato, an Indian online food delivery company, was founded in Delhi, in 2008, by Deepinder Goyal and Pankaj Chaddah, in response to the difficulties that they noticed that their office mates were having in downloading menus for restaurants. Their initial response was a simple one: they uploaded soft copies of menus of local restaurants to their website, available initially to people in their office and then to everyone in the city. As the service's popularity grew, they expanded to other large Indian cities, and in 2010, they renamed the company Zomato, with the tagline "Never have a bad meal." The business model for the company is built upon intermediation, wherein customers can connect to restaurants on the platform and order food for pickup or delivery, as well as advertising. Along the way, the company transitioned from being almost entirely an advertising company to one that became increasingly focused on food delivery. By 2021, when the company announced plans to go public, it derived its revenues primarily from four sources:

- **a.** Transaction fees from food ordering and delivery, as the company keeps roughly 20 to 25% of the total order value for itself
- **b.** Advertising, since restaurants listed on Zomato also spend more on advertising, based upon customer visits and resetting revenues, to garner additional visibility
- **c.** Subscription services, with 1.5 million members who, in return for a subscription fee, get discounts and special deals
- **d.** Restaurant raw materials, through Hyperpure, a service directed at restaurants, offering groceries and meats that are source-checked for quality

Coming into its public offering, Zomato had grown at exponential rates for much of its life, with a surge in the number of cities that it served in India from 38, in 2017, to 63, in 2018, to more than 500 in 2021, extending its reach into smaller urban settings.

While revenues had grown accordingly, the company had never made a profit, and figure 10.6 summarizes both its revenue growth and its operating losses coming into the public offering.

FIGURE 10.6 | Zomato—Operating History

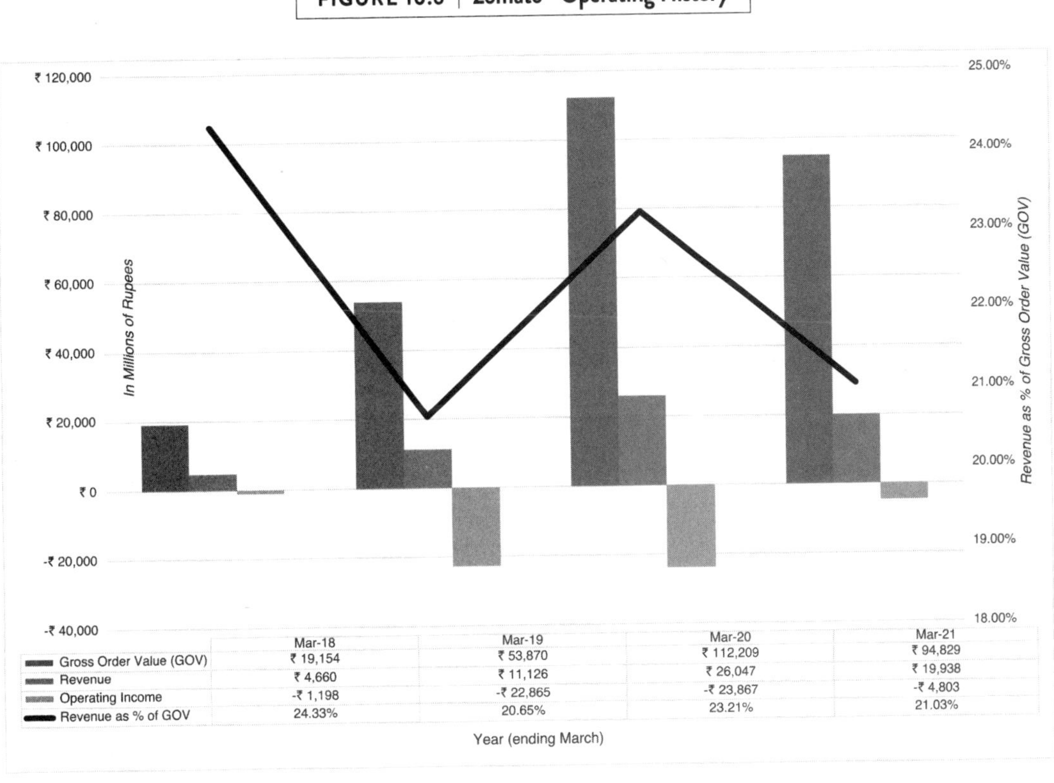

The company's gross order value increased almost sevenfold between 2018 and 2021; the drop in 2020–21 was largely due to the COVID shutdown. Along the way, the company expanded its business outside India, with the United Arab Emirates being its biggest foreign market. Between 2018 and 2020, the company claimed around 23% to 24% of gross order value as its revenues (with a drop-off to 21% in 2020–21), but it lost money every year leading into the IPO. Also, while India is a growing market for online food delivery, the overall size of the market remained small, at $4.2 billion, in 2021, relative to the much larger US or Chinese online food delivery markets, and Zomato already had a market share of close to 40% of the market, with Swiggy and Amazon Food as its biggest competitors. Its revenue growth was driven partly by acquisitions that the company made along the way, with 16 acquisitions between 2014 and 2021, and it funded its growth by drawing on venture capital, raising ₹143.75 billion in eighteen rounds over its lifetime. The ownership structure at the time of the IPO for the company reflected the dilution created by these capital raises, with the founders owning less than 10% of the company and foreign investors (Uber, Alipay, Antfin, and Info Edge) owning most of the rest.

The Zomato Story

In my Zomato story, the Indian food delivery/restaurant market will grow, as Indians become more prosperous and have increased internet access, and this market will be dominated by a handful of players, with Zomato among them. As an intermediary with strong unit economics, Zomato will see high operating margins, over time, and be able to continue to grow with relatively little reinvestment, most of which will be in the form of acquisitions. The operating risk in Zomato will be average, but as a money-losing company, it still has a non-trivial chance of failure, albeit one that will be low because of the cash buffer that the company will have after the IPO.

Valuation Inputs and Valuation:

The story that I have told about Zomato is a big one, reflecting my view on the company and its business as well as on the Indian economy and how I see it growing over time. To convert the story into valuation inputs, I will follow a familiar script:

- **Revenues:** To get a measure of market potential, I start by comparing the size of the food delivery market in India to the food delivery markets in China, the United States, and the EU in table 10.2.

Table 10.2 • Food Delivery Markets, 2021

	India	China	United States	EU
Macro Information for Economy				
GDP, 2020 (in US $ tril)	$2.71	$14.70	$20.93	$15.17
Population (in millions)	1,360	1,430	330	445
Per Capita GDP (US $)	$1,993	$10,280	$63,424	$34,090
Number of restaurants (in 000s)	1,000	9,000	660	890
Information about Food Delivery Business				
Online Access (percent of population)	43%	63%	88%	90%
Online Food Delivery Service Users (in millions)	50.00	450.00	105.00	150.00
Online Food Delivery Market (in US $ mil), 2019	$4,200	$90,000	$21,000	$15,000
Online Food Delivery Market (in US $ mil), 2020	$2,00	$110,000	$49,000	$13,800

The Indian market is smaller than its US and Chinese counterparts for three reasons: lower per-capita income, giving Indians less discretionary income to spend at restaurants; decreased digital reach, with only 43% of Indians having access to a digital device; and different eating habits, with Indians eating out less than the Chinese. To estimate how the Indian food delivery market will evolve over time, I make assumptions about growth in the Indian economy (captured in changes in per-capita income) and improvements in digital access. Table 10.3, below, captures the potential size of the Indian food delivery market for different combinations of assumptions.

Table 10.3 • Potential Indian Food Delivery Market (in US $ millions)

	Indian Per Capita GDP as % of Chinese Per Capita GDP			
	25%	50%	75%	100%
Current-level Internet access	$5,417	$10,834	$16,250	$21,667
China-level Internet access	$7,936	$15,872	$23,809	$31,745
US-level Internet access	$11,085	$22,171	$33,256	$44,342

Put simply, even if Indians had the same per-capita income and digital reach as Chinese consumers, the food delivery market in India would still be far smaller than the Chinese market, perhaps because dining out is not as entrenched in Indian eating behavior. To get from the total market to Zomato's revenues, I make assumptions about Zomato's market share, as well as the percentage of order value that the company will be able to keep for itself as revenue. I believe that the networking benefits inherent in the online food delivery business will lead to concentration, and that Zomato will be one of the dominant players in the Indian market. In the base case, I estimate that the total market in India for online food delivery will increase to $25 billion (₹2,000 billion) in a decade, with Zomato commanding a 40% market share in steady state, and that Zomato's revenues will converge on 22% of gross order value.

- **Operating margins:** To estimate Zomato's operating margins in steady state, I begin with an assessment of the company's unit economics, looking at how much a typical customer order generates in profits for the company, in figure 10.7.

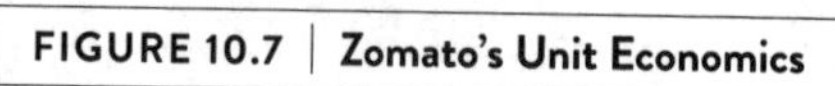
FIGURE 10.7 | Zomato's Unit Economics

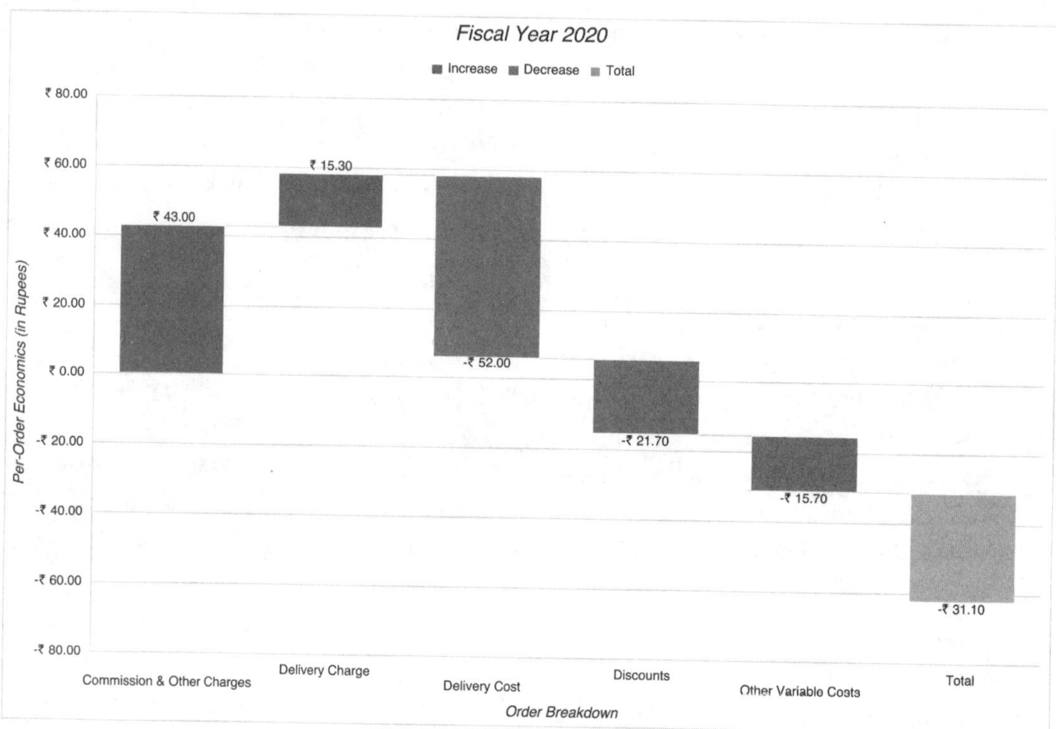

Based upon the numbers supplied for the company, the average order generated ₹20.50 in profits, in 2021, in contrast to the ₹30.50 in losses generated in 2020. As a user-based company, there is more favorable news for Zomato when you look at order volume, based upon how long a user has been using the Zomato platform, in table 10.4.

Table 10.4 • Zomato Platform Usage, by Cohort

	Relative Order Size (to Starting Year)				
Cohort	**2017**	**2018**	**2019**	**2020**	**2021**
FY 2017	1.00	1.60	2.20	3.00	2.90
FY 2018		1.00	2.00	2.70	2.40
FY 2019			1.00	1.60	1.10
FY 2020				1.00	0.70

Note that users who have been on the platform since 2017 spend almost four times as much on Zomato orders as users who joined in 2020. The combination of strong profitability on marginal orders and increased ordering, as users stay on the platform, lead me to believe that Zomato will have a high operating margin when it matures. In the base case, I assume that the pre-tax operating margin for Zomato will trend toward 35% as the company approaches maturity.

- **Reinvestment:** To estimate the reinvestment that Zomato will need to deliver its expected growth, I will assume that the company will remain an intermediary and that its reinvestment will continue to take the form of acquisitions and investments in technology. In the base case, I will assume that the company will be able to deliver ₹5 for every ₹1 of capital invested next year—largely due to the rebound from COVID—and then deliver ₹3 for every ₹1 invested in years two through five, settling at ₹2.5 for every ₹1 invested beyond.
- **Risk:** On the operating risk dimension, Zomato will remain primarily an Indian company, dependent on Indian macroeconomic growth to succeed, and the company's cost of capital should reflect that risk. Zomato is a money-losing company, but it is not a start-up, facing imminent failure risk. On the plus side, its size and access to capital, as well as its post-IPO augmented cash balance, push down the risk of failure. On the minus side, this is a company that is still burning through cash and will need access to capital in future years to continue to survive. In the base case, I will give Zomato a rupee cost of capital of 10.25% in the early years, before adjusting it down to about 9% in steady state, and attach a likelihood of failure of 10% to the company.
- **Loose ends:** Since this valuation of Zomato is for an initial public offering, I augment the cash balance of the company with the expected proceeds of ₹90 billion from the offering. I also adjust the value of equity for outstanding equity options held by management and employees.

With these inputs in place, I value Zomato's equity, for its initial public offering, as shown in figure 10.8.

FIGURE 10.8 | A Valuation of Zomato for Its IPO, July 2021

Zomato	Jul-21

The Story

Zomato will benefit as the Indian food delivery market grows, driven by overall economic growth and more digital access, and it will be one of a few (two or three) players who will dominate the market; there will be a near term COVID bounce-back effect. While Amazon Food remains the wild card, economies of scale will allow the company to generate high operating margins, and the company will continue to reinvest (acquisitions and technology) as it grows. The risk of failure is low, given the company's post-IPO cash balance and access to capital and its operating risk reflects its exposure to Indian country risk.

The Assumptions

	Base Year	Next Year	Years 2–5	Years 6–10	After Year 10	Link to Story
Indian Food Delivery	₹ 225,000	₹ 337,500	30.00%	15.27%	₹ 1,961,979	Indian food market rebounds in 2021 and grows to about $25 billion in year 10
Market Share	42.15%	41.72%	→	40.00%	40.00%	Zomato is one of two or three lead players in Indian food delivery market
Revenues as % of GOV	21.03%	22.00%			22.00%	Revenue share stabilizes at 22%
Revenues (a)	₹ 19,937.89	₹ 30,975	Total Market × Market Share × Revenue as % of GOV		₹ 172,654	COVID rebound in 2021 + growth in food delivery market in India long term
Operating Margin (b)	-24.10%	-10.0%	-10.00% →	35.00%	35.00%	Margins improve as growth wanes
Tax Rate	25.00%		25.00%	25.00%	25.00%	Indian corporate tax rate over time
Reinvestment (c)		5.00	2.50	3.00	35.42%	Acquisitions and technology investments needed to sustain growth
Return on Capital	-7.15%	Marginal ROIC =	127.01%		12.00%	Networking benefits allow for high ROIC, near and long term
Cost of Capital (d)			10.25% →	8.97%	8.97%	Cost of capital reflects Indian country risk

The Cash Flows

	Total Market	Market Share	Revenues	EBIT (1 – t)	Reinvestment	FCFF
1	₹ 337,500	41.72%	₹ 30,974.78	-₹ 3,097.48	₹ 2,207.38	-₹ 5,304.86
2	₹ 438,750	41.29%	₹ 39,852.91	₹ 498.16	₹ 3,551.25	-₹ 3,053.09
3	₹ 570,375	40.86%	₹ 51,270.19	₹ 3,293.45	₹ 4,566.91	-₹ 1,273.46
4	₹ 741,488	40.43%	₹ 65,951.07	₹ 6,182.91	₹ 5,872.35	₹ 310.56
5	₹ 963,934	40.00%	₹ 84,826.17	₹ 11,531.06	₹ 6,291.70	₹ 5,239.36
6	₹ 1,203,471	40.00%	₹ 105,905.47	₹ 16,065.01	₹ 7,026.43	₹ 9,038.57
7	₹ 1,440,555	40.00%	₹ 126,768.85	₹ 26,253.32	₹ 6,954.46	₹ 19,298.86
8	₹ 1,650,156	40.00%	₹ 145,213.72	₹ 38,118.60	₹ 6,148.29	₹ 31,970.31
9	₹ 1,805,271	40.00%	₹ 158,863.81	₹ 41,701.75	₹ 4,550.03	₹ 37,151.72
10	₹ 1,881,995	40.00%	₹ 165,615.52	₹ 43,474.07	₹ 2,250.57	₹ 41,223.50
Terminal Year	₹ 1,961,979	40.00%	₹ 172,654.18	₹ 45,321.72	₹ 16,051.44	₹ 29,270.28

The Value

Terminal Value	₹ 620,133.03		
PV (Terminal Value)	₹ 241,972.24		
PV (CF over Next 10 Years)	₹ 56,739.02		
Value of Operating Assets =	₹ 298,711.25		
Adjustment for Distress	₹ 14,935.56	Probability of failure =	10.00%
– Debt & Minority Interests	₹ 1,591.72		
+ Cash & Other Non-operating Assets	₹ 135,959.70	Includes cash proceeds from IPO of	₹ 90,000
Value of Equity	₹ 418,143.67		
– Value of Equity Options	₹ 73,244.53		
Number of Shares	7,946.68		
Value per Share	**₹ 43.40**	Stock was offered at =	₹ 70.00

With our story of growth and profitability, the value that I derive for Zomato's equity is close to ₹418 billion (about $5.4 billion), translating into a value per share of about ₹43. That may seem like a lot to pay for a money-losing company with less than ₹20 billion in revenues in the most recent year, but promise and potential have value, especially when you have a leader in a market of immense size. That said, the offering price for the IPO was set at ₹72 to ₹76 per share, making it too expensive, at least for me.

Add-ons and Augmentations

When valuing start-ups or very young companies, it is natural to feel overwhelmed by uncertainty, and many consequently give up. While there is no escaping uncertainty, there are two tools that I find useful in dealing with it in healthier ways. The first is to be explicit about how much uncertainty you face with each input and bring these explicit forecasts into play in a Monte Carlo simulation. The second is to recognize that while uncertainty brings with it many downsides, it also brings upsides, using an optionality argument.

Visualizing Uncertainty—Monte Carlo Simulations

In conventional valuation, we are called upon to make point estimates for every variable, no matter how uncertain we feel about them. As a result, we get a valuation based on these point estimates that we know has an error band around it, but we have no way of deriving how wide the band is. There is an approach that not only allows analysts to incorporate the uncertainty that they feel in their forecasts into the analysis but, as output, also delivers a range of values, reflecting that uncertainty. In this approach, called a Monte Carlo simulation, a distribution of values, rather than a point estimate, is generated for each parameter in the valuation (growth, market share, operating margin, beta, etc.). In each simulation, I draw one outcome from each distribution to generate a unique set of cash flows and estimate a value for the company. Across many simulations, I can derive a distribution for the values of investment that will reflect the underlying uncertainty I face in estimating the inputs to the valuation. In short, the more uncertainty I feel about the inputs, the greater the spread in the estimated values that emerge from the simulation. The steps associated with running a simulation are as follows:

1. **Determine "probabilistic" variables:** In any analysis, there are potentially dozens of inputs, some of which are predictable and some of which are not. At least in theory, I can define probability distributions for each input in a valuation. The reality, though, is that this will be time-consuming and may not provide much of a payoff, especially for inputs that have only marginal impact on value. Consequently, it makes sense to focus attention on a few variables that have a significant impact on value. In the case of Zomato, I will focus on the Indian food delivery market size, Zomato's market share, and operating margins as the inputs that most determine value.

2. **Define probability distributions for these variables:** This is key and is the most difficult step in the analysis. Generically, to arrive at these probability distributions, you can use a mix of historical data (for variables like inflation that have a long history and reliable data), cross-sectional data (for variables like operating margins, where the numbers can look very different for different companies in a business at a given point in time), and statistical distributions (based upon what we know about the distributions of variables). The probability distributions will be discrete for some inputs and continuous for others, based upon historical data for some and statistical distributions for others.
3. **Check for correlation across variables:** When there is strong correlation, positive or negative, across inputs, you have two choices. One is to pick only one of the two inputs to vary; it makes sense to focus on the input that has the bigger impact on value. The other is to build the correlation explicitly into the simulation; this requires more sophisticated simulation packages and adds more detail to the estimation process.
4. **Run the simulation:** For the first simulation, you draw one outcome from each distribution and compute the value based upon those outcomes. This process can be repeated as many times as desired, though the marginal contribution of each simulation drops off as the number of simulations increases. Most simulation packages allow users to run thousands of simulations, with little or no cost attached to increasing that number. Given that reality, it is better to err on the side of too many simulations rather than too few.

There have generally been two impediments to good simulations. The first is informational: estimating distributions of values for each input into a valuation is difficult to do. In other words, it is far easier to estimate an expected growth rate of 8% in revenues for the next five years than it is to specify the distribution of expected growth rates—type of distribution, parameters of that distribution—for revenues. The second impediment is computational: until the advent of personal computers, simulations tended to be too time and resource intensive for the typical analyst. Both these constraints have eased in recent years, and simulations have become more feasible.

CASE STUDY—PART 2: A MONTE CARLO SIMULATION OF ZOMATO

In our base-case valuation of Zomato, I make big assumptions about market size and profitability in estimating value, and I am sure to be wrong on all of them, though I do not know in which direction. To run a simulation, I will focus on three of our most critical assumptions in the Zomato valuation:

- **Total market size:** A major driver of Zomato's value is the expected evolution of the Indian food delivery market. While I projected the market to increase to about $25 billion (₹2 trillion) in our base case, that is based upon assumptions about economic growth and digital reach in India that could be wrong. In the simulation, I allow for a market size of between $10 billion (about ₹750 to ₹800 billion) to $40 billion (₹3 trillion to ₹3.2 trillion).
- **Market share:** In the base case, I assume that Zomato's share of the market will stabilize around 40% by year five, premised on the belief that this will be a market with two or three big players and a multitude of niche businesses. Given the regional diversity of the Indian market, it is possible that there may be more players in the market in steady state, resulting in a market share for Zomato as low as 20%, or that the niche players will get pushed out because of economies of scale, yielding a higher market share (up to 50%).
- **Operating margin:** The operating margin of 35% that I predicted in our base case for Zomato is built on the presumption that the status quo will prevail and that the delivery companies will continue to see economies of scale while holding their slice of order value stable. If one of the players decides to aggressively go for higher market share (by offering discounts or bidding more for delivery personnel), operating margins will trend lower (15% is the low end). If, on the other hand, Zomato can keep its advertising business intact as it moves forward, it could deliver a higher margin (45% is the upper limit).

The results of the simulations that I ran with distributions replacing point estimates for market size, market share, and operating margin are shown in figure 10.9.

FIGURE 10.9 | Zomato IPO Valuation—A Simulation

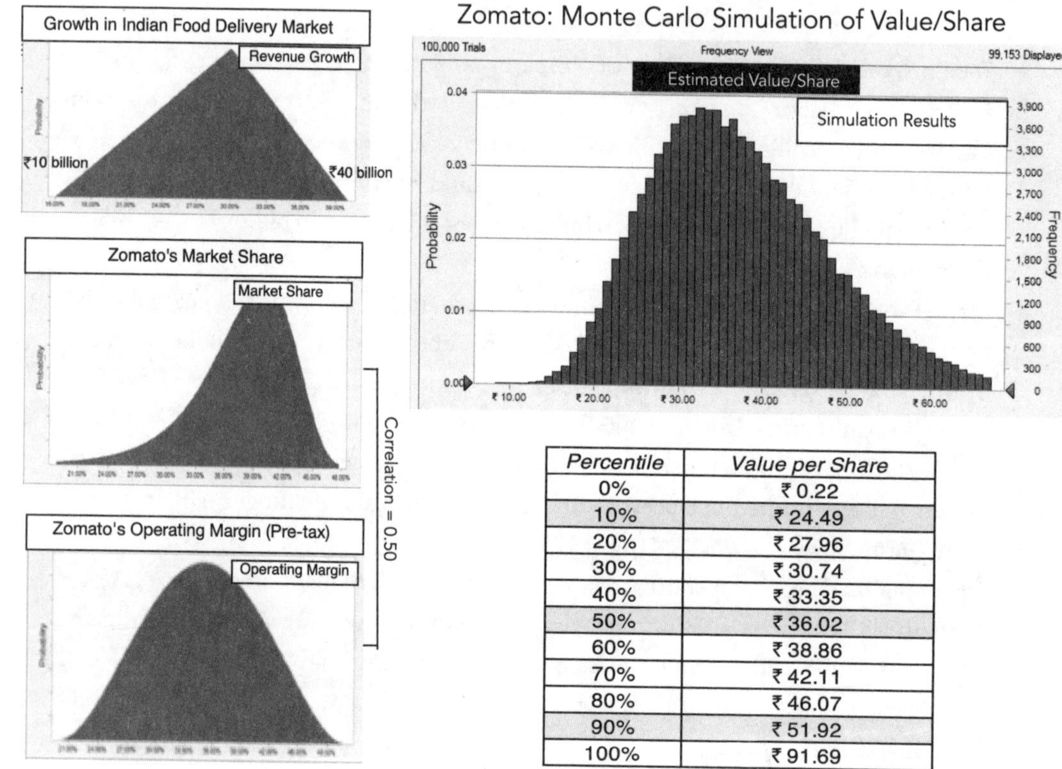

Percentile	*Value per Share*
0%	₹0.22
10%	₹24.49
20%	₹27.96
30%	₹30.74
40%	₹33.35
50%	₹36.02
60%	₹38.86
70%	₹42.11
80%	₹46.07
90%	₹51.92
100%	₹91.69

Note that the uncertainties that I face in the inputs translate into a distribution of values for Zomato, with a median value per share of ₹36.02 but a wide range of potential values (from zero to ₹91.69). It is hubris to dismiss those who invested in Zomato at ₹72 per share or higher as speculators or ill-informed, since there are plausible stories that get you to values higher than that price.

Optionality

There is a potential upside to the uncertainty that you face when valuing young businesses, and that comes from the possibility that if the stars align, and the products offered by the business find wider acceptance than expected, it can use that success to enter new businesses that do not seem viable today or are not even in consideration. This "optionality" will add a premium to the value that you estimate for the business, and that premium will increase as uncertainty becomes more rampant.

This optionality argument is not new; it was used during the 1990s, at the peak of the dot-com boom, to explain why the high prices that investors were paying for dot-com companies were justifiable, even though the fundamentals did not support them. In hindsight, many of those arguments were overwrought because, other than a few exceptions (like Amazon), most of these dot-com companies never saw the upside of risk. While the optionality argument lay dormant for a few years, it has been resuscitated in the last decade at platform companies, i.e., companies with millions or tens of millions of users or subscribers on their platforms. At these companies, the argument that is made is that while users or subscribers may be difficult to monetize and are generating only small revenues, platform companies should be able find ways to use them to enter other businesses.

There is some truth to the argument, but its weight rests not just on the number of users or subscribers on the platform but also on how loyal they are to the platform and how intense their usage is (with higher loyalty and more intense usage increasing optionality). It also depends on whether the platform company is accumulating data on its users that can be used as a competitive advantage when entering other businesses, with more data that is more exclusive to the company creating more value than data that others have access to. Thus, location data, now widely tracked by dozens of companies on your phone or other device, is less valuable than usage data that only the platform company has access to.

CASE STUDY—PART 3: OPTIONALITY AND BIG MARKET ARGUMENTS FOR ZOMATO

As a company with millions of users on its platform, if Zomato can deliver other products and services to its users, it can augment its earnings and value. This is the "optionality" that I introduced in the last section, but in Zomato's case, I would offer some caveats.

- First, as I noted in the lead-in, platforms with more intense users and more proprietary data have more value than platforms where users are transitory and there is little exclusive data being collected. Zomato's platform has the benefit of large numbers, but it falls short on both intensity and proprietary data; Zomato app users are on the system only when they order food, and their engagement is often restricted to food ordering and delivery. If Zomato plans to expand its offerings to its platform users, it is very likely that these add-on businesses will be food related—perhaps extending into grocery shopping, for example—creating some option value.
- Second, even if you believe that there is optionality in a business, attaching a numerical value to that option is one of the most difficult tasks in investment. While there

are option pricing models that can be adapted to do the valuation, getting the inputs for these models, especially before the optionality takes form, is difficult to do.

In short, if I were tempted to pay a premium over the intrinsic valuation (₹43) that I estimated for Zomato earlier, to reflect its large user base and optionality, that premium should be small, given user characteristics.

Pricing

In chapter 9, I noted that to price an asset, you look at what assets similar to it are being priced at in the market. That statement applies to young companies, but as I will show in the section to follow, there are challenges that you will face at each pricing step.

THE CHALLENGES

There are three steps to pricing a private business or publicly traded company. The first is to standardize the pricing to a common metric, with revenues, earnings, cash flow, and book value as choices. The second is to find a peer group of businesses or companies just like yours, with the "just like" left to the tender mercies of analysts. The third is to control for differences between the company you are trying to value and its peer group.

1. **Standardized price:** For a metric to be used as a scalar, it has to have a positive value, at the minimum, and ideally should have a close connection to business value. That requirement crimps your choices when pricing young companies. With pre-revenue start-ups, there are no financial metrics that can be used as scalars, since revenues are zero and all earnings numbers (from EBITDA down to net income) are negative. With companies that are further along in the life cycle and have tangible revenues, but are still losing money, the only scalar that can be used is revenues. For companies that have started making money, but are just at the beginning of the transition, there will be profits, but those profits will have little or no connection with value.
2. **Peer group assembly:** For a peer group for pricing, you first need to find businesses that are like the business that you are valuing, *and* those businesses need to be priced. With start-ups and very young businesses, almost all of the peer-group businesses can be privately owned, and the pricing information on these businesses will reflect their most recent venture capital rounds (which can be both dated and misleading). Even as these companies advance in the life cycle and become publicly traded, defining them narrowly can make it difficult to find peer groups. As an example, if you

consider Uber to be a ride-sharing company, and restrict your peer group to include only other ride-sharing companies, you would have had a sample size of two (with Lyft being the other listed company) in 2019.

3. **Controlling for differences:** Assuming that you can find a scalar for pricing and are able to assemble a peer group of businesses like yours that are priced, you will still have to determine what it is that investors are looking at when setting prices, and then figure out how to control for differences in those determinants.

In short, pricing young companies poses far more challenges than pricing more mature businesses, and many of them parallel issues that I brought up in the context of valuing young companies.

THE RESPONSES

To price start-ups and young companies, you must be pragmatic in accepting compromises that you might reject with more mature companies. I will classify some of those pragmatic choices using the same sequence that I used to present challenges:

1. **Standardized price:** As I noted in the last section, with pre-revenue or very young companies, there is nothing in the financials of the companies that can be used as a scalar. One alternative is to use an operating metric that you can observe at the business that you believe will provide you with the pathway to revenues and profitability. It was this reasoning that led analysts, in the 1990s, to scale the market capitalizations of dot-com companies to the number of website visitors that they received; more recently, it has also led to a proliferation of pricings that use subscribers, members, or users as scalars. Another alternative is to forecast the financials of a business and use the forecasted values for a key metric like revenues or earnings in the future as your scalar. This is the basis for forward multiples, where the price you pay today is scaled to what you think a company's revenues or earnings will be in the future. What you gain by forecasting is that small revenues become bigger, and losses become profits, allowing for more meaningful scaling and pricing.
2. **Peer group assembly:** If you are pricing a start-up that is still privately owned, and all of its peer group is also privately owned, you often have no choice but to stick with the flawed and frequently stale pricing from recent venture capital rounds at the peer group. That said, not all VC pricing should be weighted equally when making comparisons, with more recent rounds getting more weight than earlier rounds, larger rounds being considered more reliable than smaller rounds, and investments by VCs

with better track records outweighing investments by VCs with questionable or no records. Once a start-up is publicly traded, I would recommend defining its business broadly and loosening the criteria for "similar" firms to get more companies in the peer group, even if it means bringing in companies from other markets or sectors.

3. **Controlling for differences:** In any pricing, you should be controlling for differences in growth, profitability, and investment efficiency, and young companies are no exception. The problem is that outside of revenue growth, young businesses have profit margins and reinvestment measures that are unreliable and shifting. If your intent is to find out what the market is pricing into young businesses, you can use statistical tools to eke out correlations between market prices and observable variables. Thus, in 2013, when social media companies were first listed in the US equity markets, the variable that best explained differences in their market capitalizations was the number of users at these companies.

In a clear illustration of how everything is relative, pricing is more difficult at young companies than at more mature ones, but valuation is even *more* so, and seems like more work. Given a choice, is it any surprise that most investors only price young companies, not value them? To the extent that this pricing is shallow, with meaningless scalars and few controls for differences across firms on business models and eventual success, you will see large pricing errors across companies in a sector.

CASE STUDY—PART 4: PRICING ZOMATO, A YOUNG COMPANY

Zomato is a pioneer, in India, in the online food delivery business, and the first Indian company in the space to go public. You can see the challenges in pricing Zomato with a quick scan of the numbers. As a company with small revenues and big operating losses, the only scalars from the financials of the company that work in standardizing pricing are revenues and gross profits. I could also divide the market value by the number of platform users to get a value per user. In table 10.5, I estimate these multiples for Zomato and compare the results with the numbers that I estimated for DoorDash, a US-based online food delivery business that was closer to turning the corner in 2020.

Table 10.5 • Zomato versus DoorDash—Pricing

	DoorDash (2020)	DoorDash (2030 Forecast)	Zomato (2020)	Zomato (2030 Forecast)
Market Capitalization (US $ Mil)	$57,860		$8,600	
Enterprise Value (US $ Mil)	$53,640		$7,500	
Gross Bookings (US $ Mil)	$18,897	$72,072	$1,264	$10,038
Revenues (US $ Mil)	$3,601	$9,009	$266	$2,208
Gross Income (US $ Mil)	$1,864	$4,955	$140	$1,325
EBIT (US $ Mil)	-$412	$1,802	-$64	$773
Platform Users (in Millions)	20	50	40	200
	Current	Forward	Current	Forward
EV/GOV	2.84	0.74	5.93	0.75
EV/Revenues	14.90	5.95	28.20	3.40
EV/Gross Income	28.78	10.83	53.57	5.66
EV/User	2682.00	1072.80	187.50	37.50

If you are operating on the assumption that intrinsic valuation is subjective and pricing is not, this table should dispense with your delusions. You could make the argument that Zomato was overpriced in 2020, relative to DoorDash, by scaling the pricing to gross income, revenues, or GOV, but on a per-user basis, Zomato is much cheaper.

To get past the growing-pains effects on pricing, I estimated key numbers (from GOV to revenues to gross income to users) in ten years (2030) and scaled the market capitalization today to that value, creating forward multiples. With those numbers, Zomato looks to be fairly valued on a GOV scalar, undervalued relative to both revenues and gross income, and a massive bargain on a per-user basis.

The reason that I have only one firm in our peer group for the comparison is because DoorDash was the only publicly traded online food delivery business in 2021. Since our pricing will become better with more companies in the mix, there are two ways we can increase the peer group size. The first is to bring in non-traded food delivery businesses from around the world and evaluate how they are being priced by venture capitalists: relative to GOV, revenues, or gross income; right now or with forward estimates. The second is to expand the peer group beyond online food delivery companies to other tech-based intermediary companies, allowing us to bring Uber, Lyft, and Airbnb into the comparison.

Conclusion

The refrain from investors and traders who are required or forced to value or price start-ups and young companies is that there is too much uncertainty, and many simply give up on them (by removing them from their investment universes). In this chapter, I looked at the challenges in valuing young companies, including limited history, uninformative financials, and business models that are still in process. After dispensing with the VC approach to dealing with this problem, where a key metric such as revenues or earnings is forecast out to an arbitrary future date and then converted into a pricing, I adapted the intrinsic valuation approach around a story and used that story to extract valuation inputs and company values.

When pricing young companies, where many of the most widely used scalars in pricing (revenues, earnings, book value) are either negative or uninformative, I examined alternative scalars, including revenue drivers (like numbers of users or subscribers), and forward estimates of revenues and earnings. Finally, as much as it is tempting to define peer groups narrowly, as companies that operate in the same business and market, I noted that I will price young companies better if instead I am more expansive in what I include in these peer groups and control for differences more carefully.

11

Valuation and Pricing: High-Growth Companies

IN CHAPTER 10, I wrestled with the challenges that you face when valuing start-ups and young-growth companies and presented ways in which these companies can still be valued and priced. For the subset of these companies that make it through the travails that young companies face and emerge with functioning business models that deliver not only growing revenues but also profits, valuation does become a little simpler, with financial statements conveying more valuable information about the quality of the business model and history providing clues to its riskiness. In this chapter, I will examine these high-growth companies and look at the issues that are most likely to rise in valuing and pricing them, before presenting solutions.

The High-Growth Phase of the Corporate Life Cycle

To understand the challenges that you face when valuing high companies, it helps to begin by looking at how the operating metrics of the company shift as it moves from being a pre-revenue idea company to a start-up to a nascent business, before becoming a high-growth company. In figure 11.1, I chart out the revenues, earnings, and free cash flows through these stages of the life cycle.

FIGURE 11.1 | Operating Metrics in Early Stages of the Life Cycle

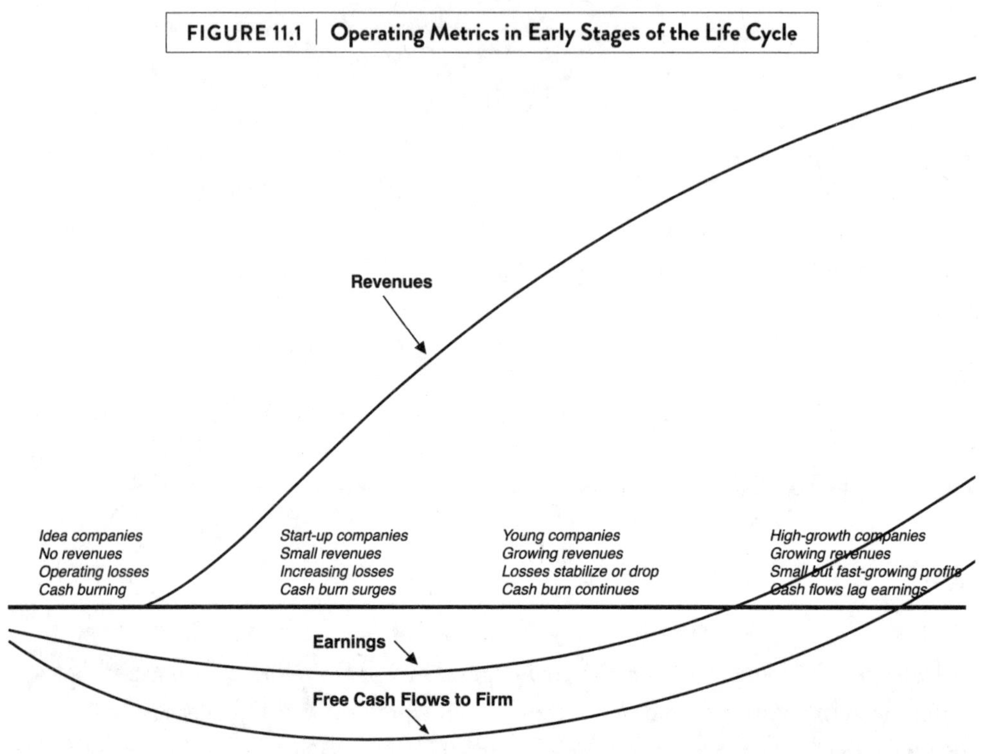

While this is a generalization, and there are numerous exceptions, start-ups and idea companies almost always have no or negligible revenues; they generate operating losses and burn through cash quickly. As their business models materialize, revenues will surge and losses will narrow, but the cash burn will continue as these businesses reinvest for future growth. High-growth companies, the focus of this chapter, have found, at least for the moment, business models that work, and with an assist from economies of scale and tweaks to these models, they can finally turn the profit corner, though the profits will be paltry early on. Since growth ambitions persist in these companies, and reinvestment is needed for that growth, it will take longer for free cash flows to turn positive.

It is easy to see why high-growth companies attract a subset of investors drawn not only by their proof of profitability but by dreams about how profits will surge as the company continues to scale up. Taking advantage of this demand, this is also the time when many of these businesses will choose to enter public markets, and if they are lucky, they will be assigned market values that seem disproportionately large, given their current fundamentals—especially when compared to their mature counterparts. For some investors, especially those in the old-time school of value investing, this is viewed as a sign of overpricing, but as I will show in the pricing section, that is too facile a conclusion to reach. A sensible assessment will require more attention to differences across companies, especially in growth and risk.

Valuation of High-Growth Companies

In the last chapter, on valuing start-ups and young companies, I noted the challenges that arise from not having historical data on performance or risk and from concerns that these companies may never develop working business models. With high-growth companies, I start with a better foundation, since there is more historical data on these businesses and working business models. That does not mean that high-growth companies are easy to value, though, because there are challenges that are, if not specific to these companies, certainly more frequently found among them.

Challenges

Assume that you are valuing a high-growth company—one that has finally unlocked its profitability door while continuing to grow its revenues at high rates. That company usually has been around for more than a year or two, and with the financials in hand, you begin your valuation. Here are some challenges that you will face:

1. **Scaling effects:** It makes sense to look at historical growth rates in revenues for any company, including a high-growth company, but you should be cautious about using those growth rates as predictors for the future, simply because percentage growth rates reflect the base on which growth occurs just as much as the growth potential of the business. To illustrate our point, let's look at Tesla's revenues and revenue growth rate over the last decade, in figure 11.2.

FIGURE 11.2 | Tesla Revenue and Revenue Growth Rate, 2011 to 2020

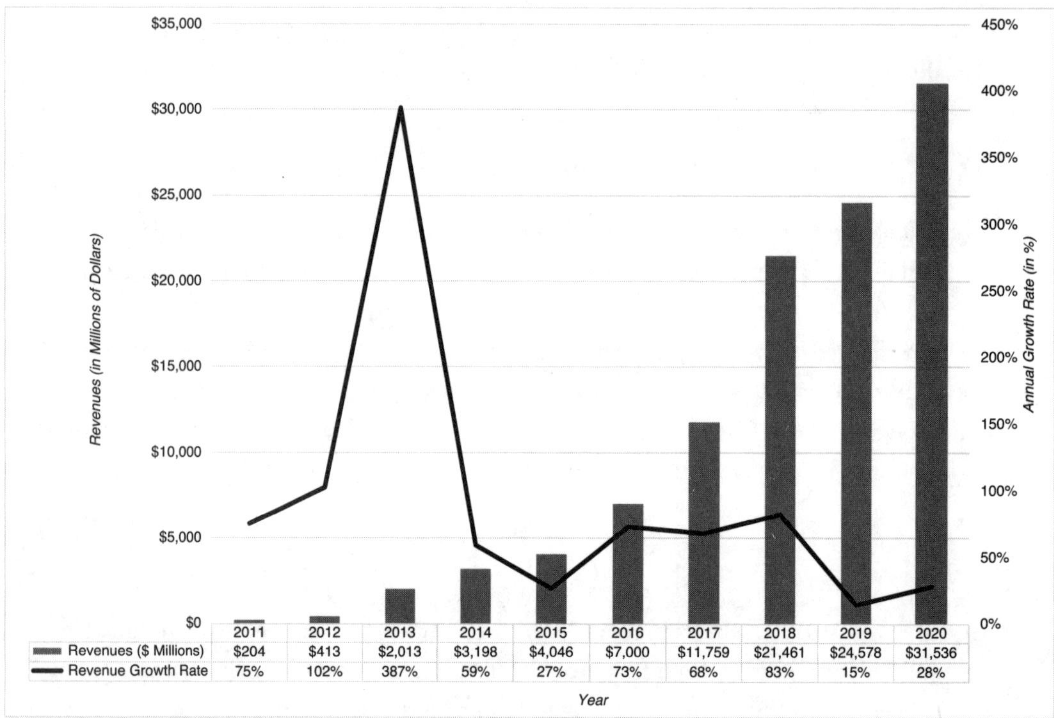

There is no denying that Tesla has had an amazing ten years of growth, posting a compounded annual growth rate over the period. That said, though, the reason the growth rate is astronomically high is because Tesla had only $204 million in revenues in 2011, and doubling or even tripling those revenues was clearly in the cards. In 2020, Tesla's revenues were $31,536 million, and even the biggest optimists on the company would be hard-pressed to explain how the company could double those revenues.

2. **Shifting financials:** One feature shared by growth companies is that the numbers in their financial statements are in a state of flux. Not only can the numbers for the latest year be very different from numbers in the prior year, they can change dramatically even over shorter time periods. For many smaller, high-growth firms, for instance, the revenues and earnings from the most recent four quarters can be dramatically different from the revenues and earnings in the most recent fiscal year (which may have ended only a few months ago). As a consequence, when valuing

these companies, you must try to get the most updated numbers that you can. Using the last annual report, for instance, when that annual report is six, nine, or twelve months old, can give you a skewed estimate of value.

3. **Questions about earnings:** With growth firms, existing assets tend to be a small part of overall value and can easily be swamped by what a firm expends to sustain and nurture its growth assets. Consider, for instance, the standard assumption that I make in discounted cash flow valuation that the existing operating income can be attributed to existing assets and thus be the basis for valuing those assets. With any company, the existing operating income (or loss) will be reached after selling, advertising, and other administrative expenses. While I assume that these expenses are associated with existing assets, that assumption may not hold up in a growth company. After all, the sales force in a growth company may be less interested in pushing existing products and more focused on cultivating a customer base for future products. By treating all sales expenses as operating expenses, I am understating earnings and, consequently, the value of existing assets.
4. **Private to public investors:** While most start-ups and very young companies are privately owned (by founders and venture capitalists), high-growth companies are far more likely to have made the transition to being publicly traded, and this helps in valuation on many dimensions. First, for some analysts, whose only pathway to estimating risk is to use past stock prices, it gives them a way of estimating a relative risk measure (beta) that they can use in valuation. Second, when you are done with your valuation of a high-growth company that is publicly traded, you have the luxury of comparing your valuation to the company's market price, to at least make sure that your valuation does not contain fatal errors. Third, having a market price for shares makes it easier to tie up loose ends in valuation, including valuing employee options (which need price and volatility as inputs).

   That said, there are valuation issues that can arise from having a market price for a high-growth company.

   - The stock prices for high-growth companies are often driven more by trading forces, such as mood and momentum, than by fundamentals. Using those stock prices as the basis for risk measures or estimating option value can be dangerous.
   - Much as I would like to preserve the myth that intrinsic valuation is an exercise where the market price never intrudes, the reality is that once you value a high-growth company and come out with a value that is very different from

the price, there will be the temptation to "play" with the inputs until the value converges on or at least gets closer to the price.

- Finally, when high-growth companies go public, the founder and venture capitalists who owned the companies prior to the IPO often stay on as investors and sometimes hold controlling stakes. That is accomplished either by offering only a small percentage of the shares to public markets, or by offering shares with lower or no voting rights to the public, while founders and insiders hold the higher-voting-rights shares.

In short, having public-market investors and market prices available for high-growth companies can help when valuing these companies but can also lead us to more biased and skewed valuations.

5. **Size disconnect:** The contrast I drew earlier in the book between accounting and financial balance sheets, with the former focused primarily on existing investments and the latter incorporating growth assets into the mix, is stark in growth companies. The market values of these companies, if they are publicly traded, are often much higher than the accounting (or book) values, because the former incorporate the value of growth assets and the latter often do not. In addition, the market values can seem discordant with the firm's operating numbers (revenues and earnings). Many growth firms that have market values in the hundreds of millions or even billions can have small revenues and negative earnings. Again, the reason lies in the fact that the operating numbers reflect the firm's existing investments, and these investments may represent a very small portion of the firm's overall value.

As you can see in figure 11.3, the shared characteristics of growth firms—including dynamic financials, a mix of public and private equity, disconnects between market value and operating data, a dependence on equity funding, and a short and volatile market history—have consequences for both intrinsic and relative valuations.

FIGURE 11.3 | Valuation Challenges—Growth Companies

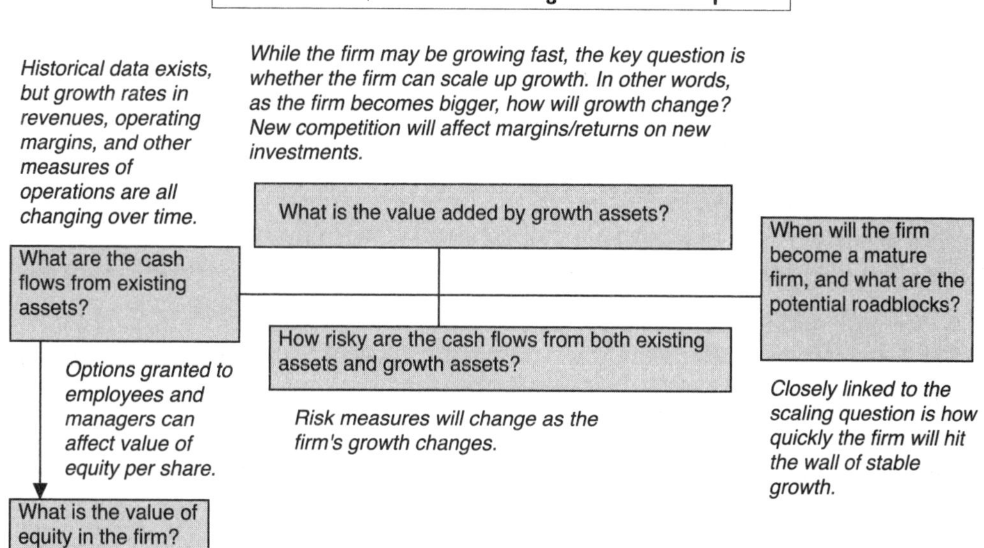

Responses

If a company's intrinsic value comes from its cash flows and risk characteristics, you will run into problems while valuing high-growth companies that can be traced back to where they are in the life cycle. In this section, I will present ways of dealing with the challenges, using the five-step process that I developed for start-ups and young-growth companies, but tweaking it to reflect the special characteristics of a high-growth company.

STEP 1: TELL A STORY

When telling business stories about start-ups and young companies, I crafted the story around potential—potential market for the proposed products or services that these companies were offering, potential management skills of its founders, and potential access to capital—and not around historical data. That was because there is little historical data available, and the data that is available is not informative. With high-growth companies, when spinning a business narrative, the focus will still stay on potential, but more weight must be given to the financial history of the company and its corporate governance structure. In some cases, this record can make you more enthusiastic about the company's prospects (revenue growth and profitability), and in others, it can lead you to scale back your story.

STEP 2: RUN THE 3P TEST (POSSIBLE? PLAUSIBLE? PROBABLE?)

While the outlines of the 3P tests do not change for high-growth companies, you can make your judgments with more information than you did when these companies were start-ups.

- On revenues, the biggest questions arise as you make assumptions that revenues can be scaled up. While management and founders can be unrestrained in their forecasts of the future, you need to bring in skepticism about whether these forecasts are pipe dreams (making them impossible) or too much of a reach (plausible, but not probable). To make this assessment, you can look at market size and at what you are giving your company as market share, given your growth assumptions and potential competition, and in making this assessment, you can look at the company's past.
- On operating profit margins, the positive trend lines in profitability at high-growth companies can lead to excessive optimism about operating profit margins. In the last decade, for instance, every high-growth company, no matter what sector it operated in, wore the mantle of a tech company, hoping to earn the 30% or 40% operating margins that tech companies earn.
- On reinvestment, assessing whether a company is reinvesting enough to deliver its expected growth can be difficult, since historical reinvestment is likely to be volatile and obscured by investments and acquisitions that are paid for with the company's stock. To evaluate the plausibility of reinvestment assumptions, you have to define reinvestment to include acquisitions and miscategorized operating expenses (like R&D), and keep track of invested capital as the company grows.

STEP 3: CONVERT THE VALUATION STORY INTO VALUATION MODEL INPUTS

Once you have a valuation story for a high-growth company that you have passed through the 3P test, the next step involves converting the story into valuation inputs:

a. **Revenue growth rate:** The biggest issue, and one I have emphasized in this chapter, is the scaling factor. Blindly using past growth rate as the growth rate assumption for the future is a recipe for overvaluation. Revenue growth rates will decrease as companies get larger—and every growth company will get larger, over time, if your forecasts of growth come to fruition. In a test of how growth changes as firms get larger, one study examined the revenue growth rate for high-growth firms, relative to growth rate in revenues for the sector in which they operate, in the immediate aftermath of their initial public offerings.* The results are shown in figure 11.4.

FIGURE 11.4 | Revenue Growth after Going Public

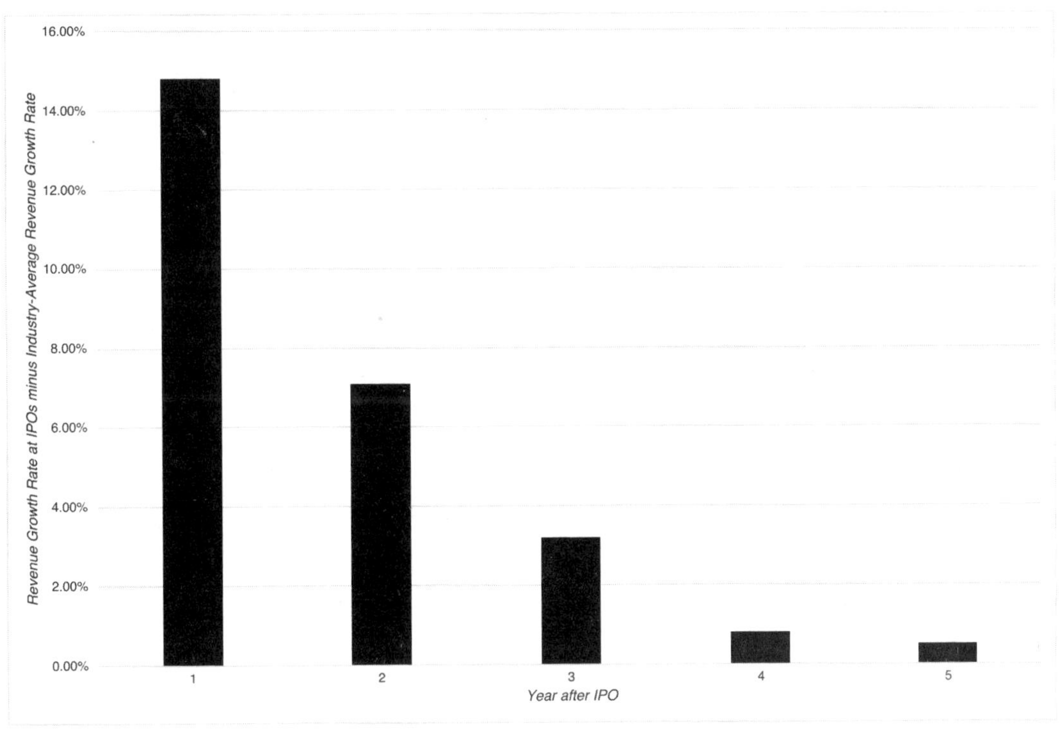

Source: Andrew Metrick

When they go public, firms have growth rates that are much higher than the industry average. Note how quickly the revenue growth at these high-growth firms moves toward the industry average: they go from a 15% higher (than the industry average) revenue growth one year after the IPO to 7% higher in year two to 1% higher in year four to the industry average in year five. I am not saying that this will happen at every high-growth firm; however, the aggregate evidence suggests that growth firms that can maintain high growth rates for extended periods are the exception rather than the rule. The question of how quickly revenue growth rates will decline at a given company can generally be addressed by looking at the company's specifics. These include the size of

* A. Metrick, *Venture Capital and the Finance of Innovation* (New York: John Wiley & Sons, 2006).

the overall market for the company's products and services, the strength of the competition, and the quality of its products and management. Companies in larger markets with less aggressive competition (or protection from competition) and with better management can maintain high revenue growth rates for longer periods. I can use a few tools to assess whether the assumptions I am making about revenue growth rates in the future for an individual company are reasonable:

- **Absolute revenue changes:** One simple test is to compute the absolute change in revenues for each period rather than to trust the percentage growth rate. Even experienced analysts often underestimate the compounding effect of growth and how much revenues can balloon over time with high growth rates. Computing the absolute change in revenues, given a growth rate in revenues, can be a sobering antidote to irrational exuberance when it comes to growth.
- **History:** Looking at past revenue growth rates, by year, for the firm in question should give us a sense of how growth rates have changed as the company size changed in the past. For those who are mathematically inclined, clues in the relationship can be used to forecast future growth.
- **Sector data:** The final tool is to look at revenue growth rates of more mature firms in the business, to get a sense of what a reasonable growth rate will be as the firm becomes larger.

In summary, expected revenue growth rates tend to drop over time for all growth companies but the pace of the drop-off will vary across companies.

b. Profitability: To get from revenues to operating income, I need operating margins over time. The easiest and most convenient scenario is one in which the current margins of the firm being valued are sustainable and can be used as the expected margins over time. In fact, if this is the case, I can dispense with forecasting revenue growth and instead focus on operating income growth, since the two are equivalent. In most growth firms, though, it is likely that the current margin will change over time. Let's start with the most likely case, which is that the current margin is either negative or too low relative to the sustainable long-term margin. This can happen for three reasons. One is that the firm has up-front, fixed costs that must be incurred in the initial phases of growth, with the payoff in terms of revenue and growth coming in later periods. This is often the case with infrastructure companies such as energy, telecommunications, and cable TV. The second reason is the mingling of expenses incurred to generate growth with operating expenses. I noted earlier that selling expenses at growth firms are often directed toward future growth rather than current sales but are included with other operating expenses. As the firm matures, this problem will get smaller, leading to higher margins and profits. The third reason is that there might be a lag between expenses being incurred and revenues being generated. If the expenses incurred this year are directed toward much higher revenues in three years, earnings and margins will be low today. The other possible scenario, where the current margin is too high and will decrease over time, is less likely, but it can occur, especially with growth companies that have a niche product in a small market. In fact, the market may be too small to attract the attention of larger, better-capitalized competitors, thus allowing the firms to operate under the radar for the moment, charging high prices to a captive market. As the firm grows, though, this will change, and margins will decrease. In other cases, the high margins may come from owning a patent or other legal protection against competitors, and as this protection lapses, margins will decrease.

In both scenarios—low margins converging on a higher value or high margins dropping to more sustainable levels—you must make judgment calls on what the target margin should be and how the current margin will change over time toward this target. The answer to the first question usually can be found by looking at both the average operating margin for the industry in which the firm operates and the margins commanded by larger, more stable firms in that industry. The answer to the second question depends on the reason for the divergence between the current and target margins. With infrastructure companies, for instance, it reflects how long it will take their investment to be operational and capacity to be fully utilized.

c. **Reinvestment:** As I noted earlier in this chapter, it is dangerous to base reinvestment assumptions on a growth company's history of reinvestment. In other words, taking the net capital expenditures and working capital changes from the most recent year and assuming that these items will grow at the same rate as revenues can result in reinvestment numbers that are both unrealistic and inconsistent with our assumptions about growth. Since high-growth firms tend to have changing margins, I will adopt the same road map I used for young-growth companies, where I estimated reinvestment based on the change in revenues and the sales-to-capital ratio:

$$\text{Reinvestment}_t = \text{Change in Revenues}_t \,/\, (\text{Sales/Capital})$$

The sales-to-capital ratio can be estimated using the company's data (which is more stable than the net capital expenditure or working capital numbers) and the sector averages. You can build lags between the reinvestment and revenue change into the computation by using revenues in a future period to estimate reinvestment in the current one. Growth firms that have already invested in capacity for future years are in the unusual position of being able to grow with little or no reinvestment for the near term. For these firms, you can forecast capacity usage to determine how long the investment pause will last and when the firm will have to reinvest. During the investment pause, reinvestment can be minimal or even zero, accompanied by healthy growth in revenues and operating income.

d. Risk profile: The components of the cost of capital—the beta(s) and the cost of equity, the cost of debt, and the debt ratio—are the same for a growth company as they are for a mature company. However, what sets growth companies apart is that their risk profiles shift over time. The key to maintaining balance in growth-company valuations is to adjust the discount rates over time to keep them consistent with the growth and margin assumptions that I make in each period. Here are two general rules:

- Growth firms should have high costs for equity and debt when revenue growth is highest, but the costs of debt and equity should decline as revenue growth moderates and margins improve.
- As earnings improve and growth drops, another phenomenon comes into play: the firm generates more cash flows than it needs, which it can use to both pay dividends and service debt financing. Firms are not required to use this debt capacity, and some of them do not, but the tax advantages of debt lead some firms to borrow, causing debt ratios to increase over time.

In summary, the cost of capital for a growth company should almost never be a number that remains unchanged over the entire time horizon. Instead, it should be a year-specific number that keeps pace with the rest of the changes you forecast at the firm. In terms of estimating risk parameters (betas), you should steer as far away as you can from using the limited price data that is available on growth companies; the standard errors on the estimates are likely to be huge. Instead, you should use estimates of betas obtained by looking at other publicly traded firms that share the same risk, growth, and cash flow characteristics as the firm being valued. If the case for using these bottom-up betas (industry average as opposed to a regression beta) is strong with any firm, it is even stronger with growth firms.

e. Stable growth: The assumptions you make about terminal value loom large with a growth company, because it comprises a much larger portion of the firm's current value than is the case with a mature firm. When will a high-growth firm become a mature, stable-growth firm? While you have a little more information than you did with young companies, making this assessment is difficult. It's akin to looking at a teenager and wondering what he or she will look like or be doing in middle age. Although no two firms are alike, the following general propositions hold.

- *Do not wait too long to put a firm into stable growth.* As I noted in the section on the dark side of valuing growth companies, analysts often allow for very long growth periods for growth firms and justify this assumption by pointing to past growth. But both scale and competition conspire to lower growth rates quickly at even the most promising growth companies. Growth periods that exceed ten years, especially when accompanied by high growth rates over these periods, are difficult to defend, because only a few companies have been able to accomplish this over time. Valuing your company as the exception, well before it has established itself, is not a good practice.
- *When you put a firm into stable growth, give it the characteristics of a stable growth firm.* In keeping with the emphasis on preserving internal consistency, in calculating terminal value, you should change the company's characteristics to reflect stable growth. With discount rates, as noted in the preceding section, this takes the form of using lower costs of debt and equity and a higher debt ratio. With reinvestment, the key assumption is the return on capital that I assume for the stable-growth phase. While some analysts believe that the return on capital should be set equal to the cost of capital in stable growth, you should preserve some company-specific flexibility. In general, the difference between return on capital and cost of capital should narrow during stable growth to a sustainable level (less than 4% or 5%).

STEP 4: VALUE THE BUSINESS

The nature of cash flows at growth companies—low or negative, in the early years, and higher later—will ensure that the terminal value is a high proportion of value, accounting for 80%, 90%, or even more than 100% of value. As I noted in chapter 10, the more-than-100% scenario will unfold when a growth company has high growth and high reinvestment needs, leading to negative cash flows for an extended part of the forecast period. Some analysts use this fact as ammunition against using discounted cash flow valuations, suggesting that assumptions about the high-growth phase will be drowned out by terminal value assumptions. This is not true. The base-year value for the terminal value calculation (earnings and cash flows in year 5 or 10) is a function of the assumptions during the high-growth phase. Changing these assumptions will have dramatic effects (as it should) on value.

STEP 5: KEEP THE FEEDBACK LOOP OPEN

In addition to keeping the process open for disagreement, as I did with start-ups and young-growth companies, there is an additional component to the feedback loop for high-growth companies that are publicly traded, and that is the market's judgment on what these companies are worth. When you estimate a value for a high-growth company that is very different from the market price, in either direction, it should be natural that you pause and consider why. The options are simple:

- **You are wrong:** The difference between price and value may be because your estimates of inputs, including revenue growth, margins, and reinvestment are wrong, and the market consensus is right.
- **The market is wrong:** The value-price difference can arise because the market, caught up in mood and momentum, has pushed the stock price to a level that does not reflect a firm's intrinsic value.
- **You are both wrong, but one of you is less wrong:** The truth is that neither you nor the market has a crystal ball, and that you are making your best estimates for the future. In hindsight, one of you will be closer to the truth, and hopefully, there will be a payoff.

If there is a lesson here, it is that you cannot adopt a knee-jerk response and assume that you are right, every time value deviates from price, or that the market is always right, which makes intrinsic valuation pointless (since you can reverse engineer the process to deliver that result). The healthiest response, in my view, when value and price are different, is to assume that you may be missing something that the market is seeing but that, having examined the data and made the appropriate tweaks, you can end up with value still being different from the price.

CASE STUDY—PART 1: VALUING TESLA, NOVEMBER 2021

The Lead-in

In November 2021, Tesla joined the rarefied ranks of companies with trillion-dollar market capitalizations, capping a decade of almost unprecedented success. Starting as a young-growth company in 2011, targeting the luxury automobile market,* Tesla made multiple transitions during the period, expanding its reach to the mass auto market while

* See my 2013 valuation of Tesla, as a luxury auto company: Aswath Damodaran, "Valuation of the Week 1: A Tesla Test," *Musings on Markets* (blog), September 4, 2013, https://aswathdamodaran.blogspot.com/2013/09/valuation-of-week-1-tesla-test.html.

disrupting the automobile business model and adding new businesses (like energy) along the way. While there were many, including me, who questioned whether its reach was exceeding its grasp, Tesla has clearly succeeded in the marketplace, as figure 11.5 shows.

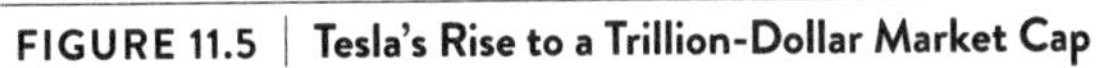

FIGURE 11.5 | Tesla's Rise to a Trillion-Dollar Market Cap

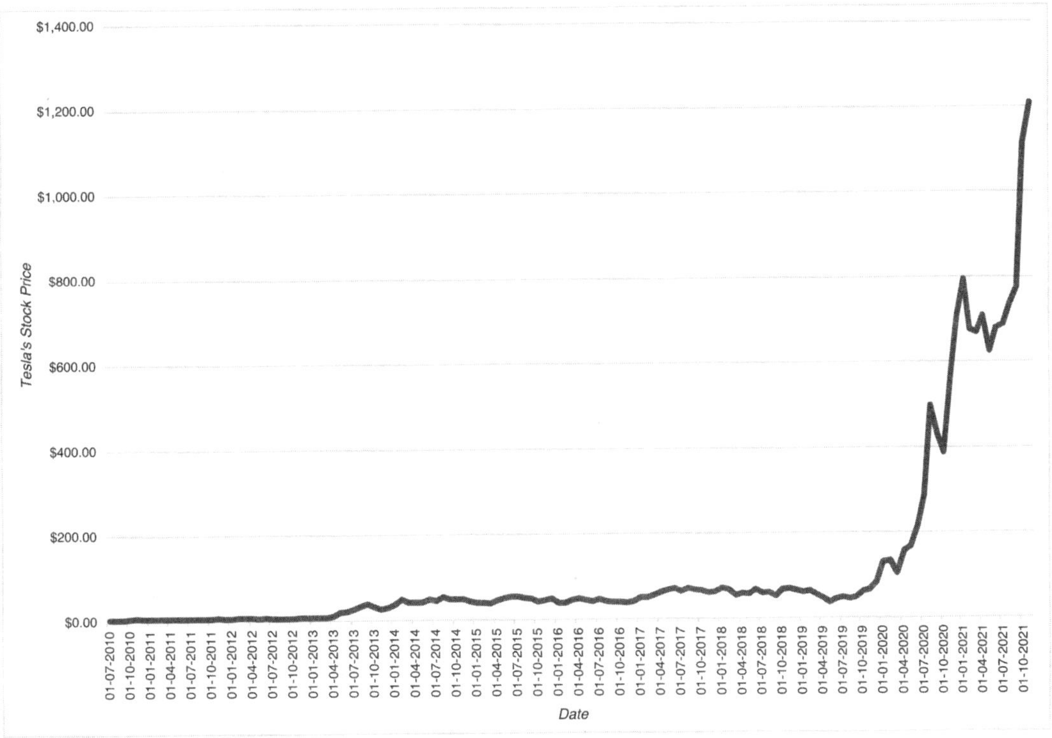

While the graph illustrates the surge in the stock price, the table embedded in the graph conveys the rise more vividly, by listing Tesla's market capitalization in millions of dollars. In sum, the company's market cap has risen from $2.8 billion, in August 2010, to more than a trillion dollars in November 2021, and along the way, it has enriched those who bought into its vision early and stayed invested in the company. While the initial rise in Tesla's market capitalization was driven by the promise of the company, and detractors were quick to note Tesla's paltry revenues and big losses, the company's more recent financials reflect how it has acquired substance over time. In figure 11.6, I report on Tesla's quarterly revenues, gross profits, and operating profits going back to 2013.

FIGURE 11.6 | Revenues and Profits at Tesla, 2013–2021

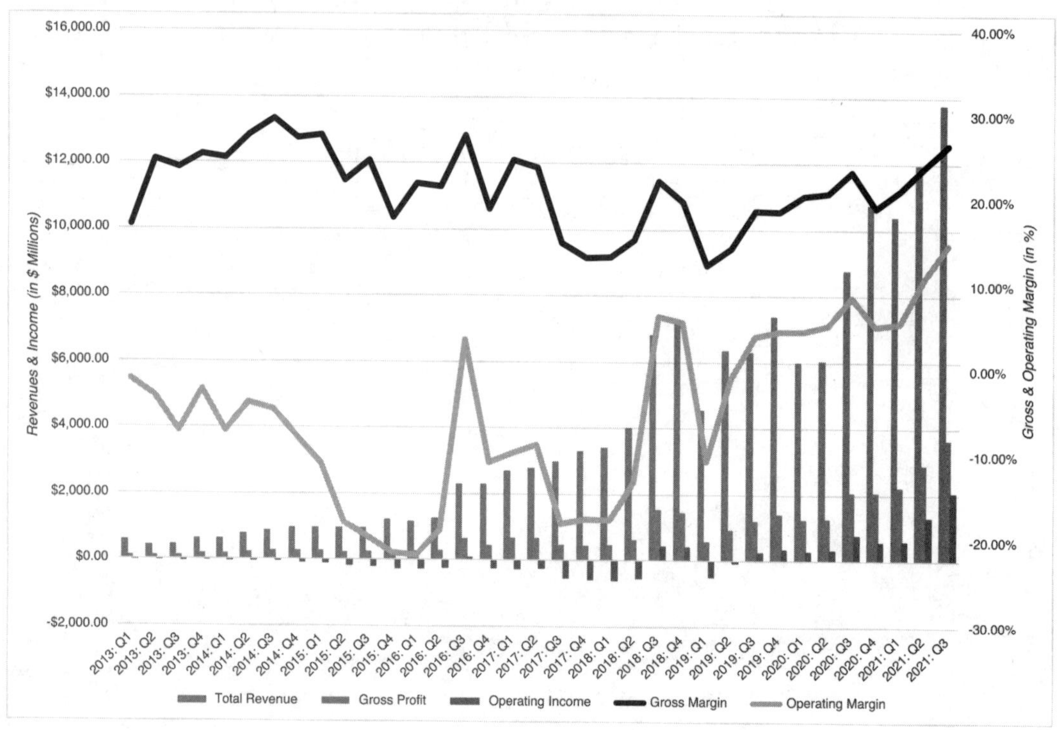

Tesla's quarterly revenues have risen from negligibly small values at the start of the last decade to almost $14 billion in the third quarter of 2021, making it the 20th largest automobile company in the world in 2020 (in revenue terms). The company spent much of the last decade losing large amounts each year, but by decade's end, it generated not only an operating profit but a healthy one, at that, with a pre-tax operating margin of close to 15% in the third quarter of 2021.

Updated Story and Valuation

Over the years, I have tried, not always successfully, to navigate between the extremes on Tesla and tell a story that reflects both the company's strengths and weaknesses. Not surprisingly, that story has changed over time, as the company, the business, and the world have all changed. In table 11.1, I list the stories that I have told, with end-year revenues, operating margins, and valuations for equity for each one, in 2013, 2017, 2019, and 2020.

Table 11.1 • Tesla Stories (and Valuations) over Time

Date	Story	Target Revenues (US $ Mil)	Target Margin	Sales/ Capital	Cost of Capital	Value of Equity (US $ Mil)	Market Cap (US $ Mil)	% Under- or Overvalued
Sep-13	Luxury auto company, with luxury car company revenues and margins	$67,000	12.50%	1.41	10.03%	$12,146	$20,496	68.75%
Aug-17	Auto/tech company, with focus primarily on high-end auto market	$93,000	12.00%	2.24	8.83%	$33,904	$57,634	69.99%
Jun-19	High-end auto/tech company with some mass-market appeal and unpredictable management	$105,000	10.00%	2.00	7.87%	$34,389	$31,756	-7.66%
Jan-20	Auto/tech company with increasing mass-market appeal	$128,000	12.00%	3.00	7.00%	$84,236	$102,837	22.08%

Over time, as you can see, my story for Tesla has become bigger (both in what I see as its potential market and the revenues from it), and I have adapted the story to reflect the company's capacity to reinvest far more efficiently than the typical automobile company that I used in my very first valuation. I know that for some, shifting stories and valuations are a sign of weakness, both in analytical capabilities and in the very idea of intrinsic valuation. For me—and this may be just my delusions talking—an unwillingness to change your valuation stories and inputs, especially for a company that delivers as many twists and turns as Tesla, is a far greater sin.

Whatever your priors were on Tesla coming into COVID, it is difficult to argue with the fact that the company benefited from the economic changes the pandemic wrought and that its story became bigger as a result. The question of how big the story is will determine value, but rather than give you my assessment at the start, I want to try an experiment. Ultimately, whatever story you tell about Tesla has to show up in five inputs that drive its value: (a) revenue growth, or what you see as end revenues for the company in steady state; (b) business profitability, reflecting what you see as unit economics, captured in the pre-tax operating margin; (c) investment efficiency, measuring how much investment will be needed to get to your estimated end revenues; (d) operating risk, incorporated into a cost of capital for the company; and (e) failure risk, the chance that the company will not make it as a going concern, gauged with a probability. If you are willing to go along with each input, I will lay out the choices (as objectively as I can) and I invite you to take your pick, given what you believe about the company. As you make these choices, though, please do not open the spreadsheet that I will provide at the end, to convert your choices into value, since that will create a feedback loop that can feed your biases.

a. **Revenue growth:** I do believe that Tesla came out of COVID with the potential for far more revenues than it had going in. As the automobile market increasingly shifts to electric cars, Tesla will hold a strong competitive advantage in that portion of the market and have the chance to be a market leader. To get a sense of what this will mean in terms of revenues by 2032, consider the choices in figure 11.7.

FIGURE 11.7 | Expected Revenues for Tesla, 2032

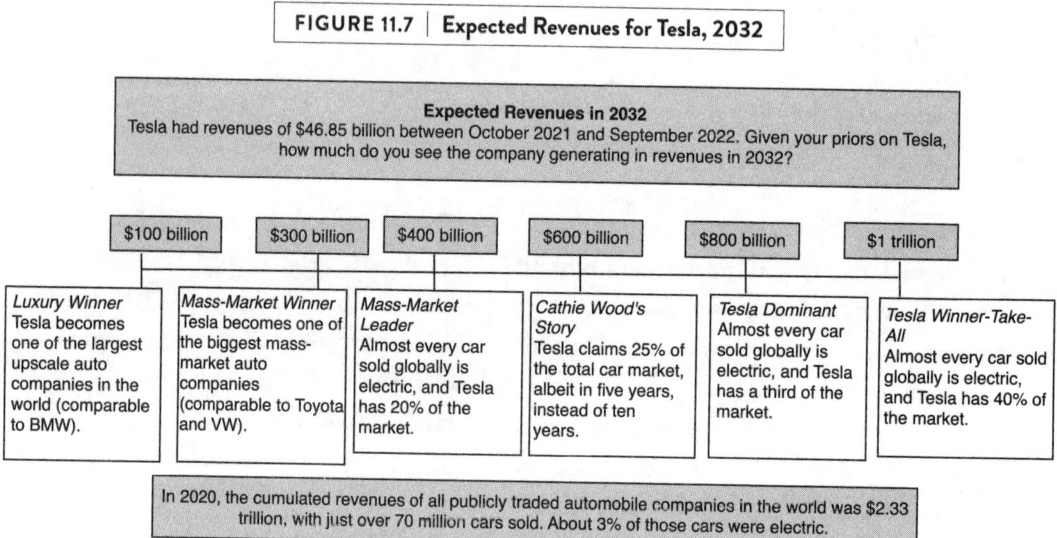

Note that if your story draws primarily on Tesla remaining an auto company, revenues of $400 billion will translate into about 10 million cars sold in 2032, more than 10 times the number of cars the company sold in 2020–21. If you believe that there are other businesses that Tesla will enter, you can augment your revenues with the added sales in those other businesses, keeping in mind that most of these businesses have far less revenue potential than the car business.

b. **Business profitability:** The biggest eye-opener for me, during COVID, was the surge in profitability at Tesla, with its operating margin nearing 15% in the third quarter of 2021. While that number is volatile, and there will be ups and downs, it looks as though the electric car business has better unit economics than the conventional automobile business, partly because of differences in assembly requirements between gas and electric cars, and partly because the battery itself is a significant component of the car. Notwithstanding Tesla's first-mover advantage, this margin will come under pressure not only through increased competition from the electric car offerings of existing automakers and new entrants (Nio, Rivian, etc.), but also from having to cut prices to increase market share in Asia, where car prices tend to be lower than in the US and Europe. Laying out the choices in terms of profitability in figure 11.8 looks like this.

FIGURE 11.8 | Expected Profitability for Tesla

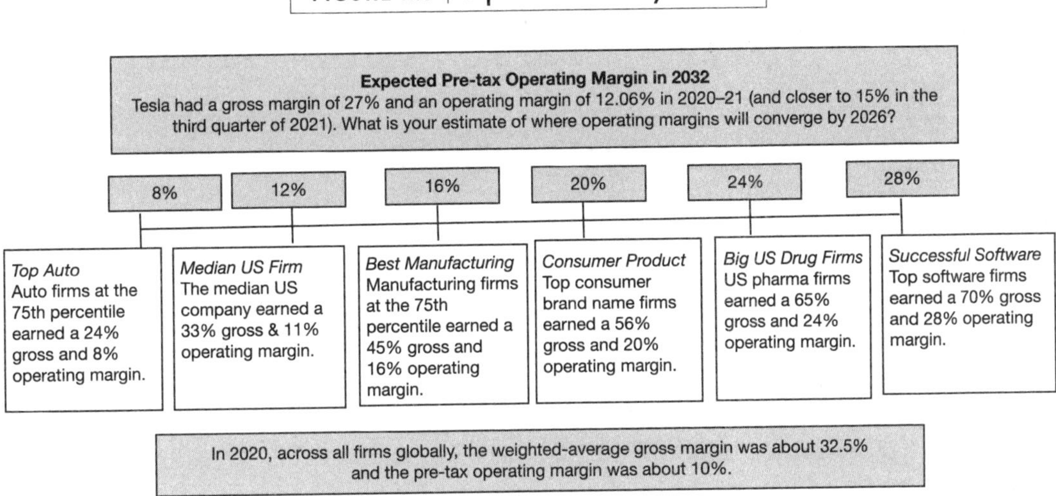

As you make this choice, recognize that, with its 30% gross margin in the last twelve months, Tesla is already approaching peak-level gross margins for a manufacturing company.

c. **Investment efficiency:** When I first valued Tesla in 2013, it had one plant, in Fremont, California, that produced all of the cars it sold. At the time, one of my concerns was that the company would need massive reinvestment in assembly plants to ramp up even to luxury-car revenue levels, and that this reinvestment would create significant cash burn. In the years since, Tesla has not only added capacity in lumps, with assembly plants/gigafactories in Storey County (Nevada), Buffalo (New York), Shanghai (China), Berlin (Germany), and Austin (Texas), it has spent far less than I originally estimated it would have to invest. That said, if you are projecting that Tesla will sell 8, 10, or 12 million cars a year a decade from now, it will need to reinvest in additional capacity. I use the sales-to-capital ratio as a proxy for investment efficiency (with higher values implying more efficient investing), and the choices appear in figure 11.9.

FIGURE 11.9 | Reinvestment at Tesla

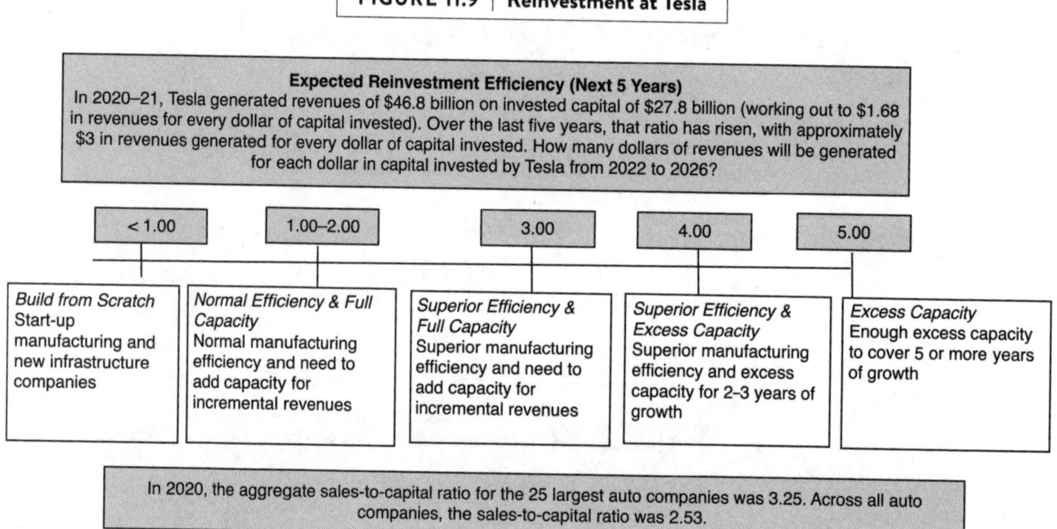

To the extent that the company has the excess capacity to cover growth for the next few years, I will allow for a higher sales-to-capital ratio in the early years but move it toward a more sustainable number thereafter.

d. **Operating and Failure risk:** In November 2021, the risk-free rate was down to 1.56%, equity risk premiums had declined to 4.62%, and the cost of capital for the median firm had drifted down to about 5.90%. The choices you have in figure 11.10 regarding cost of capital are structured around those market realities.

FIGURE 11.10 | Tesla's Cost of Capital

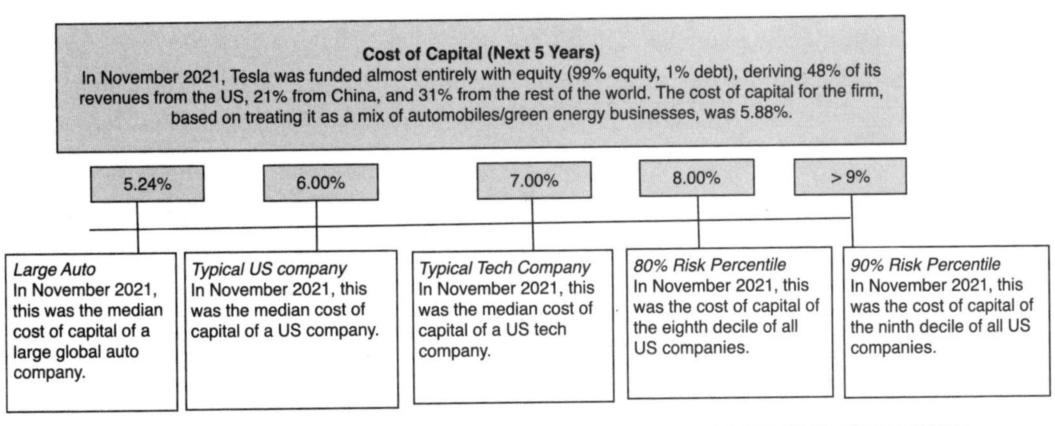

The other risk measure that will affect value is the likelihood of failure, a number that has varied over Tesla's history—partly because it used to lose money and partly because of a choice it made to borrow money in 2016. In making this assessment, recognize that Tesla now has a cash balance that exceeds its debt due and is making money, at least for the moment.

Taking to heart how closely Tesla and Elon Musk are connected, one of the concerns with Tesla has always been the sheer unpredictability of Mr. Musk. The Musk effect on value can be positive, neutral, or negative, depending on your priors, as you can see in figure 11.11.

FIGURE 11.11 | The Musk Effect

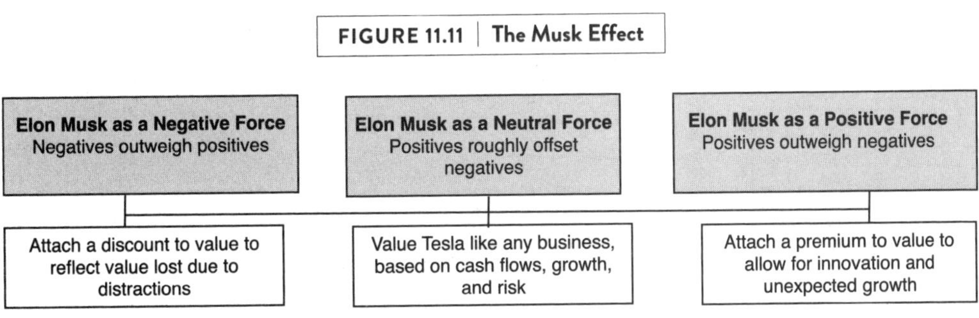

While Musk had been better behaved and more focused in the year and a half leading into this valuation (with the exception of indulging in tweeting about crypto-currencies), he seemed to revert to bad habits in the last two weeks prior to this November 2021 valuation, seeking guidance from his Twitter followers on whether to sell a significant portion of his Tesla shares and indulging in a back-and-forth with senators about the billionaire tax.

I made my choices, and in the most upbeat forecasts, I aimed for revenues of roughly $400 billion (about 10 million cars, augmented by revenues from ancillary businesses) in 2032, operating margins of 16%, and a sales-to-capital ratio of 4.00 for the next five years (making Tesla far more profitable and investment efficient than any large manufacturing company in the world). With a cost of capital of 6% (close to the median company) and no chance of failure, it should come as no surprise that my estimated value of equity for the company has increased to about $692 billion for equity in the aggregate, and $640 billion for equity in common stock, as can be seen in figure 11.12.

FIGURE 11.12 | A Valuation of Tesla, November 2021

Tesla

The Payoff to Flexibility : A Plausible Path to Auto Dominance — **Nov-21**

As the crisis handicaps its more indebted, slower-moving competitors, Tesla will consolidate its hold on the electric car market and push its production towards 10 million cars by 2032, and will also be able to deliver higher margins than conventional auto companies in steady state, using revenues from other businesses to complement auto sales. The drop in risk-free rates has reduced its cost of capital and the chance of failure. Tesla's more flexibile investment policies will allow it to be more efficient in generating growth. While other revenue sources (green energy, driverless cars in ride sharing) will supplement revenues, it will remain at its core an electric car company.

The Assumptions

	Base Year	*Years 1–5*	*Years 6–10*		*After Year 10*	*Link to Story*
Revenues (a)	$ 46,848	35.00% →	1.56%		1.56%	Growth in EV market & Tesla's early mover advantage work in its favor.
Operating Margin (b)	12.06%	12.06% →	16.00%		16.00%	Continued economies of scale & brand
Tax rate	11.99%	11.99% →	25.00%		25.00%	Global tax rate
Reinvestment (c)		Sales to Capital =	4.00	RIR =	10.40%	Capacity buildup allows for less reinvestment in the near future.
Return on Capital	17.88%	Marginal ROIC =	51.66%		15.00%	Cost of entry will limit competition.
Cost of Capital (d)		6.00% →	6.06%		6.06%	Moves to median company cost of capital

The Cash Flows

	Revenues	*Operating Margin*	*EBIT*	*EBIT (1–t)*	*Reinvestment*	*FCFF*
1	$63,245	12.85%	$ 8,126	$7,151.99	$4,099	$3,053
2	$85,380	13.64%	$ 11,643	$10,247.15	$5,534	$4,713
3	$115,264	14.42%	$ 16,626	$14,632.80	$7,471	$7,162
4	$155,606	15.21%	$ 23,671	$20,833.14	$10,086	$10,748
5	$210,068	16.00%	$ 33,611	$29,581.19	$13,616	$15,966
6	$269,542	16.00%	$ 43,127	$36,833.99	$22,303	$14,531
7	$327,828	16.00%	$ 52,453	$43,434.08	$21,857	$21,577
8	$376,793	16.00%	$ 60,287	$48,352.64	$18,362	$29,991
9	$407,871	16.00%	$ 65,259	$50,642.62	$11,654	$38,988
10	$414,233	16.00%	$ 66,277	$49,708.01	$2,386	$47,322
Terminal Year	$420,695	16.00%	$ 67,311	$50,483.45	$5,250	$45,233

The Value

Terminal Value	$1,005,182	
PV(Terminal Value)	$560,336	
PV (CF over Next 10 Years)	$126,354	
Value of Operating Assets =	$686,690	
Adjustment for Distress	$0	Probability of failure = 0.00%
– Debt & Minority Interests	$10,158	
+ Cash & Other Non-operating assets	$10,095	
Value of Equity	$692,627	
– Value of Equity Options	$51,070	
Number of Shares	1,123.00	
Value per Share	$ 571.29	Stock was trading at = $1,200.00

There are very few companies in the world that I would value at more than half a trillion dollars, and with Tesla, I get there almost entirely based upon assuming it can scale up like no other company in history while delivering on its potential profitability. That said, though, the value per share that I get of $571, even in this most upbeat of scenarios, was less than half the current stock price in November 2021, leaving me with the conclusion that the stock was overvalued, at its then prevailing stock price that exceeded $1,000 a share. Note that a five-for-one stock split occurred soon after, complicating comparisons to Tesla's current stock price.

Pricing High-Growth Companies

The process for pricing a high-growth company follows a familiar sequence: scaling the price to a common metric, finding comparable firms that are priced in the market, and then controlling for differences. In this section, I will look at the challenges associated with pricing high-growth companies and ways of overcoming them.

Challenges

The good news when pricing high-growth companies, relative to pricing start-ups, is that your scaling choices increase since, at firms with more substantial revenues and positive earnings, you have a shot at computing and using earnings multiples. The bigger challenges arise when you try to find peer-group firms and control for differences across the group:

- If the high-growth company is put into a peer group of more mature companies, with lower growth potential and different profitability profiles, the comparison will almost always lead to the conclusion that the high-growth company is overpriced. This was the conclusion that many drew about Tesla after comparing its pricing, relative to cars sold, revenues, or earnings, to that of traditional auto companies.
- If the peer group is composed of other growth companies—which is plausible only if you are in a sector where there are many high-growth companies—you must control for differences in growth and risk that will persist across the group, since not all high-growth companies follow the same glide path to profitability. In other words, while your intuition may lead you to believe that higher-growth companies should trade at higher multiples of revenues or earnings, you still need to convert that intuition into numbers.

In my intrinsic valuation of Tesla from November 2021, I noted the strong priors that people bring into assessing the company's stock, and not surprisingly, these biases find their way into pricing. An optimist on Tesla can conclude that it is underpriced, even against other auto companies, by dividing its pricing today by expected revenues or cars sold a decade from now, using inflated numbers for both metrics.

Responses

While there are clearly challenges in finding peer groups and controlling for differences across firms when pricing high-growth companies, there are a few responses that can help improve pricing.

- **Forward numbers:** The first response is to scale market values to expected operating outcomes in the future. Thus, rather than divide price per share today by current earnings per share (EPS), you can divide by expected earnings per share in five or even ten years and compare these forward multiples across the peer group. The effect of using forward numbers is illustrated in table 11.2 below, where I compare a high-growth company with a mature company in its peer group, using current and forward PE.

Table 11.2 • Current and Forward PE Comparisons

	Price per share (US $)	Current EPS	Current PE	Expected CAGR in EPS, Next 10 Years	Forward EPS, Year 10 (US $)	Forward PE
Mature firm	20	2.0	10.000	3.00%	$2.69	7.44
High-Growth firm	20	0.2	100.000	30.00%	$2.76	7.25

Using current earnings, the high-growth firm looks hopelessly overpriced relative to the mature firm, but using expected earnings per share in year 10, you get forward PE ratios that are close. This analysis is conditioned on the assumption that the expected growth rates in EPS are reasonably estimated, but that caveat would apply no matter how you tried to assess these firms.

- **Growth-adjusted multiples:** The key challenge that I face when comparing a high-growth firm to a mature firm, or even high-growth firms to each other, is that differences in growth rates should show up as differences in pricing multiples, with higher-growth companies trading at higher PE ratios. One approach that can, at least on the surface, deal with this problem is to bring the growth into the pricing multiple:

  PEG ratio = PE ratio/Expected growth rate

  In the example above, the mature firm, with a PE of 10 and an expected growth rate of 3%, would trade at a PEG ratio of 3.33, as would the high-growth firm, with a PE of 100 and an expected growth rate of 30%.

CASE STUDY—PART 2: PRICING TESLA, NOVEMBER 2021

To price Tesla in November 2021, I initially compared its pricing to that of the 20 largest auto companies in the world, in market cap terms. These values appear in table 11.3.

Table 11.3 • Auto Company Pricing in November 2021

Company	Market Cap (US $ mil)	Enterprise Value (US $ mil)	Revenues (US $ mil)	EBITDA (US $ mil)	Net Income (US $ mil)	EV/Sales	EV/EBITDA	PE
Toyota Motor Corp. (TSE: 7203)	$248,785	$398,274	$255,641	$41,072	$26,891	1.56	9.70	9.25
Volkswagen AG (XTRA: VOW3)	$142,343	$333,815	$243,016	$32,989	$21,289	1.37	10.12	6.69
Daimler AG (XTRA: DAI)	$107,839	$234,741	$162,149	$23,199	$16,044	1.45	10.12	6.72
Stellantis NV (BIT: STLA)	$63,353	$51,125	$134,751	$16,637	$9,910	0.38	3.07	6.39
Ford Motor Co. (NYSE: F)	$68,256	$181,411	$124,192	$8,274	$2,867	1.46	21.93	23.81
SAIC Motor Corp. Ltd. (SHSE: 600104)	$36,064	$25,641	$119,843	$6,590	$3,745	0.21	3.89	9.63
General Motors Co. (NYSE: GM)	$79,025	$169,913	$117,330	$17,820	$11,124	1.45	9.53	7.10
Honda Motor Co., Ltd. (TSE: 7267)	$52,485	$97,008	$109,247	$20,081	$8,658	0.89	4.83	6.06
Bayerische Motoren Werke Aktiengesellschaft (XTRA: BMW)	$65,783	$169,096	$93,942	$19,161	$13,079	1.80	8.83	5.03
Hyundai Motor Co. (KOSE: A005380)	$37,235	$99,332	$91,666	$6,533	$3,382	1.08	15.21	11.01
Nissan Motor Co., Ltd. (TSE: 7201)	$20,250	$69,304	$69,174	$2,840	$(438)	1.00	24.40	N/A
Kia Corp. (KOSE: A000270)	$28,695	$21,857	$60,285	$5,558	$3,072	0.36	3.93	9.34
Renault SA (ENXTPA: RNO)	$9,995	$58,919	$53,766	$4,509	$(429)	1.10	13.07	NA
Tesla, Inc. (NasdaqGS: TSLA)	$1,118,751	$1,112,814	$46,848	$7,267	$3,468	23.75	153.13	322.59
Tata Motors Ltd. (BSE: 500570)	$23,264	$34,004	$37,263	$3,220	$(1,273)	0.91	10.56	NA
Volvo Car AB (publ.) (OM: VOLCAR B)	$21,332	$19,247	$34,158	$3,275	$1,849	0.56	5.88	11.54
Suzuki Motor Corp. (TSE: 7269)	$22,322	$17,894	$32,424	$3,498	$2,067	0.55	5.12	10.80
Mazda Motor Corp. (TSE: 7261)	$5,762	$6,030	$29,815	$1,526	$418	0.20	3.95	13.77
BYD Co. Ltd. (SEHK: 1211)	$96,146	$97,302	$29,810	$2,815	$507	3.26	34.57	189.83
Median						1.04	**9.62**	**9.34**
Average						2.17	**17.57**	**38.21**

Note that on every pricing metric, Tesla looks not just overpriced but massively so, trading at 23.75 (322.59) times revenues (earnings) when the median auto company trades at 1.04 (9.34) times revenues (earnings).

I tried the forward PE and PEG ratio approaches, in table 11.4, with Tesla and the other auto companies, though our sample size got smaller, with some firms not having earnings growth estimates.

Table 11.4 • PEG Ratios and Forward PE—Auto Sector, November 2021

Company	Market Cap (US $ mil)	Net Income (US $ mil)	PE	Expected Net Income Growth, Next 5 Years	PEG Ratio	Expected Net Income, Year 5	Forward PE
Bayerische Motoren Werke Aktiengesellschaft (XTRA: BMW)	$65,783	$13,079	5.03	25.40%	0.20	$40,557	1.62
BYD Co. Ltd. (SEHK: 1211)	$96,146	$507	189.83	8.98%	21.14	$778	123.49
Daimler AG (XTRA: DAI)	$107,839	$16,044	6.72	33.70%	0.20	$68,545	1.57
Ford Motor Co. (NYSE: F)	$68,256	$2,867	23.81	66.90%	0.36	$37,129	1.84
General Motors Co. (NYSE: GM)	$79,025	$11,124	7.10	13.20%	0.54	$20,677	3.82
Honda Motor Co., Ltd. (TSE: 7267)	$52,485	$8,658	6.06	15.20%	0.40	$17,566	2.99
SAIC Motor Corp. Ltd. (SHSE: 600104)	$36,064	$3,745	9.63	10.50%	0.92	$6,169	5.85
Stellantis NV (BIT: STLA)	$63,353	$9,910	6.39	35.30%	0.18	$44,932	1.41
Suzuki Motor Corp. (TSE: 7269)	$22,322	$2,067	10.80	19.70%	0.55	$5,080	4.39
Tesla, Inc. (NasdaqGS: TSLA)	$1,118,751	$3,468	322.59	42.80%	7.54	$20,593	54.33
Toyota Motor Corp. (TSE: 7203)	$248,785	$26,891	9.25	3.50%	2.64	$31,938	7.79
Volkswagen AG (XTRA: VOW3)	$142,343	$21,289	6.69	15.20%	0.44	$43,193	3.30
Median			**8.18**	**17.45%**	**0.49**		**3.56**
Average			**50.33**	**24.20%**	**2.92**		**17.70**

Staying with automobile companies, there still seems to be almost no way to explain the pricing of Tesla and BYD, though pushing forward numbers to year 10 may make the mispricing look less stark. There is one final pricing option to consider, and that is to price Tesla not against auto companies but against high-growth tech companies, with the argument that Tesla is more a technology company than an auto company and that its investors therefore price it as such.

Add-ons and Addenda

In this final section, I will look at two add-ons and addenda that are particularly relevant when valuing high-growth companies. First, I will push back against the notion that growth is always good for investors and look at ways of separating good growth from bad growth. Second, I will look at techniques that can be used, after an intrinsic valuation, to explore what-if questions and to back out what the market may be pricing into a stock.

The Value of Growth

While many investors view growth as an unalloyed good, it requires a trade-off: a company invests more back into itself in the near term, denying payouts (dividends or buybacks) to its investors during that period, in exchange for higher earnings in the future. Not surprisingly, then, the net effect of growth will depend on how much is reinvested relative to what the company can harvest as future growth. While a full assessment of this value will require making explicit assumptions about growth and reinvestment, there is a shorthand that is useful in making the assessment, and that is a comparison of the returns that a company makes on its investments to the cost of funding those investments. If you use accounting returns as a proxy for project returns and the costs of equity and capital as measures of the costs of funding, you can compute excess returns to equity investors by comparing return on equity to the cost of equity, and excess returns to all capital providers by netting cost of capital from return on invested capital, as shown in figure 11.13.

FIGURE 11.13 | Excess Returns from Investments

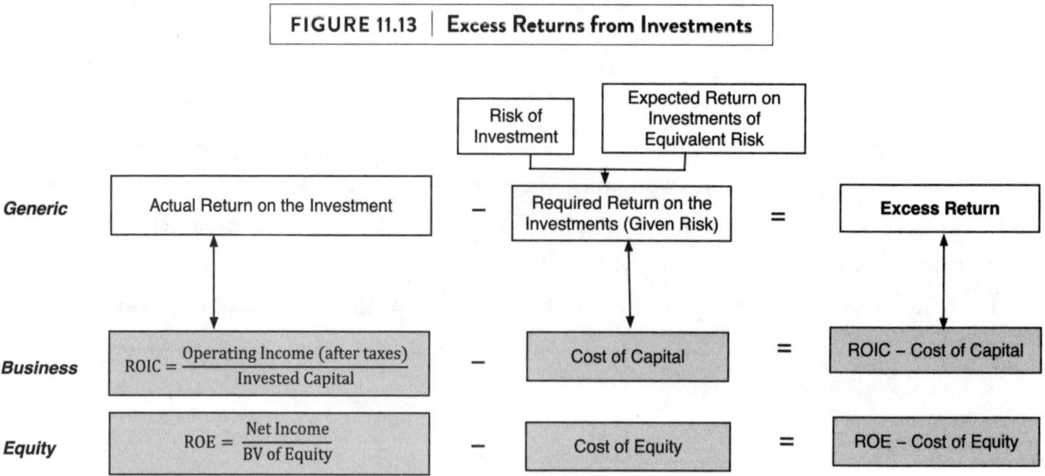

Using the accounting returns and costs of equity/capital that I computed for all publicly traded firms at the start of 2022 in chapter 6, I looked at the distribution of excess return measures across companies in figure 11.14.

FIGURE 11.14 | Excess Returns at Global Companies, 2021

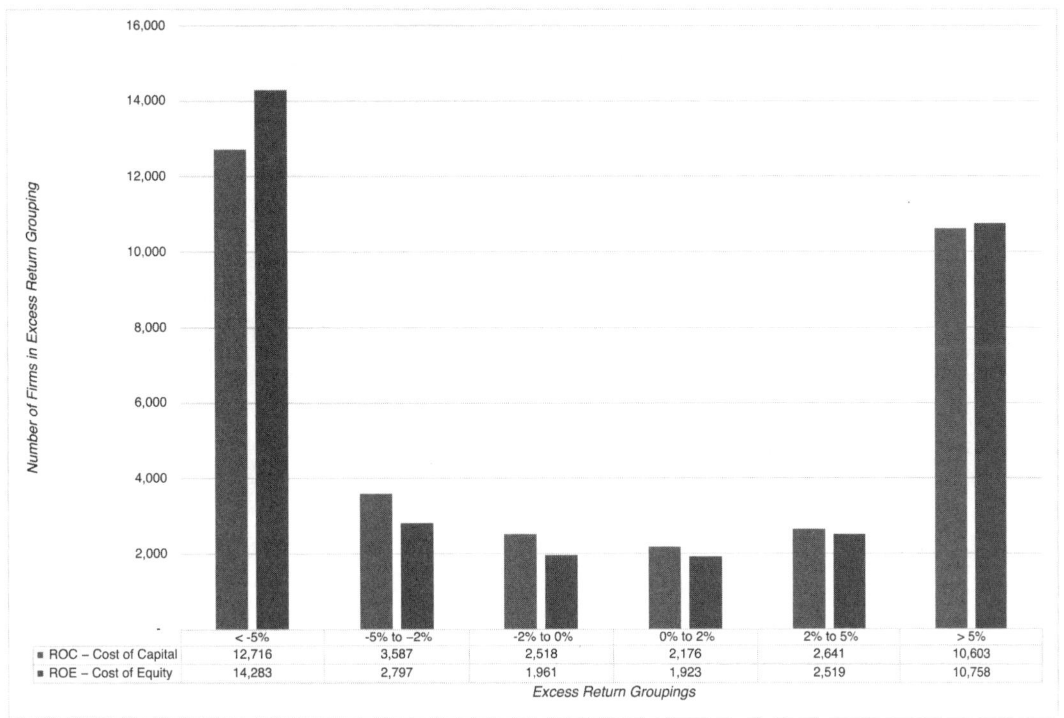

	< -5%	-5% to -2%	-2% to 0%	0% to 2%	2% to 5%	> 5%
ROC – Cost of Capital	12,716	3,587	2,518	2,176	2,641	10,603
ROE – Cost of Equity	14,283	2,797	1,961	1,923	2,519	10,758

Close to 57% of firms globally earn returns lower than their funding costs, and while this may be temporary for some, it has become a permanent feature for many businesses. It is an undeniable truth that some businesses are easier to generate value in than others, and that a bad business is one where most of the companies operating in it, no matter how well managed, have trouble earning their costs of capital. Using the excess returns estimated from 2021, I estimated the excess returns (ROIC - cost of capital) in 94 industry groups. The ten "best" and "worst" industries, in terms of median excess return, are listed in table 11.5.

Table 11.5 • Global Excess Returns—Best and Worst Industries, 2021

Bad Businesses				
			% with excess returns	
Industry Group	# Firms	Median (ROIC—WACC)	Positive	Negative
Drugs (Biotechnology)	1,223	-86.31%	42.27%	57.73%
Precious Metals	947	-24.25%	39.92%	60.08%
Metals & Mining	1,706	-21.95%	40.39%	59.61%
Air Transport	151	-12.28%	23.84%	76.16%
Hotel/Gaming	654	-10.83%	26.30%	73.70%
Oil/Gas (Production & Exploration)	642	-10.74%	46.42%	53.58%
Coal & Related Energy	206	-8.83%	46.60%	53.40%
Restaurant/Dining	385	-8.06%	37.14%	62.86%
Entertainment	734	-7.28%	53.54%	46.46%
Oilfield Svcs/Equip.	457	-5.42%	39.39%	60.61%
Good Businesses				
			% with excess returns	
Industry Group	# Firms	Median (ROIC—WACC)	Positive	Negative
Tobacco	55	13.31%	80.00%	20.00%
Retail (Building Supply)	98	7.12%	78.57%	21.43%
Information Services	266	6.98%	72.56%	27.44%
Computer Services	1,040	5.35%	69.71%	30.29%
Health Care Support Services	445	4.34%	68.76%	31.24%
Furn/Home Furnishings	359	3.85%	64.35%	35.65%
Hospitals/Health Care Facilities	223	3.40%	66.82%	33.18%
Chemical (Specialty)	898	3.28%	66.70%	33.30%
Building Materials	449	3.17%	63.25%	36.75%
Chemical (Diversified)	71	3.14%	71.83%	28.17%

Source: Excess Returns, by Industry (US, Global)

If you look at the worst businesses, there are a couple that show up every year, like airlines and hotel/gaming, where COVID exacerbated problems that are long-term and structural. The airline and hotel businesses are broken and have been for a long time, and there is no easy fix in sight. Biotechnology companies can claim, with some justification, that their presence on the bad-business list reflects the fact that many in the sector are young companies that are a breakthrough away from being blockbuster winners, and that in maturity they will resemble the pharmaceutical business (which does earn positive excess returns). I am sure that there will be ESG advocates who will claim credit for fossil fuel and mining businesses showing up on the worst-business list, but not only will these rankings change quickly if oil and commodity prices rise, the best business of all in 2021, in terms of delivering excess returns, is the tobacco business—not exactly a paragon of virtue. While the technology boom has created winners in information and computer services, building-related businesses (from materials to furnishings to retail) and chemical companies also seem to have found ways to deliver returns that exceed their costs.

Among the bad businesses, note the presence of entertainment, a historically good business that has recently seen its business model disrupted by new entrants. Netflix, in particular, has upended how entertainment gets made, distributed, and consumed, and in the process has drained value from established players. While this is a phenomenon that has played out in business after business over the last two decades, there are a couple of common themes that have emerged in the excess return data. Disruption, almost invariably, leads to lower returns for the status quo, i.e., the disrupted companies in the business—but disruptors often don't end up as beneficiaries. Consider the car service business, where ride sharing has destroyed cab and traditional car service businesses, but Uber, Lyft, DiDi, Grab, and Ola all continue to lose money. Put bluntly, disruption is easy, but making money on disruption is difficult. Disruption creates lots of losers but does not necessarily replace them with winners.

To sum up my findings, I would conclude that generating value from running a business has become more difficult, not less, in the last two decades, and that while there are companies that seem to have found pathways to sustainable, high earnings, most companies are involved in trench warfare, fighting disruptors and facing significantly more macroeconomic risk in their operations. These are lessons well worth heeding when valuing high-growth companies, since high growth while earnings are less than the cost of capital can be devastating for value. That is one reason why you should be looking at the competitive advantages that a high-growth company possesses in making your best value judgments about it.

Break-Even Analysis

When valuing high-growth companies that are publicly traded, I noted that their value and price can diverge either because you have made errors in your inputs or because the market has—and, in reality, both you and the market are likely to be wrong. Much as true believers in value like to dismiss markets as shallow and driven by herd behavior, it behooves you to at least be cognizant of what markets are pricing in, when the price of a company is different from its value. There are two ways in which you can approach this analysis:

- You can hold all else constant and change one variable (growth, revenues, risk) and then find the break-even value for that variable that will yield the current market price. The problem with this approach is that it requires you to isolate one out of many key inputs to come to your conclusion.
- A more expansive approach to backing out market expectations is to pick two or even three of the most critical inputs into valuation and look for combinations of assumptions on these variables that yield the market price.
- A third variant is to go back to the story that you built your valuation around and see how the valuation changes as you change the story.

Again, the purpose of this analysis is not to convince yourself that the market is right and you are wrong, or to come up with nonsensically wide ranges for value, but to get a sense of how much buffer you have to be wrong on key inputs.

CASE STUDY—PART 3: A BREAK-EVEN ANALYSIS FOR TESLA

There are multiple caveats that go with my valuation of Tesla, and it is possible that you may able to find a story that yields a valuation not just higher than mine but also higher than the stock price. Alternatively, you might be one of those who believes that much of what I have seen as improvements in recent years at Tesla is a mirage, and that I am being delusional in my assumptions. I would posit that almost any disagreement that two different analysts can have about Tesla ultimately becomes one about how much revenue the company can generate from the businesses one sees it operating in and how profitable it will be as a company.

1. **Revenues:** In making my revenue estimates, I assumed that Tesla would get a predominant portion of its revenues from selling cars, partly because of its history and partly because its alternative revenue sources (batteries, software, etc.) are not big revenue items. It is possible, though, that there are new businesses with ample revenues that Tesla can enter that can create new and substantial revenue streams. It is also possible that the electric car business will resemble technology businesses in their winner-take-all characteristic and that Tesla will ultimately have a dominant market share of that business. In either case, optimists will have to find ways to get to revenues far greater than my already daunting number of $414 billion in 2032. (Just for perspective, the total revenues of all publicly traded automobile companies, globally, in 2020–21 were $2.33 trillion; and this would give Tesla roughly one sixth of the overall market.)

2. **Profitability:** The other key driver of Tesla's value is its operating margin. While I think that my estimate of 16% is already at the upper end of what a manufacturing company can generate, there are a couple of ways in which Tesla might be able to earn even higher margins. One is to enter a side business, perhaps software or ride sharing (with self-driving cars), that has much higher margins than the auto business. The other is to benefit from technological advantages to reap the benefits of economies of scale in production; this would require gross margins to continue to climb from less than 30% to much higher levels.

You can check this for yourself, but the other assumptions (about reinvestment and risk) described earlier in the chapter don't have as big an impact on value. I have computed Tesla's equity value (in common stock) as a function of targeted revenues and operating margins in table 11.6.

Table 11.6 • Tesla Equity Value—Alternative Growth/Margin Assumptions

		Estimated Value of Tesla's Common Equity Per Share Today Revenues in 2032 (in US $ billions)					
		$200 (Daimler-like)	$300 (Toyota-like)	$400 (15% Mkt Share)	$600 (25% Mkt Share)	$ 800 (30% Mkt Share)	$ 1,000 (40% Mkt Share)
Target Operating Margin	12%	$257	$370	$469	$666	$857	$1,049
	16%	$346	$503	$642	$918	$1,185	$1,455
	20%	$435	$636	$814	$1,169	$1,514	$1,861
	24%	$524	$769	$986	$1,421	$1,842	$2,267
	28%	$613	$902	$1,160	$1,673	$2,170	$2,673

Shaded cells = values greater than the company market cap on November 4, 2021

As you can see, there are pathways that exist to get Tesla to its prevailing stock price and above, but they require that the company enter rarefied territory, assuming that it will have more revenues than any company (not just any automobile company) in history while delivering operating margins similar to those delivered by the largest and most successful technology stocks, none of which has the drag of substantial manufacturing costs.

Conclusion

With more historical data to work with, and with profitability as evidence of a working business model, high-growth companies should be easier to value than start-ups and very young companies—but that comfort can be deceptive. The data from a company's past will often include shifting fundamentals, as revenue growth scales down as the company gets larger and margins move from negative to positive values. The presence of a market price at many of these high-growth companies can bring benefits by making some of your valuation calculations easier, but can also distort valuations as analysts bend the numbers to bring the value closer to the price.

My advice is to stay true to the valuation process, beginning with a valuation story that fits the company's profile and history, checking your forecasted revenue growth numbers to make sure that you are not growing absolute revenues to fairy-tale levels, and ensuring that reinvestment is tied to your growth assumptions. Mechanically forecasting future values for valuation line items based upon historical trend lines is a recipe for disaster when valuing high-growth companies.

On the pricing front, while there are more measures that you can scale market prices to in this cohort, high-growth companies in sectors made up primarily of mature companies will tend to look significantly overpriced, simply because they have more growth potential than their peer groups.

12

Valuation and Pricing: Mature Businesses

IT IS CONVENTIONAL WISDOM that mature companies are the easiest ones to value, because they have long financial histories that not only provide detailed information on growth and profit margins but also frame the stories that drive company value. That is true, for the most part, but as I will argue in this chapter, the fact that mature companies are settled in their ways can sometimes lull us into a sense of complacence, blinding us to disruptors who can upend business models overnight, or to bad corporate practices wherein managers, set in their ways, make business decisions that are inimical to long-term value.

Valuation of Mature Companies

If you are mechanical in your valuation—if you just use historical data to make projections of cash flows into the future and estimate value—the segment of the life cycle where you are most likely to find success with this approach is with mature companies. In this section, I will begin by looking at the shared characteristics of mature firms, the challenges that you can face when valuing some of them, and the responses to those challenges that can put your valuations back on the right track.

The Characteristics

There are clear differences across mature companies in different businesses, but they still share some common characteristics. This section looks at what mature companies have in common, with an eye on the consequences for valuation:

1. **Convergence in growth rates:** There can be a wide divergence between growth rate in revenues and growth rate in earnings in many companies. While the growth rate for earnings for mature firms can be high because of improved efficiency, revenue growth is more difficult to alter. For the most part, mature firms register growth rates in revenues that will converge on, if not equal, the economy's nominal growth rate. As that happens, earnings growth will eventually also follow, since efficiency-driven growth comes with an expiration date.
2. **Margins are established:** Another feature shared by mature companies is that they tend to have stable margins. The exceptions are commodity and cyclical firms, where margins vary as a function of the overall economy and even mature firms exhibit volatile margins. Although I will return to take a closer look at this subgroup later in the book, even these firms have stable margins across the economic or commodity price cycle.
3. **Competitive advantages:** The dimension in which mature firms reveal the most variation is in the competitive advantages they hold, manifested by the excess returns they generate on their investments. While some mature firms see excess returns go to zero or become negative with the advent of competition, other mature firms retain significant competitive advantages (and excess returns). Because value is determined by excess returns, the latter group retain higher values relative to the former, even as growth rates become anemic.
4. **Debt capacity:** As firms mature, profit margins and earnings improve, reinvestment needs drop off, and more cash is available for servicing debt. Consequently, the capacity to borrow money should increase at mature firms, although there can be big differences in how these firms react to this surge in debt capacity. Some choose not to exploit any or most of their debt capacity and stick with financing policies they established as growth companies. Others overreact and borrow more than they can comfortably handle, given current earnings and cash flows. Still others take a more reasoned middle ground and borrow to reflect their improved financial status while preserving their financial health.

5. **Cash buildup and return:** As earnings improve and reinvestment needs drop off, mature companies generate more cash from their operations than they need. If these companies do not alter their debt or dividend policies, cash balances will start accumulating in these firms. The question of whether a company has too much cash and, if so, how it should return this cash to stockholders becomes a standard one at almost every mature company.
6. **Inorganic growth:** The transition from a growth company to a mature company is not an easy one for most companies, especially for managers. As companies get larger and find that internal investment opportunities do not provide the growth boost they used to, it is not surprising that many mature companies look for quick fixes that will allow them to maintain high growth. One option, albeit an expensive one, is to buy growth. Acquisitions of other companies can provide a boost to revenues and earnings. For larger mature companies, though, these acquisitions also have to scale up to make a difference.

One final point that needs to be made is that not all mature companies are large companies. Many small companies reach their growth ceilings quickly and essentially stay small, mature firms. Some growth companies do have extended periods of growth before they reach stable growth, though, and these companies (like Coca-Cola and Verizon) tend to be the large companies that I use as examples of typical mature companies.

The Challenges

If a firm's intrinsic value is the present value of the expected cash flows from its investments, discounted back at a risk-adjusted rate, it would seem that mature firms, where the bulk of the value comes from investments already made (assets in place), should be easiest to value on that basis. While this is generally true, problems can still lurk under the surface of these firms' long and seemingly stable histories, and I will break those challenges down here, by category.

ASSETS IN PLACE

I categorized mature companies as those that get the bulk of their value from existing assets. Consequently, measuring the value of these assets correctly becomes far more critical with mature firms than it was with the firms that I analyzed in the last two chapters. Because a key input into valuing existing assets is estimating the cash flows they generate, you may encounter two issues when valuing mature companies.

1. **Managed earnings:** Mature companies are adept at using the discretionary power offered in accounting rules to manage earnings. Note that in doing so, they are not necessarily committing accounting fraud or even being deceptive, but as a result, the earnings reported from existing assets by companies with aggressive accounting practices will be much higher than the earnings reported by otherwise similar but conservative companies. Failing to factor in the differences in accounting mindset can lead us to overvalue the existing assets of aggressive companies and undervalue those of conservative companies.
2. **Management inefficiencies**: Mature companies have long periods of stable operating history. This long history can lull us into believing that the numbers from the past (operating margins, returns on capital) are reasonable estimates of what existing assets will continue to generate in the future. However, past earnings reflect how the firm was managed over the period, and to the extent that managers might not have made the right investment or financing choices, the reported earnings will be lower than could have been generated under better or optimal management. If there is the possibility of such a management change on the horizon, you will undervalue existing assets by using reported earnings.

In summary, the notion that existing assets can be easily valued at a mature company because of its long operating history is defensible only at well-managed companies—or at companies where existing management is so entrenched that there is no chance of a management change, operating in businesses where there is little or no chance of disruption.

GROWTH ASSETS

Companies can create growth assets in two ways. One is to invest in new assets and projects that generate excess returns; this is generally called "organic" growth. The other is to acquire established businesses and companies and thus short-circuit the process; this is "inorganic" or "acquisition-driven" growth. While both options are available to companies at any stage in the life cycle, mature companies are far more likely to take the acquired-growth route, for three reasons.

- As companies mature, internal investments start to become scarce relative to cash the firm has available to invest.
- As companies get larger, the new investments they make also must be sizeable to have any impact on overall growth. Although finding multibillion-dollar internal projects is difficult, finding acquisitions of that size is easier; it also affects the growth rate almost immediately.

- The third reason applies in businesses that have a long lead time between investment and payoff. In these businesses, there will be a lag between the initial investment in a new asset and the growth generated by that investment. With an acquisition, they are in effect speeding up the payoffs.

What are the consequences of the trend toward acquisition-driven growth for intrinsic valuation? Generally, the value of inorganic growth is much more difficult to assess than the value of organic growth. Unlike organic growth, wherein firms typically take several small investments each period, acquisitions tend to be on a large scale, infrequent and lumpy. A multibillion-dollar acquisition in one year might be followed by two years of no investments, followed by another acquisition. Because how much is reinvested and what return firms make on that reinvestment should reflect both organic and acquisition-driven growth, estimating these numbers for acquisitive companies is far more difficult. If you follow the standard practice of using the reinvestment numbers from the company's most recent financial statement, you risk overstating the value (if there was a large acquisition during the period) or understating it (if it was a period between acquisitions). Computing the return on capital on investments is much more difficult with acquisition-driven growth, partly because the accounting for acquisitions creates accounting items (goodwill, acquisition-related charges) that are difficult to deal with and incorporate into accounting returns.

When estimating discount rates for mature companies, I start from a position of more strength because I have more data to work with. Most mature companies have been publicly traded for extended periods, giving access to more historical price data, as well as data on earnings variability over time. They also have settled risk profiles, which stabilizes the data and makes estimating equity risk parameters from historical data more defensible with this group of companies than it was with the companies analyzed in the preceding two chapters. In addition, many mature companies, at least in the US, use corporate bonds to raise debt, which yields two benefits. The first is that you can get updated market prices and yields on these bonds, which are an input into the cost of debt. The second is that the bonds are accompanied by bond ratings, which provide not only measures of default risk but also pathways to default spreads and costs of debt. However, there are three estimation issues that can affect discount rate estimates at mature firms.

- The first issue is that mature companies accumulate debt from multiple places, leading to complex mixes of debt: fixed-rate and floating-rate, in multiple currencies, as senior or subordinated, and with different maturities. Because these loans often carry different interest rates (and even different ratings), analysts are left with the challenge of how to deal with this complexity when computing debt ratios and costs of debt.

- The second issue is that discount rates (costs of debt, equity, and capital) are affected by the firm's mix of debt and equity. The estimates you obtain from the current price data and ratings reflect the firm's current financing mix, and if that mix is altered, the discount rate must be reestimated.
- The third factor comes into play for firms that follow the acquisitive route to growth: acquiring a firm in a different business or with a different risk profile can alter the acquiring firm's discount rate.

STABLE GROWTH AND TERMINAL VALUE

As in any intrinsic valuation, the terminal value will account for a large share of the overall value of a mature firm, albeit a smaller portion than at young or growth companies. Because mature firms have growth rates that are close to that of the economy, the computation of terminal value might seem both more imminent and simpler with a mature company than with a growth company. Although this is generally true, two factors can still cause distortions in the computation:

a. **Stable growth rates, unstable risk, and investment profile:** Many mature companies have growth rates low enough to qualify for stable growth (less than the economy's growth rate and the risk-free rate). However, other inputs into the valuation might not reflect this maturity. Thus, a firm with a 2% growth rate in revenues and earnings may qualify as a stable firm based on its growth rate, but not if its risk puts it in the 90th percentile of all firms and it is reinvesting 90% of its after-tax operating income into the business. To qualify as a stable-growth firm that can be valued using the terminal value equation, the firm should have the risk profile of a stable firm (close to average risk) and should behave like a stable firm in terms of reinvestment.
b. **Locking in inefficiencies in perpetuity:** The cash flows from existing assets and the discount rates that I obtain from past data will reflect the choices the firm makes. To the extent that the firm is not managed optimally, the cash flows might be lower and the discount rate higher than it would have been for the same firm with different management. If I lock in current values on profit margins, returns on investment, and discount rates when estimating terminal value, and the firm is poorly run, I undervalue the firm by assuming that current practices will continue forever.

In sum, the assumption that a firm is in stable growth and can be valued using a terminal value equation cannot be made easily, even for mature firms. The challenges that you face when valuing mature firms reflect concerns that, while the numbers that you see for the company reflect its history and current management, changing how it is managed can create a very different firm. If change occurs, the expected cash flows, growth, and risk characteristics for the firm will be very different, as can be seen in figure 12.1.

FIGURE 12.1 | Valuation Challenges—Mature Businesses

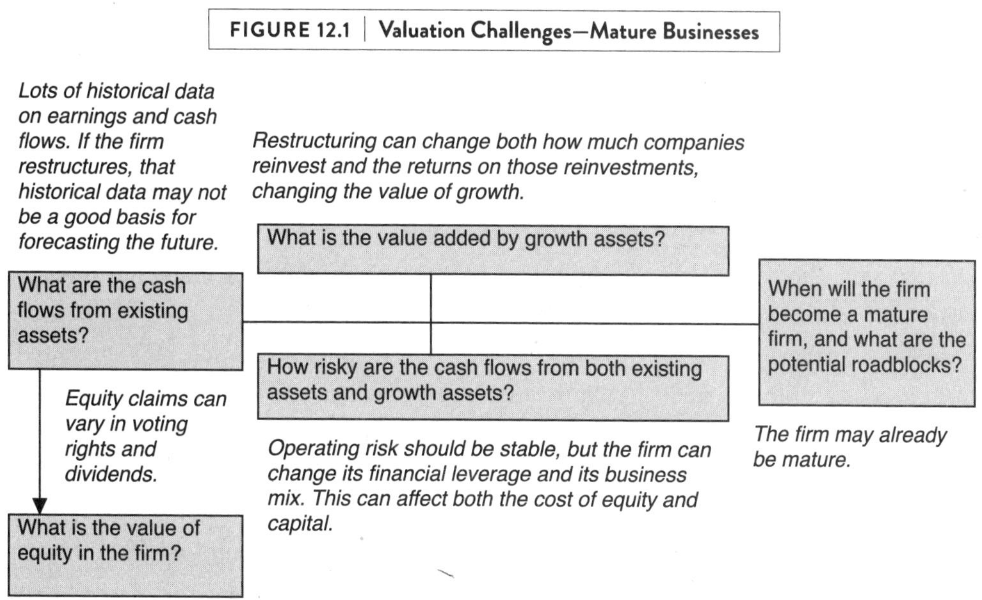

I will return to this picture later in the chapter, drawing a distinction between the status quo value of a firm, with existing management in place, and the restructured value of the same firm, with different management running it.

The Responses

To deal with these challenges, I will use the same five-step valuation template that I used for young-growth companies in chapter 10 and high-growth companies in chapter 11, but with an emphasis on mature businesses.

STEP 1: TELL A STORY

With mature companies, with their long financial history and established business models, a numbers-driven valuation is the right place to start, as you can see in figure 12.2.

FIGURE 12.2 | A Numbers-Driven Valuation Story

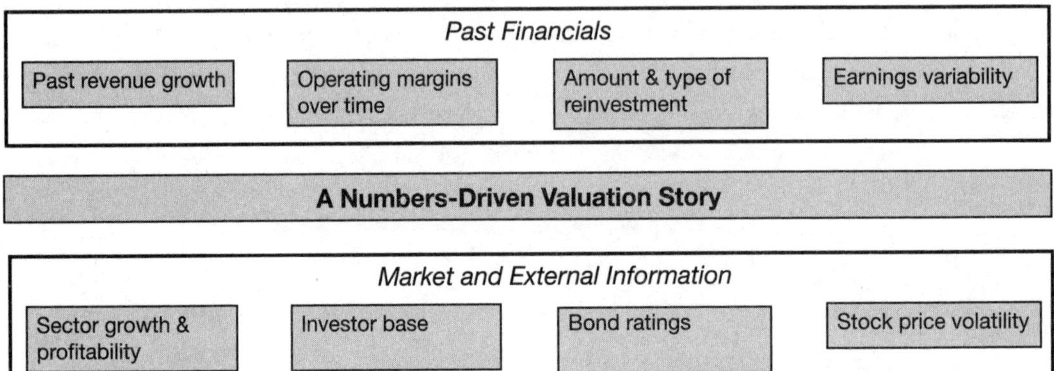

That said, though, you should probe for the weakest links in the story and consider alternative stories that might fit the company's future. Those stories come sometimes from the managers of the firm, pondering ways of returning to growth, and sometimes from investors in the company, seeking to change its business model.

STEP 2: RUN THE 3P TEST (POSSIBLE? PLAUSIBLE? PROBABLE?)

If your story for a mature business is an extension of its history, it may seem as if there is little need for a 3P test. That is true, for the most part, with two exceptions. The first is if macroeconomic or regulatory changes are imminent that could change the business economics, creating breaks with historical data. Thus, when valuing a pharmaceutical company that has a long history of solid revenue growth and high operating margins, your story that they will continue to grow and have high margins into the future will be put at risk if controls on drug pricing are on the verge of being imposed. With fossil fuel companies, climate change has put long-term business prospects at risk, and it is an open question whether you can assume that oil price cycles that characterized the market for the last century will continue in the future.

STEP 3: CONVERT THE VALUATION STORY INTO VALUATION MODEL INPUTS

Following the same path that I adopted for young-growth companies in chapter 10 and high-growth companies in chapter 11, I will break down the valuation story conversion here by input, starting with revenue growth, moving on to profitability and reinvestment, and then closing with risk.

a. **Revenue growth:** When forecasting revenue growth for a mature business, it makes sense to start with the historical growth it has recorded over the past, but you should add in the following considerations:
   - Time period: Even the most mature firms have good years, when revenues grow more than normal, and bad years, when they grow less. Consequently, when estimating revenue growth, it makes more sense to look at compounded annual growth rates over long periods, rather than growth in just the most recent year. If you are valuing a mature commodity company, you should consider where you are in the commodity price cycle, since earnings will be inflated (deflated) when the cycle is at its peak (floor).
   - Acquisition and divestiture growth effects: In their search for growth, mature companies often acquire and divest businesses, and you should break out how much revenue growth in the future will be affected by these perturbations.

   If you decide to break with historical growth rates and endow a mature business with much higher or lower growth in the future, you will need a strong storyline to explain why this might happen.
b. **Profitability:** As with revenue growth, you should start your analysis of operating margins for a mature company by looking at its history, before assessing whether change is coming, and if yes, in what form. For most mature firms, the most prudent choice is to assume that margins will stay at historic norms—i.e., averages over the last five or ten years, for instance. Unlike high-growth companies, where economies of scale and improving business models are used as an explanation for why margins in the future will be higher than they are today, it is difficult to argue with conviction that a mature company with a long history of low (high) operating margins will earn much higher (lower) margins in the future. If you do make an argument for a major shift in margins at a mature business, you must be prepared, with an explanation in terms of business model or a changing market, as to why this might happen.
c. **Reinvestment:** Firms need to reinvest to grow, and that truism applies to mature businesses as well as younger ones. However, as I noted in the challenge section, mature businesses often shift away from internal (or organic) growth to acquisitions as their primary growth mechanism. To value such businesses, you need to consider whether these acquisitions will create value, and that assessment will require that you treat acquisitions just as you would capital expenditures and forecast how much the company will spend, on average, on acquisitions in future years. To complete the

analysis, you should bring the effects of the acquisitions on revenue growth and margin predictions into future years, while also adjusting the risk profile of the firm to reflect acquisitions.

d. **Risk**: When valuing mature businesses, you start with information that can be used to assess their costs of capital and failure rates. Data on how volatile the company's stock has been on the market, the current bond rating for the company, and substantial information on its market capitalization weights for debt and equity can all be put to good use in computing the cost of capital. The caveat, though, is that cost of capital reflects the existing business and financing mixes that the mature firm is using, and if it decides to change one or both mixes, the cost of capital will have to change. An announcement by Exxon Mobil that it plans to buy back $5 billion in stock and invest $15 billion in green energy will change its business mix (since green energy has a different risk profile than fossil fuels) and its financing mix (since the buyback will reduce equity), and its cost of capital will have to be recalculated.

In sum, when valuing mature businesses, you should start with what the historical data of the company tells you about growth, profitability, reinvestment, and risk, but then you must question whether there have been or will be fundamental shifts that may lead you to expect changes to these inputs in the future.

STEP 4: VALUE THE BUSINESS

Since mature businesses derive the bulk of their value from investments that they have already made, it stands to reason that there will be less divergence of opinion, across investors, about that value. However, value will become more sensitive to two other choices that the firm makes:

- **Financing mix:** With mature businesses, changing the mix of debt and equity in running the business will have greater impact on the value you arrive at for the business than with young or high-growth businesses. That is because mature businesses often have the capacity to borrow more money, and not using that capacity can lead to higher costs of capital and lower value.
- **Cash flow return:** Young-growth and high-growth companies often cannot afford to return cash to their investors, and their need for cash makes questions about how they should return cash or what cash balances they should maintain less central to their value. Mature companies, on the other hand, generate large and positive cash

flows that they can choose to return, and if they do not, cash accumulates in these businesses. Not surprisingly, these firms will find themselves in the crosshairs of investors who feel that this cash is best returned to equity owners rather than kept in the firm. While cash by itself is a neutral asset—i.e., its presence has no effect on value—cash in the hands of management that you do not trust can destroy value, making your assessment of how much you trust incumbent managers a key valuation input.

The bottom line is that the value you estimate for a mature firm is far more dependent on your assumptions about financing and dividend policy than is the value that you estimate for a young- or high-growth firm. By extension, then, if those policies are set by existing management and you believe that the management can change, the value for the business will change as well.

STEP 5: KEEP THE FEEDBACK LOOP OPEN

With mature businesses, you will more often get intrinsic valuations that are closer to the firm's price than with young or growth companies, partly because more of their value comes from assets in place, where there should be less disagreement about value. There are, however, two exceptions:

First, with mature companies that are being disrupted, if your estimates of intrinsic value consistently stay above the market price and the market price drifts down, rather than toward your estimated value, it may be worth examining whether you are incorporating the effects of disruption sufficiently into your valuation. Put simply, markets may reflect the damaging effects of disruptions sooner than the company's financial statements, and these are the companies that become value traps—i.e., companies that look cheap, but only get cheaper over time.

Second, when you value a mature business, using its existing financial statements as the basis for forecasting cash flows and incorporating its existing financing mix and dividend policy, you are accepting incumbent management policy as a given. If an activist investor with enough funds to take a significant stake in the company takes such a position and pushes for change, that should be a trigger for you to reexamine your valuation of the business, as well.

CASE STUDY—PART 1: VALUING UNILEVER, A MATURE BUSINESS IN TRANSITION, SEPTEMBER 2022

Unilever is a company with a storied history that traces its founding back to 1929, when the Dutch company Margarine Unie and British soap maker Lever Brothers—two companies that had already been in existence for decades—merged their businesses. In the years since, the company has become a multinational with some of the most recognized consumer-product brand names in its stable. Its core business remains beauty and personal care, but it has added significant food and home care product businesses. In 2021, the company reported revenues of €52.44 billion, and pre-tax operating profits of €9.64 billion, and had a market capitalization of close to €90 billion in mid-2022.

Background

As a mature company, Unilever's financial history says a lot more about where it has come from and it might go than prognostications from analysts and managers. Figure 12.3 shows Unilever's revenues and operating income from 1998 to 2021.

FIGURE 12.3 | Unilever's Revenues and Operating Income

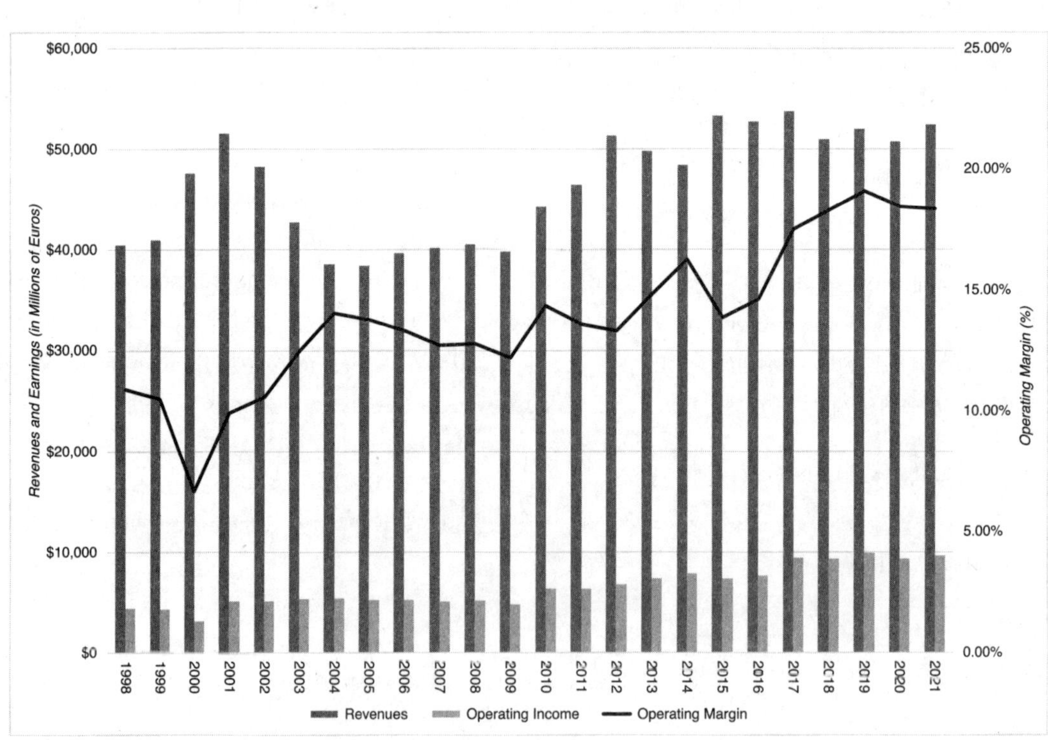

The numbers tell a compelling story of a company that has struggled to grow in recent years, with a compounded annual revenue growth rate of 1.19%, from 1998 to 2021. If there is good news in the chart, it is that the company has been able to improve its operating margins in the last decade, from 12.62% between 2001 and 2010 to 15.99% between 2011 and 2020, and especially so in the last four years, posting margins between 18% and 19%.

On the reinvestment front, Unilever has made some large acquisitions—including buying Bestfoods, the maker of mayonnaise, for $24.3 billion, in 2000; Horlicks, a drink maker, for $3.8 billion, in 2018; and Dollar Shave Club, a razor company, for $1.0 billion, in 2016—and many small ones. One measure of how active the company has been on the acquisition front is that it recorded goodwill of €21.57 billion, indicative of premiums paid, but these acquisitions clearly have not contributed to revenue growth in a noticeable way. To get a sense of how the three businesses (personal care, home care, and food) that Unilever is in are evolving, I broke down the firm's revenues and operating income between 2019 and 2021 in table 12.1, and looked at operating margins and growth by business:

Table 12.1 • Operating Results by Business—Unilever

	Revenues (in € mil)	Operating Income (in € mil)	CAGR in Revenues, 2016–21	Operating Margin, 2021
Beauty & Personal Care	€21,901	€4,742	1.66%	21.65%
Home Care	€10,572	€1,417	1.10%	13.40%
Food & Refreshment	€19,971	€3,477	-2.38%	17.41%

All three businesses are low growth, with the food business shrinking between 2016 and 2021. The beauty and personal care business is the most profitable part of the company, with an operating margin of 21.66% in 2016, while the home care business lags the most in terms of profitability.

The Story and Inputs

In constructing my valuation story for Unilever, I will stay close to what I see in its historical data. In other words, I will, at least for this iteration, assume that the company will continue its path of low revenue growth, while sustaining the higher operating margins it has been able to deliver in recent years. I will also assume no significant changes in financing and dividend policies, leaving costs of capital unchanged over time. To convert this story into specific inputs:

Revenue growth

I will assume that revenues will grow at 2% a year, which is higher than the historical growth rate but also reflective of the higher inflation expectations at the time of this valuation.

Operating margins

For next year, I expect Unilever to maintain the operating margin of 18.38% that it delivered in 2021, and I expect margins to stabilize around 18% over the next few years.

Reinvestment

With low growth, there will be relatively little reinvestment needed in the company. To estimate that reinvestment, which I expect will take the form of small acquisitions, I will assume €1.80 in revenue for every €1 invested.

Cost of capital

With Unilever's current financing mix, which is about 78% equity and 22% debt, and given its current geographic exposure for revenues, I estimate a euro cost of capital of 8.97% and assume that it will stay at that level in perpetuity.*

Failure risk

Given Unilever's history of large, positive earnings and ample cash reserves, I do not believe that there is any risk that the company will fail.

With these inputs, my valuation of Unilever is shown in figure 12.4.

* The euro risk-free rate at the time of the valuation was 2.1%, and Unilever's equity risk premium, given the regions of the world where it earns revenues, was 7.20%.

FIGURE 12.1 | Valuation of Unilever

Unilever	Sep-22
Low Growth	
Unilever is a low-growth company with solid operating margins on its businesses. The company will continue to grow at a low rate, while preserving the margins it has earned between 2017 and 2021. It does not need much reinvestment, though it will continue to do small acquisitions along the way, and it will stay with its current financing mix and dividend policy.	

The Assumptions						
	Base Year	*Next Year*	*Years 2–5*	*Years 6–10*	*After Year 10*	*Link to Story*
Revenues (a)	€ 52,444.00	2.0%	2.00%	2.00%	2.00%	Limited growth prospects
Operating Margin (b)	18.38%	18.4%	18.38% →	18.00%	18.00%	Margins stay at levels reached in most recent five years
Tax Rate	25.00%		25.00% →	25.00%	25.00%	Global/US marginal tax rate over time
Reinvestment (c)		1.80	1.80	1.80	16.67%	Maintained at global industry average
Return on Capital	14.39%	Marginal ROIC =	29.36%		12.00%	Strong brands
Cost of Capital (d)			8.97% →	8.97%	8.97%	Cost of capital based on current financing and geographic mix

The Cash Flows						
	Revenues	*Operating Margin*	*EBIT*	*EBIT (1 – t)*	*Reinvestment*	*FCFF*
1	€ 53,493	18.38%	€ 9,830	€ 7,372	€ 582	€ 6,791
2	€ 54,563	18.30%	€ 9,985	€ 7,489	€ 593	€ 6,896
3	€ 55,654	18.26%	€ 10,164	€ 7,623	€ 605	€ 7,018
4	€ 56,767	18.23%	€ 10,346	€ 7,760	€ 617	€ 7,142
5	€ 57,902	18.19%	€ 10,531	€ 7,898	€ 630	€ 7,269
6	€ 59,060	18.15%	€ 10,720	€ 8,040	€ 642	€ 7,397
7	€ 60,242	18.11%	€ 10,911	€ 8,184	€ 655	€ 7,528
8	€ 61,447	18.08%	€ 11,107	€ 8,330	€ 668	€ 7,662
9	€ 62,675	18.04%	€ 11,305	€ 8,479	€ 682	€ 7,797
10	€ 63,929	18.00%	€ 11,507	€ 8,630	€ 695	€ 7,935
Terminal year	€ 65,208	18.00%	€ 11,737	€ 8,803	€ 1,467	€ 7,336

The Value			
Terminal Value	€ 105,317.15		
PV (Terminal Value)	€ 44,628.23		
PV (CF over Next 10 Years)	€ 46,626.14		
Value of Operating Assets =	€ 91,254.37		
Adjustment for Distress	€ 0.00	Probability of failure =	0.00%
– Debt & Minority Interests	€ 36,686.00		
+ Cash & Other Non-operating Assets	€ 7,613.00		
Value of Equity	€ 62,181.37		
- Value of Equity Options	$0.00		
Number of Shares	2,569.20		
Value per Share	**€ 24.20**	Stock was trading at =	€ 45.60

As you can see, the low-growth story for Unilever, while clearly plausible and in line with its historical record, delivers a value per share of €24.20, well below the company's stock price, in September 2022, of €45.60 per share.

Pricing Mature Companies

The tailwinds that favor you when valuing mature companies include significantly more historical data and evidence of a working business model, and these also help when pricing such companies. That said, relying too much on historical data and assuming mean reversion—i.e., that variables (margins, risk, etc.) will revert back to historic norms—can be dangerous for a significant subset of mature companies, either because there is a threat of disruption or because of changing management.

The Challenges

When pricing mature companies, you start with several advantages. The first is that the long stretch of historical data on both operating metrics, like revenues and earnings, and market pricing for the company can provide perspective on how the market has priced this company in the past. The second is that in most aging sectors, such as mining, commodities, or consumer products, there will be several mature companies in the space, making it easier to construct peer groups. The third is that while markets do make mistakes on companies across the life cycle, those pricing mistakes should generally become smaller as companies mature.

You can break down the challenges that you will face when pricing mature companies by the pricing steps:

- **Scaling the price:** When scaling the pricing of mature companies, I have the luxury of choices, ranging from revenues to earnings (operating income, net income, EPS) to cash flows (EBITDA, net income + depreciation) to book value (of equity or invested capital). While choice is good, it can also become an instrument of bias, since analysts can choose the scalar that delivers the result they wanted to find.
- **Peer group construction:** As sectors age, there tend to be more mature firms that operate within them, but with globalization, those firms are often multinationals that are incorporated in different countries and operate in different regions. Thus, there are many mature businesses in mining, but as you can see on the list below, they are incorporated in multiple countries and have very different regional risk exposures:

Company	Market Cap (in US $ Bil)	Country
BHP	$132.00	Australia
China Shenhua Energy	$88.00	China
Rio Tinto	$87.00	UK
Glencore	$72.00	Switzerland
Vale	$60.00	Brazil
Nutrien	$50.00	Canada
Anglo American	$44.00	UK
Ma'aden	$44.00	Saudi Arabia
Freeport-McMoRan	$43.00	United States
Nornickel	$42.00	Russia

If your peer group is constrained to only include companies that are incorporated and traded in the same country where your company is incorporated, you will already start at a disadvantage in constructing a true peer group. If you do include all the companies in this group, which is the right path to follow, you will then need to find ways to control for differences in geographies (both in incorporation and operations) when comparing pricing.

- **Controlling for differences:** In addition to controlling for differences in geographies, there is another, more fundamental concern that you should have when pricing mature companies: Even if you control your sample to include only moneymaking mature companies, not all mature companies are equally well positioned to protect their profitability. Specifically, a company with stronger barriers to entry and competitive advantages (i.e., competitive moats), should be priced higher by markets than companies without those advantages. In addition, an imminent or ongoing disruption of the sector can shake up mature-company pricing in that sector, as historic norms fall to the wayside.

The Responses

When pricing mature businesses, I often take advantage of the additional data that I have on these businesses, but I still counsel caution on three components:

1. **Fight bias:** Much as your priors may push you to do so, you should avoid playing games with different pricing multiples until you find one that delivers the result that you hoped to find. One way to avoid this pitfall is to pick the pricing multiple that you will use in pricing a company before observing the results you get with each one. In making this choice, you should consider conventional practice (in terms of which multiple has been used most frequently in the past in a sector) as well as use business sense. In assessing project quality, scaling market capitalization to variables that are widely used within that sector makes sense, thus explaining the use of revenue multiples with retail firms, EV to EBITDA multiples with infrastructure companies, and price to book ratios with financial service companies.
2. **Go global:** As competition for mature companies is increasingly global, you should follow suit by making the peer groups that you use for pricing global as well. That will require you to (a) clean up for accounting differences across countries, when

comparing earnings or book value multiples, and (b) find ways to measure country risk from operations and incorporate it into the discount rate.

3. **Control for competitive moats and exposure to disruption:** When comparing pricing across companies in a peer group, you have to find ways of measuring competitive advantages. One widely used proxy is the return on invested capital earned by a company—a number that has the benefit of being easily computed and comparable across companies, but also the cost of being an accounting number, undermined by accounting inconsistencies and choices. Another available proxy is operating margins, especially in sectors where stronger competitive advantages lead to pricing power and higher profit margins.

CASE STUDY—PART 2: PRICING UNILEVER, SEPTEMBER 2022

The Lead-In

To price Unilever in September 2022, I looked for personal products firms with market capitalizations that exceed $10 billion, listed anywhere in the world, and arrived at a list of 21 companies. I then computed multiple pricing ratios (PE, PBV, EV to Sales, EV to EBITDA, and EV to invested capital) for each of the firms. The results are in table 12.2.

Table 12.2 • Pricing Multiples for Global Personal Product Companies, September 2022

Company	Country	PE	PBV	EV to Sales	EV/ EBITDA	EV/ Inv Cap	Pre-tax Operating Margin	Pre-tax ROIC	Expected Growth
Procter & Gamble Co. (NYSE: PG)	United States	22.36	7.21	4.42	16.50	5.01	23.31%	26.39%	4.75%
Unilever PLC (LSE: ULVR)	United Kingdom	19.13	5.54	2.47	12.72	2.92	17.50%	20.72%	5.03%
L'Oréal SA (ENXTPA: OR)	France	32.44	6.83	5.13	24.56	5.88	19.48%	22.33%	12.00%
Reckitt Benckiser Group PLC (LSE: RKT)	United Kingdom	14.47	4.93	3.89	15.52	3.00	22.85%	17.60%	8.18%
Estée Lauder Cos. Inc. (NYSE: EL)	United States	36.63	15.66	5.15	21.37	9.75	19.99%	37.85%	10.30%
Haleon PLC (LSE: HLN)	United Kingdom	14.64	0.82	3.29	15.55	0.87	19.46%	5.16%	5.49%
Colgate-Palmolive Co. (NYSE: CL)	United States	32.37	374.51	3.95	16.66	9.84	20.53%	51.20%	3.21%
Kimberly-Clark Corp. (NYSE: KMB)	United States	23.40	70.46	2.51	14.60	5.44	13.44%	29.19%	5.79%

Henkel AG & Co. KGaA (XTRA: HEN3)	Germany	22.05	1.24	1.27	10.18	1.22	9.98%	9.55%	3.41%
Hindustan Unilever Ltd. (BSE: 500696)	India	65.54	12.24	10.85	46.20	13.84	22.28%	28.42%	13.90%
Church & Dwight Co., Inc. (NYSE: CHD)	United States	24.54	5.39	4.05	18.36	3.64	18.47%	16.60%	5.46%
Beiersdorf Aktiengesellschaft (XTRA: BEI)	Germany	30.52	2.93	2.55	15.75	3.42	13.61%	18.28%	11.80%
Kao Corp. (TSE: 4452)	Japan	27.95	2.64	1.80	11.91	2.68	9.19%	13.65%	6.40%
Essity AB (publ) (OM: ESSITY B)	Sweden	23.95	2.33	1.59	11.87	1.69	8.42%	8.95%	9.97%
Shiseido Company, Ltd. (TSE: 4911)	Japan	25.17	3.16	2.08	19.48	2.61	3.48%	4.38%	21.10%
Unicharm Corp. (TSE: 8113)	Japan	42.20	4.34	2.91	15.65	7.70	13.87%	36.65%	10.70%
Clorox Co. (NYSE: CLX)	United States	38.39	31.90	2.91	21.98	5.87	10.22%	20.58%	6.59%
Unilever Indonesia Tbk PT (IDX: UNVR)	Indonesia	28.77	38.71	4.27	19.46	74.20	19.90%	345.46%	3.46%
Dabur India Ltd. (NSEI: DABUR)	India	57.34	11.92	8.97	44.95	12.44	18.02%	25.00%	9.44%
Godrej Consumer Products Ltd. (NSEI: GODREJCP)	India	55.11	8.18	7.54	39.97	8.32	17.58%	19.41%	11.00%
Yunnan Botanee Bio-Technology Group Co. Ltd. (SZSE: 300957)	China	72.06	14.61	14.54	62.66	75.46	22.76%	118.11%	31.00%
First Quartile		23.40	3.16	2.51	15.52	2.92	13.44%	16.60%	5.46%
Median		28.77	6.83	3.89	16.66	5.44	18.02%	20.72%	8.18%
Third Quartile		38.39	14.61	5.13	21.98	9.75	19.99%	29.19%	11.00%
Unilever versus Median		-33.50%	-18.84%	-36.50%	-23.64%	-46.27%	-2.89%	0.01%	-38.51%

On every multiple, Unilever comes in at below the median value for the sector, but the degree of cheapness varies across the multiples; it looks least underpriced with a price to book ratio and most underpriced with EV to sales and EV to invested capital.

In the last three columns, I highlight three variables that need to be controlled for when comparing pricing across companies: operating margins, return on capital, and expected earnings growth. Put simply, you should expect to see companies with higher margins, returns on capital, and earnings growth rates trade at higher multiples. On margins and return on capital, Unilever falls almost on the median, but it is well below the median on earnings growth, which may explain why it is priced lower than its peer group. To get a measure of how much Unilever's low growth may explain its lower pricing, I ran a regression of the PE ratios of the companies in the sector against their expected growth rates:*

$$PE = 19.30 + 152.65 \text{ (Expected Growth Rate) } R^2 = 37.94\%$$
$$(3.77)\ (3.41)$$

While the R squared of 38% of the regression may leave you unimpressed, it does indicate that in this sector, higher-growth companies earn much higher PE ratios. Plugging in the expected growth in earnings of 5.03% that analysts are predicting for Unilever to this regression, you get a predicted PE of 26.98.

$$\text{Predicted PE for Unilever} = 19.30 + 152.65\ (5.03\%) = 26.98$$

At 19.13 times earnings, Unilever still looks underpriced.

Add-ons and Addenda

The two biggest concerns that I often face with mature companies with long histories of profitability are that disruption can upend their business models and that changes in management could put the companies on different paths from their history.

Disruption's Dark Side

The last decade or two has seen a surge of disruption. Start-ups and young companies with nothing to lose have entered stable and profitable businesses with new business models and have upended the economics of these businesses in the process. These disruptions have received much attention, and I talked about how to value and price the disruptors in chapter 10—but not enough attention has been paid to the disrupted, the often mature companies that transform, almost overnight, from profitable and stable businesses to businesses on the edge of failure. I saw this with brick-and-mortar retail in the United States, when Amazon altered the retail business, and with cab service, after the entry of ride-sharing companies like Uber and Lyft.

* If your statistics knowledge is rusty, this is a simple linear regression. Differences in operating margins explain 38% (the R-squared) of the variation in EV to sales ratios, and the numbers in brackets below the regression coefficients are t statistics (with values above 2 indicating statistical significance).

If you are valuing a mature business, it is therefore prudent to at least consider the possibility that the business may be disrupted. As I see it, there are three characteristics that businesses that get disrupted seem to share:

1. **Sizeable economic footprint:** The probability of a business being disrupted increases proportionately with the amount of money that is spent by consumers on that business. Using this template, it is easy to see why financial services (active money management, financial advisory services, corporate finance) and education attract so many disruptors, and why publishing offers a smaller target.
2. **Inefficient production and delivery mechanisms:** A common characteristic that disrupted businesses share is that they are inefficiently run, and neither producers nor consumers seem happy about it. Consumers are unhappy because producers are nonresponsive to their needs and deliver substandard products, or products that don't meet their needs, at premium prices, yet producers seem to have little to show in surplus.
3. **Outdated competitive barriers and inertia:** You may wonder, if these businesses are so big and inefficiently run, what has allowed them to continue in existence for as long they have. The strongest force that they have going for them is inertia: consumers have been programmed to accept the status quo. Adding to their protections are regulatory or licensing requirements that have long outlived their original purpose and serve primarily to protect incumbents from insurgencies, and/or significant barriers (capital, knowledge, technology) to entering the business.

If a mature company operates in a business where disruption has either arrived or is imminent, you must incorporate its effects into your valuation in almost every input, as can be seen in figure 12.5.

FIGURE 12.5 | Valuing a Mature Company under Disruption Threat

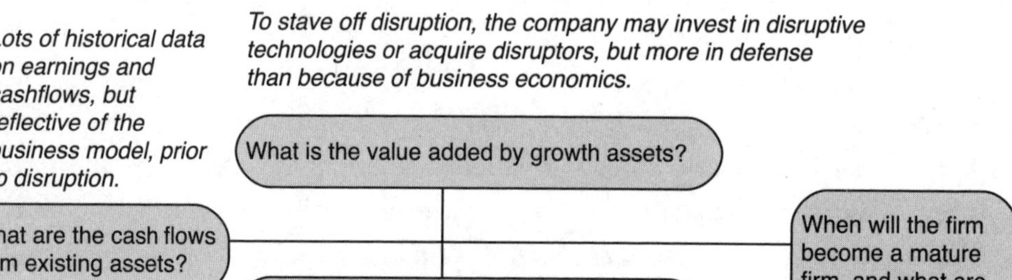

Put simply, mature companies in businesses that have been disrupted can expect to see operating margins decline and risk increase, thus reducing their value.

The Value of Control

The value of a business is determined by decisions made by its managers regarding where to invest its resources, how to fund these investments, and how much cash to return to the owners of the business. Consequently, when I value a business, I make implicit or explicit assumptions about both who will run that business and how they will run it; the value of a business will be much lower if I assume that it is run by incompetent managers rather than by competent ones. When valuing an existing company, private or public, where there is already management in place, I am faced with a choice. I can value the company run by the incumbent managers and derive what I can call a *status quo value*. I can also revalue the company with a hypothetical, optimal management team and estimate an *optimal value*. The difference between the optimal and the status quo values can be considered the value of controlling the business, as you can see in figure 12.6.

FIGURE 12.6 | The Expected Value of Control

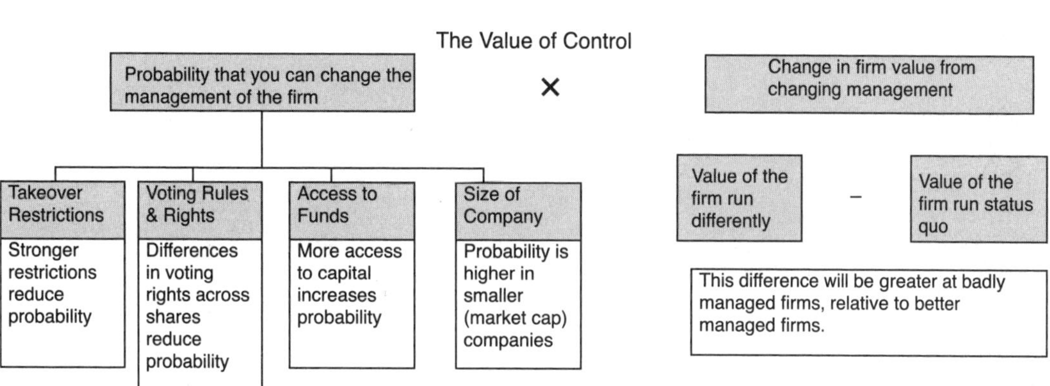

Note that for this control value to come into play, you must change a firm's management, and the likelihood of that happening can be a function of several factors, including differences in voting rights across shares, access to capital, and the size of the company.

Assuming that you can change management, what are some of the changes that you could make in the way a business is run to make it more valuable? Using the structure of valuation inputs, I looked at key questions that I can ask about how a company is run, with an eye on whether value can be changed at the company, in figure 12.7.

FIGURE 12.7 | A Template for Value Change

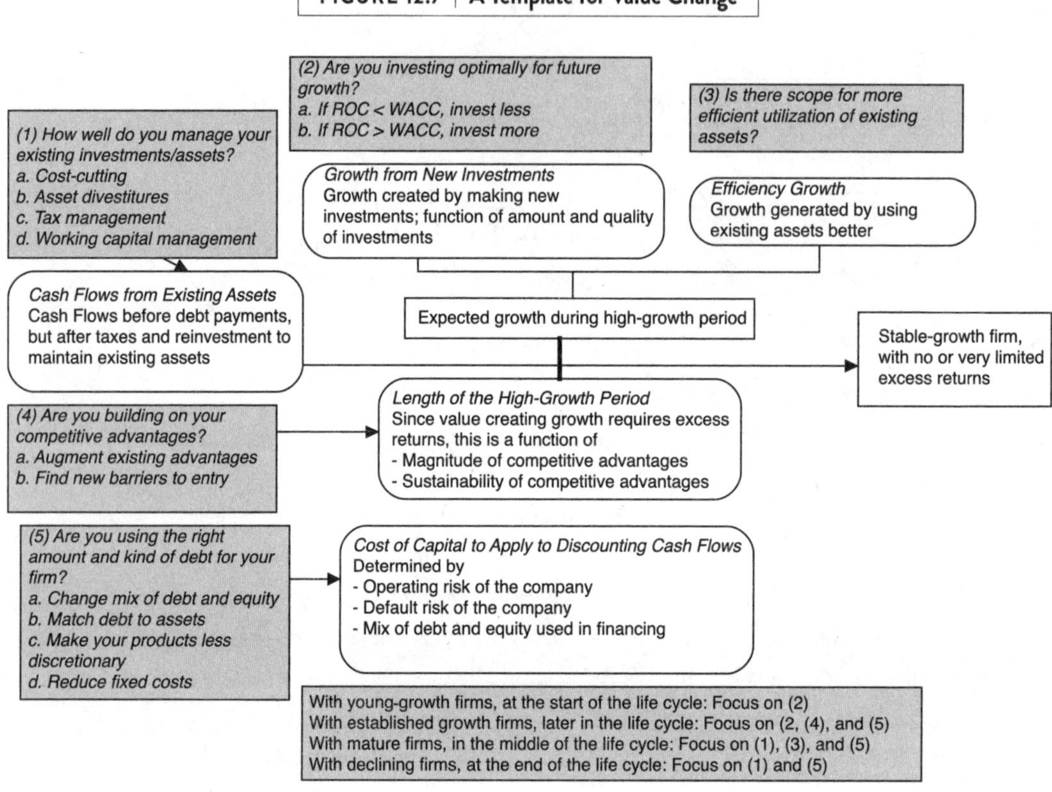

The value of control is in play for firms across the life cycle, but there are two reasons why mature firms are more likely to be targeted for its exploitation.

- There is far more potential for increasing value at mature firms than at younger firms—partly because they have more assets in place, which increase the possibilities of inefficiencies and cost cutting, and partly because they can more easily change their financing mix to reduce their cost of capital.
- The payoff, if you make these changes, tends to be more immediate and tangible, unlike the payoff from making better growth investments, which often requires patience and a long time horizon.

Retracing the steps to changing value, it is clear that the pathway to value enhancement will vary for different firms. Sub-optimal management can manifest itself in different ways at different companies. For firms where existing assets are poorly managed, the increase in value will come primarily from managing those assets more efficiently—higher cash flows from these assets and efficiency growth. For firms where investment policy is sound, but financing policy is not, the increase in value will come from changing the company's mix of debt and equity and a lower cost of capital. Table 12.3 considers potential problems in existing management, fixes to these problems, and the value consequences.

Table 12.3 • Ways of Increasing Value

Potential Problem	Manifestations	Possible fixes	Value Consequence
Existing assets are poorly managed	Operating margins are lower than peer group and return on capital is lower than the cost of capital	Manage existing assets better. This may require divesting some poorly performing assets.	Higher operating margin and return on capital on existing assets -> Higher operating income Efficiency growth -> in near term as return on capital improves
Management is underinvesting (too conservative in exploiting growth opportunities)	Low reinvestment rate and high return on capital in high-growth period	Reinvest more in new investments, even if it means lower return on capital (albeit higher than cost of capital)	Higher growth rate and higher reinvestment rate during high-growth period -> Higher value because growth is value creating.
Management is overinvesting (investing in growth that destroys value)	High reinvestment rate and return on capital that is lower than cost of capital	Reduce reinvestment rate until marginal return on capital is at least equal to cost of capital	Lower growth rate and lower reinvestment rate during high-growth period -> Higher value because growth is no longer value destroying
Management is not exploiting possible strategic advantages	Short or nonexistent high-growth period with low or no excess returns.	Build on competitive advantages	Longer high-growth period, with larger excess returns -> Higher value
Management is too conservative in its use of debt	Debt ratio is lower than optimal (or industry average)	Increase debt financing	Higher debt ratio and lower cost of capital -> Higher firm value
Management is overusing debt	Debt ratio is higher than optimal	Reduce debt financing	Lower debt ratio and lower cost of capital -> Higher firm value
Management is using wrong type of financing	Cost of debt is higher than it should be, given the firm's earning power	Match up debt to assets, using swaps, derivatives, or refinancing	Lower cost of debt and cost of capital -> Higher firm value
Management holds excess cash and is not trusted by the market with the cash	Cash and marketable securities are a large percentage of firm value; firm has poor track record on investments	Return cash to stockholders, either as dividends or stock buybacks	Firm value is reduced by cash paid out, but stockholders gain because the cash was discounted in the firm's hands
Management has made investments in unrelated companies	Substantial cross holdings in other companies that are being undervalued by the market	As a first step, try to be more transparent about cross holdings. If that is not sufficient, divest cross holdings	Firm value is reduced by divesting cross holdings but increased by cash received from divestitures. When cross holdings are undervalued, the latter should exceed the former

If control change is imminent at a company, it makes sense to value that company twice: once with the existing management in place (status quo), and once with the changes that you believe can or will be made at the company to make it more valuable (optimal).

CASE STUDY—PART 3: VALUING CONTROL IN A BUSINESS: UNILEVER

When valuing Unilever, earlier in this chapter, I pointed to its two-decades-long struggle to deliver higher growth, with acquisitions of small and large companies delivering little in terms of results. Along the way, Unilever shareholders have become restless with management, and a failed bid for GSK in 2022 crystallized their views that change was due at the company.* That dissatisfaction drew activist investors to its stock, with Nelson Peltz not only acquiring a 1.5% stake in the firm but quickly finding a slot on the board of directors.† While Peltz was opaque about the changes he would like to see at the company, in his prior investment at Procter & Gamble, a company similar to Unilever in its business profile, history, and global reach, he pushed for a simpler management structure and a shift in emphasis from its older brand names to ones that appealed to a younger market. Peltz's argument seems to be that Unilever has too many brands in its product portfolio, spread out across too many geographies and businesses, and that focusing on the right geographies can provide more growth and emphasizing the highest-margin business (personal care products) will yield better company-level margins.

Given the complexity of Unilever, and my absence of detailed knowledge about the company's operations, my hypothetical changes will be small and at company level, and are summarized in table 12.4.

Table 12.4 • Changes to Valuation Inputs from Restructuring—Unilever in 2022

Valuation Input	Status Quo	Restructured	Rationale
Revenue Growth	2% for years 1–10	3% for years 1–5, 2% in years 6–10	Higher growth in India & China
Operating Margin (Pre-tax)	18%	20%	More focus on (higher-margin) personal care division
Sales to Capital	1.80	2.50	Fewer acquisitions
Cost of Capital	8.97% -> 8.97%	8.00% -> 8.00%	Optimized financing mix

* M. Sweney, "Top Investor Castigates Unilever After Failed £50bn Bid for GSK Arm," *Guardian* (London), January 20, 2022, https://www.theguardian.com/business/2022/jan/20/top-investor-castigates-unilever-after-failed-pounds-50bn-bid-for-gsk-arm-terry-smith.

† S. Chaudhuri, "Unilever to Add Activist Investor Nelson Peltz to Board," *Wall Street Journal*, May 31, 2022, https://www.wsj.com/articles/unilever-to-add-activist-investor-nelson-peltz-to-board-11653980567.

I understand that these changes, small though they may seem in mathematical terms, nonetheless require immense work to deliver in a company as large and as complex as Unilever. If the changes can be made, the value effects will be substantial, as you can see in figure 12.8, containing the restructured valuation.

FIGURE 12.8 | Restructured Valuation of Unilever, September 2022

Unilever						Sep-22
Restructured						
Unilever is a low-growth company with solid operating margins on its businesses. Restructured, the company will be able to grow slightly faster, while improving its margins slightly (by shedding low-margin brands). It does not need much reinvestment, though it will continue to do small acquisitions along the way, and it will stay with its current financing mix and dividend policy.						
The Assumptions						
	Base Year	*Next Year*	*Years 2–5*	*Years 6–10*	*After Year 10*	*Link to Story*
Revenues (a)	€ 52,444.00	3.0%	3.00% →	2.00%	2.00%	Slight uptick in growth for next five years
Operating Margin (b)	18.38%	20.0%	20.00% →	20.00%	20.00%	Margins increase with increased focus on personal care products
Tax Rate	25.00%		25.00% →	25.00%	25.00%	Global/US marginal tax rate over time
Reinvestment (c)		2.50	2.50	2.50	16.67%	Maintained at global industry average
Return on Capital	14.39%	Marginal ROIC =	63.30%		12.00%	Strong brands
Cost of Capital (d)			8.00% →	8.00%	8.00%	Optimized financing mix leads to lower cost of capital
The Cash Flows						
	Revenues	*Operating Margin*	*EBIT*	*EBIT (1 – t)*	*Reinvestment*	*FCFF*
1	€ 54,017	20.00%	€ 10,803	€ 8,103	€ 629	€ 7,473
2	€ 55,638	20.00%	€ 11,128	€ 8,346	€ 648	€ 7,697
3	€ 57,307	20.00%	€ 11,461	€ 8,596	€ 668	€ 7,928
4	€ 59,026	20.00%	€ 11,805	€ 8,854	€ 688	€ 8,166
5	€ 60,797	20.00%	€ 12,159	€ 9,120	€ 708	€ 8,411
6	€ 62,499	19.35%	€ 12,094	€ 9,070	€ 681	€ 8,389
7	€ 64,124	19.51%	€ 12,512	€ 9,384	€ 650	€ 8,734
8	€ 65,663	19.68%	€ 12,919	€ 9,690	€ 616	€ 9,074
9	€ 67,108	19.84%	€ 13,313	€ 9,984	€ 578	€ 9,407
10	€ 68,450	20.00%	€ 13,690	€ 10,267	€ 537	€ 9,731
Terminal Year	€ 69,819	20.00%	€ 13,964	€ 10,473	€ 1,745	€ 8,727
The Value						
Terminal Value			€ 145,456.24			
PV (Terminal Value)			€ 67,374.38			
PV (CF over Next 10 Years)			€ 56,038.13			
Value of Operating Assets			€ 123,412.52			
Adjustment for Distress			€ 0.00		Probability of failure =	0.00%
– Debt & Minority Interests			€ 36,686.00			
+ Cash & Other Non-operating Assets			€ 7,613.00			
Value of Equity			€ 94,339.52			
– Value of Equity Options			€ 0.00			
Number of Shares			2569.20			
Value per Share			**€ 36.72**		Stock was trading at =	$45.60

My estimate of value per share increases from €24.20, in the status quo value, to €36.72 in the optimal value—an increase of about a third—but still trails the market price by a significant margin.

Conclusion

If the key ingredients that you need to value a company are lots of historical data and patterns that can be teased out from that data in models, you should find yourself in a sweet spot with mature companies. Often decades in the making, these companies have built up businesses that stretch across products and geographies and deliver sustained profits, albeit with limited growth. Extrapolating the past can sometimes be all you need to value these companies, dispensing with the need for subjective judgments on future growth, management quality, and competitive advantages. But that process can also lead you off the right path, if these companies are run inefficiently, with inertia rather than analysis driving investing, financing, and dividend decisions. For such firms, you should consider changes that can be made to business practices, and the value increase that would result from these changes; this is the activist investing play. In the last two decades, there has been another development that has blindsided those who value mature companies: the entrance of disruptors, who can change the profitability and growth characteristics of businesses in the blink of an eye, converting good to bad businesses. Managers in mature companies that ignore this disruption will find their business models upended, and investors in these mature companies who are blind to this disruption when valuing or pricing these firms will find themselves holding value traps, stocks that look cheap that continue to become cheaper.

13

Valuation and Pricing: Declining Businesses

I HAVE LOOKED AT, and attempted to address, the valuation challenges you face with start-ups and young companies, in chapter 10, with high-growth companies, in chapter 11, and with mature companies, in chapter 12. In this chapter, I turn my attention to valuing companies in the end stage of the life cycle—i.e., in decline. The challenges that you face when valuing declining companies are, for the most part, not mechanical but psychological. Investors and managers are hardwired for optimism. Assuming that a company's future will bring decline and perhaps even demise seems unnatural, and managing it with that expectation feels like surrender. It should come as no surprise that the greatest damage to value at these companies comes from managers desperately finding ways for the company to grow—sometimes by continuing to invest back large amounts into shrinking and bad businesses, and sometimes through acquisitions of growth businesses—and from investors who assume that these investments will pay off.

Valuation

In the chapter on mature companies, I noted that revenue growth tails down toward the growth rate of the economy and margins stabilize as companies mature. While management at these companies may not welcome these trends, preferring high growth and rising margins, there will be a point in time when these companies will have to face worse trend lines, where revenues start to shrink and margins come under pressure as changes in customer tastes, markets, and technology work against them. This section will focus on companies that are in decline and how best to value them.

Characteristics

In the last chapter on mature companies, we looked at disruptors entering businesses, and how investors valuing these companies have to consider the resulting effects on these companies—declining revenues and profits, and lower value. Let's start this chapter by looking at the characteristics that declining companies tend to share, with an eye toward the problems they create for managers running these businesses and investors trying to value or price them. Not every declining company possesses all these characteristics, but they do share enough of them to make the following generalizations:

1. **Stagnant or declining revenues:** Perhaps the most telling sign of a company in decline is its inability to increase revenues over extended periods, even when times are good. Falling revenues or revenues that grow at less than the rate of inflation indicates operating weakness. It is even more telling if these patterns in revenues apply not only to the company being analyzed but also to the overall sector, indicating problems that extend beyond the company's management to the entire business.
2. **Shrinking or negative margins:** The stagnant revenues at declining firms are often accompanied by shrinking operating margins, partly because of declining pricing power and partly because these companies are dropping the prices that they charge for their products and services to keep revenues from falling further. This combination results in deteriorating or negative operating income at these firms, with occasional spurts in profits generated by asset sales or one-time profits.
3. **Asset divestitures:** If one of the features of a declining firm is that existing assets are sometimes worth more to others, who intend to put them to different and better uses, it stands to reason that asset divestitures will be more frequent at declining firms than at firms earlier in the life cycle. If the declining firm has substantial debt obligations, the need to divest becomes stronger, driven by the desire to avoid default and to pay down debt.
4. **Acquisitions in search of growth:** In what might seem like a contradictory development, you are also more likely to see acquisitions, at least at some declining firms, with many driven by desperation. In fact, defensive acquisitions—when one company acquires another, knowing that it is paying too much but with the rationale that

if it does not do so, one of its competitors will—become more common at declining firms.

5. **Big payouts—dividends and stock buybacks:** Declining firms have few if any growth investments that generate value, and they have existing assets that might be generating positive cash flows and engage in asset divestitures that likewise result in cash inflows. Consequently, it makes sense that declining firms, and especially those with low debt burdens, not only pay out large dividends—sometimes exceeding their earnings—but also buy back stock.
6. **The downside of financial leverage:** If debt is a double-edged sword, declining firms often are exposed to the wrong edge. With stagnant and declining earnings from existing assets and little potential for earnings growth, it is not surprising that some declining firms face overwhelming debt burdens. Note that much of this debt was probably acquired when the firm was in a healthier phase of the life cycle, and at terms that cannot be matched today. In addition to difficulties these firms face in meeting their existing obligations, they face additional trouble in refinancing their debt, because lenders will demand more stringent terms.

The Challenges

A company's intrinsic value is the present value of the company's expected cash flows over its lifetime. Although that principle does not change, when valuing declining firms, there are unique challenges that I confront as I estimate cash flows and try to value them. As in the previous chapters, I will break down the challenges as they pertain to assets in place, growth assets, risk, and assumptions about stable growth.

ASSETS IN PLACE

When valuing a declining firm's existing assets, I estimate the expected cash flows from these assets and discount them back at a risk-adjusted discount rate. Although this is standard valuation practice, two characteristics of declining companies can throw a wrench into this part of the process:

a. **Earning less than cost of capital:** In many declining firms, existing assets, even if profitable, earn less than the cost of capital. The natural consequence is that discounting the cash flows back at the cost of capital will yield a value that is less than the capital invested in those assets. From a valuation perspective, this is neither surprising nor unexpected; assets that generate subpar returns can destroy value.

b. **Divestiture effects:** If existing assets earn less than the cost of capital, the logical response is to sell or divest these assets and hope that the best buyer will pay a high price for them. These divestitures of assets create discontinuities in past data and make forecasting more difficult. To see how divestitures can affect past numbers, consider a firm that divested a significant portion of its assets midway through last year. All the operating numbers from last year, including revenues, margins, and reinvestment, are affected by the divestiture, but the numbers for the year also reflect the operating results from the portion of the year before the divestiture. Similarly, risk parameters such as betas, for which you may use past prices or returns in my calculation, can be affected by divestitures of assets midway through the period. For the forecasting consequences, try estimating the revenues and earnings for a firm that is expected to divest a large portion of its assets over the next few years. Not only do you have to pinpoint the assets that will be divested and the effects of the divestiture on operating revenues and earnings, you also must estimate the proceeds from the divestitures. Put another way, a divestiture by itself does not affect value, but what you expect the company to receive in comparison to the divested assets can affect value.

In short, the failure to earn more than the cost of capital on existing assets implies that the value the company derives from these assets, as a going concern, may be lower than the value it would obtain from divesting the assets, especially if the buyers of these assets can put them to better use.

GROWTH ASSETS

Since growth assets can be expected to add little value at declining firms, you should consequently not expect the valuation of these assets to have a significant impact on value. While this is generally true, there are two twists that can have significant effects on value at individual companies:

1. **Divestitures and shrinkage:** If a firm's business has turned bad—i.e., investments earn less than the cost of capital—a sensible management team will try to shrink the firm by divesting assets that earn well below the cost of capital. Divestitures can lead to negative growth rates while bringing cash into the firm, at least for the foreseeable future. Analysts who have learned their valuation fundamentals at healthier companies often are uncomfortable with the notion of negative growth rates and cash flows that exceed earnings, but that combination characterizes many declining firms.

2. **Growth at any cost:** Some declining firms are in denial about their standing in the life cycle, and they continue to invest in new assets as if they had growth potential, with perverse effects on value. A declining firm that tries to invest larger and larger amounts in new assets with low expected returns and in overpriced acquisitions may be able to grow its revenues, but will see its value decrease as it grows.

Put simply, some declining firms may find ways to continue growing, but often at the expense of value. Others will accept their place in the life cycle and try to shrink over time. A lucky few may be able to reinvent themselves, as mature or growth companies.

RISK

If the cost of capital is a weighted average of the costs of debt and equity, what is it about declining firms that makes estimating these numbers difficult? It is a combination of a changing financing mix, a shifting asset mix, and concerns about distress.

1. The large dividends and buybacks that characterize some declining firms can have an effect on the overall value of equity and debt ratios you use in the computation. Returning large amounts of cash to stockholders reduces the market value of equity through the market price, with dividends, and the number of shares, with stock buybacks. If debt is not repaid proportionately, the debt ratio increases, which affects costs of debt, equity, and capital.
2. The divestitures of some assets, and the acquisitions of other assets, sometimes in new businesses or markets, that are typical at many declining firms also implies changing mixes of assets/businesses at these firms, leading to changes in operating risk and cost of capital.
3. The presence of distress can have significant effects on both the cost of equity and debt. The cost of debt increases as default risk increases, and some rated firms will see their ratings drop to junk status. If operating earnings drop below interest expenses, the tax benefits of debt also dissipate, leading to further upward pressure on the after-tax cost of debt. As debt-to-equity ratios climb, the cost of equity should also increase, as equity investors see much more volatility in earnings. From a measurement standpoint, analysts who use regression betas, which reflect equity risk on a lagged basis, might find themselves facing the unusual scenario of a cost of equity that is lower than the pre-tax cost of debt.*

* Regression betas are computed using long periods of historical returns. To the extent that the firm was healthy (or healthier than it is today) over some of that period, the regression beta understates the true beta.

In summary, the cost of capital for a declining firm can be a work in progress, with the operating risk affected by divestitures of key portions of the business, debt ratios changing as the company returns cash to equity investors and pays down debt, and distress, and the resulting risk of failure, being a clear and present danger at some firms.

STABLE GROWTH AND TERMINAL VALUE

The standard procedure for estimating terminal value was examined in detail in earlier chapters: You first estimate a growth rate that a firm can sustain forever—with the caveat that this growth cannot exceed the growth rate of the economy—with the risk-free rate acting as a proxy. You follow up by making reasonable assumptions about what a firm can generate as excess returns in perpetuity, and you use this number to forecast a reinvestment rate for the firm. You complete the process by estimating a discount rate for the terminal value computation, with the qualifier that the risk parameters used should reflect the fact that the company will be a more stable one. On this front, declining and distressed firms pose special challenges.

- First, you must consider the probability that the firm being valued will not make it to stable growth. Many declining firms will default and go out of business, especially if they are burdened with debt, and some will choose to liquidate themselves, even if they are not in distress.
- Second, even if a firm is expected to survive to reach steady state, not only may its growth rate in perpetuity be well below the growth rate of the economy and inflation, in some cases, it can be negative. Essentially, the firm will continue to exist, but it will get progressively smaller over time as its market shrinks.
- Third, with declining firms that are currently earning well below their cost of capital, and with incumbent management firmly in place and in denial about the state of the business, growth in perpetuity may come from these firms continuing to take projects that earn less than the cost of capital over time, essentially locking in perpetual value destruction.

In figure 13.1, I summarize the challenges that are faced in valuing declining companies, especially ones overlaid with distress.

FIGURE 13.1 | Challenges in Valuing Declining Companies

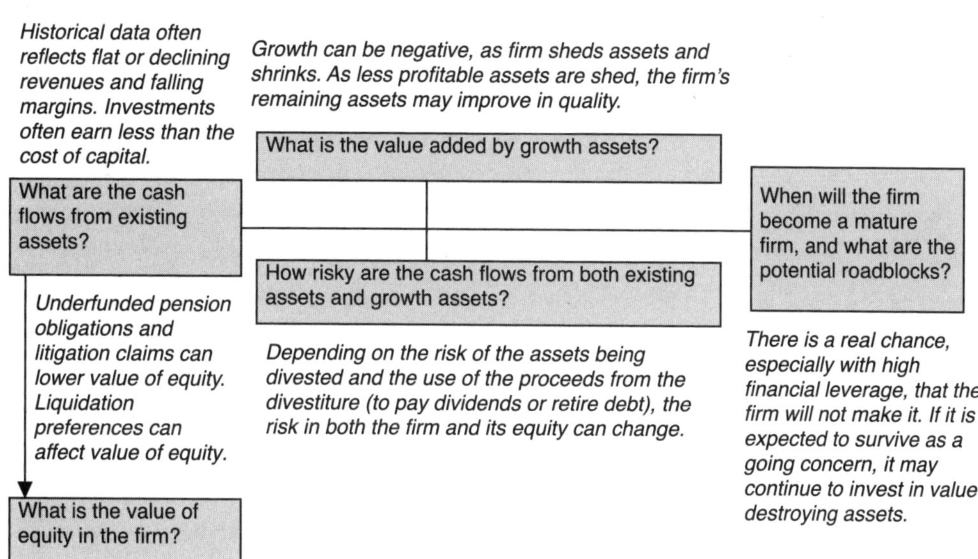

The Responses

To value declining companies, you must steer away from mechanical models in valuation, where earnings always grow over time, cash flows grow in tandem, and consequently businesses just get bigger and more valuable. As with young-growth, high-growth, and mature companies, I will break down the process for declining companies into valuation steps:

STEP 1: TELL A STORY

As with companies earlier in the life cycle, the valuation of a declining company starts with a story, albeit one that reflects the realities that the company faces. That will include a shrinking market for its products and services, increased competition for what's left of the market, and worries about survival. That story is unlikely to be uplifting or optimistic, but it should allow for differentiation between declining companies on the following dimensions:

- **Market decline:** The starting point for your story must be with a diagnosis of what is causing the company's market or revenues to shrink. In some cases, such as in the tobacco business, it may be that the products that it markets have health and societal costs, and the resulting pushback (legal, regulatory, social) is reducing demand, at least among younger consumers. In other cases, such as in brick-and-mortar retailing, it may be that disruptors (online retailers) are claiming a larger and larger share of the overall market, leaving less of the market for physical stores. Finally, at the individual company level, decline can arise because a competitive advantage that the company used in the earlier stages of the life cycle to generate growth and earn high margins has dissipated or is dissipating. This can be the case, as patent expiration approaches, for a pharmaceutical company that has been dependent on a single patent-protected blockbuster drug for its growth and high margins, or as a brand name loses its hold on consumers for a consumer-product company that draws the bulk of its revenues and profits from that brand name.

- **Management response:** Your story also should incorporate your expectations about how the management at a declining firm will respond to market decline, with four variations.
    - The first, and perhaps most frequent response, is *denial*: management refuses to face up to decline, attributing any symptoms of operating malaise (year-to-year revenue decline or stagnation, dropping margins) to temporary conditions that, once resolved, will yield to high growth and solid margins. In keeping with the definition of insanity, these firms will continue to do what they have done in the past in terms of investing and financing, even though these strategies have stopped working.
    - The second is *desperation*: management tries everything it can to reverse decline, including acquiring growth companies in other businesses and investing in the disruptive technologies that caused its decline in the first place. As an example, the initial reaction of many brick-and-mortal retailers to Amazon's success in the retail market was to acquire other online retail businesses, often at absurd premiums.
    - The third is *acceptance*: managers accept their standing in the life cycle and adopt corporate financial policies that reflect that standing. That will often mean a cessation of new investments, a pickup of divestitures, and a gradual pay-down of debt as they embark on the mission of making their firms smaller and more attuned to a smaller market.
    - The fourth is *reinvention*: managers uncover the core competencies and competitive advantages that allowed their firms to succeed in the first place and use them to create new business models or enter new markets, thus opening

the doors to fresh leases on corporate life. There may be only a few firms that succeed on this path, but their stories get told and retold as they become the subjects of case studies at business schools and props for management consulting sales pitches.

- **Company end game:** The views that you have about how management will respond to decline will also affect what you see as the end game for a declining company, with four possible outcomes.
  - In the first outcome, where the company rediscovers itself in a new business or market, your end game will be that the company returns to health—sometimes as a growth company, but even if not to high growth, at least back to being a mature company, albeit with new operating metrics.
  - In the second, where a company decides to face up to market decline and shrink itself, the end game may be either a much smaller version of the company, serving a niche market, albeit with much healthier profit margins and cash flows, or an orderly liquidation, where the remaining assets are sold to buyers who may be able to put them to better use.
  - In the third, where the company continues to invest in bad businesses, either through organic projects or acquisitions, the end game will be value destruction over the long term. If the company has significant debt outstanding, there may very well be no long term, and a distress-triggered liquidation will be the end game.

STEP 2: RUN THE 3P TEST (POSSIBLE? PLAUSIBLE? PROBABLE?)

When valuing declining companies, blindly following management stories about what they plan to do with these companies can easily lead to fairy tales. The stories of legendary business turnarounds and reincarnations, told and retold by consultants and management experts, has led many managers to believe that any narrative other than one of reinvention/reincarnation is admitting failure. It is your job to assess whether a turnaround plan, as presented by management, is a fairy tale or plausible and, if plausible, whether the management team in place is the one that can deliver on its outcomes (whether it is probable). In making this assessment, there are at least three factors that come into play:

- **Company-specific versus sector problems:** As I noted in the last section, decline can be due to company-specific factors (a fading competitive advantage, a patent approaching expiration) or due to sector-wide issues (a decline in demand for tobacco products). Generally, it is easier to map and deliver turnaround strategies for company-specific decline rather than for macro (sector-wide) decline. A fading brand name can be revitalized, perhaps by changing the target market and advertising; buying a potential blockbuster drug in the pipeline at a bargain price can breathe new life into a pharmaceutical company. In contrast, for a tobacco company to engineer a revenue-growth turnaround, it must enter a new business, either through a large investment or an acquisition, and the odds of success are much lower.

- **Competitive actions:** It is easier to map a turnaround plan when a few companies are in decline but most in the sector are healthy than it is to map turnaround plans when most companies in a sector are fighting decline at the same time. That is because declining companies often see the same pathways back to health, and if they all try to adopt those pathways, they end up competing on those pathways, reducing the chances of success for all of them. Thus, early in the years of disruption by online retail, many brick-and-mortar retailers decided that a turnaround required creating an online retail presence, but as they all attempted to create this presence, customers chose the haven of buying from Amazon over the chaos, both in terms of shopping and service, of company online retail platforms.
- **Management history and capabilities:** If you believe that a turnaround plan is plausible, you still must assess whether the company has the management in place and the resources (capital, infrastructure, personnel) that it needs to execute the plan. Some of that assessment will require looking at management's history—with a history of success, perhaps at a different firm with similar problems, working in its favor—but a great deal will remain a judgment call. As a rule, it is worth remembering that turnarounds are rare, and that the onus is on the business making the turnaround plan to convince you that it can succeed, rather than the reverse.

In sum, almost every declining company that you value will claim to have a plan to turn the business around and return to growth, but it is your job, as an investor, to make your judgment on whether the plan is possible, plausible, and probable.

STEP 3: CONVERT THE VALUATION STORY INTO VALUATION MODEL INPUTS

With your valuation story for a declining company in place, let's turn to converting that story into valuation inputs, following the same structure that I used in the earlier chapters. Since the ways companies respond to decline vary, and how the valuation inputs play out will depend on what you expect the management response to decline (denial, desperation, acceptance, or reinvention) to be, I will examine what valuation inputs will look like for each response:

1. **Revenue growth:** If a firm is in decline, you would expect the expected revenue growth rate that you use for the firm to reflect that decline, but your choice of growth rates must be attuned to how you see management responding.
   a. With management in either denial or in acceptance, you would expect revenue growth to continue to be negative, but with one significant difference in process. Management in denial is unaware of, or unwilling to look at, deterioration in its business model and, consequently, does nothing to stop the decline. Revenue shrinkage at the firm then will follow the same path that it has historically, and perhaps pick up its pace. Management that accepts the business has deteriorated might not be able to do much to change the fundamental economics of the business but can try to minimize damage by shrinking revenues where it makes the most economic sense. Thus, if you have two brick-and-mortar retailers, both of whom are facing decline, the retailer in denial will continue to open new stores and see sales slide across the board, while the retailer in acceptance starts shutting down the least profitable existing stores, and/or those with the biggest capital commitments, creating a healthier path to a smaller firm.
   b. *With management in desperation or resurrection mode*, expected revenue growth can be positive but, again, with very different outcomes for value. Management that is desperate can buy growth, especially if it is willing to pay any price, and the larger the price paid, the more growth it can add. Management in resurrection mode is going after positive revenue growth, but in a much more calculated manner, by looking at new businesses and markets that it can enter successfully. That will not only usually take more time to manifest than growth delivered in desperation mode, it will also be much more value-creating in the long term.
2. **Profitability:** Coming into valuation, declining companies often have margins that are deteriorating, and what you assume will happen in the future will depend, again, on how management responds to the deterioration. When managers are in denial, and nothing material is changing in how the company runs its business, you should expect margins to keep declining in the future. In contrast, with management in acceptance, divesting assets that generate the biggest losses (or the least profits) may give the company a shot at stabilizing or even increasing margins—if not right away,

at least over time. When managers are desperate, they can buy temporary boosts in profitability, either through acquisitions or expensive window dressing, but those boosts will come at high cost and fade quickly. When managers are reinventing a business, margins may continue to decline in the short term, but in the long term, they will move toward the margins of the new business or market being targeted.

3. **Reinvestment:** The biggest difference, and perhaps the game-changing one, when valuing declining companies is what you assume the company will reinvest in the future. With managers in denial, inertia and autopilot investment rules may induce the company to continue to reinvest as it used to when it was a mature business, even though its revenues are in decline, creating a toxic combination for value. With managers in acceptance, there will be divestitures of portions of existing businesses rather than new investments, creating a shrinking, not a growing, capital base. With desperate managers in place, there will be a great deal of reinvestment, though with no discernible objective other than to post growth and better margins in the next period. With reinvention, there can be reinvestment as well, but those investments will be driven by a vision of entering new markets or businesses and thus be more focused.
4. **Risk:** On the risk front, in the denial and acceptance cases, the company stays in its existing business. There should be little change in operating risk, but the debt load that managers in denial either take on or refuse to pay down, in the face of decline, can lead to much higher distress risk. In the reinvention case, operating risk for the company will evolve to incorporate the risk of the new business or market that the company enters, which may be higher or lower than its existing business. In desperation mode, the pursuit of growth for the sake of growth will not only have unpredictable effects on operating risk, with changes reflecting the acquisitions made along the way, but will lead to distress in the long term, especially if those acquisitions are funded with debt.

As you can see, the valuation inputs for a declining firm will vary widely, depending on what you believe about the management of the company. Table 13.1 summarizes the effects.

Table 13.1 • Valuation Inputs for Declining Companies, by Management Response

	Expected Management Response to Declining Business			
	Denial	**Desperation**	**Acceptance**	**Reinvention**
Revenue Growth	Negative	Positive blips from acquisitions or investments	Negative	Positive, but may take time to unfold
Profitability	Long-term decline	May see short-term boosts but will fade to long-term decline	Short-term decline, then stability	Decline in near term but increase over time to reflect new business margins
Reinvestment	Continue with status quo, in existing business	Significant and unpredictable reinvestment (acquisitions)	Negative (divestitures)	Negative in existing business, but positive in new business(es)
Risk	Stable operating risk, increased failure risk	Volatile operating risk, increased failure risk	Stable operating risk, stable failure risk	Melded operating risk, to reflect new business entered, with failure risk if reinvention fails

STEP 4: VALUE THE BUSINESS

Once you have a view on how you think the management of a declining company will respond to decline, and have converted your view into valuation inputs, the cash flows and value of the company will reflect those inputs.

- For management in denial, a combination of shrinking revenues and declining margins, in the long term, will cause long-term declines in earnings and cash flows, pushing the company either into distress (where equity will be worth nothing) or into a terminal value, as a bad business, where equity will be worth very little.
- For management in acceptance, revenues will shrink and margins will compress in the short term before stabilizing into a steady-state terminal value, reflective of a smaller, but healthier, company, or into a liquidation value, if that yields a higher payoff.
- For management in desperation, there is no predictable pattern to earnings and cash flows, but whatever benefits to value that may accrue from temporary surges in growth or profitability, usually from acquisitions, will fade and, over time, be more than offset by the cost of the reinvestment needed to deliver that surge, creating value destruction on steroids.
- For management intent on reinvention, there will be no short-term reprieve from shrinking revenues and margin pressure, but to the extent that the reinvention works, the firm's revenue growth, margins, and reinvestment will change over time to incorporate the effects of the new business or market entered.

STEP 5: KEEP THE FEEDBACK LOOP OPEN

The value that you estimate for a declining company will be determined, in large part, by how you think management will respond to decline, and your feedback loop must be structured around feedback on that front.

- If you are assuming, in your valuation, that management is in denial, a change in top management, a reconstruction of the board of directors, or a new CEO will constitute a break from the past and should lead to a reassessment, though you will have to decide which path the new management will be taking.
- If you have valued a company on the presumption that it is run by desperate managers, chasing growth at any cost, the entry of activist investors into the shareholder ranks creates the possibility of pushback, and perhaps even change at the company.
- If your valuation of a declining company is built on the assumption that managers will follow a sensible path, either accepting decline as an inevitable and working within its limits or reinventing the firm by pushing into new businesses or markets, there is always a chance, given that both of these strategies can take a long time to unfold, that investors won't have the faith to hold on and that these paths will be abandoned before they have a chance to deliver results.

In addition, when valuing a declining company, it is worth tracking what lenders think about the company and, if the company has bonds that are traded, what the bond market thinks about the company's chances of survival.

CASE STUDY—PART 1: VALUING BED BATH AND BEYOND, A DECLINING BUSINESS, SEPTEMBER 2022

As mentioned earlier in this chapter, the brick-and-mortar portion of the US retailing business is littered with damaged and declining businesses, and I picked Bed Bath and Beyond (BB&B), a company that surged in popularity in the 1990s and did very well in the next decade, before collapsing in the most recent one.

Background

Bed Bath and Beyond is a retail store that has always been more home goods store than a bed and bath store, carrying a huge assortment of products, from necessities to gadgets. It rose from a small linen store in New Jersey in the 1970s to become a ubiquitous presence in malls across the country. Figure 13.2 shows its operating results since 1992, the year it went public.

FIGURE 13.2 | Bed Bath and Beyond—Historical Operating Results

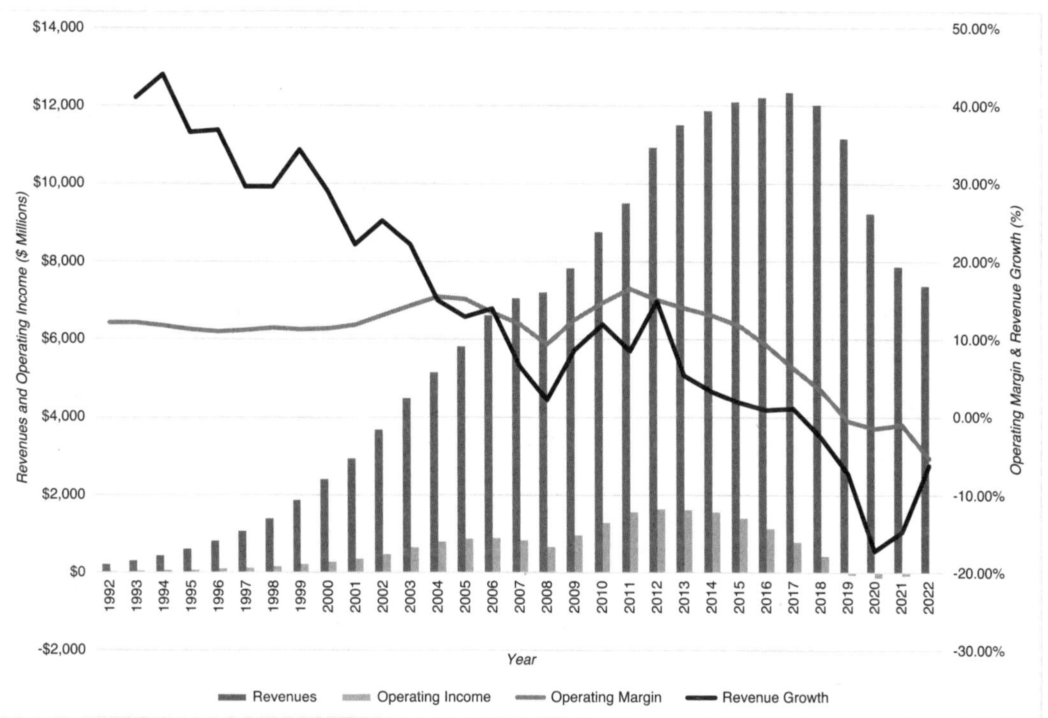

In its first decade as a public company, BB&B's revenues surged fourteenfold, from $214 million in 1992 to more than $2.9 billion in 2001, and while the growth rate scaled down, revenues continued to increase in the following decade, reaching $9.5 billion in 2011. During this two-decade run, the company posted double-digit operating profit margins, with margins increasing to 13.63% in 2002–2011, from 11.53% in 1992–2001.

The company's revenue growth rate dropped off after 2011, but it stayed positive, albeit in the single digits, and the company hit its high-water mark, with more than $12 billion in revenues, in 2017. In the subsequent four years, though, revenues fell off a cliff, with revenues in 2021 coming in at $7.8 billion, and the company lost increasing amounts every year between 2017 and 2021. While it is easy to attribute all failures in brick-and-mortar retailing to Amazon's disruptive presence, there is clearly more to the meltdown at this company, reflecting shifting customer tastes and fatigue with its retail model.

Valuation Story & Inputs

To value BB&B, I started with an assessment of the management of the company. At the start of July 2022, the company replaced its incumbent CEO, Mark Tritton, with a new CEO, Sue Gove, partly in response to criticism from key investors in the company about an "overly ambitious" strategy. If Ms. Gove has come in with a constrained mission, where reinventing BB&B is, if not off the map, at least on the back burner until the company is on more solid ground, I will assume that she is in acceptance of the company's decline. She has acted accordingly, and in September 2022, the company announced that it would close 150 stores, adding to the 240 stores that it closed during 2020 and 2021, and lay off 20% of its workforce.

In our story for BB&B, I envision continued shrinkage in revenues, but I do assume that as some of the least profitable stores are closed, there will be a pathway to operating profits, though I think it is unlikely that margins will ever revert to those of the company's glory days. If the stores being closed are also among the most capital-intensive, in terms of lease commitments, the financial pressures on the company will ease, and in steady state, I assume that there is a much smaller version of this company that can find a profitable niche in the retail business. Converting this story into valuation inputs:

- **Revenue growth/levels:** I will assume a 10% drop in revenues in year 1, followed by 5% drops every year in the following four years and, later, a gradual rise back to positive growth only in year 9. As a result of the shrinkage that I am assuming in BB&B's revenues over the next eight years, the $5.9 billion in estimated revenues in 2032 are about a third below the $7.9 billion that the company reported as revenues in 2021.
- **Operating margins:** I will assume that the stores that will be shut down are the least profitable, and that the stores that are left over will be profitable. I will assume that the operating margins at these remaining stores will converge on the average margin across US retailers of 5.54%, well below the double-digit margins enjoyed by BB&B stores in their heyday.
- **Reinvestment:** Since I am assuming that the company will shrink, there will be no new reinvestment. Instead, there will be cash flows from divestitures and store shutdowns that augment operating cash flows and will be available for return to shareholders or paying down debt.
- **Risk:** As the company shuts stores, I assume that the lease debt for the firm will decline, and as the company returns to profitability, it will be able to reduce its debt burden to manageable levels. Given that it is currently being rated at well below junk,

though, there remains a significant chance of failure, which I estimate to be 23.74%, based upon the current (Moody's) bond rating of B1.*

- **Steady State/Stable Growth:** In our story, I do see a soft landing for BB&B, assuming it makes it through the next decade, where it will be able to find a niche market as a smaller business and where it can maintain stable growth while earning a return on invested capital close to the average for mature retail firms.

A Bed Bath and Beyond Valuation

Using these inputs, I estimate the value of BB&B in figure 13.3.

FIGURE 13.3 | Valuation of Bed Bath and Beyond, September 2022

Bed Bath & Beyond						Sep-22
Incredible Shrinking Store						
Bed Bath & Beyond is in a downward spiral. There is a glimmer of hope, where the company shuts stores that require the most capital and get the least foot traffic over the next decade, shrinking already shrunk revenues further, but sees its operating margins improve to the US brick-and-mortar sector average margin over the next five years. Along the way, the divestitures and shutdowns will release cash that can be returned and used to pay down debt. By the end of the forecast period, BB&B finds a niche market, albeit with a smaller footprint, growing at the same rate as the economy and earning no excess returns.						
The Assumptions						
	Base Year	*Next Year*	*Years 2–5*	*Years 6–10*	*After Year 10*	*Link to Story*
Revenues (a)	$7,868.00	-10.0%	-5.00% →	3.00%	3.00%	Declining core business
Operating Margin (b)	-1.00%	-1.0%	-1.00% →	5.54%	5.54%	Margins improve, as worst-performing stores are shut down
Tax Rate	25.00%		25.00%	25.00%	25.00%	Global/US marginal tax rate over time
Reinvestment (c)		2.00	2.00	2.00	30.00%	Maintained at current levels
Return on Capital	-2.80%	Marginal ROIC =	-57.31%		10.00%	Minimal competitive advantages
Cost of Capital (d)			8.79% →	7.50%	7.50%	Cost of capital close to median company
The Cash Flows						
	Revenues	*Operating Margin*	*EBIT*	*EBIT (1 – t)*	*Reinvestment*	*FCFF*
1	$7,081.20	-1.00%	-$70.81	-$70.81	$0.00	-$70.81
2	$6,727.14	1.62%	$108.72	$108.72	-$177.03	$285.75
3	$6,390.78	2.92%	$186.89	$186.89	-$168.18	$355.06
4	$6,071.24	4.23%	$256.96	$256.96	-$159.77	$416.73
5	$5,767.68	5.54%	$319.56	$244.23	-$151.78	$396.01
6	$5,571.58	5.54%	$308.69	$231.52	-$98.05	$329.57
7	$5,471.29	5.54%	$303.14	$227.35	-$50.14	$277.50
8	$5,460.35	5.54%	$302.53	$226.90	-$5.47	$232.37
9	$5,536.79	5.54%	$306.77	$230.07	$38.22	$191.85
10	$5,702.90	5.54%	$315.97	$236.98	$83.05	$153.92
Terminal Year	$5,873.99	5.54%	$325.45	$244.09	$73.23	$170.86
The Value						
Terminal Value			$3,796.89			
PV (Terminal Value)			$1,695.10			
PV (CF over Next 10 Years)			$1,644.97			
Value of Operating Assets =			$3,340.07			
Adjustment for Distress			$396.47		Probability of failure =	23.74%
– Debt & Minority Interests			$3,085.00			
+ Cash & Other Non-operating Assets			$440.00			
Value of Equity			$298.60			
– Value of Equity Options			$0.00			
Number of Shares			92.50			
Value per Share			$3.23		Stock was trading at =	$8.79

With our story of recovery, albeit as a smaller company, for Bed Bath and Beyond, the value that I estimate per share is $3.23, well below the $8.79 the shares traded at on

* I have used the data on failure rates for bonds in different ratings classes to make the assessment of failure risk; about 23.74% of B1-rated bonds issued in 2008 defaulted within ten years of the issuance.

September 14, 2022. As a postscript, in the months since this valuation was completed, the company's finances deteriorated even more quickly than anticipated, perhaps as a result of higher interest rates, and it entered bankruptcy, a reminder that with declining firms, truncation or failure risk always looms large.

Pricing

Pricing declining companies is akin to trying to catch a falling knife, since the cumulated effects of declining revenues, compressing margins, and the danger of distress can make every aspect of pricing, from picking a pricing multiple to choosing peer-group companies, problematic.

The Challenges

There are three tactics used to price distressed companies. The first is to stay with current values for operations (revenues, earnings, book value) and to try and scale market value to those variables that are still viable (revenues and book value). The second is to use estimated revenues or earnings in a future year and to compute a forward multiple, which is then compared across companies. The third is to relate the market pricing of a declining company to the liquidation value of the company, with the intent of buying it at a bargain price (defined to be less than liquidation value). Each tactic poses its own challenges, but that should come as no surprise, given the disparate paths that these companies can follow.

1. **Scaling to current operating metrics:** Consider the use of current revenue or earnings multiples to price declining companies. If these companies are outliers in their sectors (if they are declining companies in sectors with primarily healthy companies), the results of this pricing will be predictable: the declining company will look cheap, because it will trade at lower multiples than the rest of the sector. To make a legitimate comparison, you must examine differences in risk, revenue growth, and expected profitability over time. If the entire sector is declining, you must control for the degree of decline across companies.
2. **Scaling to future operating metrics:** With forward pricing metrics, the problems shift to the distress issue. To see why, assume that you are valuing a firm that is in severe financial trouble, with stagnant revenues, negative earnings, and substantial debt obligations. You forecast a turnaround in the firm's fortunes and predict that EBITDA

in five years will be $150 million and that the firm will be healthy, trading at roughly the same multiple of EBITDA that healthy firms in the sector trade at right now (six times EBITDA). The forward estimate of value for this company is $900 million, but there is a catch: this works only if you assume that good health is guaranteed and that there is no chance of default. To the extent that there is a significant chance of bad things happening to the firm over the next five years, you would have to reduce the estimated value.

3. **Scaling to liquidation value:** With comparisons to liquidation value, the problems often arise in how liquidation value is estimated. If, as many do, you use the book value of assets as a proxy for their liquidation value, you should not be surprised again to see declining companies look like bargains. In a declining business, buyers will be unwilling to pay book value for assets as liquidation value, given the poor underlying business economics.

In all three cases, declining companies will tend to look underpriced—at least at first sight, or if the pricing does not control for differences or distress.

The Responses

Is there a way in which pricing can be adapted to cover declining and distressed firms? I believe so, although the adjustments will vary, depending on the declining company being priced and the sector it operates in.

SCALING VARIABLE

In scaling price at declining companies, you can use the operating numbers (revenues, earnings, etc.) it can continue to deliver as a going concern, as a scalar, or as scale against what you believe its assets will cost to replace, if replicated, or what those assets can deliver as a liquidation value, if sold.

1. **Book value:** For declining companies that have built large, tangible asset bases, it does make sense to scale their market values, representing what investors estimate the company to be worth, to their book values, indicating what accountants estimate the company has invested in its assets. In making this assessment, you have a choice of using the equity variant, relating the market value to the book value of equity, or you can scale the enterprise value of the business, which also includes net debt, to the book value of invested capital (which is book value of equity plus the book value of

net debt). The problem with book value is that it is an accounting number and, for aging firms, will reflect the cumulative effects of accounting actions or inaction over time.

2. **Replacement cost:** In a variant of the first approach, you can estimate what it would cost someone to replicate the existing assets of the business, in a replacement cost measure, and scale the enterprise value to this replacement cost. Implicitly, being able to buy a company at a market value below its replacement cost is viewed as a bargain, but that rationale works only if the declining company is in a business that is healthy and moneymaking. If the entire sector is in decline, the fact that a company trades at less than the replacement costs tells you very little.
3. **Forward operating numbers:** There is a third option—and this should be a familiar one since I also used it with start-ups and high-growth companies: rather than scale the market values of declining companies to current operating numbers, you can scale them to your future estimates of them. This approach can be useful, if you believe that a declining firm can stabilize or turn around its operations and that the market is pricing in the expectation that it will.

PEER GROUP

To come up with a peer group that you will compare your declining company to, you can look at all the companies in the peer group—with the caveat that your company will probably look cheap, at first sight—or create a peer group of declining companies in your sector.

1. **Other declining companies:** To value a distressed firm, you may be able to find a group of declining and/or distressed firms in the same business and look at how much the market is willing to pay for them. For instance, you could value a troubled telecom firm by looking at the enterprise value to sales (or book capital) multiples at which other troubled telecom firms trade. Although this approach has promise, it works only if many firms in a sector slip into financial trouble at the same time. In addition, by categorizing firms as declining or not, you run the risk of lumping together firms that are declining to different degrees, with distress adding a wild card to the mix.
2. **Healthy companies in the sector:** If you have a firm that is declining and/or distressed in a sector filled with healthy companies, you have no choice but to create a peer group of companies that are in much better operating and financial shape than your company. On the surface, using revenue earnings or book value multiples, your company will look cheap relative to the peer group, but that is because of differences in

financial health across these companies. Consequently, you should also collect data on these operating metrics, including revenue growth, profitability, and reinvestment, for all of the companies in the peer group, since you will need to control for differences.

CONTROLLING FOR DIFFERENCES

If you are comparing a declining company with a peer group composed primarily of healthy companies, you should expect to see the declining company look cheap, on whatever scalar you have picked for pricing, before you control for differences in:

1. **Operating performance**: Shrinking revenues and compressing operating margins will knock down the market pricing of a company. At the minimum, you must consider how differences in revenue growth and operating margins play out in the pricing of companies in the peer group.
2. **Distress:** Declining companies are more likely to be exposed to distress risk than healthy companies, and since distress leads to forced liquidations and bad outcomes for equity investors, you would expect their pricing to reflect that. Controlling for distress is tricky, but to the extent that you can find bond ratings for companies in your peer group, you can attempt to estimate how lower bond ratings translate into lower pricing for equity.
3. **Management:** In the intrinsic value section, I connected our estimated value to how management viewed decline. To the extent that market participants are factoring in management response, the pricing should be lower for declining companies with management in denial than with management in acceptance, and for companies with desperate rather than with purposeful management. While making these judgments on management will be difficult, you can see the rationale for why the pricing of a declining company can be affected significantly when new management is put in place.

CASE STUDY—PART 2: PRICING BED BATH AND BEYOND, A DECLINING BUSINESS

In pricing BB&B, I start by recognizing the constraints that I am operating with in September 2022. First, with current operating numbers, the only scalar that I could use for the company was revenue, since the company lost money (negative operating and net income) in 2021. Second, looking across the 96 publicly traded retail companies in the United States with market capitalizations that exceeded $100 million (BB&B's market cap was around $700 million in September 2022), I noted that many of these companies had much healthier margins than BB&B, and analysts were expecting more robust revenue growth, as you can see in table 13.2:

Table 13.2 • Bed Bath & Beyond versus US Retail, September 2022

	Market Cap (US $Mil)	Enterprise Value (US $Mil)	PE	EV/Sales	Revenue Growth (Next 2 Years)	Operating Margin, 2021
Average			11.70	1.26	5.98%	8.69%
First Quartile			5.13	0.60	0.67%	5.42%
Median			7.25	0.97	3.85%	8.22%
Third Quartile			17.22	1.74	9.78%	12.03%
Bed Bath & Beyond	$698	$3,867	N/A	0.52	-12.70%	-5.24%

Not surprisingly, given that BB&B had an operating loss in 2021 and that investors were expecting its revenues to shrink by 12.7% in the next two years, it trades at an EV to sales multiple that is about half (0.52) of its revenues, well below the 0.97 times revenues that the typical retail firm trades at.

To make at least a semblance of effort at controlling for differences, I regressed the EV to sales multiples of retail firms against revenue growth and operating margins using the data:

$$\text{EV to Sales} = \underset{(2.83)}{0.39} + \underset{(1.53)}{1.82}\ \text{Expected Revenue Growth} + \underset{(7.44)}{7.63}\ \text{Operating Margin}$$

With an R-squared of 39.4% and marginal significance on the revenue growth variable, this regression has limitations, but it does indicate that companies with higher revenue growth and/or higher operating margins trade at much higher multiples of revenues. Using this regression to price BB&B, I arrive at an estimated EV to sales ratio for the company of -0.2410:

$$\text{EV to Sales} = 0.39 + 1.82\,(-.127) + 7.63\,(-.0524) = -0.2410$$

Based upon how the market is pricing other retail companies, and BB&B's awful operating metrics, the market effectively is delivering the message that the company will not make it as a going concern. An optimist on BB&B might argue that this pricing is unfair, and that the current values for revenue growth and margins should be replaced with expected future values. There is some truth to this, but if you price BB&B with these expected future numbers, you will still need to adjust the pricing for failure risk.

Add-ons and Addenda

To complete the discussion of declining companies, I will look at two add-ons and addenda. First, I look at valuing a company as the sum of its parts, since breaking up declining companies is often an option that is considered to fix problems and unlock value. Second, I examine liquidation valuation since, for some declining companies, it may be the only viable end game. Finally, I will consider the special case of equity in a deeply distressed company, one with operating losses and substantial debt due, and argue that this equity is less a claim on expected cash flows and more of a call option on the business.

Sum of the Parts (SOTP)

One of the features of discounted cash flow valuation is that it is additive. In other words, if you have to value a company that operates in three businesses, you can either value the combined company, by adding up its cash flows across the three businesses and discounting at a rate that is a value-weighted average across the business, or you can value each of the three businesses, using the cash flows and discount rate of that business in the valuation, and then add up those values. In theory, at least, you should get the same value for the company by doing either. Here, I will term the first *aggregated valuation* and the second *disaggregated valuation* and explore the differences. If your exposure in valuation has always been to aggregated valuations, there are two reasons why it is the dominant approach.

- Investors take equity in entire companies, not in their disaggregated parts. Thus, you buy shares in General Electric (GE), the company, and not in GE Aircraft Engines or GE Capital; and in Coca-Cola, the global company, not Coca-Cola's India operations. That is perhaps why so much of valuation is built around aggregation, where you look at the revenues and cash flows of the company across geographies and businesses and discount them back at rates that reflect the weightings of these businesses and geographies.
- Most information disclosure is on an aggregated business, with firms like GE and Coca-Cola reporting full financial statements (income statements, balance sheets, and statement of cash flows) for the entire company. While there has been some attempt to improve disclosure at the level of business segment and geographic region, that information has usually been consigned to footnotes and remains spotty, with disclosure practices varying across companies and countries.

There are occasions, though, where you may want to value a company by valuing its parts separately.

- **Fundamental differences:** With multi-business companies and multinationals, one advantage of valuing each business or geographic segment separately is that you can then assign different risk, cash flow, and growth profiles to each one rather than trying to create one weighted profile for the whole company.
- **Growth differences:** If some businesses and geographic segments are growing much more quickly than others within the same company, it becomes difficult to do an aggregated valuation that reflects these different growth rates. For instance, a bottom-up beta that represents a weighted average of the businesses that a company is in will have to change, over time, if some businesses grow more than others.
- **Transactional reasons:** In some cases, you will need to value a portion of a company, rather than an entire company, because that portion will be sold or spun off and requires a value specific to it. This need becomes acute when you are valuing a company that is on the verge of being broken up into parts.
- **Management reasons:** Within a company, it makes sense to value each part of the business separately, both to monitor the performance of different divisional managers and to improve that performance.

In closing, though, if you are wondering what the difference is between liquidation and sum-of-the-parts valuation, the key distinction lies in whether individual assets are being sold (as in liquidation) or assessed as going businesses (as is the case for the sum of the parts). In liquidation value, you are selling the company's assets to other buyers who put them to their own uses, and the numbers you attach to assets will reflect what those buyers are willing to pay, i.e., a pricing. In going businesses, you will continue to run these businesses and thus have to estimate the ingredients of intrinsic value—growth, cash flows, and risk—and the resulting values.

SUM-OF-THE-PARTS (SOTP) VALUATION

The starting point in an SOTP valuation of a company is deciding the units or parts that you plan to break it down into, with the constraint that you must have access to the information you need to value these units or parts. Since many companies break down their operating metrics (such as revenues, operating income, and even assets) by division, that categorization is often used as the basis for the SOTP valuation, but with access to information, you can use geographies, user categories, or even customer groupings. In a sum-of-the-parts valuation, you estimate the intrinsic value of each sub-part of the company and then aggregate the valuations. In terms of sequencing, table 13.3 summarizes the steps in an SOTP valuation, and contrasts each one with the same step in an aggregated company valuation:

Table 13.3 • SOTP versus Company Valuation Steps

Step	Company Valuation	SOTP Valuation
Tell a story	Create a story for the entire company, based on its mix of operations and management in place.	Create a story for each part of the company, based upon that part's operations and stand-alone management of that part.
Run the 3P Test	Check the company's story to ensure it is possible, plausible, and probable.	Check each part's story to ensure it is possible, plausible, and probable.
Value the company	Convert story to valuation inputs for the company and use those inputs to estimate the value of the entire firm.	Convert story to valuation inputs for each part of the company and use those inputs to value that part. Sum up the valuations of the parts and net out the value drag from unallocated costs.* * When valuing a multi-business company, you will find some costs (G&A, corporate headquarters expenses, and others) are not allocated to the divisions/parts of the company. You have to consider the present value of these expected costs over time and net out this "value drag."
Calculate equity value	Add cash and cross holdings & net out debt.	Add cash and cross holdings & net out debt.

As you can see, the differences that may arise in your final value for the company can come either from being able to differentiate risk, growth, and cash flow characteristics across different parts of the company or from assuming that each part has its own stand-alone management that may make different choices and deliver different value from a company-wide management team. If you assume that there are inefficiencies in operations that arise when the latter is in charge, and that these will dissipate or decrease with the former in charge, your SOTP value will be higher than your consolidated company value and can be used as an argument for breaking up the company into its component parts.

SOTP PRICING

In SOTP pricing, you again follow the standard pricing sequence—where you start with pricing multiple, find comparable companies that are priced by the market, and compare your company to its peer group, controlling for differences across the companies—but you do so for each part of the company individually, rather than for the entire company. Table 13.4 summarizes the pricing sequence, drawing out the differences between SOTP and consolidated company pricing.

Table 13.4 • SOTP versus Company Pricing Steps

Step	Company Pricing	SOTP Pricing
Pick a pricing multiple	Pick a scalar (revenues, earnings, etc.) for the price and estimate the pricing multiples for the company.	Pick a scalar (revenues, earnings, etc.) for each part of the company, preserving the freedom to pick different scalars for different parts.
Find a peer group	Find other publicly traded companies that are "like" your company on valuation fundamentals (risk, growth, cash flows).	For each part of your company, find other publicly traded companies that are "like" that part on valuation fundamentals (risk, growth, cash flows).
Control for differences	Control for differences between your company and the peer-group companies on the fundamentals.	Control for differences between the part of the company you are pricing and the peer group for that part on fundamentals.
Price the company	Apply the peer-group-based pricing to your scalar to price the company.	Apply the peer-group-based pricing to the scalar chosen to price each part and then aggregate the pricing across the parts.

If you have allocated all expenses across the parts of a business, there are two main reasons why the two approaches may give you a different aggregated pricing for the company. The first is that being able to pick different scalars (revenues for some business parts, EBITDA for others, book value for still others) and peer groups that match each part, in an SOTP pricing, may sometimes lead to a more precise pricing. The second is that the market may be discounting a company, relative to the pricing of its parts, because it does not trust the holding structure or the management of the company. The conglomerate discount, which researchers have estimated to range from 7% to 15%, has almost entirely been based upon comparing consolidated to SOTP pricing for companies, often with few or no controls for differences.

Liquidation Valuation

For some declining businesses, the end game, as I noted earlier in this chapter, is not survival as a going concern but liquidation. The liquidation value of a firm is the aggregate of the value that the assets of the firm would command if sold on the market, often under duress, and net of transaction costs and legal costs. While there are some who carve out a niche for liquidation valuation, and contrast it to intrinsic valuation and pricing, note that liquidation valuation is in fact a subcategory of pricing, rather than an approach that can stand on its own. In short, to estimate what you would get in liquidation for each asset, you must estimate what investors will pay for that asset today, given how other assets like it are being priced—making it an exercise in pricing. If you are then wondering why a liquidation pricing would yield a different number for a company than a conventional pricing, wherein you price the overall company, relative to its peer group, there are three major reasons.

- The first is that when pricing a company, you are pricing it as a going concern, with the potential for growth and investments in the future, whereas a liquidation pricing looks at the pricing of the assets owned by the company. When a company's going-concern value comes under threat, it is possible that the collective proceeds you receive from selling individual assets to the highest bidder will be higher.
- The second is that a liquidation, especially if forced (because of debt coming due or distress concerns), will often result in discounted prices, as potential buyers recognize your immediate need for cash and extract bargains.
- The third is that a liquidation can create tax consequences for a company, especially when older assets that have low or even negligible book values are sold.

For most healthy firms, the going-concern value will trump the liquidation value. For growing companies, the fact that liquidation value focuses only on assets in place, since you cannot sell investments and projects you have not taken yet, will depress liquidation value even more relative to going-concern value, which includes growth potential. As companies mature, the failure to include growth assets will become less of a drag on liquidation value, but going-concern value will generally remain higher than liquidation value if the business is a good one—i.e., if it earns more than its cost of capital. As excess returns on investments fade, the liquidation value of the company will start approaching going-concern value, with the caveat that the former will still be lower because of discounts applied for illiquidity and taxes. In decline, though, there may very well be a time when continuing the business as a going concern, while earning less than the cost of capital, will deliver less value than selling the assets, individually, to the best potential bidders.

Estimating liquidation value is complicated when the assets of the firm have business entanglements and thus cannot be valued individually. If you are trying to estimate the liquidation value for a company like Disney, your task will be complicated by the reality that its broadcasting, movie, and theme park businesses are all connected to each other and cannot be priced separately. Furthermore, the likelihood that assets will fetch their fair market value will decrease as the urgency of the liquidation increases. A firm in a hurry to liquidate its assets may have to accept a discount on fair-market value as a price for speedy execution. As a note of caution, it is almost never appropriate to treat the book value of assets as the liquidation value. Most distressed firms earn subpar returns on their assets, and the liquidation value will reflect the earning capacity of the assets rather than the price paid for the assets (which is what the book value measures, net of depreciation).

Distressed Equity as an Option

When you invest in the equity of a business, it is with the hope and expectation that the business will succeed as a going concern, delivering cash flows to you. It is that view that leads us to estimate the intrinsic value of a business based upon its cash flows, growth, and risk. As a business ages, and its going-concern prospects and value wither, if the firm has borrowed money along its corporate journey, the value of its operating assets may fall below the debt outstanding. That would, in an intrinsic value world, mean that your equity is worth nothing—and that conclusion is right, if you view equity as a claim on the going concern.

Contractually, in a publicly traded firm, the equity in a firm is a *residual claim*: equity holders lay claim to all cash flows left over after other financial claimholders (lenders, preferred stockholders, etc.) have been satisfied. If a firm is liquidated, the same principle applies: equity investors receive whatever is left over in the firm after all outstanding debt and other financial claims are paid off. The principle of *limited liability* protects equity investors in publicly traded firms if the value of the firm is less than the value of its outstanding debt—they cannot lose more than their investment in the firm. Put simply, the equity value in a publicly traded company cannot drop below zero, which puts equity investors in deeply distressed businesses (where the debt due exceeds the going-concern value) in a strange position. In the worst-case scenario, they cannot lose more than they pay for their shares, but if the business finds a way to recover, leading going-concern value to rise above the debt, they generate potentially unlimited upside. That payoff combination—where your losses are limited to a known value, but your profits scale up proportionately with value and have no limit—gives equity in deeply distressed companies the characteristics of a call option, with the value of its assets yielding the value of the underlying assets, and the debt due standing in for the strike price, as can be seen in figure 13.4.

FIGURE 13.4 | **Payoff on Equity as Call Option on a Firm**

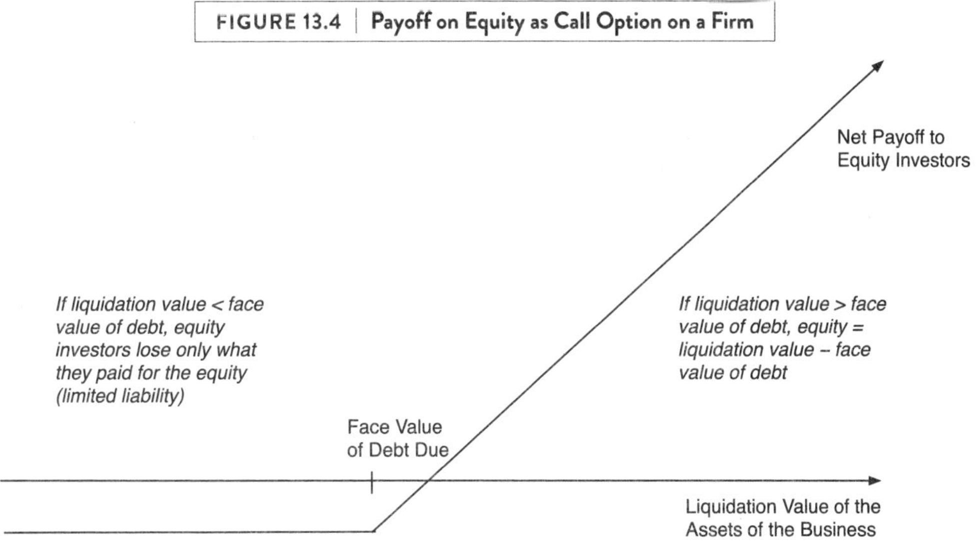

The biggest benefit of bringing in the equity-as-option perspective on distressed equity is not in valuation, since using option pricing models to value distressed equity can be complicated, but in its implications for equity investors in these companies.

1. **Basket case equities:** If you view equity as a call option on a business that has debt outstanding, it will continue to have value even if the value of the firm falls well below the face value of the outstanding debt, as long there is time left before the debt payments come due. While the firm will be viewed as troubled by investors, accountants, and analysts, its equity is not worthless. In fact, just as deep out-of-the-money traded options command value because of the possibility that the value of the underlying asset may increase above the strike price in the remaining lifetime of the option, equity commands value because of the time premium on the option (the time until bonds mature and come due) and the possibility that the value of the assets may increase above the face value of the bonds before they come due.
2. **Risk as an ally**: When investing in the equity of a going concern, increasing risk reduces value, with discount rates rising in intrinsic valuations. When a business becomes distressed enough that its equity becomes an option, risk works to the investor's benefit for a simple and intuitive reason. The most that an investor can lose is what was paid for the stock, and since the value of assets can be below the value of debt outstanding, making that value more volatile (risky) can only increase its chances of yielding upside.

3. **Debt/equity agency issues**: The equity-as-option view can also help us understand why equity investors and lenders can diverge on how best to run a business, and why that divergence will get worse as a company's operations deteriorate and it borrows more. Left to the will of equity investors, these businesses will make bigger and bigger bets on long-shot investments since, if these investments pay off, the equity investors will emerge significantly wealthier, and if they don't, they were already looking at businesses where asset value was less than debt. That is why lenders to deeply distressed firms cannot afford to be passive onlookers and need to have an active influence in the firm's operating decisions.

In sum, you are far more likely to see equity in a business take on the characteristics of an option if the company has little or no prospect of growth, significant debt, and an asset base that is risky and having trouble generating returns that match its cost of capital—all of which you would expect to see in the declining phase of the life cycle.

Conclusion

In chapter 10, I highlighted the reasons that young companies are difficult to value, with shaky base-year financials, uncertainty about business models, and concerns about failure risk at the top of the list of challenges. In this chapter, looking at declining companies—and especially those burdened with debt—I found myself facing the same set of problems, albeit with different causes. First, while declining companies often have long financial histories, assuming that operating metrics will revert back to historic norms is not viable if the underlying business itself has changed for the worse. Second, the management response to decline—ranging from denial to acceptance to desperation to reinvention—can lead to a wide range of outcomes, thus creating significant uncertainties about how the future will look at these companies. Third, deteriorating operations, when combined with significant debt loads, increase the likelihood of distress and failure risk.

As with young companies, the answers to these challenges do not lie in mechanical models but come from making measured judgments regarding the reasons for decline at a company (which can range from company-specific to sector-wide challenges), what management will do in response, and whether you believe that the response will be sufficient to turn the company's fortunes around. Those judgments will determine what value you attach to the company, and its equity, and how you price the company, relative to its peer group.

Investing Philosophies and Strategies across the Life Cycle

14

Investment Philosophies 101: A Life Cycle Overview

WE ALL DREAM OF being super investors, and some of us spend an inordinate amount of time and resources in this endeavor. Despite our best efforts, though, most of us fail in our attempts to be more than "average." Nonetheless, we keep trying, hoping that we can be more like the investing legends—another Warren Buffett, George Soros, or Peter Lynch. As you study the success of such super investors, you will quickly realize that they have different views on how markets work (and don't), and they have different templates for investment success, but what they share is an adherence to investment philosophies that reflect their personalities and their beliefs about markets.

In this chapter, I will start with a definition of what an investment philosophy is, drawing a contrast with investment strategies and processes, and then use this definition to present a wide array of philosophies that investors adhere to. I also try to make connections between investment philosophies and the corporate life cycle, arguing that your choice of investment philosophy will determine where you look for investments in the life cycle, with some investors seeking out young and growth companies as their best investments, and others looking for bargains among mature and declining companies.

What Is an Investment Philosophy?

An investment philosophy is a coherent way of thinking about markets, how they work (and sometimes do not), and the types of mistakes that you believe consistently underlie investor behavior. Why does an investment philosophy need to make assumptions about investor mistakes? Most active investment strategies are designed to take advantage of errors made by some or all investors in pricing stocks. Those mistakes themselves are driven by far more basic assumptions about human behavior, and that behavior plays out as market mistakes that you hope to exploit for profits. In this section, I will look at what goes into an investment philosophy, starting with market beliefs, working through how those beliefs translate into behavior, examining what investors can do to take advantage of that behavior, and closing with a tie-in to personal traits.

Step 1: Identify Human Behavior (or Misbehavior) in Markets

Underlying every investment philosophy is a view about human behavior. In fact, one weakness of conventional finance and valuation has been the short shrift given to human behavior. Conventional financial theory does not assume that all investors are rational, but it does assume that irrationalities are random and cancel out: for every investor who tends to follow the crowd too much (a momentum investor), it assumes an investor who goes in the opposite direction (a contrarian) and posits that their push and pull in prices will ultimately result in a rational price. While this may, in fact, be a reasonable assumption for the very long term, it may not be a realistic one for the short term.

Academics and practitioners in finance who have long viewed the rational investor assumption with skepticism have developed a branch of finance called behavioral finance, which draws on psychology, sociology, and finance to try to explain both why investors behave the way they do and the consequences for investment strategies. Every investment philosophy, not surprisingly, begins with a view of market misbehavior that eventually plays out as profits to more discerning investors. To illustrate the diversity of market misbehavior, consider the following:

- **Individual versus group misbehavior:** If investor mistakes arise from individualized irrationalities, there is a much greater chance that they will average out across all investors. In fact, as I noted in the lead-in, this is the assumption that underlies "efficient markets," not the much more dubious one that all investors are rational. However, if investors are induced to misbehave because others around them are misbehaving, a crowd effect arises, and there is a far greater chance that the misbehavior will affect market prices—and perhaps be exploitable for gain.
- **Learning-speed-related mistakes:** When markets are called on to price new businesses, unanticipated macro or political developments, or new investment products, investors

must learn about these phenomena to price them. In a rational market, the learning occurs almost instantaneously, albeit with error. If markets learn slowly, they will make pricing errors during the learning period, though there is disagreement about whether they will overshoot or undershoot.

- **Reaction to information:** One of the functions of markets is to incorporate the effects of new information—either macroeconomic or from companies—into prices. Thus, when a company reports earnings or announces its intent to acquire another firm, investors have to make judgments about how this information will affect the company's future earnings and risk and reprice its shares. There are two contrasting views of how, in doing so, they may misbehave. In the first, investors overreact to news announcements, pushing prices up too much on good news and down too much on bad news. In the second, they underreact to news announcements, pushing prices up too little on good news and down too little on bad news.
- **Dealing with uncertainty:** Uncertainty is part and parcel of business and investing, but investors often cope with it in unhealthy (and irrational) ways. Some go into denial, effectively erasing uncertainty from their analysis because they are uncomfortable dealing with it. Some become paralyzed by uncertainty and find themselves unable to act. Some choose avoidance, completely removing investments with too much uncertainty from their choice sets. While all of these behaviors are understandable, they can sometimes lead to pricing errors that those who are more comfortable dealing with uncertainty can exploit.
- **Framing:** Behavioral finance has shone a bright light on how investor misbehavior can emerge from framing bias, which looks at how investor decisions can vary as a function of how choices are presented. Thus, if investors are amply provided with the facts on the upside of an investment, and given very little information on the downside, they are far more likely to take the investment than if the same investment had been presented with the downside risks highlighted. In what they termed "loss aversion," Daniel Kahneman and Amos Tversky, pioneers in the behavioral finance field, noted that investors are prone to weight losses more than equivalent gains when investing, and argued that this explained why they tend to hold on to losing investments too long.

This is not meant to be a comprehensive list of market misbehaviors, but every investment philosophy must start with a view on human frailty.

Step 2: Market Misbehavior to Market Mistakes

Unless market misbehavior shows up as a mispricing in the market that you can exploit, it cannot be the basis for an investment philosophy. In this second step of developing an investment philosophy, you must expand on how the misbehavior that you believe characterizes markets will play out as market mispricing. Thus, if you believe that markets overreact to new information, you have to reason through whether that overreaction is more likely to occur for company-specific developments (earnings or acquisition announcements), as opposed to market-wide or macro announcements (an unanticipated increase in inflation, or a report that the economy is weakening)—and, if it is the former, whether it will be greater for some companies (smaller, less followed by analysts, less liquid) than others. If slow learning is your market misbehavior, you should consider not only whether that slow learning is more exaggerated with new investment products or new business models but also whether how long it takes varies across different environments.

To exploit mispricing in most markets, that mispricing eventually has to be corrected, and to develop an investment philosophy that has coherence, you need to have beliefs about both why and when the correction must happen. In some cases, you may be able to find a way to lock in a mispricing today for a guaranteed profit in the future—arbitrage—but in most cases, there must be a catalyst for the correction. If you have enough capital at your disposal, *you* may be the catalyst, as is the case for an activist hedge fund or investor that targets a mispriced investment. If you cannot be the catalyst, you must rely on outside forces, and in a well-constructed investment philosophy, these forces will be identified.

While all active investment philosophies assume that markets make mistakes, they differ in their views on where in the market the inefficiencies are most likely to show up and how long they will last. Some investment philosophies assume that markets are correct most of the time but that they overreact when new and key pieces of information are released about individual firms—they go up too much on good news and down too much on bad news. Other investment philosophies are founded on the belief that markets can make mistakes in the aggregate—the entire market can be under- or overvalued—and that some investors (mutual fund managers, for example) are more likely to make these mistakes than others. Still other investment philosophies may assume that while markets do a good job of pricing stocks where there is a substantial amount of information—financial statements, analyst reports, and financial press coverage—they systematically misprice stocks on which such information is not available.

Step 3: Develop Investment Tactics and Strategies

Once you have an investment philosophy in place, you must develop investment strategies that build on the core philosophy. Consider, for instance, the divergent views on market overreaction that I expounded in the last section, where you might have two investors who both believe that markets overreact, but one believes that it is more likely with company-specific information and the other that it occurs more frequently with macroeconomic news stories. The first investor, who believes that markets overreact to company news, may develop a strategy of buying stocks after large, negative earnings surprises (when announced earnings come in well below expectations) and selling stocks after positive earnings surprises. The second investor, who believes that markets make mistakes in response to macroeconomic news stories, will buy (sell) stocks (perhaps even the entire index) right after unexpectedly bad (good) macroeconomic news.

It is worth noting that the same investment philosophy can spawn multiple investment strategies. Thus, a belief that investors consistently overestimate the value of growth and underestimate the value of existing assets can manifest in several different strategies, ranging from a passive one of buying low PE ratio stocks to a more activist one of buying cheap companies and attempting to liquidate them for their assets. In other words, the number of available investment strategies will vastly outnumber the number of investment philosophies.

Step 4: A Test of Fit

In the abstract, you could look at investment philosophies, pick the one that has delivered the most winners in the past, and make it your own—and that is what many investors choose to do. They also tend to find, very quickly, that past success notwithstanding, the "winning" philosophy does not deliver the returns that they thought that it would. After all, more books have been written about Warren Buffett than any investor in history, but I would wager that the readers of these books, many of whom have tried to replicate his investment philosophy and strategies, have not shared in his success. One reason for that is that for each philosophy, success will require not just a blind replication of methods but a set of personal characteristics. The old-time value-investing philosophy that Buffett adheres to requires patience, since winning may require holding unloved companies for long periods and a willingness to stand up to peer pressure. Investors who are naturally impatient and are easily swayed by crowd views may start off on the Buffett path, but they will have no staying power. As another example, you may buy in to the investment philosophy that the best way to lock in profits is to buy poorly run companies and put pressure on them to change, which is what activist investors like Carl Icahn or Bill Ackman do, but you are unlikely to succeed with that philosophy if you don't have hundreds of millions of dollars of capital at your disposal.

Notwithstanding claims to the contrary from advocates for value investing or trading on momentum, there is no one "best" investment philosophy that fits all investors—but there is an investment philosophy that best fits *you*. If your end game is to be a successful investor, you should perhaps spend less time understanding what makes Buffett or Lynch tick and more time understanding yourself.

Why Do You Need an Investment Philosophy?

Most investors have no investment philosophy, and the same can be said about many money managers and professional investment advisors. They adopt investment strategies that have worked, at least in recent periods, for other investors and then abandon them when they do not. If this is possible, why, you might ask, do you need an investment philosophy? The answer is simple: in the absence of an investment philosophy, you will tend to shift from strategy to strategy simply based upon a strong sales pitch from a proponent or a perceived recent success. There will be three negative consequences for your portfolio:

- Lacking a rudder or a core set of beliefs, you will be easy prey for charlatans and pretenders, each claiming to have found the magic strategy that beats the market.
- As you switch from strategy to strategy, you will have to change your portfolio, resulting in high transaction costs and increased taxes.
- While a given strategy may work for some investors, it may not be appropriate for you, given your objectives, risk aversion, and personal characteristics. In addition to having a portfolio that underperforms the market, you are likely to find yourself with an ulcer, or worse.

With a strong sense of your core investing beliefs, you will have far more control over your destiny. You will be able not only to reject strategies that do not fit your core beliefs about markets but also to tailor investment strategies to your needs. In addition, you will obtain much more of a big-picture view of what is truly different across strategies and what they have in common.

In my view, most portfolio managers—including many who claim to have deeply held investment philosophies—lack core investment philosophies, mistaking investment strategies for philosophies and imitation of others for authenticity. Not surprisingly, their track records reflect this failing, with excessive trading and turnover in portfolio and no coherence in their portfolio decisions.

Categorizing Investment Philosophies

Since investment philosophies are not the core of this book, rather than providing a laundry list of investment philosophies, with details and criteria for success, I will look at broad categories of investment philosophies and tie them closely to the corporate life cycle.

Market Timing versus Security Selection (Stock Picking)

The broadest categorization of investment philosophies is made according to whether they are based upon timing overall markets or finding individual assets that are mispriced. The first set of philosophies can be categorized as *market timing* philosophies, while the second can be viewed as *security selection* philosophies.

Within each group, though, are numerous strands that take very different views about markets. Consider market timing first. While most of us consider market timing only in the context of the stock market, you can extend market timing to include a much broader range of markets—currency markets, commodities markets, bond markets, and real estate markets come to mind. The range of choices among security selection philosophies is even wider and can span charting and technical indicators, fundamentals (earnings, cash flows, or growth) and information (earnings reports, acquisition announcements). While market timing has allure to all of us—because it pays off so well when you are right—it is difficult to succeed at, for exactly that reason. There are all too often too many investors attempting to time markets, and succeeding consistently is very difficult to do. If you decide to pick securities or individual assets, though, how do you choose whether to pick them based upon charts, fundamentals, or growth potential? The answer, as you will see in the next section, will depend not only on your views of the market and what works but also on your personal characteristics.

What is the link from these two kinds of investment philosophy to the corporate life cycle? While the overall market goes through up and down cycles, and all stocks are impacted, it turns out that the effect varies for companies at different stages in the life cycle. Generally, when the market is buoyant, and investors are seeking out risky investments, young companies benefit the most, since they are the riskiest and most in need of capital.

Conversely, when markets are down, and risk capital moves to the sidelines, it is more mature companies that hold their value better, as investors are drawn to safety. If you are a good market timer, you can magnify the benefits of timing by also shifting your holdings from older to younger companies, ahead of up markets, and from younger back to more mature companies, if you expect down markets. As I noted in chapter 3, sectors often stand in as proxies for the corporate life cycle (tech for young companies, utilities for mature ones); sector rotation, a strategy of moving across sectors depending on where you are in the market cycle, is an example of the interplay between market timing and the corporate life cycle.

Investing versus Trading

When talking about investing, you often hear talk about "value" and "price" as if they are interchangeable, but they are not. Value, as I noted in chapter 9, is driven by cash flows, growth, and risk—i.e., the fundamentals—but price is determined by demand and supply, which incorporate mood, momentum, and a host of behavioral forces. That confusion between value and price lies at the heart of why it is impossible to have a conversation about how much a stock is worth, when the parties to the conversation come from different camps. The difference becomes visible in how you play markets, in what I loosely call the *pricing game* and the *value game*. In table 14.1, I look at the differences between the two.

Table 14.1 • Investing versus Trading

	The Pricing Game	The Value Game
Underlying Philosophy	The price is the only real number that you can act on. No one knows what the value of an asset is, and estimating it is of little use.	Every asset has a fair or true value. You can estimate that value, albeit with error, and price must converge on value (eventually).
Playing the Game	You try to guess which direction the price will move in the next period(s) and trade ahead of that movement. To win the game, you must be right more often than wrong about direction and exit before the winds shift.	You try to estimate the value of an asset, and if it is priced under (over) value, you buy (sell) the asset. To win the game, you must be right about value (for the most part), and the market price has to move to that value over time.
Key Drivers	Price is determined by demand and supply, which in turn are affected by mood and momentum.	Value is determined by cash flows, growth, and risk.
Information Effect	Incremental information (news, stories, rumors) that shifts the mood will move the price, even if it has no real consequences for long-term value.	Only information that alters cash flows, growth, or risk in a material way can affect value.
Tools of the Game	1. Technical indicators 2. Price charts 3. Multiples and comparable firms 4. Investor psychology	1. Ratio analysis 2. DCF valuation 3. Excess return models
Time Horizon	Can be very short-term (minutes) to mildly short-term (weeks, months).	Long-term.
Key Skill	Be able to gauge market mood/momentum shifts earlier than the rest of the market.	Be able to "value" assets, given uncertainty.
Key Personality Traits	1. Market amnesia 2. Quick acting 3. Gambling instincts	1. Faith in "value" 2. Patience 3. Immunity from peer pressure
Biggest Danger(s)	Momentum shifts can occur quickly, wiping out months of profits in a few hours.	Price may not converge on value, even if your value is "right."
Added Bonus	Capacity to move prices (with lots of money and lots of followers).	Can provide the catalyst that can move price to value.
Most Delusional Player	A trader who thinks he is trading based on value.	A value investor who thinks he can reason with markets.

If you play the pricing game, you are a trader, and if you play the value game, you are an investor. I am not passing judgment when I make this statement, because unlike some, I don't view traders as shallow or somehow less critical to the functioning of markets than investors. After all, a trader who makes a million-dollar profit can buy just as much with that money as an investor who makes the same profit. Ultimately, which avatar (price or value) best fits you will depend not only on your level of comfort with the tools but also on your personal traits. In our experience, naturally impatient people who are easily swayed by peer pressure almost never succeed as good value players, and excessively cerebral folks who must weigh everything in the balance before they make decisions are incapable of being successful traders.

This black-and-white view of the world may strike some of you as extreme. After all, why not allow for shades of gray—traders who are interested in value and investors who think about the pricing process? Tempting though that might sound, it generally does not work, for two reasons. The first is that many self-proclaimed hybrid investors are nothing of the sort: they are traders who merely pay lip service to value, while using it to back their momentum plays, or investors who claim to respect markets, but only until they start moving in the wrong direction. The second is that there is a danger in playing on unfamiliar turf: traders who delude themselves into believing that they understand value can undercut their own effectiveness just as much as investors who think that they can get in and out of markets when it suits them. A healthy market needs both traders and investors, in the right balance. A market that has no traders, only investors, will have no liquidity; one that has only traders, and no investors, will have no center of gravity. Ironically, each group needs the other for sustenance. Trading and momentum cause prices to move away from value, creating the bargain opportunities that investors try to exploit—and in the process of exploiting them, they create the corrections and momentum shifts that traders exploit.

It is true that there are both traders and investors in companies at every stage of the life cycle, but the mix will shift as companies age. To see why, go back to chapter 9, where I argued that it is easier to both price and value mature companies, relative to young companies. With uncertainty running rampant on every dimension of the business model and little historical data, there are few who are willing to even try valuing young companies, leaving the arena almost entirely to traders. As companies mature, and uncertainty lessens, investors are more likely to enter the process, and traders may leave, as volatility in stock prices drops and trading opportunities decrease.

Trading: Momentum, Information, and Arbitrage

If the essence of trading is to take advantage of market mood, momentum, and overreaction, you can already see that there are a variety of philosophies that fit under the trading umbrella. In this section, I will look at these subsets, again with the intent of connecting them to corporate life cycles.

MOMENTUM TRADING

Momentum is a force to reckon with in markets, as past pricing trends often continue, but with a significant chance of reversal thrown into the mix. For as long as there have been markets, there have been traders trying to take advantage of the information in past pricing trends, by using either pricing indicators (such as relative strength) or price charts. While academic finance and much of practitioner finance have tended to be dismissive of the idea of predictive patterns in past prices, there are clearly some traders who have learned to play the game well enough to deliver profits.

Accepting momentum trading as a viable philosophy, it is still worth noting why it is so difficult to hold on to the winnings from a momentum philosophy. The reason lies in the mixed evidence on price patterns in financial markets. Research on past prices, especially from the equity markets, is supportive of price patterns, yet it produces contradictory findings:

- If you define the short term as ranging from minutes to hours to even a few days, there is evidence of mild positive correlation, with prices continuing to move in the same direction. The correlation is low enough that it is difficult to make trading profits on predictions, but that does not stop investors from trying, especially when they are backed by data and high-powered computers.*
- If you extend the short term to weeks, rather than days, there seems to be some evidence that prices reverse. In other words, stocks that have done well over the last month are more likely to do badly in the next one, and stocks that have done badly over the last month are more likely to bounce back.† The reasons given are usually rooted in market overreaction—i.e., the stocks that have gone up (down) the most over the most recent month are ones where markets have overreacted to good (bad) news that came out about the stock. The price reversal then reflects markets correcting themselves.
- In the medium term, defined as multiple months or even a year, there seems to be a tendency again toward positive serial correlation. Narasimhan Jegadeesh and Sheridan Titman present evidence of what they call price momentum in stock prices over time periods of several months—stocks that have gone up in the last six months tend to continue to go up, whereas stocks that have gone down in the last six months tend to continue to go down.‡ Between 1945 and 2008, if you classified stocks into deciles based upon price performance over the previous year, the annual return you would

* In the middle of the last decade, high-frequency trading, wherein institutional investors used powerful computers and timely data to make very large trades, enjoyed a moment in the limelight. The profits made by those traders quickly faded as data and computer power evened out across competing traders.

† N. Jegadeesh, "Evidence of Predictable Behavior of Security Returns," *Journal of Finance* 45, no. 3 (July 1990): 881–98; B. N. Lehmann, "Fads, Martingales, and Market Efficiency," *Quarterly Journal of Economics* 105, no. 1 (February 1990): 1–28.

‡ N. Jegadeesh and S. Titman, "Returns to Buying Winners and Selling Losers: Implications for Stock Market Efficiency," *Journal of Finance* 48, no. 1 (March 1993): 65–91; N. Jegadeesh and S. Titman, "Profitability of Momentum Strategies: An Evaluation of Alternative Explanations," *Journal of Finance* 56, no. 2 (April 2001): 699–720.

have generated by buying the stocks in the top decile and holding for the next year was 16.5% higher than the return you would have earned on the stocks in the bottom decile. To add to the allure of this strategy, the high-momentum stocks also had less risk (measured as price volatility) than the low momentum stocks.*

- When the long term is defined in terms of many years, there is substantial negative correlation in returns, suggesting that markets reverse themselves over very long periods. Eugene Fama examined five-year returns on stocks from 1941 to 1985 and present evidence of this phenomenon.† He found that serial correlation is more negative in five-year returns than in one-year returns and is much more negative for smaller stocks rather than larger stocks.

The push and pull between momentum (positive correlation) and reversal (negative correlation) across time horizons also provides an explanation for why price-based trading is never monolithic.

Building on the argument, introduced in the last section, that almost all the market activity in young companies comes from traders rather than investors, I would expect momentum, if it exists, to be stronger at young companies than at mature firms, and reversals, when they happen, to be more drastic as well. Thus, the price swings that you see at young companies are not just a reflection of the underlying business uncertainties at these companies but are magnified by the dominance of traders in these firms' shareholder mix.

INFORMATION-BASED TRADING

There are some traders whose focus is trading around information announcements, especially ones like earnings reports or acquisition announcements, with the intent of taking advantage of what they perceive to be errors either in expectations or in market responses to announcements. On the latter, the simplest way of assessing market efficiency is to look at how quickly and how well markets react to new information in terms of fairly reassessing value changes that result from that information. The value of an asset should increase when new information that positively affects any of the inputs into value—the cash flows, the growth, or the risk—reaches the market. In an efficient market, the price of the asset will adjust instantaneously and, on average, correctly to the new information, as shown in figure 14.1.‡

* K. Daniel, "Momentum Crashes," Working Paper, SSRN #1914673, 2011.

† E. F. Fama, "Market Efficiency, Long Term Returns and Behavioral Finance," *Journal of Financial Economics* 49, no. 3 (September 1, 1998): 283–306.

‡ K. C. Brown, W. V. Harlow, and S. M. Tinic, "Risk Aversion, Uncertain Information, and Market Efficiency," *Journal of Financial Economics* 22, no. 2 (December 1988): 355–85.

FIGURE 14.1 | Price Adjustment in an Efficient Market

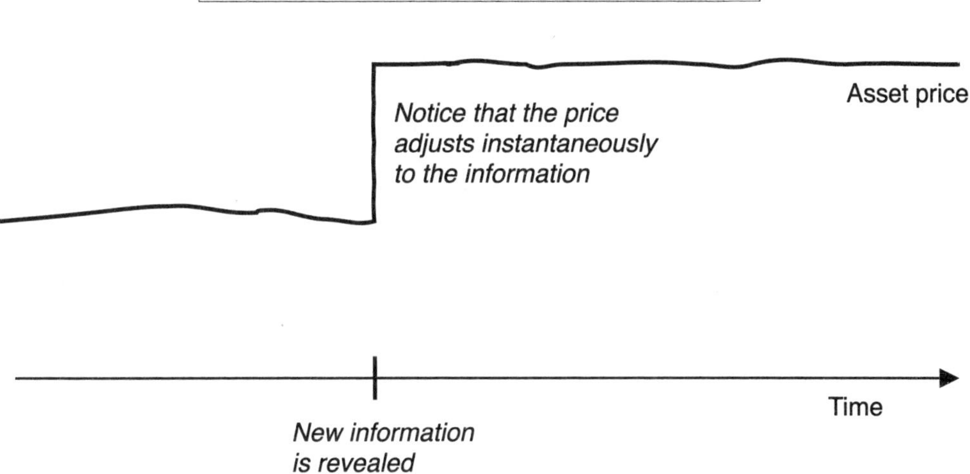

The adjustment will be slower if investors are slow in assessing the impact of the information on value. In figure 14.2, I show the price of an asset adjusting slowly to new information. The upward drift in price after the information arrives is indicative of a slow-learning market.

FIGURE 14.2 | Price Adjustment in a Slow-Learning Market

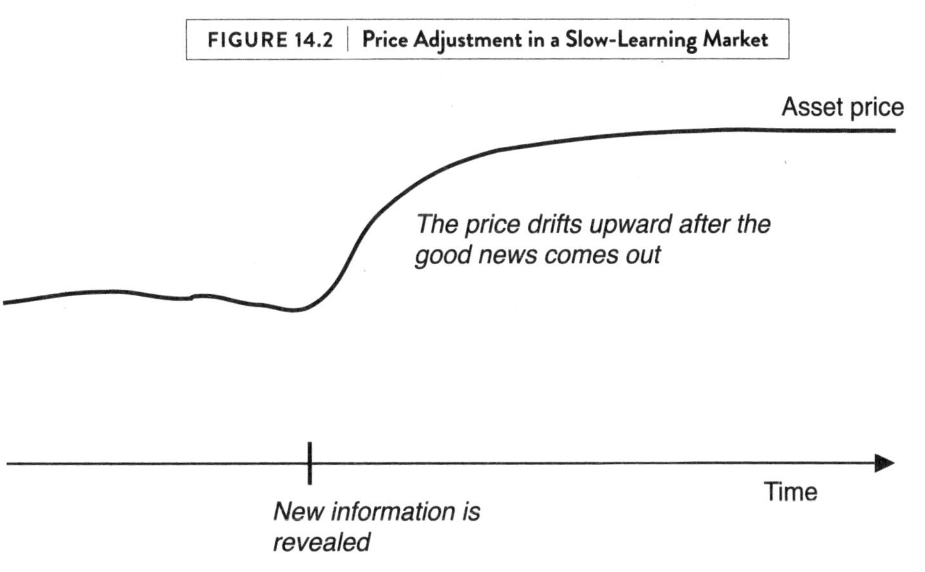

The market could also adjust instantaneously to the new information but overestimate the effect of the information on value. Then the price of the asset will increase by more than it should, given the effect of the new positive information on value, or drop by more than it should on negative information. Figure 14.3 shows the drift in prices in the opposite direction, after the initial reaction.

FIGURE 14.3 | Price Adjustment in an Overreacting Market

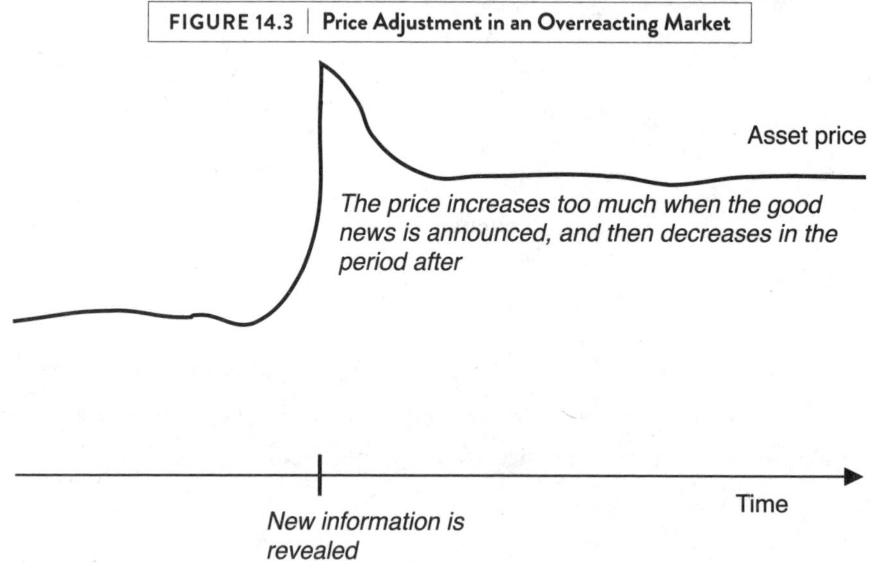

The research on which of these behaviors (underreacting or overreacting) is more commonly found in markets comes back with mixed results. For instance, figure 14.4 provides a graph of price reactions to earnings surprises that are classified, based on magnitude of surprise, into different classes from "most negative" earnings reports (Group 1) to "most positive" earnings reports (Group 10).*

* The original study of this phenomenon was in R. Ball and P. Brown, "An Empirical Evaluation of Accounting Income Numbers," *Journal of Accounting Research* 6, no. 2 (Autumn 1968): 159–78. That study was updated by Bernard and Thomas, with daily data around quarterly earnings announcements. See V. Bernard, and J. Thomas, "Post-Earnings Announcement Drift: Delayed Price Response or Risk Premium?" *Journal of Accounting Research* 27 (1989): 1–48. This graph is developed from an update of that study by D. C. Nichols and J. M. Wahlen, "How Do Accounting Numbers Relate to Stock Returns: A Review of Classic Accounting Research with Updated Numbers," *Accounting Horizons* 18, no. 4 (January 2005): 263–86.

FIGURE 14.4 | **Excess Returns around Earnings Announcements**

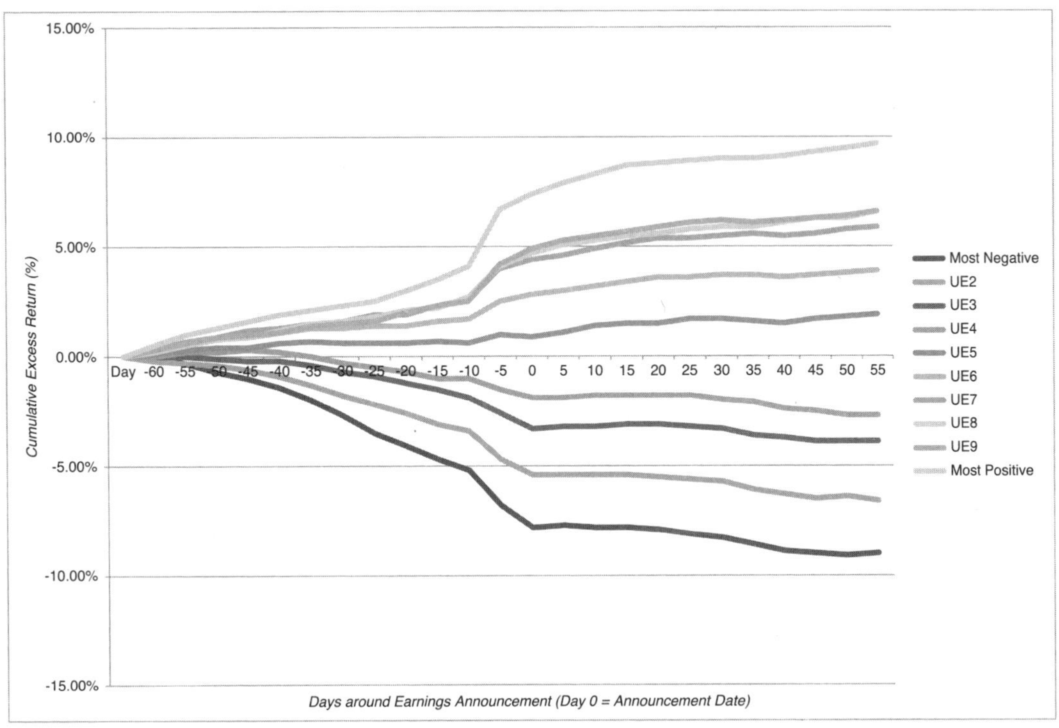

Source: D. Craig Nichols and James Wahlen

The evidence contained in this graph is consistent with the evidence in most earnings announcement studies.

- The earnings announcement clearly conveys valuable information to financial markets; there are positive excess returns (cumulative abnormal returns) around positive announcements and negative excess returns around negative announcements.
- There is some evidence of a price drift in the days immediately prior to the earnings announcement that is consistent with the nature of the announcement, i.e., prices tend to go up in the days before positive announcements and down in the days before negative announcements. This can be viewed as evidence of either insider trading or prescient trading, ahead of reports.
- There is some evidence of a price drift in the days following an earnings announcement. This can be seen by isolating only the post-announcement effect of earnings reports, in figure 14.5.

FIGURE 14.5 | Excess Returns after Earnings Announcements

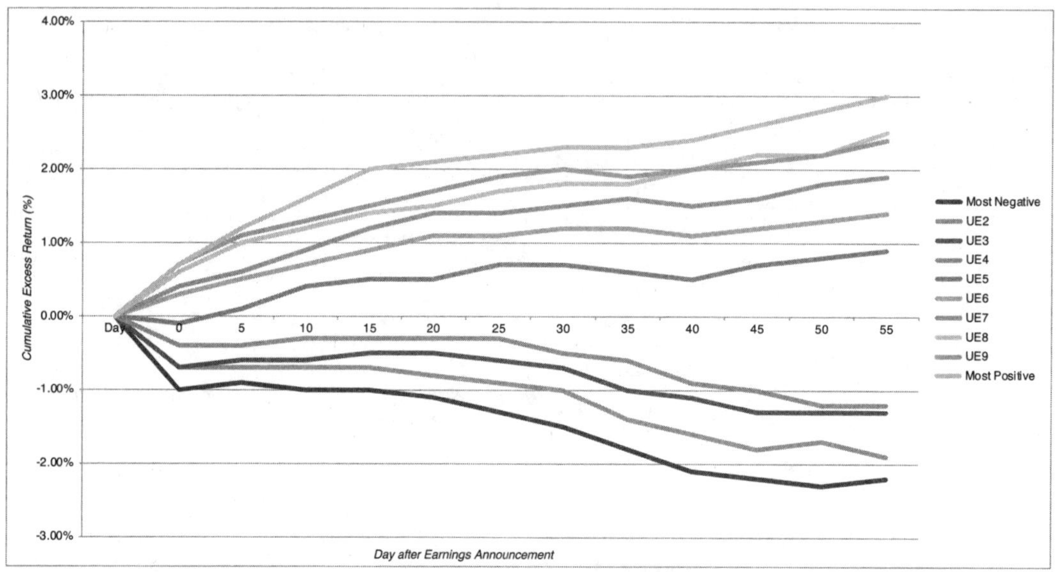

Source: D. Craig Nichols and James Wahlen

Thus, a positive (negative) report evokes a positive (negative) market reaction on the announcement date, and there are positive (negative) excess returns in the days and weeks following the earnings announcement. In short, there is some evidence in this graph to back different trading views. For those who believe that there is profit to be made by trading ahead of earnings announcements, based upon price momentum, there is evidence to back up that view in figure 14.4, looking at the price drift before the announcements. For other traders, the drift in prices that continues after the report is supportive of the view of a slow-learning market and a trading strategy of buying (selling short) shares in companies after extremely positive (negative) earnings reports.

What is the link between information-based trading and the corporate life cycle? I would argue that the market learning mistakes that I observe across all companies can be greater at young businesses than at their mature counterparts. Studies of the market reaction to earnings reports note that the post-announcement drift is greater at small firms than larger ones,* at firms where there is greater uncertainty about future earnings,† and

* V. Bernard and J. Thomas, "Post-Earnings Announcement Drift: Delayed Price Response or Risk Premium?" *Journal of Accounting Research* 27 (1989): 1–36.

† C. Y. Liang and R. Zhang, "Post-Earnings Announcement Drift and Parameter Uncertainty: Evidence from Industry and Market News," *Review of Quantitative Finance and Accounting*, 55 (2020): 1–44.

at firms where institutional investors hold a smaller percentage of the shares.* Though it may be coincidental, young firms tend to have smaller market capitalizations and greater uncertainty about future earnings, and are less held by institutions.

ARBITRAGE TRADING

Arbitrage represents the holy grail of investing, because it allows traders to invest no money, take no risk, and walk away with sure profits. In other words, it is the ultimate money machine that investors hope to access, and it can take three forms:

- The first is *pure arbitrage*, where, in fact, you risk nothing and earn more than the riskless rate. For pure arbitrage to be feasible, you need two assets with identical cash flows, different market values at the same point in time, and a given point in time in the future at which their values must converge. This type of arbitrage is most likely to occur in derivatives markets—options and futures—and in some parts of the bond market.
- The second is *near arbitrage*, where you have assets that have identical or almost identical cash flows trading at different prices, but there is no guarantee that the prices will converge and there exist significant constraints on forcing convergence.
- The third is *speculative arbitrage*, which is not arbitrage in the first place. Here, investors take advantage of what they see as mispriced and similar (though not identical) assets, buying the cheaper one and selling the more expensive one. If they are right, the difference should narrow over time, yielding profits. It is in this category that I consider hedge funds in their numerous forms.

In all its forms, arbitrage trading is focused more on the short than the long term and is more dependent on efficient execution (trade quickly, while keeping costs low) and pricing than on investing.

While dreams of arbitrage and guaranteed profits animate a lot of investing and trading, it is difficult to find in practice. What looks like arbitrage on the surface is often not, for the following reasons:

1. **Illusory identicalness:** For arbitrage, you need two investments that are identical that trade at different prices at the same point in time. In practice, though, many settle for

* E. Bartov, S. Radhakrishnan, and I. Krinsky, "Investor Sophistication and Patterns in Stock Returns After Earnings Announcements," *Accounting Review* 75, no. 1 (January 2000): 43–63.

close or very similar, rather than identical, investments, and while the differences between the investments may be small, they can still explain price differences.

2. **Non-tradability:** To lock in profits from arbitrage on two investments that you believe are identical, but are listed at different prices, you must be able to trade both investments. This can explain why some emerging-market companies with dual listings trade at different prices in domestic and foreign markets, if the foreign-listed shares cannot be converted into domestic shares.
3. **Trading costs:** In a related challenge, there are some arbitrage opportunities, wherein identical assets trade at different prices, where the costs of trading on the differences, including transaction costs and price impact, are large enough to overwhelm the observed price difference.

A more insidious side effect of the search for arbitrage is that those looking for it become prime candidates for scams. From Charles Ponzi to Bernie Madoff, the common denominator for investment frauds has been promising investors that they can earn guaranteed returns that exceed the prevailing risk-free rate, without taking risks.

The link between arbitrage profits and the corporate life cycle is complicated. While the lower profiles and lighter liquidity at younger firms make arbitrage opportunities more likely to show up on their traded securities, the higher transaction costs (bid ask spreads and price impact) that you face in trading these securities may also mean that you will find it more difficult to convert these opportunities to profits. To the extent that some investors can create cost or information advantages over the rest of the market on these stocks, though, they may be able to still find ways to generate arbitrage profits.

Investing: Value versus Growth

Investing is built on the presumption that you can value individual assets and take advantage of price deviations from the value, eventually profiting when the gap between price and value disappears. Note that there is nothing in this definition that suggests that investing is skewed toward young or old companies, growth or mature companies. In practice, though, most investors prefer one grouping over the other and are subsequently classified into value investors and growth investors.

No investment philosophy has been written about more and has more adherents, at least on the surface, than value investing, for two reasons. First, the academic research on investing success (I will present the evidence in chapter 16) seems to back the thesis that value investing has done significantly better than growth investing, its competing philosophy, in US equity markets over much of the last century. Second, a disproportionately large number of investors who have been consistently successful over long periods seem to come from its ranks. While I will return, in chapter 16, to look at whether value investing's success is as overwhelming as its adherents claim, I will lay the groundwork in this chapter by defining what I see as value investing. It is not, as some contend, that value investors care about value and growth investors do not, which is absurd. Rather, the difference lies in where they find value. Using the financial balance sheet construct that I introduced in this book, where I broke a firm's value down into assets in place and growth assets, figure 14.6 presents the contrast between value and growth investors.

FIGURE 14.6 | Value versus Growth Investing

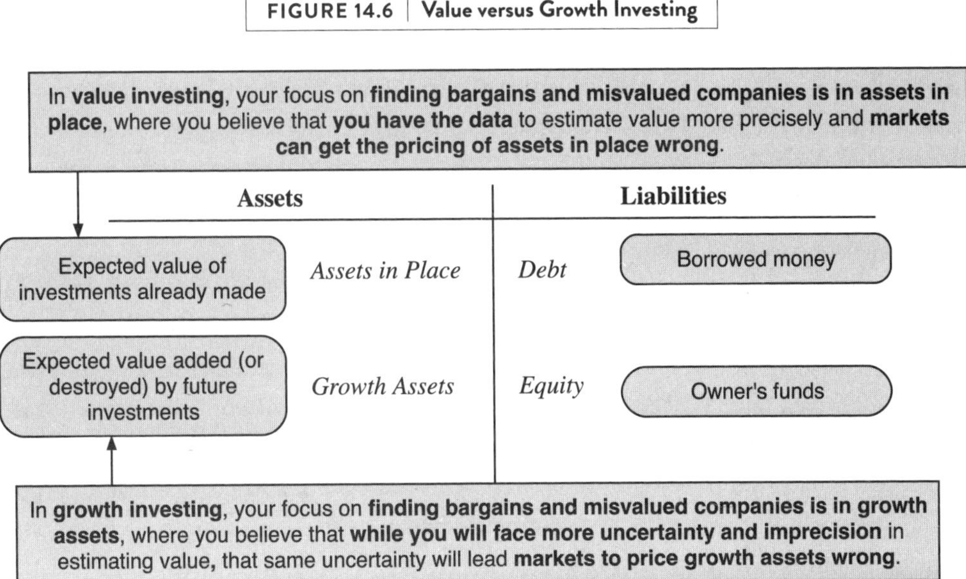

Put simply, the contrast between value and growth investing is not that one cares about value and the other does not, but is where in the company the investor believes the "value error" lies. Value investors believe that their tools and data are better suited to finding mistakes in valuing assets in place, and that belief leads them to focus on more mature companies that derive the bulk of their value from existing investments. Growth investors, on the other hand, accept that valuing growth is more difficult and more imprecise, but argue that it is precisely because of these difficulties that growth assets are more likely to be misvalued. This distinction also connects these two philosophies directly to the corporate life cycle, with value investors drawn to mature companies, which derive much or all of their value from assets in place, and growth investors to younger companies, where the bulk of the value comes from growth assets.

Activist versus Passive Investing

At the broadest level, investment philosophies can also be categorized as activist or passive strategies. In a *passive strategy*, you invest in a stock or company and wait for your investment to pay off. Assuming that your strategy is successful, this payoff will come from the market recognizing and correcting a misvaluation. Thus, a portfolio manager who buys stocks with low PE ratios and stable earnings is following a semi-passive strategy. So is an index fund manager, who essentially buys all stocks in the index—an all-passive strategy. In an *activist strategy*, you invest in a company and then try to change the way the company is run to make it more valuable. Venture capitalists can be categorized as activist investors, since they not only take positions in promising young companies but also provide significant inputs into how these firms are run. Investors who have the capital wherewithal sometimes bring this activist philosophy to publicly traded companies, using the clout of large ownership positions to change the way companies are run.

I should hasten to draw a contrast between activist investing and *active* investing. In the popular vernacular, active investing includes any strategy where you try to beat the market by steering your money to undervalued asset classes or individual stocks/assets. Any investor who tries to beat the market by picking stocks is viewed as an active investor. Thus, active investors can adopt passive strategies or activist strategies.

Finally, there is a link between activism in investing and where a firm is in the corporate life cycle. As I noted earlier, the venture capitalists in start-ups and very young companies are almost never passive investors, for many reasons. First, their input to the management of the company may be critical in helping it convert an idea into a product and a product into a business model. Second, since their returns depend on exiting the investment on favorable terms, they will try to steer the firm toward pathways that generate better exit valuations. Thus, if VCs believe that a user-based company will generate a higher pricing at exit if it has more users, they may push the company to prioritize adding users over building business models. Finally, since VC ownership can be easily diluted by subsequent rounds of capital raised, venture capitalists have to build protections against this dilution into their investments. As companies mature, this activism will tend to fade, especially as the shareholder base for the company becomes more institutional and passive; most institutional investors who dislike how a firm is run tend to vote with their feet—i.e., sell their holdings and move on. As companies enter decline, you are likely to see activism pick up again, as investors try to alter a firm's operating direction, in some cases buying them out and making changes themselves, and in others, pushing them to liquidate or break up.

Investment Philosophies in Context

I can consider the differences between investment philosophies in the context of the investment process, described in figure 14.7.

FIGURE 14.7 | The Investment Process

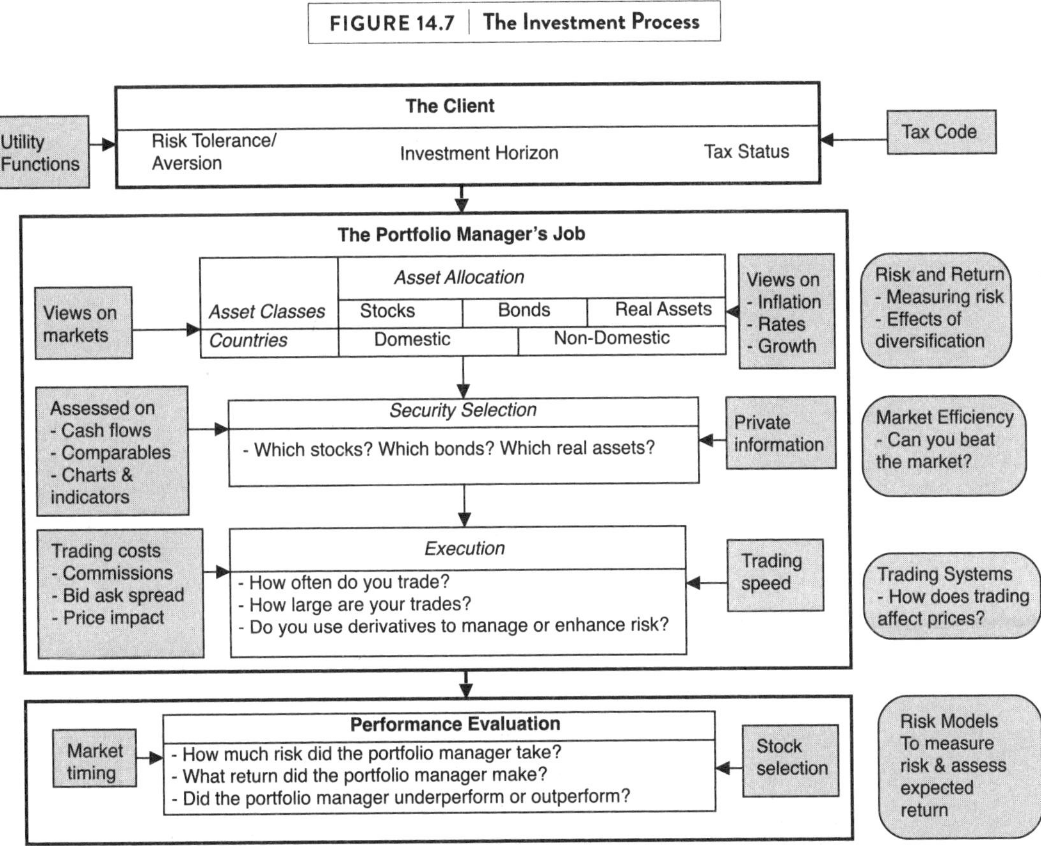

As you can see, the investment process begins with an assessment of the client—with the caveat that the client can be yourself, if you are managing your own investments—and an understanding of how much risk the client is willing to bear, the time horizon on the portfolio, and the tax status. The portfolio creation process has three steps (which do not always occur in the sequence shown in the picture), with asset allocation determining how much of the portfolio is invested in different asset classes and geographies, security selection specifying which individual investments are chosen within each class, and execution looking at trading choices and costs. The final part of the process (albeit one that some active investors would avoid) is a performance evaluation, where you compare the returns earned on a portfolio with the returns that you should have made, given risk exposure and actual market performance.

The investment philosophies that I broadly contrasted above all fit into the investment process. Market timing strategies primarily affect the asset allocation decision, since a strong view that an asset class (equities, real estate, etc.) is undervalued (overvalued) will shift the portfolio toward (against) that asset class. Security selection strategies, in all their forms—technical analysis, fundamentals, or private information—all center on the security selection component of the portfolio management process. You could argue that strategies that are not based upon grand visions of market efficiency but are designed to take advantage of momentary mispricing of assets in markets (such as arbitrage) revolve around the execution segment of portfolio management. It is not surprising that the success of such opportunistic strategies depends upon trading quickly to take advantage of pricing errors and keeping transaction costs low. Figure 14.8 presents the different investment philosophies in the context of where they fit into the portfolio construction part of the investment process.

FIGURE 14.8 | Investment Philosophies and Investment Process

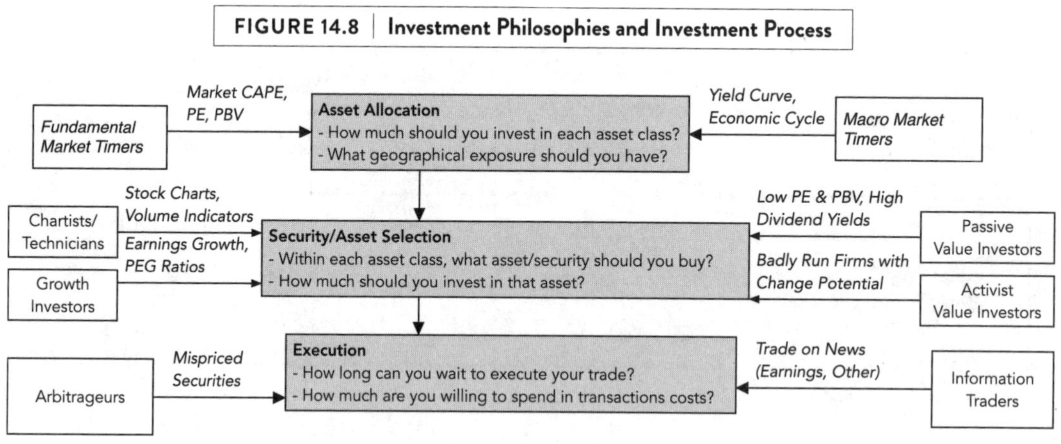

One of the most fascinating aspects of investment philosophy is the coexistence of investment philosophies based upon contradictory views of the markets. Thus, you can have market timers who trade on *price momentum* (suggesting that investors are slow to learn from information) and market timers who are *contrarians* (based on the belief that markets overreact). Among security selectors who use fundamentals, you can have *value investors* who buy value stocks because they believe markets overprice growth, and *growth investors* who buy growth stocks using exactly the opposite justification. The coexistence of these contradictory impulses for investing may strike some as irrational, but it is healthy and may be responsible for keeping the market in balance. In addition, you can have investors with contradictory philosophies coexisting in the market because of their different time horizons, views on risk, and tax status. For instance, tax-exempt investors may find stocks that pay large dividends a bargain, while taxable investors may reject these same stocks because their dividends are taxed at the ordinary tax rate.

Investment Philosophies and the Corporate Life Cycle

With the lead-in on investment philosophies, I can now make connections to the corporate life cycle and show how investors at different stages in the life cycle make choices on whether to trade or invest and, within each group, in what types of stocks. Using the breakdown from the last section, and superimposing the characteristics of companies across the life cycle, I arrive at the following:

1. **Price versus value:** If the value process is driven by fundamentals, and the pricing process by demand and supply, the gap will be reflective of the divergence between the two. While that divergence will exist for companies no matter where they are in the life cycle, I would expect the gap between price and value to be larger and more volatile at young companies, where uncertainty abounds, historical data is absent or untrustworthy, and there are wide differences across investors on the valuation story.
2. **Investing versus trading:** In chapter 10, I noted that many investors avoid valuing young companies, using the excuse that there is too much uncertainty about business models and future projections to bother. Not surprisingly, they abandon these companies almost entirely to traders, some of whom benefit from the wild swings in prices that characterize these companies. As companies mature and their financials take form, you are more likely to see investors enter the arena, creating more of a balance between traders and investors in the shareholder mix.
3. **Trading focus:** There arc traders operating in every segment of the corporate life cycle, but the basis for their trading will shift. With start-ups and very young companies, where venture capitalists set prices, that pricing is almost entirely based upon how

other venture capitalists have priced these companies, or companies very much like them, in the past—i.e., momentum. When these companies are first listed in public markets, the trading is still mostly driven by momentum, which explains why research finds the power of momentum to be greater at growth than mature companies. As these companies stay in public markets, and the market pricing settles in, trading shifts toward information events, with analysts expending resources forecasting the numbers in the earnings report, and traders buying or selling ahead of or after the report. With mature companies, where neither markets nor information announcements deliver much in the way of surprises, traders search for mispricing across markets, small though it might be, that they can arbitrage.

4. **Investing focus:** Investing's divide into growth and value already gives you a sense of its link to the life cycle. With growth investing, the search for bargains will be in younger companies, where a greater portion of the value comes from future growth. With value investing, your investing universe will be predominantly mature companies, since you are looking for mistakes that the market may be making in valuing assets in place. In chapters 15 and 16, I will explore this divide and argue that this self-selection may handicap both philosophies.
5. **Activist versus armchair:** Within investing, I looked at the contrast between passive "armchair" investing—where you find bargains, buy them, and hope that the market correction happens—and activist investing, where you try to not only speed up the market correction but also change the way a company is run. In connection with the life cycle, being an armchair investor in a start-up or very young company is extraordinarily dangerous, since founders need both guidance and oversight. As companies age, go public, and become mature, you can afford to be an armchair investor, with the hope that disclosure rules and strong corporate governance systems will keep managers in check. In decline, as I showed in chapter 13, the need for activism rises again, since managers in denial or desperation can do serious damage to your wealth as an investor.
6. **Passive versus active:** If you buy in to the proposition that active investing has a greater chance of a payoff in markets where there are frictions and uncertainties that you can parlay into competitive advantages, it stands to reason that active investing has a greater likelihood of paying off for companies at either end of the life cycle—very young and steeply declining companies—than at stable and mature companies, which have more investment consensus on business model and the future.

In figure 14.9, I consider changes in investment philosophies across the life cycle.

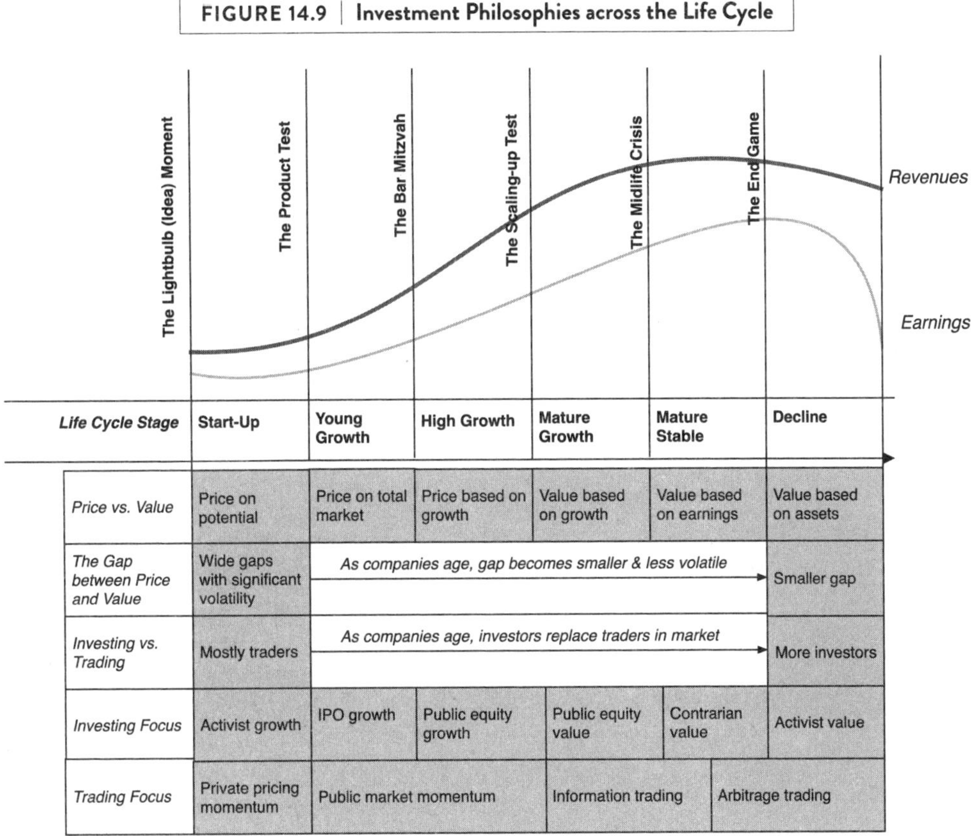

FIGURE 14.9 | Investment Philosophies across the Life Cycle

As you can see, at young companies, you are far more likely to see trading be dominant, but much of that trading will be driven by momentum. As companies mature, you are more likely to see at least a subset of people trying to value these companies and invest in them, and the focus will shift to trading around information announcements. Activism, where investors are actively involved in changing how businesses are run, will have its biggest payoffs at either end of the corporate life cycle, with venture capitalists putting pressure on founders in young companies and private equity and activist investors trying to push declining companies to divest, liquidate, or split up.

Conclusion

An investment philosophy, at its core, is a set of beliefs about markets and investors that determine where you see the payoff from investing and, through that determination, drive the investment strategies that you use. Within that broad construct, there is an extraordinarily wide range of choices, covering everything from technical analysis and charting, at one end of the spectrum, to data-based quantitative investing at the other. While there is no one best investment philosophy for all investors, there is an investment philosophy that best fits you. Once you find a philosophy that fits you, you will also find your preferred habitat in the corporate life cycle, with some philosophies leading you toward young- and high-growth companies and others pushing you toward mature or even declining companies.

15

Investing in Youth

IN THE CORPORATE FINANCE and valuation assessment chapters, I noted that uncertainty is a feature at young companies, and that no amount of wishful thinking or elaborate modeling will make that uncertainty go away. For some investors, that uncertainty is a roadblock to investing in these companies, but for others, it operates as a clarion call, offering upside and drawing them to invest. In this chapter, I will start with a look at those who invest in the youngest companies, mostly before they go public, as venture capitalists, and examine the history of success and failure in VC investing. I will then look at VCs' public-market counterparts, who make their bets on growth companies, hoping for payoffs—either from investing in or trading on them—and evaluate their history of success and failure. With each group, I will use what I have learned about young and growth companies in earlier chapters to create checklists for success.

Venture Capital

For start-ups and very young companies, it is venture capitalists who help founders build these businesses, supplying capital in exchange for receiving shares of ownership in these companies. In chapter 4, I noted that venture capitalists play a key role in the transition from idea businesses to successful moneymakers, but do they generate returns commensurate with the risk that they are exposed to in these investments? In this section, I will begin by arguing that venture capitalists are more traders than investors, playing the pricing game, and then look at the winners and losers in that game.

A Pricing Game

Using as a starting point the contrast between price and value that I made both in chapter 9 and chapter 14, I posit that venture capitalists (VCs) don't value companies, they price them. This is less a critique of what venture capitalists do and more a recognition of reality. In fact, not only is pricing exactly what you should expect from VCs, it lies at the heart of what separates the elite from the average venture capitalist. Earlier, in chapter 10, I saw this divide play out in our examination of the VC valuation approach, which I noted was more pricing than valuation, with an arbitrary target rate used as a discount rate. In fact, when VCs price companies, they look at:

1. **Recent pricing of the same company:** In the most limited version of this game, a prospective or existing investor in a private business looks at how investors in the most recent prior funding round have priced the company to gauge whether they are getting a reasonable price. Thus, for Uber, in June 2016, this would imply that a pricing close to the $62.5 billion that the Saudi sovereign fund priced the company at, when it invested $3.5 billion, would become the benchmark for a reasonable price for others investing close to that date. The dangers in following this path are numerous, including the possibility of pricing mistakes, when a new investor over- or underprices the company, causing that mistake to spiral up and down the pricing chain. Put simply, one new round of overpricing or underpricing can spawn many more rounds of overpricing or underpricing.
2. **Pricing of "similar" private companies:** In a slightly more expanded version of the above process, a VC would look at what investors are paying for similar companies in the "same business,"—with all the necessary subjective judgments of what comprises a "similar," or the "same," business—scale this price to revenues (or, lacking that, a common metric for that space, like users, subscribers, downloads, etc.), and price your company. Staying in the ride-sharing space, you could price Lyft, in 2016, based upon the most recent Uber transaction, by scaling the pricing of the company to its revenues (relative to Uber), or to the number of riders served.
3. **Pricing of public companies, with post-value adjustments:** In the rare cases where a private business has enough operating substance today, in the form of revenues or even earnings, in a space where there are public companies, a VC could use the pricing

of public companies as the basis for pricing private businesses. Thus, if a private company is in the gaming business and has $100 million in revenues, and publicly traded companies in that business trade at 2.5 times revenues, its estimated pricing would be $250 million. That pricing, though, assumes that the company is liquid (as publicly traded companies tend to be) and held by investors who can spread their risks across portfolios. Consequently, a discount for lack of liquidity and, perhaps, diversification is applied, though the magnitude (20%, 30%, or more) is one of the tougher numbers to estimate and justify in practice.

It is not just venture capitalists who play the pricing game. Most investors in public markets (including many who call themselves value investors) are also in the pricing game, though they use pricing metrics of longer standing (from PE to EV/EBITDA) and have larger samples of publicly traded firms as comparable firms. The challenges with adapting this pricing game to venture capital investments are primarily statistical:

- **Small samples:** If your pricing is based upon other private-company investments, your sample sizes will tend to be much smaller if you are a VC than if you are a public-company investor. As an investor in a publicly traded oil company, in 2021, one could draw on 351 publicly traded firms in the US, or even the 1029 publicly traded companies globally, when making relative value or pricing judgments. A VC investor pricing a ride-sharing company is drawing on a sample of fewer than ten ride-sharing firms globally.
- **Infrequent updating:** The small-sample problem is exacerbated by the fact that unlike public companies, where trading is frequent and prices are updated for most of the companies in the sample almost continuously, private-company transactions are few and far between. In many ways, VC pricing is closer to real estate pricing, where you must price a property based upon similar properties that have sold in the recent past, than conventional stock pricing.
- **Opaque transactions:** There is a third problem that makes VC pricing complicated. Unlike with public equities, where shares of equity give you identical claims and the company's total market value is the share price times the number of shares outstanding, extrapolating from a VC investment for a share in a company to the overall value of its equity can be and often is complicated. Why? As I noted in chapter 10, the VC investment at each stage of funding is structured differently, with a myriad of options embedded in it, some designed for protection (against dilution and future equity rounds), and some for opportunity (allowing future investments at favorable prices).

Consequences

If venture capitalists price companies, and that pricing is often based upon small samples, with infrequently updated and tough-to-read data, there are predictable consequences:

- **VC pricing estimates will have more noise (error) attached to them**: The pricing that you obtain for Lyft, in 2016, based upon the pricing of Uber, Didi, and Grab at the time, will have a larger band around the estimate, and there is a greater chance that you will be wrong.
- **VC pricing will be more subjective**: VCs have the freedom to choose their comparable firms and often can use discretion to adjust for the infrequent data updates and the complexity of their equity investments. While that may seem to just be a restatement of the first critique, there is also a much greater potential for bias to enter the process. Not surprisingly, therefore, not all VC returns are created equal—especially when it comes to the unrealized portion, with more aggressive VCs reporting "higher" returns than less aggressive VCs.
- **The pricing will lag the market**: It is a well-established fact that the capital coming into the VC business ebbs and flows across time, with the number of transactions increasing in up markets and dropping in down markets. When there is a severe correction (as was the case just after the dot-com bust), transactions can come to a standstill, making repricing difficult, if not impossible. If VCs hold off on full repricing until transactions pick up again, there can be a significant lag between when prices drop at young companies and those price drops being reflected in returns at VC firms.
- **There is a price feedback loop**: Since VC pricing is based upon small samples with infrequent transactions, it is susceptible to feedback loops, where one transaction that's badly priced (in either direction) can trigger many more badly priced transactions. Price spirals, if they occur, will be more pronounced in both directions.
- **There is a time horizon issue**: The lack of liquidity and small samples that get in the way of pricing VC holdings also introduce a constraint into the pricing game. Unlike public-market investing, where the pricing game can be played in minutes, or even fractions of a minute, on liquid stocks, private-market pricing requires patience, and more of it the younger a company is. Put differently, winning at the VC pricing game may require that you take a position in a start-up and bide your time until you build it up and find someone who will find it attractive enough to offer you a much higher price for it.

There is one final point that also needs to be made. Much as I like to talk about the VC market and the public market as separate, populated by different species, they are linked at the hip. To the extent that a venture capitalist must plot an investment exit strategy, either in an initial public offering or by selling to a publicity traded company, if the public market catches a cold, the venture capital market will get pneumonia, though the diagnosis may come much later.

VC Returns: Winners and Losers

Do venture capitalists earn higher returns than other investors, and do those higher returns cover the additional risk that they are exposed to on their investments? Before looking at the evidence on this proposition, it is worth drawing attention to a weak link in the test, which is the measurement of returns. Unlike public-market investments, where the unrealized returns are based upon observed market prices for traded stocks and can be converted to realized returns relatively painlessly, the unrealized returns at venture capital funds are based upon estimates, and these estimates are themselves based upon opaque VC investments in other companies in the space and not easily monetized. Consequently, unrealized returns at VC funds are subject not only to estimation error but also to bias, and should thus be viewed as softer than realized returns. With those caveats in place, here is what the research shows:

1. **The average VC does better than the average public-market active investor:** Both VC and public-market investors play the pricing game, with the latter having the advantage of more and better data, but over time, venture capitalists seem to deliver better results than public-market investors, as seen in figure 15.1.

FIGURE 15.1 | Returns on US VC, Private Equity, and Public Equity, 2002–2021

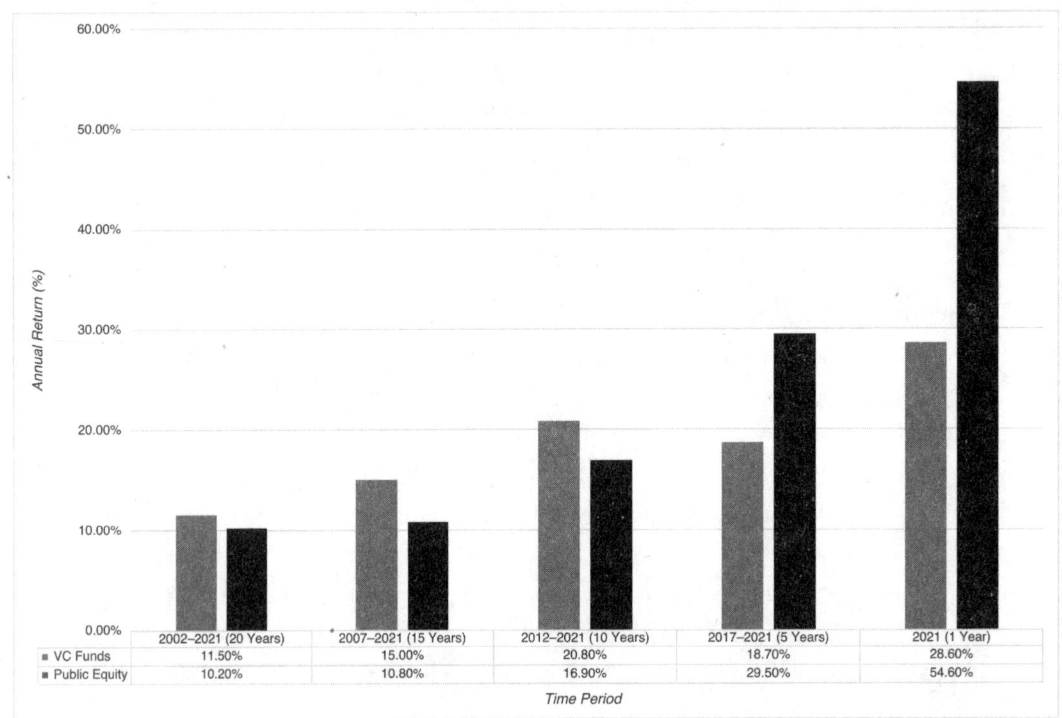

	2002–2021 (20 Years)	2007–2021 (15 Years)	2012–2021 (10 Years)	2017–2021 (5 Years)	2021 (1 Year)
VC Funds	11.50%	15.00%	20.80%	18.70%	28.60%
Public Equity	10.20%	10.80%	16.90%	29.50%	54.60%

Source: Cambridge Associates

These are raw returns, and I do realize that you must adjust for risk, but the biggest risk in venture capital (failure risk) has already been incorporated into long-term returns. As you can see, venture capitalists collectively earn modestly higher returns, over the long term (10, 15, and 20-year periods), but underperform public-equity investors in the shorter time periods. Even in the long term, it is an open question as to whether the extra returns in earnings (1.3% a year for the 20-year returns, or 4.20% a year for 15-year returns) is enough to cover the extra risk in venture capital investing.

2. **Venture capital has skewed payoffs:** The nature of VC investing is that even the most successful VCs lose on a large proportion—even a majority—of their investments, but their big winners make enough to cover all their losers and more. Figure 15.2 provides a breakdown of returns to early-stage venture capitalists from 2004 to 2013.

FIGURE 15.2 | Early-Stage Venture Capital Returns, 2004–2013

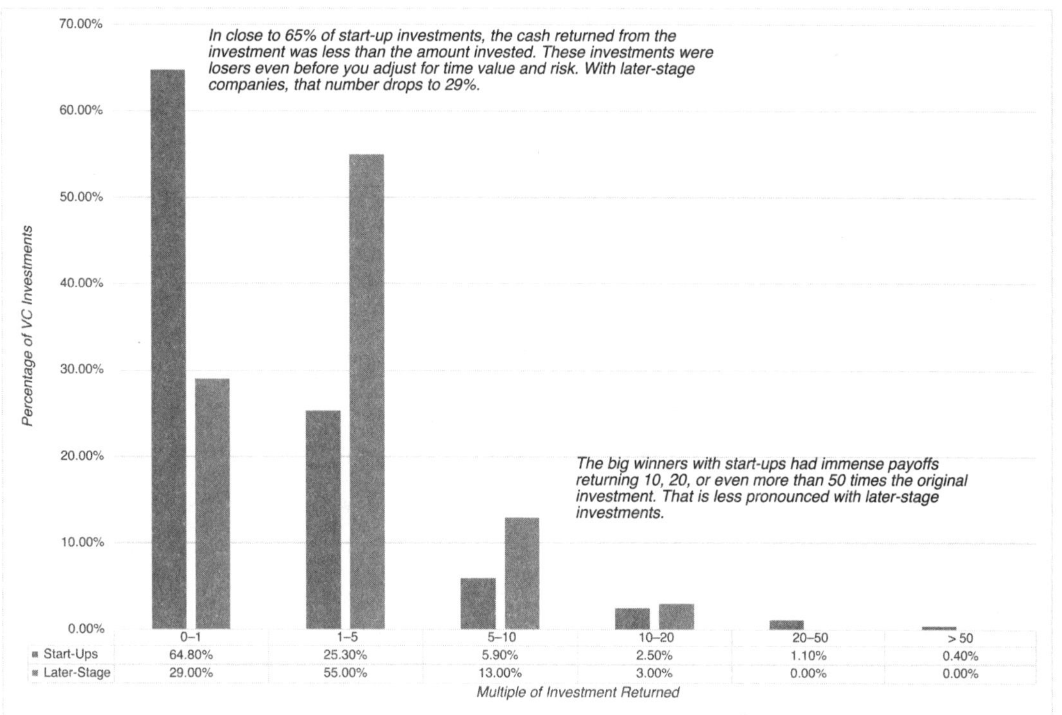

While these are returns over a single ten-year period, they capture the nature of payoffs from VC investing. To see how corporate aging changes this distribution, comparing early-stage VC returns to those earned by later-stage VC investors, you get fewer losers with the latter, as well as less upside on winners.

3. **Elite venture capitalists have staying power:** Not only do the most successful VCs earn higher returns than the top public-market investors, there is more consistency in the VC business, insofar as the best of the VCs are able to generate higher returns across longer time periods. That would suggest that venture capitalists bring more durable competitive advantages to the investing game than public-market investors.

How do I reconcile our argument that the VC pricing game is inherently more error-prone and noisy with the fact that VCs seem to make money at it? I think that the very factors that make it so difficult to price and profit off a VC investment are what allow venture capitalists, collectively, to earn excess returns, and the very best to set themselves apart from the rest. In particular, the best in the venture capital business distinguish themselves on three dimensions:

1. **They are better at pricing (relatively):** The price that you can attach to a VC investment can vary widely across investors, and while all these prices are undoubtedly wrong (because they are estimates), some of them are less wrong than others. Having even a slight edge in the pricing game can give a venture capitalist a significant advantage over the long term, and, on this dimension, success may feed itself and create continuity. A start-up may give more successful venture capitalists better pricing terms just to get them on board, so that they can be used to attract other investors to the firm.
2. **They have more influence in the companies that they invest in:** Unlike public-market investors, who for the most part can observe company metrics but not change them, venture capitalists can take a more active role in the companies that they invest in, from informally advising managers to more formal roles as board members, helping these companies decide what metrics to focus on, how to improve these metrics, and how (and when) to cash in on them (through an IPO or a sale).
3. **They have better timing:** The pricing game is all about timing, and the VC pricing game is more emphatically so. To be successful, VCs not only have to time your entry into a business right but, even more critically, they have to time their exit from it. The most successful VCs are better at gauging mood and momentum and timing their investment entries and exits.

If you are an investor in a VC fund, therefore, you should of course look at both realized returns and unrealized returns, but you should also look at how the fund measures its unrealized returns and how it has generated its returns. A realized return that comes primarily from one big hit is clearly less indicative of skill than a return that reflects multiple hits over longer time periods. After all, if separating luck from skill is difficult in the public marketplace, it can become even more so in the venture capital business.

Determinants of Success

While venture capital is not a recipe for guaranteed high returns, there are some venture capital investors who succeed and earn extraordinary returns. What sets them apart, and how can you partake in their success? The keys seem to be the following:

1. **Good judges of narrative:** In chapter 10, I argued that when valuing start-ups and very young companies, it is the story that drives the valuation, not historical financials or numbers. If you are an investor in young companies, you not only have to be good at assessing founder stories and passing them through the 3P test, you must also craft your own narrative for the company, to drive your investment in it.
2. **Good judges of managers/founders:** In a young company, you are entirely reliant on the founder and management team to deliver on the valuation story, and what sets the very best venture capitalists apart is their capacity to gauge the capacity and trustworthiness of a founder to deliver on a story.
3. **Protective of their investments as the firm grows:** As the firm grows and attracts new investment, you, as the venture capitalist, will have to protect your share of the business from the demands of those who bring in fresh capital.
4. **Good assessors of failure risk:** Most small private businesses fail, either because the products or services they offer do not find a ready audience or because of poor management. Good venture capitalists seem to have the capacity to find the combination of ideas and management that makes success more likely, albeit not guaranteed.
5. **Spread their bets wisely:** That said, the rate of failure will remain high among venture capital investments, making it critical that you spread your bets. The earlier the stage of financing you work in—seed money, for example—the more important it is that you diversify your investments.

As a successful venture capitalist, your portfolio will be a risky one, but relatively undiversified, with large stakes in several small and volatile business, often in the same sector or industry group. The bottom line is that success at venture capital comes just as much from trading skills, where you gauge mood and momentum to time entry and exit, as it does from your skills at evaluating business narratives and founder capabilities.

Growth Investing and Trading: Public Equities

Public-market growth investors use proxies and screens to find high-growth stocks that are undervalued by the market. Some invest in initial public offerings, with the intent of capturing any excess returns associated with the stock going up after the offering. Others design investment strategies that seek companies that are expected to deliver the highest growth in revenues or earnings. Still others consider a more nuanced strategy of buying growth stocks, but only at a reasonable price.

Initial Public Offerings (IPOs)

In chapter 4, I looked at the process that private companies use in going public, noting that discontent with the banker-led IPO process is opening the door for change. That said, it is young and growth companies that are most likely to go through this process, and there are public-market investors who have sought to beat the market by exploiting market frictions and mistakes around the process of going public.

THE OFFERING DAY AND AFTERMATH

In banker-led IPOs, bankers, driven partially by the offer-price guarantee that they offer issuing companies, underprice companies for the offering and do so openly. In figure 15.3, I look at the average underpricing of IPOs, based upon how the company's stock does on the offering date.

FIGURE 15.3 | Return on Offering Day for US IPOs

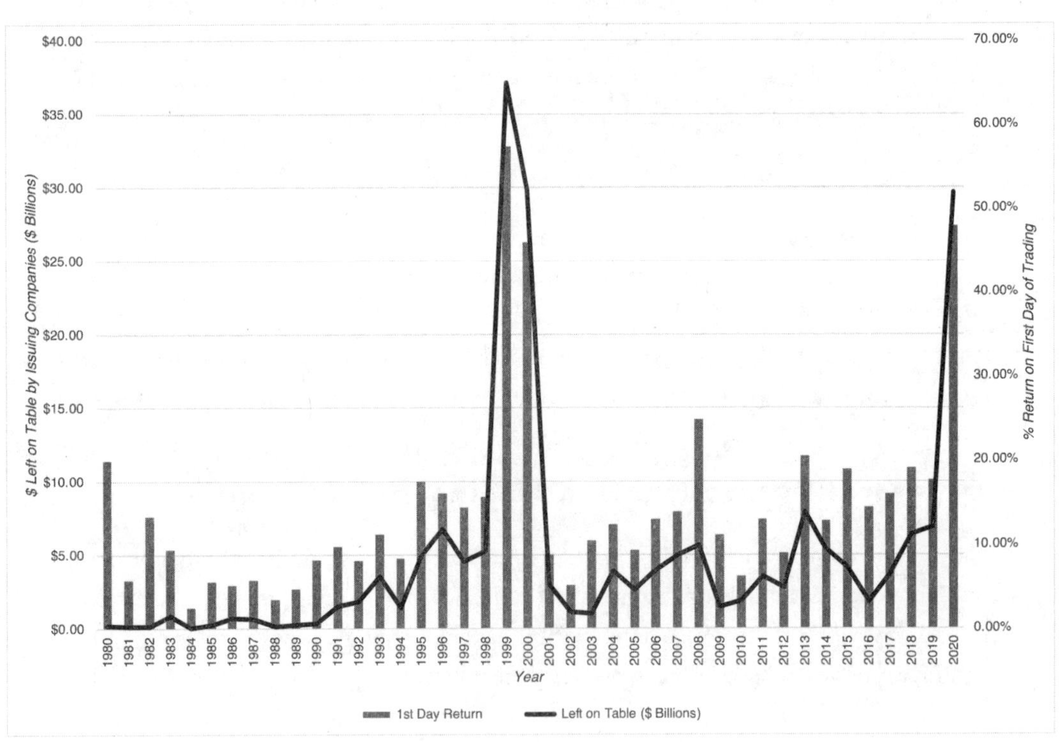

You can see that in every single year, the average percentage change in the stock price on the offering day has been a large positive value. Since this offering-price discount is effectively money left on the table by the founders and owners of the VC company, I have also computed the dollar value of this loss.

While the payoff to trading ahead of initial public offerings is questionable, might there still be a payoff to trading on IPOs on the offering date and in the days after? Since much of the buying and selling in the first few days that a stock is listed comes from traders trying to take advantage of short-term price movements, not investors gauging its long-term value, you would expect momentum to be a dominant price driver in these windows. That said, there is little documented evidence of consistent payoffs to all the frenetic trading that I see around offerings.

POST-IPO RETURNS

While the evidence that initial public offerings go up on the offering date is strong, it is not clear that these stocks are good investments in the years after. Tim Loughran and Jay Ritter tracked returns on 5,821 IPOs in the five years after the offerings and contrasted them with returns on non-issuers in figure 15.4.

FIGURE 15.4 | Returns after Initial Public Offerings

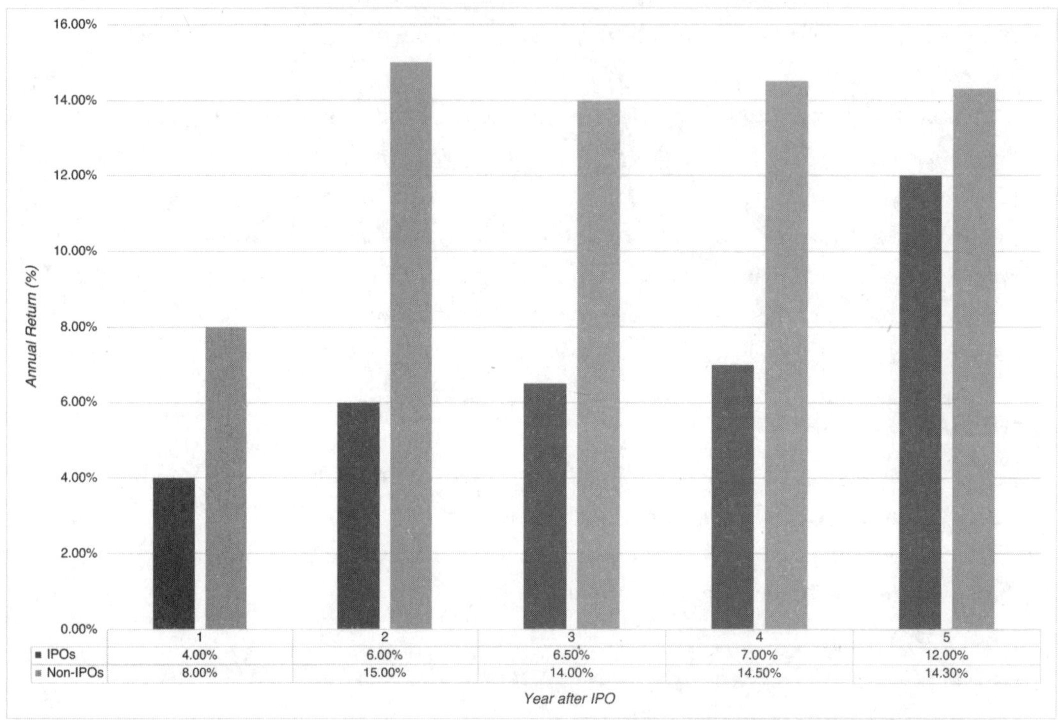

	1	2	3	4	5
IPOs	4.00%	6.00%	6.50%	7.00%	12.00%
Non-IPOs	8.00%	15.00%	14.00%	14.50%	14.30%

Source: Tim Loughran and Jay Ritter

Note that the IPO firms consistently underperform the nonissuing firms, and that the underperformance is greatest in the first few years after the offering. While this phenomenon is less pronounced for larger initial public offerings, it persists. Put succinctly, the primary payoff to investing in IPOs comes from having the shares in hand when the stock opens for trading on the offering day. I update this study and look at the returns in the three years after the IPO, for IPOs from 1980 to 2019, in figure 15.5.

FIGURE 15.5 | Market- and Risk-Adjusted Returns in 3 Years Post-IPO

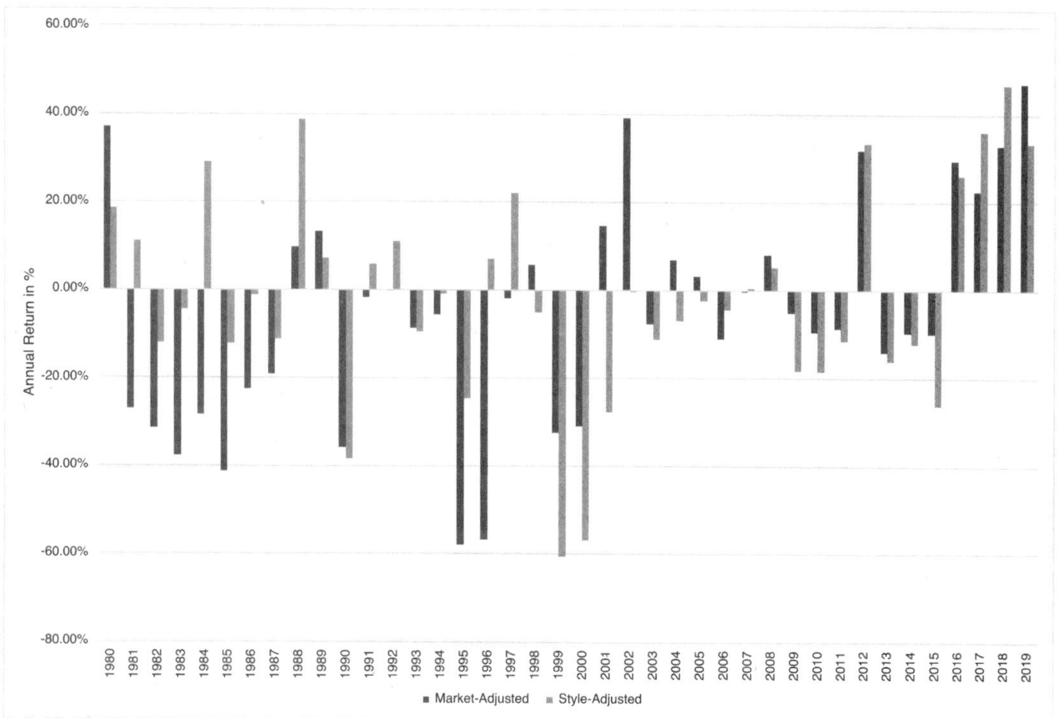

Like the earlier study that I quoted, this one indicates that investing in IPOs at the offering and holding on for long time horizons is not a winning strategy, delivering, on average, 6.45% less, on an annualized basis, than the market and 3.45% less, on an annualized basis, than a growth investing index fund.

INVESTMENT STRATEGIES

Given the evidence on underpricing of IPOs and the substandard returns in the years after, are there investment strategies that can be constructed to make money on IPOs? In this section, I will consider three. In the first, I adopt the bludgeon approach, trying to partake in every initial public offering and hoping to benefit from the offering-day jump (chronicled in the studies above). In the second, I adopt a variant of momentum investing, riding IPOs in hot markets and avoiding them in cold markets. In the last, I look at refinements that allow us to invest selectively in those IPOs where the odds best favor investors.

THE BLUDGEON STRATEGY: INVEST IN EVERY IPO

While there is substantial evidence that IPOs are, on average, underpriced at their offerings, the evidence on investors being able to take advantage of these pricing errors and frictions is much weaker. That anomaly can be explained by bringing in trading costs and details of the offering process. If initial public offerings, on average, are underpriced, an obvious investment strategy is to subscribe to many initial public offerings and to construct a portfolio based upon allotments of these offerings.

There is, however, a catch in the allotment process that may prevent this portfolio from earning the excess returns from the underpricing. When investors subscribe to initial public offerings, the number of shares that they are allotted will depend upon whether and by how much the offering is underpriced. If it is significantly underpriced, you will get only a fraction of the shares that you requested. On the other hand, if the offering is correctly priced or overpriced, you will get all the shares that you requested. Thus, your portfolio will be underweighted in underpriced initial public offering and overweighted in overpriced offerings. Is there a way in which you can win this allotment game? There are two strategies that you can adopt, though neither guarantees success. The first is to be the beneficiary of a biased allotment system, where the investment bank gives you more than your share of your requested shares in underpriced offerings. The second is to bet against the herd and sell short on IPOs just after they go public, hoping to make money from the price decline in the following months. The peril with this strategy is that these stocks are driven by mood and momentum, and the stocks may get significantly more overpriced for long periods before there is a correction.

RIDE THE WAVE: INVEST ONLY IN HOT MARKETS

Initial public offerings ebb and flow with the overall market, with both the number of offerings and the degree of underpricing moving in waves. There are periods where the market is flooded with initial public offerings, with significant underpricing, and periods where there are very few offerings, with a concurrent drop-off in underpricing as well. In chapter 4, I showed the ebbs and flows in IPOs (in figure 4.9) and contrasted the salad days of the late 1990s, when firms went public at an extraordinary pace, and 2001, when the number slowed to a trickle. A strategy of riding the IPO wave would therefore imply investing when the IPO market is hot, with lots of offerings and significant underpricing, and steering away from IPOs in the lean years.

This strategy is effectively a momentum strategy, and the risks are similar. First, while it is true that the strategy generates returns, on average, across the entire "hot" period, whether you make money or not depends largely upon how quickly you recognize the beginning of a hot IPO market (with delayed entry translating into lower returns) and its end (since the IPO listings toward the very end of the hot market are the ones most likely to fail). Second, the initial public offerings during any period tend to share a common sector focus. For instance, the bulk of the initial public offerings during 1999 were of young technology and telecom firms. Investing only in these public offerings will result in a portfolio that is not diversified in periods of plenty, with an overweighting in whichever sector is in favor at that point in time.

THE DISCRIMINATING IPO INVESTOR

If the biggest danger of an IPO investment strategy is that you may be saddled with overpriced stocks (either because you received your entire allotment of an overpriced IPO or because you are approaching the end of a hot IPO cycle), incorporating a value focus may allow you to avoid some of the risk. Thus, rather than invest in every IPO listing across time or in hot markets, you might invest only in those IPOs where the odds of underpricing are greatest. This will require an investment of time and resources prior to the offering, wherein you use the information in the prospectus and other public filings to value the company, using either intrinsic or relative valuation models. You would then use the value estimates from your analysis to decide which IPOs to invest in and which ones to avoid.

There are two potential pitfalls with this strategy. The first is that your valuation and pricing skills must be well honed, because valuing or pricing a company going public is generally much more difficult than doing the same with one that is already listed. While companies going public must provide information on their financial standing and what they plan to use the offering proceeds for, they also tend to be younger, high-growth firms. As I noted in chapters 10 and 11, valuing these companies requires a combination of narrative and number skills that can be difficult to find. The second is that, as I noted in the last section, IPO markets go through cycles, with the number of underpriced offerings dropping to a handful in cold markets. Thus, your task may end up being to find the least overpriced IPOs, rather than underpriced ones, and then work out an exit strategy for selling these stocks before the correction hits.

Growth Investing

If you are a portfolio manager whose choices come from a very large universe of stocks, your most effective way of building a portfolio may be to screen stocks and pick those that pass specific screens. In other words, you look for companies that have earnings that you expect to continue to grow at high rates in the future, implicitly assuming that this will pay off in higher returns. In making assessments of growth, you can look at growth in the past—i.e., historical growth—or expectations of growth in the future, with the former being easier to access and the latter offering the benefit of being forward-looking.

HISTORICAL GROWTH

For companies with any historical financial data, estimating the rates at which they have been able to grow revenues, if they are money losing, or earnings, if they are moneymaking, is generally easy to do. For investors seeking high growth, these historical growth rates are often used as screens for growth stocks. But is the growth rate in the past a good indicator of growth in the future? Past growth rates may be used by many investors as forecasts of future growth, but there are three problems:

- **Limited history:** To estimate past growth, you need a financial history, and for some of the highest-growth companies, especially early in the life cycle, that historical data can be limited and, even if available, not particularly informative. For companies that do have a significant financial history, the growth rate that you estimate can vary depending on time periods used, the operating metric being looked at (revenues, operating income, net income, earnings per share), and even the averaging approach (arithmetic versus geometric averages can yield very different estimates).
- **Noisy predictors:** In a 1962 study of the relationship between past growth rates and future growth rates, Ian Little coined the term "higgledy piggledy growth" because he found little evidence that firms that grew fast in one period continued to grow fast in the next period.* In the process of running a series of correlations between growth rates in earnings in consecutive periods of different length, he frequently found negative correlations between growth rates in the two periods, and the average correlation across the two periods was close to zero (0.02). If past growth in earnings is not a reliable indicator of future growth at the average firm, it becomes even less so at smaller firms. The growth rates at smaller firms tend to be even more volatile than growth rates at other firms in the market. The correlation between growth rates in earnings in consecutive time periods (five-year, three-year, and one-year) for firms in the United States, categorized by market value, is reported in figure 15.6.

* I. M. D. Little, "Higgledy Piggledy Growth," *Oxford Bulletin of Economics and Statistics* 24, no. 4 (November 1962): 387–412.

FIGURE 15.6 | Time Correlations in Earnings Growth, by Market-Cap Class

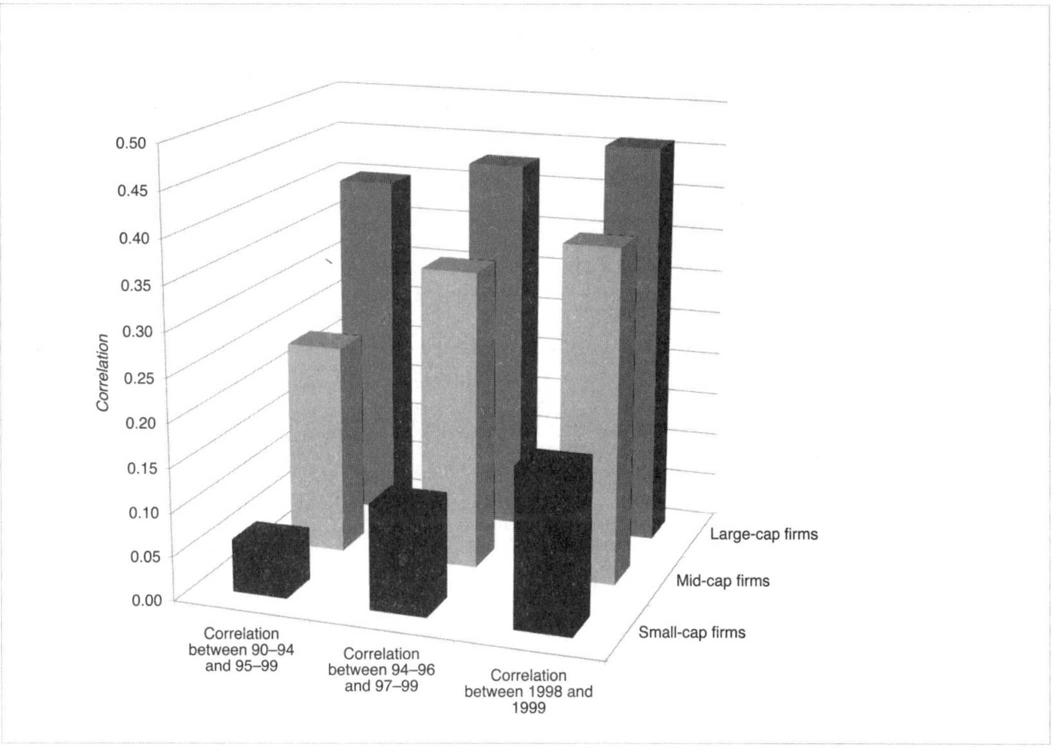

Source: Capital IQ

While the correlations tend to be higher across the board for one-year growth rates than for three- or five-year growth rates in earnings, they are also consistently lower for smaller firms than they are for the rest of the market. This would suggest that you should be more cautious about using past growth, especially in earnings, to forecast future growth at these firms.

- **Reversion to the mean:** Companies that are growing at rates much higher than the industry average growth rate will generally see their growth rates decline toward the market or industry average. This tendency is chronicled by David Dreman and Eric Lufkin when they track companies in the highest- and lowest-earnings-growth classes for five years after the portfolios are formed.* While the highest-earnings-growth companies have an average growth rate which is 20% higher than the average growth rate for the lowest-earnings-growth companies in the year the portfolio is formed, the difference is close to zero five years later.

If you have no choice but to use past growth as a predictor, revenue growth tends to be more persistent and predictable than earnings growth. This is because accounting choices have a far smaller effect on revenues than they do on earnings. The implication is that historical growth in revenues is a far more useful number when it comes to forecasting than historical growth in earnings. In summary, past growth is not a reliable indicator of future growth, and there is no evidence that I am aware of that investing in companies with high past growth yields significant returns. In fact, if there is mean reversion and you have paid a large premium for companies with high growth, you will find yourself with a losing portfolio.

EXPECTED EARNINGS GROWTH

Value is ultimately determined by future growth, not past growth. It seems reasonable, therefore, that you would be better served investing in stocks where expected growth, rather than historical growth, is high. Here, too, you run into a practical problem. In a market with thousands or even hundreds of listings, you cannot estimate expected growth for each firm in the market. Instead, you must rely on analyst estimates of expected growth for companies. That information, though, is accessible now to most investors, and you could choose to buy stocks with high expected growth rates in earnings. For this strategy to generate high returns, the following conditions must hold: First, analysts must be proficient at forecasting long-term earnings growth. Second, the market price must not already reflect or price this growth, since if it does, your portfolio of high-growth companies will not generate excess returns. On both conditions, the evidence works against the strategy. When it comes to forecasting growth, analysts tend to overestimate growth, and these forecast errors are not only high, for long-term forecasts, but highly correlated across analysts following the same stock. In fact, some studies find that just using historical growth rates, from a time series model, matches or even outperforms analyst estimates when it comes to long-term growth. As for pricing growth, markets

* D. Dreman and E. Lufkin, "Do Contrarian Strategies Work Within Industries?" *Journal of Investing* 6, no. 3 (Fall 1997): 7–29; D. Dreman and E. Lufkin, "Investor Overreaction: Evidence That Its Basis Is Psychological," *Journal of Psychology and Financial Markets* 1, no. 1 (2000): 61–75.

historically have been more likely to overprice growth than underprice it, especially during periods of high earnings growth for the market.

GROWTH INVESTOR TRACK RECORD

When assessing whether investors in companies with high growth generate market-beating returns, you must start with a finding that seems to push against an affirmative answer. Given that expected growth in earnings and PE ratios are correlated, with higher-growth companies usually trading at high PE ratios, one simplistic test of growth investing is to look at returns earned by stocks, classified based upon PE ratios. In figure 15.7, I look at the difference in annual returns from buying low EP (high PE) stocks and high EP (low PE) portfolios from 1951 to 2021.*

FIGURE 15.7 | Annual Returns on US Stocks, by Earnings/Price Decile, 1951–2021

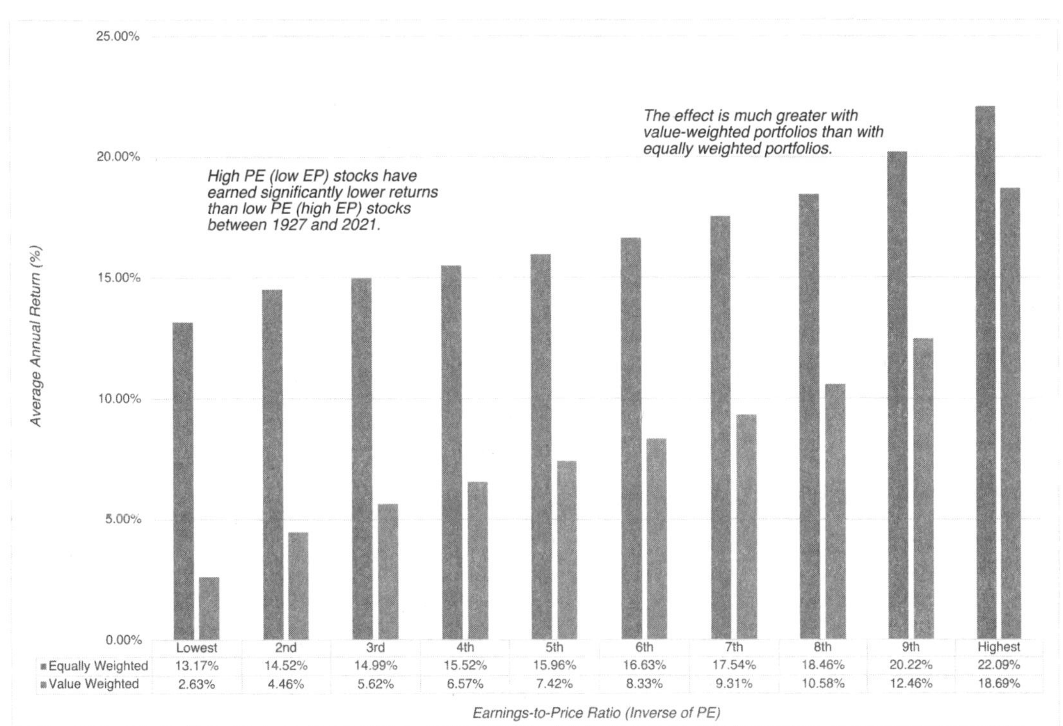

Source: Raw data from Kenneth French

* One reason that stocks are classified based on earnings to price ratios, instead of PE ratios, is to prevent the loss of money-losing firms from the sample. A company that has a stock price of $10 and an earnings per share of -$0.50 has a PE ratio that is "not meaningful" or cannot be computed, but its earnings to price ratio of -5% (EPS/price per share) can still be computed and used.

On both an equally-weighted and a value-weighted basis, low EP (high PE) stocks have underperformed high EP (low PE) stocks.

Given this sorry performance, what, you might wonder, attracts investors to this strategy? The answer lies in market cycles. There have been extended time periods when high PE stocks outperformed low PE stocks. For instance, as you can see in figure 15.8, there seems to be a link between the returns you earn on high PE stocks, relative to low PE stocks, and the earnings growth rate.

FIGURE 15.8 | Returns to Growth Investing and Earnings Growth Levels

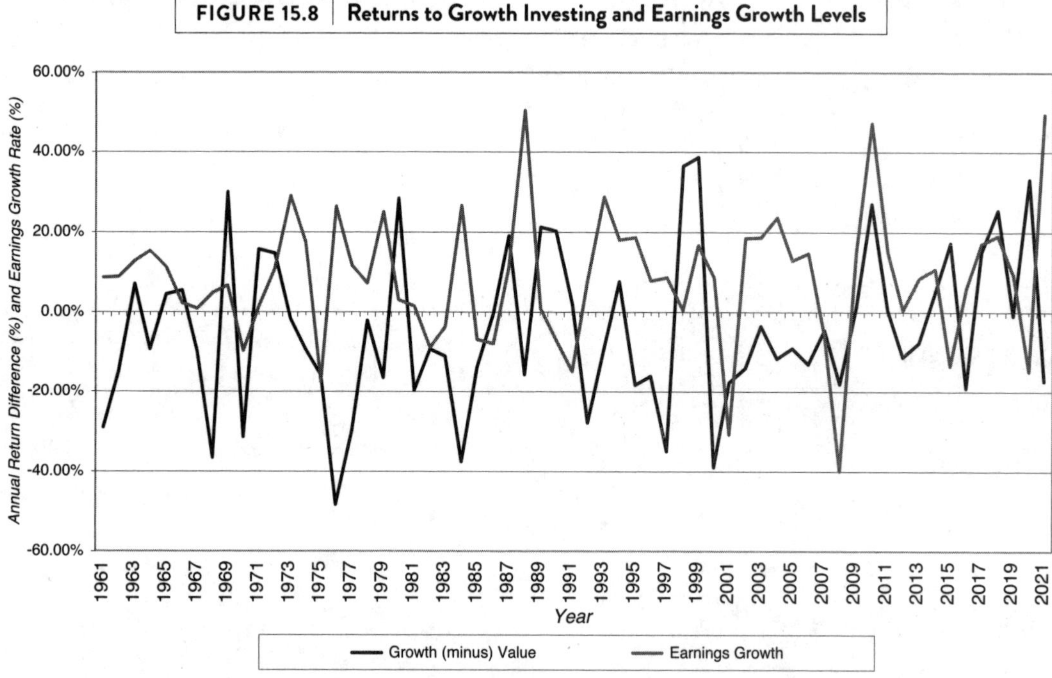

Source: Raw data from Kenneth French, S&P

I measure the performance of growth versus value by looking at the difference between the returns earned on a portfolio of stocks in the top decile in terms of PE (growth) and a portfolio of stocks in the lowest decile (value). Thus, a positive value indicates that high PE stocks outperformed low PE stocks in that year. *Growth investing does better in years when earnings growth is low*, perhaps because growth stocks are more desirable in periods when earnings growth is low—i.e., growth is scarce.* By the same token, when all

* Though statistically significant, the correlation between how growth stocks do and earnings growth is about 6%, indicating that this strategy may make money in the long term, but with lots of hits and misses along the way.

companies are reporting high earnings growth, investors seem to be unwilling to pay a premium for growth.

Growth investing also seems to do much better when the yield curve is flat or downward sloping, whereas value investing does much better when the curve is much more upward sloping. Figure 15.9 presents the relationship between the slope of the yield curve, using the difference between the ten-year T. bond rate and the three-month T. bill rate as proxy, and the performance of growth investing, measured as the difference in annual returns between the top and bottom PE ratio deciles.

FIGURE 15.9 | Returns to Growth Investing and Yield Curve

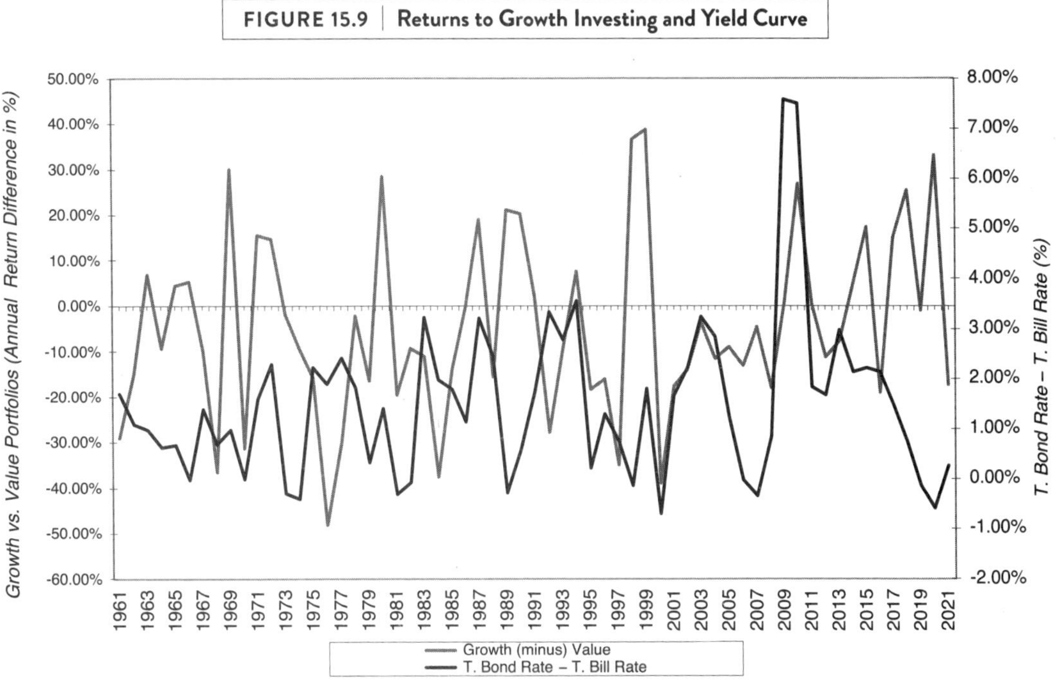

Source: Raw data from Kenneth French, Federal Reserve

Again, while the relationship is weak, there is evidence that high PE stocks do better during periods when the yield curve is strongly upward sloping—generally a precursor to strong economic growth in future periods—than when it is flat or downward sloping.

The most interesting evidence on growth investing, however, lies in the percentage of active money managers who beat their respective indices. When measured against their respective indices, active growth investors seem to beat growth indices more often than active value investors beat value indices. In his paper on mutual funds in 1995, Burton

Malkiel provides additional evidence on this phenomenon.[*] He notes that between 1981 and 1995, the average actively managed value fund outperformed the average actively managed growth fund by only 16 basis points a year, while the value index outperformed a growth index by 47 basis points a year. He attributes the 31-basis-point difference to the greater value-added of active growth managers, relative to value managers.

Growth Trading Strategies

In chapter 14, I talked about price momentum strategies, where investors buy stocks that have gone up the most in recent periods, expecting the momentum to carry forward into future periods. You could construct similar strategies based upon earnings momentum—-i.e., the rate of change in earnings growth, rather than the growth rate itself—where you would trade stocks that have high earnings momentum and ride the stock price up on that momentum. Thus, a company that reports an increase in growth rate from 10% to 15% would be viewed more favorably than one whose growth rate remains stagnant at 20%. While some of these strategies are based purely upon earnings growth rates, most of them are based upon how earnings measure up to analyst expectations. In fact, one momentum strategy is to buy stocks where analysts are revising earnings forecasts upward, and hope that stock prices follow these earnings revisions.

THE EVIDENCE

Several studies in the United States conclude that it is possible to use forecast revisions made by analysts to earn excess returns. In one of the earliest studies of this phenomenon, Dan Givoly and Josef Lakonishok created portfolios of 49 stocks in three sectors, based upon earnings revisions, and reported earning an excess return of 4.7% over the following four months on the stocks with the most positive revisions.[†] Eugene Hawkins, Stanley Chamberlin, and Wayne Daniel reported that a portfolio of stocks with the 20 largest upward revisions in earnings on the I/B/E/S database would have earned an annualized return of 14%, as opposed to the index return of only 7%.[‡] In another study, Rick Cooper, Theodore Day, and Craig Lewis report that much of the excess return is concentrated in the weeks around the revision—1.27% in the week before the forecast revision, and

[*] B. G. Malkiel, "Returns from Investing in Equity Mutual Funds 1971 to 1991," *Journal of Finance* 50, no. 2 (1995): 549–72.

[†] D. Givoly and J. Lakonishok, "The Quality of Analysts' Forecasts of Earnings," *Financial Analysts Journal* 40, no. 5 (September–October 1984): 40–47.

[‡] E. H. Hawkins, S. C. Chamberlin, W. E. Daniel, "Earnings Expectations and Security Prices," *Financial Analysts Journal* 40 no. 5 (September/October 1984): 20–38.

1.12% in the week after—and that analysts that they categorize as "leaders" (based upon timeliness, impact, and accuracy) have a much greater impact on both trading volume and prices.* In 2001, John Capstaff, Krishna Paudyal, and William Rees expanded the research to look at earnings forecasts in other countries and concluded that you could have earned excess returns of 4.7% in the U.K, 2% in France, and 3.3% in Germany from buying stocks with the most positive revisions.†

As researchers probe the earnings revision data, some interesting facts are coming to the fore.

- First, forecast revisions that diverge more from the consensus—i.e., bold forecasts—have a much bigger impact on price and are more likely to be accurate than forecast revisions that stay close to the pack. However, bold forecasts are uncommon, since most analysts tend to go with the herd, revising earnings in the same direction and by about the same magnitude as others following the stock.‡
- Second, timeliness matters, with analysts who revise their earnings estimates earlier having a much bigger price impact than those whose revisions occur later in the cycle.
- Third, earnings revisions made by analysts who work at bigger banks/brokerage houses have a much bigger price impact, perhaps because they have wider reach and exposure, than those made by analysts who work with smaller entities.

In sum, there is evidence that companies for which analysts are revising earnings upward can ride momentum to generate higher returns, though how much of those returns will persist, after transaction costs and trading frictions, remains an open question.

POTENTIAL PITFALLS

The limitation of an earnings-revision strategy is its dependence on two of the weakest links in financial markets: earnings reports that come from firms and analyst forecasts of these earnings. In recent years, I have become increasingly aware of the capacity of firms not only to manage their earnings but also to manipulate them using questionable accounting ploys. At the same time, I have discovered that analysts' forecasts are biased, partly because of their closeness to the firms that they follow.

* R. A. Cooper, T. E. Day, and C. M. Lewis, "Following the Leader: A Study of Individual Analysts Earnings Forecasts," *Journal of Financial Economics* 61, no. 3 (September 2001): 383–416.

† J. Capstaff, K. Paudyal, and W. Rees, "Revisions of Earnings Forecasts and Security Returns: Evidence from Three Countries," Working Paper, SSRN #253166, 2000.

‡ C. Gleason and C. M. C. Lee, "Analyst Forecast Revisions and Market Price Discovery," *Accounting Review* 78, no. 1 (January 2003): 193–225.

Even if the excess returns persist, you also need to consider why they might exist in the first place. To the extent that analysts influence trades made by their clients, they are likely to affect prices when they revise earnings. The more influential they are, the greater the effect they will have on prices, but the question is whether the effect is lasting. One way you may be able to earn higher returns from this strategy is to identify key analysts and build an investment strategy around forecast revisions made by them, rather than looking at consensus estimates made by all analysts. Focusing on more influential analysts and trading on bolder, more timely revisions offers greater odds for success.

Finally, you should recognize that earnings revision is a short-term strategy that yields small excess returns over investment horizons ranging from a few weeks to a few months. The increasing skepticism of markets toward both earnings reports from firms and forecasts by analysts bodes ill for these strategies. While forecast revisions and earnings surprises by themselves are unlikely to generate lucrative portfolios, they can augment other, more long-term screening strategies. One way you may be able to earn higher returns from this strategy is to identify key analysts who are both independent and influential and build an investment strategy around forecast revisions made by them, rather than looking at consensus estimates made by all analysts.

Growth at a Reasonable Price (GARP) Investing

There are many growth investors who would blanch at the strategy of buying high PE stocks, arguing that their mission is to buy high-*growth* stocks, where growth is undervalued. To find these stocks, they have developed several strategies wherein they consider both expected growth and the current pricing of the stock. I will consider two of these strategies in this section—buying stocks with a PE less than the expected growth rate, and buying stocks with a low ratio of PE to growth (called a PEG ratio).

PE LESS THAN GROWTH RATE

The simplest GARP strategy is to buy stocks that trade at a PE ratio less than the expected growth rate. Thus, a stock that has a PE ratio of 12 and an expected growth rate of 8% would be viewed as overvalued, whereas a stock with a PE of 40 and an expected growth rate of 50% would be viewed as undervalued. While this strategy clearly has the benefit of simplicity, it can be dangerous for several reasons.

- **Interest rate effect:** Since growth creates earnings in the future, the value created by any given growth rate will be greater when interest rates are low (which makes the present values higher) than when interest rates are high. It is not surprising, therefore, that portfolio managers who use this strategy not only find far more underpriced stocks when interest rates are high but also find many stocks in many emerging markets (where interest rates tend to be high) to be cheap. The effect of interest rates on the relationship between PE and growth can be best illustrated by looking at the percentage of firms that trade at less than their expected growth rate as a function of the treasury bond rate. In 1981, when T. bond rates hit 12%, more than 65% of firms traded at PE ratios less than the expected growth rate. In 1991, when rates had dropped to about 8%, the percentage of stocks trading at less than the expected growth rate also dropped, to about 45%. By the end of the nineties, with the T. bond rate dropping to 5%, the percentage of stocks that traded at less than the expected growth rate had dropped to about 25%, and in 2021, when the treasury bond rate was less than 2%, the percentage of stocks with PE ratios less than their expected growth had dropped to 10%.

- **Growth rate estimates:** When this strategy is used for a large universe of stocks, you have no choice but to use analyst estimates of expected growth, with consensus values across many analyst estimates. When you do this, you have to wonder about both the differences in the quality of the growth estimates across different analysts and their comparability (timing and time horizon).

PEG RATIOS

An alternative approach that seems to offer more flexibility than just comparing the PE ratio to expected growth rates is to look at the ratio of the PE ratio to expected growth. This ratio is called the PEG ratio and is widely used by analysts and portfolio managers following growth companies.

$$\text{PEG ratio} = \frac{\text{PE ratio}}{\text{Expected Growth Rate}}$$

For instance, a firm with a PE ratio of 40 and a growth rate of 50% is estimated to have a PEG ratio of 0.80. There are some who argue that only stocks with PEG ratios less than one are desirable, but this strategy is equivalent to the strategy of comparing the PE to the expected growth rate.

Consistency requires that the growth rate used in this estimate be the growth rate in earnings per share. Given the many definitions of the PE ratio, which one should you use to estimate the PEG ratio? The answer depends upon the base on which the expected growth rate is computed. If the expected growth rate in earnings per share is based upon earnings in the most recent year (current earnings), the PE ratio that should be used is the current PE ratio. If it based upon trailing earnings, the PE ratio used should be the trailing PE ratio. The forward PE ratio should generally not be used in this computation, since it may result in a double-counting of growth.* Building upon the theme of uniformity, the PEG ratio should be estimated using the same growth estimates for all firms in the sample; you should not, for instance, use five-year growth rates for some firms and one-year growth rates for others. One way of ensuring uniformity is to use the same source for earnings growth estimates for all the firms in the group. For instance, both I/B/E/S and Zacks provide consensus estimates from analysts of earnings per share growth over the next five years for most US firms. Many analysts who use PEG ratios, though, prefer to use short-term growth rates in earnings to compute them.

How do analysts use PEG ratios? A stock with a low PEG ratio is considered cheap because you are paying less for the growth. The PEG ratio is viewed as a growth-neutral measure that can be used to compare stocks with different expected growth rates. In a study concluded in 1998, Morgan Stanley found that a strategy of buying stocks with low PEG ratios yielded returns that were significantly higher than what you would have made on the S&P 500. They came to this conclusion by looking at the 1,000 largest stocks on the US and Canadian exchanges each year, from January 1986 through March 1998, and categorizing them into deciles based upon the PEG ratio. They found that the 100 stocks with the lowest PEG ratio earned an annual return of 18.7% during the period, much higher than the market return of about 16.8% over the period. While no mention was made of risk adjustment, it was argued that the difference was larger than could be justified by the risk adjustment.

I updated this study to examine how this strategy would have done from 1991 to 2021, creating five portfolios at the end of each year based upon the PEG ratio and examining the returns in the following year. Figure 15.10 summarizes the average annual returns on PEG ratio classes in the 1991–1996, 1997–2001, 2002–2011, and 2012–2021 time periods.

* If the forward earnings are high because of high growth in the next year, and this high growth results in a high growth rate for the next five years, you will understate your PEG ratio.

FIGURE 15.10 | Returns across PEG Ratio Classes—US Stocks

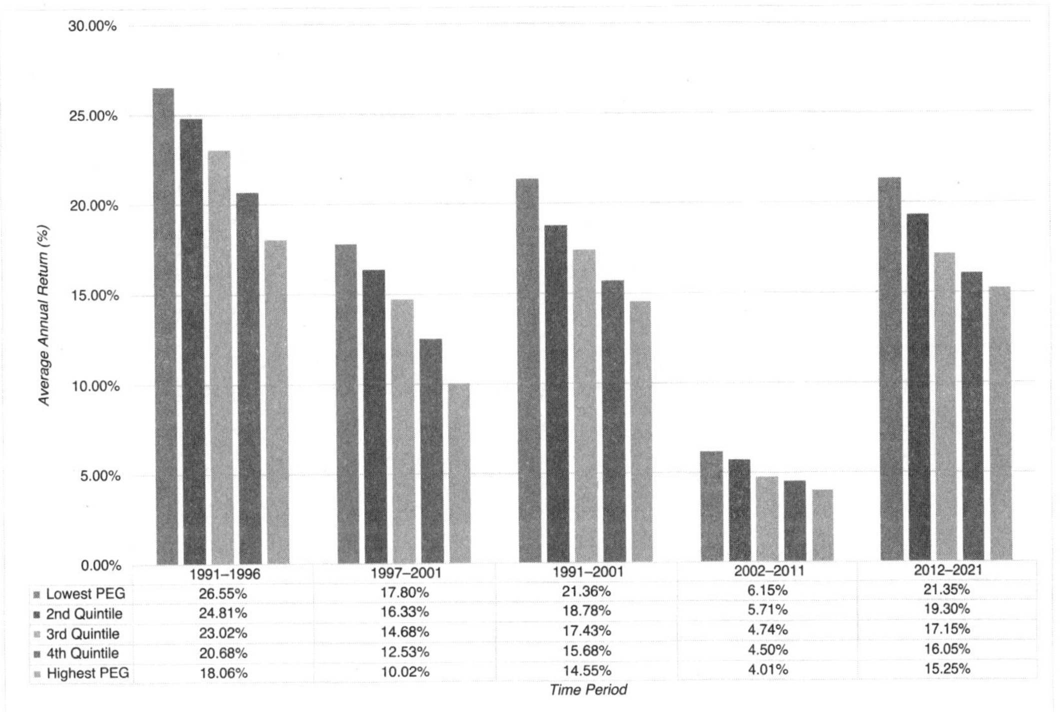

	1991–1996	1997–2001	1991–2001	2002–2011	2012–2021
Lowest PEG	26.55%	17.80%	21.36%	6.15%	21.35%
2nd Quintile	24.81%	16.33%	18.78%	5.71%	19.30%
3rd Quintile	23.02%	14.68%	17.43%	4.74%	17.15%
4th Quintile	20.68%	12.53%	15.68%	4.50%	16.05%
Highest PEG	18.06%	10.02%	14.55%	4.01%	15.25%

Source: Value Line

A strategy of investing in low PEG ratio stocks would have generated an average return about 2% to 3% higher than the average returns on a high PEG ratio portfolio, before adjusting for risk, during all the time periods studied.

While that excess return looks attractive at first sight, the PEG ratio strategy has a flaw, perhaps even a fatal one, and that is its failure to adjust for risk. A simple assessment of the drivers of PEG ratios will show that higher-risk stocks should trade at lower PEG ratios than lower-risk stocks. Put simply, the higher returns earned by low PEG stocks may be entirely due to their higher risk, making them fair, rather than excess, returns.

Determinants of Success at Growth Screening

The overall empirical evidence on the efficacy of screens is much less favorable for growth screens than it is for value screens. While there are cycles during which growth screens like low PEG ratios and high PE ratios yield excess returns, they are trumped over longer periods by value screens, such as low PE or low price to book value ratios. From our perspective, there are three key determinants of success at this strategy:

- **Better growth estimates:** Since growth is the key dimension of value in these companies, obtaining better estimates of expected growth should improve your odds of success. If you are a growth investor following a small set of companies, you may try to estimate growth yourself. If you can estimate growth more precisely than the overall market, you should get a payoff. If this is not a feasible option because you do not have the resources to estimate expected growth rates for the hundreds of firms that you follow, you should compare the different sources that you have for this input to see which one has the best track record.
- **Long time horizon:** While a long time horizon improves your odds of success, as an investor, across all companies, it is even more critical when investing in younger and growth companies. That is because, as I noted in chapter 14, a much higher proportion of the trading in high-growth stocks comes from traders, playing mood and momentum games, than from investors, and these traders can take a stock that is undervalued, or overvalued, and make it even more so in the short term.
- **Macro forecasting skills:** There are extended cycles during which the growth screens work exceptionally well and other cycles when they are counterproductive. If you can time these cycles, in earnings or overall economic growth, you could augment your returns substantially. Since many of these cycles are related to how the overall market is doing, this boils down to your market timing ability.

As you can see, investing successfully in growth companies requires a great deal of those who try, and it should come as no surprise that, at least in the short term, the biggest winners in growth stocks are traders who play off momentum and its shifts.

Conclusion

Investing successfully in high-growth companies requires a very different set of skills and mental makeup than investing in mature companies. First, at growth companies, you must be willing to face up to uncertainty and make your best estimates for the future, knowing well that you will be wrong (and sometimes strongly so) in hindsight. Second, assuming that you are right in your overall assessment of a growth company, you must be patient and have a strong stomach, since the price can push away from your estimated value for extended periods. Third, when investing in growth companies, you are far more exposed to overall macroeconomic conditions, and your returns can be augmented if you have the skills to forecast interest-rate and economic-growth trends in the market.

If you are willing to meet these more strenuous requirements for investing in growth companies, there does seem to be a payoff to active investing. That evidence is stronger for investment in the earliest stages in the life cycle, with venture capitalists generating high returns, at least on average, and the most successful of the group being able to do so consistently. It is weaker for public-market investors in growth companies, at least in the aggregate, but even in that group, there is some evidence that being active provides more benefits than it does in mature companies.

16

Investing in Middle Age

MANY INVESTORS, IF ASKED to describe their investment philosophies, characterize themselves as value investors, but what is value investing? In this chapter, I begin by addressing this question, arguing that value investors come in many forms. Some value investors use specific criteria to screen for what they categorize as cheap stocks and invest in these stocks for the long term. Other value investors believe that bargains are best found in the aftermath of a sell-off and that the best time to buy a stock is when it is down. Still others contend that the key to investing success is finding companies in good businesses, run by competent management, and buying and holding these companies for the long term. The one thing that all these investors seem to share is that they tend to find their bargains mostly among mature companies, and an assessment of the successes and failures of value investing is, by extension, an assessment of investing in mature businesses.

Value Investing: Variants

In chapter 14, I presented my definition of value investing, using the financial balance sheet as the vehicle for contrasting it with growth investing. Specifically, I argued that value investors believe that their best chance of finding market mistakes lies in how markets value assets in place, not growth assets, and that the focus should therefore be on a firm's existing investments. That definition alone explains why value investing is so focused on mature companies in its search for bargains. That said, there are three variants on value investing that I have seen used in practice, with each one drawing on a different perspective on what types of mature companies the market is mispricing.

1. **Screeners:** Investors in this camp believe that mature companies, especially those with stable earnings and solid cash flows, are often undervalued by investors because they are boring and predictable. In the most simplistic variation on this approach, they screen for the cheapest stocks in the market, using pricing multiples like PE or price to book, and invest in stocks that trade at low PE or low price to book ratios. In extensions of this approach, they not only screen the market for companies that are trading at low pricing multiples but also add screens for low risk and high profitability to find bargains. As the data that we have on companies has become richer and more accessible, the screens used by passive value investors have similarly grown to include some of this data.
2. **Contrarians:** Contrarian value investors start with the presumption that mature companies are, for the most part, fairly valued by the market, but that they get misvalued in the aftermath of big information announcements (earnings reports, changes in management, etc.), with markets overreacting to the news in these announcements. Thus, mature companies become cheap (expensive) after bad news (good news) announcements, making them attractive buys (sells) to contrarian investors.
3. **Buy-and-Holders:** Adherents to this third strand of value investing believe that companies in good businesses, run by superior managers, will outperform the market over the long term. The key to success in this strategy then becomes finding these great companies and, once you find them, buying and holding them for the long term.

These approaches are not mutually exclusive, and there are some investors who use melded versions of them. While Ben Graham fell into the first category and developed a long list of screens to find bargains, Warren Buffett's annual letters to shareholders posit that good value investing starts by looking at cheapness but has to be further based on other criteria such as good management and solid moats, or competitive advantages. For better or worse, the way value investing has been practiced over the last few decades has linked it closely to investing in mature companies, and it is for that reason that this chapter's examination of value investing pluses and minuses becomes an examination of investing in mature companies.

The Case for Value Investing

While it is not uncommon for investors of all stripes to express confidence that their approach to investing is the best one, it is our experience that value investors express not just confidence but an almost unquestioning belief that their approach to investing will win in the end. To see where this confidence comes from, it is worth tracing out the history of value investing over the last century, in which two strands, one grounded in stories and practice and the other in numbers and academia, connected to give it a strength that no other philosophy can match.

The Story Strand

When stock markets were in their infancy, investors faced two problems. The first was that there were almost no information disclosure requirements, and investors had to work with whatever information they had on companies, or with rumors and stories. The second was that investors, more used to pricing bonds than stocks, drew on bond pricing methods to evaluate stocks, giving rise to the practice of paying dividends (as replacements for coupons). That is not to suggest that there were not investors who were ahead of the game, and the first stories about value investing come out of the damage of the Great Depression, amid which a few investors, like Bernard Baruch, found a way to preserve and even grow their wealth. However, it was Ben Graham, a young associate of Baruch, who laid the foundations for modern value investing by formalizing his approach to buying stocks and investing in 1934 in *Security Analysis*, a book that reflected his definition of an investment as "one which thorough analysis, promises safety of principal and adequate return."[*] In 1938, John Burr Williams wrote *The Theory of Investment Value*, introducing the notion of present value and discounted cash flow valuation.[†] In Graham's subsequent book, *The Intelligent Investor*, he elaborated his more developed philosophy of value investing as well as a list of screens, built around observable values, for finding undervalued stocks.[‡]

While Graham was a successful investor, putting many of his writings into practice, Graham's greater contribution to value investing came as a teacher at Columbia University. Many of his students acquired legendary status, but one of them, Warren Buffett, has

[*] B. Graham, *Security Analysis: The Classic 1934 Edition* (New York: McGraw-Hill Education, 1996 reprint).
[†] J. B. Williams, *The Theory of Investment Value* (Flint Hill, VA: Fraser Publishing Company, 1997 reprint).
[‡] B. Graham, *The Intelligent Investor* (New York: Harper Business, 2007).

come to personally embody value investing. Buffett started an investment partnership that he dissolved, famously, in 1969, arguing that given a choice between bending his investment philosophy to find investments and not investing, he would choose the latter. These words from his final letter to partners in May 1969,* more than any others, have cemented his status in value investing: "I just don't see anything available that gives any reasonable hope of delivering such a good year and I have no desire to grope around, hoping to 'get lucky' with other people's money." He did allow his partners a chance to receive shares in a struggling textile maker, Berkshire Hathaway—and the rest, as they say, is history, as Berkshire Hathaway morphed into an insurance company, with an embedded closed-end mutual fund investing in public and some private businesses, run by Buffett. While Buffett has been generous in his praise for Graham, his approach to value investing has been different, insofar as he has been more willing to bring in qualitative factors (management quality, competitive advantages) and to be more active (taking a role in how the companies he has invested in are run) than Graham was. If you had invested in Berkshire Hathaway in 1965 or soon after, and had continued to hold through today, you would be incredibly wealthy, as you can see in figure 16.1.

* W. E. Buffett to Limited Partners, May 29, 1969, Buffett Partnership Letters, Ivey Business School, 129, accessed December 13, 2023, https://www.ivey.uwo.ca/media/2975913/buffett-partnership-letters.pdf

FIGURE 16.1 | The Berkshire Hathaway Story

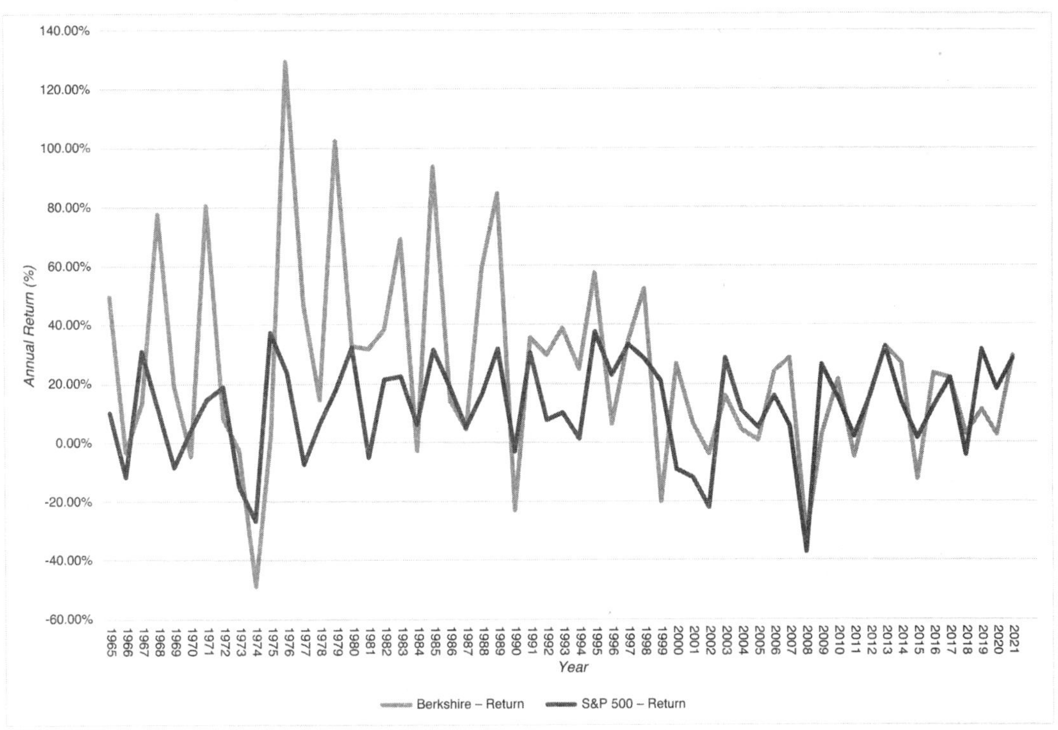

Source: Berkshire Hathaway Annual Report for 2019 (with a 2022 Update)

The numbers speak for themselves, and you don't need measures of statistical significance to conclude that these are not just unusually good but also cannot be explained away as luck or chance. Not only did Berkshire Hathaway deliver a compounded annual return that was double that of the S&P 500, it did so with consistency, outperforming the index in 38 out of 57 years. (It is true that the returns have looked a lot more ordinary in the last two decades, and I will come back to examine those years in later in this chapter.)

Along the way, Buffett proved to be an extraordinary spokesperson for value investing, not only because he delivered mind-blowing returns but also because of his capacity to explain value investing in homespun, catchy letters to shareholders each year.* In 1978, he was joined by Charlie Munger, whose aphorisms about investing have been just as effective at getting investor attention and were captured well in a book called *Poor Charlie's*

* "Berkshire Hathaway Inc., Shareholder Letters," Berkshire Hathaway, accessed November 28, 2023, https://www.berkshirehathaway.com/letters/letters.html.

Almanack.[*] There have been others who have worn the value-investing mantle successfully, and I don't mean to discount them, but it is difficult to overstate how much value investing, as we know it, has been built around the teachings of Graham and Buffett. The Buffett legend has been burnished not just with flourishes like the 1969 partnership letter but by the stories of the companies that he picked along the way. Even novice value investors will have heard the story of Buffett's investment in American Express in 1963, after its stock price collapsed following a disastrous loan to a scandalous salad oil company, and quickly doubled his investment.

The Numbers Strand

It has to be said that value investing has more going for it than the stories of great value investors and their exploits. It would not have the punch that it does without the help of a numbers strand—delivered, ironically, by the very academics whom value investors hold in low esteem. To understand this contribution, I need to go back to the 1960s, when finance as we know it developed as a discipline, built around strong beliefs that markets are, for the most part, efficient. In fact, the capital asset pricing model so despised by value investors also was developed in 1964, and for much of the next 15 years, financial researchers worked hard trying to test the model. To their disappointment, the model not only possessed clear weaknesses, it consistently misestimated returns for particular classes of stock. In 1981, Rolf Banz published a paper showing that smaller companies (in terms of market capitalization) delivered much higher returns, after adjusting for risk with the CAPM, than larger companies.[†] Over the rest of the 1980s, researchers continued to find other company characteristics that seemed to be systematically related to "excess" returns, even though theory suggested that they should not. It is interesting that in the early days, these systematic irregularities were called "anomalies," not "inefficiencies," suggesting that it was not markets that were mispricing these stocks but researchers who were erroneously measuring risk.

In 1992, Eugene Fama and Kenneth French pulled all these company characteristics together in a study in which they reversed the research order: rather than ask whether betas, company size, or profitability were affecting returns, they started with the returns

[*] C. T. Munger, *Poor Charlie's Almanack: The Wit and Wisdom of Charlie T. Munger* (Marceline, MO: Walsworth Publishing Company, 2005).

[†] R. W. Banz, "The Relationship between Return and Market Value of Common Stocks," *Journal of Financial Economics* 9, no. 1 (March 1981): 3–18.

on stocks and looked for the characteristics that were strongest in explaining differences in returns across companies.* Their conclusion was that two variables, *market capitalization* (size) and *book to market ratios*, explained the bulk of the variation in stock returns from 1963 to 1990, and that the other variables were either subsumed by these or played only a marginal role in explaining differences. For value investors, long attuned to book value as a key metric, this research was vindication of decades of work. In fact, the relationship between returns over time and book to market ratios still takes pride of place in any sales pitch for value investing. Kenneth French has updated and made accessible the data on the Fama-French factors, allowing us to update the link between returns and price to book ratios through 2021, in figure 16.2.

FIGURE 16.2 | Returns on PBV Deciles, 1927–2021

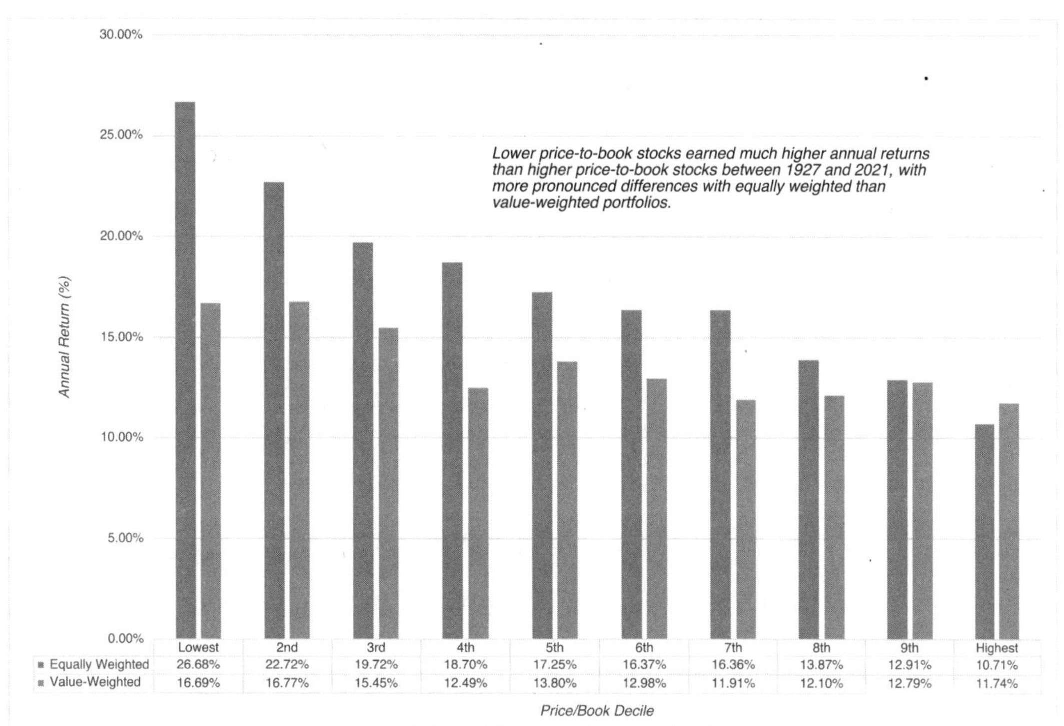

	Lowest	2nd	3rd	4th	5th	6th	7th	8th	9th	Highest
Equally Weighted	26.68%	22.72%	19.72%	18.70%	17.25%	16.37%	16.36%	13.87%	12.91%	10.71%
Value-Weighted	16.69%	16.77%	15.45%	12.49%	13.80%	12.98%	11.91%	12.10%	12.79%	11.74%

Source: Kenneth French

* E. F. Fama and K. R. French, "The Cross-Section of Expected Return," *Journal of Finance* 47, no. 2 (June 1992): 427–65.

Not only has that study been replicated multiple times with US stocks, there is evidence that low price to book stocks earn premium returns in much of the rest of the world. Elroy Dimson, Paul Marsh, and Mike Staunton, in their annual update on global market returns, note that the value premium (the premium earned by low price to book stocks relative to the market) has been positive in 16 of the 24 countries where they have studied returns for more than a century and amounted to an annual excess return of 1.8% on a global basis.*

While value investors are quick to point to these academic studies as backing for value investing, they are slower to acknowledge the fact that among researchers, there is a clear division in what they see as the reason for these value premiums:

1. **It is a proxy for missed risk:** In their 1992 paper, Fama and French argued that companies that trade at low price to book ratios are more likely to be distressed and that risk and return models were not doing an adequate job of capturing that risk. They were arguing that rather than serving as a stamp of approval for value investing, these studies indicate risks that may not show up in near-term returns or in traditional risk and return models but eventually will manifest themselves and explain the excess returns. Put simply, in their world, value investors will look as though they are beating the market until these unseen risks show up and mark down their portfolios.
2. **It is a sign of market inefficiency:** During the 1980s, as behavioral finance became more popular, academics also became more willing to accept and even welcome the notion that markets make systematic mistakes and that investors less susceptible to these behavioral quirks could take advantage of these mistakes. For these researchers, the findings that low price to book stocks were being priced to earn higher returns gave rise to theories of how investor irrationalities could explain these higher returns.

It is the latter group that reinforces the value investors' opinion have that they are better than the rest of the market and that the excess returns that they earn are a reward for their patience and careful research—i.e., for being the grown-ups in a world filled with juvenile and impulsive traders.

In the chapters on valuing companies, I talked about how value is a bridge between stories and numbers, and how the very best and most valuable companies represent an uncommon mix of strong stories backed up by strong numbers. In the realm of invest-

* Credit Suisse Global Investment Returns Yearbook 2022, Credit Suisse.

ment philosophies, value investing has had that unique mix work in its favor, with stories of value investors and their winning ways backed up by numbers on how well value investing performs, relative to other philosophies. It is therefore no surprise that many investors, when asked to describe their investment philosophies, describe themselves as "value investors," not just because of the philosophy's winning track record but also because of its intellectual and academic backing.

The Pushback on Value Investing

For some value investors, the graph showing that low price to book stocks have outperformed high price to book stocks by 5% a year, going back to 1926 in the US, is all the proof they need to conclude that value investing has won the investing game—but that rosy history has warts that need closer examination.

The Volatile Value Premium

In figure 16.3, I look at the year-to-year movements in the value premium, i.e., the difference between the annual returns on the lowest and highest deciles of price to book ratios.

FIGURE 16.3 | **Annual Returns on Value (Lowest PBV Decile) and Growth (Highest PBV Decile), 1927–2021**

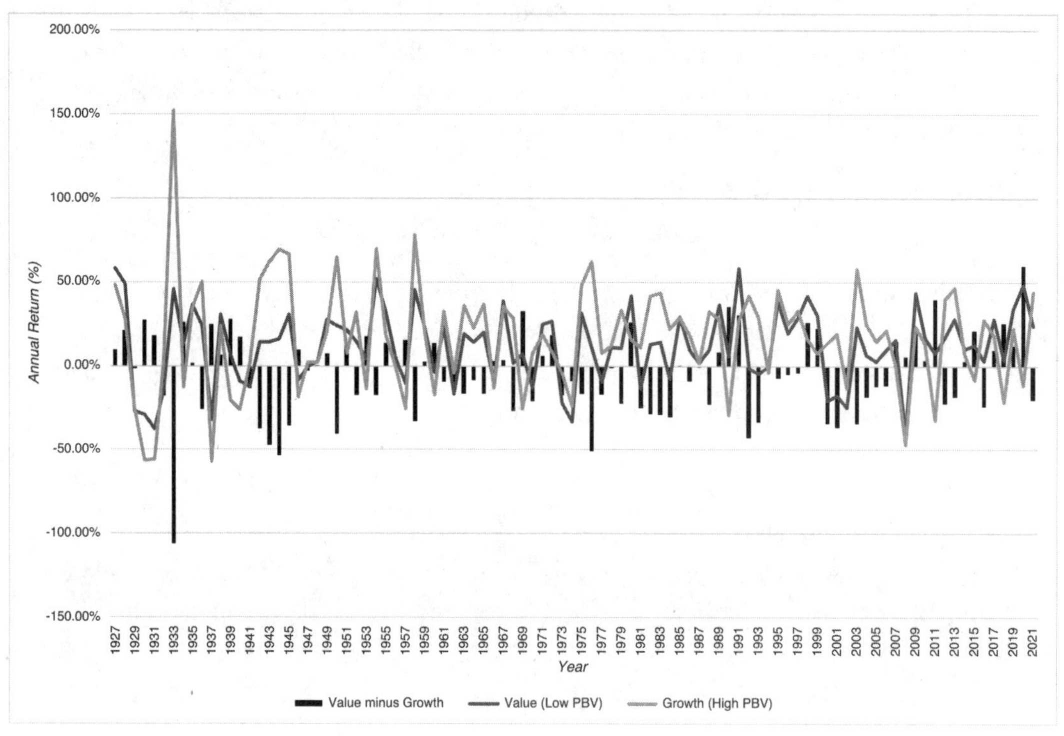

Source: Kenneth French

While it is true that low price to book stocks earned higher annual returns than high price to book stocks, on average, between 1926 and 2021, note that there is significant variation over time and that the high price to book stocks delivered higher returns in 45 of the 95 years studied. In fact, one of the pitches that growth investors made, with some success, during the glory days of value investing was that you could still succeed as a growth investor if you had the capacity to time the value/growth cycle.

In short, the fact that value stocks, at least based upon the price to book proxy, delivered higher returns than growth stocks (again using that proxy) obscures the reality that there were periods of time, even in the twentieth century, where the latter won out. Not only do growth stocks beat value stocks almost half the time, there have been extended periods in history when they have done so every year.

FIGURE 2.3 | New Business Applications by Industry Grouping, 2005–2021

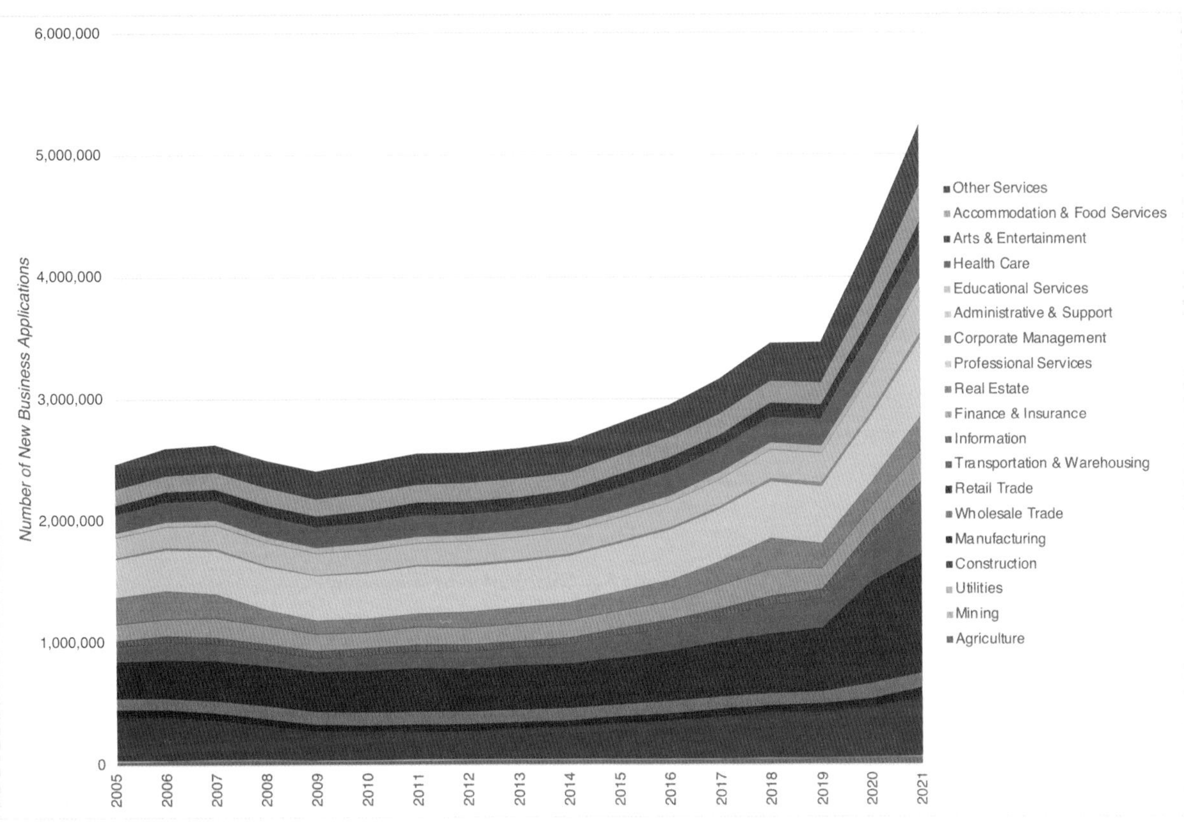

Source: US Census Bureau

FIGURE 2.4 | Number of Start-ups, by Country, 2021

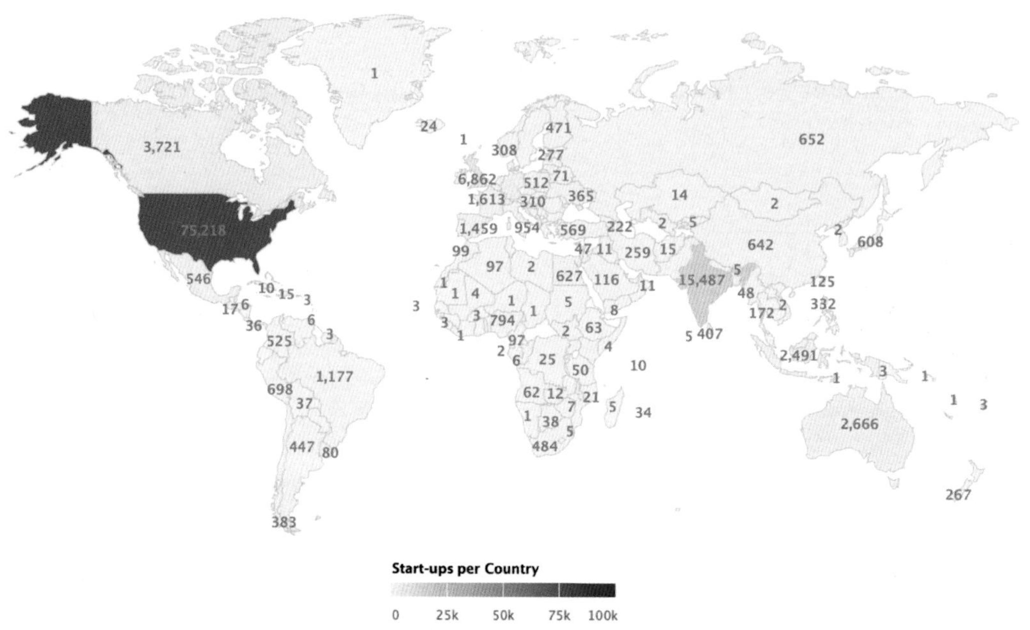

FIGURE 3.1 | Corporate Age Distribution by Geography

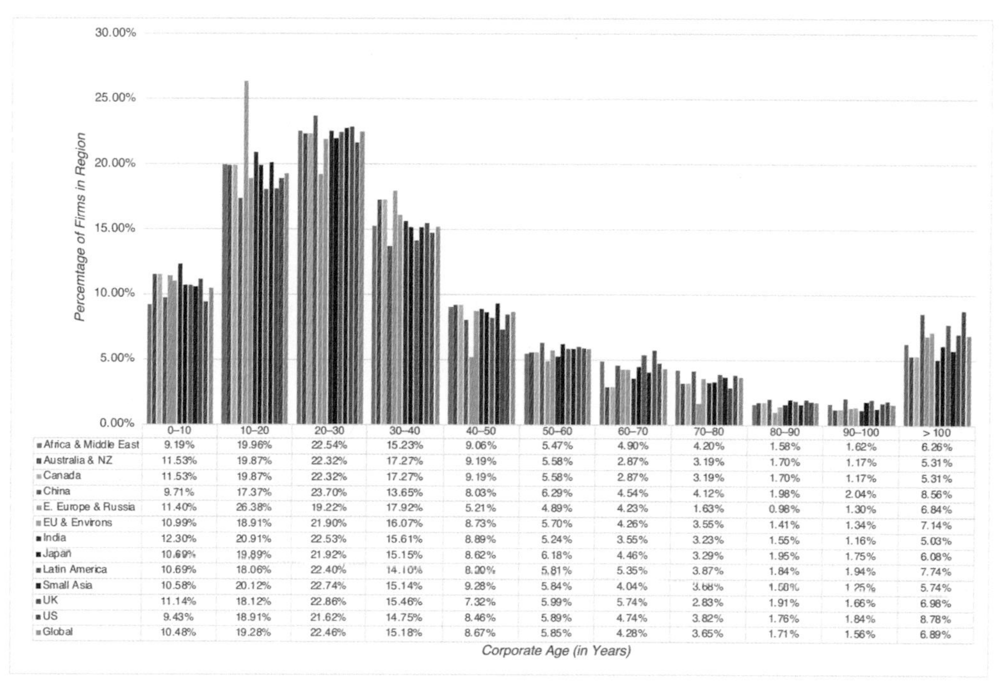

	0–10	10–20	20–30	30–40	40–50	50–60	60–70	70–80	80–90	90–100	> 100
Africa & Middle East	9.19%	19.96%	22.54%	15.23%	9.06%	5.47%	4.90%	4.20%	1.58%	1.62%	6.26%
Australia & NZ	11.53%	19.87%	22.32%	17.27%	9.19%	5.58%	2.87%	3.19%	1.70%	1.17%	5.31%
Canada	11.53%	19.87%	22.32%	17.27%	9.19%	5.58%	2.87%	3.19%	1.70%	1.17%	5.31%
China	9.71%	17.37%	23.70%	13.65%	8.03%	6.29%	4.54%	4.12%	1.98%	2.04%	8.56%
E. Europe & Russia	11.40%	26.38%	19.22%	17.92%	5.21%	4.89%	4.23%	1.63%	0.98%	1.30%	6.84%
EU & Environs	10.99%	18.91%	21.90%	16.07%	8.73%	5.70%	4.26%	3.55%	1.41%	1.34%	7.14%
India	12.30%	20.91%	22.53%	15.61%	8.89%	5.24%	3.55%	3.23%	1.55%	1.16%	5.03%
Japan	10.69%	19.89%	21.92%	15.15%	8.62%	6.18%	4.46%	3.29%	1.95%	1.75%	6.08%
Latin America	10.69%	18.06%	22.40%	14.10%	8.20%	5.81%	5.35%	3.87%	1.84%	1.94%	7.74%
Small Asia	10.58%	20.12%	22.74%	15.14%	9.28%	5.84%	4.04%	3.68%	1.50%	1.25%	5.74%
UK	11.14%	18.12%	22.86%	15.46%	7.32%	5.99%	5.74%	2.83%	1.91%	1.66%	6.98%
US	9.43%	18.91%	21.62%	14.75%	8.46%	5.89%	4.74%	3.82%	1.76%	1.84%	8.78%
Global	10.48%	19.28%	22.46%	15.18%	8.67%	5.85%	4.28%	3.65%	1.71%	1.56%	6.89%

Corporate Age (in Years)

FIGURE 3.5 | Corporate Life Cycle—Three Common Variations

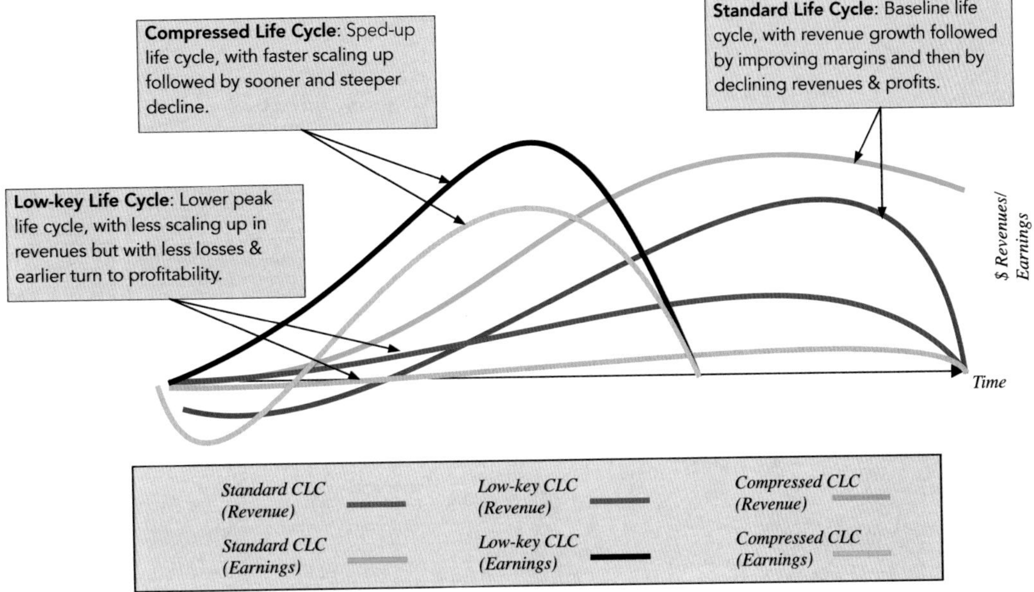

FIGURE 6.5 | Default Spreads by Bond Ratings Class

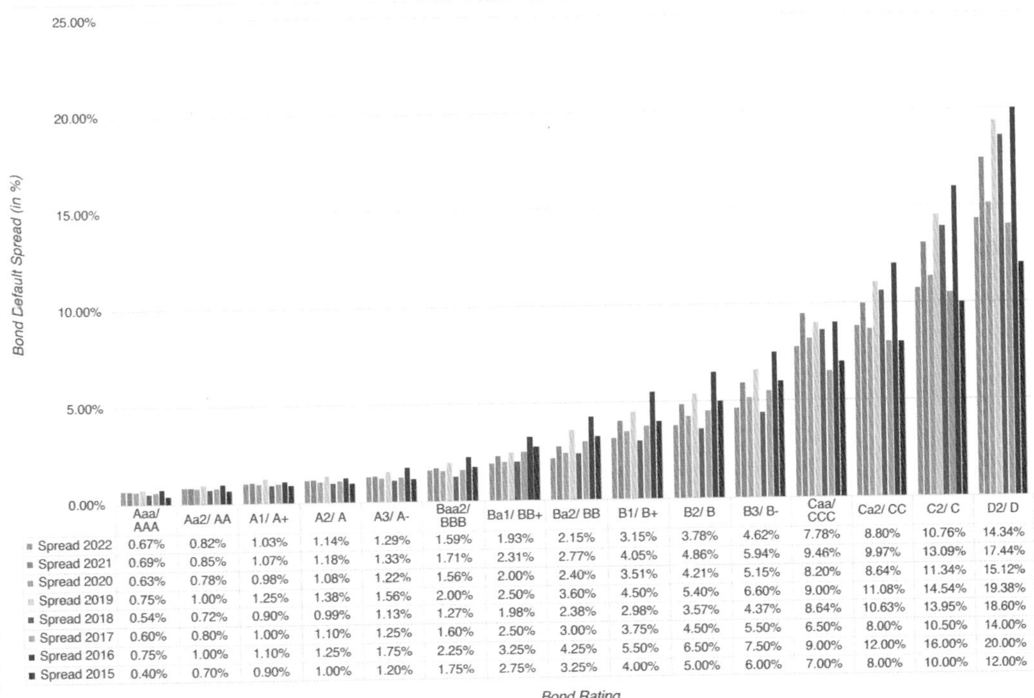

	Aaa/ AAA	Aa2/ AA	A1/ A+	A2/ A	A3/ A-	Baa2/ BBB	Ba1/ BB+	Ba2/ BB	B1/ B+	B2/ B	B3/ B-	Caa/ CCC	Ca2/ CC	C2/ C	D2/ D
Spread 2022	0.67%	0.82%	1.03%	1.14%	1.29%	1.59%	1.93%	2.15%	3.15%	3.78%	4.62%	7.78%	8.80%	10.76%	14.34%
Spread 2021	0.69%	0.85%	1.07%	1.18%	1.33%	1.71%	2.31%	2.77%	4.05%	4.86%	5.94%	9.46%	9.97%	13.09%	17.44%
Spread 2020	0.63%	0.78%	0.98%	1.08%	1.22%	1.56%	2.00%	2.40%	3.51%	4.21%	5.15%	8.20%	8.64%	11.34%	15.12%
Spread 2019	0.75%	1.00%	1.25%	1.38%	1.56%	2.00%	2.50%	3.60%	4.50%	5.40%	6.60%	9.00%	11.08%	14.54%	19.38%
Spread 2018	0.54%	0.72%	0.90%	0.99%	1.13%	1.27%	1.98%	2.38%	2.98%	3.57%	4.37%	8.64%	10.63%	13.95%	18.60%
Spread 2017	0.60%	0.80%	1.00%	1.10%	1.25%	1.60%	2.50%	3.00%	3.75%	4.50%	5.50%	6.50%	8.00%	10.50%	14.00%
Spread 2016	0.75%	1.00%	1.10%	1.25%	1.75%	2.25%	3.25%	4.25%	5.50%	6.50%	7.50%	9.00%	12.00%	16.00%	20.00%
Spread 2015	0.40%	0.70%	0.90%	1.00%	1.20%	1.75%	2.75%	3.25%	4.00%	5.00%	6.00%	7.00%	8.00%	10.00%	12.00%

FIGURE 6.7 | Equity Risk Premium, by Country, July 2022

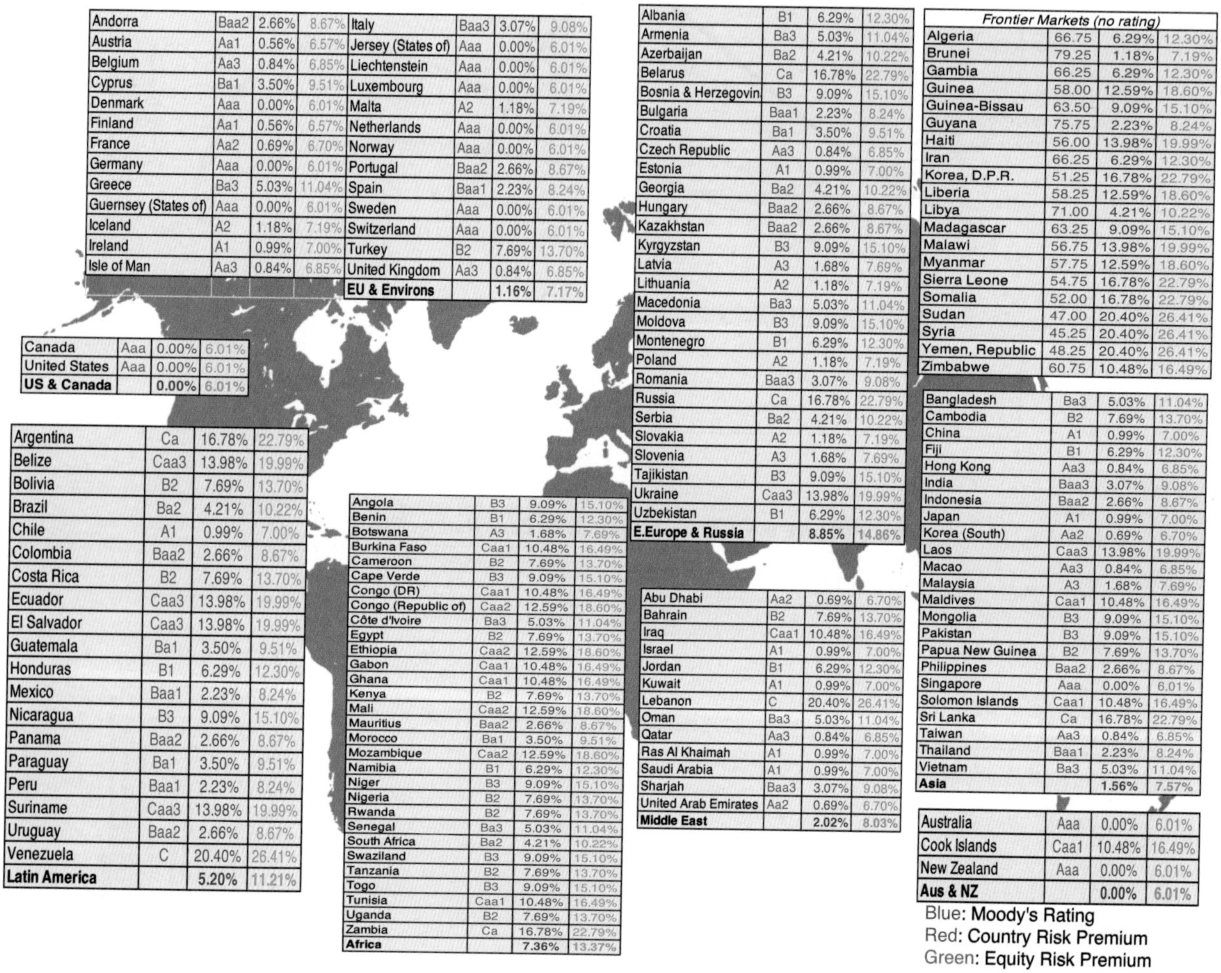

Country	Rating	CRP	ERP	Country	Rating	CRP	ERP
Andorra	Baa2	2.66%	8.67%	Italy	Baa3	3.07%	9.08%
Austria	Aa1	0.56%	6.57%	Jersey (States of)	Aaa	0.00%	6.01%
Belgium	Aa3	0.84%	6.85%	Liechtenstein	Aaa	0.00%	6.01%
Cyprus	Ba1	3.50%	9.51%	Luxembourg	Aaa	0.00%	6.01%
Denmark	Aaa	0.00%	6.01%	Malta	A2	1.18%	7.19%
Finland	Aa1	0.56%	6.57%	Netherlands	Aaa	0.00%	6.01%
France	Aa2	0.69%	6.70%	Norway	Aaa	0.00%	6.01%
Germany	Aaa	0.00%	6.01%	Portugal	Baa2	2.66%	8.67%
Greece	Ba3	5.03%	11.04%	Spain	Baa1	2.23%	8.24%
Guernsey (States of)	Aaa	0.00%	6.01%	Sweden	Aaa	0.00%	6.01%
Iceland	A2	1.18%	7.19%	Switzerland	Aaa	0.00%	6.01%
Ireland	A1	0.99%	7.00%	Turkey	B2	7.69%	13.70%
Isle of Man	Aa3	0.84%	6.85%	United Kingdom	Aa3	0.84%	6.85%
				EU & Environs		1.16%	7.17%

Country	Rating	CRP	ERP
Albania	B1	6.29%	12.30%
Armenia	Ba3	5.03%	11.04%
Azerbaijan	Ba2	4.21%	10.22%
Belarus	Ca	16.78%	22.79%
Bosnia & Herzegovin	B3	9.09%	15.10%
Bulgaria	Baa1	2.23%	8.24%
Croatia	Ba1	3.50%	9.51%
Czech Republic	Aa3	0.84%	6.85%
Estonia	A1	0.99%	7.00%
Georgia	Ba2	4.21%	10.22%
Hungary	Baa2	2.66%	8.67%
Kazakhstan	Baa2	2.66%	8.67%
Kyrgyzstan	B3	9.09%	15.10%
Latvia	A3	1.68%	7.69%
Lithuania	A2	1.18%	7.19%
Macedonia	Ba3	5.03%	11.04%
Moldova	B3	9.09%	15.10%
Montenegro	B1	6.29%	12.30%
Poland	A2	1.18%	7.19%
Romania	Baa3	3.07%	9.08%
Russia	Ca	16.78%	22.79%
Serbia	Ba2	4.21%	10.22%
Slovakia	A2	1.18%	7.19%
Slovenia	A3	1.68%	7.69%
Tajikistan	B3	9.09%	15.10%
Ukraine	Caa3	13.98%	19.99%
Uzbekistan	B1	6.29%	12.30%
E.Europe & Russia		8.85%	14.86%

Frontier Markets (no rating)			
Algeria	66.75	6.29%	12.30%
Brunei	79.25	1.18%	7.19%
Gambia	66.25	6.29%	12.30%
Guinea	58.00	12.59%	18.60%
Guinea-Bissau	63.50	9.09%	15.10%
Guyana	75.75	2.23%	8.24%
Haiti	56.00	13.98%	19.99%
Iran	66.25	6.29%	12.30%
Korea, D.P.R.	51.25	16.78%	22.79%
Liberia	58.25	12.59%	18.60%
Libya	71.00	4.21%	10.22%
Madagascar	63.25	9.09%	15.10%
Malawi	56.75	13.98%	19.99%
Myanmar	57.75	12.59%	18.60%
Sierra Leone	54.75	16.78%	22.79%
Somalia	52.00	16.78%	22.79%
Sudan	47.00	20.40%	26.41%
Syria	45.25	20.40%	26.41%
Yemen, Republic	48.25	20.40%	26.41%
Zimbabwe	60.75	10.48%	16.49%

Country	Rating	CRP	ERP
Canada	Aaa	0.00%	6.01%
United States	Aaa	0.00%	6.01%
US & Canada		0.00%	6.01%

Country	Rating	CRP	ERP
Argentina	Ca	16.78%	22.79%
Belize	Caa3	13.98%	19.99%
Bolivia	B2	7.69%	13.70%
Brazil	Ba2	4.21%	10.22%
Chile	A1	0.99%	7.00%
Colombia	Baa2	2.66%	8.67%
Costa Rica	B2	7.69%	13.70%
Ecuador	Caa3	13.98%	19.99%
El Salvador	Caa3	13.98%	19.99%
Guatemala	Ba1	3.50%	9.51%
Honduras	B1	6.29%	12.30%
Mexico	Baa1	2.23%	8.24%
Nicaragua	B3	9.09%	15.10%
Panama	Baa2	2.66%	8.67%
Paraguay	Ba1	3.50%	9.51%
Peru	Baa1	2.23%	8.24%
Suriname	Caa3	13.98%	19.99%
Uruguay	Baa2	2.66%	8.67%
Venezuela	C	20.40%	26.41%
Latin America		5.20%	11.21%

Country	Rating	CRP	ERP
Angola	B3	9.09%	15.10%
Benin	B1	6.29%	12.30%
Botswana	A3	1.68%	7.69%
Burkina Faso	Caa1	10.48%	16.49%
Cameroon	B2	7.69%	13.70%
Cape Verde	B3	9.09%	15.10%
Congo (DR)	Caa1	10.48%	16.49%
Congo (Republic of)	Caa2	12.59%	18.60%
Côte d'Ivoire	Ba3	5.03%	11.04%
Egypt	B2	7.69%	13.70%
Ethiopia	Caa2	12.59%	18.60%
Gabon	Caa1	10.48%	16.49%
Ghana	Caa1	10.48%	16.49%
Kenya	B2	7.69%	13.70%
Mali	Caa2	12.59%	18.60%
Mauritius	Baa2	2.66%	8.67%
Morocco	Ba1	3.50%	9.51%
Mozambique	Caa2	12.59%	18.60%
Namibia	B1	6.29%	12.30%
Niger	B3	9.09%	15.10%
Nigeria	B2	7.69%	13.70%
Rwanda	B2	7.69%	13.70%
Senegal	Ba3	5.03%	11.04%
South Africa	Ba2	4.21%	10.22%
Swaziland	B3	9.09%	15.10%
Tanzania	B2	7.69%	13.70%
Togo	B3	9.09%	15.10%
Tunisia	Caa1	10.48%	16.49%
Uganda	B2	7.69%	13.70%
Zambia	Ca	16.78%	22.79%
Africa		7.36%	13.37%

Country	Rating	CRP	ERP
Abu Dhabi	Aa2	0.69%	6.70%
Bahrain	B2	7.69%	13.70%
Iraq	Caa1	10.48%	16.49%
Israel	A1	0.99%	7.00%
Jordan	B1	6.29%	12.30%
Kuwait	A1	0.99%	7.00%
Lebanon	C	20.40%	26.41%
Oman	Ba3	5.03%	11.04%
Qatar	Aa3	0.84%	6.85%
Ras Al Khaimah	A1	0.99%	7.00%
Saudi Arabia	A1	0.99%	7.00%
Sharjah	Baa3	3.07%	9.08%
United Arab Emirates	Aa2	0.69%	6.70%
Middle East		2.02%	8.03%

Country	Rating	CRP	ERP
Bangladesh	Ba3	5.03%	11.04%
Cambodia	B2	7.69%	13.70%
China	A1	0.99%	7.00%
Fiji	B1	6.29%	12.30%
Hong Kong	Aa3	0.84%	6.85%
India	Baa3	3.07%	9.08%
Indonesia	Baa2	2.66%	8.67%
Japan	A1	0.99%	7.00%
Korea (South)	Aa2	0.69%	6.70%
Laos	Caa3	13.98%	19.99%
Macao	Aa3	0.84%	6.85%
Malaysia	A3	1.68%	7.69%
Maldives	Caa1	10.48%	16.49%
Mongolia	B3	9.09%	15.10%
Pakistan	B3	9.09%	15.10%
Papua New Guinea	B2	7.69%	13.70%
Philippines	Baa2	2.66%	8.67%
Singapore	Aaa	0.00%	6.01%
Solomon Islands	Caa1	10.48%	16.49%
Sri Lanka	Ca	16.78%	22.79%
Taiwan	Aa3	0.84%	6.85%
Thailand	Baa1	2.23%	8.24%
Vietnam	Ba3	5.03%	11.04%
Asia		1.56%	7.57%

Country	Rating	CRP	ERP
Australia	Aaa	0.00%	6.01%
Cook Islands	Caa1	10.48%	16.49%
New Zealand	Aaa	0.00%	6.01%
Aus & NZ		0.00%	6.01%

Blue: Moody's Rating
Red: Country Risk Premium
Green: Equity Risk Premium

FIGURE 10.6 | Zomato—Operating History

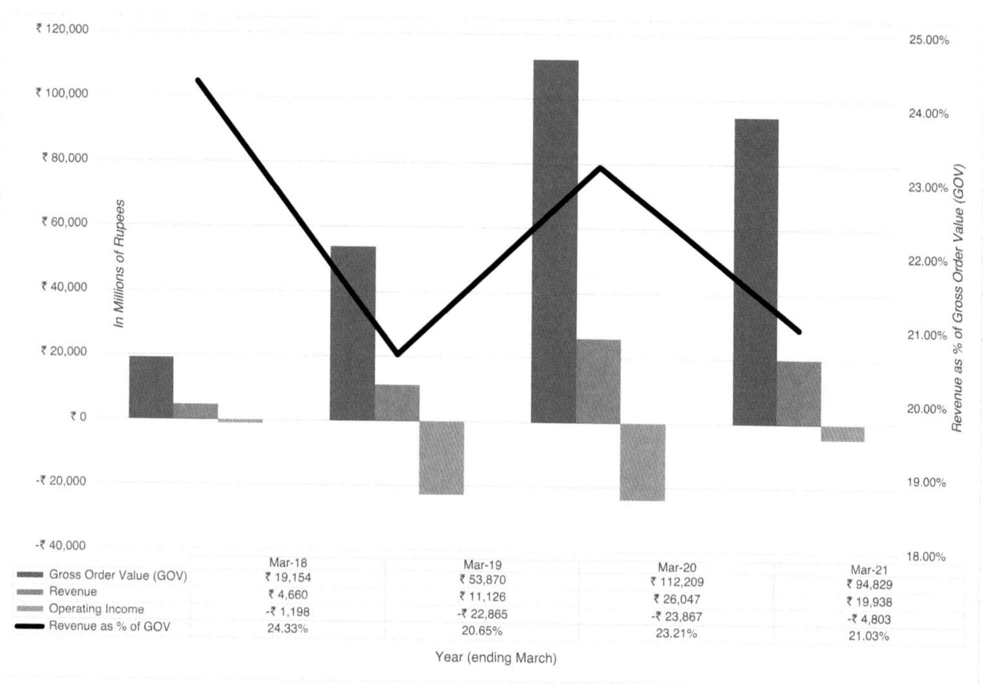

	Mar-18	Mar-19	Mar-20	Mar-21
Gross Order Value (GOV)	₹ 19,154	₹ 53,870	₹ 112,209	₹ 94,829
Revenue	₹ 4,660	₹ 11,126	₹ 26,047	₹ 19,938
Operating Income	-₹ 1,198	-₹ 22,865	-₹ 23,867	-₹ 4,803
Revenue as % of GOV	24.33%	20.65%	23.21%	21.03%

FIGURE 10.7 | Zomato's Unit Economics

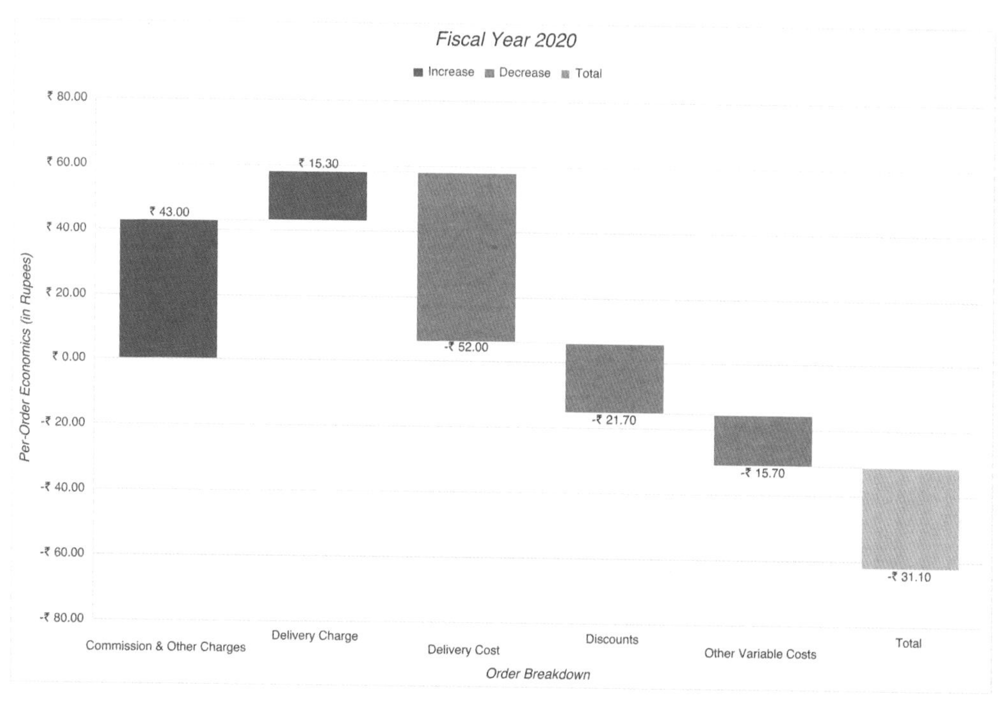

FIGURE 11.6 | Revenues and Profits at Tesla, 2013–2021

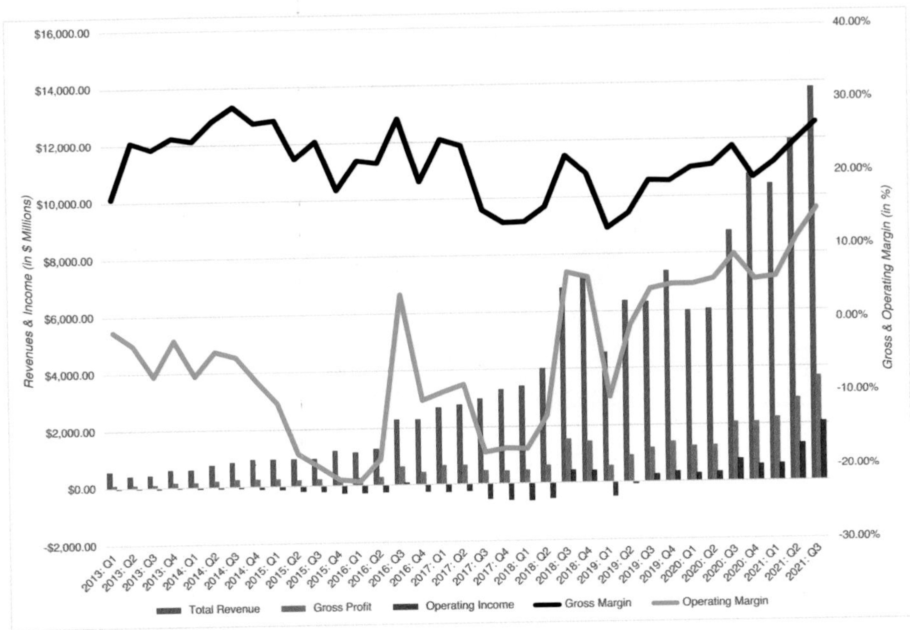

FIGURE 14.4 | Excess Returns around Earnings Announcements

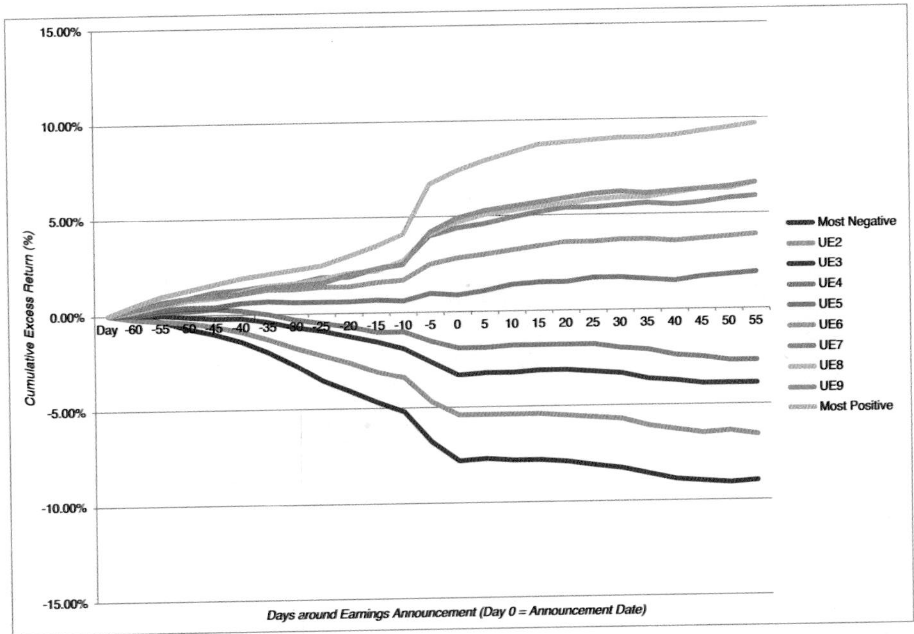

Source: D. Craig Nichols and Wahlen

FIGURE 14.5 | Excess Returns after Earnings Announcements

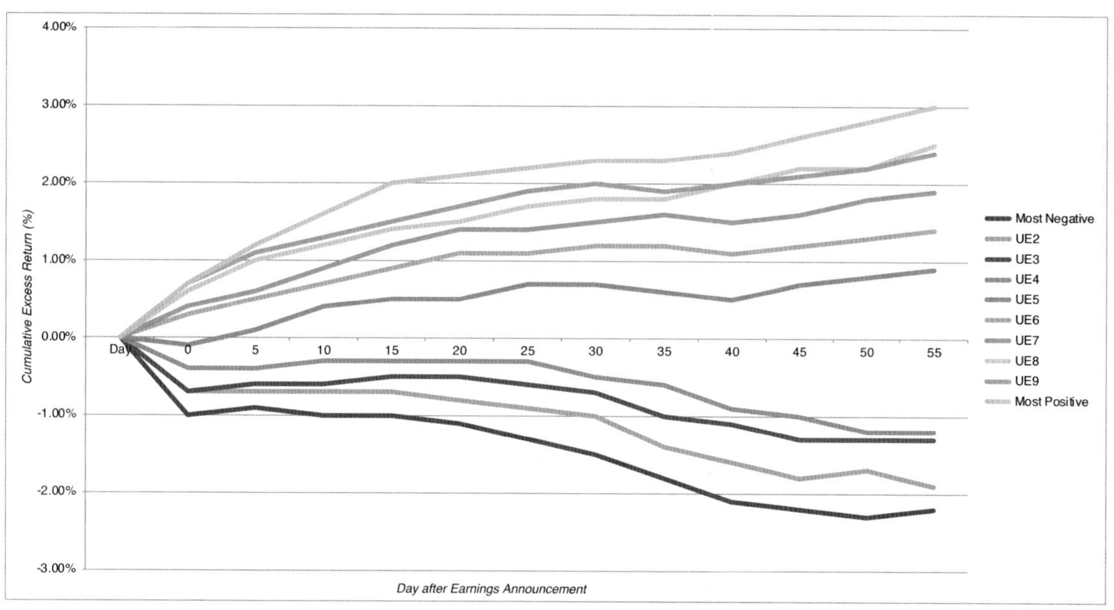

Source: D. Craig Nichols and Wahlen

FIGURE 15.10 | Returns across PEG Ratio Classes—US Stocks

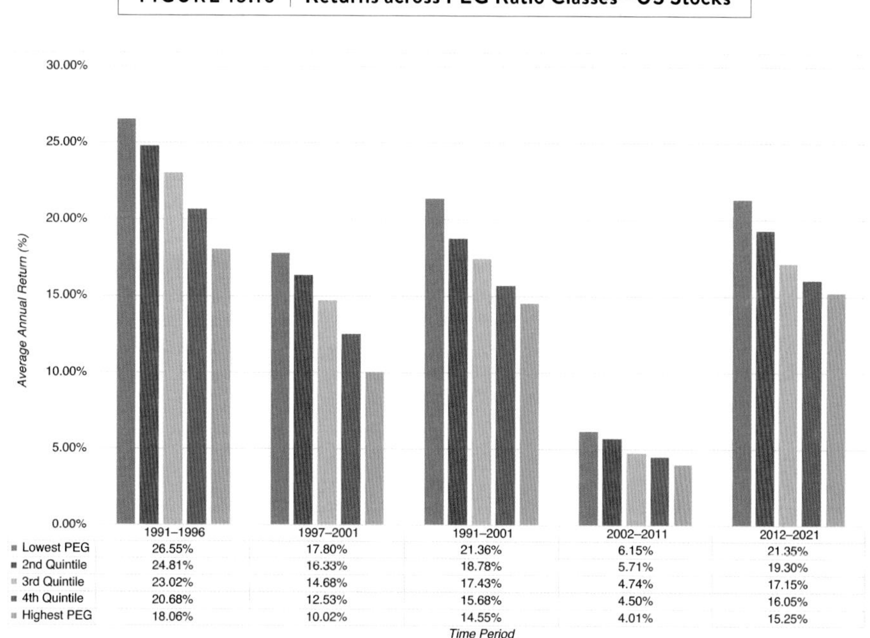

	1991–1996	1997–2001	1991–2001	2002–2011	2012–2021
Lowest PEG	26.55%	17.80%	21.36%	6.15%	21.35%
2nd Quintile	24.81%	16.33%	18.78%	5.71%	19.30%
3rd Quintile	23.02%	14.68%	17.43%	4.74%	17.15%
4th Quintile	20.68%	12.53%	15.68%	4.50%	16.05%
Highest PEG	18.06%	10.02%	14.55%	4.01%	15.25%

Source: Value Line

FIGURE 18.6 | **Dual Class Shares in IPOs, 1980–2021**

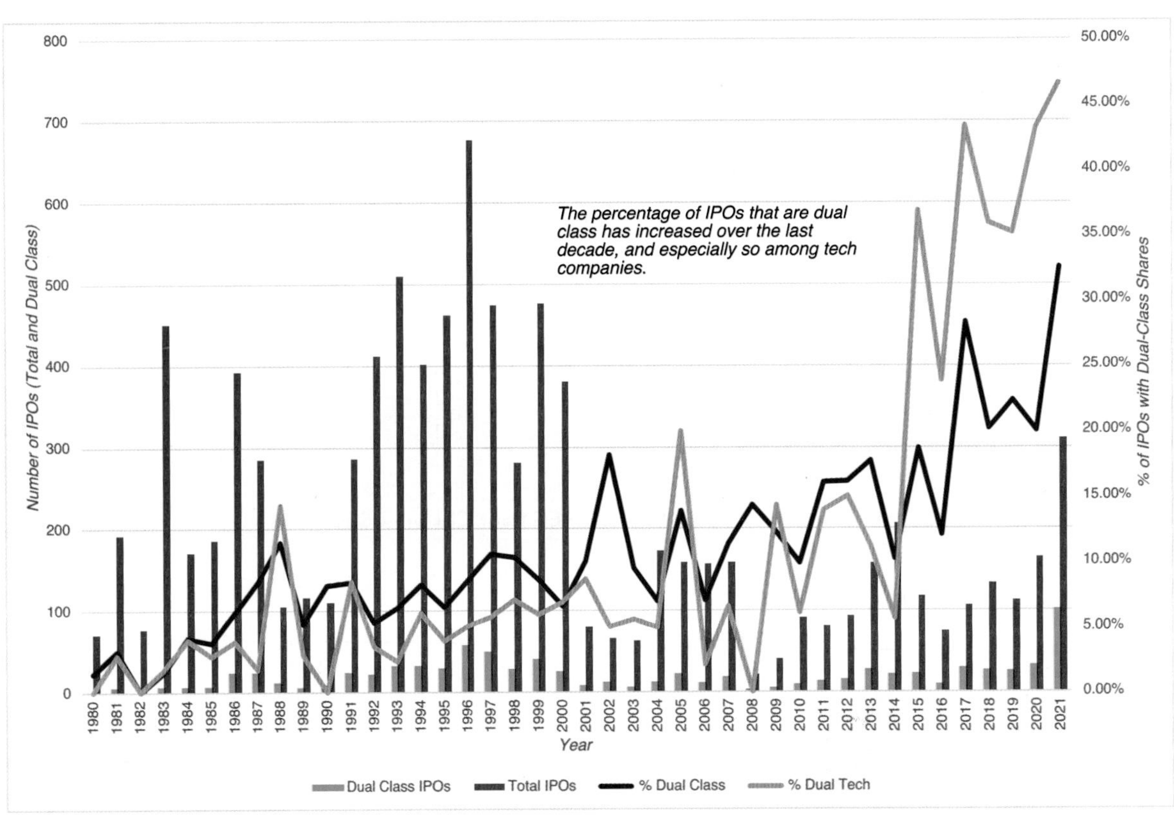

Source: Jay Ritter

Payoff to Active Value Investing

Investing in low PE or low PBV stocks would not be considered true value investing by most of the movement's adherents. In fact, most value investors would argue that while you may start with these stocks, the real payoff to value investing comes from additional analysis, bringing in other quantitative screens (following up on Ben Graham) and/or qualitative ones (like Buffett's focus on good management and moats). If I call this *active value investing*, the true test of value investing then becomes whether following value investing precepts and practices and picking stocks generates returns that exceed the returns on a value index fund, created by investing in an index fund that trades low price to book or low PE stocks. Defined thus, the evidence that value investing works has always been weaker than just looking at the top lines, though the strength of the evidence varies depending upon the strand of value investing examined.

THE SCREENERS

Since Ben Graham provided the architecture for screening for cheap stocks, it should be no surprise that some of the early research looked at whether Graham's screens worked in delivering returns. Henry Oppenheimer examined the returns on stocks, picked using the Graham screens, between 1970 and 1983 and found that they delivered average annual returns of 29.4% a year, as opposed to 11.5% of the index. There are other studies that come to the same conclusion, looking at screening over the period, but they all suffer from two fundamental problems.

- The first is that one of the value screens invariably used is low PE and low PBV. We already know that these stocks delivered significantly higher returns than the rest of the market for much of the last century, and it is unclear from these studies whether all the additional screens (Graham gives a dozen or more) add much to returns.
- The second is that the ultimate test of a philosophy is not in whether its strategies work on paper but in whether the investors who use those strategies make money on actual portfolios. There is many a slip between the cup and the lip when it comes to converting paper strategies to practical ones, and finding investors who have consistently succeeded at beating the market by using screening is difficult to do.

In short, what should give you pause is how easily academics seem to make money on paper with value investing, evidenced by the hundreds of papers chronicling the connection of alphas (excess returns) to screens or factors, and how difficult it is for practitioners who must actually deliver these returns.

THE CONTRARIANS

The early evidence on contrarian investing came from looking at loser stocks—i.e., stocks that have gone down the most over a prior period—and chronicling the returns you would earn if you bought these stocks. One of the earliest studies, from the mid-1980s, presented the eye-catching graph in figure 16.4, backing up the thesis that loser stocks are investment winners.*

FIGURE 16.4 | Cumulative Abnormal Returns—Winners versus Losers

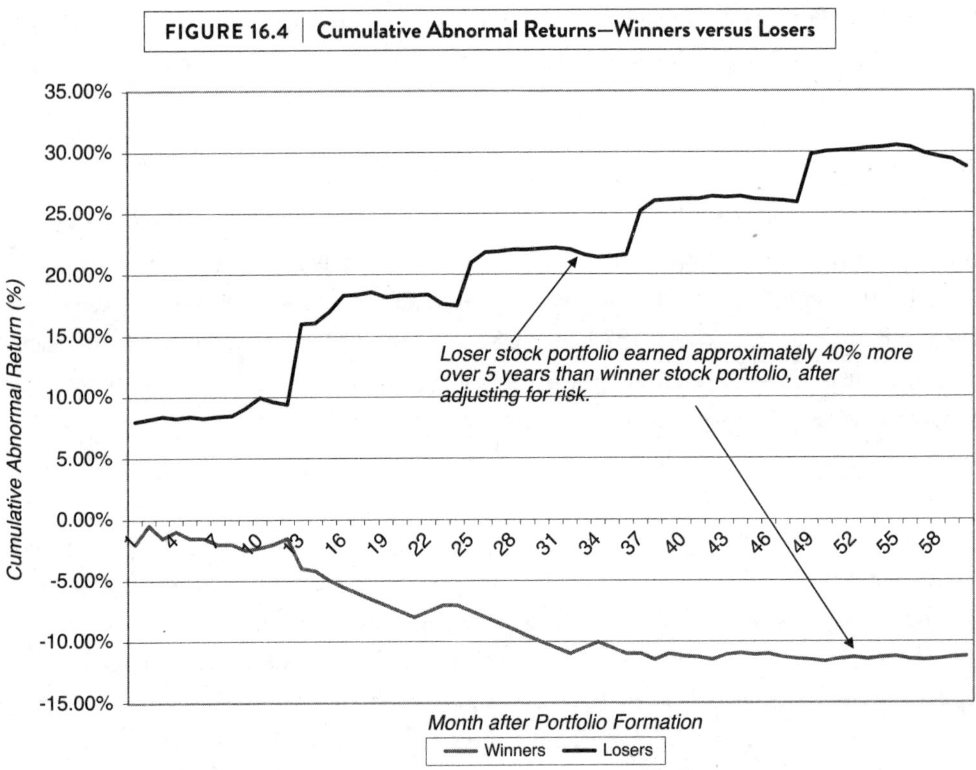

Loser stocks, defined as the stocks that have gone down the most in the last year, deliver almost 45% more in returns than winner stocks, defined as stocks that have gone up the most in the last year. Before you start buying loser stocks based on this study, though, note that research in subsequent years pointed to two flaws. The first was that

* W. F. M. DeBondt and R. Thaler, "Does the stock market overreact?" *Journal of Finance* 40, no. 3 (July 1985): 793–805.

many of the loser stocks in the study traded at less than a dollar per share, and once transaction costs were factored in, the payoff to buying these stocks shrank significantly. The second came in a different study, which made a case for buying winner stocks with figure 16.5.*

FIGURE 16.5 | Differential Returns—Winner versus Loser Portfolios

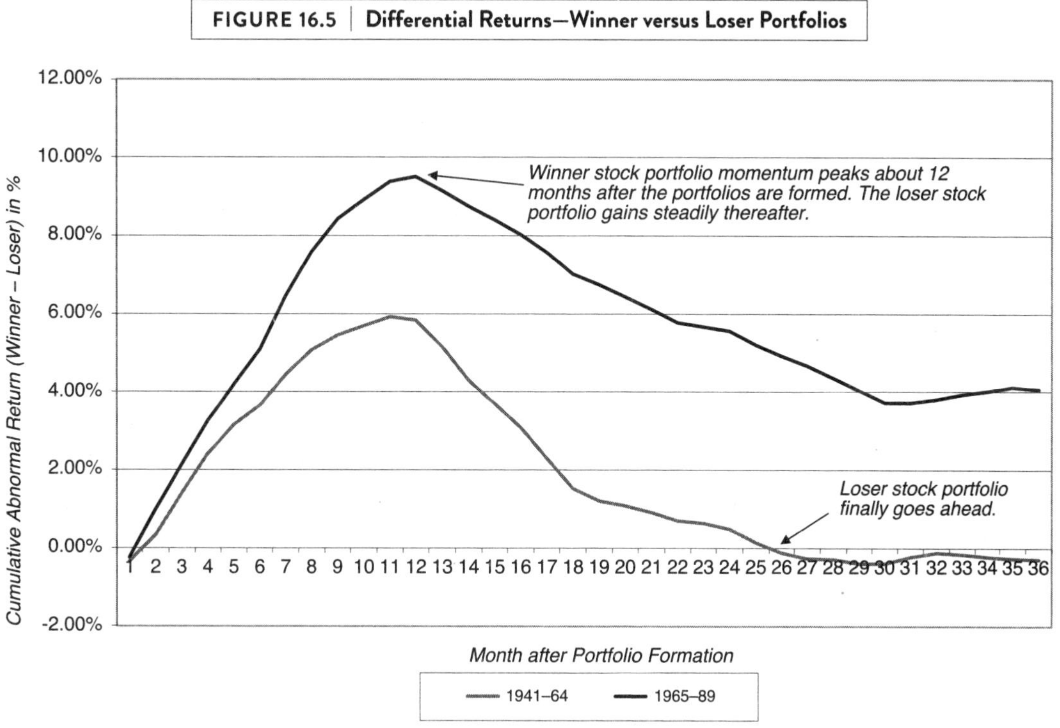

Note that winner stocks continue to win, in both time periods examined, in the first twelve months after the portfolios are created, though those excess returns fade in the months thereafter. Put simply, if you invest in loser stocks and then lose your nerve or your faith and sell too soon, your loser-stock strategy will not pay off.

THE VALUE INDEXERS

Many value investors will blanch at the idea of letting indexed value investors into this group, but there can be no denying the fact that funds have flowed into tilted index funds, with many of the tilts reflecting historical value factors (low price to book, small cap, low

* N. Jegadeesh and S. Titman, "Returns to Buying Winners and Selling Losers: Implications for Stock Market Efficiency," *Journal of Finance* 48, no. 1 (March 1993): 65–91.

volatility). The sales pitch for these funds is often that you can get not only a higher return, because of your factor tilts, but also a bigger bang (return) for your risk (standard deviation), rather than a higher return per se (higher ratios of returns to standard deviation). The jury is still out, and my view is that tilted index funds are an oxymoron, and that these funds should be categorized as "minimalist value funds," which try to minimize your activity, in order to lower your costs.

The most telling statistics on the failure of active value investing come from looking at the performance of mutual fund managers who claim to be its adherents. While the earliest studies of mutual funds looked at them as a group, and concluded that they collectively underperformed the market, later studies have looked at mutual funds grouped by category (small cap versus large cap, value versus growth) to see if fund managers in any of these groupings performed better than managers in other groupings, compared to index funds for each category. None of these studies found any evidence that value fund managers are more likely to beat their index counterparts than their growth fund counterparts. It is telling that value investors, when asked to defend their capacity to add value to investing, almost never reference that research (partly because there is little that they can point to as supportive evidence) but instead fall back on Warren Buffett as their justification for value investing. There is no doubt about Buffett's success over the decades, but it is worth asking whether the continued use of his name is more a sign of weakness in value investing than of strength.

Wandering in the Wilderness?: Value Investing in the Last Decade

Looking at my analysis of value investing over the last century, you can accuse me of perhaps nitpicking an overall record of success, but the last decade has, in my view, tested value investing in ways that have never been seen before. To see how much of an outlier this period (2010–2019) has been, look at the returns to low and high PBV stocks, by decade, in table 16.1.

Table 16.1 • Value versus Growth: US Stocks by Decade, 1930–2019

	Lowest PBV	Highest PBV	Difference	Lowest PE	Highest PE	Difference
1930–39	6.04%	4.27%	1.77%	N/A	N/A	N/A
1940–49	22.96%	7.43%	15.53%	N/A	N/A	N/A
1950–59	25.06%	20.92%	4.14%	34.33%	19.16%	15.17%
1960–69	13.23%	9.57%	3.66%	15.27%	9.79%	5.48%
1970–79	17.05%	3.89%	13.16%	14.83%	2.28%	12.54%
1980–89	24.48%	12.94%	11.54%	18.38%	14.46%	3.92%
1990–99	20.17%	21.88%	-1.71%	21.61%	22.03%	-0.41%
2000–09	8.59%	-0.49%	9.08%	13.84%	0.61%	13.23%
2010–19	11.27%	16.67%	-5.39%	11.35%	17.09%	-5.75%

Source: Kenneth French

While it is true that the dot-com boom allowed growth stocks to beat out value stocks in the 1990s, the difference was small and bunched up in the last few years of that decade. In the 2010–2019 period, in the battle between value and growth, it was no contest, with growth winning by a substantial amount in seven of the ten years.

To make things worse, active value investors—at least those that run mutual funds—found ways to underperform even these badly performing indices. Rather than use risk and return models or academic research to back up this proposition, and thereby open the debate about portfolio theories, I will draw on a much more simplistic but perhaps more effective comparison. One of S&P's most informative measures is SPIVA, where S&P compares the returns of fund managers in different groupings to indices that reflect that grouping (value index for value funds, growth index for growth funds, etc.) and reports on the percentage of managers in each grouping that beat the index. In figure 16.6, I report on the SPIVA measures for 2005–2019 for value managers in different market cap classes (large, mid-sized, small).

FIGURE 16.6 | **Payoff to Active Value Investing—SPIVA Measures**

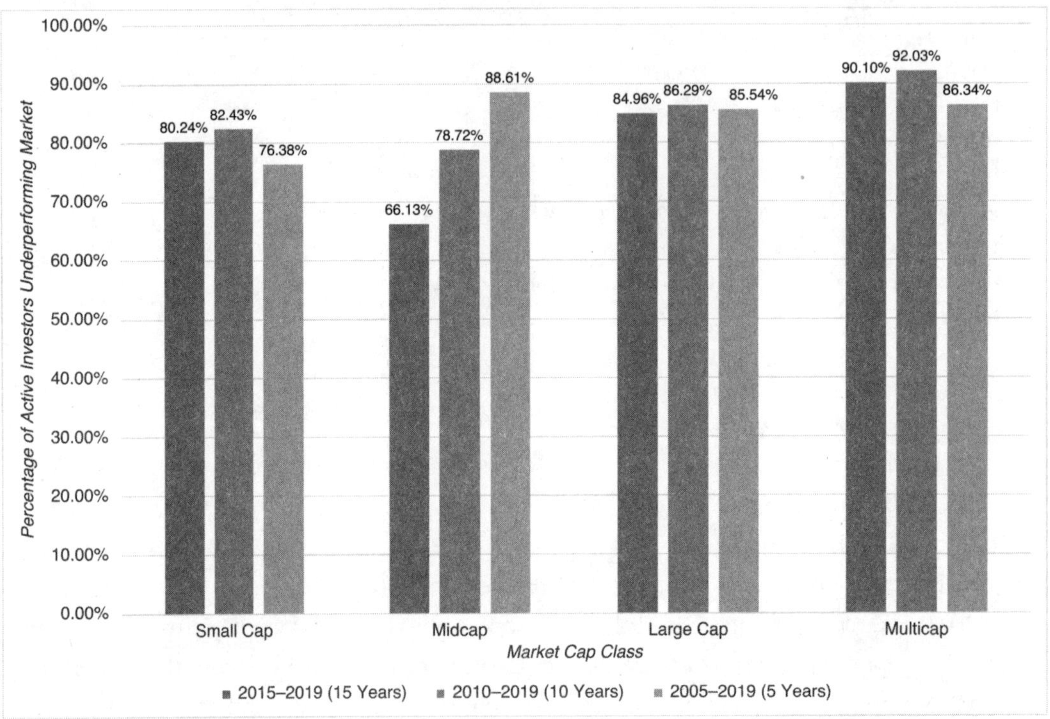

Put simply, most value fund managers have had trouble beating the value indices, net of fees. Even gross of fees, the percentage of fund managers underperforming their indices stays well above 50%.

Legendary value investors lost their mojo during the decade, and even Warren Buffett's stock picking delivered average returns. He abandoned long-standing practices, such as using book value as a basis for estimating intrinsic value and never doing buybacks, for good and bad reasons. The best indicator of how the market has also lowered the value it attaches to Buffett's stock picking is in a number that has the Buffett imprimatur, the ratio of price to book at Berkshire in the last few years, as seen in figure 16.7.

FIGURE 16.7 | The Buffett Premium at Berkshire Hathaway

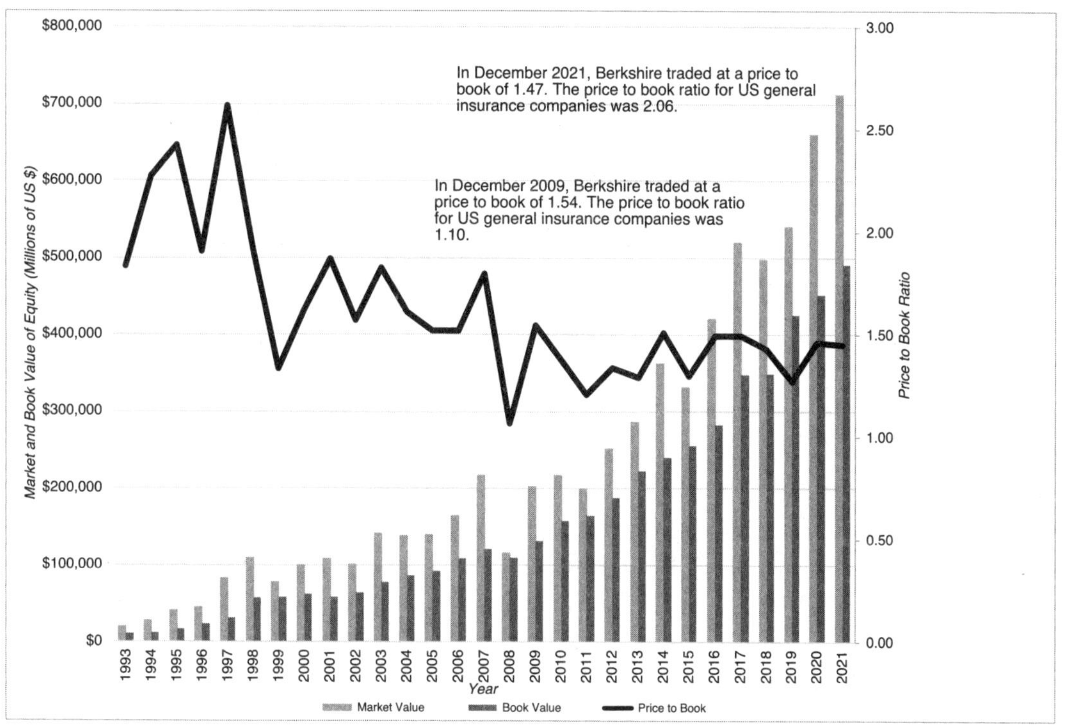

Since Berkshire's assets are primarily in publicly traded companies, and these investments have been marked to market for all this period, one way to look at a portion of the premium that investors are paying over book value is to consider it to be the *stock picker premium*. Since some of the premium can also be explained by its presence in the insurance business, I compared the price to book for Berkshire to that of general insurance companies listed and traded in the United States. At the start of 2010, Berkshire traded at a price to book ratio of 1.54, well above the US insurance company industry average of 1.10. A decade later, at the end of 2021, the price to book ratio for Berkshire had dropped to 1.47, below the average of 2.06 for US insurance companies. The loss of the Buffett premium may seem puzzling to those who track news stories about the man, since he is still not only treated as an investing deity but viewed as the person behind every Berkshire Hathaway decision, from its investment in Apple in 2017 to its more recent one in the Snowflake IPO. My reading is that markets are less sentimental and more realistic in assessing both the quality of Buffett's investments (that he is now closer to the average investor than he has ever been) and the fact that at his advanced age, it is unlikely that he is the lead stock picker at Berkshire anymore.

Explanations and Excuses

The attempt to determine what happened to value investing in the last decade is not just about explaining the past, since the rationale you provide will inform whether you will continue to adhere to old-time value investing rules, modify them to reflect new realities, or abandon them entirely in search of new ones. There are four explanations that I have heard from value investors for what has gone wrong during the last decade, and I will list them in their order of consequence for value investing practices, from most benign to most consequential.

1. *This is a passing phase!*

   Diagnosis: Even in its glory days, during the last century, there were extended periods (like the 1990s) when low PE and low PBV stocks underperformed relative to high PE and high PBV stocks. Once those periods passed, value stocks regained their rightful place at the top of the investing heap. The last decade was one of those aberrations, and as with previous aberrations, it too shall pass.

   Prescription: Be patient. With time, value investing will deliver superior returns.

2. *The Fed did it!*

   Diagnosis: Starting with the 2008 crisis and stretching into the last decade, central banks around the world have become much more active players in markets. With quantitative easing, the Fed and other central banks have not only contributed to keeping interest rates lower (than they should be, given fundamentals) but also provided protection for risk-taking at the expense of conservative investing.

   Prescription: Central banks cannot keep interest rates low in perpetuity, and even they do not have the resources to bail out risk-takers forever. Eventually, the process will blow up, causing currencies to lose value, government budgets to implode, and inflation and interest rates to rise. When that happens, value investors will find themselves less hurt than other investors.

3. *The investment world has become flatter!*

   Diagnosis: When Ben Graham listed his screens for finding good investments in 1949, running those screens required data and tools that most investors did not have access to, or the endurance to run. All the data came from poring over annual reports, which often used very different accounting standards; the ratios had to be computed with slide rules or on paper; and the sorting of companies was done by hand. Even into the 1980s, access to data and powerful analytical tools was restricted to professional money managers and thus remained a competitive advantage. As data has become easier to get, accounting more standardized, and analytical tools more accessible, the competitive advantage to computing ratios (PE, PBV, debt ratio, etc.) from financial statements and running screens to find cheap stocks has become very little.

Prescription: To find a competitive edge, value investors must become creative in finding new screens that are either qualitative or go beyond the financial statements, or in finding new ways of processing publicly accessible data to find undervalued stocks.

4. *The global economy has changed!*

   Diagnosis: At the risk of sounding clichéd, the shift in economic power to more globalized companies, built on technology and immense user platforms, has made many old-time value investing nostrums useless.

   Prescription: Value investing must adapt to the new economy, with less of a balance sheet focus and more flexibility in how practitioners assess value. Put simply, investors may have to leave their preferred habitat (mature companies with physical assets bases) in the corporate life cycle to find value.

When I listen to value investors across the spectrum, I don't yet hear a consensus on what ails the philosophy, but the evolution in thinking has been clear. As the years of underperformance have stretched on, there are fewer value investors who believe that this is a passing phase and that all that is needed is patience. There are many value investors who still blame the Fed (and other central banks) for their underperformance, and while I agree with them that central banks have overreached and skewed markets, I also think that this belief has become a convenient excuse for not looking at the very real problems at the heart of value investing.

Having never made the pilgrimage to a Berkshire Hathaway shareholder meeting, nor counted myself among the value investing faithful, I believe that the troubles in value investing are deep and can be traced back to three developments:

1. **It has become rigid:** In the decades since Ben Graham published *Security Analysis*, value investing has developed rules for investing that have no give to them. Some of these rules reflect value investing history (screens for current and quick ratios), some are throwbacks in time, and some just seem curmudgeonly. For instance, value

investing has been steadfast in its view that companies that do not have significant tangible assets, relative to their market value, are cheap, and that view has kept many value investors out of technology stocks for most of the last three decades. Similarly, value investing's focus on dividends has caused adherents to concentrate their holdings in utilities, financial service companies, and older consumer product companies, as younger companies have shifted to returning cash in buybacks.

2. **It has become ritualistic:** The rituals of value investing are well established, from the annual trek to Omaha to the claim that your investment education is incomplete unless you have read Ben Graham's *The Intelligent Investor* and *Security Analysis*, to an almost unquestioning belief that anything said by Warren Buffett or Charlie Munger must be right.
3. **It has become righteous:** While investors of all stripes believe that their "investing ways" will yield payoffs, some value investors seem to feel entitled to high returns because they have followed all the rules and rituals. In fact, they view investors who deviate from the script as shallow speculators and are convinced that they will fail in the "long term."

Put simply, value investing, at least as practiced by some of its advocates, has evolved into a religion rather than a philosophy, viewing other ways of investing as not just misguided but wrong and deserving of punishment.

Good Companies versus Good Investments

An adage of value investing is that management matters and, by extension, investing in companies that are well managed will generate good returns. This is the rationale that induces many value investors to buy mature companies, with good management and solid financials, and to avoid companies that are poorly managed, with shaky financials. In this section, I will argue that this view is flawed and explain how the missing variable is the price that the market has attached to the company.

What Is a "Good" Company?

Let's start with what makes a company a good one. There are various criteria that get used, but every one of them comes with a catch. You could start with profitability, arguing that a more profitable business is better than a less profitable one, but that may not be true if the business is capital-intensive (and the profits generated are small relative to the capital invested) or a risky business, in which you are always waiting for the other shoe to drop. You could look at growth—but growth, as I noted earlier in this book, can be good, bad, or neutral, and a company can have high growth while destroying value. To me, the best measure of corporate quality is a high excess return, i.e., a return on capital that is vastly higher than the company's cost of capital.

It is dangerous to attribute all excess returns in a company to its management, in good scenarios or bad. The "goodness" or "badness" might just reflect the aging of the company, its endowed barriers to entry, or macro factors (exchange rate movements, country risk, or commodity price volatility). Good management is realistic about assessing where a company is in the life cycle and adapting to it. As we noted in the corporate finance chapters earlier in this book, the future of a company is determined by three broad groups of decisions: *investment decisions* (deciding where to invest scarce resources), *financing decisions* (deciding how much debt to take on and in what form), and *dividend decisions* (deciding how much cash to return to the owners of the business and in what form). For a young-growth company, "good" management usually is about optimizing investment decisions—finding and taking great investments to deliver growth—and the firm should steer away from debt or paying dividends. As the company matures, "good" management may shift to playing defense, protecting brand name and franchise value from competitive assault, and using financing and dividend decisions to tweak value. In a declining company, the essence of "good" management is to preside over the liquidation of the company by not just avoiding taking on more investments but also extricating the company from its existing investments. My way of capturing the quality of management is to value a company twice, once with the management in place (status quo) and once with new (and better) management.

The Expectations Game

Now that I have working definitions of good companies and good managers, let's think about "good" investment. For a company to be a good investment, it must be trading at the right price, given its business and management characteristics. If you have a very good company with capable management in place, and the market is valuing the company as a great company with exceptional managers, it is a bad investment. Conversely, if you have a company that is not just badly managed but in a bad business (where earning less than the cost of capital is par for the course), which is priced as an even worse firm, it would be a good investment.

Put simply, investing is about buying a company at a price that is less than its value, and to make an investment assessment, you must bring in what the market is expecting a company to do and, consequently, pricing in. In figure 16.8, I use the value and pricing processes that I introduced in chapter 9 to lay out how your expectations, as an investor, for a company must be compared with what the market is expecting for that same company.

FIGURE 16.8 | **Good (Bad) Companies versus Good (Bad) Investments**

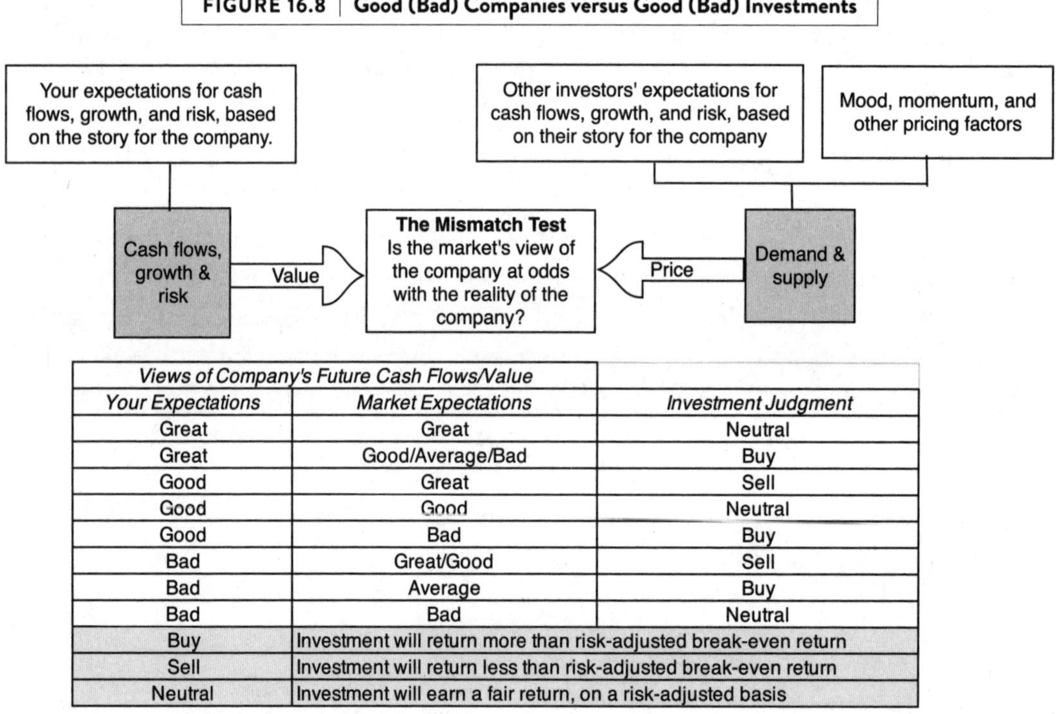

Views of Company's Future Cash Flows/Value		
Your Expectations	*Market Expectations*	*Investment Judgment*
Great	Great	Neutral
Great	Good/Average/Bad	Buy
Good	Great	Sell
Good	Good	Neutral
Good	Bad	Buy
Bad	Great/Good	Sell
Bad	Average	Buy
Bad	Bad	Neutral
Buy	Investment will return more than risk-adjusted break-even return	
Sell	Investment will return less than risk-adjusted break-even return	
Neutral	Investment will earn a fair return, on a risk-adjusted basis	

As you can see, there is a wide range of outcomes, depending on how your expectations for a company and the market expectations for that company match up.

- In all the scenarios where your expectations are in sync with those of the market, whether the company is bad, average, good, or great, the investment becomes a neutral one, since the company will be priced, given those expectations, to deliver a fair rate of return.

- In the scenarios where your expectations for a company are that it will be better run than and deliver results superior to what the market is anticipating for that company, you have the makings of a good investment, since the company will be priced too low and so will be well positioned to deliver excess returns.
- In the scenarios where you expect a company to be less well managed and deliver worse operating results than what the market is anticipating for the company, the pricing for the company will be too high, and buying it will be a pathway to below-market returns.

Put simply, investing is a game of expectations, and when expectations are set too high, even great companies will struggle to deliver on them, making them questionable investments.

Screening for Mispricing

If you take the last section to heart, you can see why multiples like PE ratio and EV/EBITDA and screens for cheap stocks are so embedded in investment practice. In effect, to be a successful investor, you must find market mismatches; a very good company in terms of business and management that is being priced as a bad or even average company will be your "buy." With that mission in hand, let's consider how you can use multiples in screening, using the PE ratio to illustrate the process. Starting with a very basic valuation model, you can back out the fundamental drivers of the PE ratio, as in figure 16.9.

FIGURE 16.9 | The Fundamental Determinants of PE ratios

Start with a simple dividend discount model

$$\text{Value of Equity per Share} = \frac{\text{Expected Dividends per Share Next Year}}{(\text{Cost of Equity} - \text{Expected Growth Rate})}$$

Divide both sides of the equation by earnings per share

$$\frac{\text{Value of Equity per Share}}{\textit{Earning per Share}} = \text{PE} = \frac{\text{Payout Ratio}}{(\text{Cost of Equity} - \text{Expected Growth Rate})}$$

Payout Ratio = Dividends per Share/Earnings per Share

PE Ratio = f (Payout Ratio, Cost of Equity, Expected Growth Rate)
Higher growth → Higher PE
Higher risk (cost of equity) → Lower PE
Higher ROE (payout ratio) → Higher PE

Now what? This equation links PE to three variables: growth, risk (through the cost of equity), and the quality of growth (in the payout ratio or return on equity). Plugging in values for these variables into this equation, you will quickly find that companies that have low growth, high risk, and abysmally low returns on equity should trade at low PE ratios, and those with higher growth, lower risk, and solid returns on equity should trade at high PE ratios. If you are looking to screen for good investments, where the pricing is mismatched to the company, you need to find stocks with low PE, high growth, a low cost of equity, and a high return on equity.

Using this approach to deconstruct other pricing multiples, I list multiples and the screening mismatches that characterize cheap and expensive companies in table 16.2.

Table 16.2 • Mismatched Multiples and Mispricing

Multiple	Cheap Company	Expensive Company
PE	Low PE High growth Low equity risk High payout	High PE Low growth High equity risk Low payout
PEG	Low PEG Low Growth Low equity risk High payout	High PEG High growth High equity risk Low payout
PBV	Low PBV High growth Low equity risk High ROE	High PBV Low growth High equity risk Low ROE
EV/Invested Capital	Low EV/IC High growth Low operating risk High ROIC	High EV/IC Low growth High operating risk Low ROIC
EV/Sales	Low EV/sales High growth Low operating risk High operating margin	High EV/sales Low growth High operating risk Low operating margin
EV/EBITDA	Low EV/EBITDA High growth Low operating risk Low tax rate	High EV/EBITDA Low growth High operating risk High tax rate

If you are wondering about the contrast between equity risk and operating risk, the answer is simple. Operating risk reflects the risk of the businesses that you operate in, whereas equity risk reflects operating risk magnified by financial leverage; the former is measured with the cost of capital, whereas the latter is captured in the cost of equity.

Investing Lessons

Separating good companies from bad ones is easy, determining whether companies are well or badly managed is slightly more complicated, but the biggest challenge is defining which companies are good investments. Good companies bring strong competitive advantages to a growing market, and their results (high margins, high returns on capital) reflect these advantages. In well-managed companies, the investing, financing, and dividend decisions reflect what will maximize value for the company—thus allowing for the possibility that you can have good companies that are sub-optimally managed and bad companies that are well managed.

Good investment requires that you be able to buy at a price that is less than the value of the company, given its business and management. Thus, you can have good companies become bad investments (if they trade at too high a price) and bad companies become good investments. Given a choice, it is true that we would all like to buy great companies with great managers at bargain prices, but greatness on all fronts will attract investors and often push up prices to make this infeasible.

I will settle for a more pragmatic end game: At the right price, I will buy a company in a bad business, run by indifferent managers. At the wrong price, I will avoid even superstar companies. Table 16.3 summarizes the combinations that emerge from examining the quality of a company's business and its management, along with its market pricing, to make investment decisions.

Table 16.3 • Business, Management, and Markets—Investment Decisions

Company's Business	Company's Managers	Company Pricing	Investment Decision
Good (strong competitive advantages, growing market)	Good (optimize investment, financing, dividend decisions)	Good (price < value)	Emphatic buy
Good (strong competitive advantages, growing market)	Bad (sub-optimal investment, financing, dividend decisions)	Good (price < value)	Buy & hope for management change
Bad (no competitive advantages, stagnant or shrinking market)	Good (optimize investment, financing, dividend decisions)	Good (price < value)	Buy & hope that management does not change
Bad (no competitive advantages, stagnant or shrinking market)	Bad (sub-optimal investment, financing, dividend decisions)	Good (price < value)	Buy, hope for management change, and pray company survives
Good (strong competitive advantages, growing market)	Good (optimize investment, financing, dividend decisions)	Bad (price > value)	Admire but don't buy
Good (strong competitive advantages, growing market)	Bad (sub-optimal investment, financing, dividend decisions)	Bad (price > value)	Wait for management change
Bad (no competitive advantages, stagnant or shrinking market)	Good (optimize investment, financing, dividend decisions)	Bad (price > value)	Sell
Bad (no competitive advantages, stagnant or shrinking market)	Bad (sub-optimal investment, financing, dividend decisions)	Bad (price > value)	Emphatic sell

A New Paradigm for Value Investing

For value investing to rediscover its roots and reclaim its effectiveness, I believe that it must change in fundamental ways. Some of these changes may sound heretical, especially if you have spent decades in the value investing trenches.

1. **Be clearer about the distinction between value and price:** While "value" and "price" are used interchangeably by some market commentators and investors, they are the re-

sults of very different processes and require different tools to assess and forecast. As I noted in chapter 9, value is a function of cash flows, growth, and risk, and any intrinsic valuation model that does not explicitly forecast cash flows or adjust for risk is lacking core elements. Price is determined by demand and supply, and moved by mood and momentum, and you price an asset by looking at how the market is pricing comparable or similar assets. I am surprised that so many value investors seem to view intrinsic valuation as a speculative exercise and instead pin their analysis on comparing on pricing multiples (PE, price to book, etc.). After all, there should be no disagreement that the value of a business comes from its future cash flows and the uncertainty you feel about those cash flows. It is true that in intrinsic valuation you are forecasting future cash flows and trying to adjust for risk, and that both exercises expose you to error, but I don't see how using a pricing ratio or a shortcut makes that error or uncertainty go away.

2. **Rather than avoid uncertainty, face up to it:** Many value investors view uncertainty as "bad" and something to be avoided, and it is this perspective that has led them away from investing in growth companies, which require you to grapple with forecasting the future, and toward investing in mature companies with tangible assets. The truth is that uncertainty is a feature of investing, not a bug, and that it always exists, even with the most mature, established companies (albeit in smaller doses). In fact, I looked at uncertainty, as it plays out across the life cycle, and noted that it changes, both in terms of magnitude and type, as companies age. While it is true that there is less uncertainty when valuing more mature companies in stable markets, you are more likely to find market mistakes investing in companies where the uncertainty about the future is greatest, either because they are young or distressed or because the macroeconomic environment is challenging. In fact, uncertainty underlies almost every part of intrinsic value, whether it be from micro or macro sources. To deal with that uncertainty, value investors need to expand their toolboxes to include basic statistical tools, from probability distributions to decision trees to Monte Carlo simulations.
3. **Margin of safety is not a substitute risk measure:** I know that value investors view traditional risk and return models with disdain, but there is nothing in intrinsic valuation that requires swearing allegiance to betas and modern portfolio theory. In fact, if you don't like betas, intrinsic valuation is flexible enough to allow you to replace them with your preferred measures of risk, whether it be based upon earnings, debt, or accounting ratios. For those value investors who argue that the margin of safety is a better proxy for risk, it is worth emphasizing that the margin of safety comes into

play only *after* you have valued a company, and to value a company, you need a measure of risk. When used, the margin of safety creates trade-offs, wherein you avoid one type of investment mistake for another, as can be seen in figure 16.10.

FIGURE 16.10 | Margin of Safety—The Trade-off

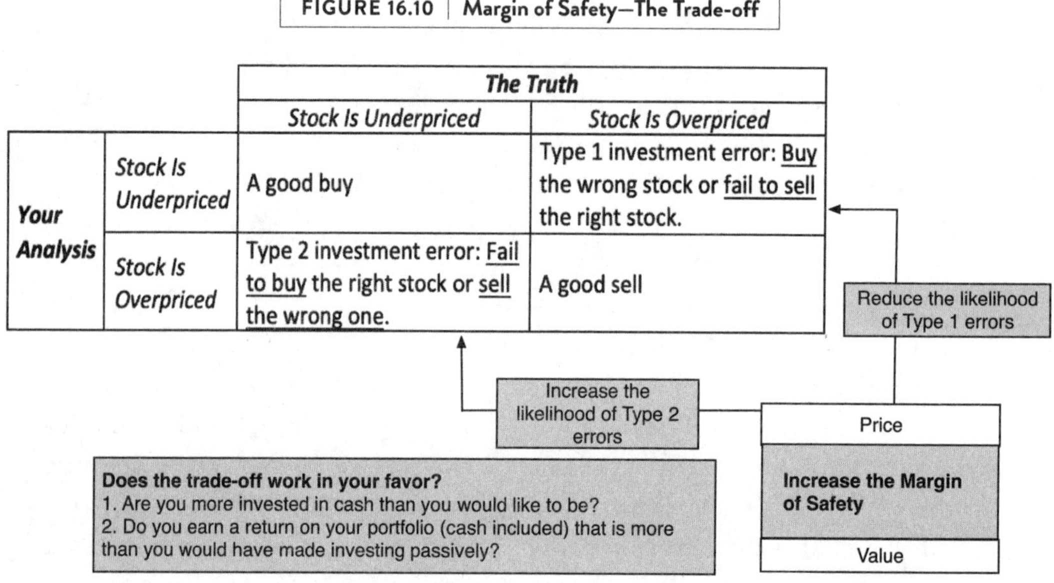

Whether having a large margin of safety is a net plus or minus depends in large part on whether value investors can afford to be picky. One simple measure that the MOS has been set too high is a portfolio that is disproportionately in cash, an indication that you have set your standards so high that too few equities pass through.

4. **Don't take accounting numbers at face value:** It is undeniable that value investing has an accounting focus, with earnings and book value playing a central role in investing strategies. There is good reason to trust those numbers less now than in decades past, for a few reasons. One is that companies have become much more aggressive in playing accounting games, using pro forma income statements to skew the numbers in their favor. The second is that as the center of gravity in the economy has shifted away from manufacturing companies to technology and service companies, accounting has struggled to keep up. In fact, the accounting treatment of R&D has resulted in the understatement of book values of technology and pharmaceutical companies.
5. **You can pick stocks and be diversified at the same time:** While not all value investors make this contention, a surprisingly large number seem to view concentrated port-

folios as a hallmark of good value investing, arguing that spreading your bets across too many stocks will dilute your upside. The choice of whether you want to pick good stocks or be diversified is a false one, since there is no reason you cannot do both. After all, you have thousands of publicly traded stocks to pick from, and all that diversification requires is that, rather than put your money in the very best stock or the five best stocks, you should hold the best 20, 30, or even 40 stocks. The reasoning for diversification is built on the presumption that any investment, no matter how well researched and backed up, comes with uncertainty about the payoff, either because you missed a key element when valuing the investment or because the market may not correct its mistakes. In figure 16.11, I present the choice between concentration and diversification in terms of those two uncertainties—i.e., about value and about the price/value gap closing.

FIGURE 16.11 | **Concentrated Portfolios versus Diversified Portfolios**

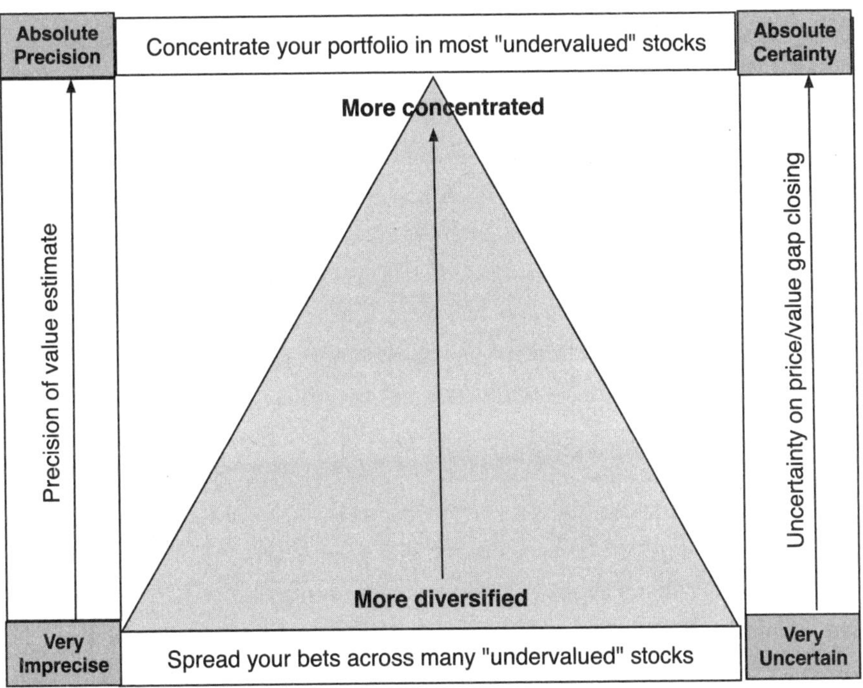

I think that value investors are on shaky ground assuming that doing your homework and focusing on mature companies will yield precise valuations, and on even shakier ground assuming that markets will correct these mistakes in a timely fashion.

In a market where even the most mature of companies are finding their businesses disrupted and market momentum is augmented by passive trading, having a concentrated portfolio is foolhardy.

6. **Don't feel entitled to be rewarded for your virtue:** Investing is not a morality play, and there are no virtuous ways of making money. The distinction between investing and speculating is not only a fine one but very much in the eyes of the beholder. To hold any investing philosophy as better than the rest is a sign of hubris and an invitation for markets to take you down. If you are a value investor, that is your choice, but it should not preclude you from treating other investors with respect and borrowing tools to enhance your returns. Respecting other investors and considering their investment philosophies with an open mind can allow value investors to borrow components from other philosophies to augment their returns.

Conclusion

Investors, when asked to pick an investment philosophy, gravitate toward value investing, drawn by both its way of thinking about markets and its history of success in markets. While that dominance was unquestioned for much of the twentieth century, when low PE/PBV stocks earned significantly higher returns than high PE/PBV stocks, the last decade has shaken the faith of even die-hard value investors. While some in this group see this downturn as a passing phase or the result of central banking overreach, I believe that value investing has lost its edge, partly because of its dependence on measures and metrics that have become less meaningful over time and partly because the global economy has changed, with ripple effects on markets. To rediscover itself, value investing needs to get over its discomfort with uncertainty and be more willing to define value broadly, to include not just countable and physical assets in place but also investments in intangible and growth assets.

17

Investing in Decline and Distress

FOR MANY, THE NOTION of investing in declining businesses sounds counterintuitive. After all, what is to be gained by buying a piece of a company when you expect revenues to decline in the future and margins to stay stagnant or shrink, and when the risk of distress is real and sometimes imminent? As I will show in this chapter, notwithstanding these negatives, a declining company can sometimes be a good investment, for many reasons. The first is that its problems may be fixable and that, once salvaged, the company may be able to reclaim a large portion of its value. That is the promise of private equity investors in the buyout space, where poorly performing companies are targeted for restructuring. The second is that there are some companies that may be worth more for their liquidation or break-up value than as ongoing businesses, and investors with the resources and the power to push for this change may gain from doing so. The third is that markets may be mispricing the company's equity or debt offerings, and traders may be able to take advantage of that mispricing.

Private Equity and Activist Investors: The Fixer Uppers?

Private equity, defined broadly, includes equity invested in privately owned and unlisted businesses. Therefore, it also includes venture capital, which I considered as part of the chapter on investing in young companies. In this section, our focus will be on the segment of private equity that invests in mature and declining companies (many of them public), often in partnership with incumbent management at these companies, and I will build on the introduction that I provided to private equity in chapter 4. These equity holders invest with the intent of taking these companies private, fixing their problems, and then exiting the investments by taking them back into public markets again.

The Life Cycle Connection

To understand how private equity works, let us begin with what many view as the natural sequence in which, as a young business transitions to being a mature one, it moves from being a private business to a publicly traded company and, as it ages, its ownership structure changes from being primarily owned by founders and insiders to being mostly owned by public-market investors, many of them institutional. In figure 17.1, I capture this shift in ownership as companies age.

FIGURE 17.1 | Ownership Structure and Corporate Aging

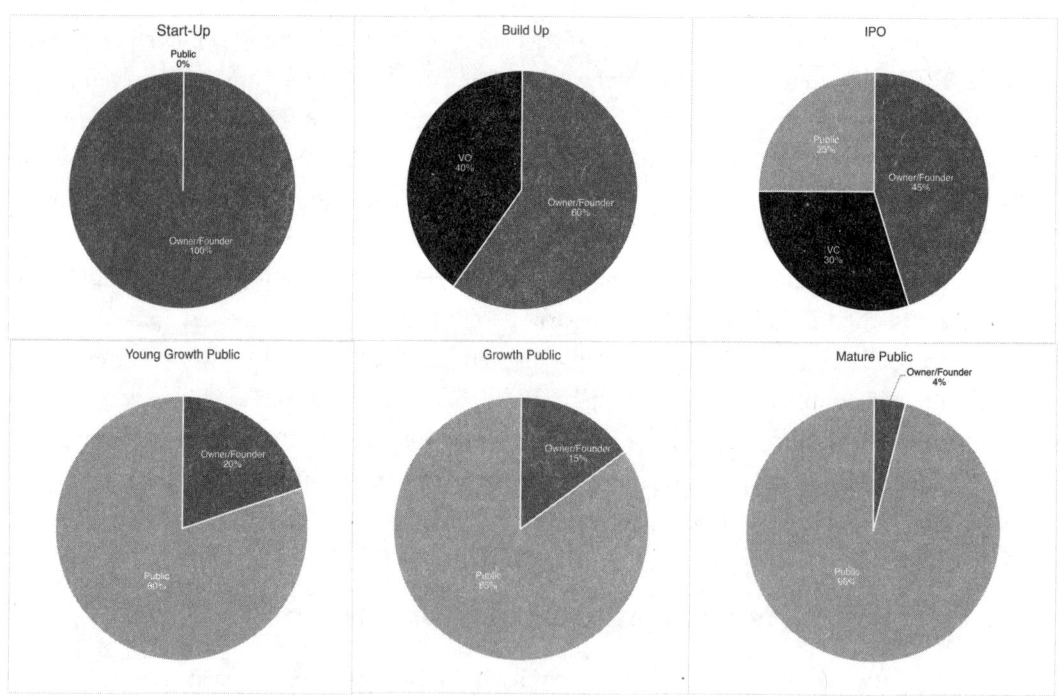

As the founders' shares and control of companies fade over time, the separation between those running the publicly traded firm (i.e., its managers) and those who own the firm (i.e., its shareholders) becomes greater. That corporate governance gap exists at all firms, but in their growth phase, it is often less an issue, because founder/owners are part of management, investment opportunities abound, and financing/dividend decisions matter less. Toward the later stages of the mature phase, and more so in decline, the management-ownership separation has a far greater potential to create dysfunction, and in chapter 13, I addressed the value destruction that occurs when declining company managers act in denial or desperation.

In chapter 4, I provided a description of the private equity process and established a timeline for the buyout and the exit (in figure 4.16). I argued that the role of private equity is first to find firms that are operating in dysfunctional ways, and then to gain effective control of these firms. In some cases, the changes that need to be made at the firm may be accomplished quicker and cheaper if the firm becomes private, and the capital needed for this conversion may require the use of debt, sometimes in disproportionate amounts. When all three pieces—the buyout, a high debt load, and going private—come together, you have the phenomenon of leveraged buyouts.

If the end game in buyouts is changing the way a business is run, removing inefficiencies created either by inertia or by the separation of management from ownership, activist investing shares the same objective, with key differences. The first is that activist investors often acquire small stakes in companies, rather than entire companies, and use those stakes to push for the changes that they perceive will add to value. Since the company remains publicly listed, it is through proxy fights and representation on the board of directors that activist investors try to accomplish their objectives.

While there is no reason why private equity, in its non-VC form, and activist investors cannot target companies across the life cycle, the nature of how they add value will tend to result in them targeting mature and declining firms for their buyouts. First, the increased use of debt as a pathway to value creation, a key component in buyouts and part of many activist investor agendas, requires positive cash flows, and these are more likely to be present in mature and declining firms than in growth firms. Second, while firms at every stage of the life cycle can be inefficiently run, the fixes that provide payoffs quickly will be those that are made to existing investments, again skewing buyouts and activism toward firms that are aging.

Trends in Private Equity and Activism

Private equity—at least in its generic form, where investors take positions in or buy out publicly traded businesses and then try to change the way they are run—has always been part of markets. However, the institutional form of private equity is of more recent origin and saw explosive growth in the 1980s, with firms like KKR, Blackstone, and the Carlyle Group targeting large, high-profile publicly traded companies for leveraged buyouts (LBOs). While these three entities remain large players in the private equity space, private equity has widened and deepened its reach in recent years.

To see the growth in the buyout component of private equity, I look at the dollar value of leveraged buyouts of publicly traded companies in the United States—admittedly a subset of the private equity deal-making space—over time in figure 17.2.

FIGURE 17.2 | Leveraged Buyouts by Year, 2000–2021

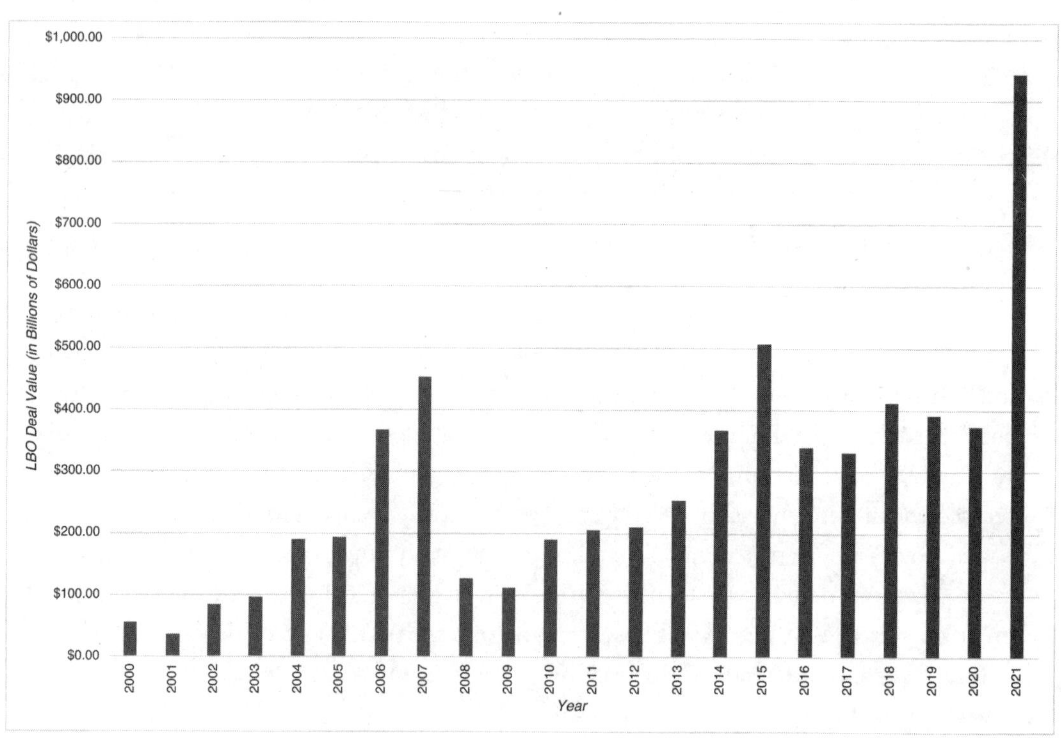

In 2021, close to $900 billion was invested in LBOs in the United States—and that number, large though it is, captures only a subset of the money invested by PE firms. For instance, private equity firms have increasingly targeted private businesses, many family-owned, for the same restructuring reasons that they target public companies. In 2021, there were almost 8,600 private equity deals in the United States, with a total deal value of $1.2 trillion, if you include both publicly listed and privately owned businesses.

In the last decade, the typical deal has also changed, with larger companies being targeted, and the number of private equity dealmakers has surged. The ten largest buyout funds, at the start of 2022, are listed in table 17.1.

Table 17.1 • Largest Buyout PE Funds in 2021

Institution	Headquarters	Capital Raised ($ Mil)
KKR	New York	$126,508
Blackstone	New York	$82,457
EQT	Stockholm	$57,287
CVC Capital Partners	Luxembourg	$55,414
Thoma Bravo	San Francisco	$50,257
Carlyle Group	Washington, DC	$48,441
General Atlantic	New York	$44,832
Clearlake Capital Group	Santa Monica, CA	$42,350
Hellman & Friedman	San Francisco	$40,925
Insight Partners	New York	$40,131

It is worth noting not only how much capital these firms have access to but also that some of these firms—including KKR and Blackstone, the two biggest—are themselves publicly traded companies now.

Some of these institutions, in addition to investing in buyouts, operate as activist investors, pushing for change in public companies (in either operations or capital structure) but without acquiring them and converting them to private companies. They are supplemented by other activists, like Carl Icahn and Bill Ackman, who target firms with specific agendas of change. While activist investing initially was focused on US companies, it has globalized over time, as can be seen in figure 17.3, where I report on the number of global firms targeted by activists each year, as well as the percentage of these firms that are non-US-based.

FIGURE 17.3 | Activist Target Numbers, by Year

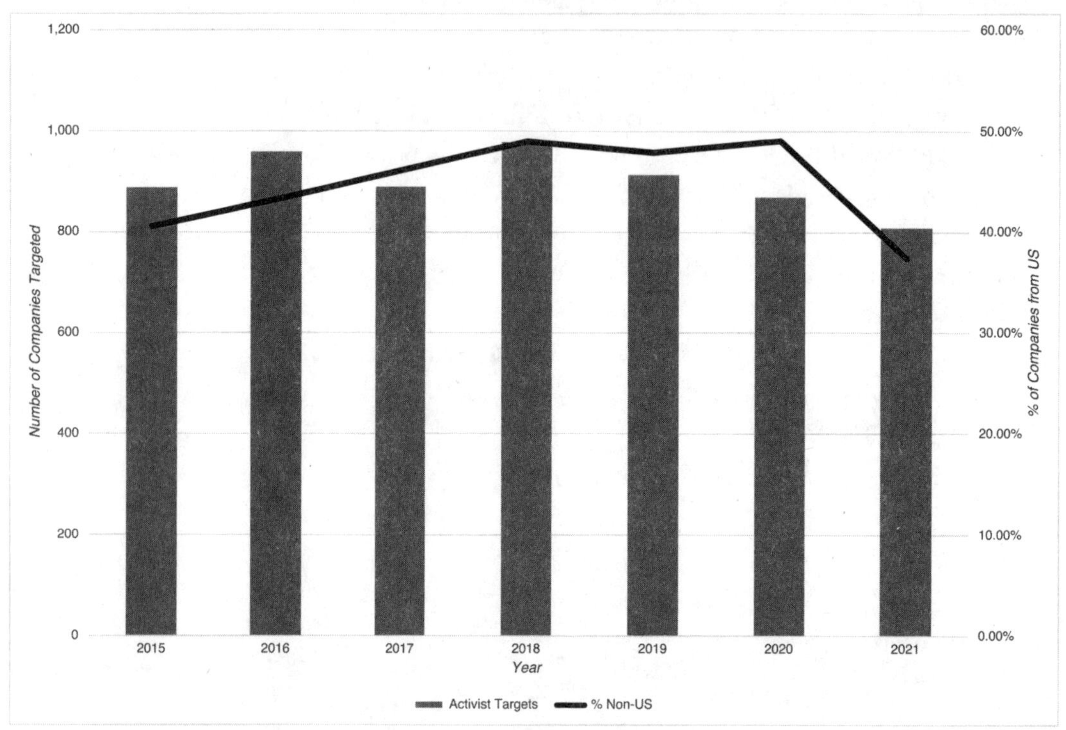

Source: Insightia (2022)

As I will show in the sections to come, activism has developed more sophisticated tools to put pressure on management to change, and management has learned to push back better against activism. In short, activist investing is growing up!

The Right Targets in Buyout and Activist Investing

If activist investors hope to generate returns from changing the way companies are run, they should target poorly managed companies for their campaigns. Institutional and individual activists do seem to follow the script, targeting companies that are less profitable and have delivered lower returns than their peer group, but private equity seems to have a different focus.

Let us start with the research on the typical firms, in public markets, that are targeted for buyouts. Starting in the 1980s, the target firms in leveraged buyouts have been studied with the intent of unearthing the primary motives for these buyout deals. While there is nothing resembling overwhelming consensus in these studies, there are a few characteristics that these targeted firms seem to share:

1. **Free cash flows:** Given that many buyouts are funded with debt, it should come as no surprise that one of the common characteristics across target firms in buyouts is large positive free cash flows from operations that can be used to service and pay down debt.
2. **Cheap prices:** While the objective in a buyout may be to fix up a poorly run firm and flip it back to the market at a much higher price, private equity firms improve their odds of high returns if they can acquire target firms at low prices. Targeted firms in leveraged buyouts commonly trade at lower pricing multiples, with enterprise value to EBITDA among the more widely used metrics. Since companies become cheap after extended periods of market underperformance, many of the targeted firms have also underperformed their peer group in the years leading in to the buyout.
3. **Potential for operating improvement:** One simple, and flawed, measure of the potential for operating improvement is a comparison of the operating margins or returns on invested capital of the targeted firm to that of its peer group, and the evidence is supportive of the notion that companies that lag their peer group in profitability and investment returns are more likely to be targeted in buyouts.

Early in the buyout boom, in the 1980s and the early 1990s, private equity and targeted managers were often on opposite sides of the deal, and many buyouts were hostile acquisitions. Later studies indicate changes in both the LBO process and in targeting, finding managers in targeted firms cooperating with private equity funds in buyouts.

The research on the types of firms that are targeted by activist investors for change seems to find more consensus on motives and targeting, though the results seem to vary depending upon whether you are looking at activist hedge funds or individual activists:

- A study of 888 campaigns mounted by activist hedge funds between 2001 and 2005 finds that typical target companies are small- to mid-cap companies, have above-average market liquidity, trade at low price to book value ratios, are profitable with solid cash flows, and pay their CEOs more than other companies in their peer group.
- Another study of the motives of activist hedge funds uncovered that their primary motive is undervaluation, as evidenced in figure 17.4.*

* A. Brav, W. Jiang, and H. Kim, "Hedge Fund Activism: A Review," Columbia Business School Research Archive, 2010, accessed November 28, 2023, https://business.columbia.edu/faculty/research/hedge-fund-activism-review.

FIGURE 17.4 | Motives behind Targeting in Buyouts

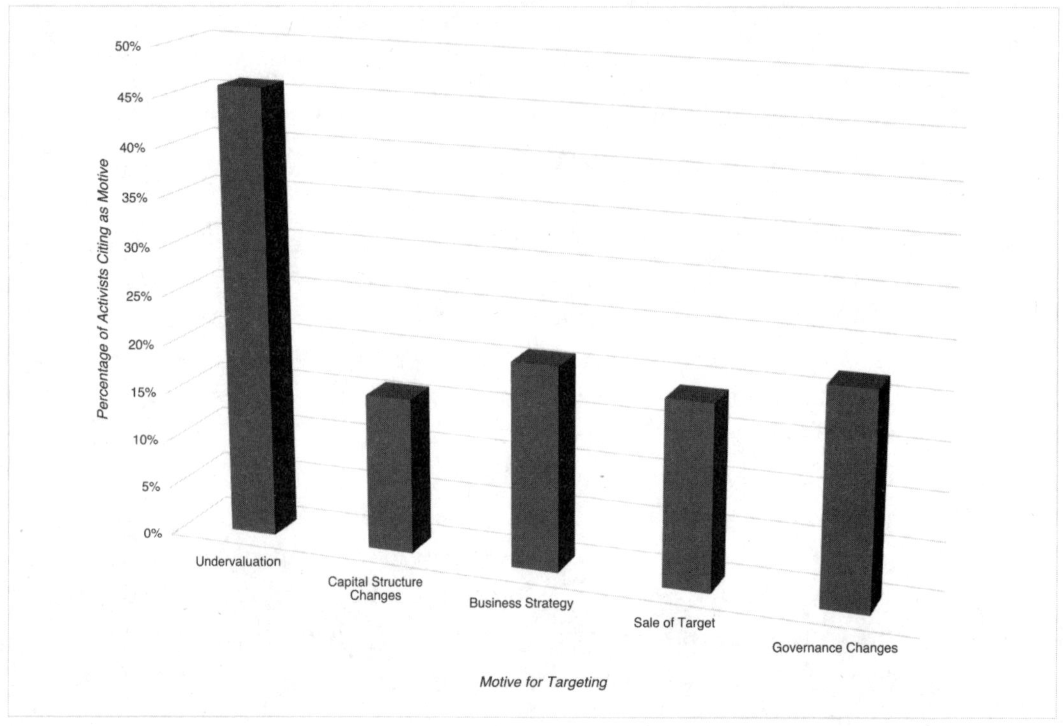

Source: Brav, Jiang, and Kim (2010); some firms cite more than one motive

In summary, the typical activist hedge fund behaves more like a passive value investor, looking for undervalued companies, than like an activist investor, looking for poorly managed companies. Activist individuals are more likely to target poorly managed companies and push for change.

- While activism occurs across sectors and market-cap classes, you should expect to see it more focused on sectors that are aging and where companies are having trouble growing and maintaining margins, as well as on smaller companies, where acquiring a large equity stake costs less and change is more deliverable. Table 17.2 provides a breakdown of firms targeted by activists in recent years, by sector and market cap.

Table 17.2 • Private Equity Targets, by Sector and Market Cap, 2018–2021

Activist Targets (by Sector)			
Sector	**2018**	**2019**	**2020**
Basic Materials	9%	11%	9%
Communication Services	3%	4%	3%
Consumer Cyclical	16%	15%	13%
Consumer Defensive	5%	6%	4%
Energy	6%	5%	4%
Financial Services	11%	12%	13%
Investment Funds	3%	5%	5%
Health Care	10%	10%	10%
Industrials	17%	14%	18%
Real Estate	5%	4%	5%
Technology	11%	12%	12%
Utilities	3%	3%	4%
Activist Targets (by Market Cap)			
	2018	**2019**	**2020**
Large Cap (>$10 Bil)	23%	21%	27%
Mid Cap ($2—$10 Bil)	17%	18%	16%
Small Cap ($250 Mil—$2 Bil)	23%	24%	25%
Micro Cap ($50—$250 Mil)	18%	19%	18%
Nano Cap (< $50 Mil)	18%	18%	14%

The numbers are surprising, insofar as the targeted companies cut across sectors, and a surprisingly large number are companies with larger market caps.

What Do Private Equity Firms and Activists Do at (or to) These Targeted Companies?

Let us start with buyouts and examine the changes that private equity firms make to target companies after they take them private. The evidence will make neither advocates nor critics of PE happy. The early studies of buyouts indicated value creation from both the use of debt (and the resultant tax savings) and improved operations, but later studies have provided more mixed results, especially on operating improvements.

- **Asset deployment:** Critics accuse private equity firms of being asset strippers who hollow out target companies by selling assets and starving them of new investments. While that undoubtedly occurs in some buyouts, there is little evidence of this rapacious behavior, at least in the aggregate. Research on buyouts indicates that firms that are bought out by private equity investors reduce capital expenditures only marginally and do not cut back on R&D or other investments. Rather than extract capital from target firms and shrink them, private equity investors seem more likely to redeploy capital from non-core businesses back into core or new businesses.

- **Profitability:** If private equity firms target companies with inefficient operations, and the changes do make a difference in operating efficiency, you should expect to see improvement in operating metrics, such as operating profit margins, after buyouts. The early studies* of LBOs found evidence that target firms improve operating profitability after buyouts, as you can see in table 17.3:

Table 17.3 • Percentage Change in Operating Income & Margins at Buyout firms

	Operating Income		Operating Margin	
YEAR	Buyout firms	Adjusted for Industry	Buyout firms	Adjusted for Industry
-2 to -1	11.40%	-1.20%	-1.70%	-1.90%
-1 to +1	15.60%	-2.70%	7.10%	12.40%
-1 to +2	30.70%	0.70%	11.90%	23.30%
-1 to +3	42.00%	24.10%	19.30%	34.80%

Source: Kaplan (1989), from a sample of 48 buyouts, 1980–1986

In this study, which looked at 48 buyouts from 1980 to 1986, firms that were bought out experienced much larger percentage increases in operating income and margins in the three years after buyouts than the rest of the industry. That evidence, though, has been contested in later studies, which found little difference in operating metrics at firms that were bought out relative to benchmark firms in the sector. In a 2014 study that looked at 192 buyouts completed between 1990 and 2006, the gains in operating performance at the bought-out firms were matched or exceeded by benchmark firms that were not bought out, and much of the value creation at bought-out firms came from increasing leverage.†

* S. Kaplan, "The Effects of Management Buyouts on Operating Performance and Value," *Journal of Financial Economics* 24, no. 2 (1989): 217–54.

† S. Guo, E. Hotchkiss, and W. Song, "Do Buyouts (Still) Create Value?" *Journal of Finance* 66, no. 2 (April 2011): 479–517.

- **Financial leverage**: Since many buyouts are funded disproportionately with debt, the debt loads at targeted firms jump after a buyout, as can be seen in table 17.4:*

Table 17.4 • Debt to Total Assets at Buyout Firms

	Excess CF LBOs		Cash Shortfall LBOs		All Firms	
Year	Mean	Median	Mean	Median	Mean	Median
Year -2	45.30%	40.00%	48.80%	41.70%	47.50%	41.00%
Year -1	41.30%	40.80%	46.80%	44.10%	44.70%	43.20%
Year of LBO	73.10%	69.50%	75.80%	77.50%	74.80%	75.40%
Year +1	74.80%	69.60%	76.70%	78.70%	76.00%	77.60%
Year +2	80.00%	76.00%	84.50%	77.60%	82.70%	77.50%

Source: Cohn, Mills, and Towery (2014), from a study of 317 LBOs, 1995–2007

Note the jump in debt ratios in the year of the buyouts, which is to be expected, but note also that debt ratios stay elevated in the years after the buyout, which cuts again a prevailing belief that debt gets paid down quickly in the years soon after buyouts are done. This additional debt brings with it tax benefits, and the value created by these tax benefits represents a significant part of the value creation in most leveraged buyouts, but it does increase distress risk at the targeted firm and the likelihood of default.

- **Dividends and cash return**: The buyout itself represents a significant return on cash to shareholders in the pre-buyout firm, but there are some who fear that PE investors pay themselves large dividends right after they take over target firms. The evidence suggests that special dividends remain rare. A study of 788 private equity targets, tracked from 1993 to 2009, found only 42 instances of special dividends paid to PE investors.

In summary, in most buyouts, private equity investors deliver on the promise of change, but more so on the capital structure front, by increasing debt to harvest tax benefits, than when it comes to improved operations. To the extent that these investors get their biggest returns on those companies that they can relist on markets as public com-

* J. B. Cohn, L. F. Mills, and E. M. Towery, "The Evolution of Capital Structure and Operating Performance after Leveraged Buyouts: Evidence for US Corporate Tax Returns," *Journal of Financial Economics* 111, no. 2 (February 2014): 469–94.

panies, there is a basis for believing that the payoff in many buyouts comes as much from timing deals well as it does from real changes made to companies.

Let's move on to activist investing. The essence of the approach is challenging incumbent management, but on what dimensions is the challenge mounted, and how successfully? A 2013 study of 1,164 activist investing campaigns between 2000 and 2007 documents the demands that activists make at companies and the success rate of each one (see table 17.5):*

Table 17.5 • Activist Demands and Success Rates

Activist Demand	# Campaigns	% of Sample	% Success Rate
Strategic and Operating Changes			
Sale of company to third party	159	31.55%	32.08%
Operating restructuring	69	13.69%	34.78%
Convert to private (from public)	52	10.52%	40.38%
Capital Structure and Dividend Policy			
More dividends & buybacks	78	15.48%	16.67%
Increase debt load	22	4.37%	31.82%
M&A			
Back out of announced merger	63	12.50%	28.57%
Corporate Governance			
Remove CEO, separate CEO from board chair	27	5.36%	18.52%
Reduce executive compensation	20	3.97%	15.00%
Increase disclosure	14	2.78%	35.71%

As you can see, activist demands range from changes in operations to increased disclosure, and the rate of success varies substantially across demands. In addition, the paper also presents some interesting facts about activism:

1. The failure rate in activist investing is very high, with two thirds of activist investors quitting before making any formal demands of the target.
2. Among those activist investors who persist, less than 20% request a board seat, about 10% threaten a proxy fight, and only 7% carry through on that threat.
3. Activists who push through and make demands of managers are most successful (success % rate in parentheses next to each action) when they demand the taking private of a target (41%), the sale of a target (32%), restructuring of inefficient oper-

* N. Gantchev, "The Costs of Shareholder Activism: Evidence from a Sequential Decision Model," *Journal of Financial Economics* 107, no. 3 (March 2013): 610–31.

ations (35%), or additional disclosure (36%). They are least successful when they ask for higher dividends/buybacks (17%), removal of the CEO (19%), or executive compensation changes (15%). Overall, activists succeed about 29% of the time in their demands of management.

This paper also finds that the median holding for an activist hedge fund is about 7%, with little difference between friendly and hostile campaigns. Thus, most activist hedge funds try to change management practices with relatively small holdings, and they have average holding periods of about two years, though the median is much lower (about 250 days).

As with buyouts, looking at companies that have been targeted and sometimes controlled by activist investors, I can classify the changes that they make into four groups as potential value enhancement measures:

- **Asset deployment and operating performance:** There is mixed evidence on this count, depending upon the type of activist investor group looked at and the period. Divestitures of assets do pick up after activist investment in targeted firms, albeit not dramatically. There is evidence that firms targeted by individual activists do see an improvement in return on capital and other profitability measures relative to their peer groups, whereas firms targeted by hedge fund activists don't see a similar jump in profitability measures.
- **Capital structure:** On financial leverage, there is a moderate increase (about 10%) in debt ratios at firms that are targeted by activist hedge funds, but the increase is not dramatic, nor is it statistically significant. There are dramatic increases in financial leverage at a small subset of firms that are targets of activism, but the conventional wisdom that activist investors go overboard in their use of debt is not borne out in the overall sample. One study does note a troubling phenomenon, at least for bond holders in targeted firms, with bond prices dropping about 3% to 5% in the years after firms are targeted by activists, as well as a higher likelihood of bond rating downgrades.
- **Dividend policy:** The firms that are targeted by activists generally increase their dividends and return more cash to stockholders, with the cash returned as a percentage of earnings increasing by about 10% to 20%.
- **Corporate governance:** The biggest effect of activist investing is on corporate governance. The likelihood of CEO turnover jumps at firms that have been targeted by activists, increasing 5.5% over the year prior to the activism. In addition, CEO compensation decreases in the targeted firms in the years after the activism, with pay tied more closely to performance.

In sum, private equity investors push for change at the companies they target, but many seem to settle for too little or give up too soon. Only a small subset of activist investors has the wherewithal and the stomach to stay engaged with incumbent managers to create real change at companies.

Do Private Equity Firms and Activist Investors Make High Returns?

After this long lead-in on buyouts and activist investors, you are probably wondering whether private equity firms and activist investors make higher returns than public-market investors.

PRIVATE EQUITY

To look at whether private equity collectively generates excess return for its investors, I looked at the annual returns to private equity and compared them to returns on public equities, in figure 17.5.

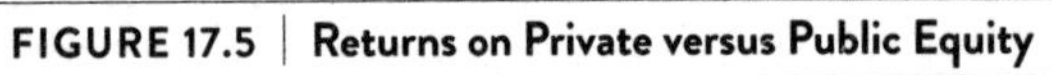

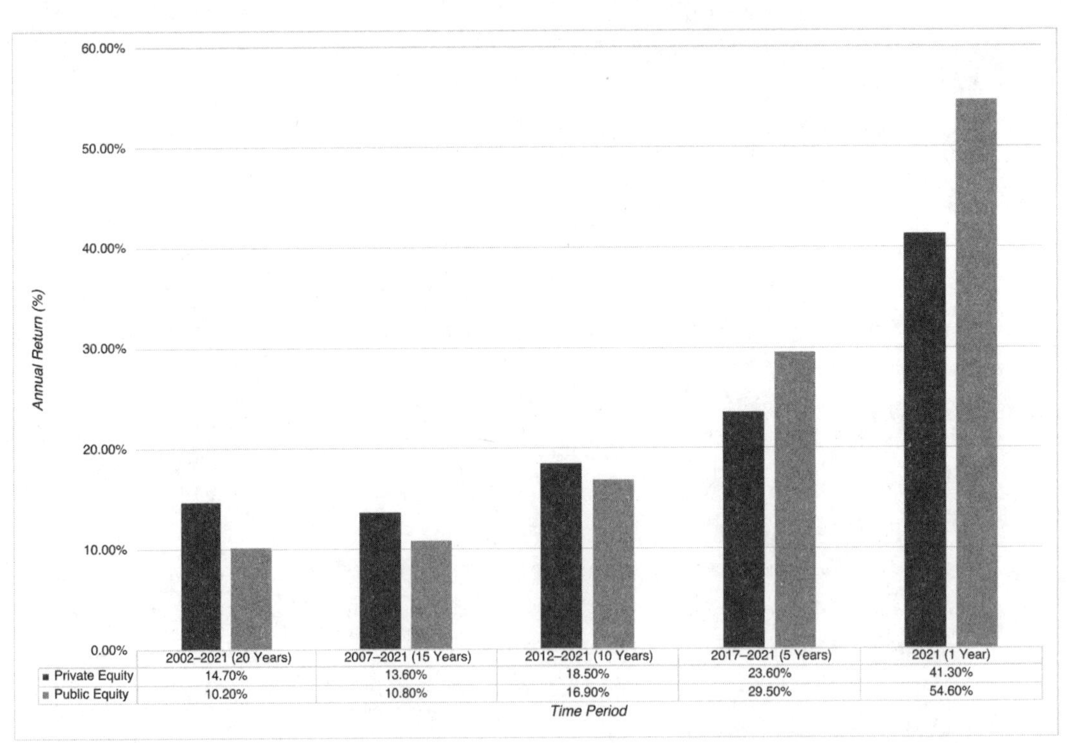

	2002–2021 (20 Years)	2007–2021 (15 Years)	2012–2021 (10 Years)	2017–2021 (5 Years)	2021 (1 Year)
■ Private Equity	14.70%	13.60%	18.50%	23.60%	41.30%
■ Public Equity	10.20%	10.80%	16.90%	29.50%	54.60%

As you can see, private equity has outperformed public equity over longer periods, ranging from 10 to 20 years, but has underperformed public equity in recent years. In fact, there is evidence that any excess returns that private equity investors may have posted, especially in their early years of existence, have been eroded as the private equity space has become more crowded and competitive. A 2015 study of buyout fund returns reinforces this conclusion, noting that while buyout funds earned almost 3% to 4% more than public equity funds prior to 2005, those excess returns have faded, putting them on par with public equity since. You can see this effect in figure 17.6, graphing alphas on private equity, relative to the S&P 500.*

FIGURE 17.6 | Excess Returns (Alphas) for Private Equity versus S&P 500, 1993–2015

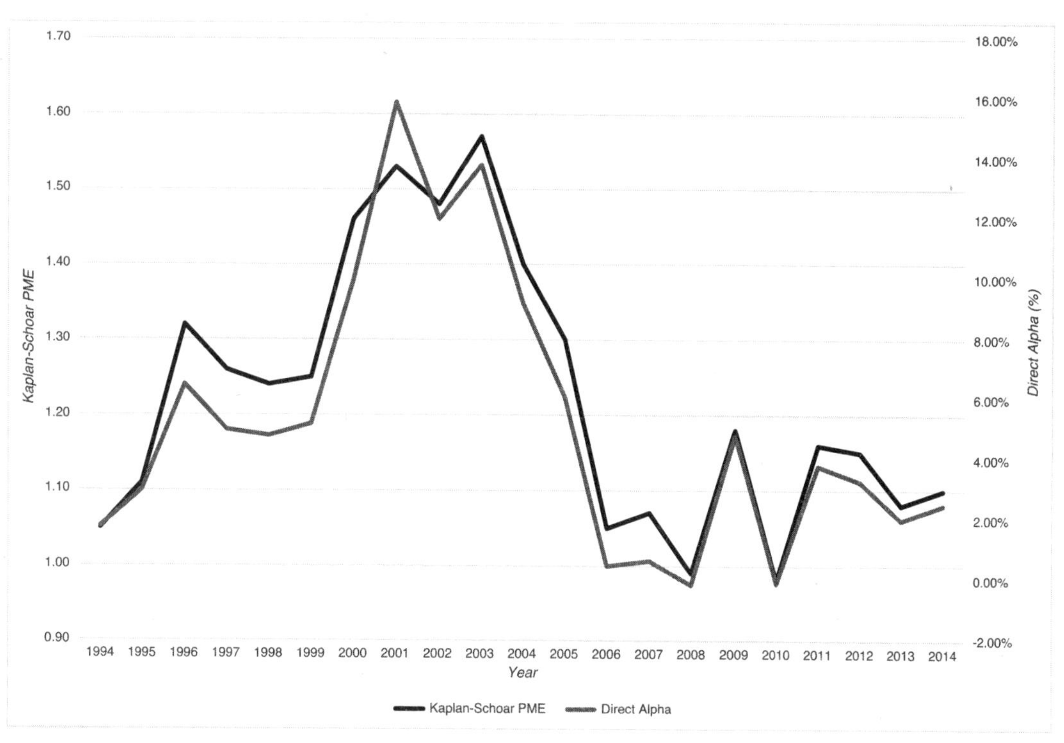

Source: Brown and Kaplan, 2019

This is, of course, across all private equity investors, and it is possible that, as in venture capital, the best private equity funds have done much better and done so more con-

* G. W. Brown and S. N. Kaplan, "Have Private Equity Returns Really Declined?," *Journal of Private Equity*, no. 22 (2019): 11–18.

sistently than the averages suggest. Again, the research seems to suggest that while private equity investors showed evidence of persistence, with winners continuing to win, in the pre-2000 data, that persistence has largely disappeared since 2000.* As you assess private equity returns, it is worth noting that these returns are based upon assessed values for non-traded investments in their portfolios and, as with returns reported by venture capitalists, there is reason to be cautious about accepting these figures at face value.

ACTIVIST INVESTING

The overall evidence on whether activist investors make money is mixed and varies depending upon which group of activist investors are studied and how returns are measured.

1. Activist mutual funds seem to have had the lowest payoff to their activism, with little change accruing to the corporate governance, performance, or stock prices of targeted firms. Markets seem to recognize this, with studies that have examined proxy fights finding that there is little or no stock price reaction to proxy proposals by activist institutional investors. Activist hedge funds, on the other hand, seem to earn substantial excess returns, ranging from 7% to 8% on an annualized basis at the low end to 20% or more at the high end. Individual activists seem to fall somewhere in the middle, earning higher returns than institutions but lower returns than hedge funds.
2. While the average excess return earned by hedge funds and individual activists is positive, there is substantial volatility in these returns, and the magnitude of the excess return is sensitive to the benchmark used and the risk adjustment process. Put in less abstract terms, activist investors frequently suffer setbacks in their campaigns, and the payoff is neither guaranteed nor predictable.

Targeting the right firms, acquiring stock in these companies, demanding board representation, and conducting proxy contests are all expensive, and the returns made across the targeted firms must exceed the costs of activism. While none of the studies that I have referenced hitherto factored these costs, one study that did concluded that the cost of an activist campaign at an average firm was $10.71 million, and that the net return to activist investing, if these costs are considered, shrinks toward zero. The average return across activist investors obscures a key factor, which is that the distribution is skewed, with the most positive returns being delivered by the activist investors in the top quartile; the me-

* R. S. Harris, T. Jenkinson, S. N. Kaplan, and R. Stucke, "Has Persistence Persisted in Private Equity? Evidence from Buyout and Venture Capital Funds," Working Paper, SSRN #2304808, 2020.

dian activist investor may very well just break even, especially after accounting for the cost of activism.

No matter what you think about activist investing as a source of excess returns, if you are a stockholder in a publicly traded company, the entry of an activist investor into your stockholder ranks is good news, since stock prices go up substantially on the announcement of a buyout and continue their drift upward. Figure 17.7 is from a study of the returns on activist investing, and it provides a measure of how a target company's stock responds to announcements of an activist campaign, usually in the form of a filing (13D) with the SEC.*

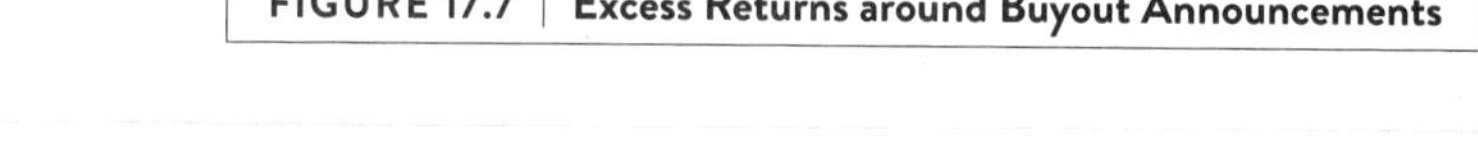
FIGURE 17.7 | Excess Returns around Buyout Announcements

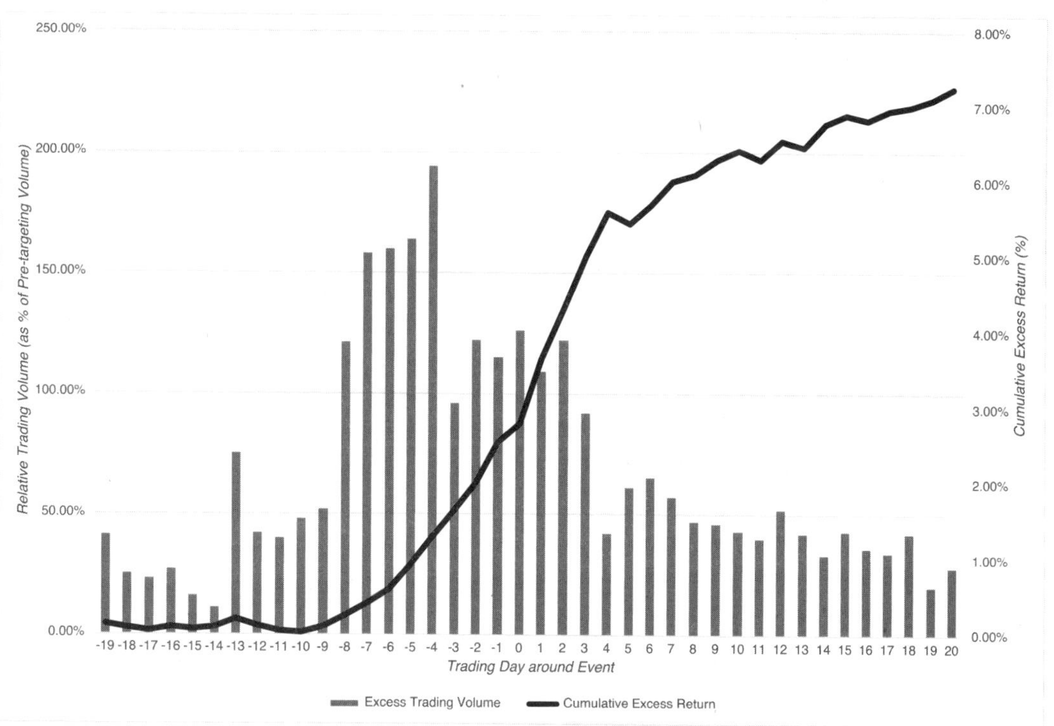

Note that not only do stock prices jump on the 13D filing—effectively the time when markets become aware of activist activity—they also drift up in the days before and after

* A. Brav, W. Jiang, F. Partnoy, and R. Thomas, "Returns to Hedge Fund Activism," *Financial Analysts Journal* 64, no. 6 (November/December 2008): 45–61.

that date; the drift in the days before is perhaps indicative of insider trading and the drift after an effect of momentum trading. In the same paper, the researchers examine the returns to activism by comparing the returns earned on activist hedge funds to returns on all hedge funds and on public equity. The results are in figure 17.8.

FIGURE 17.8 | Returns on Activist Hedge Funds, 1995–2007

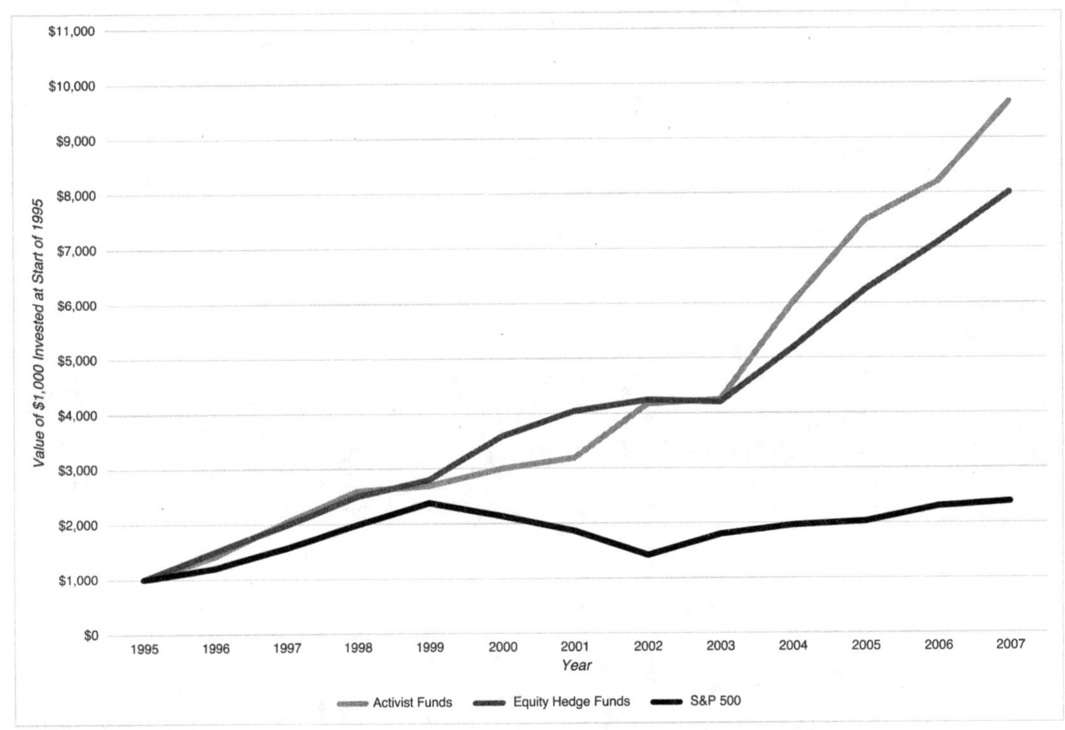

The cumulative payoff from investing in activist hedge funds exceeds the returns on hedge funds overall, and public equity returns lag both.

As a final note, I should say that as with venture capital, there is some evidence that the very best activist investors earn higher returns than the average and can do so consistently. A study of activist investing campaigns between 2008 and 2014 documents that hedge funds that acquire a reputation for clout and expertise, based upon their demonstrated ability to not only target the right firms but also have the staying power to force changes at those firms, have much bigger price impacts when they target new firms and earn higher returns from their targeting.[*]

Vulture Investing

Private equity and activist investors focus on changing the way their targeted companies are run, and this search leads them to look more frequently at mature and declining companies, but there is another group of investors that are drawn to these same companies, albeit with different motives. Rather than try to change the way their target companies operate and are funded, this group looks for companies that they believe are worth more liquidated or broken up and tries to profit by pushing for those actions.

What Is Vulture Investing?

Vulture investors come in many forms, but what they share is an affinity for investing or trading in declining and distressed companies, with the belief that these investments can deliver high risk-adjusted returns. Below are several common types of vulture investors.

1. **Liquidators:** In chapter 13, where I valued distressed and declining companies, I noted that the values of some of these companies as going concerns, run by management in denial, can be lower than the values of their assets in liquidation. There are investors who notice this disparity, target these companies for acquisition and, once acquired, liquidate them. If they are right in their initial judgment—i.e., that the company's liquidation value is greater than its going-concern value—and can pay a price that is less than the liquidation proceeds, they will keep the difference. There are three challenges that they face in delivering on this premise. First, they may be wrong in their initial assessment about going-concern value being less than liquidation value. Second, even if they are right in their initial assessment, they may push up share prices as they acquire the company, so much that they leave themselves no surplus value. Third, the liquidation process can be costly and time-consuming, and waiting too long to liquidate or accepting too much of a liquidation discount can also wipe out excess returns.

[*] C. N. V. Krishnan, F. Partnoy, and R. S. Thomas, "The Second Wave of Hedge Fund Activism: The Importance of Reputation, Clout, and Expertise," *Journal of Corporate Finance* 40 (October 2016): 296–314.

2. **Break-up specialists:** Break-up specialists start with the same premise as liquidators do—i.e., that their targeted companies should not continue as going concerns—but rather than liquidate assets, they aim to split up, break up, or spin off the company into smaller parts, each of which continues to operate as a going concern. Success in this approach lies, again, in targeting the right companies, but also requires making the right judgments on whether to spin off, split off, or divest businesses.
3. **Traders:** This group of vulture investors includes those who believe that while declining companies may face a dark future, there are trading profits to be made during decline and distress. In some cases, those profits can come from understanding the legal process of bankruptcy and the restructuring of companies that occurs around the process, and trading ahead of the market on developments in both, either on equity or on debt. In other cases, trading profits can come from trading different securities issued by a declining company that you believe are being mispriced relative to each other. Thus, if a declining company has stocks, bonds, and convertible bonds that are outstanding and trading, you may be able to assess the pricing of these securities and create close-to-riskless positions by going long on the underpriced and selling short on the overpriced securities.

Trends in Vulture Investing

To get a measure of how many investors follow the liquidation route, you can start by looking at all corporate liquidations, but many of these liquidations are forced liquidations driven by bankruptcies, where courts oversee timing and the liquidation process. It is voluntary corporate liquidations—i.e., companies that choose to liquidate their assets on their own, rather than due to legal or lender pressure—that are at the heart of liquidation investing, and there is reason to believe that the subcategory ebbs and flows over time with overall liquidations. As for spin-offs and split-offs, the statistics are cleaner, and figure 17.9 summarizes the number of spin-offs, by year, from 2008 to 2021.

FIGURE 17.9 | Number of Global Spinoffs, by Year, 2008–2021

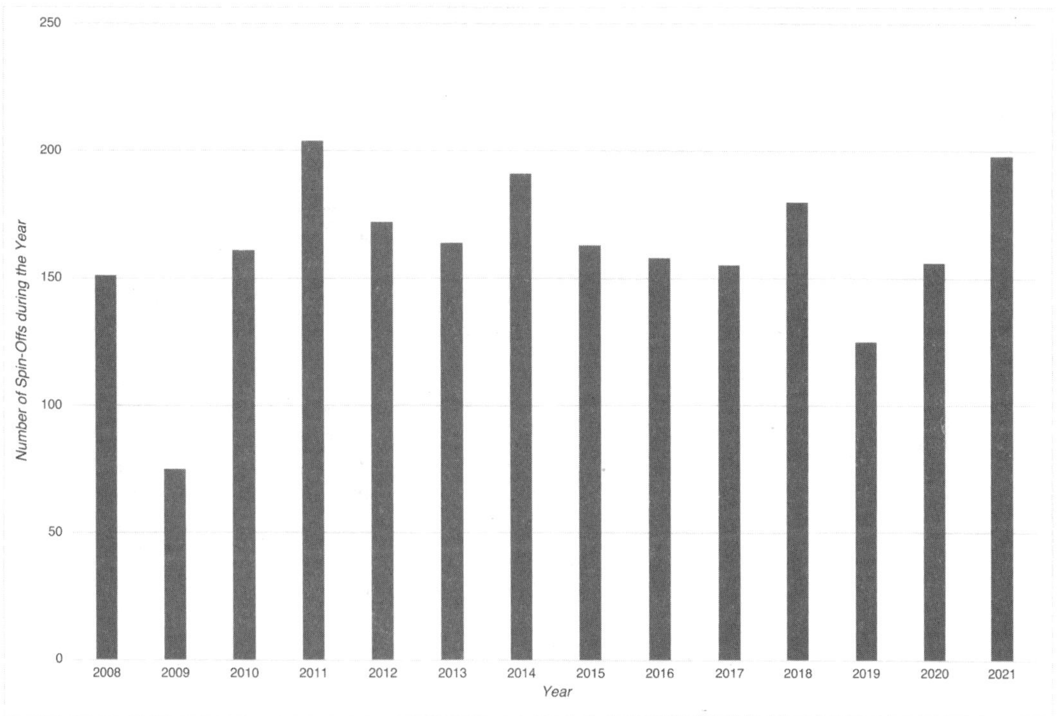

There are many high-profile companies on the list of recent spin-off participants, with diverse motives for doing so. For some, like Altria Group, which spun off its food unit (Kraft Heinz), it was concerns about one business (tobacco) contaminating another. For others, like HP, it was an attempt to reclaim a pathway to growth, in the face of growth and profitability challenges that it faced as a company. For a few, like Dell, the spin-off (in this case, of VMware) was an attempt to capture the high pricing that was being attached by investors to the business being spun off.

On the trading front, where investors buy or sell short debt and equity in distressed companies, the market for those securities, especially on the debt side, has grown significantly over the last few years, with original issuances of high-yield debt supplementing seasoned bonds that have slipped into distress. Figure 17.10 provides a picture of the different components of low-rated corporate debt across the years.

FIGURE 17.10 | Growth of Low-Rated Corporate Debt Market

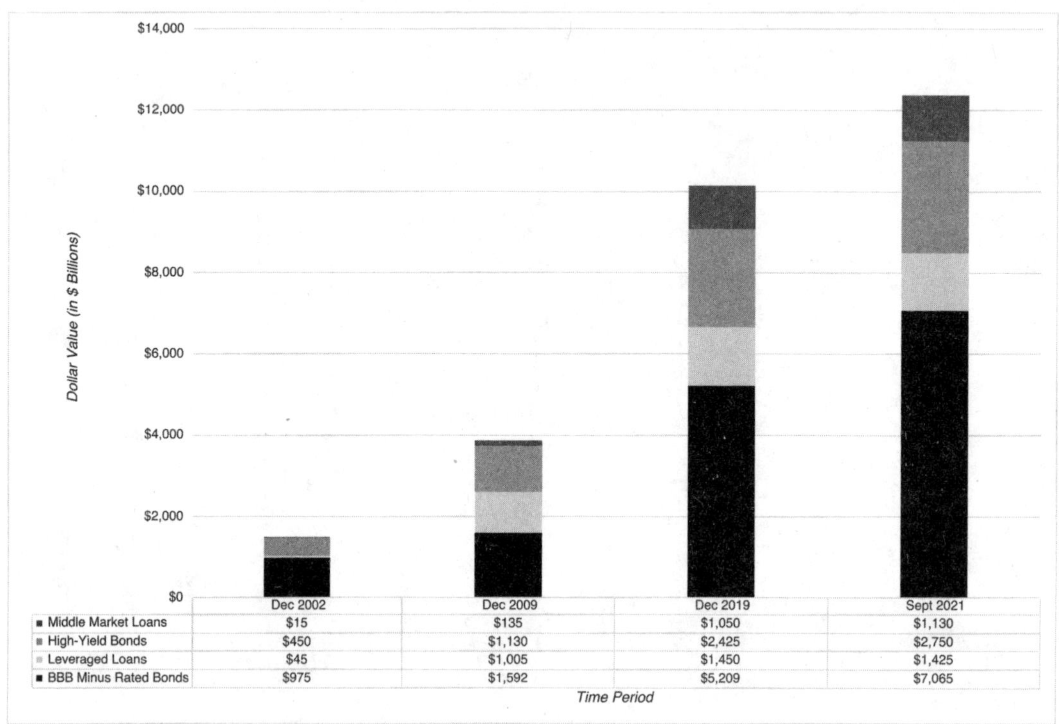

	Dec 2002	Dec 2009	Dec 2019	Sept 2021
Middle Market Loans	$15	$135	$1,050	$1,130
High-Yield Bonds	$450	$1,130	$2,425	$2,750
Leveraged Loans	$45	$1,005	$1,450	$1,425
BBB Minus Rated Bonds	$975	$1,592	$5,209	$7,065

As the potential market for distressed debt trading has grown, so have the funds intended for this market. Figure 17.11 summarizes the assets under management (AUM) that distressed funds had from 2000 to 2020.

FIGURE 17.11 | Assets under Management at Distressed Debt Funds, 2000–2020

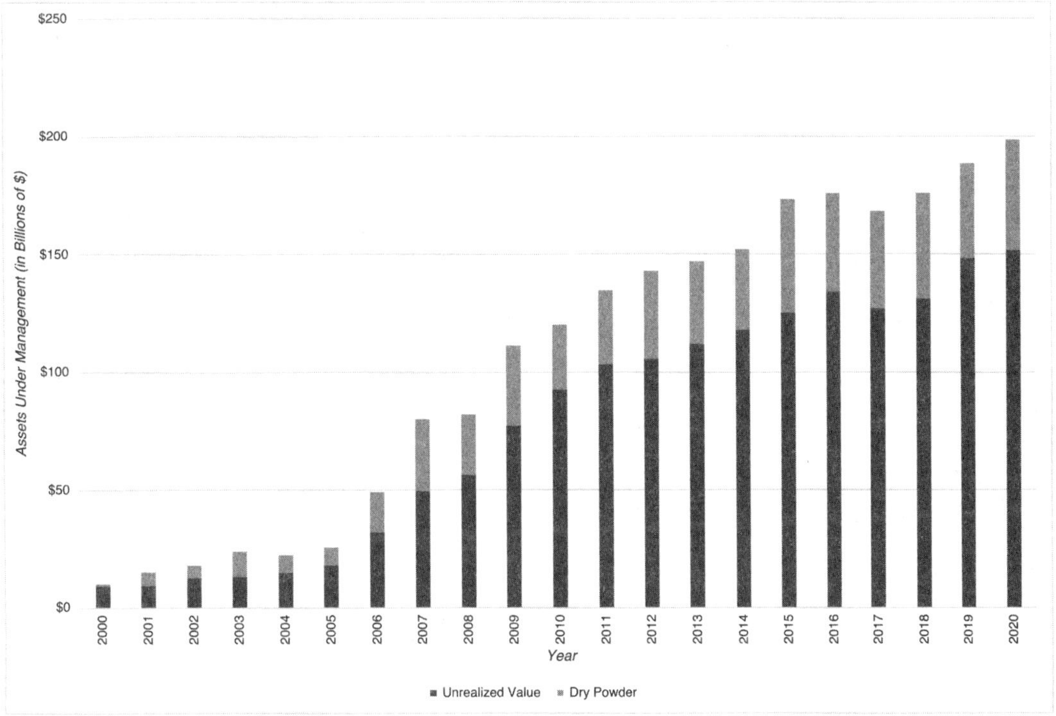

In sum, vulture investing, in all its forms, has seen growth over the last decade, but with a diverse set of actors playing for different end games.

Modus Operandi

Following the corporate life cycle, I noted that investing in start-up and very young companies is seldom passive, and that venture capital investors, in addition to providing capital to firms, also must provide support and advice as companies struggle to create working business models. As you move through the life cycle, and more firms become publicly traded, you can invest more passively, finding stocks that are cheap and buying and holding them. In the declining phase of the life cycle, the investing strategies described once again require more activism, since the changes that you are pushing for, whether it be in operations and capital structure, as a private equity firm, or liquidation and spin-offs, as a "vulture," will not happen without investors asserting their power.

LIQUIDATION (VOLUNTARY)

If your end game is to liquidate a firm because you believe that its liquidation value exceeds it going-concern value, there is a sequence to follow after you have gained control of the company.

1. First, the board of directors will have to assent to the liquidation; once consent is received, a liquidator is appointed.
2. The liquidator sells the assets in the market for cash and equivalents and usually has the legal power to act on behalf of the company.
3. Once the assets have been liquidated, the liquidator will follow the order of obligations, starting with the most senior debt first, then subordinated debt and mezzanine financing. The residual cash goes to equity investors.

The keys to profiting from this strategy follow this sequence. First, as you acquire the target firm, you must ensure that you do not bid up the price to a level that is higher than liquidation value—an obvious requirement, but one that is often difficult to meet in practice. The second key is that costs associated with liquidation, including any discounts that you may have to offer for speedier asset sales and taxes due, must be controlled to leave you with excess profits. Finally, liquidation investing is more likely to succeed when the target company's assets are more liquid to begin with, and when the market value of the distressed company is much lower than the liquidation value of what it owns.

SPIN-OFFS AND SPLIT-UPS

The other action that investors targeting declining firms take is to push for spinning off some or a large portion of the company's businesses, or splitting up the company into its parts, with the expectation that these actions will unearth hidden value. To understand the choice among a spin-off, a split-off, and a split-up, I will delineate what they share, as well as the differences across these actions:

a. **Spin-off:** In a spin-off, the parent company takes a portion of its business (a subsidiary, a geography, etc.) and creates an independent company with a stand-alone governance structure. The shareholders in the parent company receive a proportional shareholding in the spun-off entity.
b. **Split-off:** A split-off follows the same script as a spin-off, in terms of the parent company creating an independent company that owns a portion of its business. How-

ever, shareholders in the parent company are then given a choice of exchanging their shares in the parent company for the split-off company's shares or staying on as shareholders in just the parent company.

c. **Split-up:** In a split-up, the parent company is broken down into two or more entities and the parent company is liquidated, with its shareholders receiving shares in the new entities that emerge.

Put simply, the most significant differences across spin-offs, split-offs, and split-ups is in the ownership stakes that parent company shareholders have after the transactions, with tax consequences.

The benefits from breaking up a company, with a spin-off, a split-off, or a split-up, can range the spectrum:

a. **Market mistakes:** The simplest rationale for a breakup is that the market is mistakenly valuing the whole company at less than the sum of its pieces.
b. **Contaminated parts:** One division of a company may be saddled with actual, perceived, or potential liabilities that are so large that they drag down the valuation of the rest of the company. This was the rationale for tobacco companies, faced with potential billion-dollar payouts on lawsuits brought by smokers, spinning off their non-tobacco businesses. In the same vein, a company with a heavily regulated or constrained subsidiary may find that the regulations and constraints on that subsidiary spill over into its other businesses, rendering them less profitable.
c. **The efficiency story:** In the 1960s and 1970s, some companies were built to span multiple businesses, on the presumption that conglomerates would have significant advantages over their smaller competitors. Studies over the last three decades suggest that this optimism was misplaced and that conglomerates are often less efficient than competitors, earning lower returns and profit margins. If multi-business companies are less well-run than the competition, perhaps because managers are spread too thin across businesses or because there is cross-subsidization, then breaking them up into their individual businesses should increase efficiency, profits, and value.
d. **The simplicity story:** Multi-business companies are not only more difficult to manage, they are also more difficult to value. With companies like GE and United Technologies, different businesses within each company can have very different risk, cash flow, and growth characteristics, and coming up with a consolidated number can be cumbersome. In good times, investors may overlook the complexities of valuation,

trust the managers, and value these multi-business companies highly. In bad times, they will not be as charitable and will punish complex companies by discounting their value. Breaking up the companies into bite-sized pieces that are easier to value may increase what investors are willing to pay, especially if you are in a "crisis" market.

e. **The tax story:** When tax codes are complex, companies may be able to lower their tax bills by breaking themselves up. For instance, let us assume that the US government decides to tax all income generated by US corporations, anywhere in the world, at the US corporate tax rate in the year in which the income is generated (rather than when it is repatriated back to the US, as is the current law). Multinationals like GE and Coca-Cola that generate a significant portion of their taxes in foreign locales, with lower tax rates, will be able to lower their tax bill by breaking up into independent domestic (US) and international entities, with different stockholders, managers, and corporate governance structures.

On the other side of the ledger, there are costs to breaking up as well:

a. **Loss of economies of scale:** Combining businesses into a larger company can create cost savings. Thus, a group of consumer product businesses may benefit from being consolidated into one unit, with shared advertising and distribution costs. Breaking up will result in a loss of these savings.
b. **Reduced access to capital (and higher cost):** If external capital markets (stock and bond) are undeveloped or under stress, combining businesses into a consolidated company can provide access to capital. The excess cash flows from cash-rich businesses can be used to finance reinvestment needs in cash-poor businesses.
c. **Lost synergies:** In some multi-business companies, businesses feed off each other's successes, thus making the whole greater than the sum of its parts.

In sum, the payoff to breaking a company down into parts will depend on whether the positives outweigh the negatives.

DISTRESS AND BANKRUPTCY

For investment strategies built around distress and bankruptcy, you need to understand the sequence of events in distress, as shown in figure 17.12.

FIGURE 17.12 | **Distress Sequence**

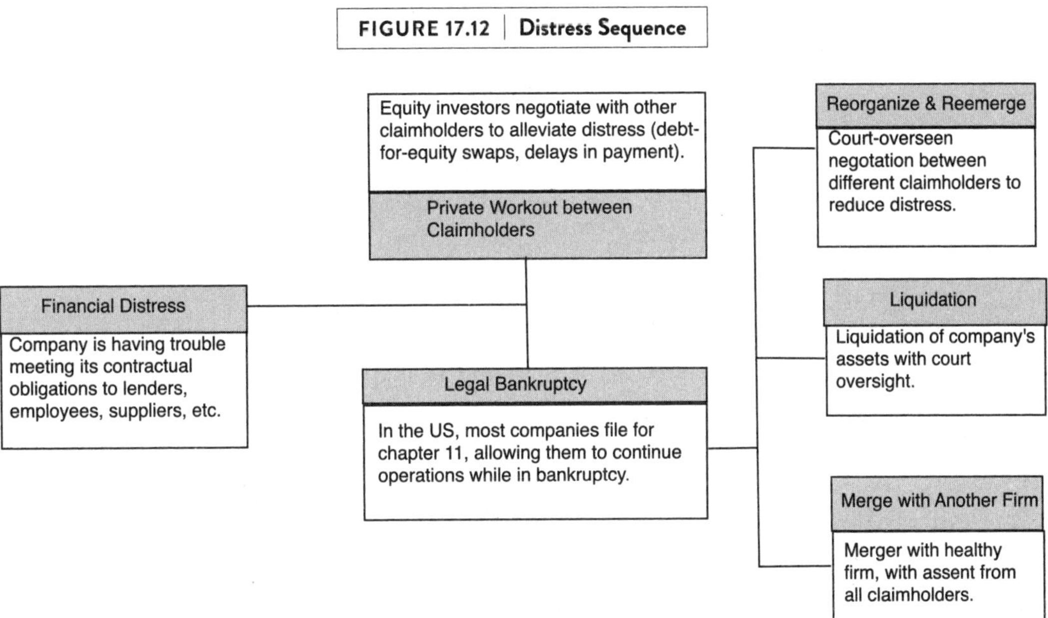

The least painful route for a distressed firm is a financial restructuring that fixes its problems, either in a private workout or as a public company, without court involvement. If the restructuring does not work, the firm must file for bankruptcy, under either chapter 7 (where it must cease operations) or chapter 11 (where it can continue operating, with legal protections but under court supervision) of the US Bankruptcy Code. While chapter 7 is followed by liquidation, here are three possible exit strategies from chapter 11:

a. **Liquidation:** The liquidation process under bankruptcy is similar in structure to a voluntary liquidation, with two potentially significant differences. First, the liquidator is appointed by and answerable to the bankruptcy court, rather than the board of directors or equity investors. Second, court-driven liquidations tend to be more costly, with liquidation costs becoming a bigger drag on proceeds.
b. **Reorganization:** In the aftermath of a bankruptcy filing, the different claimholders in the firm may try to restructure their claims in a way that relieves distress, with the pressure coming from court-driven liquidation being the alternative. Any plan that emerges must be voted on and accepted by creditors, bondholders, and shareholders and confirmed by the court. Ultimately, the court can disregard the vote and still confirm the plan if it finds that the plan treats creditors and stockholders fairly.

c. **Merger**: There is a third option, albeit only in a subset of cases, where a merger with a healthy firm reduces distress in a company or makes it less imminent and allows for an exit from the bankruptcy process.

In the context of this structure, there are four possible pathways that investors can use to generate excess returns:

1. **Operating comeback:** The most painless way out of bankruptcy is a return to operating profitability, perhaps even with growth, at the distressed firm. In some cases, this recovery can be driven by a stronger economy or a sector-wide boom; in others, it can come from changes made at the company that turn operating fortunes around. Investors who buy distressed companies, on the expectation of operating recovery, will benefit if they are right by owning either the company's debt or its equity.
2. **Liquidation/merger valuation:** In cases where an operating comeback is not in the cards, investors in a distressed company can benefit if a liquidation delivers much more in proceeds than expected, or if a potential buyer of the business is willing to pay a premium.
3. **Reorganization sweepstakes:** In both private and court-overseen reorganizations, there will be a restructuring of claims, and some claimholders will be made better off at the expense of others. If you are a claimholder and can find a way to be a beneficiary of a restructuring, you should be able to profit from your claim.
4. **Market mispricing:** When companies are in chapter 11, the securities that they have issued in the market can continue to trade, with investors attaching prices to these securities, reflecting how they expect distress to play out. To the extent that markets make mistakes on their price judgments, traders can exploit these differences by buying underpriced securities or selling short on overpriced securities. In some cases, traders may even be able to lock in the mispricing and deliver guaranteed profits, i.e., arbitrage.

Returns on Vulture Investing

As interest in investing in declining and distressed firms has grown over time, and more funds have followed that interest, it is worth asking whether investors in this group beat, match, or lag the market. The studies that examine this question fall broadly into two groups, with the first examining how shares in companies do around announcements or occurrences of liquidations or spin-offs, and the second looking at the returns earned by investors who are focused on investing in distressed companies.

For an example of the first group of studies, where stock price reactions to events are tracked and recorded, consider how the stock prices of companies react to a spin-off, as in figure 17.13, where researchers looked at all spin-offs between 2010 and 2016.

FIGURE 17.13 | Stock Price Reaction to Spin-Offs

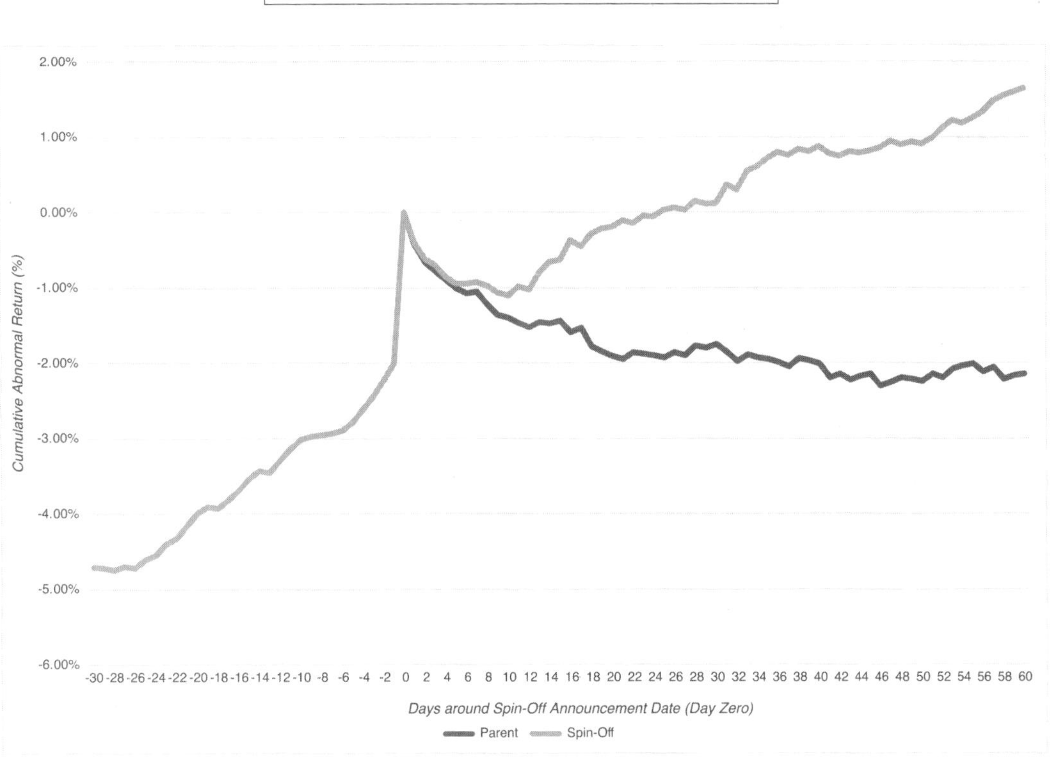

The results are mixed, with the stock price of the spin-off rising, but that of the parent company falling, leaving the parent company shareholders, who receive shares in the spin-off as well, with a wash. Another example is from a study that looks at how stock and bond prices of distressed companies behave around the onset of distress, as seen in figure 17.14.*

* D. Avramov, T. Chordia, G. Jostova, and A. Philipov, "The Distress Anomaly Is Deeper than You Think: Evidence from Stocks and Bonds," *Review of Finance* 26, no. 2 (March 2022): 355–405.

FIGURE 17.14 | **Stock and Bond Prices, around Onset of Distress**

Source: Avramov, Chordia, Jostova, and Philipov (2022)

Not surprisingly, stock and bond prices in the most distressed firms drop ahead of the onset of distress, but they also recover to almost match the returns on the least distressed firms. While that would leave investors for the long term unmoved, it does provide the basis at least for traders to make profits, if they can time their trades in distressed companies well.

In the second group of studies are those that look at the returns that investors focused on distress deliver, relative both to the markets and to investors in healthy firms. Figure 17.15 compares returns generated by hedge funds investing in distressed debt with returns on corporate-bond hedge funds and equity hedge funds over different time periods.

FIGURE 17.15 | Returns on Investing in Distress, 2012–2022

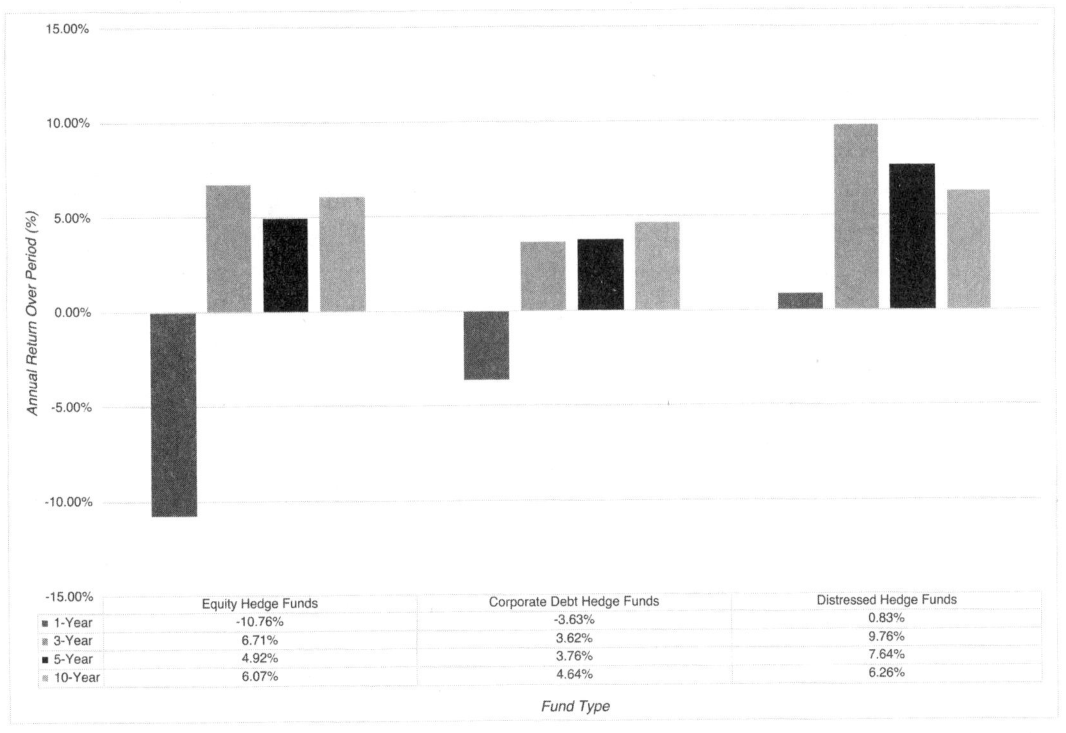

	Equity Hedge Funds	Corporate Debt Hedge Funds	Distressed Hedge Funds
1-Year	-10.76%	-3.63%	0.83%
3-Year	6.71%	3.62%	9.76%
5-Year	4.92%	3.76%	7.64%
10-Year	6.07%	4.64%	6.26%

The results, as you can see, show that distressed-debt hedge funds have outperformed, at least on average, both equity and corporate-debt funds, though the difference narrows as you look at longer time periods.

Conclusion

Declining companies, especially with distress added to the mix, are not appealing businesses, but they can still be good investments for some. In this chapter, I looked at the investors who inhabit this space, starting with private equity funds that target firms that they believe are cheap but need fixing, and then buy them out, fix them, and take them public again. A close variant is activist investors who take stakes in these firms and put pressure on managers to change the way they are run. With both groups, I present evidence that while in the aggregate, these groups make excess returns, those returns have declined over time and are earned by a small subset of each group.

In the second part of the chapter, I focused on investors who target declining and distressed firms with a different end game, starting with liquidators, whose intent is to acquire businesses that they believe are worth more either liquidated or as the sum of their parts than as going concerns. Finally, I looked at companies in distress and bankruptcy, and the traders who try to exploit pricing mistakes or frictions in the bankruptcy process for profits. From an investing standpoint, the evidence on whether this group of investors makes money remains mixed, with excess returns accruing often to the subset of these investors who have an edge in the legal arena, where many of these companies end up in liquidation.

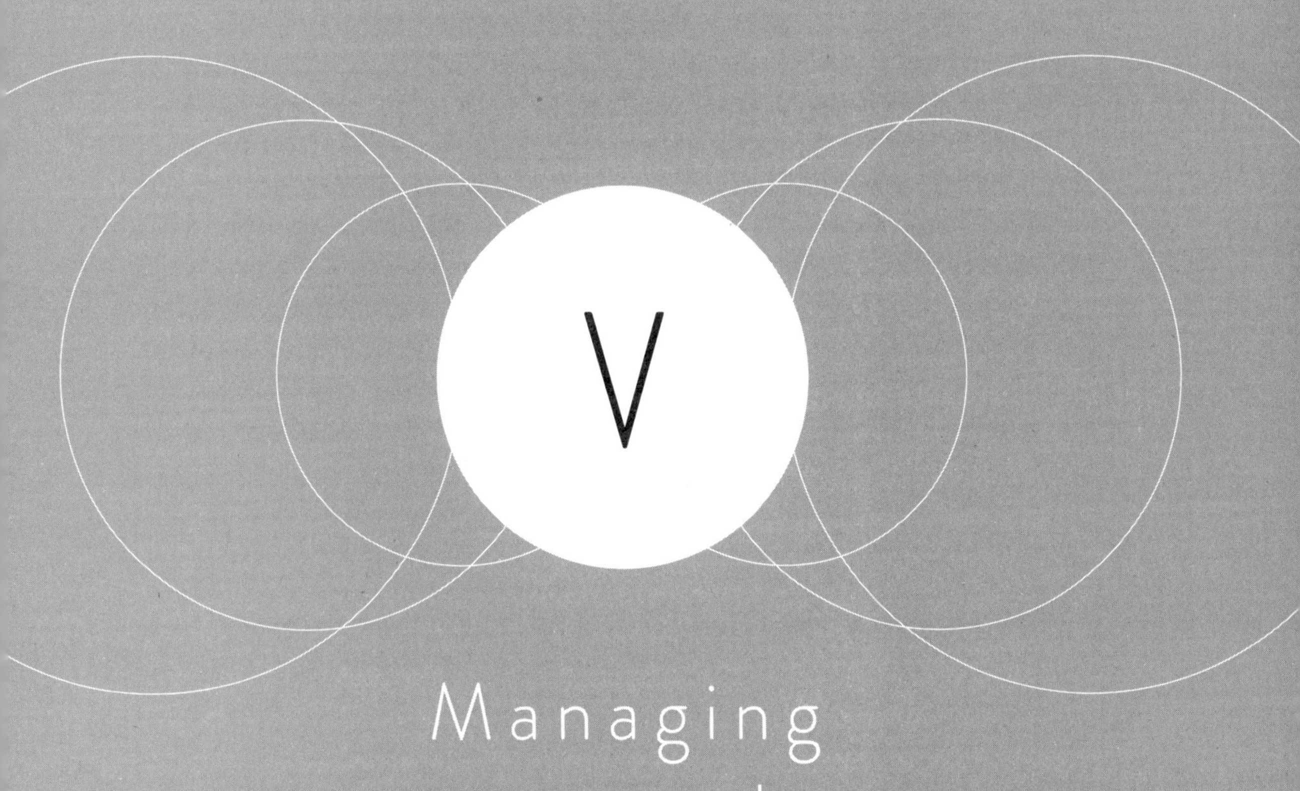

V
Managing across the Life Cycle

18

Managing 101: A Life Cycle Overview

IF THERE IS A theme that should have emerged as I have looked across the corporate life cycle on different dimensions, it is that one size does not fit all. In the chapters on corporate finance, I noted that not only the focus of a firm, but also how it makes investing, financing, and dividend decisions, changes as it goes through the life cycle. In the chapters on valuation, I argued that the challenges you face in valuation shift as you move from valuing young businesses to valuing mature and declining firms, and in the investing chapters, I examined how investors with different views on how markets make mistakes and correct these mistakes target firms at different stages of the life cycle for their investments.

In this chapter, I look at the management challenges that companies face as they move through the life cycle and argue that the qualities that make for good management will be different in young, as opposed to mature or declining, companies. I also look at management mismatches, where the management has competencies that do not match up to those required in the companies that they manage. After looking at some reasons why these mismatches occur, I examine the follow-up question that lies at the heart of corporate governance, which is whether these mismatches can be corrected, and if yes, how.

Management across the Life Cycle

In this section, I begin with a discussion of the many functions and roles played by the top management of a company and, in particular, its CEO. I then follow by examining the significance of each of the functions/roles as a company moves through the life cycle, as the basis for arguing that, mythology notwithstanding, there is no one template for a great CEO, and the right CEO for a company will reflect its special standing and where it stands in the youth-to-old-age corporate spectrum.

What Do Managers Do?

What do managers do at a business? Given the many tasks that go into creating, building, and running a business, it should come as no surprise that the list is long, but I will classify managerial duties into broad groups:

1. **Storyteller:** As I noted in chapter 9, every business is built around a story, and that story drives its valuation and sometimes its pricing. While that story is grounded in the company's products and the markets that it seeks, it is the top manager's job to craft and tell the story to investors, employees, and consumers. Clearly, the significance of this component of a CEO's job will shift depending on where the company is in its life cycle, with its importance being greatest at either end of the cycle.
2. **Business manager:** It is, of course, top management's job to manage the business that they are put in charge of, but that can span the spectrum from building a business model, for young companies, to working on ways to scale up a business, for high-growth firms, to defending a business model, for mature businesses, to scaling down the model, as the company enters the declining phase.
3. **People leader:** Organizations are composed of people, including suppliers, employees, and customers, and it is top management's job to lead these people, though the nature of that leadership will also shift as a company ages. Early on, when a company is still seeking out a business model and faces failure risk, leadership should inspire people with vision and direction. As companies grow and mature, it should create a corporate culture that retains employees, while competitors try to lure them away. In decline, when a company is shedding employees and shrinking, leadership should find a way to do so as humanely as possible and perform a soft landing, without destroying morale.

4. **Public face:** For better or worse, the CEO is the public face of the company for investors, regulators, and others, and the role they play will vary across groups and across the life cycle. With investors, top managers frame the vision/narrative for young companies and are key to drawing in fresh capital, whereas with mature firms, especially if they are publicly traded, managers' interactions are with institutional investors, wherein they try to manage expectations and frame results. With regulators and politicians, top management's role is sometimes to play defense, when their company is in the crosshairs and facing regulatory questioning, and sometimes to play offense against competitors.
5. **Succession planner:** There is a final aspect of top management responsibility that is often ignored but can be key to extending a company's life cycle, and that is preparing for a succession, wherein a new management is readied for a handover when it comes due. Clearly, the importance of creating succession plans increases as top managers age, and especially so at companies that are transitioning from one stage of the life cycle to the next.

In sum, while the list of roles that top managers play and the functions that they perform is long, the role and functions that get emphasized will shift as companies move through the life cycle. This understanding of what management will be called on to do, as companies age, is critical as you try to find the right top management for a company.

How Much Does Management Matter?

A hundred years of formalized business education has been built on the premise that managers matter, and that having good management at the top of a business can make the difference between success and failure. While I do not disagree with that broad premise, the effect of good management can be greater at some firms and smaller at others, based on four determinants:

1. **Macro versus micro:** Businesses that are driven more by macroeconomic movements, such as those in interest rates or commodity prices, will be less affected by who manages them than companies whose success can be traced to company-specific decisions on which products to produce, how to price them, and where to market them. Thus, management will matter more at a consumer product company than at a commodity company, since the former's success will depend upon its management decisions a great deal more than the latter's.

2. **Corporate life cycle:** At the risk of generalizing, management matters more at start-ups and very young companies, since it must deliver not just on vision but on business building, than at mature firms that have strong competitive advantages and are in good financial position, where management can be on autopilot. As firms go into decline, management will matter again, since management in denial or desperation can cost shareholders a great deal.
3. **Competitive advantage:** The nature of the competitive advantages possessed by a business can also affect how much management matters. In companies with long-standing and legacy competitive advantages, management has more of a caretaking role than at companies that constantly need to reinvent their competitive advantages. While I do not intend to downplay the challenges that managers at Coca-Cola and Aramco face, it is less of a challenge than managers at Costco, a company in an intensely competitive business facing disruption, or at NVIDIA, a semiconductor company that has to keep rediscovering its technological edge.
4. **Transition:** Management matters more when businesses are at transition points—i.e., start-ups that are seeking out venture capital for the first time, companies on the verge of an initial public offering, mature/declining firms ahead of a restructuring—since not only can management actions make a significant difference between success and failure, investor reactions can also be governed by how much investors trust management.
5. **Upside and downside:** There is one final parameter that management at companies can be judged upon, and that is whether they operate in businesses where success is keyed by creating upside or by protecting against downside, with the former falling under the category of taking advantage of opportunities and the latter under risk management. In young companies, it is the former that will dominate, but as companies mature, the latter will become more important.

In sum, management always matters, but the extent to which it matters will vary across companies, with the life cycle playing a significant role.

The Myth of the Great CEO

Is there a set of qualities that makes for a great CEO? To answer this question, I looked at two institutions, one academic and one practitioner, that are deeply invested in the idea of a "great" CEO and spend considerable time advancing it.

- The first is the Harvard Business School, where every student who enters the MBA program is treated as a CEO-in-waiting, notwithstanding the reality that there are too few openings to accommodate their collective ambitions. The *Harvard Business Review*, over the years, has published multiple articles about the characteristics of the most successful CEOs, including a 2017 article that highlights four characteristics they share: (a) deciding with speed and conviction, (b) engaging for impact with employees and the outside world, (c) adapting proactively to changing circumstances, and (d) delivering reliably.*
- The second is McKinsey, the consulting firm described by some as a "CEO factory" because so many of its consultants go on to become CEOs of their client companies. In an article, McKinsey lists the mindsets and practices of the most successful CEOs shown in figure 18.1.†

FIGURE 18.1 | CEO Mindset and Practices (according to McKinsey)

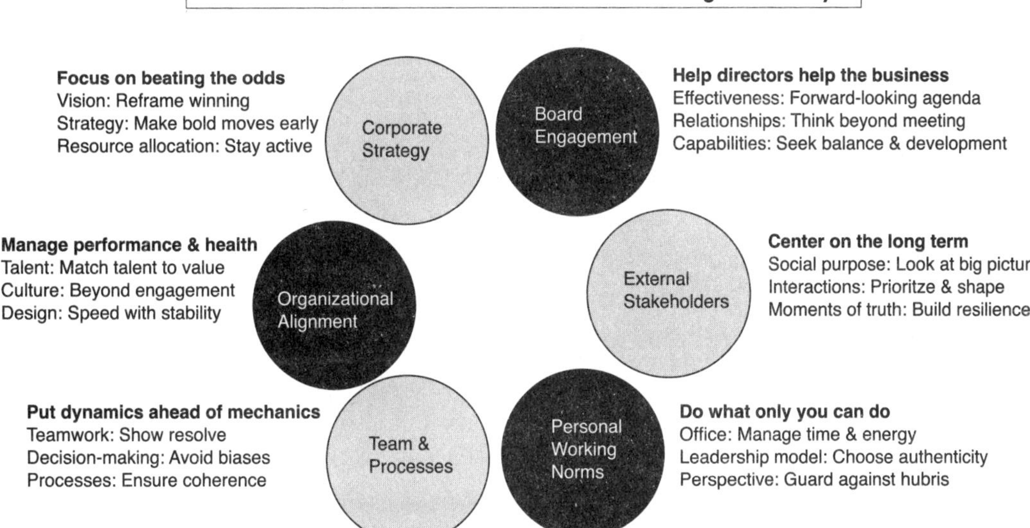

Given how influential these organizations are in framing public perception, it is no surprise that most people are convinced that there is a template for a great CEO that

* E. L. Botelho, K. R. Powell, S. Kincaid, and D. Wang, "What Sets Successful CEOs Apart," *Harvard Business Review*, May/June 2017, https://hbr.org/2017/05/what-sets-successful-ceos-apart.

† C. Dewar, M. Hirt, and S. Keller, "The Mindsets and Practices of Excellent CEOs," McKinsey, October 25, 2019, https://www.mckinsey.com/capabilities/strategy-and-corporate-finance/our-insights/the-mindsets-and-practices-of-excellent-ceos.

applies across companies, and that boards of directors in search of new CEOs should use this template.*

That perspective also gets fed by books and movies about successful CEOs, real or imagined. Consider Warren Buffett, Jack Welch, and Steve Jobs, very different men who have been mythologized in business literature and popular culture as great CEOs. Many of the books about Buffett read more like hagiographies than true biographies, given how starstruck the writers of these books are by the man, but by treating him as a deity, they do him a disservice. The fall of GE has taken some of the shine from Jack Welch's star, but at his peak, he was viewed as someone that CEOs should emulate. With Steve Jobs, the picture of an innovative, risk-taking disruptor comes not just from books about the man but from movies that gloss over his first, and rockier, stint as founder CEO of Apple in the 1980s.

The problem with the one-size-fits-all "great CEO" model is that it does not hold up to scrutiny. Even if you take the HBS and McKinsey criteria for CEO success at face value, there are four fundamental problems or missing pieces.

1. **Selective and anecdotal evidence:** Even if all successful CEOs share the qualities listed in the *HBR*/McKinsey papers, not all people or even most people with these qualities become successful CEOs. So, is there a missing ingredient that allowed some of them to succeed? If so, what is it? There is a clear selection bias at work here, and until it is addressed, the template is unconvincing.
2. **All good qualities:** I find it odd that there are no questionable qualities listed on the successful CEO list, especially given the evidence that overconfidence seems to be a common feature among CEOs, and that it is this overconfidence that allows them to act decisively and adopt long-term perspectives. When those bets, often made in the face of long odds, pay off, their makers are perceived as successful, but when they do not, the decision-makers are consigned to the ash heap of failure. Put simply, it is possible that the quality that binds together successful CEOs the most is luck, a quality that neither Harvard Business School nor McKinsey can pass on or teach.
3. **Exceptions to the rule:** There are clearly some successful CEOs who not only do not possess many of the listed qualities but often have inverse ones. If you believe that Elon Musk and Marc Benioff (CEOs of Tesla and Salesforce, respectively) are great CEOs, how many of the *HBR*/McKinsey criteria do they possess?

* S. Ireland, "What Makes a Great CEO," *CEOWORLD*, October 12, 2020, https://ceoworld.biz/2020/10/12/what-makes-a-great-ceo/.

4. **Flawed success:** Finally, even the CEOs cited as success stories in magazine articles have had to deal with failure during their lifetimes, or have seen their legacies tarnished in hindsight. Steve Jobs had a failed first stint at Apple, when his arrogance on design and stubbornness in refusing to admit mistakes almost drove the company to bankruptcy, before the legendary turnaround that he engineered on his second go-around as CEO of the company. Jack Welch's success at GE, much celebrated during his time, also laid the groundwork for the failures at the company in the years after he left, leading to a retrospective questioning of Welch's tenure.

While it may serve the purposes of management academics and consultants to sell the monolithic idea of a great CEO, the reality is far more complex. In fact, there seems to be very little binding together successful CEOs, who come in all shapes, sizes, and types, and even the most successful CEOs have flaws and failures.

The Right CEO: A Life Cycle Perspective

I believe that the discussion of what makes for a great CEO is flawed for a simple reason: there is no one template that works for all companies. One way to see why is to look at how the challenges in managing companies change as they go through a life cycle, from start-ups (birth) to maturity (middle age) to decline (old age). At each stage of the life cycle, the focus in the company changes, as do the qualities that top managers need to contribute for success:

- Early in the life cycle, as a company struggles to find traction with a business idea that meets an unmet demand, you need a CEO-as-visionary, capable of thinking outside the box and with the capacity to draw employees and investors to their vision.
- In converting an idea to a product or service, history suggests that pragmatism wins out over purity of vision, as compromises must be made on design, production, and marketing to convert an idea company into a business. As the products/services offered by the company take form, the capacity to build a business becomes front and center, as production facilities must be built and supply chains put in place—critical for business success, but clearly not as exciting as selling visions.
- Once the initial idea has become a business success, the need to keep scaling up may require coming up with extensions of existing product lines or geographies into which to grow, where an opportunistic, quick-acting CEO can make a difference.

- As companies enter the late phases of middle age, the imperative will shift from finding new markets to defending existing market share, in what I think of as the "trench warfare" phase of a company, where shoring up moats takes priority over new product development.
- The most difficult phase for a company is decline, as the company is dismantled and sells or shuts down its constituent parts, since anyone who is put in charge of this process has only pain to mete out, and bad press to go with it.

I capture the different phases of a company, with the keys to business and management success at each phase and the right CEO for that phase, in figure 18.2.

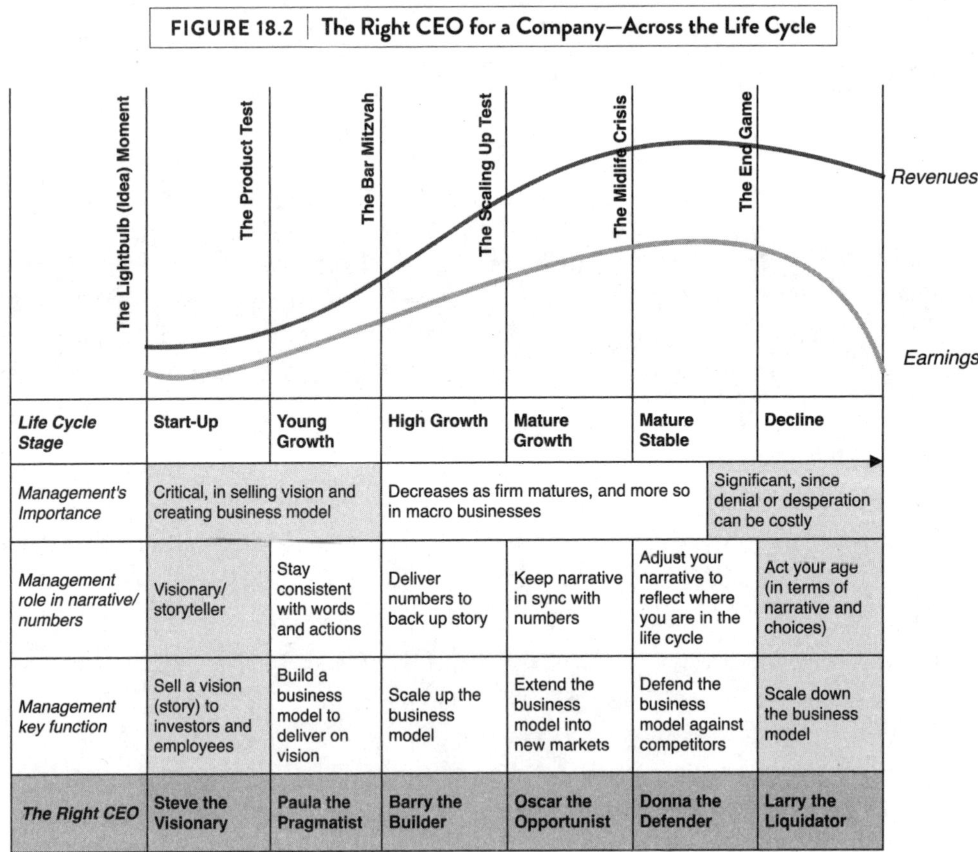

Life Cycle Stage	Start-Up	Young Growth	High Growth	Mature Growth	Mature Stable	Decline
Management's Importance	Critical, in selling vision and creating business model		Decreases as firm matures, and more so in macro businesses			Significant, since denial or desperation can be costly
Management role in narrative/ numbers	Visionary/ storyteller	Stay consistent with words and actions	Deliver numbers to back up story	Keep narrative in sync with numbers	Adjust your narrative to reflect where you are in the life cycle	Act your age (in terms of narrative and choices)
Management key function	Sell a vision (story) to investors and employees	Build a business model to deliver on vision	Scale up the business model	Extend the business model into new markets	Defend the business model against competitors	Scale down the business model
The Right CEO	Steve the Visionary	Paula the Pragmatist	Barry the Builder	Oscar the Opportunist	Donna the Defender	Larry the Liquidator

FIGURE 18.2 | The Right CEO for a Company—Across the Life Cycle

A great CEO at a young business, with the skill to frame the company's story and to use it to induce investors to risk their capital on it and inspire employees to follow, may be a misfit at a mature company, where the skill set needed for a successful CEO may come from protecting existing competitive advantages and playing defense against competitors and regulators.

Management Mismatches

If the right management for a company reflects its value drivers and its standing in the corporate life cycle, it stands to reason that even if management is well regarded, you can end up with mismatches between management and business. In this section, I will start by looking at the reasons for these mismatches in the first place, and then look at how these mismatches play out for companies (and CEOs) as they age and become publicly traded, as well as at businesses that stay privately owned and/or are family businesses.

Mismatch Reasons

Can management personnel measure up to the standards of competence and still be mismatched with the companies that they are asked to manage? Absolutely. There are many reasons why these mismatches can occur:

1. **Aging management and/or company:** Companies and managers age, and as they do, they change. With companies, I noted that as they move from start-ups to growth to maturity, the focus shifts from building business models to defending them, and from more risk-taking to less. With top managers, aging creates its own dynamics, with studies showing that as managers age, they are generally less likely (or willing) to take risks or engage in innovations that may undercut existing products.* In the uncommon scenario where both the CEO and business change at the same rate, you could have the same management for the company, as it goes from start-up to decline, with no loss of efficiency, but in the more likely scenario, where their aging and shifting risk preferences occur at different rates, you can get mismatches. In supportive evidence, a study that looks at the link between firm value and CEO tenure finds that with long-tenured CEOs, value increases, on average, for the first decade of tenure, peaks at about 12 years, and drops off thereafter.†

* D. C. Hambrick and P. A. Mason, "Upper Echelons: The Organization as Reflection of Its Top Managers," *Academy of Management Journal* 9, no. 2 (April 1984): 193–206.

† F. Brochet, P. Limbach, M. Schmid, and M. Scholz-Daneshgari, "CEO Tenure and Firm Value," *Accounting Review* 96, no. 6 (November 2021): 47–71.

2. **A changing business, static management:** There is a more subtle problem, where a company is well matched to its CEO at a certain point in time but then evolves across the life cycle, while the CEO does not. The firm's evolution in the life cycle can come from changes in its makeup, perhaps as its business model evolves, or from disruption of the overall business by an external force, which can convert a mature and predictable business into a risky and declining business. A good example would be Yahoo!, an early pioneer in the search engine game, whose founders, Jerry Yang and David Filo, went from being hailed as visionary successes to written off as failures over the course of a decade, as Google upended the business. The same can be said of a host of brick-and-mortar retail firms at the start of this century, with entrenched and often well-regarded managers, who found themselves lost as Amazon disrupted the retail business.
3. **Hiring mistakes:** When looking for replacements for top managers who are stepping down, boards of directors often look for executives who they believe will be successful stewards of the company, but they can make mistakes. If the board of directors hires someone who has been a successful CEO, but that success came at another company at a very different stage in its life cycle, it risks a mismatch. I think Uber dodged a bullet in 2017, when they decided not to hire Jeff Immelt as CEO for the company. Even if you had believed that Immelt was successful at his prior job as CEO for GE—and that is arguable—he would have been a bad choice as CEO at Uber, a company that was as different from GE as you could get in every aspect, not just corporate age.
4. **A gamble on rebirth:** In some cases, a board of director picks a mismatched CEO intentionally, with the hope that the CEO's characteristics rub off on the company. This is often the case when you have a mature or declining company that thinks hiring a visionary as a CEO will lead to its reincarnation as a growth company. While the impulse to become young again is understandable, the odds are against this gamble working, leaving the CEO tarnished and the company worse off. This was the reason that Yahoo! hired Marissa Mayer as its CEO in 2012, hoping that her success at Google would rub off on the company, an experiment that did not end well for either Yahoo! or Ms. Mayer.

In any case, a CEO/company mismatch is a problem, though the consequences can range from benign to malignant, as can be seen in figure 18.3.

FIGURE 18.3 | Company/CEO Mismatches and Value Effects

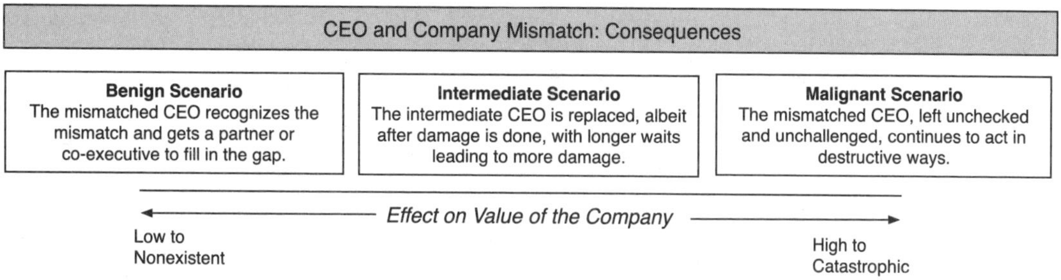

In the most benign case, a mismatched CEO recognizes the mismatch, sets ego aside, and finds a partner or co-executive with the skills needed for the company. In my view, the difference between the first iteration of Steve Jobs, during which he let his vision run riot and almost destroyed Apple as a company, and the second iteration, during which he led one of the most impressive corporate turnarounds in history, was his choice of Tim Cook as his chief operating officer in his second go-around, and his willingness to delegate operating authority. In short, Jobs was able to continue to put his visionary skills to work while Cook made sure that the promises Jobs made were delivered as products on the ground. In the most malignant instances, a badly mismatched CEO is entrenched in his or her position, perhaps because the board of directors has become a rubber stamp or because voting rules (shares with different voting rights) have been titled in favor of incumbency, and continues down a pathway that takes the company to ruin. In the intermediate case, the board of directors, perhaps with a push from activist investors and large stockholders, engineers a CEO change, albeit only after some or a great deal of damage has been done.

Mismatch Types

As you review the reasons for business/management mismatches, you can see why mismatches can occur at every stage of the corporate life cycle, from youth to decline, and across all types of businesses, from privately owned to family controlled to publicly traded.

ACROSS THE LIFE CYCLE

At each stage in the life cycle, there will be cases where the top management of a business is ill-equipped to handle the challenges that it faces, and being aware of these cases can equip them better to deal with the resulting mismatches.

1. **Start-ups and young businesses:** With start-ups and young businesses, mismatches are common, since neither the founder/manager nor the business comes in with a track record that can be used to ensure a good fit.
   a. **Purist founder:** The first common mismatch occurs at a start-up with a purist founder, who refuses to change or adapt the planned product or service to meet either market or business needs. In technology companies, this problem can sometimes come from founders who are technocrats, whose objective becomes creating the "perfect" software or hardware product rather than a "good enough" one that meets customer demands and is easier to build a business model around.
   b. **Control fixation:** Start-ups and young companies need cash flows to convert ideas to products and then to build business models, but they lack the capacity to carry debt. Consequently, success often requires founders to give up ownership shares to investors in return for capital. Founders who are focused on maintaining complete control will either raise capital in dysfunctional ways or starve themselves of funds, sacrificing business promise for control.
   c. **Low interest/skill in business building:** Once an idea has been converted into a product or service that consumers want, management must work on building business models to deliver that product. That task often involves grunt work and attention to detail, and that is not what some founders want to spend their time on or have the skills to do. Without someone in charge of business building, businesses will not be able to commercialize their product or service offerings.

2. **High-growth businesses:** In high growth, the test is whether and how much a business that has worked on a smaller scale can be scaled up, and there are founders who overreach in both directions.
   a. **Scaling up at any cost:** In some companies, managers become so centered on growing revenues that this urge becomes the driver of every business decision. These companies will succeed in delivering on growth, but often at the expense of finding pathways to profitability, and with huge investments in acquisitions or new products.
   b. **Refusing to scale:** At the other extreme, an obsession with turning earnings and cash flow positive can result in managers turning aside value-creating opportunities to scale up their businesses because it may mean losing money or having negative cash flows for longer.

3. **Mature-growth businesses:** In mature-growth business, growth rates will start to decrease, but high growth is still reachable if managers are opportunistic. It is in this phase that managers face choices between revenue growth and profitability, with higher growth sometimes going with lower profitability, generating value consequences that can be positive or negative.
    a. **Scaling over profits:** Since mature-growth businesses come into this phase after periods of high growth, where growth was always given priority over profits, top managers at these businesses can sometimes stay stuck in that paradigm. That will lead them to invest more than they should in new projects or big acquisitions and create companies that are growing too much and earning too little.
    b. **Chasing the past:** When businesses are in high growth, they usually have more investment opportunities than they have capital available, have light or no debt loads, and return no cash to investors. As they transition to mature growth, those circumstances will change, as improving earnings give rise to debt capacity as well as allow for cash return (via dividends or buybacks) to owners. Managers at these businesses sometimes fight these trends, choosing not to borrow or return cash, because that is what has worked for them in the past.

4. **Mature stable businesses:** In mature and stable businesses, the sensible and prudent route for top management is to accept lower growth, while defending and augmenting the moats (competitive advantages) that allow these businesses to continue to generate profits.
    a. **Growth delusions:** While low growth is the outcome that you should expect to see at most mature businesses, there are some that are run by top managers who yearn for a return to high growth and act accordingly. Lacking internal projects of enough size to make a growth difference, they seek out acquisitions, skewing toward bigger deals. In so doing, they set in motion a process where overpaying becomes the rule rather than the exception, and the mistakes get larger and more expensive over time.
    b. **Empire builders:** There are some companies where top managers become more intent on building empires, rather than viable and profitable businesses. This is especially the case when you have CEOs, with long tenure and a captive board of directors, who are interested in expanding company size (defined in terms of revenues or even employees) at any cost. In the 1970s, it was the model used by Charles Bluhdorn to convert Gulf and Western into a conglomerate, largely

through acquisitions. There are some who look back at Jack Welch's tenure at GE and question whether he was reinventing the company or building an empire.

c. **Moat mix-ups and neglect:** If the key drivers of value in a mature business are its moats or competitive advantages, it behooves the management of the business to be aware of, track changes in, and protect these advantages. If top management misidentifies the moats in a business—believing, for instance, that brand name is its competitive advantage when it is really economies of scale—its actions will reflect that misidentification and put its competitive advantages at risk.

5. **Declining businesses:** In the chapters on valuing and investing in declining businesses, I noted how difficult it can be for management to accept decline, even if it is inevitable and obvious. Consequently, the are many dysfunctional paths that top management at these businesses can follow.
   a. **Denial:** When management of a declining business is in denial about its permanence, attributing the decline in revenues and profit margins to extraordinary circumstances, macro developments, or luck, it will act accordingly, staying with past practices on investing, financing, and dividends. If that management stays in place, the truth will eventually catch up with the company, but not before more money has been sunk into a business that is uninvestable.
   b. **Desperation:** Management may be aware that the business is in decline but may be incentivized, by money or fame, to make big bets with long odds, hoping for a hit. While the owners of these businesses lose much of the time, the managers who get hits become superstars (and get labeled as "turnaround specialists") and increase their earning power, perhaps by moving to other firms.
   c. **Survival at any cost:** In some declining businesses, top managers believe that it is corporate survival that should be given priority over corporate health, and they act accordingly. In the process, they create zombie or walking-dead companies that survive, but as bad businesses that shed value over time.

THE COMPRESSED LIFE CYCLE EFFECT

In chapter 3, I noted that while every company goes through the process of starting up, aging, and eventually declining, the speed at which it does so will vary depending on the business it is in. More specifically, the more capital it takes to enter a business and the more inertia there is among the existing players (producers, customers), the longer it will take for a company to get from start-up to mature growth—but the same forces will play out in reverse, allowing the company to stay mature for a lot longer and decline a lot more gradually.

Also in chapter 3, I argued that corporate life cycles have become compressed in the last few decades, as technology companies, specifically, have made their presence felt in both markets and the economy. The great companies of the twentieth century took decades to ramp up, facing big infrastructure investments and long lags before expansion, and had long stints as mature firms, milking cash flows, before embarking on long and mostly gradual declines. To illustrate, Sears and GE had century-long runs as successful companies before time and circumstances caught up with them, and GM and Ford struggled for three decades setting up manufacturing capacity and tweaking their product offerings before enjoying the fruits of their success. In contrast, consider Yahoo!, a company that was founded in 1994 and managed to reach $100 billion in market capitalization by the turn of the century, but enjoyed only a few years of dominance before Google's arrival and conquest of the market, until finally it was acquired by Verizon in 2017.

I believe that this compressed life cycle has consequences for management mismatches. With the long-life-cycle companies that characterized the twentieth century, companies and managers both aged over time, allowing for transitions to occur more naturally. To see why, consider how corporate governance played out at Ford, a twentieth-century corporate giant. Henry Ford—undoubtedly a visionary, but also a crank on some dimensions—was Ford's CEO from 1906 to 1945. His vision of making automobiles affordable to the masses, with the Model T, was a catalyst in Ford's success, but by the end of his tenure in 1945, his management style was already out of sync with the company. With Ford, time and mortality solved the problem, and his grandson, Henry Ford II, was a better custodian for the firm in the decades that followed. Put simply, when a company lasts for a century, the progression of time naturally takes care of mismatches and succession. In contrast, consider how quickly Blackberry, as a company, soared, how short was its stay at the top, and how steep its descent proved to be as other companies entered the smartphone business. Mike Lazaridis, one of the cofounders of the company, and Jim Balsillie, the CEO he hired in 1992 to guide the company, presided over both its soaring success, gaining accolades for their management skills for doing so, and its collapse, drawing jeers from the same crowd. By the time a change in top management happened, in 2012, it was viewed as too little, too late.

This compression of the life cycle and its potential for creating management mismatches is illustrated in figure 18.4.

FIGURE 18.4 | Compressed Life Cycles and Management Mismatches

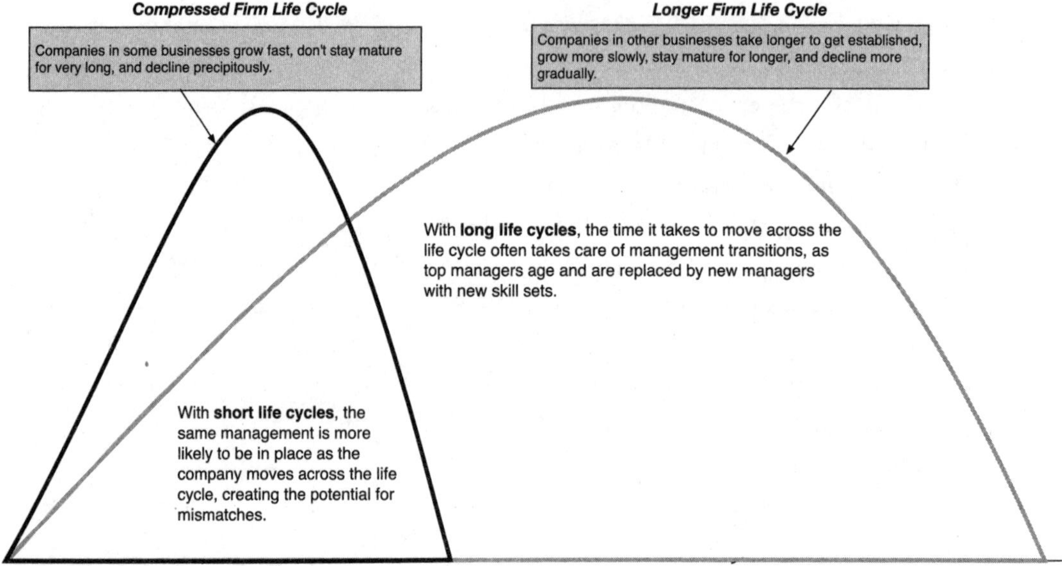

In short, tech companies age in dog years, with a 20-year tech company often resembling a 100-year-old manufacturing company, saddled with creaky business models and facing disruption. In my view, the next decade will bring forth more conflict, rooted in the compressed life cycle of today's companies. If I were a case study writer, I would not rush to write case studies or books about successful tech company CEOs, because many of those same CEOs will become case studies in failure within a few years.

Fixing Management Mismatches

I know that corporate governance covers a whole host of details, from how boards should be constructed to who should vote at annual meetings, but at its core, as I see it, corporate governance is about the power that owners have, or don't have, to replace the management of a company when it is mismatched with the company's needs. In this section, I will explore the process by which management is replaced at businesses, private and public, and examine the consequences of this process for firms across the life cycle.

Changing Management: The Process

When the top management is mismatched to the firm, the obvious solution is to change managers, but not only may that not happen—and I will look at the variables that determine whether it does in the next section—the process of changing management is not always easy or timely.

1. **Private businesses:** When a business is privately owned and has a management mismatch, you face a quandary if the owner of the business is also the manager. That is often the case with both start-ups and very young companies, before they go public, and with family-owned businesses. While the owner-manager overlap can make change impossible in some cases, there are processes for change in both founder-run and family-owned businesses. With founder-run businesses, change can sometimes come from venture capitalists and outside investors who have ownership stakes in the business and can use those stakes to remove and replace founder-managers. A study of founder replacement at start-ups notes that in 11,929 VC-backed start-ups founded from 1995 to 2008, at least 15% had at least one founder replacement during the period.* With family-run businesses, the change must come from the family, motivated by poor performance in the business, and can involve replacing family member managers either with other family members or with outsiders.
2. **Public companies:** Once companies become publicly traded, the management change process must go through the board of directors of the company. To the extent that board members are picked by incumbent managers, there will be a built-in bias toward preserving existing management. The pressure to change management, though, will increase as companies underperform, both in market and stock price terms, and if it reaches a tipping point, the board will replace managers. One metric of the ebbs and flows of corporate governance in a market is the number of CEOs who are removed by boards of directors, and that statistic for the S&P 1500 companies, from 1993 to 2018, is shown in figure 18.5.

* Ewens, M. and M. Marx, "Founder Replacement and Startup Performance," *Review of Financial Economics* 31, no. 4 (2018).

FIGURE 18.5 | Number of Forcible CEO Removals at S&P 1500, 1993–2018

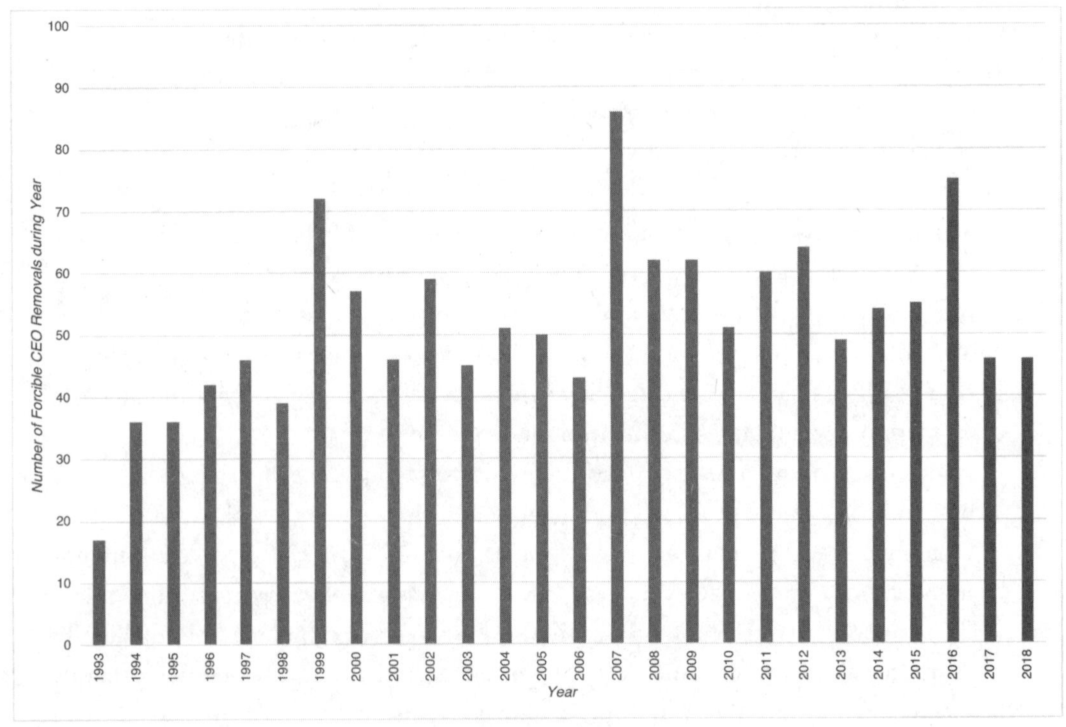

Source: Florian Peters

As you can see, the number of forced removals (or firings) of CEOs changes over time, with a peak occurring in 2007. That said, even in peak years, the number of forcible removals remains a low number, suggesting that there are strong forces keeping incumbent managers in place at most companies, and I will examine those forces in the next section.

Changing Management: The Catalysts and Challenges

When there is a mismatch between management and the skill set needed in the company that they manage, why is it that change occurs quickly at some companies, slowly at others, and never at some? In this section, I will address this question by looking at the catalysts that create management change and the forces arrayed against change, and examine why both (catalysts and challenges) can change over the life cycle.

THE CATALYSTS

Even when there is widespread acceptance that change is needed at a company, for that change to occur there must be catalysts that come into play, and it is the presence or absence of these catalysts that explain why changes are more frequent in some phases of the life cycle than in others.

- With *start-ups and very young companies* in the private domain, the catalyst for change is often a venture capitalist or a group of venture capitalists with skin in the game—i.e., significant amounts invested in the company—and a view that the existing management, often the founder or founders, is ill-equipped to run the company.
- With *young-growth companies*, right after they go public and in the early years as a public-market company, the push for change usually comes from inside investors in the companies—shareholders who own large stakes in the company, either because of a pre-IPO holding or because of stakes acquired in the public offering.
- With *high-growth companies*, change is often pushed to the forefront by individual or institutional investors with a large stake and an activist tilt. The large stake is necessary to be heard, and the activism is needed to convince other shareholders to join the push for change. The success of the movement will depend in large part on how successful the company has been in its scaling up endeavors, with less success in scaling up creating more pressure for change.
- With *mature-growth companies*, the catalyst for change can come as the result of natural transitions, wherein the existing CEO retires or dies. While most new CEOs in this position follow the path that the prior CEO has laid, constrained by a board picked by the old CEO and by a calcified corporate culture, a few use the transition as an opportunity to reset direction. When Steve Ballmer retired in 2013 and Satya Nadella took his place, few expected Microsoft to make major changes in its business model and mix, but the changes that Nadella made have put Microsoft on a new, and much more lucrative, path.
- With *mature companies* that are publicly traded, the catalyst for change will be activist investors and hedge funds, often in response to disappointing operating and stock market performance. The changes they push for will usually be more restraint on new investments, especially acquisitions, more debt in capital structure, and more cash returned to shareholders.
- With *declining firms*, private equity firms become catalysts pushing to buy out these firms and take them private while they make operating and financial changes. In some

cases, the push can be for liquidation, if the company's assets are worth more liquidated than as part of a going concern, while in others, the firm may be spun off or split off, if private equity firms believe that the firm is worth more in parts than as a whole.

THE CHALLENGES

There is a strong bias toward preserving incumbent management at firms, even when there is widespread agreement that the management is mismatched to the business that it is managing. In this section, I will start by looking at institutional constraints on changing management that apply across all firms, and then look at company-level constraints that can get in the way of change, which will shift as you move through the life cycle.

a. Institutional Constraints

The first group of constraints on challenging incumbent management in companies is institutional and affects all publicly traded companies, albeit to different degrees. Some of these constraints can be traced to difficulties associated with raising the capital needed to fund the challenge, some to state restrictions on hostile takeovers, and some to inertia.

1. **Capital constraints:** The quickest, and sometimes most decisive, way to change management is to raise capital to acquire firms that are poorly managed, and any constraints on that process can impede change. It should come as no surprise that management changes are less frequent in economies where capital markets—equity and debt—are not well developed; in fact, for much of the last century, badly managed companies in Europe were at least partially shielded from change by the absence of an active corporate bond market and the reliance of companies on bank loans. In general, then, I would argue that the likelihood of changing the management in badly managed firms is greater when financial markets are open and funds are accessible to a wide variety of investors (and not just to large corporations with good credit standing). Capital constraints do have disproportionate effects, providing greater protection for larger market cap companies than for smaller ones, and to the extent that younger companies have smaller market capitalizations than older ones, this constraint is more likely to slow or stop management change at the latter.
2. **State constraints on takeovers and shareholder votes:** In many countries, the state takes the side of incumbent managers, making it more difficult to change management. In some countries, there are restrictions or even outright bans both on hostile acquisitions and on activist investing. In other countries, the restrictions are on shareholder voting, perhaps tying it to tenure, with the votes of longer-term shareholders carrying

more weight than those of more recent entrants into the shareholder pool. While the rationale for these restrictions is to create a more long-term perspective in decision-making, it does work in favor of incumbency, at least at publicly traded companies.

Capital and state-imposed constraints that impede management change can explain why change is less frequently seen in companies in some geographies than in others, as well as in some periods than in others. These constraints can also explain why management changes occur more frequently early in the life cycle, when businesses are still private and often small, rather than later in the life cycle, as firms mature and become publicly traded.

b. Firm-Specific Constraints

There are some firms where incumbent managers, no matter how mismatched to the company, are protected from stockholder pressure by actions taken by these firms that skew the rules of the corporate governance game. This protection can take the form of amendments to the corporate charter, elaborate cross-holding structures, the creation of shares with different voting rights, and large insider holdings of shares, but the challenges to change will vary across companies and geographies. As I will show in the next section, the types of constraints that impede management change will vary across the life cycle, and that is precisely why corporate governance reforms often end up failing. The types of reforms that open management to change at mature companies may not help as much in young companies.

Finally, the push toward stakeholder wealth maximization and ESG at some companies has made it more difficult for shareholders to make changes at these companies. With stakeholder wealth, making managers accountable to all stakeholders (from employees to lenders to society) dilutes their accountability to shareholders and, in effect, makes them accountable to no one. As for ESG, you may be puzzled that a concept that has governance in its name can weaken corporate governance, but that is because the governance in ESG is expanded to all stakeholders.

THE LIKELIHOOD OF CHANGE

The pathway to fixing management mismatches is to change management, and you need catalysts that push you toward change while overcoming market-wide and company-specific barriers to changes. A practical question that has relevance to both managers and investors is whether you can assess the likelihood of change at a company ahead of the change happening. One statistical approach that is promising is a logit, or probit, where you assess the probability of management change by contrasting the characteristics of firms where management has changed in the past with firms where that has not occurred. Researchers have applied this technique to look at both hostile acquisitions and forced CEO change, to eke out the characteristics of the companies where these events are most likely to happen. The research on hostile acquisitions points to the following:

- In one of the first papers to assess the likelihood of takeovers by comparing target firms in acquisitions to firms that were not targets, Krishna Palepu (1986) noted that target firms in takeovers were smaller than non-target firms and invested inefficiently.[*]
- In a later paper, David North (2001) concluded that firms with low insider/managerial ownership were more likely to be targeted in acquisitions.[†] Neither paper specifically focused on hostile acquisitions, though. Robin Nuttall (1999) found that target firms in hostile acquisitions tended to trade at lower price to book ratios than other firms, and Charlie Weir (1997) added to this finding by noting that target firms in hostile acquisitions also earned lower returns on invested capital.[‡]
- Finally, Lee Pinkowitz (2003) finds no evidence to support the conventional wisdom that firms with substantial cash balances are more likely to become targets of hostile acquisitions.[§]

In summary, then, target firms in hostile acquisitions tend to be smaller, trade at lower multiples of book value, and earn relatively low returns on their investments.[¶]

In recent years, researchers have also examined when forced CEO turnover is most likely to occur.

- The first factor is stock price and earnings performance, with forced turnover more likely in firms that have performed poorly relative to their peer group and to expecta-

[*] K. G. Palepu, "Predicting Take-Over Targets: A Methodological and Empirical Analysis," *Journal of Accounting and Economics* 8, no. 1 (March 1986): 3–35.

[†] D. S. North, "The Role of Managerial Incentives in Corporate Acquisitions: The 1990s Evidence," *Journal of Corporate Finance* 7, no. 2 (June 2001): 125–49.

[‡] R. Nuttall, "Take-Over Likelihood Models for UK Quoted Companies," Working Paper, SSRN #155168, 1999; C. Weir, "Corporate Governance, Performance and Take-Overs: An Empirical Analysis of UK Mergers," *Applied Economics* 29, no. 11 (1997): 1465–75.

[§] L. Pinkowitz, "The Market for Corporate Control and Corporate Cash Holdings," Working Paper, SSRN #215191, 2003. This study of hostile acquisitions between 1985 and 1994 concludes that firms with large cash balances are less (not more) likely to be targets of hostile acquisitions.

[¶] In a contrary finding, Julian Franks and Colin Mayer (1996) find no evidence of poor performance in target firms in hostile acquisitions in the UK; see J. Franks and C. Mayer, "Hostile Takeovers and the Correction of Management Failure," *Journal of Financial Economics* 40, no. 1 (January 1996): 163–81.

tions.[*] One manifestation of poor management is overpaying for acquisitions, and there is evidence that CEOs of acquiring firms that pay too much for acquisitions are far more likely to be replaced than CEOs who do not make such acquisitions.[†]

- The second factor is the structure of the board, with forced CEO changes more likely to occur when the board is small,[‡] when it is composed of outsiders,[§] and when the CEO is not also the chairman of the board of directors.[¶]
- The third and a related factor is the company's ownership structure; forced CEO changes are more common in companies with high institutional and low insider holdings.[**] They also seem to occur more frequently in firms that are more dependent upon equity markets for new capital.[††]
- The final factor is industry structure, with CEOs more likely to be replaced in competitive industries.[‡‡]

In summary, firms where you see forced CEO change share some characteristics with firms that are targets of hostile acquisitions—they are poorly managed and run—but they tend to have much more effective boards of directors and more activist investors who can change management without turning over the firm to a hostile acquirer.

Governance across the Life Cycle

Building on the themes that management mismatches are at the heart of the push for management change, and that corporate governance is the structure that determines

[*] J. Warner, R. Watts, and K. Wruck, 1988, "Stock Prices and Top Management Changes," *Journal of Financial Economics* 20, no. 1–2 (1992): 461–92; K. Murphy and J. Zimmerman, "Financial Performance Surrounding CEO Turnover," *Journal of Accounting and Economics* 16, no. 1–3 (January–July 1993): 273–316; S. Puffer and J. B. Weintrop, "Corporate Performance and CEO Turnover: The Role of Performance Expectations," *Administrative Science Quarterly* 36, no. 1 (March 1991): 1–19.

[†] K. Lehn and M. Zhao, "CEO Turnover after Acquisitions: Are Bad Bidders Fired?" Working Paper, SSRN #444360, 2006.

[‡] O. Faleye, "Are Large Boards Poor Monitors? Evidence from CEO Turnover," Working Paper, SSRN #498285, 2003. Using a proportional hazard model, Olubunmi Faleye finds that every additional director on the board reduces the probability of a forced CEO change by 13%.

[§] M. Weisbach, "Outside Directors and CEO Turnover," *Journal of Financial Economics* 20 (January–March 1988): 431–60.

[¶] V. K. Goyal and C. W. Park, "Board Leadership Structure and CEO Turnover," *Journal of Corporate Finance* 8, no.1 (January 2002): 49–66.

[**] D. J. Denis, D. K. Denis, and A. Sarin, "Ownership Structure and Top Executive Turnover," *Journal of Financial Economics* 45, no. 2 (August 1997): 193–221.

[††] S. Linn, D. Hillier, and P. McColgan, "Equity Issuance, Corporate Governance Reform and CEO Turnover in the UK," Working Paper, SSRN #484802, 2003. The study finds that CEOs are more likely to be forced out just before new equity issues or placings.

[‡‡] M. L. DeFondt and C. W. Park, "The Effect of Competition on CEO Turnover," *Journal of Accounting and Economics*, 27, no. 1 (February 1999): 35–56.

whether there will be management change, let us trace out how corporate governance takes shape at each stage in the life cycle.

START-UPS AND YOUNG COMPANIES (PRE-PUBLIC)

Companies have always had founders, and while the conflicts between founders and others in the company have been around for decades, the compressed corporate life cycle has exacerbated these tensions and magnified problems. In particular, the research on founder CEOs has yielded two disparate findings.

The first is that in the early stages of companies, founder CEOs either step down or are pushed out at much higher rates than in more established companies.

The second is that those founder CEOs who nurse their companies to more established status, and to public offerings, are more entrenched than their counterparts at mature companies.

To understand the first phenomenon (i.e., the high displacement rate among founder CEOs of very young companies), I draw again on the work of Noam Wasserman, who has focused intensively on this topic.* Using data on top management turnover at young firms, many of them non-public, he concludes that almost 30% of CEOs at these firms are replaced within a few years of inception, usually at the time of new product development or fresh financing. Much of this phenomenon can be explained by venture capitalists with large ownership stakes pushing for change in these companies, but a portion of it is voluntary, and to explain why a founder CEO might willingly step down, Wasserman uses the concept of the founder's dilemma, wherein founders trade off full control of a much less valuable firm (with themselves in charge) for lesser control of a much more valuable firm (with someone else at the helm). In the corporate life cycle structure, there is a recognition on the part of founders or capital providers that the skills needed to take a company forward require a different person at the top of the organization, especially as a firm transitions from one stage of the life cycle to the next.

YOUNG AND GROWING PUBLICLY TRADED COMPANIES

When private businesses transition to being publicly traded, the founders of these companies, if they survive the VC purges, stay at the helm when companies debut in public markets. They are often put on a pedestal, relative to CEOs of established companies—and while that may be understandable, in some cases, it can take the dangerous form of

* N. Wasserman, "Founder-CEO Succession and the Paradox of Entrepreneurial Success," *Organizational Science* 14, no. 2 (March–April 2003): 149–172.

founder worship, wherein founders are viewed as untouchable and any challenge to their authority is viewed as bad, making it more difficult to change management at these firms.

That process has been skewed even more by efforts to change the rules of the game to prevent these challenges. In the United States, prior to 1980, it was unusual to see shares with different voting rights in the same firm. Such an arrangement is now more the rule than the exception, and especially so at tech companies, as can be seen in figure 18.6.

FIGURE 18.6 | Dual Class Shares in IPOs, 1980–2021

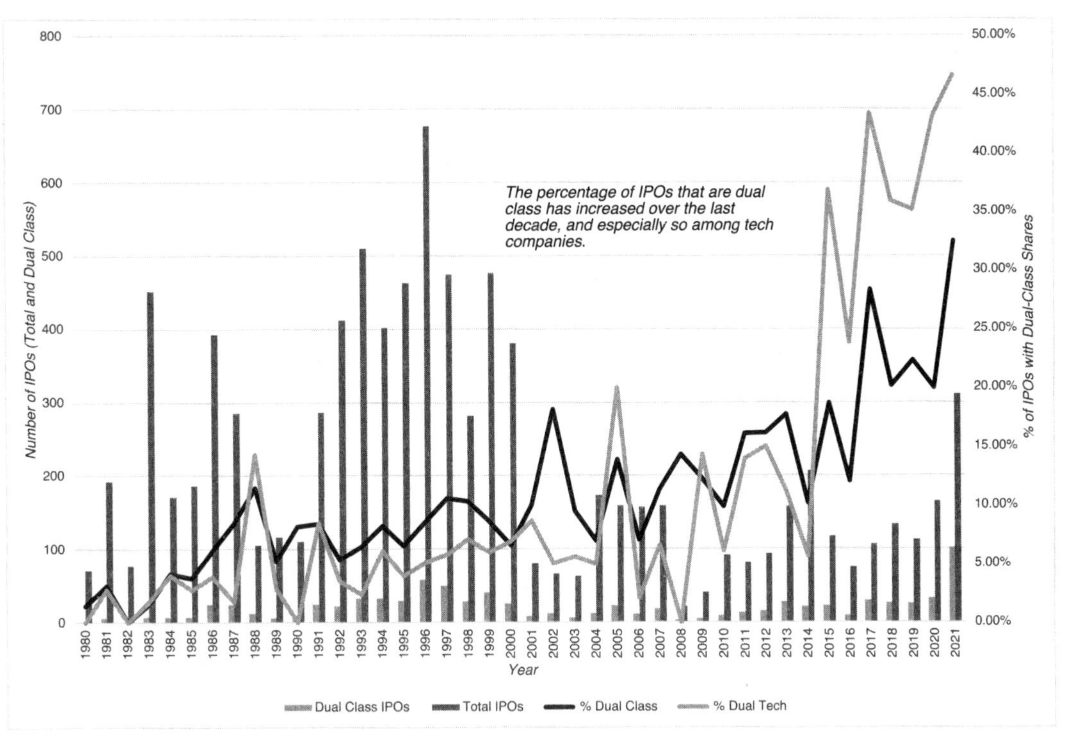

Source: Jay Ritter

In 2021, close to half of all tech firms that went public did so with shares with different voting rights, endowing the management of these firms with increased power to fend off governance challenges. That seems like a particularly bad idea at companies with compressed life cycles, since, as I noted earlier, they are likely to create more, rather than fewer, management mismatches between companies and their founder CEOs—and sooner, rather than later. In my view, the next decade will bring forth more such conflict, rooted in the compressed life cycle of companies. I have long argued that when investing in young tech companies, you are investing in a story about the company, not an extrapolation of numbers. The compressed corporate life cycle, and the potential for CEO/company mismatches that it creates, in conjunction with the stickiness that comes from the existence of voting and non-voting shares, adds a layer of additional uncertainty to valuation. In short, when assessing the value of a young company's story, you are also assessing the capacity of the management of the company to deliver on that story, with the caveat that if you are wrong about incumbent management, you may be still stuck with its decisions.

As young companies transition to become mature-growth companies, the presence of a large stockholder as a manager is often a significant impediment to a management change. Consider a firm like Oracle, where the founder CEO, Larry Ellison, owned almost 25% of the outstanding stock, even as the company aged and moved through the life cycle to become a mature-growth firm. With that holding, he could effectively stymie hostile acquirers and activist investors. In addition, when mature-growth companies come to the crossroads between pushing for more growth (with more investment) and acting more mature (with more debt and cash return), investors in the company will disagree on the right path forward, making it difficult to establish consensus on change. Mature-growth companies also acquire protection from their successes in the past, in delivering both operating growth and high returns, making shareholders more likely to defer to management.

MATURE PUBLIC COMPANIES

It has always been difficult to change managers at mature firms, and here, it is the share ownership structure of the firm that becomes the biggest challenge to overcome, as more shares are held by institutions and fewer by insiders and individuals. Institutional stockholders, for the most part, are passive and vote with their feet (by selling stock in firms that they believe are not well managed). Consequently, rather than push against incumbent managers and its decisions,* they tend to go along, voting with managers most of the time. To add to the challenge, many mature firms modify their corporate charters, adding

* R. Parrino, R.W. Sias, and L. T. Starks, "Voting with Their Feet: Institutional Ownership Changes around Forced CEO Turnover," *Journal of Financial Economics* 68, no. 1 (April 2003): 3–46. The study finds that aggregate institutional ownership drops by about 12% in the year prior to a forced CEO change, and that individual ownership increases. Institutional investors who are better informed and more concerned about prudent stocks are more likely to sell during this period.

staggered board elections, whereby only a portion of the board can be replaced each year, and supermajority clauses requiring more than majority approval for changes to happen. These amendments, no matter what the motivations behind them, ultimately make change more difficult at these firms.

That said, the likelihood of changing management has increased over the last few decades, for many reasons. The first is that the capital that private equity and hedge funds control is much greater than it was three or four decades ago, making it easier for them to target for change not only more firms but also much bigger ones. The second is that technology and information sharing has made it easier to build coalitions for change. For instance, the proxy solicitation fight, whereby investors challenging management try to gain control of enough proxy votes to change management, is now largely fought online and with direct access to shareholders. In the same vein, social media can now be tapped by investors who want to challenge management narratives and offer counternarratives.

There is another force at play that is opening the market for corporate control, and that is globalization. As investors in a company become global, you find companies that would not have faced questioning and challenges from their local-market investors being exposed to those questions from a global investor base. In Europe, prior to the creation of the EU, most investors in companies were from the countries in which these companies were incorporated, and management challenges were uncommon. As the investor bases for these companies have become more European, you do see more challenges of management; German (French) investors seem to have fewer qualms about challenging French (German) companies.

DECLINING AND DISTRESSED PUBLIC COMPANIES

There are two significant hurdles to change in declining companies, even if it is desperately needed for these companies to survive. The first is in the nature of the changes that will be delivered by new management, since decline implies layoffs and shutdowns, both of which create side costs for stakeholder groups and society. It is no surprise that Hollywood's biggest villains in business-centered movies are private equity investors doing leveraged buyouts of companies. The challenge with changing the ways declining companies are run is not in the changes themselves but in the packaging and presenting of those changes, many of which create pain for stakeholders in the firm (employees, suppliers) or for society. It is one of the reasons that private equity firms, which are often the agents of change in this space, buy out public firms in decline and try to make them private firms, where the changes they plan to implement receive less scrutiny and perhaps less backlash. In recent years, private equity has expanded its reach from publicly traded firms to privately owned businesses that they perceive as constrained or in need of change.

The second hurdle to change is that in decline, especially if accompanied by distress, firms become entangled in the legal system, which slows down change. A company that declares bankruptcy and enters chapter 11 is buying itself time, but the legal system becomes part of the change process since, once a company declares bankruptcy, any changes must get court approval. If the bankruptcy process is slow and costly enough, change will become uneconomical, and these companies will be left to fend for themselves, using up resources and capital that could find better uses. In fact, investors seeking change at these companies are put through an endurance test, and only those with staying power remain.

FAMILY-OWNED AND FAMILY-CONTROLLED BUSINESSES

In much of the world, businesses, even if they are publicly traded, are run by family groups. To the extent that the top management of these businesses are members of the family, these companies are uniquely exposed to company/CEO mismatches, especially as second or third generations of a family enter the management ranks and/or these families enter new businesses. To see how the corporate life cycle structure story plays out in family-group companies, it is worth remembering that family groups often control companies that spread across many different business, effectively resembling conglomerates in their reach but structured as individual companies. Consequently, it is not only possible, but likely, that a family group will control companies at different stages in the corporate life cycle, ranging from young, growth companies at one end of the spectrum to declining companies at the other end. In fact, one of the reasons family groups survived and thrived in economies where public markets were underdeveloped was their capacity to use cash generated in their mature and declining businesses to cover capital needs in their growing businesses. This intra-group capital market becomes trickier to balance as family-group companies go public, since you need shareholder assent for these capital transfers. With weak corporate governance, more the rule than the exception at family-group companies, it is entirely possible that shareholders in the more mature and cash-generating companies in a family group will be forced to invest in younger, growth companies in that same group.

There is research on CEO turnover in family-group companies, and the results are not surprising. In a study, researchers looked at 4,601 CEOs in companies, classifying them based on whether they were family CEOs or outside CEOs, and found that forced turnover was much less frequent in the first group.* In other words, family CEOs are less likely to be fired and more likely to stay around until a successor is found, often within the family. While this is good news in terms of continuity, it is bad news if there is a company/CEO mismatch, since that mismatch will wreak havoc for far longer before it is fixed.

What can family groups do to deal with such a mismatch—especially as the potential for mismatch increases, as disruption turns some mature and growing businesses into declining ones and capital gets shifted to new businesses in the green energy and technology spaces? First, power must become more diffuse within the family, spreading away from a powerful family leader and more toward a family committee, to allow for the different perspectives needed to become successful in businesses at other stages in the life cycle. Second, there must be a serious reassessment of where different businesses within the family group are in the life cycle, with special attention devoted to those that are transitioning from one phase to another.

If top management positions are restricted to family members, the challenge for the family will be finding people with the characteristics needed to run businesses across the life cycle. For example, as many family groups enter the technology space, drawn by its potential growth, the limiting constraint might be finding a visionary storyteller from within the family. If one does not exist, the question becomes whether the family will be willing to bring in someone from outside and give that person enough freedom to run the young, growth business. Finally, if a mismatch arises between a family member CEO and the business he or she is responsible for running, there has to be a willingness to remove that family member from power, even though it may be sure to raise family tensions and create fights.

To address why family control can help in some cases and hurt in others, it is again useful to bring in the corporate life cycle. In the portions of the corporate life cycle where patience and a steady hand are required, the presence of a family member CEO may increase value, since he or she will be more inclined to think about long-term consequences for value, rather than short-term profit or pricing effects. On the other hand, if a family CEO is entrenched in a company that is transitioning from growth to mature, or from mature to declining, and is not adaptable enough to modify the way he or she manages the company, it is a negative for value. Family-group companies composed primarily of

* B. H. Hamilton, S. Hanna, A. Hincapié, and N. Lyman, "Family CEOs, Turnover, and Firm Performance," Working Paper, Washington University of St. Louis, 2020.

companies in the former grouping will therefore trade at premiums, whereas family group companies that include a disproportionately large number of disrupted or new businesses will be handicapped.

In the subset of companies that are publicly traded but family controlled, the weapon of choice against change is more complex holding structures, including pyramids and cross holdings. In a pyramid structure, an investor uses control in one company to establish control in other companies. In a cross-holding structure, companies own shares in each other, thus allowing the group's controlling stockholders to run all the companies involved with less than 50% of the outstanding stock. With both structures, change becomes more difficult. Most Japanese companies (*keiretsu*) and Korean companies (*chaebols*) in the 1980s and 1990s were structured as cross holdings, immunizing management at these companies from stockholder pressure.

Life Cycle and Management Change: A Summary

During this chapter, I looked at why mismatches happen at companies, the catalysts that push companies toward changing management, and the challenges that they may face in making those changes. With each topic, I have argued that there are differences across companies, with the corporate life cycle a key factor in those differences.

Figure 18.7 brings together both the catalysts and challenges that you face in changing a firm at each stage in the life cycle.

FIGURE 18.7 | Management Mismatches and Changes across the Corporate Life Cycle

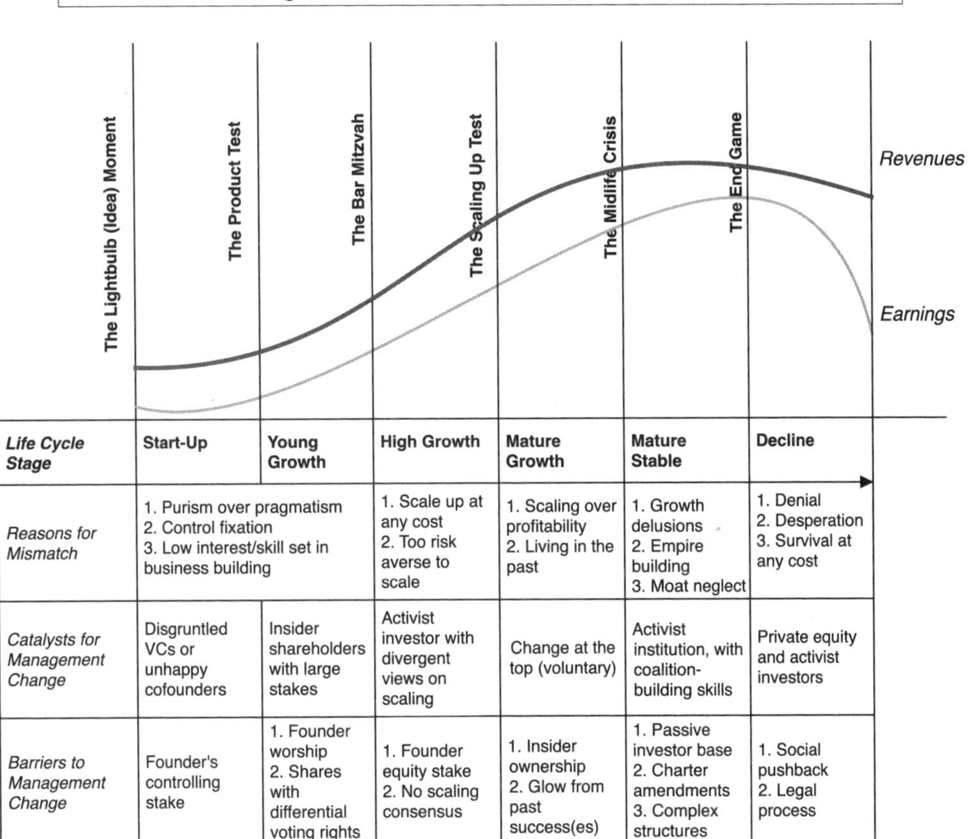

Life Cycle Stage	Start-Up	Young Growth	High Growth	Mature Growth	Mature Stable	Decline
Reasons for Mismatch	1. Purism over pragmatism 2. Control fixation 3. Low interest/skill set in business building		1. Scale up at any cost 2. Too risk averse to scale	1. Scaling over profitability 2. Living in the past	1. Growth delusions 2. Empire building 3. Moat neglect	1. Denial 2. Desperation 3. Survival at any cost
Catalysts for Management Change	Disgruntled VCs or unhappy cofounders	Insider shareholders with large stakes	Activist investor with divergent views on scaling	Change at the top (voluntary)	Activist institution, with coalition-building skills	Private equity and activist investors
Barriers to Management Change	Founder's controlling stake	1. Founder worship 2. Shares with differential voting rights	1. Founder equity stake 2. No scaling consensus	1. Insider ownership 2. Glow from past success(es)	1. Passive investor base 2. Charter amendments 3. Complex structures	1. Social pushback 2. Legal process

As you can see, finding management that fits a company properly is an ongoing task as companies and their managers age. While it is important at every stage of the life cycle, it is most critical at either end of the life cycle, with start-ups and young companies at one end and declining and distressed companies at the other.

Conclusion

There is no one template for great management, since the roles that managers play and their key functions will vary as a company goes from a start-up to mature and, eventually, into decline. Early in the process, CEOs will be judged on storytelling (vision) and business building skills; as firms mature, they are more likely to be evaluated on their skills in protecting competitive advantages (moats) and delivering on numbers. The right CEO for a company will therefore reflect where it is in the life cycle.

With that lead-in, I noted that management, even if it is competent and qualified, can be mismatched with the company that it is given to manage because of the passage of time, during which the company and manager changed, because of bad choices regarding replacement managers by the board of directors, or because of macroeconomic changes that alter risk exposures. A mismatch between management and company, if allowed to persist, will have negative consequences for growth and profitability and, in extreme cases, can cause business failure. The process of fixing the mismatch is the essence of corporate governance, and I examined how the catalysts for management change and obstacles to change shift as a company goes through the life cycle.

19

Fighting Aging: The Upside and Downside

IF THERE IS A theme to this book, it is that for most companies, the best response to aging is to accept that it is happening and run the company to reflect its aging. I will argue in this chapter that from the perspective of the owners or shareholders of a business, this is the strategy that offers not only the best odds but the best risk/return trade-off. That said, there are several factors that induce companies to fight aging, sometimes with success. Some are rooted in psychology, where shrinking a business is viewed as a failure while growing one is considered a success, and some in management incentives, where there is upside to managers risking it all on low-odds, high-payoff bets made with other people's money. In this chapter, I look at pathways that companies follow to stop or even reverse the aging process, from cosmetic makeovers to revolutionary changes in business models, and examine the commonalties across firms that have succeeded. To provide balance and perspective, I also look at what happens to businesses that try to make these changes and fail, and how failure can create steep falls, sudden death, and walking-dead companies.

Accepting Aging

In the chapters leading in, I talked about how, as companies age, the focus within the business changes from how much and where to invest to whether to fund those investments with debt or equity and how much cash (if any) should be returned to shareholders. If a company accepts aging, its managers will adapt to where it is in the life cycle and adjust investing, financing, and dividend decisions to reflect its age—even if means low, no, or even negative growth for the business and, in some cases, leads to demise. Growth for the sake of growth, and survival for the sake of survival, is not a good end game for any business.

The Acceptance Playbook

For a company to age gracefully, its management must start by accepting its age and redefining what success and failure will look like at the company. Put simply, if high growth is defined to be a prerequisite for success, mature and even declining businesses will find ways to fight their fates and grow, no matter what the cost. That is one reason I argued, in chapter 18, that the top management and CEO of a mature or declining firm must bring in a very different mindset about business, one that is less ambitious, and more anchored in reality, than that of the top management or CEO of a firm earlier in the life cycle. If you have management that matches where the company is in the life cycle, the rest of the playbook unfolds:

1. **Narrative that fits:** If one of the roles of top management is to create and convey a narrative for the company that is in their custody, an accepting management will tell a corporate story that reflects where the company is in the life cycle. With a mature business, that story will be one of low growth, perhaps with optimistic takes on margins and returns; with a declining business, it will be one where the company reduces its asset base and becomes smaller, in response to a shrinking market.
2. **Consistency in investing policy:** A business story that is grounded in reality has credibility only if it is backed up by actions that reflect management's belief in the story. Thus, the mature company management that tells a "mature business story" will be credible only if it steers away from making big acquisitions or investing in new businesses. In the same vein, managers telling a growth story will lose credibility if they refuse the investments needed to scale up, even if those investments are financially sound.
3. **Consistency in financing and cash return:** In the chapters on financing and dividend policy, I noted the transitions in both as firms age, from no debt in the early stages, to more debt in maturing, and from being dependent on cash inflows from equity when young, to large dividends and buybacks in maturity. A management in acceptance will follow this script, refusing to borrow money, or doing so only if it has no

other option, when managing young-growth companies and borrowing more, while buying back stock, as managers of mature firms.

4. **With investors who buy in to that narrative:** In chapters 14 through 17, I looked at how investors with different preferences for risk and growth pick companies in different phases of the life cycle. When companies are at peace with where they are in the life cycle, they will tend to attract investors who are like-minded, making it easier to maintain policies that make sense. In fact, these companies will repel investors whose preferences do not match what they can deliver, given where they are in the life cycle, even if it means lower share prices in the near term. Companies that seek out investors who want what they cannot deliver, often because these investors have capital, are setting themselves up for failure and friction. Thus, young, growth companies that seek out investors who like and want dividends, or mature companies that draw in investors who want high earnings growth, are creating stresses that will leave both the companies and its investors worse off.

In short, management that accepts where the company it manages sits in the corporate life cycle does not overreach on either operating or financing decisions. It does not overpromise on growth and profitability and seeks out an investor clientele that not only is comfortable with what the firm can deliver but may actually pay a premium for it.

Why Is Acceptance So Difficult to Achieve?

Acceptance of where a business is in the life cycle makes management simpler and less error-prone, but for many companies, that acceptance remains elusive, as their managers craft plans and act in ways that are out of sync with where they are in the life cycle. This disconnect occurs for many reasons:

1. **Boredom:** It is undeniably more exciting being at the helm of a growing company than a mature or declining one. Like moths drawn to a flame, managers at mature and even declining companies are drawn to the excitement of growth.
2. **Hope:** Human beings are hardwired for optimism and to hope that things will get better, and managers at many mature and declining companies believe that they are merely victims of circumstance or extraordinary events. Change, they tend to believe, is just around the corner, which will allow them to reverse, or at least stop the clock on, corporate aging.

3. **Management incentives:** In publicly traded companies, especially in the mature and declining phases of the life cycle, managers operate with different incentives and interests than the owners of these companies. To the extent that compensation is tied to absolute levels of earnings or revenues, or to growth in those numbers, managers will be incentivized to push for growth, even if it costs too much, leaving shareholders worse off.
4. **Peer-group pressure:** Even if managers can overcome these barriers to acceptance, they will face an additional barrier to staying on the path of acceptance, and especially so if they operate in businesses where most of their competitors continue to strive for growth. With muted ambitions on revenue growth and scaled down plans for reinvestment back into the business, the companies that these managers run will be outliers in their peer group. A casual analyst who equates higher growth with higher value will tag the firm as a laggard on growth and attach a negative recommendation to it, and investors who go along with that line of reasoning can push down share prices, increasing the pressure on the company to conform.

Finally, there is an ecosystem in business that will be brought to bear on companies that accept their mature or declining status to change their perspective. At the risk of being cynical, I would note that management consultants and bankers generate a large portion of their fees from their capacity to convince companies that they can reverse the aging process and getting them to act on that belief.

Examples of Acceptance

It is a testimonial to the forces that are arrayed against acceptance that there are so few examples of companies that adapt to where they are in the life cycle, especially in the mature or declining phases, and make decisions accordingly. Put differently, even in sectors where there is clear and incontrovertible evidence of business decline, individual companies aspire for growth, even if it never manifests. One example of a company that countered this trend is Severstal, a Russian steel company, which responded to a collapse in profitability in the global steel business by divesting a large chunk of its non-Russian holdings and becoming a smaller, albeit more profitable, business between 2011 and 2016, as can be seen in figure 19.1.

FIGURE 19.1 | Revenues, Operating Income and Operating Margins—Severstal

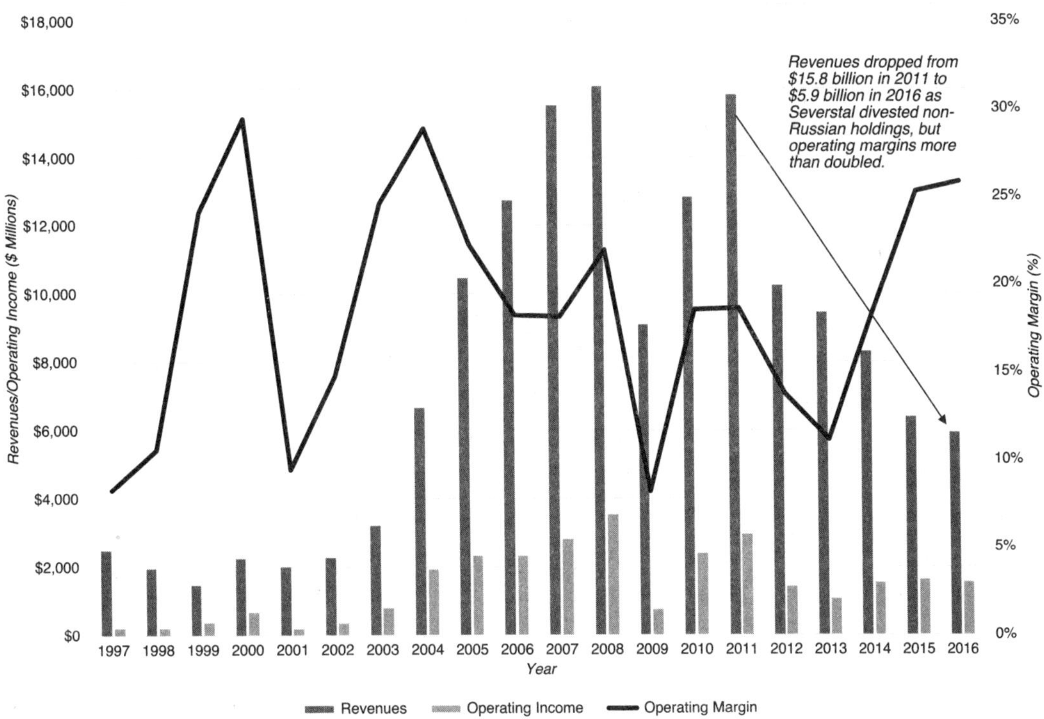

As you can see, revenues shrank by more than 60% between 2011 and 2016 as Severstal sold off a large chunk of its non-Russian operations, leaving itself with a domestic market that was dramatically more profitable. The net effect was that Severstal became a much smaller, but more profitable and valuable, company as a result of its actions.

For most companies, acceptance comes only after they have tried more ambitious plans to reclaim growth and reverse aging. An example of how much it takes for management to arrive at acceptance is General Electric, a company with a storied past and a history of success coming into the twenty-first century. For much of this century, the company has struggled to make its multiple businesses, spread across geographies, succeed. In 2001, Jeff Immelt took the reins of the company from his legendary predecessor, Jack Welch, who had been largely responsible for building the corporate behemoth, and he felt the pressure not only to keep the company intact but to continue the path of acquisitions and growth that Welch had forged. By 2017, when Immelt stepped down as CEO, it was clear that GE was heading for a cliff, but it took two more CEOs and three more years of operating pain before the company announced plans to break itself up and become a smaller business.

DETERMINANTS OF ACCEPTANCE

To understand why Severstal responded as quickly as it did to changing steel market economics and why GE took decades, it is worth looking at the factors that determine how quickly companies move toward acceptance, as well as how aggressively they respond with action:

1. **Skin in the game:** One characteristic often shared by companies that respond quickly to changed circumstances is that that they are either privately or family owned or, if they are public, their managers hold significant shares of ownership in these companies. Going back to the Severstal example, the company was majority-owned and controlled by an individual, Alexey Mordashov, during the 2011 to 2016 period. In contrast, GE's shareholder base was primarily institutional, and top managers held a very small percentage of outstanding shares there.
2. **Extended operating pain:** When companies report poor operating performance, the initial response that many managers have is to attribute it to extraordinary circumstances or macroeconomic events and stay with tried and true business practices. As the poor operating performance stretches into many years, it becomes more and more difficult to sustain these excuses, and the truth eventually comes through.
3. **Pressure from investors:** In companies that are mature or in decline, but where managers are in denial, acceptance is speeded up if you have investors pushing for change. It is for this reason that it is healthy for a market to have activist investors, challenging management and holding them accountable. Since this principle is at the core of corporate governance, it follows that you are far less likely to see companies refusing to act their age in markets with strong corporate governance than in markets where corporate governance is weak or absent.
4. **Market mood and momentum:** In good times, when markets are buoyant and stock prices are rising, companies will find themselves with more slack, and the cost of pushing for growth by taking bad investments, even if you are a mature or declining company, may be overlooked. As market mood changes and share prices drop, that buffer disappears quickly, and corporate weaknesses and limitations are more likely to be exposed.
5. **Access to and use of debt:** In the 1980s, as the first wave of leveraged buyouts hit the market, Michael Jensen argued that debt could operate as a disciplining force in

some companies. While he did not make mention of corporate life cycles explicitly, his point was that the managers of mature and declining firms would become more disciplined in their investing decisions. Implicitly, he was arguing that borrowing more and burdening themselves with interest expenses that they were contractually obligated to meet would make managers at these firms less likely to overreach and take investments in bad businesses.

In sum, if companies are mature or declining, are run by managers with little skin in the game, and face little pressure from investors to change their ways, it is very likely that these companies will refuse to act their age. They will invest like growth companies, impoverishing their shareholders and using up capital that would be used far more productively by younger, growth businesses.

Fighting Aging

The forces arrayed against acceptance are powerful, and it should come as no surprise that most firms facing maturity or decline look for ways to stop or reverse aging. In some cases, they succeed, providing big payoffs for their shareholders and burnishing the reputations of their top managers. In others, they crash and burn, wiping out the value that they built up over their lifetimes.

Renewals, Revamps, and Rebirths

Fighting aging is difficult to do, but at least in the corporate life cycle, it can be done. In this section, I will look at the range of actions that companies take to reverse the aging process, starting with *renewals*, where firms try to "fix" their existing businesses to make them grow again; moving on to *revamps*, where they extend their businesses into new markets and new products; and closing with *rebirths*, where they change their businesses, hoping to restart the corporate aging clock. I confess that the lines between renewals, revamps, and rebirths are often blurred, and a corporate action, like an acquisition, may fall into more than one of these categories. What starts as a renewal or revamp in a company can become a rebirth over time.

RENEWALS

In a renewal, a company stays largely within its existing business, which is maturing or even in decline, but makes changes that allow it to go back to growth, at least in the near term. Renewal includes some of the least aggressive anti-aging actions that a company can pursue, with the benefit that failing carries smaller costs.

ACTS OF RENEWAL

The actions that fall under this grouping can range from cosmetic changes, which occur mostly on the surface and change little in terms of substance, to more tangible changes, whereby a company can alter how a product is made or marketed and perhaps even perceived by its customers.

1. **Corporate name changes:** Companies do sometimes change their names, for a variety of reasons, but one that falls into the renewal grouping is if the name change is designed to change perceptions of the company and perhaps allow it to expand its market. Since companies spend significant amounts trying to build recognition of their names, there is an obvious cost to abandoning a recognizable name, but there are cases where the benefits can exceed the costs.
    a. **Expand or update product offerings:** If a business name is narrowing the market for its products and services, and the name change will allow for a broader market, it may make sense. One example was when Boston Chicken, which had expanded its fast-food offerings from just chicken to an array of other food, decided to change its name to Boston Market, to reflect its diversified product mix.
    b. **Toxic connections:** Sometimes a corporate name has become toxic, due to either news stories around it or corporate actions, and that toxicity affects the company's capacity to run its businesses. One reason Philip Morris, the largest tobacco company in the world, changed its name to Altria was the hope that the name change would reduce the taint of being associated with a cancer-causing product and the lies the company told about its dangers. It may also partially explain why Facebook, perhaps the one of the most recognized corporate names on the planet, decided to change its name to Meta in the aftermath of years of negative stories about the company.
    c. **Hot sectors:** During the dot-com boom in the 1990s, and the more recent social media explosion in the last decade, many companies tried to reframe their stories for both their investors and consumers by changing their names to make themselves appear to be part of hot sectors. A study of companies that added ".com" to their names during the 1990s found that their stock prices soared on the name change, even with no operating changes at these firms.*

* M. J. Cooper, O. Dimitrov, and P. R. Rau, "A Rose.com by Any Other Name," *Journal of Finance* 56, no. 6 (December 2001): 2371–88.

2. **Strategic makeovers:** "Strategic" is a fuzzy word and, in my view, it is often used to justify decisions that cannot be justified with the numbers. That said, the road map that guides a company in its choices on investing, financing, and dividend policy is a strategic one, and changes in that road map are indicative of changes to come in how a company makes those choices. In some companies facing a low-growth future, the first step in altering that future is to provide blueprints to investors and consumers of the changes they plan to make. The reaction will depend largely on the credibility of the management mapping out changes, and it is often more credible when a new CEO and management, rather than the incumbent management, are making the claim. In 2013, for instance, Alcatel-Lucent, with a new CEO in Michel Combes, announced that it would shift its focus from telecom equipment to networking products and broadband and saw its shares jump 7% in response.*
3. **Remarketing and rebranding:** In some cases, the seeds for a company's return to growth lie in marketing an existing product or service differently, with the hope of either getting existing customers to buy more or attracting new customers. This approach is more likely to be attempted in consumer product companies, and especially when brand names and consumer perception of products, rather than tangible differences across competitive products, determine market share and success. It worked at Abercrombie & Fitch, a company that was founded as a store for outdoor gear but used marketing to great effect to become a destination for young mall shoppers in the 1990s.†
4. **Product redesign:** For some companies with aging brands, the key to growth is redesigning their products and services to make them appealing to different customer bases. This is the path that Lego adopted in 2003, when it took a product that had largely remained the same for much of the company's life and adapted with sets based upon movies (Star Wars, Marvel, and its own Lego movies) or targeted to gaming afficionados (Minecraft Legos) and others to get a new lease on life. Just for balance, it is worth noting that this is also the path that Coca-Cola followed in 1985 when it introduced New Coke, to disastrous effect.

* Leila Abboud, "New CEO Begins Alcatel Makeover," Reuters, June 19, 2013, https://www.reuters.com/article/us-alcatel-reorganisation/new-ceo-begins-alcatel-makeover-idUKBRE95I06O20130619.

† Filling in the rest of the Abercrombie & Fitch story, the company's soaring success in the 1990s came to a crashing end, as it was accused of racial discrimination a decade later. See A. Horton, "'Discrimination Was Their Brand': How Abercrombie & Fitch Fell Out of Fashion," *Guardian*, April 19, 2022, https://www.theguardian.com/film/2022/apr/19/abercrombie-fitch-netflix-documentary-fashion-discrimination.

PAYOFF TO RENEWAL

Most companies that face slowing growth map out renewal plans, and while some succeed, many end up with little to show for the millions or billions of dollars that are spent on them. I would argue that the following factors determine the likelihood and extent of success from renewal plans:

1. **Cosmetic versus real change:** Cosmetic changes at companies, such as corporate name changes, can have effects on investor perception, but in my view, those effects will fade over time. The companies that saw their stock prices soar when they added ".com" to their names in the late 1990s saw all that price surge disappear in 2001, with the dot-com crash. Strategic plans, like the one announced by Alcatel, can evoke favorable market reactions, but if the company does not follow through with operating changes that are in line with the plan, not only will those stock price increases fade, the management will lose credibility, affecting its capacity to make changes in the future.
2. **Market price versus operating focus:** On a related point, for many publicly traded companies making renewal changes, the focus seems to be on convincing investors that change is coming and that it will add value, rather than on actual operating changes and what can be done to add to growth and value. While I understand why investors need to be part of any renewal process, the more a renewal plan is grounded in operating changes that add value, the greater will be its chance of success in returning the firm to growth.
3. **Individual or herd behavior:** In some cases, the impetus for renewal comes to individual firms that are struggling in sectors that are doing well; in others, it is a collective problem, where many or most firms in a sector are facing operating challenges at the same time. It is easier to map out renewal plans when the problems are company-specific than if are they sector-wide, for a simple reason: when many firms in a sector or group are facing slowdown in growth at the same time, the plans for renewal that they come up with will tend to be very similar, and that can affect the payoffs. When Amazon disrupted the retail business, the renewal plans for most brick-and-mortar retailers followed the same script—usually involving cutting costs at existing stores and expanding their online retailing—thereby undercutting the benefits. The lesson for renewal plans is that success is more likely if you have plans that are original and different and that build on strengths that are unique to your company.
4. **Old versus new customers:** In service of an understandable desire to draw in new customers, companies sometimes make changes that alienate existing customers,

creating net negative effects for the firm. For instance, the Gap, facing a slowdown in growth in the 1990s, decided to rebrand itself to appeal to a younger, hipper market, but in the process lost its hold on the older customers that formed its core market. In general, renewal plans that result in changing the core market for a company are riskier than ones that build on that market.

REVAMPS

In the continuum of actions taken by companies that seek to fight aging, revamps require more change than renewals. Not surprisingly, they are both more costly to undertake and have much bigger positive payoffs, if they work. In this section, I will discuss ways in which companies approaching maturity or decline can revamp themselves.

ACTS OF REVAMPING

In a revamp, a company augments its product portfolio with new products, or expands from its current markets into new ones. In some cases, this can include changes in business models to deliver better operating results, and perhaps more growth, from existing products and services.

1. **New products/services:** When a company finds itself hitting a wall in growth, because of either competition or disruption, it can sometimes find a pathway back by expanding its offerings. As newspapers have lost advertising revenues to online advertisers, the *New York Times* has found a pathway to survive, and even grow, with an online presence that draws on its strengths. In an experiment still in progress, Lululemon, a company that benefited from the growth of exercise wear among women but has found that growth lagging as competition picked up, is trying to rediscover itself with casual dress clothes for women and men.
2. **New markets:** For some companies, the key to rediscovering growth comes from finding new markets for its products, either in the form of new customers for its existing products or new geographies in which to grow. As an example of the former, Goya, a US-based food manufacturer that catered primarily to the Hispanic market until the 1980s, found growth by marketing its products more aggressively to non-Hispanics.* As an example of the latter, Bajaj Auto, an Indian company that was built around selling scooters in its domestic market, used globalization to expand its reach into other geographies and extend its growth.

* "Goya Sales Target: Not Just Hispanic," *New York Times*, March 26, 1984, https://www.nytimes.com/1984/03/26/business/goya-sales-target-not-just-hispanic.html.

3. **New business models:** In some cases, a company may be able to alter its growth trajectory by modifying the business model that it uses to make and sell its products or services. Consider Adobe, a long-standing maker of software, which shifted its business model, in 2013, from selling software and updates to a subscription model. That shift allowed the company to reclaim its growth status, while making its revenues more stable.

It is worth noting that these revamp choices are not mutually exclusive; a company can introduce new products, expand into new markets, and/or adopt new business models at the same time, though it risks trying to do too much.

PAYOFF TO REVAMPS

Do revamps pay off? The answer, again, lies in the nature of the revamp and what the company doing the revamp brings to the table in terms of competitive advantages. Consider again the success stories that I quoted in the last section and what they share.

- The *New York Times* has succeeded with its online entry, while most other newspapers that have tried have failed, because it built on the content that the paper gets from its unparalleled staff of reporters around the world, opinion columnists with wide followings, and even its puzzle content (crosswords, Wordle). Most regional and national newspapers, in contrast, have spent years reducing original content in their newspapers, often because they want to cut costs, and so have little to offer online readers.
- Goya's successful expansion in the 1980s came from its unique positioning as one of the only Hispanic food manufacturers in the US market and its strong brand-name identification in its core market. In short, consumers were more likely to buy Goya canned black beans than an equivalent offering from Campbell or Kraft because of the company's pedigree.
- For Bajaj Auto, the lower cost structure in its Indian manufacturing facilities gave it a leg up, especially when competing with Italian or Japanese scooter manufacturers, and explains why it was able to capture market share so quickly in the global market.
- With Adobe, the subscription model caught on quickly because its software was already dominant in the market and its products (Photoshop, Acrobat, etc.) benefited broadly from the online shift.

If there is a lesson here, it is that companies planning revamps must begin with an assessment of their moats (competitive advantages) and strengths and try to exploit them when developing new products/services, seeking out new markets, or creating new business models. A mistake that many companies and investors make in assessing growth plans is that they pay too much attention to the size of the market that a company is targeting and far too little to what the company can bring as unique strengths that will allow it to capture a tangible share of the targeted market. That is a lesson worth remembering as artificial intelligence (AI) becomes the big buzzword of the moment and every company claims to be developing a pathway to making money in that space.

REBIRTHS

In a renewal, a company tries to find new growth opportunities with its existing products and business model, using rebranding and redesign to expand its market. In a revamp, a company reaches further, with new products and services, new markets, and new business models driving growth. In a rebirth, a company remakes itself in a new business, perhaps very different from its original one.

THE ALLURE OF REBIRTHS

The Chinese saying 生, 老, 病, 死 ("you are born, get old, get sick, and die") is a reality check for human beings, but it is not exactly an uplifting calling, and it is no wonder that many look for an escape from its strictures. One option that almost every religion offers is the possibility of an afterlife, cleverly tied to how closely you follow that religion's edicts. For corporations approaching the end stages of their life cycle, this option is a nonstarter, since there is no corporate heaven (unless you count starring in a Harvard case study as heavenly) or hell (though bankruptcy court comes awfully close). The other option is the possibility of a rebirth or reincarnation, wherein you manage to redefine yourself. After all, I am uplifted by stories of people who have experienced that rebirth—athletes who transition to successful businesspeople or actors who become presidents. On this count, corporations have an advantage over individuals, since they are legal entities that can reinvent themselves while holding on to their corporate identities.

There are companies that have beaten the odds of the business life cycle, fought off decline, and been reborn as successful ventures. Two examples that come to mind are IBM, in its fall from glory in the 1980s and its subsequent rebirth as a healthy, profitable firm in the 1990s, and Apple, with its climb back from the dark days of 1997 to the top of the market capitalization table in 2012. As I think of these and other examples, it is worth noting that the very fact that I can name these companies suggests that they are the exceptions rather than the rule. Notwithstanding that sobering reality, it is still useful to put these success stories under the microscope, not only to gain an understanding of what allowed these companies to succeed but also to develop forward-looking criteria that I may be able to use in investing.

THE INGREDIENTS FOR SUCCESS

At the outset, I must admit my trepidation about this exercise. First, I am not a corporate historian or strategist, and I am sure that there is much that I am glossing over as I make a list of "rebirth" criteria. Second, I am wary of drawing big lessons from anecdotal evidence, recognizing how easy it is to reach the wrong conclusions. Nevertheless, there are common factors that I see in successful rebirth stories:

1. **Acceptance that the old ways don't work anymore:** To have a corporate rebirth, a company must come to an acceptance that the old ways, successful though they might have been in the past, don't work anymore. That acceptance, as I noted earlier in this chapter, does not come easily or quickly, and the longer and hoarier the history of the company, the longer it takes for acceptance to set in. With IBM, in the late 1980s, a series of CEOs at the company raised denial to an art form and almost pushed the company into irrelevance. Acceptance also requires more than lip service to change and must be backed up by actions that indicate that the company is indeed willing to jettison big portions of its past.
2. **A change agent:** This is a cliché, but change starts at the top. At IBM, the rebirth really began when Lou Gerstner became CEO of the company, in 1993, and at Apple, the change agent was obviously Steve Jobs, a man who had been banished from Apple for his lack of focus a decade prior but returned as CEO in 1997. It would be simplistic to say that the change agent always must come from outside the company, because there have been companies where insiders who have spent a lifetime in the company have nonetheless been willing to shake it up. I think it is safe to say, though, that change agents are usually not shrinking violets and that they are ready to jettison the status quo.
3. **A plan for change:** Pointing out that the existing ways don't work anymore is important, but it is futile unless accompanied by a new mission and focus. At IBM, Gerstner changed the mindset of the company (and its employees) early in his tenure, an incredible accomplishment given how deeply entrenched it was in its existing ways. Coming from RJR Nabisco, he brought both a customer focus and a willingness to let

go of IBM's past mistakes (anyone remember OS/2?), and this allowed him to create the modern IBM. Steve Jobs shocked Apple employees by entering a détente with Microsoft wherein, in return for $150 million in cash and a promise by Microsoft that it would continue producing Office for the Mac, he essentially gave Microsoft a free legal pass to borrow from the Mac operating system in updating Windows. He used the breathing room that this agreement gave him to redefine Apple as an entertainment company rather than a computer company, and the rest, as they say, is history.

4. **Building on a company's strengths:** If there is a common theme that runs across renewals, revamps, and now rebirths, it is that a company that is trying to reinvent itself in a new business must build around its strengths. Microsoft's successful foray into the cloud business, under Satya Nadella, was fueled by the expertise of the software engineers at Microsoft, just as Apple's success in smartphones, with Steve Jobs at the top, was built around the company's strengths in design and proprietary operating systems.
5. **Shake up existing businesses:** At many companies, rebirth will mean that you may have to give up revenues and earnings that you generate from existing product businesses, and those who run those businesses will push back, pointing to cannibalization as a reason to go slow on new businesses. It is this behavior that led Clayton Christensen to argue that disruption, if it happens in a business, almost always comes from new entrants with nothing to lose rather than the largest and most successful players in that business. In successful rebirths, it is critical that the decision-makers who are given the responsibility of transitioning a company to a new business have disruption mindsets, as well as a CEO who protects them from backlash from those in charge of the company's existing businesses.
6. **Luck:** Much as I would like to attribute success uniquely to great skill and failure to poor management, it remains true that the X factor in successful rebirth is luck. Gerstner was lucky that he made his changes at IBM in the 1990s, a decade of robust economic growth overall, but especially so for technology companies. Steve Jobs was helped by the ineptitude of his competition, so blinded by their investment in the status quo (music companies selling us music on CDs, cell phone companies thinking of cell phones as extensions of landline phones) that they either did not react or reacted too slowly to Apple's innovations.

I am sure that this is not a comprehensive list and that I have missed a few items, but it is a start. Companies that have been value traps or are destined to become walking-dead businesses can become great investments if they can find a path to rebirth; an investor who bought IBM shares in 1993 or Apple shares in 1997 would have profited immensely from their reincarnations. As an investment exercise, you could prepare a list of the companies where stock prices have stagnated for long periods and check to see which of them have the ingredients in place for rebirth: an acceptance that the old ways don't work (with tangible evidence in investment, financing, and dividend decisions to back it up), a change agent (new management), and a new focus (with actions to back it up). The last factor, luck, is immune to assessment, but you can consult your astrological signs or read the tea leaves if it helps you to make the right choices.

The Downside: Steep Falls, Sudden Death, and Zombieland

If the dream of every mature and declining company is to find a path to a renewal, a revamp, or rebirth, the actions taken to push toward that dream can sometimes give rise to the nightmare scenarios, where a company falls steeply from its historical operating path or, in some cases, has to shut down. In this section, I look at these bad endings for firms, as well as some of the factors that explain why some companies are more exposed to them than others.

STEEP FALLS

There are cases where firms with a seemingly long and profitable future ahead of them face a steep falloff and a precipitous decline from growth or mature status to being in decline. There are a multitude of reasons for steep falls, some of which are easier to defend against than others.

1. **Personality driven:** If a business is built around a personality, such as a founder CEO who operates as the public face of the company and who plays the lead role in every significant decision made by the business, it is exposed to the danger that losing that person will make the company less valuable and, in some cases, not salvageable. That has been my concern with investing in Tesla, a company built around and nurtured by a personality; the company is so built around the entwining of its interests with those of its CEO that any shareholder who is bullish about the company is making a joint bet on Tesla and Elon Musk. In contrast, whatever you may think of Microsoft's Bill Gates and Amazon's Jeff Bezos, they built companies with trillion-dollar market capitalizations and created professional management teams that would outlast them at the companies. In small businesses, especially those built around personal services,

this is called the key person effect, and the value of these businesses will be conditioned on the presence or absence of the key person.

2. **Political connections:** In some parts of the world, one of the biggest competitive advantages that a company can bring to its business is political connections, which can be used to get licenses to operate and approval for expansion/acquisition. When the connections are with those in power, they can used to pump up growth and profitability, but there is a caveat: being labeled a company that works well because of its connections with one side of a political divide can create danger if the other side ever claims power, or if those connections weaken. Consider Didi, Alibaba, and Tencent, large and very successful companies with Chinese operations, whose valuations were buoyed for much of their lives by the assumption that the Chinese government was in their corner, supporting and subsidizing them. In the last two years, the Chinese government has moved from ally to adversary, and as it has, the operating metrics and market valuations of these companies have gone into steep falls.
3. **Concentrated success (of product, geography, customer):** There are some large and very successful companies that can trace their operating and market success to one or two of their products, or to sales to one or two very large customers. That concentration may reduce marketing costs and generate more predictable revenues and profitability, but any threat to one of the products or customers can cause a steep drop-off in profitability and value. As an Apple shareholder, I am concerned that Apple's dependence on one product—the iPhone—for so much of its value exposes it to a risk of a meltdown.
4. **Disruption of business:** The first three factors exposing companies to steep falls are largely self-inflicted, but there are also forces outside a firm that can cause steep fall-offs in revenues, and I can loosely lump them together under the heading of "disruption." As an example, consider the revenues from taxicab businesses in New York in 2008, when taxis effectively had a monopoly on car service. A yellow cab medallion, needed to operate a taxicab in the city, sold for more than $1.5 million, with owners justifying the price by noting the barriers to entry in the business. Then Uber, Lyft, and other ride-sharing business devastated the taxicab business, with the value of a medallion dropping to less than $150,000.
5. **Acts of God:** For much of human existence, the biggest threats to businesses came from acts of God, as natural disasters such as floods, fires, and hurricanes laid waste to thriving businesses. With access to sophisticated insurance and risk-management products, some believed that we had put those days behind us, but the COVID shutdown in 2020 was a reminder that these risks still exist. While most businesses that

saw a slowdown during COVID could expect an eventual comeback post-virus, there were some businesses, like cruise lines, where the damage may well last into the long term.

There are clearly actions that companies can take on the first three counts, to make themselves less likely to take steep falls. They can work on replacing solo top manager acts with management teams, steer away from being too closely tied to one portion of the political spectrum, and diversify their product portfolios and customer revenues. In the process, though, they may have to give up profits, sometimes in significant amounts, in the short term. Companies may not be able to do much about natural disasters or disruption that is unanticipated, but they can build more resilience into their business models. Note that when revenues fall steeply and there are no early warnings, companies with high fixed costs and lots of debt are most exposed to risk. Creating more flexible cost structures where, as revenues drop, costs can also be scaled down quickly, can help companies survive significant shocks to their businesses.

SUDDEN DEATH

Can a company in high growth or in the mature phase face sudden death? It is uncommon, but it can happen, and the catastrophic event that causes it can come from within the firm, from a macro development, or from a combination of the two.

Companies fail all the time, but in most cases, those failures reflect long-term decline in their core businesses or rash attempts to lever up. What sets apart sudden-death companies is that failure comes, often while they are in the growth or mature phase of the life cycle. There are at least three reasons that I can point to, though I am sure that there are more that I have missed:

1. **Legal jeopardy:** As I have shown several times in the last few decades, a company that is growing and profitable, with a high value attached to its business, can lose it all in the face of a large lawsuit that lays claim to its primary assets or contends that the products and services sold by the company have created significant costs for consumers and society. Lawsuits related to asbestos, a lightweight construction product that led to cancer among those who worked around it for extended periods, put Johns Manville into bankruptcy in 1981. Litigation costs are so common in the tobacco and drug businesses that companies in these businesses have developed business models that incorporate this risk or try to hedge against it.

2. **Regulatory actions:** In businesses like financial services and telecom, where companies need regulatory approval to stay in business, violating a regulatory constraint or rule can lead to not just punishment but a shutdown. During the 2008 crisis, some banks were forcibly shut down, or forced to merge with other banks, in response to concerns that they did not have enough regulatory capital to keep going.
3. **Fraud and criminal behavior:** A third reason for corporate shutdown is fraud, either legal or accounting, wherein companies have been misleading or lying to investors and consumers for years and the lies are eventually exposed. Consider how quickly Enron went from being a company with a market capitalization of $70 billion to a corporate shell with no assets and no business in the aftermath of its bad behavior in the 1990s.

How do you defend against sudden death? One obvious way is to build safety buffers into constraints, so that you can ride out the effects of a shock. In the context of banking, prudent banks came out of the 2008 crisis with the recognition that having just enough capital to meet regulatory minimums will expose you to sudden death. If there is another lesson that all companies should take to heart, it is that there is a benefit to building "good citizen" constraints into business decision-making. Put simply, there may be investments that a company should choose not to make, even though these investments are profitable and value creating, because they will push the company too close to the line between legal and illegal, or right and wrong.

ZOMBIELAND

While I have drawn parallels between human beings and corporations on the life cycle, there is a key difference. Human beings die, no matter how heroic the attempts to keep them alive may be. Corporations, on the other hand, can survive well after their business models have expired, becoming the walking dead of the business world, and can create damage to those vested in and closest to them.

I have talked off and on in this book about these companies and the management and investor incentives that may keep them in operation after death, but to recap, they tend to share the following characteristics.

1. **A broken business model:** The company's business model is dead, with the causes varying from company to company: management ineptitude, strong competition, macroeconomic shocks, or just plain bad luck. Whatever the reason, there is little hope of a turnaround and even less of a comeback. The manifestations are there for

all to see, including sharply shrinking revenues, declining margins, and repeated failures in new business ventures/products/investments.

2. **Management entrenched and in denial:** The managers of these companies, though, act as if they can turn the ship around, throwing good money after bad, introducing new products and services, and claiming to have found the fountain of youth. They are fortified by weak or nonexistent corporate governance systems and sometimes by family ties (if the business is family controlled or owned).
3. **Enabling ecosystem:** Managers in denial are aided and enabled by consultants (who collect fees from selling their rejuvenating tonics), bankers (who make money off desperation ploys), and journalists (either out of ignorance or because there is nothing better to write about than a company thrashing around for a solution).
4. **Resources to waste:** While almost all declining companies share the three characteristics listed above, walking dead companies are set apart by the fact that they have access to the resources to continue on their path to nowhere and must be kept alive for legal, regulatory, or tax reasons. The needed resources can take the form of cash on hand, lifelines from governments, and/or capital markets that have taken leave of their senses.

The challenge that you face as an investor in a walking dead company is that you cannot assess its value based upon the assumption that managers in the company will take rational actions: make good investments, finance them with the right mix of debt and equity, and return unneeded cash to stockholders. As I noted in chapter 13, to get realistic assessments of value, you have to assume that managers will sometimes take perverse actions, investing in low-probability, high-possible-payoff investments (think lottery tickets), financing them with odd mixes of debt and equity (if you are on the road to nowhere, you don't particularly care about who you take down with you), and holding back cash from owners. Incorporating these decisions into your valuation will yield lower values for these companies, with the extent of the discount depending upon the separation of management from ownership (it is easier to be destructive with other people's money), the capacity of managers to destroy value (which will depend on the cash/capital that they have access to and will increase with the size of the company) and the checks put on managers (by covenants, restrictions, and activist investors). At the limit, managers without any checks on their destructive impulses, given enough time, can erase all of a company's value. For value investors, these companies are often value traps, looking cheap on almost every value-investing measure but never delivering the promised returns, as managers undercut their plans at every step.

In December 2011, I wrote about Blackberry (then called Research in Motion) and argued that it needed to act its age, accept that it would never be a serious mass-market competitor in the smartphone market, and settle for being a niche player.* That piece, which I published when Blackberry had a market capitalization of $7.3 billion, argued that Blackberry should give up on introducing new tablets or phones and revert to a single model (which I termed the "Blackberry Boring"), catering to paranoid corporates (who do not want their employees accessing Facebook or playing games on smartphones). I also suggested that Blackberry settle on a five-year liquidation plan to return cash to stockholders.

I was accused of being morbid and overly pessimistic, but when I looked at Blackberry three years later, its market cap had dropped to $5.3 billion, and in the three years since the first post, the company had spent $4.3 billion on R&D, while its annual revenues dropped from $18.4 billion in 2011–12 to $4.1 billion in 2014–15 and its operating income of $1.85 billion in 2011–12 became an operating loss of $2.7 billion in 2014–15. Blackberry's new model may have been a technological marvel, but the smartphone market had moved on, to where a phone is only as powerful as the ecosystem of apps and other accessories available for it. If it was true in 2011 that Blackberry could not compete against Apple and Google in the operating system world, it was even truer in 2015, when either of these mammoth companies could have used petty cash to buy Blackberry. (Apple's cash balance was $163 billion, Google's cash balance was $63 billion, and Blackberry's enterprise value was $4.1 billion). Perhaps I was missing something here, but I really did not see any light at the end of the smartphone tunnel for Blackberry.

By 2015, the options for Blackberry, in my view, were even fewer than they were in 2011, to the point where even the niche market option did not seem viable anymore. In fact, I saw only two ways to encash whatever value was left in the company. The first was to hope that a strategic buyer with deep pockets would see some value in the Blackberry technology and buy the company. The second was a more radical idea: In a world where social media companies like Facebook, Twitter, and LinkedIn command immense value, with each user generating about $100 in incremental market cap, Blackberry could consider relabeling itself as a social media company and create a Blackberry Club, where those with Blackberry thumbs could stay connected.

In sum, the problems at walking dead companies get worse the longer they stay alive, as do their options.

* Aswath Damodaran, "Living within Your Limits: Thoughts on Research In Motion (RIM)," *Musings on Markets* (blog), December 16, 2011, https://aswathdamodaran.blogspot.com/2011/12/living-within-your-limits-thoughts-on.html.

Making Your Choice

As a manager of a business, you must play the hand you have been dealt, not the one that you wish you had; that discipline is at the heart of good management. If you are lucky enough to be at the helm of a high-growth business with strong competitive advantages and a growing market, you clearly will have an easier time delivering operating success than if you are running a company that operates in a declining business, with few competitive advantages left and debt weighing you down. This commonsense insight yields the following implications:

- **Measuring management quality:** In financial analyses, I am trained to take numbers from financial statements, compute operating measures and ratios (such as revenue growth rates, operating margins, and returns on invested capital), and use those to judge not only business success but also management quality. It is worth emphasizing that management quality is captured not in the levels of these ratios but in how the presence and actions of management change those ratios. There are companies with endowed competitive advantages, such as access to low-cost natural resources or a centuries-old brand name, where management really adds very little to success and, if anything, can do more harm than good. Conversely, there are companies with little or no competitive advantage, struggling to earn returns that match their cost of capital in mature markets, where a good management team might be able to eke out a meager excess return. A simplistic solution is to compare a company's margins or returns to industry averages, but this is a crude fix, since it assumes that all companies in an industry share the same characteristics.
- **The dangers of anecdotal evidence:** Over the decades, the most successful companies and the biggest business failures have become pet subjects of researchers, who pore over every aspect of each grouping, looking for commonalities that they can use to create a template for the next great business success or avoid the next catastrophic failure. While there is value in storytelling, especially with a skillful narrator, I believe not only that the lessons from both successes and failures have limited extrapolative power but also that luck and timing may be sometimes all that separates the two groups.
- **The expectations game:** Financial markets provide fairer assessments of management impact because expectations level out the investing game, making it more difficult to win in contrast to judging business success. This is the point I made far more elaborately in chapter 16, where I drew the contrast between good companies and good

investments. In some ways, managers will have an easier time delivering market success at a company that is in decline, with little or no competitive advantage, than at a company that is at peak profitability and growing strongly, since investors will expect very little of the first and a great deal of the latter.

Conclusion

In the late stages of the mature phase, or at the precipice of decline, companies face a choice. For most of them, the choice that both offers the best odds and requires the fewest contortions is acceptance, wherein managers adapt to being mature or declining businesses and act accordingly. Many of these firms, though, will look for alternate pathways designed to either stop aging, or better still, reverse it, for two reasons. The first is that incentive systems are designed to reward managers who take this route, with success cementing their status as super managers and failure, especially with other people's money, carrying fewer consequences. The second is the presence of an ecosystem of consultants selling metrics and tools that promise to reverse aging and bankers who generate fees from acquisitions and deals.

Firms that try to stop or reverse aging can take actions that range from the cosmetic, such as a corporate name change, to complete makeovers, wherein they change businesses and business models, hoping to rediscover their youth. While the odds of success are low, firms that build on their strengths in their renewal, revamp, or rebirth attempts have a greater likelihood of success. At the other end of the spectrum, firms also must be aware of the risks of steep falls—if they are built around key persons or personalities, are dependent upon a single product or a few customers, or use political connections as their prime competitive advantage—or sudden death, where a legal or regulatory ruling or disruption in their core businesses can truncate life. If there is a lesson that should have been learned over the last two decades of crises and disruptions, it is that there is a benefit to building more adaptable businesses.

Aging Gracefully: In Search of Serenity

THE CORPORATE LIFE CYCLE has been the centerpiece of this book, and I have used it to talk about how the focus in managing a business changes as it moves from starting up to maturity to decline, in the chapters on corporate finance; why the challenges that you face in valuation are likely to be different when valuing young businesses as opposed to more mature companies, in the chapters on valuation; what are the determinants of investment success at each stage of the life cycle, in the chapters on investment philosophy; and how the qualities that make a good manager change as a company ages. I will wrap up the discussion in this chapter by first arguing that the quality that you aspire to, when managing, valuing, or investing in any business, is serenity. I will also summarize the arguments of the book in the form of "lessons from the corporate life cycle," first for managers or owners of businesses and then for investors in these businesses. I will close with broad lessons that can be learned by market regulators and economic policymakers from understanding corporate life cycles.

The Essence of Serenity

Serenity is a sought-after quality, not just in spiritual retreats but also in almost every major religion in the world. In Buddhism, it is serenity (samatha-bhavana) that opens the door to insight (vipassana-bhavana); in Hinduism, serenity is a quality that you aspire toward to get on the road to enlightenment. In Christianity, its most visible presence, at least in daily life, is in the serenity prayer, created by Reinhold Niebuhr, an American theologian, but the search for serenity has deeper roots in biblical teachings.

Notwithstanding its ubiquitous appeal, serenity is still misdefined and misunderstood by many who claim to be in search of it. First, it is not, as some argue, a belief that nothing bad will happen to you (as an individual or a business). In fact, you are just as exposed to the good and the bad outcomes in life if you are serene as if you are not, but serenity lets you deal with both possibilities in a much healthier way. Second, it does not imply that you have given up and will simply let bad things happen to you, a distorted and defeatist view of karma—but it does imply that you will not exhaust yourself in unwinnable fights. In fact, the words of the serenity prayer capture the concept's essence, with the acceptance of the things that you cannot change, the courage to change the things you can, and, most critically, the wisdom to know the difference.

How does this definition of serenity work in a business setting? If there is a lesson that I hope that I have been able to convey in this book, it is that as businesses age, they need to find the right balance between fighting all aspects of aging tooth and nail and giving up, whereby they effectively ascribe everything that happens to aging and capitulate. The wisdom that leads businesses to differentiate between the aspects of aging that they can change and the aspects they cannot comes from understanding their customers, their competition and, most importantly, their own strengths and weaknesses.

Serenity Lessons for Managers and Owners

If you own a business or are a manager at a publicly traded company, I noted in chapters 5 through 8 how the focus in corporate finance changes as the company ages. In chapter 18, I looked at the skill sets that managers need at different stages of the life cycle. In this section, I will summarize this learning into a series of lessons for managers and owners of businesses.

Growing Old Is Neither Effortless Nor Easy

It was said of Joe DiMaggio, the Yankees great, that he made playing baseball look effortless, but I am sure that that that the ease with which he swung the bat or patrolled center field was the result of hard work and practice. Businesses need to recognize that not only is aging inevitable, it comes with adjustments that are not pain-free. First, as businesses transition from one stage of the life cycle to the next, there are not only costs to transitioning but changes in the way the business has to be managed. Thus, the owners of start-ups that get their first venture capital investments will have to give up ownership stakes and must allow venture capitalists input on business decisions. Moving from being a privately owned business to becoming a publicly traded company, via an initial public offering, will bring new disclosure and investor relationship requirements. Second, as businesses age, they will find themselves facing limits, some the result of scaling up and getting bigger, and some coming from competition, that they might not have faced when they were younger. Third, as companies age, they acquire histories, and if these include significant successes, there will be nostalgia for past glory that may then feed into poor operating and business decisions. For instance, a retailer making the transition from high growth to maturity may continue with a historical practice of opening dozens of new stores each year, even though the market has changed.

> **LESSON** *As businesses age, they should expect discomfort, acknowledge their limits, even if they have plans to push past them, and celebrate their pasts while not trying to relive them.*

You Have to Survive to Deliver on Potential

In most businesses, failure is not a word that is talked about openly, either because of the hope that denial will make it go away or due to the perception that talking about or planning for bad outcomes is a sign of weakness. While this may not be a problem when a firm is stable (growth or mature), it can be one at either end of the life cycle.

- With young firms, as I have noted multiple times, the risk of failure is real and significant. Ignoring the existence of failure risk, or blithely building it into discount rates, as some investors tend to do, will not make it go away and in fact may increase exposure to it. Acknowledging the existence of failure risk and examining what is causing it can help managers make decisions that reduce the likelihood of failure. For young firms, for example, taking large investments in stages or seeking out a deep-pocketed venture capital partner may reduce upside, if these investments pay off, but also could reduce failure risk substantially.
- With declining firms, the first challenge in dealing with failure is defining what it means. After all, a firm in a declining business that liquidates its assets and returns cash to its owners may be failing if success is defined as staying in business, but it is taking the right course of action given its prospects. If failure means bankruptcy or default, a declining firm can reduce its exposure to that risk by selling its least productive assets and paying down debt as it shrinks.

- For all firms, there are macroeconomic forces that can push them into failure risk territory, as is the case with cyclical firms amid a severe economic recession, or commodity companies when commodity prices drop dramatically. Again, being aware of that exposure can reduce the risk of it happening; cyclical firms should borrow based upon what they generate as earnings in the middle of the economic cycle, not at its peaks or floors.

> **LESSON** *Acknowledge the existence of failure risk, consider the factors that determine the likelihood of failure, and then take actions that reduce the business's exposure to the risk, including preserving buffer debt capacity, using risk management products, and building business models that are more adaptable and flexible.*

Business Is about Making Trade-offs, and There Are No Costless Choices

Managing a business is all about making trade-offs, and there are almost no actions that are all upside. Being aware of the trade-offs, and explicitly considering how they will play out over time, is a key step toward aging with grace. The types of trade-offs that you face will change as a company ages. To provide a few examples:

- At the beginning of the life cycle, when faced with a choice of business models, you may have to choose between a low-capital-intensity model (where less investment is needed to enter a market, allowing you to grow much more quickly, but with fewer barriers to entry for competitors) or a high-capital-intensity model (where the need for more investment up front slows down growth, while creating a more defensible business model in the long term).
- For a young company facing the question of whether to give priority to scaling up (high growth) or building a better business model (longer life), it is worth noting that that ambition and longevity can be at odds with each other. Some of the longest-lived businesses in the world are family-owned, niche businesses that have stayed small and focused.
- For a mature company operating in a competitive business and in a large, albeit mature market, the trade-off can be between scaling up revenues, by growing faster, and increasing profitability, since the higher growth may require keeping product prices low and competing for market share.

- For a declining company, facing a market that is shrinking and becoming less profitable, the choice can be between continuing as a going concern—struggling to earn returns that match, let alone exceed, the cost of capital or potential proceeds from liquidating assets—and ending the business.

Faced with trade-offs, there is no choice that works for everyone, but there is one that is right for a specific company. Thus, if it is a family business that you would like to last for the long term, you may go slow on growth and be more cautious about entering new markets, whereas the manager of a publicly traded company may feel under more pressure to deliver results quickly. As the decision-maker in a business, you should be clear about your end game and act accordingly.

LESSON *View any decision or action that is presented as all to the good, with no downside, with skepticism. There is always a trade-off to consider.*

Business Building Is Mostly Perspiration, Not Inspiration

As a business goes from idea to product, the focus shifts from idea generation and raising capital to business building—and, in general, building businesses is more about grunt work than it is about creativity, requiring an attention to detail and a willingness to get in the weeds. For founders who feed off the excitement of idea generation and crave the adrenaline rush of selling their visions to investors and employees, finding more cost-efficient means of production and working on supply chains can be a letdown. Yet if founders decide to put these activities on the back burner because of their tedium, there is a substantial risk that the business will be stillborn. As I noted earlier in the book, this is the lesson that serial entrepreneurs learn, often after harsh lessons on survival and failure on their first attempts at starting businesses, and incorporate into their subsequent attempts. It is also the lesson that Steve Jobs learned the hard way in his first stint at Apple, and solved by hiring Tim Cook, to whom business building came easier, as his chief operating officer in his second and more successful stint at the company.

LESSON *As a founder, if you don't want to spend your time on business building, find someone who does and give that person freedom to make big operating decisions, without second-guessing those decisions.*

Scaling Up Is Hard to Do, and Not Always Sensible

We live in a world where growth is glorified, and where making a business bigger is prized far more than scaling it down. The heroes of the business world are empire builders, whether they be CEOs of companies or founders of new businesses, and they are held up for acclaim in academia and in practice. In this book, I have pushed back against that conventional wisdom, noting that scaling up a business comes with costs, one of which is a delay in turning the corner on profitability and another of which is the reinvestment needed to generate the scaling up. There are some businesses that should stay small and can be profitable businesses at that scale, and there are others where scaling up makes sense not because the business gets bigger, but because it gets more valuable. In the chapters on valuation, I made the link between scaling up and value explicit by bringing in the benefits of scaling up into revenues and the costs of scaling up into lower profit margins and higher reinvestment, and then computing the net effect on value.

The incentives to scale up a business get stronger if you have managers who are rewarded based on scale or growth, and if they are investing other people's (shareholders') money, and this sets up the scenarios where private equity investors and activist hedge funds are drawn in to level the playing field.

> **LESSON** *Be clear-eyed about the costs and benefits of scaling up, and if the net effect is negative and you choose to scale up anyway, be honest about whose interests are being served by that action.*

Good Offense Builds Businesses, Good Defense Preserves Them

When you are a start-up or young company disrupting a market or entering a new business, you are playing offense almost all the time, simply because you have nothing to defend yet. You can afford to take big risks, because you get dramatic upside if they pay off and have little to lose if they do not. As your business matures and grows, you create assets of substance, but the potential loss of those assets can now entail a downside from risk-taking. It is this dynamic that led to Clayton Christensen's thesis that disruption, when it happens in a business, almost always comes from new entrants and not existing players.

As a firm moves through the life cycle, its management will be judged just as much or more on its capacity to defend what has already been built as on its skills in going after new markets or growth. Using a sports analogy, while there is always valuc to having a good offense, the importance of playing defense rises at mature firms.

> **LESSON** *As the owner or manager of a business, you need to assess, given where the company is in its life cycle, whether you should be playing offense or defense and, if the latter, the competitive advantages or moats that you will be defending.*

Corporate Immortality Is Not the End Game

"Sustainability" is the new buzzword in business, and while there are benign versions of the concept, in its most malignant form, it is about what businesses can do to live longer, or even forever. With that objective in mind, consultants and bankers come up with action plans that extend the life of a business, sometimes at the expense of profitability and value, yielding the prototype for a walking dead company. If you are tempted by the prospect of a longer life for your business, it is worth remembering two simple truths. The first is that no matter how creative and clever your consultants are, no business lasts forever. The second is that a corporation is a legal entity, and if the reason for its existence (running a viable, profitable business) disappears, the most prudent path to follow is to let it disappear as well. Taking a corporate shell and refilling it with new content is generally neither efficient nor productive.

> **LESSON** *To paraphrase the lyrics of a legendary country song, when running a business, you have to know when to hold 'em and know when to fold 'em. Don't be a zombie company.*

Rebirth and Reincarnation

Despite the odds against success, I understand the draw of rebirth and reincarnation for companies that are aging. After all, who doesn't want to be young again? For managers who choose this path, though, I have three pieces of advice. First, for a rebirth plan to work, you need a host of other factors that work to your advantage, including being at the right place at the right time and having competitors who make bad choices. Second, to improve your odds of success, you need to build around strengths you already have as a company and recognize there are no shortcuts. Third, you should not surround yourself with consultants and bankers offering advice on the best rebirth plan, because what's best for them will not be what's best for you.

> **LESSON** *If you decide to take the path of rebirth, build on your strengths, don't be in a rush, and pray for good luck.*

Business Aging Does Not Follow the Chronological Clock

The tricky part of corporate aging is that it does not follow a chronological clock. As I noted in our discussion of the compressed life cycle, a firm in a low-capital-intensity business, where scaling up is easy, will grow much faster, stay at the top for a much shorter period, and decline more quickly than a firm in an infrastructure business. In addition, as disruption becomes a clear threat in more and more businesses, the life cycle can be sped up for disrupted companies, with many moving from mature to near-death over short periods. While I have used corporate age as a proxy for where a company is in the life cycle, it is the operating metrics (revenue growth, operating margins, and reinvestment) that are more indicative of true aging. A forward-looking management team will track these metrics over time to receive advance notice that aging is slowing the firm down.

> **LESSON** *Since aging is less about how old your business is and more about your growth and profitability metrics, the best way to slow aging is to work on holding revenue growth at reasonable levels, while preserving and growing profit margins.*

The Fate of a Business Is Not Always in Its Own Hands

I have been taught to believe that the fates of businesses lie in the hands of their managers and, by extension, that good companies are run by good managers and bad companies by managers of dubious quality. That assertion may serve business schools well, since it justifies the nosebleed prices that they charge for what they claim is accreditation to be a good manager, but the truth is more complicated. Much of what happens in a business is driven by movements in macroeconomic variables, country risk shifts, and political changes, none of which are controlled by managers. In some cases, a business can benefit from the misfortunes or missteps of a competitor or can be set back by a regulatory change or legal development. As I noted in chapter 18, the effect that management can have on a company is greatest (in both good and bad ways) at either end of the corporate life cycle and becomes much more muted in the middle of the life cycle. At the risk of being branded a cynic, there are businesses that could be run just as well by autopilot rules or a robot as by the existing (and expensive) management team.

> **LESSON** *While managers cannot foresee acts of God or unexpected macroeconomic developments, they can stay vigilant and watchful and build adaptable businesses that can react quickly to change.*

Lessons for Investors

There are lessons in the life cycle for investors in businesses, since the challenges that you face when investing or trading shift as companies age. While I examined these challenges in detail in chapters 9 through 17, first in the sections on valuing these companies and later in the chapters on investing in these companies, I will summarize what I have learned as lessons for investors in this section.

Uncertainty Is a Feature, Not a Bug

When valuing or investing in companies, investors always face uncertainty in trying to forecast the future, but the magnitude and types of uncertainty that they face will change as companies age. Uncertainty is greatest at young companies with little operating history and unformed business models and will tend to decrease as companies age. If you view uncertainty as a problem to be avoided, you will find yourself investing only in or primarily in mature companies, and while you may view that as a positive, it does constrain you. If, at the other extreme, you deny the existence of uncertainty and/or adopt arbitrary rules to deal with it, like the target rates made up by venture capitalists, you will invest in young companies, but without a serious assessment of the risks that you face.

The path forward is to face up to uncertainty, making your best estimates given the information that you have, and then using statistical tools like scenario analysis and simulations to deal with the uncertainty of various outcomes. In chapter 10, when I valued start-ups, and again in chapter 15, where I discussed investing in start-ups, I tried to put this precept into practice. Ignoring uncertainty will not make it go away, and the irony in investing is that your biggest payoffs will come from those investments where you face the most uncertainty.

> **LESSON** *Face up to uncertainty, accept its existence, and try to turn its presence to your advantage.*

Don't Deny Your Biases

Investors and analysts have a fetish about being objective when, in truth, they are always biased. With young companies, you will like some founders more than others, and you will sometimes fall in love with their business stories. When that occurs, and you want a business story to be true, you will gather facts, often selectively, to back up your beliefs. With more mature firms, your bias may come from your past investment experiences, good or bad, holding its shares, or from reading about or listening to what investors you respect think about these firms. In both cases, being biased makes you a worse investor, since your biases will lead you to either not do your homework or ignore contradictory data, making you incapable of acting sensibly until it is too late.

While there is little that you can do about your biases, being open about them will make you aware of how your assumptions and decisions are being altered by your priors and perhaps make you more cautious about following through on your own analysis. It also helps if you listen to those who disagree with you on an investment and consider or even incorporate their points of view.

> **LESSON** *Be open about your biases, even though you may be unable to do much about them, and keep the feedback loop open by surrounding yourself with people who don't think like you.*

Investing Is a Skewed Game

Even if you are a successful investor, most of your investments will lag the market, but your big winners will be what push your overall portfolio ahead of the market. This asymmetry in returns exists for companies across the life cycle, but it is greater for younger firms than for older firms. As you may recall from chapter 15, successful venture capitalists in start-up companies lose on almost 60% of their investments, but their very best investments do well enough not only to cover their losses but to yield a surplus. This asymmetry in returns also applies when you look across investors, since most lag the market, and there are only a few consistent winners. Again, that asymmetry is more extreme with investors in young companies, with a wider gulf between the most and least successful venture capitalists, than it is with investors in mature companies.

The skewed nature of investment returns should make investors cautious about widely repeated nostrums in investing and trading. The notion that holding a concentrated portfolio, where you put all your money in a small number of companies, is a sign of investor conviction is a part of value investing lore, but if your strict criteria for stock selection lead you to miss the biggest winners, you will lag the market. At the other extreme, the traders' argument that you can use charts and technical indicators to time when you buy and sell stocks can lead you to sell your biggest winners just before they start winning, or buy your biggest losers just before they go down.

> **LESSON** *Be cautious about adding to or pruning your portfolio based upon short-term performance or for emotional reasons. If you are entrusting your money to someone else, look for consistency as much as outperformance.*

Be Realistic about the Management Effect

When investing in a company, there are two concerns that you should have about its management. The first is management quality, with good management adding to a company's value and bad management doing the opposite. The second is conflicts of interests between management and ownership; what's good for managers at these firms may or may not be what's good for shareholders.

If you are an investor in young companies, where founders or insiders hold significant ownership stakes and management can make a much bigger difference to value, your focus should be on management quality and finding ways to better assess it, especially given the paucity of historical performance data. As I noted in chapter 15, this is the reason that the most successful venture capitalists tend to be better at judging founders on their capacity to convert ideas into businesses.

In more mature companies, where management generally makes less of a difference to value and managers often have smaller ownership stakes, your bigger challenge will be evaluating corporate governance. The recognition that managerial and shareholder interests diverge will not only reduce your frustration from seeing companies not acting their age but also allow you to direct your money to companies where owners run the business or where the managers are incentivized to act more in the interest of shareholders.

> **LESSON** *The data that you collect and the assessments that you make about management will shift from management quality to corporate governance as companies age.*

Mean Reversion Works, Until It Does Not

The essence of mean reversion is that a company's operating metrics and pricing converge on averages, either historical or across companies, and investors draw on its power in developing investment strategies, with key differences.

- In some cases, investors assume that the reversion will be to historical averages, either on operating metrics like growth and operating margins, or on commodity prices. It leads them to buy oil companies when oil prices are low and consumer product companies when their margins drop below historic norms, expecting to make money when they bounce back.
- In others, the reversion is to industry averages, again either on operating metrics (margins, return on capital) or pricing (PE ratios, EV/EBITDA). Much of active investing, in fact, is built on the presumption that when a company trades at a pricing multiple very different (either higher or lower) than the industry average, there will be a correction, where its pricing multiple will converge on the average. Thus, buying a stock that trades at a lower PE ratio than its peer group pays off as the company's PE converges on the industry average.

While mean reversion is a strong force and works a significant portion of the time, there are two limits to it. The first is timing, since convergence in the long term will not work in your favor if your time horizon is much shorter. Second, mean reversion works only if there is no structural change in the underlying process or system. In the first decade of this century, assuming that operating margins and growth at brick-and-mortar retail companies would revert back to historical averages would have been disastrous for investors, since Amazon's disruption of retail changed the dynamics.

While mean reversion as a force exists across the life cycle, its allure increases with the amount of historical data available, making it a bigger driver of investments in mature companies and sectors with long histories. In fact, it can be blamed for one of value investing's most dreaded scenarios, the value trap, where you invest in a company because it looks cheap (relative to history or the sector) and it only becomes cheaper over time, partly because its fundamentals have deteriorated.

LESSON *When there are structural changes, as is the case with disruption or macroeconomic shifts, falling back on mean reversion is false comfort.*

Assessing Company Quality Is Easy, Assessing Investment Quality Is Hard

In chapter 16, when examining value investing, I drew a distinction between good companies and good investments, arguing that while the former is based on operating metrics like growth, margins, and returns on invested capital, the latter is a function of how the investment is priced. The way this distinction plays out will vary depending on whether your investment focus is on young or more mature companies:

- With start-ups and young companies, the quality of businesses can be measured based upon potential market size, unit economics, and competitive advantages, but there are some investors who seem to believe that any price is justifiable for high-quality businesses with potential. That is, of course, not true, and I can see it play out in corrections in pricing at these companies, as expectations come down to match reality.
- With mature companies, the focus when measuring company quality is on earnings power, with more earnings (and cash flows) leading to higher value, and business moats, with more value attached to bigger and more long-lasting moats. If your investment analysis stops there, you risk overpaying for great companies, especially if there is market consensus around that greatness.

It is for this reason that I argued that the best investments are in companies where there is a mismatch between its business and investment qualities. With young companies, your best investments will be when the consensus view is that they don't have much growth potential, when their true markets are much bigger. With mature companies, your best investments will be in companies where the consensus view is that they have no moats, when, in fact, they have strong and sustainable competitive advantages.

> **LESSON** *Investment success does not come just from assessing business or management quality but also from your assessments of a company deviating from the consensus view.*

The Less You Bring to the Investing Table, the Less You Should Expect to Take Away

To win at investing, I believe that you must bring something unique or at least uncommon to the table. If you are using the same data as everyone else, and working with the same tools, why would you expect whatever you are doing to deliver an investing payoff? Investors who succeed have a niche or an edge that they cultivate, and that niche/edge can be different for investors at different stages in the life cycle.

- With young companies, being able to gauge founder quality, failure risk, and potential market size (for products or services that are still unformed) will give investors who are better at doing this a leg up on their competition.
- With high-growth businesses, being able to better separate those companies that can scale up more quickly and with better profitability from those that will either struggle on scaling or do so at the expense of profitability is the defining factor separating investment success from failure.
- With more mature businesses, it is superior assessments of competitive advantages or moats, in conjunction with the capacity to foresee disruption, that is the key to investment success.

In each of these cases, though, there are personal qualities that investors bring to the table, like patience and willingness to withstand peer pressure, that can augment investing payoffs.

LESSON *Find your niche or edge, build an investment philosophy around it, and then find a way to monetize it.*

Taking on Risk Does Not Entitle You to Rewards

Risk is part of investing, and every risk and return model in finance is built on linking higher risk to higher expected returns. That linkage, though, is not an entitlement, and investors who take risk, expecting higher returns, are not entitled to those returns, even if they do their homework and have long time horizons. That is a point worth making, because investors who believe that they are entitled to rewards because of the hard work that they have put in and don't get that reward not only become embittered, blaming markets for the shortfall, but also act accordingly. They double down on bad bets, make worse returns, and become more frustrated—and the cycle continues.

The way this dynamic plays out will vary depending on the companies that investors target in their investment philosophies. When investments in young companies underperform, investors blame macroeconomic forces or short-term thinking on the part of others who don't see the growth potential in these firms. If short selling is a factor in prices falling, labeling those sellers as speculators, who benefit from destruction, becomes an easy out. With investors in mature businesses, underperformance is attributed to the rest of the market being in a bubble, with traders and shallow investors pushing up prices.

> **LESSON** *If you do your homework and find "good" investments, do so on the expectation of rewards, but don't feel entitled to those rewards.*

Investor or Trader?

In chapter 14, I used the contrast between value, determined by fundamentals, and price, driven by mood and momentum, to explain what sets investors apart from traders. Investors, I argued, assess value, try to buy at a price less than that value, and make money from convergence. Traders, I noted, play a simpler game, buying at a low price and selling at a higher one, using whatever tools they can to harness momentum strength and shifts. Investors and traders exist in every phase of the life cycle, but the balance between the two will tend to shift as you move through the life cycle. With younger companies, it is traders who will dominate markets as investors stay away, unwilling or unable to deal with the uncertainties that are endemic to these companies. As companies mature, you will see more investing, as investors become more comfortable making estimates and dealing with uncertainties.

If you choose to invest rather than trade, you can go the conventional route, focusing entirely on mature companies, or you can go against the grain and look for undervalued firms in the earlier stages of the life cycle. You are likely to find more market mistakes, but you will face a steeper climb in valuing these companies and a greater concern that trading can drive the price away from the value in the near term, rather than toward it. If you are a trader, your trading focus will change for companies across the life cycle, with more momentum/reversal trading earlier in the life cycle and information-based trading (around earnings or merger announcements) for more mature companies.

> **LESSON** *Choose the game that you want to play, with a sense of why you think you can win at that game, and stop deluding yourself. In short, if you are trading, don't masquerade as an investor or talk about value, and if you are investing, stay clear of pricing plays.*

Luck Trumps Skill

Over the last century, many have tried to make investing into a discipline, with some even using the vast amounts of data that comes out of investing to argue that it is a science. The truth, though, is that there is far too much that investors don't control for it to ever resemble a science. In practical terms, this means that separating luck from skill, when assessing investment performance, is very difficult—perhaps even impossible—to do. This is especially the case with younger companies, with the skewed distribution of a few big winners and lots of losers among them, since any investor or trader who buys a winner, no matter how absurd the reason, will emerge looking like a winner.

There are two lessons investors can draw from this. First, being honest with yourself, as an investor, about how much of your success comes from being in the right place at the right time will make you a better investor. Second, humility in the face of investment success is the most prudent response. Not only will this make you more likeable as a person, it will allow you more protection when you fail, since claiming full credit for success will also mean that you are fully accountable for failure.

LESSON *View investment success and failure as two sides of the same coin, accepting neither as a measure of your worth as a person or an investor.*

Lessons for Security Regulators

Over the course of this book, I have looked at companies across the life cycle, but primarily from the perspective of managers of and investors in these companies. These companies operate in markets, where what they disclose and how they are structured is determined by regulatory rules and restrictions. In this section, I will argue that regulators must modify rules on disclosure, corporate governance, and investor protections to reflect where a company is in the life cycle.

Disclosure

Over the last few decades, we have seen an explosion in disclosure requirements, especially so at publicly traded companies. While the motivation for these increased disclosures is to inform investors, in many ways it has been counterproductive and led to investors being less informed, rather than more informed. I believe that this is because disclosure rules, as they have evolved, have been written with two beliefs:

1. **One size fits all:** The prevailing orthodoxy in disclosure is "one size fits all," where all companies are covered by disclosure requirements, even if they are only tangentially exposed. Though that practice is defended as fair and evenhanded, it adds to disclosure bloat, since disclosures that are useful for assessing some firms will be required even for firms where they have little informative value. As I will argue later in this section, the types of information that investors in young companies want, or need, to assess value are very different from the types that investors in mature businesses may demand.
2. **More is better:** Is more disclosure always better than less? There are some who believe so, arguing that investors always have the option of ignoring the disclosures that they don't want to make use of and focusing on the disclosures that they do. Not surprisingly, this view on disclosure tends to be expansive, since if someone, somewhere, can find a use for disclosed data, it should be disclosed. The research accumulating on information overload suggests that this is wrong, and that more data can lead to less rational and reasoned decisions, for three reasons:
   a. The human mind is easily distracted and, as filings get longer and more rambling, it is easy to lose sight of the mission on hand and get lost on tangents.
   b. As disclosures mount up in multiple dimensions, it is worth remembering that not all details matter equally. Put simply, separating the information that matters from the many data points that do not becomes more difficult when you have 250 pages in a 10-K or S-1 filing.
   c. Behavioral research indicates that as people are inundated with more data, their minds often shut down, and they revert to "mental shortcuts," simplistic decision-making tools that throw out much or all of the data designed to help them make that decision.

   Put simply, investors are drowning in disclosures and are becoming less informed along the way. The way out of the disclosure maze requires turning these building blocks on their heads.
3. **Less is more:** We are well past the point of diminishing returns on more disclosure, and disclosures need slimming down. That is easier said than done, since it is far more difficult to pull back disclosure requirements than it is to add them. There are three suggestions that I would make, though there will be interest groups that will push

back on each one. First, one way to prune disclosures is to ask investors (not accountants or lawyers) whether they find these disclosures useful. (A more objective test of the value to investors of these disclosures is to look at the market price reaction to them and, if there is none, to assume that investors are not helped by them.) Second, when a new disclosure requirement is added, an old one of equivalent length must be eliminated—which of course will set up a contest between competing disclosure needs, but that is healthy. Third, any disclosures that draw disproportionately on boilerplate language (risk sections are notorious for being filled with legalese that is completely useless) need to be shrunk or even eliminated.

4. **Triggered disclosures:** At first sight, the requirements to make disclosures slimmer and more informative may seem at war with each other, since disclosure bloat has largely come from well-intentioned attempts to make companies reveal more about themselves. Triggered disclosures, where disclosures are tailored to a company's makeup and stories, are one solution, where what is disclosed by a company will be reflective of what investors in that company believe matters most in assessing its value. The corporate life cycle can help in tailoring disclosures to where a company is in the life cycle, as can be seen in figure 20.1.

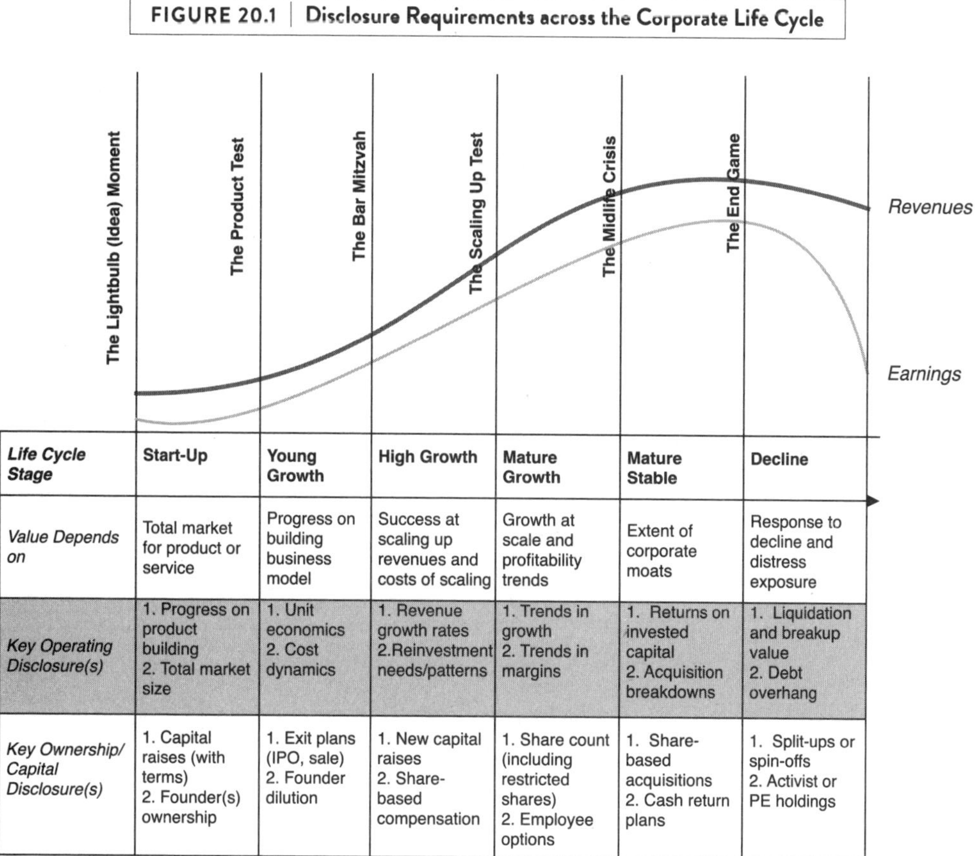

Life Cycle Stage	Start-Up	Young Growth	High Growth	Mature Growth	Mature Stable	Decline
Value Depends on	Total market for product or service	Progress on building business model	Success at scaling up revenues and costs of scaling	Growth at scale and profitability trends	Extent of corporate moats	Response to decline and distress exposure
Key Operating Disclosure(s)	1. Progress on product building 2. Total market size	1. Unit economics 2. Cost dynamics	1. Revenue growth rates 2.Reinvestment needs/patterns	1. Trends in growth 2. Trends in margins	1. Returns on invested capital 2. Acquisition breakdowns	1. Liquidation and breakup value 2. Debt overhang
Key Ownership/ Capital Disclosure(s)	1. Capital raises (with terms) 2. Founder(s) ownership	1. Exit plans (IPO, sale) 2. Founder dilution	1. New capital raises 2. Share-based compensation	1. Share count (including restricted shares) 2. Employee options	1. Share-based acquisitions 2. Cash return plans	1. Split-ups or spin-offs 2. Activist or PE holdings

FIGURE 20.1 | **Disclosure Requirements across the Corporate Life Cycle**

Investors in start-ups are much more interested in how an idea is moving toward becoming a product or service and how big the potential market for that product or service will be than in a breakdown of working capital into its constituent parts on the balance sheet. In terms of disclosures about ownership and capital, knowing how much venture capital has been raised by a firm, and on what terms, is critical in judging the value of a start-up. In young companies, the value of a company depends on unit economics, where the information that is most useful in valuing the firm relates to how much it costs to manufacture a unit (or acquire a new user or subscriber) and what the marginal costs are of providing that unit (or servicing the user). Knowing the owners' exit plan for that young business—i.e., whether they aim for it to stay a going private concern, for sale to a public company, or for an initial public offering—can also help in valuing a young company.

The notion of triggered disclosure does not require a complete rewrite of disclosure laws. Businesses at every stage in the life cycle will still need to provide full financial statements (income statement, balance sheet, cash flow statements), but the additional disclosures demanded should reflect where the company is in the life cycle. In a paper looking at disclosures in initial public offerings, I argue that this additional information, for a user- or subscriber-based company, should include detailed information on user economics, whereas, for an infrastructure company, that detail should be on infrastructure project timelines.*

Corporate Governance

The regulatory push toward better corporate governance moves in fits and starts, with corporate scandals increasing the pressure to make managers more accountable to shareholders. In the United States, it was the Enron, Tyco, and WorldCom fiascos that pressured lawmakers to pass the Sarbanes-Oxley Act, a detailed set of rules designed to strengthen corporate governance at companies, and the SEC to tighten rules on proxy voting and shareholder activities. However, much of what we have seen as corporate governance reform, in the United States and elsewhere, is built on the presumption that the core conflict of interest that needs addressing comes from managers not owning enough shares in a company, and thus not thinking like shareholders. The solutions offered therefore try to fix this conflict by offering managers either carrots, in the form of stock-based compensation, or sticks, which try to make boards of directors more representative of and responsive to shareholders (by requiring directors to be independent and restricting director tenure).

That type of corporate governance reform may work in more mature firms, where managers do tend to have no or very small ownership stakes and consequently tend to put their interests, as managers, ahead of those of shareholders. But as you look across the life cycle, you can see that the governance challenge changes. At start-up and young companies, it is founders or inside shareholders who hold large ownership stakes and are entrusted with the management of the firm. That removes the core conflict that conventional corporate governance is trying to resolve but replaces it with a different conflict between that which is good for inside shareholders/founders and that which is good for outside shareholders. It is revealing that in the twenty years since Sarbanes-Oxley was written, ostensibly to protect shareholders, we have seen young companies, especially in the technology space, shift to shares with different voting classes, giving inside shareholders a profound advantage in the control game.

* M. Cohen, A. Damodaran, and D. McCarthy, "Initial Public Offerings: Dealing with the Disclosure Dilemma," Working Paper, SSRN #3936750, 2021.

Investor Protection

Finally, let's consider the third part of regulatory concern, which is protecting investors. Here again, much of what we see as investor protection stems from three assumptions about risk and investor sophistication:

1. **Risk awareness:** A fundamental premise in both disclosure and regulation seems to be the belief that the reason investors who choose to invest in very risky businesses do so is because they are unaware of how much risk there is in these companies. Put differently, regulators seem to believe that if these investors were made fully aware of the risks, they would not invest. That misses the reality that risk is both upside and downside, and that investments with high downside risk also offer the most upside. In short, those investors who choose to put their money in risky companies do so precisely because they are risky, and having a hundred-page risk disclosure to that effect will not change a single mind.
2. **Investor sophistication:** Much of the regulatory action on investor protection takes a paternalistic view of individual and retail investors. Specifically, regulators seem to believe not only that individual investors are incapable of informing themselves and making reasoned judgments on risk/return trade-offs but also that they should be protected from their own mistakes. The truth, again, is much more complex. Individual investors have access to much of the same fundamental information that institutional investors do, and not only are they just as capable of using this information to make buy and sell decisions, they are less subject to emotional and panic-driven trading than institutions.
3. **Company risk versus portfolio risk:** Regulators seem to view their job as regulating company-specific risk, even though investors have the option of diversifying across multiple companies and most of them take advantage of that opportunity. Why does that matter? Rather than spend the bulk of their resources containing and regulating company-level risk, which will average out across the portfolio, regulators should place a greater focus on exposure to macroeconomic or market-wide risks that will flow through into portfolios.

At the risk of stating the obvious, investor protections must be written with the investors that they are trying to protect in mind. Investors in young companies are more risk-takers and traders, who are hoping to use mood and momentum to make money, and informing them that their investments are risky is both futile and insulting. In mature companies, investors are more institutional, and the protections that they seek are more from managerial overreach than from operating mistakes or risks.

In Summary

I have argued in this section that regulatory rules and restrictions on disclosure, corporate governance, and investor protection are rooted in fundamental misconceptions about both the companies that are being regulated and the investors in these companies. In defense of the regulators, it is worth noting that many of the core regulations were put in place to regulate US equity markets in the last century, when most firms, at least in public markets, were mature or close to mature, with homogeneous investor bases. The problem for regulators is that markets have changed, and publicly traded companies today not only are more diverse in terms of where they are in the life cycle but also have heterogenous investor bases. Regulators can either change the way they approach their jobs or risk irrelevance.

Lessons for Policymakers

Should economic policymakers care about the corporate life cycle? I think so, and in this closing section, I will consider why. If you consider an economy as composed of a portfolio of all businesses that are in it, you can see that the mix of businesses, based upon where they are in the life cycle, can be different in different economies. Consider three scenarios:

- If you have an economy composed primarily or entirely of mature businesses, you will gain the benefit of overall economic stability, but at the expense of innovation and growth.
- If your economy is made up almost entirely of start-up and young-growth companies, you will have more innovation and excitement in both the economy and markets, but at the cost of much bigger swings as you move from good to bad times.
- If your economy has primarily or only businesses in decline and distress, it is difficult to see how the economy will not reflect those characteristics as well.

A healthy economy will have balance across the life cycle, with mature firms forming the anchor for economic stability, but with innovation coming from young firms and start-ups, and with the necessary pruning occurring as firms in declining businesses are liquidated or broken up.

With the objective of creating an economy composed of firms spread across the life cycle, we can map out the challenges that policymakers may face in transitioning to that ideal from an economy's current standing. If you are faced with an economy of mature or declining businesses and you are trying to increase the number of start-ups and young-growth companies, there are a few lessons that I have learned from looking at countries or regions that have attempted to accomplish this:

1. **Risk capital versus subsidy capital:** Many countries that are in a hurry to develop an entrepreneurial class have tried to do so by offering capital directly to these businesses, often as subsidized loans or grants. Unfortunately, that does not seem to do much other than burn through billions of dollars over time, enriching several entities along the way, but with no payoff in terms of new businesses that are self-supporting. The long-term solution that has staying power is for investors to be willing to put their money into the risky businesses (start-ups and young companies) on the expectation that they will earn high returns, but also with the recognition that these companies will fail often. I believe that this risk-taking culture can be cultivated in any setting, but for it to happen, you must work on building liquidity in markets and fairness into the legal system.
2. **Top down versus bottom up:** Policymakers tend to overestimate their capacity to change the way investors and businesspeople think, leading them to believe that pronouncements and policy tweaks change behavior. Just as the risk culture is slow to build on the investor side, the entrepreneurial drive, where an individual or individuals leave well-paying jobs to start new businesses, must occur from the bottom up. One factor that seems to make a difference is examples of entrepreneurial success close to home. To illustrate, the Indian economy, for much of its existence, was dominated by family businesses where risk-taking was frowned upon, earnings power was revered, and social/political connections were the ultimate barrier to entry. It was the success of a handful of technology entrepreneurs in the 1980s and 1990s, who started companies with little more than human capital and turned them into successful and valuable businesses, that changed perceptions about risk-taking.
3. **Timelines:** Policymakers usually work with timelines that have more to do with election cycles and bureaucratic tenure than they do with reality. Creating artificial and completely unreasonable deadlines for economic transformation will not only kill any chance of success early on but will convert these exercises into boondoggles for consultants, scams, and shady operations masquerading as businesses. This is one more reason to be skeptical about government plans for economic transformation.

Conclusion

I started this book by introducing the corporate life cycle as a construct that can be used to explain much of what I see in businesses and markets. Knowing where companies are in the life cycle can explain what aspect of corporate finance (investing, financing, or cash return) they should be most focused on, the methods they use for analysis, and the consequences of not acting their age. Understanding the key drivers of value, as well as the information (or absence of it) when you make your best estimates, becomes a key component of valuing companies across the life cycle. Understanding the differences across investment philosophies can also make clear why investors in young companies can have very different mindsets than investors in mature companies. In this chapter, I have come full circle, with corporate life cycle lessons for managers and investors, as they manage or invest in companies; for regulators, as they write new rules on disclosure, corporate governance, and investor protection; and for policymakers intent on building growing, vibrant economies. If you, as a person or business, are tempted to fight aging, it is worth remembering that growing old is mandatory, but growing up is optional.

ACKNOWLEDGMENTS

To Noah and Lily, who are starting on their own life cycles, with the hope and prayers that they will see joy and success as they grow up.

INDEX

NOTE: *Italic page numbers indicate figures*